Application (Re)Engineering
Building Web-Based Applications and Dealing with Legacies

Amjad Umar, Ph.D.
Bell Communications Research (Bellcore)
Piscataway, New Jersey

To join a Prentice Hall PTR Internet mailing list,
point to **http://www.prenhall.com/mail_lists/**

Prentice Hall PTR
Upper Saddle River, NJ 07458
http://www.prenhall.com

Acquisitions editor: *Paul Becker*
Editorial assistant: *Maureen Diana*
Editorial/production supervision
    and composition: *Eileen Clark*
Cover design director: *Jerry Votta*
Cover design: *Design Source*
Manufacturing manager: *Alexis Heydt*
Marketing Manager: *Dan Rush*

Prentice Hall books are widely used by corporations and government agencies for training, marketing, and resale. The publisher offers discounts on this book when ordered in bulk quantities.
For more information, contact:

    Corporate Sales Department
    Phone: 800-382-3419 Fax: 201-536-7141
    E-mail: corpsales@prenhall.com
or write: Prentice Hall PTR
    Corp. Sales Dept.
    One Lake Street
    Upper Saddle River, NJ 07458

Printed in the United States of America
10   9   8   7   6   5   4   3   2

ISBN 0-13-750035-1

Prentice-Hall International (UK) Limited, *London*
Prentice-Hall of Australia Pty. Limited, *Sydney*
Prentice-Hall Canada Inc., *Toronto*
Prentice-Hall Hispanoamericana, S.A., *Mexico*
Prentice-Hall of India Private Limited, *New Delhi*
Prentice-Hall of Japan, Inc., *Tokyo*
Simon & Schuster Asia Pte. Ltd., *Singapore*
Editora Prentice-Hall do Brasil, Ltda., *Rio de Janeiro*

Book at a Glance

Trademark Acknowledgments

The following list recognizes the commercial and intellectual property of the trademark holders whose products are mentioned in this book. Omission from this list is inadvertent:

Adapt/X Harness is a trademark of Bellcore

Adapt/X Traxway is a trademark of Bellcore

AIX is a trademark of IBM Corporation

CORBA is a trademark of Object Management Group

DB2 is a trademark of IBM Corporation

DCE is a trademark of Open Software Foundation

DSOM is a trademark of IBM Corporation

EDA/SQL is a trademark of Information Builders, Inc.

Encina is a trademark of IBM Corporation

Flowmark is a trademark of IBM Corporation

HotJava is a trademark of Sun Microsystems

IPX/SPX is a trademark of Novell Corporation

Java is a trademark of Sun Microsystems

Lotus Notes is a trademark of IBM Corporation

NetBIOS is a trademark of IBM Corporation

NetWare is a trademark of Novell Corporation

ODBC is a trademark of Microsoft Corporation

OLE is a trademark of Microsoft Corporation

OpenMail is a trademark of Hewlett-Packard

Orbix is a trademark of Iona Technologies

UNIX is a registered trademark licensed exclusively through X/Open Company, Ltd.

WebObjects is a trademark of NeXT Corporation

Windows is a trademark of Microsoft Corporation

Dedicated to my family:

my loving wife Dolorese, fond memories of my parents, and the rest of the gang.

About the Author

Dr. Amjad Umar is a Senior Scientist at Bell Communications Research, Inc. (Bellcore) and an Adjunct Professor at Rutgers University, Stevens Institute of Technology, and Fordham Graduate School of Business. At Bellcore, he specializes in distributed systems and consults/leads projects in electronic commerce, Web-based applications, Web access to corporate resources, data warehouses, and legacy system reengineering. As an Adjunct Professor, he teaches graduate-level courses in distributed systems, networks, and object-oriented technologies. He has also developed and taught numerous industrial seminars in client/server systems, distributed computing, networks, and databases for the telecommunications industry, the Society of Manufacturing Engineers, U.S. Department of the Navy, and Frost and Sullivan (England). He is the author of two other books: *Distributed Computing and Client-Server Systems* (Prentice Hall, 1993), and *Object-Oriented Client/Server Internet Environments* (Prentice Hall, 1997). Before joining Bellcore, he was on the faculty at the University of Michigan (Dearborn and Ann Arbor campuses) where he received the Distinguished Faculty award. His prior work experience includes management of a statewide computing network and development/consulting assignments with manufacturing organizations, educational institutions, and organizations in England, Singapore, China, and Canada. He has an M.S. in Computer, Information and Control Engineering and a Ph.D. in Industrial and Operations Engineering (major in Information Systems Engineering) from the University of Michigan.

Disclaimer

This book presents a broad picture of information technologies as they relate to distributed systems. The material has been compiled and prepared as a textbook for computer and information systems students and as a reference for information technology practitioners and managers. The views and opinions presented in this book are solely those of the author and do not represent the views of Bell Communications Research, Inc. (Bellcore). The names of the vendor products mentioned should not be construed as a recommendation from Bellcore. Bellcore does not provide comparative analysis or evaluation of products or suppliers. Any mention of products or suppliers in this book is done where necessary for the sake of scientific accuracy and precision, or for background information to a point-of-technology discussion, or to provide an example of a technology for illustrative purposes, and should not be viewed or construed as either positive or negative commentary on that product or supplier, neither should the inclusion of a product or a supplier in this book, nor the omission of a product or supplier on the part of the author.

Table of Contents

Chapter 3: Methodology Overview: Planning and Modeling

PART II: APPLICATION ENGINEERING—BUILDING WEB APPLICATIONS

Chapter 4: Building New (Web-Based) Applications

Chapter 5: Enterprise Data Architectures

Chapter 6: Web-Based Application Software Architectures

Chapter 7: Implementation Concepts and Examples
(Web, CORBA, ActiveX, DCE, Encina, PowerBuilder)

Chapter 10: Data Warehouses

Preface

This book explores the issues in building the new breed of Web-based applications that exploits object technologies, and deals with the large embedded base of legacy applications. The book is intended as a guide and a tutorial for the IT managers and practitioners who are involved in engineering of new applications and reengineering of existing (mostly legacy) applications.

The first part of the book reviews application (re)engineering issues, scans the IT infrastructure, and develops a general methodology for application (re)engineering. The second part concentrates on building Web-based object-oriented applications and explores enterprise-critical areas such as data architectures, application software architectures, and implementation issues (e.g., Web-Java, CORBA, ActiveX, OSF DCE). The third part presents critical examination of approaches to deal with legacy applications such as access/integration of legacy applications through the Web, data warehouses, and rearchitecture/migration strategies.

Several examples are presented and a single case study is developed throughout the book to illustrate the key points. Extensive references for additional information are provided.

Key Features of the Book

Focus on Applications. While many books are being written on the infrastructure (e.g., networks, World Wide Web, Groupware, CORBA, etc), this book concentrates on *using* the infrastructure to build applications for modern enterprises. In particular, application engineering as well as reengineering issues are discussed.

Web-Based Object-Oriented Applications View. We are interested in the class of enterprisewide applications that leverage powerful technologies such as the Web (e.g., Java, CGI), distributed objects (CORBA, ActiveX), and data access middleware (e.g., SQL gateways) to provide business value. These applications, termed object-oriented, client/server, Internet-based (OCSI) applications, are a special class of distributed applications for the enterprises of the 1990s and beyond. These three technologies are viewed as complementing each other to provide business value and not as replacements for each other.

Strategies to Deal with Legacy Applications. New applications must coexist with the large embedded base of existing (mostly legacy) applications. A systematic approach is suggested for dealing with legacy systems with discussion and analysis of legacy data access, data warehousing, and application migration/transition strategies.

Merging of Case Studies, Industrial Products, and Research Efforts. Each chapter is written as a self-contained tutorial with several case studies and examples to illustrate the key points throughout. State-of-the-market and state-of-the-art trends are noted in each chapter with numerous references for additional studies.

Integration with Infrastructure, in Particular Middleware, Issues. This book builds upon and uses the infrastructure and middleware discussed in the companion book ("Object-Oriented Client/Server Internet Environments," A. Umar, Prentice Hall, 1997). Together, these two books form an invaluable source of information for modern enterprises.

Practical Hints, Guidelines, Checklists. Numerous practical hints, guidelines, and checklists are highlighted throughout the book as sidebars for quick reference.

A Systematic Framework for Study. A framework for discussion and a general methodology is introduced early in the book to serve as a roadmap for study. The framework provides a basis for analysis and synthesis of the wide range of issues such as data architectures and application architectures.

In short, the reader of this book should develop a thorough understanding of how to engineer new applications and databases, and how to reengineer the existing terminal-host systems in an object-oriented client/server Internet world.

BOOK OUTLINE

PART I: GETTING STARTED

Chapter 1: Application (Re)Engineering—The Big Picture
Chapter 2: Object-Oriented Client/Server Internet Environments
Chapter 3: Methodology Overview: Planning and Modeling

PART II: APPLICATION ENGINEERING: BUILDING WEB APPLICATIONS

Chapter 4: Building New (Web-Based) Applications
Chapter 5: Enterprise Data Architectures
Chapter 6: Web-Based Application Software Architectures
Chapter 7: Implementation Concepts and Examples (Web CORBA, ActiveX, DCE, Encina, PowerBuilder)

PART III: APPLICATION REENGINEERING: DEALING WITH LEGACIES

Chapter 8: Dealing with Legacy Applications: An Overview
Chapter 9: Access and Integration of Legacy Applications through the Web
Chapter 10: Data Warehouses
Chapter 11: Migration Strategies

Intended Audience and Recommended Usage

This book is based on a synthesis of experience gained from three different sources. First, extensive project management, consulting, and system integration assignments in recent years in client/server systems, object-oriented technologies, Web-based applications, middleware evaluation, legacy data access, data warehousing, and data migration. Second, development and teaching of industrial training courses on client/server technologies and distributed systems that have been taught several times in the telecommunications industry and general IT community. Finally, teaching of graduate-level special topics courses in distributed systems for IT majors and computer-science students. This experience has indicated that this book should be useful as a reference for almost all IT managers and practitioners and also as a textbook for university courses and industrial training seminars. Specifically, this book should be of value to:

- Architects and designers of information services (application designers, database designers, network designers)

- Analysts and consultants of information technologies

- Planners of IT infrastructure and platforms

- Technical support personnel

- Managers of information technologies (CIO, MIS managers, database administrators, application development managers)

- System integrators who combine databases, networks, and applications between different platforms

- Teachers of university courses in information technologies

- Technical trainers for professional development courses in information technology

- Researchers in computing and information technologies who need a broad coverage of the subject matter

- Students for an introduction to the subject matter with numerous references for additional studies.

Depending on the background and interest of the reader, the book can be used in a variety of ways. This book has been, and can be, used in academic courses as well as in corporate training. Outlines of a university course and a two-day professional training course are suggested on the next page (the companion book "Object-Oriented Client/Server Internet Environments" is used as a reference book). These outlines are based on experience of teaching several university courses and industrial seminars in the last three years. Specifically:

> **University Courses.**[1] This book can be used in the information systems concentration in business schools and industrial engineering departments at most universities. The courses, usually graduate level, have been attended by students from management, computer science and industrial engineering departments.

> **Professional Seminars and Corporate Training**. This book has been used as a foundation for a two-day professional seminar under the title "Building Web-Based Applications."

---

1. I taught a graduate-level course on distributed systems where both books (this book and the companion book) were covered. Although the course went well, some students felt that too much material was covered. Depending on student background, it is possible to cover both books in one comprehensive course on distributed systems (roughly the first seven weeks are spent on the infrastructure and the last seven weeks cover application (re)engineering).

University Course Outline: Distributed Application Systems

Week	Topic	Reading
1	Introduction	Chapter 1
2	IT platforms (Web technologies)	Chapter 2
3	Middleware	Chapter 2
4	OO Concepts	Chapter 2
5	A General Methodology	Chapter 3
6	Web-based applications	Chapter 4
7	Enterprise Data Architectures	Chapter 5
8	Midterm Examination (or Project 1 Due)	
9	Application Software Architectures	Chapter 6
10	Implementation Examples and Concepts	Chapter 7
11	Legacy applications: The challenge	Chapter 8
12	Access and Integration through the Web	Chapter 9
13	Data Warehouses	Chapter 10
14	Migration Strategies	Chapter 11
15	Final Examination (or Project 2 Due)	

Professional Training Course: Building Web-Based Applications

Session	Topic	Duration	Reading
1	Introduction	1.0 Hour	Chapter 1
2	IT Building Blocks: The Middleware	2.0 Hours	Chapter 2
3	Web and distributed objects	1.5 Hours	Chapter 2
4	A General Methodology	1.0 Hour	Chapter 3
5	Web-based applications	1.5 Hours	Chapter 4
6	Data and Application Architectures	1.5 Hours	Chapters 5, 6
7	Implementation Examples and Concepts	1.0 Hour	Chapter 7
8	Legacy applications: The challenge	1.0 Hour	Chapter 8
9	Access and Integration through the Web	1.0 Hour	Chapter 9
10	Data Warehouses	0.5 Hour	Chapter 10
11	Migration Strategies and wrapup	1.0 Hour	Chapter 11

Acknowledgments

Many of my colleagues and friends at Bellcore graciously agreed to review specific chapters for content and/or style. Here is an alphabetical list of the reviewers who commented on at least one chapter (some reviewed 4 to 5): Dr. Aloysius Cornelio, Prasad Ganti, Bret Gorsline, Dr. Jon Kettering, Tom Knoble, Frank Marchese, Dr. Paul Matthews, Mike Meiner, KJ Shah, and Dr. Gomer Thomas. I really feel fortunate to have access to so many experts who are also very nice folks.

In addition, many of my university friends read early drafts and made numerous suggestions. Professor Nabil Adams of Rutgers Graduate School of Business, Professor Ahmed Elmagarmid of Purdue University, Professor Peter Jurkat of the Stevens Institute of Technology, and Professor Jerry Luftman of Stevens Institute of Technology gave valuable suggestions about different topics.

I should not forget the contribution of many university students at Stevens Institute of Technology, Rutgers, and Fordham who "suffered" through very rough drafts of many chapters. In addition, many attendees of professional-training seminars volunteered to review different chapters. The list of topics included in this book is based on extensive discussions with the university students and seminar attendees.

I want to express my gratitude toward my management (Dr. Satish Thatte, Rich Jacowleff, and Jac Simensen) for their understanding and support.

Conventions Used

We will use the following conventions in this book. *Highlighted italics* are used to indicate definition of new terms, *italics* are used for emphasis and **bold letters** are used for subject headings.

Interrelationships Between Books and Personal Remarks

Several people, especially faculty members from different universities, in the past few months have asked me how this book relates with my first book *Distributed Computing and Client/Server Systems* (Prentice Hall, 1993) and how/why did I decide to write two companion books instead of one large one. The following discussion, somewhat anecdotal, should help.

My first book covered a broad range of issues in distributed computing (networks, middleware, applications, and management issues). Due to the size (it exceeded 700 pages), I eliminated about 100 pages of application related topics from that book. During 1993 and 1994, I became involved in numerous application engineering/reengineering and IT infrastructure projects and wrote a few tutorials, as part of my practice, on emerging topics such as data warehouses, application architectures, distributed objects, and legacy data access. During a 1994 year-end conversation with my friend Paul Becker, a senior editor at Prentice Hall, we both concluded that the world could most certainly use another book by me that concentrated on the distributed application issues (the first book had only one chapter on this topic).

I started developing the manuscript at the end of 1994 but soon found that I needed to explain many of the IT infrastructure components, especially the perplexing middleware, before delving into the applications issues. So I did. The end result was that the new book was huge (more than 800 pages with roughly half on middleware and the other half on applications). After several conversations with Paul Becker, we both decided to break the material into two companion books: one on middleware and the other on application (re)engineering. This seemed to be a good idea because distributed computing is a vast and rapidly evolving field and it is difficult to discuss everything in one book. The following table attempts to show the interrelationships between my three books in terms of the following building blocks of distributed computing:

- **Networks** to provide the transport services in distributed computing environments
- **Middleware** to enable the distributed applications
- **Applications** to provide business value
- **Management and support issues** to deal with administrative aspects of distributed computing

Topics Discussed in Books on Distributed Computing

Topics	"Distributed Computing and Client/Server Systems" (1993)	"Object-Oriented Client/Server Internet Environments" (1997)	"Application (Re)Engineering: Building Web-based Applications and Dealing with Legacies" (1997)
Networks	Extensive coverage (6 chapters)	Light coverage (1 chapter)	No coverage
Middleware	Moderate coverage (3 chapters)	Extensive coverage (9 chapters)	Light coverage (1 chapter)
Applications	Light coverage (1 chapter)	No coverage	Extensive coverage (10 chapters)
Management and Support	Moderate coverage (2 chapters)	No coverage	No coverage

I received a great deal of help during this process from several people at Prentice Hall. Of particular note are Eileen Clark as the production editor of both books, Maureen Diana as an administrative assistant and fire fighter, and Paul Becker as an overall "spiritual leader."

Of course, my best friend and my wife, Dolorese, valiantly saw me through this undertaking. She has, as always, shown exceptional patience and tolerance for which I am greatly indebted to her. She continues to advise me and helps me in editing and preparing the material. It is a good example of teamwork.

P A R T   I

GETTING STARTED

Chapter 1: Application (Re)Engineering—The Big Picture

Chapter 2: Object-Oriented Client/Server
Internet Environments—The IT Infrastructure

Chapter 3: Methodology Overview: Planning and Modeling

1

Application (Re)Engineering
—The Big Picture

3

1.1   Introduction

Profound changes are taking place in the business world today. Increased demands for flexibility, pressures to respond quickly to market conditions, intense local and global competition, and continued business process reengineering and improvement for enterprise efficiency are the typical characteristics of enterprises circa 1997. Driven by these, and other pressures, companies are using Information Technologies to fundamentally transform the way they organize work and conduct business [Baster 1997], [Cronin 1996], [Hayashi 1996], [Davenport 1995], [Henderson 1993], [Keen 1991], and [Charan 1991]. In particular, enterprises are relying on applications that are leveraging the following key technologies to deliver business value:

- **World Wide Web (Web)**. This Internet-based technology is widespread because it allows ubiquitous and easy access to a very wide range of resources (e.g., files, databases, programs) from Web browsers. For example, Boeing's IT managers reportedly reach 20 times more customers with their new Web-based parts sales system [Varney 1996, August].

- **Object-orientation**. Adoption of object-oriented technologies is common as a foundation for increased productivity in the initial deployment and subsequent changes. For example, extensive analysis of over 5,000 products by Capers Jones of Software Productivity Research, Inc. indicates that reuse of OO programs increases to 80 percent in the third year [Sutherland 1994].

- **Client/server**. Distributed systems, especially based on the client/server architectures, are commonly being used for improving flexibility through widespread employment of remote servers (database servers, transaction servers, object servers). For example, a 1996 Gartner Group report indicates that client/server architectures will continue to play a strong role and largely coexist/mesh with World Wide Web in the modern enterprises.

These applications, termed *object-oriented, client/server, Internet-based (OCSI) applications,* are a special class of distributed applications for the enterprises of the 1990s and beyond. In fact, most of the new applications being developed at present and in the near future will be based on the OCSI paradigm due to the interest in Web technologies, distributed objects, and widely distributed servers. The basic contention of this book is that these three powerful technologies should be viewed as complementing each other and not as replacements for each other. This view is being echoed by others due to the synergies between these three appealing technologies [Robicheaux 1996]. According to this paradigm, the knowledge workers have access to Web browsers residing on desktop computers that are interconnected over fast digital networks. The resources (databases, programs, HTML pages) dispersed among different sites around the globe appear as objects that can be created, viewed, invoked, modified, and deleted on an as-needed basis. For example, a worker can perform the following operations from his/her desktop or mobile computer:

- Review "inbox" that displays e-mail, voice mail, magazines received (i.e., simulate a real mail box).

- Respond to urgent matters (these may appear as red flashing icons).

- Query the status of his/her projects and browse through a variety of information sources (e.g., documents, databases).

- Interact with multiple applications that may be dispersed around the globe (many of these applications and resources are "encapsulated" as objects).

- Invoke a multitude of operations (e.g., business transactions and data analysis) which may involve client/server interactions and bulk data transfers between a variety of computers (PCs, UNIX machines, mainframes).

- Participate in conference calls, telephone conversations, faxes, and videoconferences over the Internet/Intranet.

This new paradigm shift is raising the following questions for the IT community:

- How can one build (i.e., engineer) new applications to take full advantage of these paradigms?

- What strategies are needed to deal with (i.e., reengineer) existing (legacy) systems?

- How can one understand and analyze the ever-evolving infrastructure, especially the middleware, needed to support this paradigm?

The focus of this book is on the first two questions; the third question is addressed in the companion book (*Object-Oriented Client/Server Internet Environments*, A. Umar, Prentice Hall, 1997). This book is not concerned with "static" Web applications that allow you to simply browse through hypertext information (e.g., HTML pages). Instead, we are interested in the class of enterprisewide Web-based applications that utilize the OCSI paradigm. In particular, the goal is to explore, with an enterprise view, the interrelationships and trade-offs between several "hot" areas such as distributed objects, Web-based applications, data warehousing, enterprise data architectures, application software architectures, integration and access of legacy applications through Web, and application migration strategies. In other words, we will help guide you through the application (re)engineering jungle shown in Figure 1.1 and will suggest an approach that synthesizes enterprise business issues and technological considerations into a single framework.

This chapter gives a broad overview of the subject matter and attempts to set the tone for the rest of this book by answering the following questions:

- What are the key building blocks and classifications that can be used as a framework for discussion (Section 1.2)?

- How can IT be aligned with business needs (Section 1.3)?

- What is application (re)engineering; how does it interrelate to business process reengineering and what are its core activities (Section 1.4)?

- What are the main objectives of this book and what is the overall approach to discuss the various topics (Section 1.5)?

- What is the overall state of the art, state of the market, and state of the practice in this field (Sections 1.6 through 1.8)?

Key Points

- Application (re)engineering = application engineering and/or reengineering

- Object-oriented, client/server, Internet-based applications are expected to meet the demands of the businesses of the 1990s and beyond. Client/server architecture provides the fundamental framework to allow the object-orientation, Web, and other emerging technologies to plug in for the applications of the 1990s and beyond.

- Tying BPR (business process reengineering) with application (re)engineering aligns IT with business and should be an essential aspect of modern IT practice.

- Modern enterprises use a broad range of applications (decision support, operational support, real time) which can operate within departments, within the boundaries of an enterprise, or between enterprises.

- Application engineering/reengineering efforts must respond to business needs by effectively utilizing the IT infrastructure and the embedded legacy systems.

Figure 1.1 The Application Jungle

Web Applications   Distributed Objects   Legacy Systems

Object-Oriented Distributed Applications   Application Architectures

Legacy Application Reengineering   Three-Tiered Architectures

Data Architectures   Legacy Data Access   Data Warehousing

Data Allocation   Legacy System Migration   Mediation Technologies

Web Access to Corporate Information

Object-Oriented Client/Server Internet Environments

? ? ? ? ?

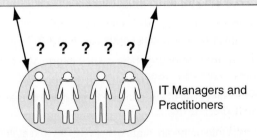

IT Managers and Practitioners

1.2   Concepts and Definitions

1.2.1   A General Framework

Figure 1.2 shows a simple framework that depicts three high level components and their role as drivers and enablers in the contemporary enterprises:

- Business processes
- Applications
- IT infrastructure

Figure 1.2 Interrelationships Between Key Components

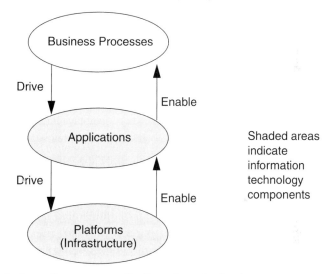

Note: This framework shows the common situation where the business processes drive the technology (i.e., application and platforms). We will consider other situations where the technology can drive the business processes in Section 1.3 "Aligning IT with Business Needs."

Business processes represent the day-to-day business related activities of an enterprise (e.g., manufacturing a car, book publishing, operating a cable TV company, operating an airline, running a bank, providing mail delivery, teaching students, etc.). For example, if you want to open a training business, then business processes need to be established for advertising, enrolling students, scheduling class rooms, etcetera. Business processes support corporate goals and thus establish the requirements and the business drivers for the lower level technology utilization. Business processes may be centralized or distributed—most medium to large organizations distribute business processes among multiple sites (e.g., cars are designed in one place, assembled in many places, and shipped to dealers at several places).

Internet, Intranet, Extranet, and the Web

Due to the popularity of these terms, let us quickly define them here (more details are given in Chapter 2):

- *Internet, also known as the "Public Internet,"* is a network of unrestricted/unregulated networks that are interconnected to give the appearance of a large global network.Technically, Internet is based on the IP (Internet Protocol) stack.

- *Intranet* is a private Internet used by a corporation for its internal use (i.e., an internal IP network). Intranets are used to provide corporate services and they use the Web technologies, in addition to others (e-mail, database access).

- *Extranet* is the Internet (privately or collaboratively owned) that is used exclusively for business-to-business communications. Extranets are becoming popular because the public Internet is not suitable for serious business-to-business activities (e.g., electronic commerce).

- In reality: Internet = Public Internet + Intranets + Extranets.

- *World Wide Web (WWW)*, also known as *Web*, operates on top of the Internet to support users and applications.

- World Wide Web is based on the following concepts and technologies:
  - Web servers that house the resources (data, application programs).
  - Uniform Resource Locator (URL) is an address used by the Web to locate resources.
  - Hypertext Transfer protocol (HTTP) is a protocol used by the Web browsers and Web servers to exchange information.
  - Hypertext Markup Language (HTML) is a language used to create hypertext documents that can be displayed on the browsers.
  - Web browsers are ubiquitous GUI tools, available on almost all computing platforms, that exploit HTTP, URL, and HTML to access the Internet resources in a generic fashion.
  - Web navigation and search tools are used to "surf" the Internet.
  - Web gateways to non-Web resources are used to allow Web users to access non-Web resources (e.g., corporate databases).

- WWW's unique feature is that it makes hypermedia available on the Internet in what has evolved into a global information system.

- The same Web interface can be used for applications that cross the company, industry, and country boundaries.

- Java is a programming language designed to work on the Web. The main thing is that Java applications (known as Java *applets)* can run on the Web browsers (i.e., the user desktops). This allows Web browsers to run applications at the user desktops instead of relying on remote Web servers.

- Web access to relational databases is provided through "relational gateways" that serve as translators and mediators between Web browsers and relational database managers.

Business Scenarios and Short Examples

Businesses are regularly using Internet home pages to advertise their products and services to the Internet users. Some companies, such as SAS Institute, are planning to put all of their documentation on Web [Fryer 1996]. The following scenarios exemplify how businesses are exploiting the object-oriented client/server Internet environment at present (also see the sidebars on the next few pages on electronic commerce, data warehouses, and intelligent agents):

- **Web based purchasing systems** that allow users to search company catalogs for certain price ranges and then place orders for chosen product(s). For example, the Chrysler Web site built by NeXT Corporation allows customers to search the site for several specific models of cars, at different price ranges, in different colors, and sorted in different ways. Each time, the user is instantly presented with a Web page that includes all the cars requested.

- **Modern database applications** that are invoked from Web browsers. For example, a company has a Human Resource application that operates as a client/server model. The Human Resources application uses the clients on desktops that access remotely located data that may be located in Oracle or mainframe DB2 database. The Web access to Human Resource applications is provided through Web browsers.

- **Electronic shopping malls** that allow Web users to shop and purchase products over the Internet. For example, the Internet Shopping Network is a start-up company that sells about 35,000 computer hardware and software products over the Internet. These systems combine the catalogs and legacy data access.

- **Communities of Interest** (COI) users rely on Web access for exchanging messages, transferring files, sending mail and using EDI (Electronic Data Interchange) transactions for the COI. For example, the real estate COI users access real estate documents and databases through Web browsers. COIs are becoming more sophisticated with incorporation of work flows and multimedia presentations.

- **Image processing applications** that require sending, processing and editing of images such as X rays for the medical industry, photographs used in claims processing for the insurance industry, proofs and advertisements in the publication industry, and visualization of systems dynamics in the aerospace industry.

- **Groupware systems** that allow users to prepare documents, exchange files and use electronic mail. More recent systems use Web browsers to exchange voice, data, and video for numerous office applications. For example, new teleconferencing systems display text, pictures, and video/voice on different windows of a work station.

- **Collaborative computing applications** that go beyond the computer conferencing and groupware software to cooperatively solve problems. These systems may include high definition TV and "artificial life" animations. An example is the extensive "decision support systems" that allow location-independent teams to work cooperatively as if they were in the same room (talk, see each other, review each other's documents, etc.). It is important to provide all these facilities through one common user interface (i.e., the Web).

Applications provide automated support to the business processes. Applications, for the purpose of this book, are *business aware*. For example, an airline reservation system contains business logic and data that is not the same as a hotel reservation system (business awareness). Applications also *provide business value to an enterprise*. Obviously, an airline reservation system provides business value to the airline business. Applications use the information technologies to support the enterprise and thus are enablers to the business processes. Modern enterprises use applications such as marketing support systems, automated order processing and tracking systems, electronic commerce systems, telecommunications provisioning systems, and real-time manufacturing control systems. Applications consist of a user database (a pool of data), a set of programs to access and manipulate the database, and user interfaces to execute the programs. An application may also be centralized (all of its components at one site) or distributed (its components reside at different computers on a network).

The *IT platforms* are used to build, deploy, and operate the applications. IT infrastructure, also known as computer-communication platform, consists of technologies such as computers, networks, databases, and transaction managers (we will discuss IT infrastructure in the next chapter). IT infrastructure enables the applications and is *business unaware*. For example, the same type of networks and computers are used in airline reservation systems and hotel reservation systems. An important part of the platform is *middleware*, an increasingly crucial and, at the same time, bewildering component of the modern IT infrastructure. Middleware is needed to interconnect and support applications and users across a network. Middleware services typically include directories, facilities to call remotely located procedures, and software to access and manipulate remotely located databases. Middleware services are typically provided by specialized software packages (for example, Lotus Notes is a middleware package that supports groupware applications). However, middleware services may reside in a combination of database management systems, computer operating systems, and transaction management systems. Middleware is explained in great detail in [Umar 1997].

Figure 1.3 refines the simple framework presented in Figure 1.2 and highlights the following key points that are essential for IT managers and practitioners:

- The business processes provide the requirements that should drive the applications and the IT infrastructure.
- Applications enable the business processes and IT infrastructure enables the applications. This must be kept in mind while making IT infrastructure choices.
- IT infrastructures (this includes middleware), does not add any direct business value. For example, installing a fast network may not help a company unless the network is used effectively to meet business needs.
- IT infrastructure enables applications and, if not handled properly, can disable applications and business processes. For example, New York Stock Exchange trading traffic topped out at 608 million shares due to computer and network congestion instead of reaching the daily maximum of 1.4 billion shares on October 20, 1987.[1]

---

1. Hayes, M., "The Tale of Two Cities," *Information Week,* December 1995, pp. 58–64.

Voice over the Internet—Talking Applications

Making phone calls over the Internet is gradually gaining popularity. According to a 1996 International Data Corp (IDC) report, about a half million users are already using voice over the Internet; this number could go as high as 63 million users if RBOCs (the Regional Bell Operating Companies) get into the Internet business. Software is becoming commercially available that converts voice into data packets that are shuffled across the Internet like any other data packets (e.g., e-mail messages, hypertext pages, database queries). Many Internet service providers (ISPs) are adding voice options to their services.

Although many companies are considering voice over the Internet as an alternative to telephone services, some are beginning to develop "talking applications." For example, a corporate home page may include an audio icon which, if clicked, connects the user to an operator or to an application that uses audio input/output. Some products are beginning to appear that combine phone services with e-mail systems. Many interesting talking applications are currently being envisioned in marketing and customer support.

Users of these applications need powerful desktops (minimum 25 MHz 486 PC), 14.4 Kbps modem (26.8 Kbps is preferable), Internet access, sound card, speakers, microphone, and the client software that converts audio to/from data packets. Most of the voice systems are currently directory-based, that is, each service provider maintains a directory of users that are voice enabled. Users log onto the server, review the list of other users who are logged on (the receiving party must be logged on to receive a call), and then clicks on a user address to initiate a call. Once again, the other party may be a human being or an application.

There are a few roadblocks that stand in the way to the explosion of Internet telephony. Examples of these roadblocks are lack of common standards (so what is new!), poor transmission quality, and regulation problems. But most of these problems can be solved.

Sources:

   IDC Report, "Voice over the Internet," 1996.

   Gareiss, R., "Voice over the Internet," *Data Communications,* September 1996, pp. 93–100.

   Levy, S., "The Rise of Internet Telephony," *Datamation,* August 1996, pp. 64–67.

- A key role for the IT infrastructure in the 1990s and beyond is to enable enterprisewide distributed applications to support the distributed business processes. For example, business processes are typically distributed to support a dispersed business topology (e.g., different branch and local offices). However, many applications that support these distributed business processes are still centralized due to lack of adequate IT infrastructure (e.g., slow/congested networks and lack of tools to manage and support distributed applications).

Figure 1.3 A Framework for IT's Role

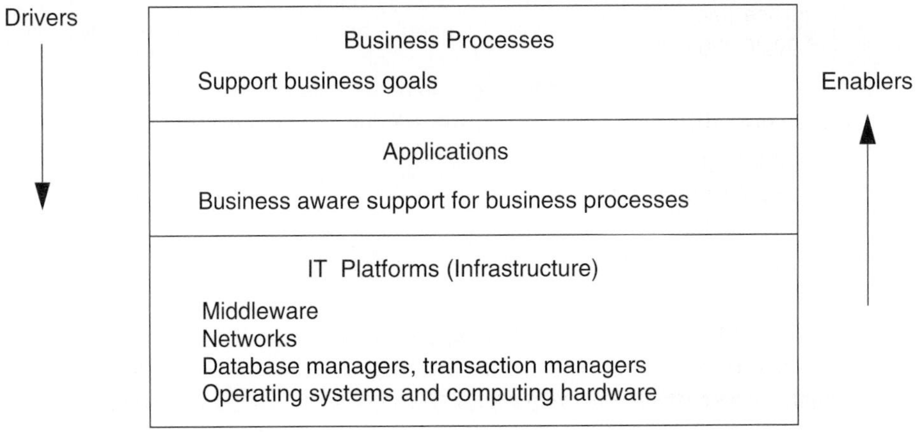

Drivers

Business Processes Support business goals
Applications Business aware support for business processes
IT Platforms (Infrastructure) Middleware Networks Database managers, transaction managers Operating systems and computing hardware

Enablers

1.2.2 Application Concepts and Components

Applications are a crucial aspect of modern enterprises because they can enable, and if not handled properly, disable business processes. As stated previously, an application represents the *business aware* functionality and data. Examples of applications are business aware systems such as airline reservation systems, inventory control systems, financial planning systems, material handling systems, and the like. These systems are used by organizations to gain/retain competitive edge, reduce costs, and improve management decision making. From a business point of view, systems such as e-mail, word processors, text editors, operating systems and Web browsers are not applications, because they are not business aware.

An application consists of three components:

- *Application datasets* D = (d1,d2 . . .) that contain the information needed by the enterprise activities. Examples of this information are customer information, payroll information, design data, product information, and corporate plans. This data may be physically stored in flat files, relational databases, object-oriented databases, or under any other database management system. More and more applications are beginning to store enterprise "knowledge" in the form of rules in databases. In addition, some real-time databases may be stored in main memory for fast access.

- *Application programs* P = (p1, p2 . . .) to perform business operations (e.g., bookkeeping, credit checking), engineering/scientific functions (solid modeling, simulations, animations, drawings), manufacturing operations (e.g., robotics), and/or expert systems inferences. The programs code the business rules, also known as business intelligence, that represent the functional logic unique to the user organization (not the data, not the user interface).

- ***User presentation programs*** U = (u1, u2 . . .) to process the user access to the application data and programs. The user interfaces may be simple text command/response systems, pull-down menus, graphical user interfaces, speech recognition systems, and video systems with a pointing device (mouse). With the expected growth of multimedia applications, the user interfaces are beginning to include sophisticated combinations of voice, text, and video on the same screen.

Figure 1.4 shows how different applications can be configured in terms of data, processing, and user interface components. These components of an application may be centralized or distributed. In a ***distributed application,*** the application components (user interface, user data, and programs) reside at different computers on a network. On the other hand, all application components of a ***centralized application*** are restricted to one computer. In this book, we are primarily interested in distributed applications that employ object-orientation and World Wide Web. In these applications, the user interface processing resides on Web browsers, the user data typically resides on remote data servers, and the application logic can reside on the data server, Web browser site, another "middle tier" machine, or some combination thereof.

Figure 1.4 Conceptual View of Different Applications

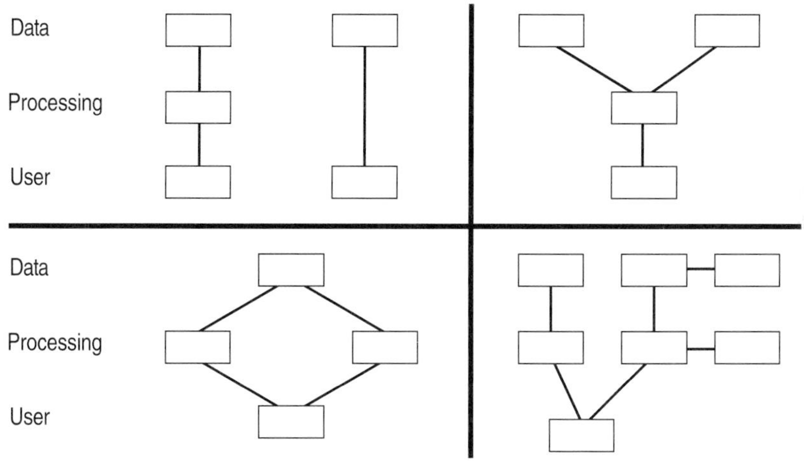

Note: Applications can be simple (few components) or complex (many components). Application components can be assigned to different machines and can employ different technologies (e.g., Web technologies in user interfaces, object-orientation in processing logic, and relational databases for data storage and retrieval).

1.2.3   A Classification of Applications

Applications in modern enterprises are multidimensional and complex. For our purpose, we focus on two dimensions of applications: **type** and **span** (see Table 1.1). Application types, for the purpose of our discussion, are subdivided into operational support, decision support/ retrieval, and real-time applications. The span indicates the level of usage (e.g., departmental applications, enterprisewide applications, and interenterprise applications). The sidebars on the next five pages exemplify a few interesting applications.

This two dimensional view of applications will help us in determining the most appropriate strategies for engineering of new and reengineering of existing applications. Why? Mainly because there is "no one size fits all" approach. Some approaches and tools work well for decision support applications while others work for operational support applications. In addition, some technologies work quite well for small departmental applications but not for large interenterprise applications of the same type. We will present a methodology in Chapter 3 that will allow us to systematically deal with the wide range of issues related to (re)engineering of applications of different types at different spans.

TABLE 1.1 A CLASSIFICATION OF APPLICATIONS

SPAN \ TYPE	Operational Support (Transaction Processing)	Decision Support (Browsal and Analysis)	Real Time (Embedded in Real Life)
Group/ Departmental	Example: Regional inventory control	Example: Regional marketing information system	Example: Videoconferencing within a group
Enterprisewide	Example: Enterprise-wide cash management systems	Example: Corporate data warehouses	Example: Enterprise-wide desktop video conferencing and network management
Interenterprise	Example: Electronic commerce over the Internet and "Extra-nets" (business to business transactions over Internet)	Example: Databases to support browsing for Communities of Interest	Example: "Talking applications" over the Internet and distributed multimedia over the Internet

Electronic Commerce Takes Off

Electronic commerce, the conducting of business over a network, has taken off due to the availability of Web technologies over the Internet. A 1996 survey conducted by the Giga Information Group indicates that US companies already buy $500 billion worth of goods electronically each year—a small fraction (about 10 percent) of their total purchases (Source: Verity, J., "Invoice? What's an Invoice?" *Business Week,* June 10, 1996, pp. 110–112).

Most of the electronic commerce activities are concerned with buying and selling over the networks.However, numerous other business activities (e.g., exchanging legal business documents) are included within the scope of electronic commerce. In particular, different industry segments (known as "communities of Interest") are engaging in increased business activities over the networks. Here are some examples from different industry segments.

Automotive: ANX (Automotive Network eXchange) between AIAG, Caterpillar, Chrysler, Ford, GM, John Deere for information common to the automotive industries.

Healthcare: HOST (Healthcare Open Systems and Trials) for work flows among doctors, hospitals, insurance companies

Government: Numerous bidding and procurement projects in the Department of Navy and Department of Defense.

Telecommunications: Bell Atlantic's evaluated receipt and billing system linking BA to its suppliers

Banking: MCI's Rapid*EDI for immediate fund transfer and notification

Publishing: Museum on-line (French Ministry of Cultures)

Education: Education brokerages being formed for "just-in-time" education

Others: Real estate, military, local governments, financial, insurance, etc.

To support these and other activities, a large number of vendors have gotten into the electronic commerce business (e.g., IBM's Electronic Commerce Center) and many Business Schools have started offering courses and concentration in electronic commerce.

Major Sources of Information:

Kalakota, R. and Whinston, A., *Frontiers of Electronic Commerce,* Addison Wesley, 1996.

Adam, N., and Yesha, Y., editors, *Electronic Commerce,* Springer, 1996

Communications of the ACM, June 1996 (Special issue on Electronic Commerce)

Electronic Commerce World (an online journal at http://ecworld.utexas.edu)

IDC Industry Reports on Electronic Commerce

Health Industry Goes High-Tech

The $1 trillion health-care industry is under siege due to new competitors and pressures to contain costs. There is reportedly 10 to 20 percent waste in this industry (this amounts to $100 to $200 billion). To respond to these pressures, health-care companies are embracing a range of technologies such as the Internet, data mining tools, data warehouses, object-orientation, and high-speed private networks. These technologies are being employed to restructure the businesses, enter new markets, improve customer relations, develop products and services, streamline distribution, and reduce bottom line. The main idea is to interconnect hospitals, doctors, drug makers, and drug distributors through Internet and then provide powerful object-based querying and transactional capabilities to minimize paperwork.

Source:

> Gambon, J., "Healthcare Gets Technology Transfusion," *Information Week*, July 1, 1996, pp. 14–19.

Operational Support applications support the day-to-day operational activities of an organization. A large number of operational support applications are categorized as OLTP (on-line transaction processing). As the name implies, these applications support on-line users and require robust transaction processing facilities such as logging, integrity control, and backup/recovery. OLTP applications are typically involved in the day-to-day operational activities such as order processing, purchasing, shipping, and inventory control. As a result, they tend to update data frequently and require immediate response. Examples of the operational support applications are shown in Table 1.1. The major characteristics of these applications are:

- Operations are performed on current values of data
- Data is updated frequently by a large number of users
- Operations on data are predictable (nondiscovery and not ad hoc)
- Majority of users are line workers and clerical staff
- Data integrity and concurrency requirements are high (usually hundreds of concurrent users need to access the most current information)
- Stringent response time requirements (usually subsecond)
- Detailed, and usually small, amount of data is accessed

Decision support (retrieval) applications are primarily intended for a class of users known as "knowledge" workers and managers. A large body of management literature on decision support systems has accumulated since the mid-1980s (see for example, the textbooks by [Sauter 1997], and [Turban 1993]). Decision support applications focus on informational data to drive the business and not on operational data to help in the day-to-day operation of a company. Examples of decision support applications are data warehouses, marketing information systems, executive information systems, and business planning systems. The characteristics of these applications are:

- Operations are performed on archival data

- Data is not application captive, instead it is integrated across different applications (enterprise data)

- Data is queried frequently and updated very infrequently

- Queries are ad hoc and used in a discovery and browsing mode

- Users are typically decision makers and knowledge workers

- Data integrity and concurrency requirements are low (for example, data can be slightly outdated for long range planning)

- Response time requirements are typically not stringent

- Large amounts of data (typically joins between very large relational tables) are processed

---

Data Warehouses and Data Mining Become Big Business

Data warehousing, initially popularized by IBM as "Information Warehouse," is receiving a great deal of industrial attention at present. Many conferences and seminars are devoted to the planning, development, and deployment of data warehouses. An IDC survey conducted at the end of 1994 indicated that 10 percent of the companies surveyed expressed an interest in data warehouses. At the end of 1995, the same survey indicated that 90 percent of the companies were interested in data warehouses.

Data warehouses are being established in many organizations to provide access to operational data by creating a repository instead of providing "universal" access to operational data through mediators. Initial implementations of data warehouses concentrated on simple query and analysis tools. But data mining tools are increasingly playing a key role in data warehousing because they utilize statistical analysis and pattern recognition techniques to answer business questions. These tools exploit a combination of AI and statistical analysis to discover information that is hidden or not apparent through typical query and analysis tools. The availability of massive amounts of corporate data in data warehouses has provided a rich field for these tools to mine.

Data warehouses—typically large relational databases—are becoming increasingly accessible from Web. The users of the warehouses are employing Web browser based tools for querying and analysis. An example of the data warehouse Web tools is the OLAP (On-line Analytical Processing) Web Gateway from Arbor Software. Web-based data mining is a natural area of growth.

Data warehouses are discussed in detail in Chapter 10.

Real-time applications are embedded in real life activities such as manufacturing processing. While the operational support and decision support applications provide information to users, the real-time applications *are part of* a real life process. Due to this, these applications impose stringent requirements for performance (subsecond response time) and availability (continuous and often fault tolerant). Examples of real-time applications are voice applications over the Internet, manufacturing control systems, real-time market data monitoring and analysis systems, command and control systems, and telecommunications network managers. The main characteristics of real-time applications are:

- Application processes are closely tied to real life
- Response time and availability requirements are "hard" (must be met)
- Most data is kept in main storage to improve performance
- Data integrity requirements are low (data change several times per second, so if you do not like the current value—wait for a second!)

These applications can be used at different span levels: **group/departmental level, enterprisewide,** and **interenterprise**. The group/departmental applications are developed and used within a work group or a department of an enterprise. These applications are typically developed around LANs and can use the latest technologies (e.g., C/S, OO) effectively. The enterprisewide applications are used throughout an enterprise. These applications use the LAN as well as WAN technologies and are typically heterogeneous because they span across a diverse array of computers (PCs, Macs, UNIX, Mainframes), networks (LANs, WANs), and database managers (Informix, Oracle, DB2). Utilization of new technologies for large enterprise networks is more challenging. However, the use of Internet within organizations (known as "Intranets"), is spreading rapidly. Interenterprise applications are used between enterprises. A good example of these applications are the Communities of Interest that are being formed between vertical industry segments (health industry participants) to share common information.

1.3   Aligning IT with Business Needs

It is essential to use information technology (IT) effectively to engineer/reengineer business applications. Basically, information technology must be aligned with the business needs of an organization. For example, Michael Hammer [1990] defines business process reengineering (BPR) as the use of the power of modern IT to radically redesign business processes in order to achieve dramatic improvements in performance. In essence, IT must enable the organization to survive and prosper in the competitive global economy. While there is a general agreement on the importance of aligning IT with business, the approaches and views differ widely. This short discussion is intended to establish an overall context within which the issues of application engineering/reengineering can be presented.

Intelligent Agents: Another Frontier

Intelligent agents (IAs) provide an interesting area of research to use artificial intelligence in Internet and the World Wide Web (WWW). Intelligent agents, also known as Virtual Agents and Knowbots, are intelligent software entities that simulate the behavior of "capable" human agents such as an experienced travel agent or an insurance agent. In particular, IAs are capable of autonomous goal-oriented behavior in a heterogeneous computing environment. An example of an IA is a software entity that extracts, organizes, and presents information on a given topic (e.g., ancient history). Another example is an intelligent agent that makes travel arrangements (e.g., makes reservations, purchases tickets) for a trip within time and money constraints. Yet another example is a buyer agent that might travel across the Internet to find the seller agent offering the best possible deal for a given commodity.

The key characteristics of Intelligent Agents are:

- Knowledge representation (rules, semantic networks)
- Learning capabilities (acquire new knowledge)
- Goal specification and reasoning (backward/forward reasoning)
- Interaction with environment (e.g., network, databases)
- Interact with other agents (human or software)
- Object orientation (each IA is an object)
- Deal with unexpected situations
- Use mobile code where needed (e.g., Java)

IAs have many potential applications in Internet because of the large volume of information that needs to be organized and presented in a wide variety of ways. Many research prototypes at present are directed towards making the Internet intelligent by using IAs. Examples of the research projects are: the Internet Softbot at the University of Washington that roams around the Internet collecting information; and Infosleuth at MCC that combines the Web with OO and AI to enable electronic commerce between large numbers of DOD (Department of Defense) participants. A practical example is the DHL tracking system that uses agent software to track where a particular package is [Varney, August 1996].

Sources:
A good source of information for IAs is the *IEEE Expert,* December 1996 Special Issue on Intelligent Agents. For IAs in Internet, the *IEEE Expert,* August 1995 Special Issue on Intelligent Internet Services is a good source (it also contains a large number of references on this topic). *Communications of the ACM,* 37(7), 1994, is a Special Issue on Intelligent Agents and *Object Magazine,* July/August 1995, has a special section on Intelligent Agents.

Different views and models for aligning IT with business needs have been discussed widely in the management literature [Davidson 1993], [Boar 1994], [Henderson 1990], [Keen 1991], [Luftman 1996], [Luftman 1993], [Teng 1995], and [Venkatraman 1984]. For example, Peter Keen [Keen 1993] proposes a "fusion map" between the information technology, business processes, and people and management. Keen's basic premise is that top management challenge is to make sure that technology, business processes, and people are meshed together, instead of being dealt with as separate elements in planning and implementation. Keen's "fusion map" describes the steps to enable such a strategy. William Davidson [Davidson 1993] presents a three phase transformation approach to effectively utilize information technology to reengineer business. His three-phase transformation process starts with structured automation of existing activities, builds on this automation to extend and enhance the original business, and then redefines the business itself (e.g., spawns new businesses).

While the models and approaches differ between IT management scholars, the basic principles of aligning business and IT are the same. Let us discuss a model presented by Henderson and Venkatraman [Henderson 1994] to illustrate the key concepts. This model is accepted in the IT management research community and has been used by many researchers as a framework for further work (see for example, [Luftman 1996, Luftman 1993]). In addition, this model has been adopted by IBM for management training and is used by the IBM Consulting Group. The basic Henderson-Venkatraman model views business and IT in terms of strategy and infrastructure (see Figure 1.5). The four closely interacting components of this model are: business strategy, IT strategy, business infrastructure, and IT infrastructure.

Figure 1.5 Henderson-Venkatraman (H-V) Strategic Alignment Model

	Business	IT
Strategy	Business Strategy	IT Strategy
Infra-structure	Business Infrastructure	IT Infrastructure

Henderson-Venkatraman (H-V) propose that IT can be aligned with business by involving not less than three components of the alignment model. The effort can be initiated (driven) from any component and then involve the other two. For example, the following scenarios for aligning IT with business processes can be envisioned (see Figure 1.6):

- **Business strategy->IT strategy->IT infrastructure.** In this case, the business strategy drives the IT strategy, which in turn influences the IT infrastructure. This common approach is depicted in Figure 1.6A.

- **Business strategy->Business infrastructure->IT infrastructure.** In this case, the business strategy drives the business infrastructure, which in turn influences the IT infrastructure (Figure 1.6B). This is the traditional BPR model.

- **IT strategy->Business strategy->Business infrastructure.** In some cases the IT strategy drives the Business strategy, which in turn influences the Business infrastructure. This scenario, shown in Figure 1.6C, is used in cases where organizations initiate new businesses due to their expertise in IT (this is happening in the telecommunications industry where the Baby Bells are entering the Internet market to take advantage of their networking know-how).

- **IT strategy-> IT infrastructure->Business infrastructure.** In this case, the IT strategy influences the IT infrastructure, which in turn influences the business infrastructure (Figure 1.6D).

Figure 1.6 Aligning IT with Business—A Few Scenarios

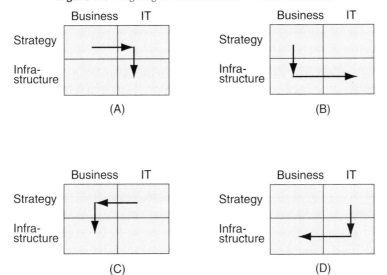

These scenarios show some of the interactions between IT and business. Naturally, other scenarios and interactions can be envisioned. An extensive discussion of these scenarios with different applications can be found in Luftman [1996].

1.4   What Is Application (Re)Engineering?

1.4.1   Responding to Business Needs—Tying BPR to IT

Simply stated, *application (re)engineering is concerned with development of new applications and the strategies to deal with existing (in many cases, legacy) applications.* The primary goal of this activity is to respond to business needs and align IT to business by exploiting the most appropriate technologies.[2] This activity ties the business process reengi-

---

2. Notice that we did not say the latest technologies. Appropriate technologies do not have to be the latest.

neering to application (re)engineering. Real strategic and sizable business gains do not result from (re)engineering only the applications but come from the combination of business (re)engineering along with the supporting application (re)engineering.

The mainframe-based systems developed in the 1970s and 1980s used the terminal host model where all business logic and data are restricted to one machine. These systems may not be flexible enough for the changing business needs of today. However, the life of IT personnel in the old days was quite simple—they focussed on new application logic because most of the platform issues were nonexistent (after all, you used whatever was available on the mainframe), the business needs and end-user expectations did not change quickly, very few off-the-shelf applications were available, and the issues of dealing/interfacing with existing applications were virtually nonexistent. The situation is considerably more complicated nowadays, illustrated in Figure 1.7, due to several reasons: (a) a very large number of platform options (i.e., large numbers of middleware and networking options), (b) an ever-increasing list of tools, (c) a significant embedded base of existing applications that may partially satisfy your needs, (d) an almost unlimited number of off-the-shelf applications, (e) changing business needs, and (f) high user expectations. At a high level, the contemporary enterprises face two key application-related questions:

> ***Application engineering.*** How can the *new* applications be developed efficiently by using the latest technologies (i.e., how do the new infrastructures help me in developing new applications)?

Some Cautions

- Real strategic and sizable business gains do not result from (re)engineering only the applications but come from the combination of business (re)engineering along with the supporting application (re)engineering. See the sidebar "Case Study: Federal Express Reengineers Business and Applications."

- IT should be used to enable business decisions and processes. Make sure that there are clear business drivers before you get carried away with the technology.

- Many new technologies that claim to eliminate existing N technologies themselves become $N+1$.

- The life cycle for the reason for undertaking an effort should be longer than the life cycle of the undertaking itself. In other words, if you undertake a two-year reengineering effort to save hardware cost, but hardware costs change in 6 months, you may be looking at a very tough year and a half.

- Distribution is not always good. Replacing a mainframe with multiple PCs may be like replacing a horse with 100 chickens to pull a cart. You face similar coordination problems!

- There is a thin line between vision and hallucination. You should know when you cross it.

Application reengineering. How can the existing applications be dealt with (i.e., how can new applications be integrated with existing applications, and when/how/if the existing applications should be transitioned)?

This book addresses both of these questions (application (re)engineering = application engineering and/or reengineering).We will discuss application engineering in Part II and application reengineering in Part III of this book. Figure 1.8 illustrates the application engineering/reengineering challenges in terms of databases and application software. For example, application engineering requires new databases and new software (the shaded area). Application reengineering, however, can occur due to the need to utilize existing databases and/or software.

Figure 1.7 The Application (Re)Engineering Challenge

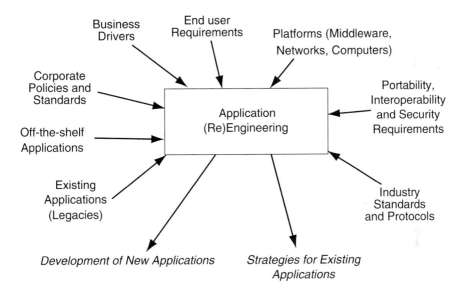

Figure 1.8 The Engineering/Reengineering Dilemma

	New Database(s)	Existing Database(s)
New Application Software	Application Engineering	Reengineer existing database(s)
Existing Application software	Reengineer existing application software	Reengineer application software plus database(s)

Case Study: Federal Express Reengineers Business and Applications

The Optically Recorded Information Online Network (ORION) project at Federal Express is a good example of utilizing new information technologies while reengineering their business processes.

ORION was conceived in response to the inability of alternative methods (paper, microfilm, microfiche) to cope with the massive documentation needed for its more than 90,000 employees worldwide. Instead of just an archiving system, ORION has virtually eliminated all manual data and has allowed secure and instant access to documents worldwide. This was accomplished through systematically combining technological innovation with organizational changes. In particular, the project was conducted in three stages of reengineering that systematically replaced the character-based with GUI devices. In each stage, the customers, input devices, output devices, indexing schemes, and network were clearly specified. In addition, the work flow was reengineered in each stage and the organizational/staff issues were carefully taken into account. The key factors for the success of this project are:

- Strong sponsorship from senior management

- Information systems group served as enabler and facilitator instead of leader

- Focus on integration with existing systems

- Effective staging of technical and organizational changes

- Constant review and analysis of evolving technologies

- High initial investment on nontechnical issues such as end-user training

Source:
   Candler, J., et al., "The ORION Project: Staged Business Process Reengineering at FedEx," *Communications of the ACM,* February 1996, pp. 99–107.

The engineering/reengineering of applications and databases may be initiated due to business process reengineering, introduction of new services/products, business realignment, mergers/acquisitions, etc. For example, in order to improve customer order processing, a new application may need to be developed or existing applications or databases may need to be reengineered. A common example of application (re)engineering at present is the melding of Web technologies with the existing applications and databases.

The following subsections discuss the application engineering and reengineering issues. We will tie these issue together into a single methodology in Chapter 3.

1.4.2   Application Engineering—Building New Applications

Simply stated, application engineering is concerned with architecting, implementing, testing, and deploying all components of an application (i.e., databases, business logic, and user interfaces). Engineering of new applications, discussed in detail in Part II of this book, is an important area because many new applications are being developed at present. Our particular interest, as stated previously, is in the class of new applications that are being developed by combining three core technologies (we will discuss these concepts in more detail in Chapter 2):

- **Client/server.** This technology allows communications between computing processes, typically at different machines, which are classified as service consumers (**clients**) and service providers (**servers**). Simply stated, client/server environments allow application processes (business aware programs and subroutines) at different sites to interactively exchange information (e.g., transfer funds, query a database, send a request to a remote program).

- **Object-orientation.** Object-oriented technology is currently being widely used to develop reusable software. The basic idea is to view software systems in terms of "natural" objects such as customers and sales regions that can be easily created, viewed, used, modified, reused, and deleted over time. The goal is that the users view applications in terms of objects through graphical user interfaces; programmers develop code that performs operations on objects; and database managers store, retrieve, and manipulate objects.

- **Internet.** World Wide Web over the Internet allows access to resources located around the world. For all practical purposes, the Web provides a GUI interface called the browser, which can access information by pointing and clicking through hypertext linkages that chase unique resource identifiers called **Uniform Resource Locators (URLs)**. Most of the Internet work at present is document-centric—however, Web gateways are being developed rapidly for providing access to corporate databases and applications through Web browsers.

These ***object-oriented, client/server, Internet-based (OCSI)*** applications are a special class of Web-based applications (see the sidebar "Classes of Web-Based Applications"). Figure 1.9 shows an idealized view of OCSI applications. This view illustrates the following key points:

- Web browser is used to access hypertext documents, databases, and programs that may be located anywhere in the network.

- The application programs are becoming increasingly OO with the popularity of OO programming languages such as C++, Smalltalk, and Java. These programs appear as objects that can reside anywhere in the network and communicate with each other by using OO paradigm.

- The databases are largely non-OO. The databases are accessed from programs typically through SQL or other data access technologies.

- Object-orientation is used in at least one component of the application architecture. Most of the OO concepts are being used more on the client side of business logic, because OO technology is very useful for GUI programming.

- Client/server paradigm is used in at least one component of the application. In other words, user interfaces, application programs, and databases of an application are split across at least two machines.

Figure 1.9 Ideal View of Object-Oriented Client/Server Internet Applications

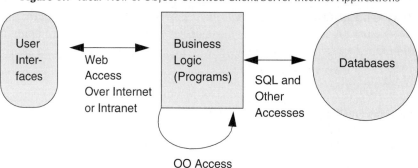

OO Access

The main idea is that you can use the cheap, ubiquitous, and user-friendly Web software as the integrating layer that sits on top of other layers of information. There is no need to abandon or retrofit existing investments. The "Web gateway" provides the necessary glue between the Web and non-Web world.

OCSI applications provide many benefits to IT by allowing the various computing activities to be dispersed across a network to maximize flexibility and availability. Given a suitable IT infrastructure, IT planners and architects can configure the applications by using mixtures of mainframes, microcomputers, and minicomputers to meet different business requirements and to respond to competitive pressures quickly. However, OCSI applications introduce many challenges in management, performance, and security, among others (see the sidebar "Why OCSI Applications: Promises and Pitfalls"). An application engineering approach, presented in Part II of this book, is needed that consists of the following main steps:

- Clearly understand and analyze the OCSI application issues (Chapter 4)
- Establish a data architecture (Chapter 5)
- Develop a software architecture (Chapter 6)
- Implement the application (Chapter 7)

Classes of Web-Based Applications

Static applications that retrieve, display, and browse precreated hypertext pages.

Web server-based applications that retrieve, display, and browse remote database information and/or invoke remote programs from Web servers through Web gateways.

Web browser-based applications that invoke Java applets that run on the Java-enabled browsers.

Object-oriented client/server (OCSI) applications that combine Web technologies with distributed objects and client/server middleware. Thus Web browsers may interact with objects that encapsulate back-end legacy systems or database servers. These three technologies provide a natural synergy for enterprisewide applications where object-orientation promote reusability, client/server promotes placement of resources where they are needed, and the Web browsers support ubiquitous access.

Why Object-Oriented Client/Server Internet-based Applications: Promises and Pitfalls

According to a 1996 Sentry Market Research survey report, almost 50 percent of the respondents are integrating Web into their client/server applications; the other 50 percent are planning to do so in the next 18 months [Fillon 1996]. In addition, distributed objects are moving into mainstream client/server applications with Web interfaces. For example, Netscape has reportedly shipped 20 million copies of CORBA-enabled browsers in 1996 [Linthicum 1997], and Microsoft has made ActiveX (a Web-distributed object technology) its main product direction. Why? Here are some potential promises and pitfalls.

Potential Promises

- Flexibility and scalability in supporting growing and ever-changing enterprises by offering desktop processing, departmental services, and corporate services through Web browsers.

- Give more end-user control and access to all users by allowing specialized clients on machines of their choice through ubiquitous Web browsers.

- Potential for improved availability and performance through duplicate servers and configuration options that can be offered as remote objects.

- More suitable for newer applications with different user interfaces (GUIs, voice, and other multimedia presentations).

- Industrial attention and interest leading to off-the-shelf Web-based servers, clients, tools, and applications, and resultant cost reductions.

Potential Pitfalls

- More "behind the scene" complexity due to:

    Multiple computing platform technologies
    Multiple network technologies and architectures
    Many new components (e.g., "middleware")
    Multiple suppliers
    Many interfaces, standards and protocols

- Many difficult management and support challenges, especially in end-user support (e.g., end-user effort in learning and operating desktops is higher, end-user help desks require more support, and many hidden costs at end-user sites emerge).

- Increased interdependencies and points of failures between numerous components arise because distributed applications are more complex.

- Software and staffing costs can be higher due to multiple licenses and environments, especially for middleware.

- Numerous security, performance, and interoperability issues arise.

- Several disciplines need more coordination (databases, networks, operating systems).

OCSI Application Engineering Issues. Adoption of OCSI paradigms should be evaluated very carefully. The best approach is to clearly specify the business drivers and application requirements. Based on this, a judgment needs to be made about how well the OCSI approach enables these drivers and requirements (not every application needs to be blindly developed by using Web, object-orientation and client/server technologies). If chosen, then the potential pitfalls need to be managed as risks. Chapter 4 gives an overview of the various issues and presents an approach for the engineering of OCSI applications.

Enterprise Data Architecture Considerations. This activity is a crucial undertaking for new applications because the requirements for many new applications may be satisfied by designing, developing, and deploying a new database. The new application functionality may be available through off-the-shelf packages or end-user tools such as GUI or Web-based spreadsheets, data browsers, and report writers. Data architectures are the primary activity for decision support applications, because decision support information is stored in a database that is accessed by desktop tools. Data architecture involves decisions such as how to partition the data, where to allocate the databases, and what will be the data interconnectivity software/hardware. We will discuss these issues in detail in Chapter 5.

Application Software Architecture Considerations. If new application software needs to be developed, then we can assume that this software will use object-orientation, C/S, and Web technologies. Establishing software architectures of such applications is a nontrivial task with a very wide range of options and trade-offs. For example, the architect has to divide the application logic between client and server modules, determine the communication paradigm to be used between clients and servers, decide on a two versus three-tiered architecture, and select appropriate infrastructure services. Chapter 6 discusses the application software architecture issues in detail.

Implementation Considerations. Ideally, applications should be implemented by using the most appropriate infrastructure services. However, the infrastructure services (e.g., networks, middleware, computing platforms) are evolving at the time of this writing. In particular, there are many middleware products that are becoming available as enablers of the new applications (see Umar [1997] for an extensive discussion of middleware). The architects/developers of new applications have to know how to choose and use the existing middleware. Chapter 7 discusses the concepts used in implementing new applications and illustrates the key concepts by using Web, DCE, Encina, Powerbuilder, and CORBA middleware.

1.4.3   Application Reengineering—Dealing with Legacies

Application reengineering is concerned with restructuring (i.e., interfacing, integration, migration) of existing application components (i.e., databases, business logic, user interfaces). Many of these applications can be "legacy" systems that are old, unstructured, and monolithic. According to Webster, legacy is something of value that is passed along to the next generation. Dealing with legacy applications, discussed in detail in Part III of this book, is a dominant concern of IT management at present. If possible, the IT management would like to keep the legacy systems as they are primarily because they provide vital services (e.g., billing) that are very risky to disrupt. However, something must be done about these systems because these systems are inflexible and are becoming increasingly expensive to maintain and operate. The core of the application reengineering challenge is: How should the existing (mostly legacy) databases and/or application software be used to satisfy the ever- evolving information needs of modern businesses?

Specific approaches to deal with legacy applications are:

- Understand the application reengineering problem and develop a reengineering strategy (Chapter 8)
- Combine and, if possible, integrate legacy applications with new (mostly Web-based) applications and tools (Chapter 9)
- Provide "shadow" systems (e.g., develop data warehouses) (Chapter 10)
- Migrate legacy systems to the new OCSI applications (Chapter 11)

Understanding Application Reengineering. Figure 1.10 shows the reengineering options in terms of databases and software. For example, application reengineering can occur due to the need to utilize existing databases and/or software. Some requirements can be satisfied by interfacing existing application software with existing databases. For example, an inventory control system may benefit by interfacing with different vendor databases that contain vendor product information. In particular, this type of linkage between existing databases and applications is a prerequisite for electronic order processing. Approaches to deal with legacy applications include a combination of application and data reengineering activities such as legacy data access, data migration, application migration, application reconstruction, and development of shadow databases and code.

Choice of appropriate approach depends on several factors such as business value of the legacy system, its technical value, and flexibility requirements. Chapter 8 discusses these approaches and outlines a methodology that can be used to choose an approach. Let us briefly review these strategies.

What Is a Legacy System—An Anecdote

Early in 1996, I attended a presentation on Java. The presenter mentioned legacy systems during his presentation in somewhat confusing contexts. I couldn't control myself and asked him: "What is a legacy system (according to you)?"

Without hesitation, the presenter said: "Anything that is not Java is legacy."

I was greatly amused.

Figure 1.10 Application Reengineering (Shaded Area)

	New Database(s)	Existing Database(s)
New Application Software	Application Engineering	Reengineer existing database(s)
Existing Application software	Reengineer existing application software	Reengineer application software plus database(s)

Access/Integration of Legacy Applications with Web. Interfacing and integrating the existing databases and applications with new object-oriented client/server Internet-based applications is a very desirable strategy for many business situations. This coexistence of old with new leverages the enterprise investment in existing systems and takes advantage of new technologies. For example, many new Web-based applications and tools need information that resides in existing (in many cases, legacy) databases. Providing Web access to the existing databases through "Web gateways" is an area of a great deal of activity at present. We will discuss these approaches in Chapter 9.

Data Warehousing. A data warehouse is a repository of information (data) for decision support. Data warehousing is receiving a great deal of industrial attention at present as a viable approach to access legacy data, that is, instead of using gateways to access legacy data, the needed data are extracted and loaded into a data warehouse. The activities involved in designing a data warehouse are in principle similar to the database design activities. The differences are in determining the level of detail to be stored in the warehouse and the frequency with which the warehouse data are synchronized with the original data. Chapter 10 presents an overview of the data warehouse concepts, technologies, and development/ deployment issues.

Migration Strategies. In several cases, the legacy applications may need to be migrated partially or fully to the new platforms. Data migration, a popular approach, involves movement of data from one format/platform to another. In practice, data migration may include a wide range of issues such as data conversion (from nonrelational to a relational database), data transformation (the creation of summaries and views), data movement (the movement of mainframe databases to UNIX platforms), and data allocation (the determination of the locations where the data will be assigned and if redundant copies are needed). If data migration is not enough, then other portions of applications may need to be migrated. Application migration includes, in addition to data migration, code conversion, reengineering of user interfaces (e.g., replacement of existing user interfaces with Web browsers), and gradual migration of applications. Chapter 11 discusses the migration issues of large and mission-critical applications.

Many Faces of Reengineering

Reengineering means different things to different people. We will use the following definitions of reengineering:

- **Business process reengineering** is concerned with rethinking and redesigning business processes instead of automating existing processes [Hammer 1993].

- **Software reengineering** is concerned with conversion of the form and not of the functionality of the software [Chikofsky 1990].

- **Data reengineering** is concerned with conversion of data format and not its content [Aiken 1994].

- **Application reengineering** means that the application functionality does not change but its form changes. Application reengineering can involve data and/or software reengineering and may result in complete restructuring of an application.

- **Legacy application reengineering** concentrates on restructuring of legacy applications. In practice this means a combination of access, integration, re-architecture, and migration strategies.

1.5 Why This Book?

This book is intended to serve as a tutorial and a guide on developing (i.e., the engineering of) new applications and establishing/implementing strategies to deal with (i.e., the reengineering of) legacy applications in the emerging object-oriented client/server Internet (OCSI) environments. In particular, we attempt to answer the following questions:

- What are the key characteristics of modern distributed applications that use the OCSI paradigm and why are they important?
- What are the various issues in building new OCSI applications?
- What are legacy systems and why should they be dealt with?
- What are the strategies needed to deal with existing (legacy) applications?
- Where can additional information be found?

This book does not discuss platforms (e.g., middleware and networks) on which the modern applications reside. The relevant platform issues are discussed in detail in the companion book [Umar 1997]. Due to the widespread industrial applications and continuing research efforts in application engineering/reengineering, our discussion will include

- **State-of-the-Art** approaches, which are prototypes and/or research and development reports and papers
- **State-of-the-Market** information to show commercial availability of the approaches as products
- **State-of-the-Practice** information to show that the approaches/products are actually being actually used by organizations.

A coverage of all three aspects is important because, due to the delays and filters built into the industry, only a few of the state-of-the-art ideas become state of the market, and even fewer become state of the practice (Figure 1.11). Focus on one area only (state of the art) does not give the reader the necessary breadth. The book will intentionally cover different views, perspectives, and interrelationships. The approach used in this book is shown in Figure 1.12 (i.e., a coverage of the terms, concepts, building blocks, and interrelationships instead of detailed discussion of one topic or a broad, brush discussion).

Figure 1.11 Different States of Technologies

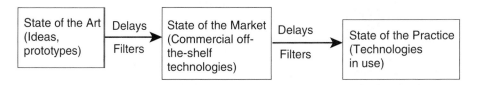

Figure 1.12 Different Views of Application Engineering/Reengineering

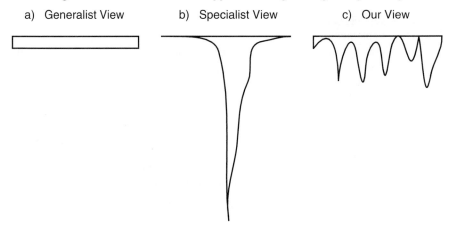

Figure 1.13 shows the book roadmap. The first part of this book consists of three chapters that introduce the subject matter (this chapter), describe the main building blocks of an OCSI environment, and suggest a general application engineering/reengineering methodology. Part II consists of four chapters that explore the detailed issues in building new applications. Strategies to deal with legacy applications are discussed in four chapters of Part III of this book. Each chapter is written as a self contained tutorial on the subject matter. Different levels of discussion are included in each chapter (conceptual overviews, management summaries, trends, and technical details) to support different audiences. Each chapter concludes with a brief discussion of state of the practice (examples and case studies), state of the market (vendor products and relevant standards), and state of the art (research notes). Numerous references for additional study are provided at the end of each chapter.

Figure 1.13 Book Roadmap

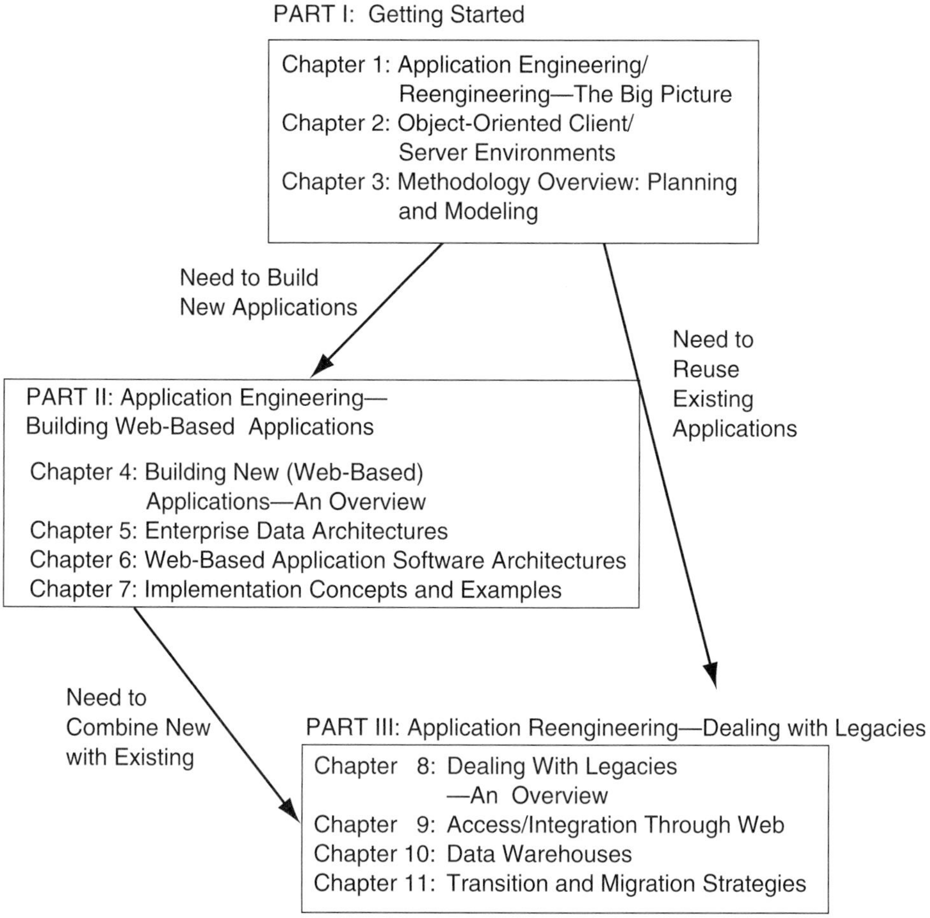

PART I: Getting Started

Chapter 1: Application Engineering/
         Reengineering—The Big Picture
Chapter 2: Object-Oriented Client/
         Server Environments
Chapter 3: Methodology Overview: Planning
         and Modeling

Need to Build
New Applications

Need to
Reuse
Existing
Applications

PART II: Application Engineering—
Building Web-Based Applications

Chapter 4: Building New (Web-Based)
         Applications—An Overview
Chapter 5: Enterprise Data Architectures
Chapter 6: Web-Based Application Software Architectures
Chapter 7: Implementation Concepts and Examples

Need to
Combine New
with Existing

PART III: Application Reengineering—Dealing with Legacies

Chapter 8: Dealing With Legacies
         —An Overview
Chapter 9: Access/Integration Through Web
Chapter 10: Data Warehouses
Chapter 11: Transition and Migration Strategies

1.6   State of the Practice: General Observations

Many new applications currently being engineered are either using or planning to use the object-oriented client/server Internet architectures to some extent. In addition, many efforts to reengineer legacy applications are underway. Success stories and future plans are published in the trade literature (e.g., *Datamation, Client/Server Today, Database Programming and Design, Information Week),* are advertised over the Internet and appear in the vendor literature. Failures are rarely reported for obvious reasons (who will allow their employees to advertise that their corporate effort failed). However, a few moments of truth do trickle through. In particular, the initial euphoria about client/server seems to be somewhat moderated. See the sidebar "Failures—Lessons from the Client/Server Wave."

Failures—Lessons from the Client/Server Wave

No new technology is risk free. What we are calling OCSI is no exception. Although, this technology offers many promises, there are several potential pitfalls (see the sidebar "Promises and Pitfalls of OCSI"). Unfortunately, many pitfalls are discovered after the fact and are usually not paid attention to initially.

The client/server technology wave hit us all around 1992 as a cure for all the evils of the old mainframe-based systems. There have been, admittedly, several well documented C/S success stories (see, for example, the Client/Server Journal, *Computerworld,* June 1995 Special Issue, which contains 20 C/S success stories that have been reviewed and selected by a panel of experts). However, there have been numerous failures, albeit not well documented. Here are some examples of failures intended as lessons to be more cautious:

- *Information Week* C/S backlash survey conducted at the end of 1995 indicated that 80 percent of the respondents had to reevaluate, cancel, or pull back from a C/S development project. The reasons include lack of management support, poor system performance, and costs higher than expected [DePompa 1995].

- Early examples of failures are given in "Dirty Downsizing," *Computerworld,* Special Report, August 10, 1992. These examples show how some companies suffered major losses when they tried to replace their mainframes with Unix and/or PC-based C/S systems. Other examples of failures are presented by Simpson [1997], DePompa [1995], McGee]1996], and Jenkins [1996]. Reasons for these failures are repeatedly lack of management direction, difficulties of working with vendors, and immature technologies.

- A Gartner Group report [Dec 1995] includes a report card on C/S computing. Basically, the report card gives C/S computing failing grades on lowering costs (costs go up), higher availability (C/S systems tend to fail more often), and serviceability (too many components to service).

- The hidden costs of C/S have been much more than expected [Latch 1996]. According to a study conducted by the University of California at Berkeley's School of Business, every $1,000 spent on server hardware/software needs to be matched with $9,000 of management and maintenance costs [Jenkins 1995].

Sources:

Dec, K., "Client/Server—Reality Sets in," *Gartner Group Briefing,* San Diego, February 22–24, 1995.

DePompa, B., "Corporate Migration: Harder Than It Looks," *Information Week,* December 4, 1995, pp. 60–68.

Jenkins, A., "Centralization Strikes Again," *Computerworld Client/Server Journal,* August 1995, pp. 28–31.

Latch, C., "The Hidden Costs of Client/Server Computing," *Data Management Review,* November 1996, pp. 16–20.

McGee, M. and Bartholomew, D., "Meltdown," *Information Week,* March 11, 1996, pp. 14–15.

Simpson, D., "Are Mainframes Cool Again?" *Datamation,* April 1997, pp. 46–53.

How do typical IT environments look while all this application engineering/reengineering is going on. Figure 1.14 shows a conceptual view of a typical configuration of a typical organization. Private corporate networks were developed in the 1970s and 1980s to support the terminal-mainframe applications. These networks started supporting many new applications in the early 1990s to support the C/S paradigm. This introduced many database servers that are accessed from clients such as desktop browsers, report writers and the like. More recently, a few applications have started using distributed objects thus introducing object servers and object clients. Now, the Internet/Intranet "craze" has introduced Web browsers and servers around the corporate networks. In the meantime, some mainframe-based legacy applications have been migrated ("downsized") to client/server paradigms, and a few have been interfaced with new applications. In addition, data warehouses have been developed by many organizations to extract and store legacy data in relational databases for decision support users. The corporate networks are also typically connected to the Public Internet due to the resources available on the Public Internet. Figure 1.14 shows the result of this evolution.

Figure 1.14 Conceptual View of Typical Environments

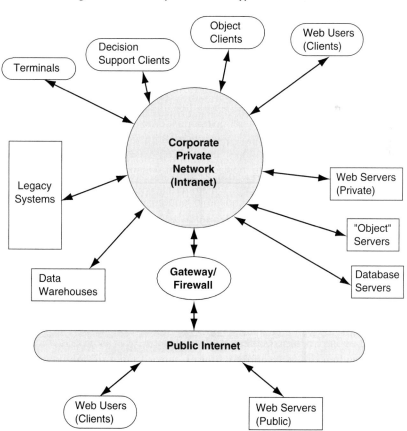

1.7　State of the Market: General Observations

A multitude of products from a diverse array of vendors are becoming available to support application engineering/reengineering. For example, middleware products and computer-aided software engineering (CASE) tools that allow application components, distributed across machines, to communicate with each other are readily available. The two-dimensional view of applications introduced in Section 1.2.3 can be used to understand the overall state of the application engineering/reengineering market at present. Table 1.2 shows the type of products that are available and being used for different classes of applications. This picture will change with time.

TABLE 1.2 STATE OF THE MARKET —A SUMMARY

TYPE / SIZE	Operational Support	Decision Support	Real Time
Group/Departmental	PC Windows-based transaction processing and OO products are still evolving	Many off-the- shelf products (mainly SQL-based) available for querying and browsing	Multimedia technology is maturing
Enterprisewide	OLTP over private corporate Internets (known as "Intranets") are gaining popularity	Web-based products for warehouses and group-ware for Intranets is becoming popular	Products becoming commercially available
Interenterprise	Electronic commerce is becoming popular	Web products for document centric work (e.g., HTML documents) are very mature	Good products not generally available

1.8　State of the Art: General Trends

The need for flexible and portable applications will continue to grow. The following interrelated trends are worth noting:

- Continuing application trends
  - Pressure to provide business value
  - Pressure to conform to business topology (i.e., businesses are distributed thus applications should be distributed too)
  - Increased use of object-oriented C/S systems over the Internet

- Continuing IT platform (infrastructure) trends
  - Middleware getting more sophisticated and intelligent
  - Networks getting faster
  - Computing hardware becoming faster, cheaper, more reliable
  - Operating systems becoming more efficient
  - Relational database managers becoming more efficient (object-oriented databases are still looming around)
  - Transaction managers (TMs) becoming portable and interoperable (e.g., TM from one vendor interoperating with database managers from different vendors)
  - Many off-the-shelf tools for decision support (4GL, spreadsheets, data browsers, etc.) growing
  - Computers becoming more personal and not shared
  - Integration of multimedia (e.g., text, voice, moving videos) for user presentations
  - Increased use of AI concepts to facilitate agent-based computing

Standardized APIs will play an important role because without standards each new middleware component will add more complexity (see Figure 1.15). A potential future scenario is the three-tiered architecture shown in Figure 1.16. In this scenario, the Web browser is used as a front-end to access Web resources over the public Internet or private Internet (Intranet). The middle tier will house Web resources and also serve as a gateway to the back-end corporate resources. The back-end corporate resources are accessed from the middle tier by using the traditional middleware such as remote procedure calls, remote SQL, and file transfers. The middle tier can serve as a transition gateway to gradually migrate the corporate resources to employ the distributed object technologies. This marriage of object-orientation with the Web is being recognized in the industry and convergence was initiated at the World Wide Web Consortium and Object Management Group (OMG) meeting held in June 1996. At present, platforms from different vendors are moving in this direction. For example, Netscape has announced distributed objects support for Netscape browsers and Microsoft has introduced the Active Platform that combines Web technologies with distributed objects and desktop tools (see Chapter 2 for more details).

Figure 1.15 The Role of Standardized APIs

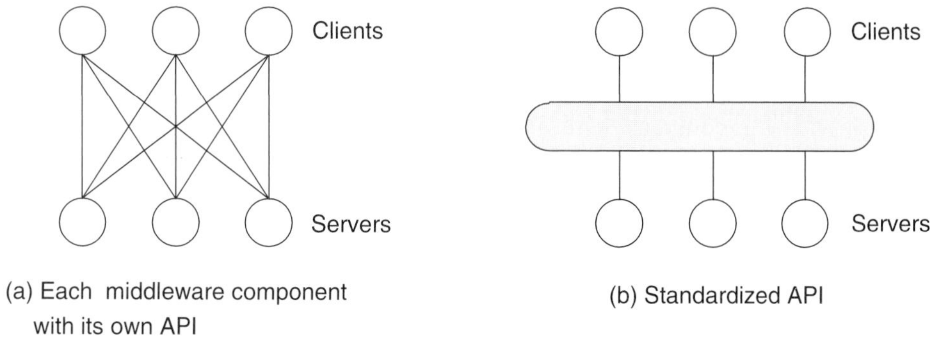

(a) Each middleware component
with its own API

(b) Standardized API

Several publications and articles discuss research and industry trends frequently. For example, *Communications of the ACM,* February 1997, is a special issue on the next 50 years of computing and contains many interesting articles on the social as well as technical aspects of computing. The *IEEE Computer Magazine,* October 1996, is also devoted to the long range computing issues. General industrial trends are discussed in Vaughn-Nichols [1997].

Figure 1.16 A Potential Future Scenario

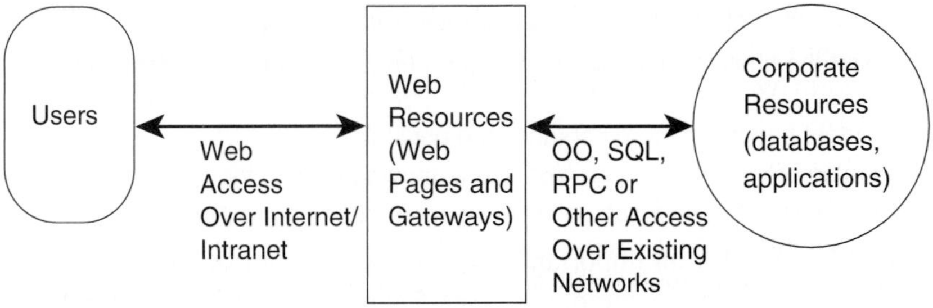

1.9   Summary

Most of the new applications being developed at present and in the near future will be based on the object-oriented, client/server, Internet-based (OCSI) paradigm that combines Web technologies with distributed objects and SQL-based middleware to deliver business value. The focus of this book is on how to build (i.e., engineer) new applications to take full advantage of this paradigm and how to deal with (i.e., reengineer) existing (legacy) applications. In this chapter we have presented a broad overview of the subject matter and have attempted to set the overall tone for rest of this book.

1.10   A Case Study

We will use the following case study, introduced in the companion book [Umar 1997], at the end of each chapter to illustrate the concepts introduced in this book.

XYZCorp was formed by Ms. Jones to provide technology solutions to a diverse array of industries. Ms. Jones believes that the latest OO, Web-based products that utilize C/S concepts, will provide the company with a competitive edge in a relatively crowded market. Here is her basic idea: build and market middleware and applications that allow different databases residing over different computers (mainframes, minis, desktops) to be accessed over different networks. The long range focus of the company is on Web-based distributed object applications (for internal use and external marketing). The company will also develop/acquire and market a variety of desktop tools. XYZCorp company wants to "field test" most of its services by trying them in-house. If needed, the company could also start offering consultation and training services.

The company headquarters are in Chicago with branch offices in the United States, Europe, and Asia. The company has currently about 3000 employees with a great deal of growth expected in the next two years. XYZCorp has recently acquired a company that builds desktops, laptops, "network computers," and personal digital assistants, has formed partnerships with numerous other computer hardware/software vendors and has acquired several retail electronic stores that sell and service microcomputers, televisions, VCRS, radios, and calculators. These stores will be used to market and service the company products.

The company operates many regional offices: Southern (Headquarters, Atlanta), Western (Headquarters, San Francisco), Eastern (Headquarters, New York), Midwestern (Headquarters, Detroit), North Western (Headquarters, Seattle), European (Headquarters, Paris), and Asian (Headquarters, Tokyo). Each region supports ten local offices (some of these offices are stores, the others are marketing, training, consulting, and support centers), with an average of 200 staff members per region. At present, many applications are operational at XYZCorp. Examples of some of the applications are:

- MVS-IMS-based administrative systems (payroll, accounts receivable, accounts payable)
- MVS-DB2-based financial system
- An old Unix-indexed file system for customer support
- Many Unix-Oracle-based regional systems
- Novell-based Human resource system at PC LANs

Ms. Jones has been thinking a lot lately. A corporate planning committee has been formed to establish an IT infrastructure that will allow the company to develop and support the variety of applications and services needed by the company that could also be marketed externally. The committee has recommended a major initiative to extend and integrate the applications that support the business processes (payroll, accounts receivable/accounts payable, order processing, marketing information systems, and computerized checkout systems), engineering processes (computer-aided design, computer-aided engineering, computer-aided process planning), and manufacturing processes (material requirement planning, production scheduling, and flexible manufacturing systems). The committee also has to decide what to do with the existing applications, including legacy. In particular, the planning committee will initiate and supervise the completion of a series of projects. As a starting point, the following projects have been initiated (we will discuss these projects in the chapters indicated):

- Review the IT infrastructure architecture that will support the XYZCorp applications and services. Specifically, is the existing infrastructure suitable to support OCSI applications? See Chapter 2.

- Adopt a methodology for the engineering of new applications and reengineering of existing (mostly legacy) applications for XYZCorp. In other words, how should the corporation approach the issues involved in building new Web-based applications and establish suitable strategies for dealing with its embedded base of mainframe-based legacy applications? See Chapter 3.

The initiative has identified a wide range of new applications that will use the OCSI paradigm. Examples of the new applications are: a new "advanced" inventory management system for integrated order processing/inventory management, a management planning system that will support the management decisions in marketing and product planning, and a flexible manufacturing system to automate the manufacturing of electronic products. The following application engineering projects have been initiated:

- Establish the requirements and an overall plan for these applications. What are the benefits and risks to develop these applications? What is the strategy to manage the risks? See Chapter 4.

- Develop the enterprise data architectures for the three applications. What will be the data allocation strategies? How will the data be accessed and shared across the XYZCorp network? See Chapter 5.

- Develop the application software architecture for the three applications. What are the logical components of these applications? How many tiers will be used? What will each tier do? What type of middleware components will you use? See Chapter 6.

- Implement the systems by using the chosen middleware components and develop detailed architecture diagrams that map the system to the underlying platform. These diagrams should show the pieces of the systems, where they reside, and how they interact with each other (i.e., middleware). See Chapter 7.

The initiative involves many legacy applications. Examples of the legacy applications are: a financial information system that processes financial data (e.g., personnel costs, materials costs, etc.) stored on the IBM mainframe in a DB2 Relational database, a mainframe-based corporate material requirement planning (MRP) system that contains a bill of materials (raw materials), information in IMS databases and outside vendor information in DB2 databases, and a UNIX-based order processing system that was developed in the 1980s to receive orders, verify them, and send them to mainframe for shipping/receiving and billing purposes. The following application reengineering projects have been initiated to establish:

- An overall strategy and a plan to deal with the existing legacy applications. In particular, which strategy will be selected and why (i.e., ignore, access/integrate in place, data warehousing, gradual migration, or "cold turkey"). See Chapter 8.

- An approach to access/integrate the MRP application with the inventory management system. In particular, how will you access the mainframe databases (IMS and DB2) through Web? See Chapter 9.

- A data warehouse to help within the scope of this initiative. What steps will you take to develop a data warehouse and why? See Chapter 10.

- A detailed migration plan for the re-architecture and transition of the order processing application to an OCSI paradigm. What specific steps in tools/techniques will be employed in this migration? See Chapter 11.

We will discuss these projects at the end of each chapter and give hints and guidelines about how these projects can be completed.

1.11 Problems and Exercises

1. In your view, what is the main strength of combining OO, C/S, and Web to deliver business value? What is the main weakness (risk)?

2. Give three specific examples to illustrate the OCSI applications.

3. How is the three-layered framework (Section 1.2) influenced by the Henderson-Venkatraman Strategic Alignment model (Section 1.3) scenarios where IT drives the business strategy?

4. Suppose that you have been asked to develop a two-day management training program in application (re)engineering in the modern distributed environments. What topics will you cover in this program?

1.12 Additional Information

Literature on different aspects of application engineering and reengineering is growing steadily. The sidebars on the following pages point you to books, technical journals and trade magazines where you can find additional information about this growing area. We will present numerous other sources of additional information as we go along.

Andrews, G., "Paradigms for Interprocess Interactions in Distributed Programs," *ACM Computing Surveys,* March 1991, pp. 49–90.

Aiken, P., Muntz, A., and Richards, R., "DOD Legacy Systems—Reverse Engineering Data Requirements," *Communications of the ACM,* May 1994.

Baster, G., "Business Components for End-User Assembly," *Object Magazine,* January 1997, pp. 38–45.

Boar, B., *Practical Steps for Aligning Information Technology With Business Strategies,* John Wiley, 1994.

Bernstein, P., "Middleware: A Model for Distributed Systems Services," *Communications of the ACM,* February 1996, pp. 86–98.

Chikofsky, E., and Cross, J., "Reverse Engineering and Design Recovery—A Taxonomy," *IEEE Software,* January 1990, p. 13.

Cronin, M., *The Internet Strategy Handbook,* Harvard Business School Press, 1996.

Davenport, T., *Process Innovation: Reengineering Work Through Information Technology,* Harvard Business School Press, 1993.

Davenport, T., "Cultivating an Information Culture," *CIO Magazine,* January 1995.

Davenport, T., and Short, J., "The New Industrial Engineering: Information Technology and Business Process Reengineering," *Sloan Management Review,* Vol. 31 (No. 4), pp. 11–27.

Davidson, W., "Beyond Re-engineering: The Three Phases of Business Transformation," *IBM Systems Journal,* Vol. 32, No. 1, 1993, pp. 65–79.

Dec, K., "Client/Server—Reality Sets in," *Gartner Group Briefing,* San Diego, February 22–24, 1995.

DePompa, B., "Corporate Migration: Harder Than It Looks," *Information Week,* December 4, 1995, pp. 60–68.

Eckerson, W., "Searching for the Middleground," *Business Communications Review,* April 1995, pp. 46–50.

Fillon, M., "What's Ahead for 1997," *Client/Server Computing,* December 1996, pp. 32–43.

Fryer, B., "Intranet Mania," *Datamation,* June 15, 1996, pp. 54–57.

Hackathorn, R., and Schlack, M., "How to Pick Client/server Middleware," *Datamation,* July 15, 1994, pp. 52–56.

Hammer, M., "Reengineering Works: Don't Automate, Obliterate," *Harvard Business Review,* Vol. 68, No. 4, pp. 104–112, 1990.

Hammer, M., "Hammer Defends Reengineering," *The Economist,* November 5, 1994, p. 70.

Hammer, M., and Champy, J., *Reengineering the Corporation: A Manifesto for Business Revolution,* Harper Collins Publishers, 1993.

Hayashi, A., and Varney, S., "Six Hot Technologies for the 21st Century," *Datamation,* August 1996, pp. 68–73.

Henderson, J., "Plugging into Strategic partnership: The Critical IS Connection," *MIT Sloan Management Review,* Vol. 31, No. 3, 1990, pp. 7–18.

Henderson, J., and Venkatraman, "Strategic Alignment: Leveraging Information Technology for Transforming Organizations," *IBM Systems Journal,* Vol. 32, No. 1, 1993, pp. 4–16.

Javenpaa, S., and Ives, B., "The Global Network Organization of the Future: Information Management Opportunities and Challenges," *Journal of Management Information Systems,* Spring 1994, pp. 25–57.

Jenkins, A., "Centralization Strikes Again," *Computerworld Client/Server Journal,* August 1995, pp. 28–31.

Keen, P., *Shaping the Future,* Harvard Business School Press, Boston, 1991.

Keen, P., "Information Technology and the Management Difference: A Fusion Map," *IBM Systems Journal,* Vol. 32, No. 1, 1993, pp. 17–39.

Latch, C., "The Hidden Costs of Client/Server Computing," *Data Management Review,* November 1996, pp. 16–20.

Linthicum, D., "Distributed Objects Get New Plumbing," *Internet Systems,* January 1997, pp. 4–5.

Luftman, J., *Competing in the Information Age: Strategic Alignment in Practice,* Oxford University Press, 1996.

Luftman, J., Lewis, P., and Oldach, S., "Transforming the Enterprise: The Alignment of Business and Information Technology Strategies," *IBM Systems Journal*, Vol. 32, No. 1, 1993, pp.198–221.

McGee, M. and Bartholomew, D., "Meltdown," *Information Week*, March 11, 1996, pp. 14–15.

Ozsu, M., and Valduriez, P., *Distributed Database Systems*, Prentice Hall, 1991.

Richter, J., "Distributing Data," *Byte*, June 1994, pp. 139–145

Robicheaux, M., "Client/Server/Web: Extending Your Reach," *Object Magazine*, July 1996, pp. 50–53.

Sauter, V., *Decision Support Systems*, John Wiley, 1997.

Sutherland, J., "Business Objects Architecture: Key to Client/Server Development," *Data Management Review*, November 1994, pp. 46–50.

Teng, J., and Kettinger, W., "Business Process Redesign and Information Architecture: Exploring the Relationships," *Database Advances*, February 1995, pp. 30–42.

Turban, E., *Decision Support and Expert Systems*, 2nd ed., Macmillan, 1993.

Umar, A., *Distributed Computing and Client/Server Systems*, Prentice Hall, 1993.

Umar, A., *Object-Oriented Client/Server Internet Environments*, Prentice Hall, 1997.

Vaughan-Nichols, S., "Object Futures: The Ten Trends of 1997," *Object Magazine*, January 1997, pp. 54–55.

Varney, S., "IS Takes Charge of Customer Service," *Datamation*, August 1996, pp. 46–51.

Varney, S., and McCarthy, V., "E-commerce: Wired for Success," *Datamation*, October 1996, pp. 42–50.

Venkatraman, N. and Camillus, J., "Exploring the Concept of 'Fit' in Strategic Management," *Academy of Management Review*, Vol. 9, 1984, pp. 513–525.

State-of-the-Art Periodicals and Conference Proceedings

The following conference proceedings and technical periodicals publish articles on technical and research issues related to middleware.

- International Conference on Distributed Platforms (held once a year; 1996 conference was held in Dresden, Germany, February, 1996)
- The International Conference on Distributed Computing Systems. This conference is held every year.
- IEEE Conferences on Data Engineering
- IEEE *Computer Magazine*
- IEEE *Software Magazine*
- IEEE Transactions on Software Engineering
- ACM Computing Surveys
- Communications of the ACM
- ACM Standard View

Related Books

At present, no single book covers different aspects of application engineering/ reengineering needed for the contemporary organizations (why do you think this book was written?). The following books discuss several topics that could be clustered under the general umbrella of application engineering/reengineering.

- Berson, A., *Client/Server Architectures*, McGraw Hill, 1993.

- Brodie, M.L., and Stonebroker, M., *Migrating Legacy Systems: Gateways, Interfaces & the Incremental Approach,* Morgan Kauffman, 1995.

- Cronin, M., *The Internet Strategy Handbook,* Harvard Business School Press, 1996.

- Inmon, W., *Developing Client/Server Applications,* QED, 1993.

- Khanna, R., *Distributed Computing: Implementation and Management Strategies*, Prentice Hall, 1993.

- Luftman, J., *Competing in the Information Age: Strategic Alignment in Practice,* Oxford University Press, 1996.

- Martin, J., and Leben, J., *Client/Server Databases,* Prentice Hall, 1995.

- Mowbray, T., and Zahavi, R., *The Essential CORBA,* John Wiley, 1995

- Mullender, S., Editor, *Distributed Systems*, ACM Press, Addison Wesley, 2d ed., 1993

- Orfali, R., Harkey, D., and Edwards, J., *Essential Client/Server Survival Guide,* John Wiley, 1994.

- Orfali, R., Harkey, D., and Edwards, J., *The Essential Distributed Objects Survival Guide,* John Wiley, 1996.

- Peterson, M., *DCE: A Guide to Developing Portable Applications,* McGraw Hill, 1995.

- Ryan, H., et al., *Practical Guide to Client/Server Computing*, Auerbach, 1997.

- Ryan, T., *Distributed Object Technology,* Prentice Hall, 1996

- Umar, A., *Distributed Computing and Client/Server Systems,* Prentice Hall, Revised Edition, 1993.

- Vaskevitz, D., *Client/Server Strategies: A Survival Guide for Corporate Reengineers*, IDG Books, 1993.

State of the Market/Practice Magazines and Periodicals

The following trade magazines publish case studies and new products:

- *Byte Magazine*
- *Client/Server Today*
- *Client/Server Computing*
- *Computerworld,* Weekly (section on networks and standards)
- *Database Programming and Design*
- *Data Management Review*
- *Datamation* (Cahners Publication)
- *Database Advisor*
- *Distributed Computing Monitor,* Patricia Seybold Group Publications
- *Gartner Group Reports on Client/Server*
- *IDC Industry Reports*
- *Information Week*
- *Infoworld,* Weekly (section on networks)
- *Internet Advisor*
- *Object Magazine*
- *Software Industry Report* (Computer Age Publication)
- *UNIX World*
- *Web Week*

2

Object-Oriented Client/Server Internet Environments—The IT Infrastructure

2.1   Introduction

Simply stated, an object-oriented client/server Internet (OCSI) environment provides the IT infrastructure (i.e., middleware, networks, operating systems, hardware) that supports the OCSI applications—the breed of distributed applications of particular interest to us. The purpose of this chapter is to explore this enabling infrastructure before digging deeply into the details of application engineering and reengineering in Parts II and III of this book, respectively. Specifically, we review the following three core technologies of the modern IT infrastructure:

- **Client/server** that allows application components to behave as service consumers (**clients**) and service providers (**servers**). See Section 2.2.

- **Internet** for access to application components (e.g., databases, business logic) located around the world from Web browsers. See Section 2.3.

- **Object-orientation** to let applications behave as objects that can be easily created, viewed, used, modified, reused, and deleted over time. See Section 2.4.

In addition, we will attempt to answer the following questions:

- How are the key technologies combined to support the modern applications (Section 2.5)?

- What type of general observations can be made about the state of the art, state of the market, and state of the practice in OCSI environments (Sections 2.6, 2.7, 2.8)?

- What are the sources of additional information on this topic (Section 2.13)?

The information in this chapter is intentionally high level and is an abbreviation of the companion book [Umar 1997] that discusses the infrastructure issues, in particular the middleware, in great detail.

Figure 2.1 will serve as a general framework for discussion. This framework, introduced in Chapter 1, illustrates the role of the following main building blocks of OCSI environments:

- Client and server processes (applications) that represent the business logic as objects that may reside on different machines and can be invoked through Web services

- Middleware that supports and enables the OCSI applications (see the sidebar "What is Middleware?")

- Network services that transport the information between remote computers

- Local services (e.g., database managers and transaction managers)

- Operating systems and computing hardware to provide the basic scheduling and hardware services

We will quickly scan these building blocks and illustrate their interrelationships in multivendor environments that are becoming common to support enterprisewide distributed applications.

Figure 2.1 Object-Oriented Client/Server Internet Environments

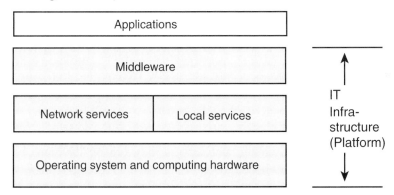

2.2 Client/Server Fundamentals

2.2.1 Definitions

Client/server model is a concept for describing communications between computing processes that are classified as service consumers (*clients*) and service providers (*servers*). Figure 2.2 presents a simple C/S model. The basic features of a C/S model are:

1. *Clients and servers are functional modules with well defined interfaces (i.e., they hide internal information).* The functions performed by a client and a server can be implemented by a set of software modules, hardware components, or a combination thereof. Clients and/or servers may run on dedicated machines, if needed. It is unfortunate that some machines are called "servers." This causes confusion (try explaining to an already bewildered user that a client's software is running on a machine called "the server"). We will avoid this usage as much as possible.

2. *Each client/server relationship is established between two functional modules when one module (**client**) initiates a service request and the other (**server**) chooses to respond to the service request.* Examples of service requests (SRs) are "retrieve

customer name," "produce net income in last year," etc. For a given service request, clients and servers do not reverse roles (i.e., a client stays a client and a server stays a server). However, a server for SR R1 may become a client for SR R2 when it issues requests to another server (see Figure 2.2). For example, a client may issue an SR that may generate other SRs.

3. *Information exchange between clients and servers is strictly through messages (i.e., no information is exchanged through global variables).* The service request and additional information is placed into a message that is sent to the server. The server's response is similarly another message that is sent back to the client. This is an extremely crucial feature of C/S model.

The following additional features, although not required, are typical of a client/server model:

4. *Messages exchanged are typically interactive.* In other words, C/S model does not support an off-line process. There are a few exceptions. For example, message queuing systems allow clients to store messages on a queue to be picked up asynchronously by the servers at a later stage.

5. *Clients and servers typically reside on separate machines connected through a network.* Conceptually, clients and servers may run on the same machine or on separate machines. In this book, however, our primary interest is in *distributed client/ server systems* where clients and servers reside on separate machines.

The implication of the last two features is that C/S service requests are real-time messages that are exchanged through network services. This feature increases the appeal of the C/S model (i.e., flexibility, scalability) but introduces several technical issues such as portability, interoperability, security, and performance.

Figure 2.2 Conceptual Client/Server Model

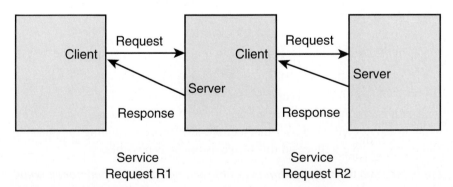

What Is Middleware?

Middleware is a crucial component of modern IT infrastructure. We will use the following definition of middleware in this book:

Definition: Middleware is a set of common business-unaware services that enable applications and end users to interact with each other across a network. In essence, middleware is the software that resides above the network and below the business-aware application software.

The services provided by these routines are available to the applications through *application programming interfaces (APIs)* and to the human users through commands and/or graphical user interfaces (GUIs).

A common example of middleware is e-mail because it provides business-unaware services that reside above networks and interconnect users (in several cases applications also). Other examples are groupware products (e.g., Lotus Notes), Web browsers, Web gateways, SQL gateways, Electronic Data Interchange (EDI) packages, remote procedure call (RPC) packages, and "distributed object servers" such as CORBA. We will briefly discuss these middleware components in this chapter.

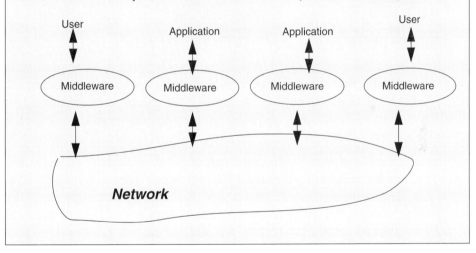

Client/server applications, an area of vital importance to us, employ the C/S model to deliver business aware functionalities. C/S applications provide a powerful and flexible mechanism for organizations to design applications to fit the business needs. For example, an order processing application can be implemented using the C/S model by keeping the order processing databases (customers, products) at the corporate office and developing/customizing the order processing logic and user interfaces for different stores that initiate orders. In this case, order processing clients may reside on store computers to perform initial checking and preprocessing, and the order processing servers may exist at the corporate mainframe to perform final approval and shipping. Due to the critical importance of C/S applications to business enterprises of the 1990s and beyond, we will focus on C/S applications in this book.

2.2.2   Client/Server—A Special Case of Distributed Computing

Figure 2.3 shows the interrelationships between distributed computing and client/server models. Conceptually, client/server model is a special case of distributed-computing model.

Figure 2.3 Interrelationships between Computing Models

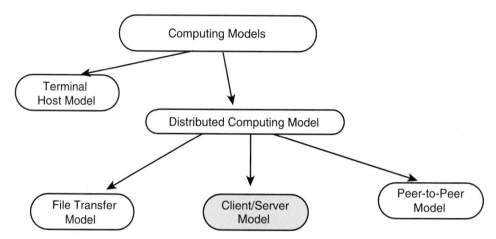

A *Distributed Computing System (DCS)* is a collection of autonomous computers intercon-nected through a communication network to achieve business functions. Technically, the computers do not share main memory so that the information cannot be transferred through global variables. The information (knowledge) between the computers is exchanged only through messages over a network.

The restriction of no shared memory and information exchange through messages is of key importance because it distinguishes between DCS and shared memory multiprocessor com-puting systems. This definition requires that the DCS computers are connected through a network that is responsible for the information exchange between computers. The definition also requires that the computers have to work together and cooperate with each other to sat-isfy enterprise needs (see Umar [1993, Chapter 1] for more discussion of DCS).

Distributed computing can be achieved through one or more of the following:

- File transfer model
- Client/server model
- Peer-to-peer model

File transfer model is one of the oldest models to achieve distributed computing at a very minimal level. Basically, programs at different computers communicate with each other by using file transfer. In fact, e-mail is a special case of file transfer. Although this is a very old and extremely limited model of distributed computing, it is still used to support loosely coupled distributed computers. For example, media clips, news items, and portions of corporate databases are typically exchanged between remote computers through file transfers; and e-mail is used frequently to exchange files through embeddings and attachments.

The C/S model is state of the market and state of the practice for distributed computing at the time of this writing. C/S model, as stated previously, allows application processes at different sites to interactively exchange messages and is thus a significant improvement over the file transfer model. Initial versions of C/S model utilized the remote procedure call paradigm that extends the scope of a local procedure call. At present, the C/S model is increasingly utilizing the distributed objects paradigm that extends the scope of local object paradigm (i.e., the application processes at different sites are viewed as distributed objects).

Peer-to-peer model allows the processes at different sites to invoke each other. The basic difference between C/S and peer-to-peer is that in a peer-to-peer model the interacting processes can be a client, server, or both while in a C/S model one process assumes the role of a service provider while the other assumes the role of a service consumer. Peer-to-peer middleware is used to build peer-to-peer distributed applications.

In this book, we will primarily concentrate on a C/S model. File transfer model is older and does not need additional discussion. We will also not dwell on the peer-to-peer model because peer-to-peer applications are not state of the market and state of the practice at the time of this writing.

2.2.3   Client/Server Architectures

Client/server architecture provides the fundamental framework that allows many technologies to plug in for the applications of 1990s and beyond. Clients and servers typically communicate with each other by using one of the following paradigms (see [Umar 1997, Chapter 3] for detailed discussion and analysis of these and other paradigms):

> *Remote Procedure Call (RPC).* In this paradigm, the client process invokes a remotely located procedure (a server process), the remote procedure executes and sends the response back to the client. The remote procedure can be simple (e.g., retrieve time of day) or complex (e.g., retrieve all customers from Chicago who have a good credit rating). Each request/response of an RPC is treated as a separate unit of work, thus each request must carry enough information needed by the server process. RPCs are supported widely at present.

> *Remote Data Access (RDA).* This paradigm allows client programs and/or end-user tools to issue ad hoc[1] queries, usually SQL, against remotely located databases. The key technical difference between RDA and RPC is that in an RDA the size of the result is not known because the result of an SQL query could be one row or thousands of rows. RDA is heavily supported by database vendors.

---

1. The term ad hoc for most of our purposes indicates improvised, spur of the moment activity.

Queued Message Processing (QMP). In this paradigm, the client message is stored in a queue and the server works on it when free. The server stores ("puts") the response in another queue and the client actively retrieves ("gets") the responses from this queue. This model, used in many transaction processing systems, allows the clients to asynchronously send requests to the server. Once a request is queued, the request is processed even if the sender is disconnected (intentionally or due to a failure). QMP support is becoming commonly available.

Initial implementations of client/server architecture were based on the "two-tiered"[2] architectures shown in Figure 2.4 (a) through Figure 2.4 (e) (these architectural configurations are known as the "Gartner Group" configurations). The first two architectures (Figure 2.4 (a) and Figure 2.4 (b) are used in many presentation intensive applications (e.g., XWindow, multimedia presentations) and to provide a "face lift" to legacy applications by building a GUI interface that invokes the older text-based user interfaces of legacy applications. Figure 2.4 (c) represents the distributed application program architecture in which the application programs are split between the client and server machines, and they communicate with each other through the remote procedure call (RPC) or queued messaging middleware. Figure 2.4 (d) represents the remote data architecture in which the remote data is typically stored in a "SQL server" and is accessed through ad hoc SQL statements sent over the network. Figure 2.4 (e) represents the case where the data exist at client as well as server machines (distributed data architecture).

Figure 2.4 Traditional Client/Server Architectures

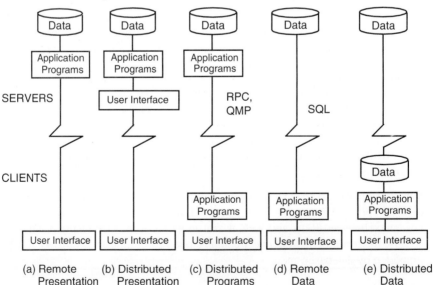

(a) Remote Presentation (b) Distributed Presentation (c) Distributed Programs (d) Remote Data (e) Distributed Data

---

2. We will discuss the tiers in great detail in Chapter 6.

Although a given C/S application can be architected in any of these configurations, the remote data and distributed program configurations are used heavily at present. The remote data configuration at present is very popular for departmental applications and is heavily supported by numerous database vendors (as a matter of fact this configuration is used to represent typical two-tiered architectures that rely on remote SQL). Most data warehouses also use a remote data configuration because the data warehouse tools can reside on user workstations and issue remote SQL calls to the data warehouse (we will discuss data warehouses in Chapter 10). However, the distributed programs configuration is very useful for enterprisewide applications, because the application programs on both sides can exchange information through messages.

2.2.4   OSF DCE—A Client/Server Environment

The Open Software Foundation (OSF) Distributed Computing Environment (DCE) packages and implements "open" and de facto standards into an environment for distributed client/server computing. OSF DCE, also commonly known as DCE, is currently available on a wide range of computing platforms such as UNIX, OS/2, and IBM MVS. Figure 2.5 shows a conceptual view of OSF DCE. The applications are at the highest level and the OSI transport services are at the lowest level in DCE (at present, DCE uses the TCP/IP transport services). The security and management functions are built at various levels and are applicable to all components. The distributed file access to get at remotely located data, naming services for accessing objects across the network, remote procedure calls (RPCs), and presentation services are at the core of DCE. As can be seen RPCs are at the core of DCE. Additional information about DCE can be found in Rosenberry [1993].

Figure 2.5 OSF DCE

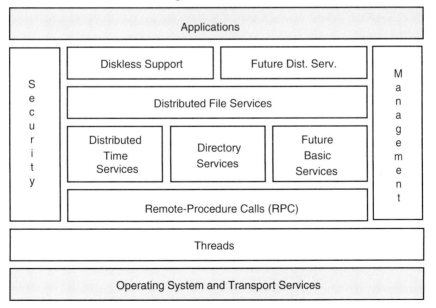

2.3   Internet and the World Wide Web (WWW)

Origin of the Internet is the ARPANET (Advanced Research Projects Agency Network) that was initiated in 1969 to support researchers on DOD (Department of Defense) projects. For many years, Internet had been used mainly by scientists and programmers to transfer files and send/receive electronic mail. The users of Internet relied on text-based user interfaces and tedious commands to access remote computing resources. In 1989, this changed with the introduction of World Wide Web (WWW), commonly referred to as the Web. The Web has been a major contributor in turning the Internet, once an obscure tool, into a household word. Why? Mainly because the Web allows users to access, navigate, and share information around the globe through GUI clients ("Web browsers") that are available on almost all computing platforms. The Web browsers allow users to access information that is linked through hypermedia links. Thus a user transparently browses around, or "surfs" around, different pieces of information that are located on different computers in different cities and even in different countries.

2.3.1   Internet, Intranets, and Extranets

Simply stated, Internet is a network of networks. Technically, however, Internet is a collection of networks based on the IP (Internet Protocol) stack. This protocol stack, initially referred to as the DOD (Department of Defense) or ARPANET Protocol Suite and commonly referred to as the TCP/IP[3] (Transmission Control Protocol/Internet Protocol) was designed to support e-mail, file transfer, and terminal emulation for ARPANET users. The services and protocols supported by IP have dramatically grown in popularity and have become the de facto standards for heterogeneous enterprise networks. At present, the term Internet is used to symbolize the IP (or loosely speaking, TCP/IP) networks in the following situations:

- **Public Internet,** or just the Internet, that is not owned by any single entity—it consists of many independent IP networks that are tied together loosely. Initially, the public Internet was used to tie different university networks together. With time, several commercial and private networks have joined the public Internet. The computers on the public Internet have publicly known Internet Protocol (IP) addresses that are used to exchange information over the public Internet (see discussion on addressing below). The public Internet at present consists of thousands of networks.

- Private Internets, or **Intranets**, are the IP networks that are used by corporations for their own businesses. Technically, an Intranet is the same as the public Internet, only smaller and privately owned (thus hopefully better controlled and more secure). Thus any applications and services that are available on the public Internet are also available on the Intranets. This is an important point for WWW, because many companies are using WWW technologies on their Intranets for internal applications (e.g., employee information systems).

---

3. Strictly speaking, TCP is one of the protocols that runs in the IP stack (see Figure 2.6). However, it is used most frequently, so the IP stack is commonly known as TCP/IP. Although imprecise, the term TCP/IP is so popular that we will have to use it.

- Business-to-business Internets, or **Extranets**, are the TCP/IP networks that are used for business-to-business activities. Technically, an Extranet is the same as the public Internet but is better controlled and more secure. Many electronic commerce applications between business partners are beginning to use Extranets. Any applications and services that are available on the public Internet are also available on the Extranets.

Basically: Internet = Public Internet + Intranets + Extranets

The following protocols (the first three belong to the original DOD Suite) are among the best known application protocols[4] in the Internet (see Figure 2.6):

- **Telnet:** This protocol is used to provide terminal access to hosts and runs on top of TCP.

- **File Transfer Protocol (FTP)**: This TCP-based protocol provides a way to transfer files between hosts on the Internet.

- **Simple Mail Transfer Protocol (SMTP)**: This TCP-based protocol is the Internet electronic mail exchange mechanism.

- **Trivial File Transfer Protocol (TFTP)**: This UDP-based protocol also transfers files between hosts, but with less functionality (e.g., no authorization mechanism). This protocol is typically used for "booting" over the network.

- **Network File System (NFS) Protocol**: This UDP-based protocol has become a de facto standard for use in building distributed file systems through transparent access.

- **Xwindow:** This is a windowing system that provides uniform user views of several executing programs and processes on bit-mapped displays. Although Xwindow is supposedly network independent, it has been implemented widely on top of TCP.

- **SUN Remote Procedure Call (RPC)**: This protocol allows programs to execute subroutines that are actually at remote sites. RPCs, similar to Xwindow, are supposedly network independent but have been implemented widely on top of TCP. SUN RPC is one of the oldest RPCs. Examples of other RPCs are OSF, DCE, RPC, and Netwise RPC.

- **Domain Naming Services**: This protocol defines hierarchical naming structures that are much easier to remember than the IP addresses. The naming structures define the organization type, organization name, etc.

- **SNMP (Simple Network Management Protocol):** This is a protocol defined for managing (monitoring and controlling) networks.

- **Kerberos**: This is a security authentication protocol developed at MIT.

- **Time and Daytime Protocol**: This provides machine-readable time and day information.

The **World Wide Web (WWW)** has introduced additional application protocols and services. For example, the Web browsers, the Web servers, and the HTTP protocol used in WWW reside on top of the IP stack (see next section). As the use of Internet grows, more services and protocols for the IP application layer will emerge.

---

4. An application protocol is a protocol that is used to exchange information between applications and users residing on different computers.

Figure 2.6 Technical View of Internet and World Wide Web

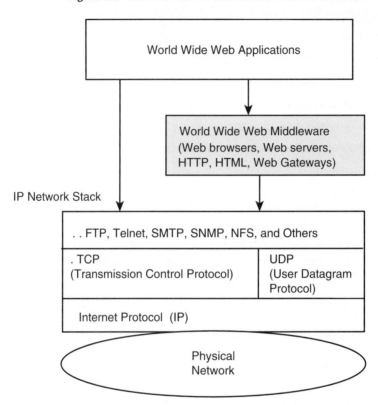

Note: The IP stack is commonly known as TCP/IP
because of the popularity of TCP to support
higher level services & applications

2.3.2   Overview of World Wide Web

World Wide Web (WWW) is a wide area information retrieval project that was started in 1989 by Tim Berners-Lee at the Geneva European Laboratory for Particle Physics (known as CERN, based on the laboratory's French name) [Berners-Lee 1993] and [Berners-Lee 1996]. The initial proposal suggested development of a "hypertext system" to enable efficient and easy information sharing among geographically separated teams of researchers in the High Energy Physics community.

Technically speaking, *WWW is a collection of middleware that operates on top of IP networks (i.e., the Internet).* Figure 2.6 shows this layered view. The purpose of the WWW middleware is to support the growing number of users and applications ranging from entertainment to corporate information systems. Like many other (successful) Internet technologies, the WWW middleware is based on a few simple concepts and technologies such as the following (see Figure 2.7):

- Web servers
- Web browsers
- Uniform Resource Locator (URL)
- Hypertext Transfer Protocol (HTTP)
- Hypertext Markup Language (HTML)
- Web navigation and search tools
- Gateways to non-Web resources

Figure 2.7 Conceptual View of World Wide Web

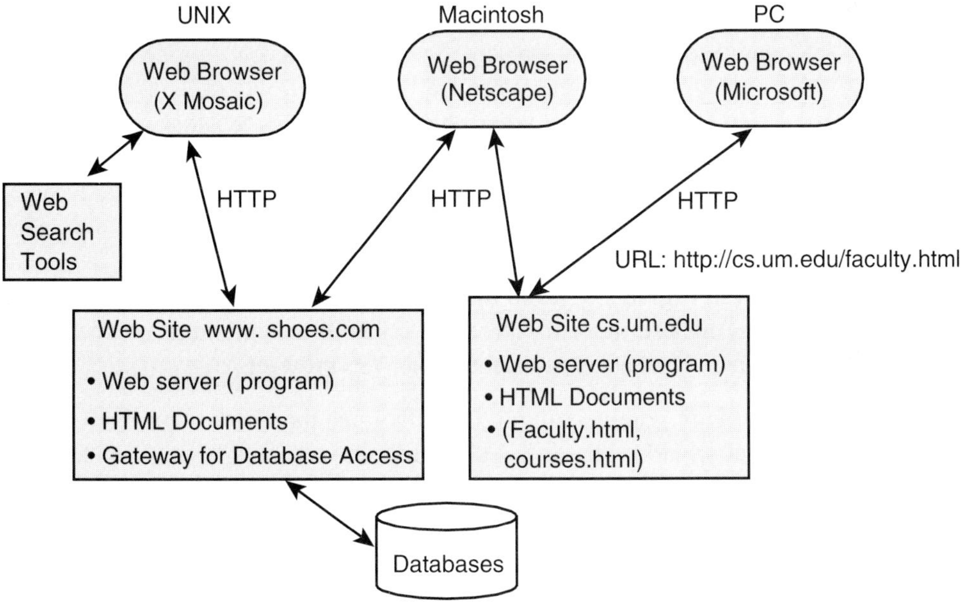

Let us briefly review these components and show how they tie with each other through an example.

Web sites provide the content that is accessed by Web users. Web sites are populated and in many cases managed by the ***content providers***. For example, Web sites provide the commercial presence for each of the content providers doing business over the Internet. Conceptually, a Web site is a catalog of information for each content provider over the Web. In reality, a Web site consists of three types of components: a Web server (a program), content files ("Web pages"), and/or gateways (programs that access non-Web content). A ***Web server*** is a program (technically a server process) that receives calls from Web clients and retrieves Web pages and/or receives information from gateways (we will discuss gateways later). Once again, a Web user views a Web site as a collection of files on a computer, usually a UNIX or Windows NT machine. In many cases, a machine is dedicated/designated as a Web site on which Web accessible contents are stored. As a matter of convention, the entry point to a Web site is a "home page" that advertises the company business. Very much like storefront signs in a shopping mall, the home pages include company logos, fancy artwork for attention, special deals, overviews, pointers to additional information, etc. The large number of Web sites containing a wide range of information that can be navigated and searched transparently by Web users is the main strength of WWW. Figure 2.7 shows two Web sites—one for a shoe shop (www.shoes.com) and the other for a computer science department for a university (cs.um.edu).

Web browsers are the clients that typically use graphical user interfaces to wander through the Web sites. The first GUI browser, Mosaic, was developed at the National Center for Supercomputer Applications at the University of Illinois. Mosaic runs on PC Windows, Macintosh, UNIX, and Xterminals. At present, Web browsers are commercially available from Netscape, Microsoft and many other software/freeware providers. These Web browsers provide an intuitive view of information where ***hyperlinks*** (links to other text information) appear as underlined items or highlighted text/images. If a user points and clicks on the highlighted text/images, then the Web browser uses HTTP to fetch the requested document from an appropriate Web site. Web browsers are designed to display information prepared in a markup language, known as HTML. We will discuss HTTP and HTML later. Three different browsers are shown in Figure 2.7. Even though these are different browsers residing on different machines, they all use the same protocol (HTTP) to communicate with the Web servers (HTTP compliance is a basic requirement for Web browsers).

Most browsers at present are relatively dumb (i.e., they just pass user requests to Web servers and display the results). However, this is changing very quickly because of Java, a programming language developed by Sun Microsystems. Java programs, known as ***Java applets,*** can run on Java-compatible browsers. This is creating many interesting possibilities where Java applets are downloaded to the Java enabled browsers where they run producing graphs/charts, invoking multimedia applications, and accessing remote databases.

Uniform Resource Locator (URL) is the basis for locating resources in WWW. A URL consists of a string of characters that uniquely identifies a resource. A user can connect to resources by typing the URL in a browser window or by clicking on a hyperlink that implicitly invokes a URL. Perhaps the best way to explain URLs is through an example. Let us look at the URL "http://cs.um.edu/faculty.html" shown in Figure 2.7. The "http" in the URL tells the server that an HTTP request is being initiated (if you substitute http with ftp, then an FTP session is initiated). The "cs.um.edu" is the name of the machine running the Web server. (This is actually the domain name used by the Internet to locate machines on the Internet.) The "/faculty.html" is the name of a file on the machine cs.um.edu. The "html" suffix indicates that this is an HTML file. When this URL is clicked or typed, the browser initiates a connection to the "cs.um.edu" machine and initiates a "Get" request for the "faculty.html" file. Depending on the type of browser you are using, you can see these requests flying around in an appropriate window spot. Eventually, this document is fetched, transferred to, and displayed at the Web browser. You can access any information through the Web by issuing a URL (directly or indirectly). As we will see later, the Web search tools basically return a bunch of URLs in response to a search query. The general format of URL is:

protocol://host:port/path

where

> *protocol* represents the protocol to retrieve or send information. Examples of valid protocols are HTTP, FTP, Telnet, Gopher, and NNTP (Network News Transfer Protocol)
>
> *host* is the computer host on which the resource resides
>
> *port* is an optional port number (this is not needed unless you want to override the HTTP default port, port 80)
>
> *path* is an identification, typically a file name, on the computer host

Hypertext Markup Language (HTML) is an easy to use language that tags the text files for display at Web browsers. HTML also helps in creation of ***hypertext link***s, usually called hyperlinks, which provide a path from one document to another. The hyperlinks contain URLs for the needed resources. The main purpose of HTML is to allow users to flip through Web documents in a manner similar to flipping through a book, magazine, or a catalog. The Web site "cs.um.edu" shown in Figure 2.7 contains two HTML documents: "faculty.html" and "courses.html." HTML documents can imbed text, images, audio, and video.

Hypertext Transfer Protocol (HTTP) is an application-level protocol designed for Web users. It is intended for collaborative, distributed, hypermedia information systems. HTTP uses an extremely simple request/response model that establishes connection with the Web server specified in the URL, retrieves the needed document, and closes the connection. Once the document has been transferred to your Web browser, then the browser takes over. Keep in mind that every time you click on a hyperlink, you are initiating an HTTP session to transfer the needed information to your browser. The Web users shown in Figure 2.7 access the information stored in the two servers by using the HTTP protocol.

Web navigation and search services are used to search and surf the vast resources available over the "cyberspace." The term cyberspace, as stated previously, was first introduced through a science fiction book by Gibson [1984] but currently refers to the computer-mediated experiences for visualization, communication, and browser/decision support. The general search paradigm used determines that each search service contains an index of information available on Web sites. This index is almost always created and updated by "*spiders*" that crawl around the Web sites chasing hyperlinks for different pieces of information. Search engines support key-word and/or subject-oriented browsing through the index. Result of this browsing is a "hit list" of hyperlinks (URLs) that the user can click on to access the needed information. For example, the Web users in Figure 2.7 can issue a keyword search by using a search service for shoe stores in Chicago. This will return a hit list of potential shoe stores that are Web content providers. You then point and click till you find a shoe store of your choice. Many search services are currently available on the Web. Examples are Yahoo, Lycos, and Alta Vista. At present, many of these tools are being integrated with Web pages and Web browsers. For example, the Netscape Browser automatically invokes the Netscape home page that displays search tools that you can invoke by just pointing and clicking. It is beyond the scope of this book to describe the various Web navigation and search tools. Many books on Internet describe these search tools quite well.

Gateways to non-Web resources are used to bridge the gap between Web browsers and the corporate applications and databases. Web gateways are used for accessing information from heterogeneous data sources (e.g., relational databases, indexed files, and legacy information sources) and can be used to handle almost anything that is not designed with an HTML interface. The basic issue is that the Web browsers can display HTML information. These gateways are used to access non-HTML information and convert it to HTML format for display at a Web browser. The gateway programs typically run on Web sites and are invoked by the Web servers. At present, Common Gateway Interface (CGI) is used frequently. "Relational gateways" that provide access to relational databases from Web browsers are an area of active work.

2.3.3 A Simple Example

Figure 2.8 illustrates how the Web components can be used for a department store "Clothes-XYZ." This store wants to advertise its products on the Web (i.e., it wants to be a Web content provider). The store first designates a machine or buys services on a machine called "clothes.com" as a Web site. It then creates an overview document "overview.html" that tells the potential customers of the product highlights (think of this as the first few pages of a catalog). In addition, several HTML documents on the Web site for different types of clothes (men.html, women. html, kids.html) are created with pictures of clothes, size information, etc. (once again think of this as a catalog). We can assume that the overview page has hyperlinks to the other documents (as a matter of fact, it could have hyperlinks to other branches of Clothes-XYZ). In reality, design of the Web pages would require a richer, deeper tree structure design as well as sequential links for alphabetical and keyword searches needed to support the "flipping through" catalog behavior.

Once HTML documents have been created on the Web server, then an Internet user can browse through them as if he/she is flipping through a catalog. The customers typically supply the URL, directly or indirectly, for the overview (http://clothes.com/overview.html) and then use the hyperlinks to look at different types of clothes. Experienced customers may directly go to the type of clothes needed (e.g., men may directly go to "men.html" document). As shown in Figure 2.8, the URL consists of three components: the protocol (http), the Web server name (clothes.com), and the needed document (overview.html). HTTP provides the transfer of information between the Web users (the clients) and the Web Servers.

At first, Clothes-XYZ is only using Web to store an electronic catalog. After a customer has browsed through the catalog and has selected an item, he/she calls the store and places an order. Let us say that Clothes-XYZ wants to be more forward-looking and wants the customers to purchase the items over the Internet. In this case, a "Purchasing Gateway" software is developed and installed at the Web site. This gateway program gets into action when a user clicks on the "purchase" button on his screen. It prompts the user with a form (HTML supports forms) that the user fills out. The gateway program uses this form information to interact with a purchasing system that processes the purchase (see Figure 2.8). The purchasing system can be an existing system that is used for traditional purchasing. The role of the gateway is to provide a Web interface to the purchasing system.

Figure 2.8 A Simple Web Example

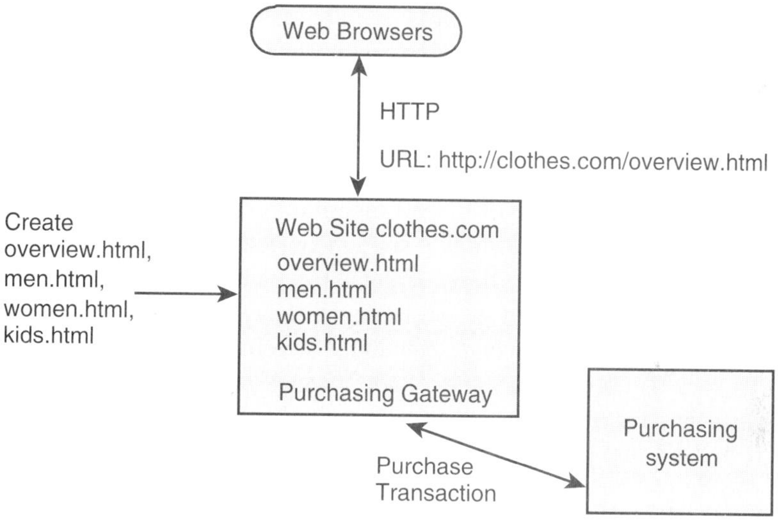

2.4   Objects and Distributed Objects

In addition to client/server and Internet, we are in the midst of object orientation (OO), with names like OO programming, OO design, OO databases, OO user interfaces, and so on. Most new software being developed at present and in the future will use some level of OO (at least in the user interface displays). Let us discuss the core OO technologies (e.g., OO user interfaces, OO programming languages, OO databases), and introduce the distributed object concepts. We will discuss only those topics that are of relevance to object-oriented client/server Internet environments. For the uninitiated, a short tutorial in Section 2.12 ("Appendix 2A: Object-Oriented Concepts" at the end of this chapter), gives the basic information. Extensive discussion of OO concepts can be found in the books by Booch [1994], Rumbaugh [1994], Taylor [1994].

2.4.1   Core Object-Oriented Technologies

The basic object concepts are comprised of object, message, class, and inheritance. When used in building software systems, these concepts can be of great value in developing reusable and flexible systems. In particular, OO concepts are being used in OO user interfaces, OO programming languages, and OO databases.

Object Oriented User Interfaces. At present, almost all new applications provide user interfaces that are either *GUI* (graphical user interface) or *OOUI* (object oriented user interface). GUI provides graphic dialogs, menu bars, color, scroll boxes, and pull-down and pop-up windows. GUI dialogs use the object/action model where users can select objects and then choose the actions to be performed on the selected objects. Most GUI dialogs at present are serial in nature (i.e., perform one operation at a time). OOUIs are highly iconic, object oriented user interfaces to support multiple, variable tasks whose sequence cannot be predicted. Examples include multimedia-based training systems, executive and decision-support systems, and stockbroker workstations. OOUIs are supported by commercial products such as NextStep, OS/2 Workplace Shell, and Macintosh.

Object-Oriented Programming. A significant proportion of software at present is being developed in object-oriented or object-based programming languages. Object-based programming languages such as ADA and Modula support objects as a language feature but do not support the concept of inheritance. Object-oriented programming languages (OOPLs) support inheritance. Several object-oriented programming languages have been introduced over the years. The first object-oriented language, Smalltalk, was introduced in the 1960s. Since then, several OOPLs such as C++, Objective C, and Object Pascal have been introduced. A more recent example is the Java programming language. An early review of some of these and many other OOPLs can be found in the OOPL survey by Saunders [1989]. More recent reviews can be found in Meade [1995], and Pancake [1995]. For continued developments in OOPL, the *Journal of Object Oriented Programming Languages* should be consulted.

Object-Oriented Databases. Simply stated, *object-oriented databases* allow storage and retrieval of objects to/from persistent storage (i.e., disks). Object-oriented databases, also known as *object databases*, allow you to store and retrieve nontraditional data types such as bitmaps, icons, text, polygons, sets, arrays, and lists. The stored objects can be simple or complex, can be related to each other through complex relationships, and can inherit properties from other objects. *Object-oriented database management systems (OODBMS)*, which can store, retrieve and manipulate objects, have been an area of active research and exploration since the mid-1980s. The initial work in OODBMSs was driven by the computer-aided design and computer-aided manufacturing (CAD/CAM) applications [Spooner 1986].

Relational databases are suitable for many applications and SQL use is widespread. However, it is not easy to represent complex information in terms of relational tables. For example, a car design, a computing network layout, and software design of an airline reservation system cannot be represented easily in terms of tables. For these cases, we need to represent complex interrelationships between data elements, retrieve several versions of design, represent the semantics (meaning) of relationships, and utilize the concepts of similarities to reduced redundancies. Additional information about object-oriented databases can be found in Davis [1995], Kim [1990], and Loomis [1995].

In addition to these, many new OO technologies are emerging, and market segments are evolving for reusable software that can be assembled to quickly build new applications (see the sidebars on "Object Frameworks" and "Component Software and Applets"). However, these technologies are introducing new terms and jargon. Due to ever-growing object-oriented "things," many groups are trying to figure out what to do. An example is the Object Management Group (OMG) that has been formed as a nonprofit consortium of more than 500 software and systems manufacturers and technology information providers. OMG is specifying a set of standard terms and interfaces for interoperable software by using the object-oriented concepts.

Component Software and Applets

Components are high-level "plug-and-play" software modules that perform a limited set of tasks within an application. Components are essentially small applications, also known as **"applets,"** that are *recognizable* by the users (i.e., they do not perform internal programming tasks such as initializing internal memory locations). For example, Microsoft Draw is an applet within Microsoft applications. This particular component is high level enough to perform end-user type functions (it draws boxes, arrows, circles, etc.). However, it is not a stand-alone application, it only works with other applications components.

Does everybody agree upon what a component is? Of course not (that would be a miracle!). However, most agree that (a) it is an independently delivered software and (b) it has an interface. A component may not have all the features of an object (i.e., inheritance and polymorphism) but it may be constructed from objects ("Components are molecules, objects are atoms," [Frye 1996]). Components are very much like objects; however, the emphasis is on recognition by users (many objects are oriented towards programming tasks).

Why are components important? The reason is simple—they can be used as plug-and-play to build complete applications. It is possible that components could finally realize the long-term dream of many pundits, that is, assemble software as you assemble cars instead of custom building each application. Many predictions are pointing to component-based software assemblies as being the norm in the next millennium [Vaughan-Nichols 1997], [Fingar 1996], and [Frye 1996].

At present, Microsoft appears to lead the component software by producing applets for Windows environments that draw, produce charts, perform calculations, etc. Depending on the size of the application, the components may be small or large. Many desktop tools are currently becoming available as components. Examples of typical desktop components are spell-checkers, SQL query builders, and print managers (conceptually, each icon on your toolbar can be a separate component). This will change quickly as more components become available for Web applications (this is the basic philosophy of Microsoft's ActiveX). Other vendors are naturally joining in.

Object Frameworks

Object frameworks, also known as "Frameworks," are essentially descendents of object oriented class libraries. Class libraries are collections of predefined object classes that define commonly used presentation, business processing logic, and data management structures and methods. An object framework simply defines how given sets of classes are related and arranged for different application domains. Let us use an example to explain the object frameworks. Suppose that you want to build a car. You have the following choices:

- Custom build all parts (wheels, seats, engine parts, etc.) yourself and then assemble these parts into a car. This is the old fashioned way of building a system from the scratch.
- Buy as many pre-fabricated parts as possible and then extend-assemble them into a car. This is analogous to the class libraries for building applications.
- Buy a pre-fabricated frame which already has the basic components already assembled (e.g., the engine is already installed, and the places where you need to plug in new components are clearly marked). This is like object frameworks.

In essence, object frameworks contain class libraries that have been integrated for certain domains Additionally, frameworks are extensible and can talk to other frameworks. It is possible to view frameworks at the following levels.

Foundation classes provide fine grained data and control statements, I/O functions, GUI structures, memory management functions, and database access functions.

Middleware framework covers an extensive set of C/S middleware services such as transaction processing, database access, directory services, telephony, authentication and systems management.

Application frameworks, also known as desktop frameworks, provide programmer productivity tools for compound documents, multimedia, groupware, mail, 3D graphics, and decision support applications.

Frameworks provide a convenient mechanism for component software. Basically, components can be integrated into frameworks and new components can be added to frameworks to build applications [Wooding 1997], and [Pree 1996].

Microsoft's Active Platform is an example of object frameworks. Web-based development environments from vendors such as Netscape are touting to be frameworks [Burr 1996]. Another example is the IBM object frameworks strategy that is expected to create "seas of objects" with object frameworks as the glue to tie these objects into applications. Examples of other players in this market are ParcPlace Systems, Rogue Wave, ILOG, Next, Sun Microsystems, Easel, and others. Frameworks for domains such as manufacturing are also evolving [Appley 1996].

2.4.2   Distributed Objects for Enterprisewide Applications

The trend at present is to extend the OO concepts to enterprisewide distributed applications. Simply stated, ***distributed objects*** are objects that can be dispersed across the network and can be accessed by users/applications across the network. Conceptually, enterprisewide applications are decomposed into objects that can reside around the network. An object on one machine can send messages to objects on other machines thus viewing the entire network as a collection of objects. This concept naturally extends the notions of object frameworks, business objects, and component software to distributed systems. Distributed objects present a very powerful technology that has the potential of addressing many problems facing the IT community today (i.e., reuse, portability, and interoperability). This is because applications can be constructed by using reusable components that encapsulate many internal details and can interoperate across multiple networks and platforms.

Technically, distributed applications can be viewed as a collection of objects (user interfaces, databases, application modules, customers). Each object has its own attributes, and has some methods that define the behavior of the objects (e.g., an order can be viewed in terms of its data and the methods that create, delete, and update the order object). Interactions between the components of an application can be modeled through "messages" that invoke appropriate methods. In particular, classes and inheritance are extremely useful in modeling distributed applications, because these concepts lead to reuse and encapsulation—critical to managing the complexity of distributed systems. For example:

- A customer can be defined as a class from which other business classes that define different types of customers can inherit properties.

- An inventory can be defined as a class from which other properties of specific inventory items can be inherited.

- An entire legacy application can be viewed as an object (or a class) by using object wrappers that mediate between legacy systems and OO users (we will discuss object wrappers in later chapters).

Figure 2.9 shows a conceptual view of a distributed object model:

- ***Objects*** are data surrounded by code with properties such as inheritance, polymorphism, encapsulation, and the like. Objects can be clients, servers, or both.

- ***Object brokers*** allow objects to dynamically find each other in a distributed environment and interact with each other over a network. Object brokers are the backbone of distributed object-oriented systems.

- ***Object services*** allow the users to create, name, move, copy, store, delete, restore, and manage objects.

Most of the applications so far have used OO technologies at the client side to implement GUIs. However, there is no reason why this technology should not be equally valuable to servers also. In fact, the reuse and encapsulation features of OO technologies should be of value to manage the complexity of server implementations. It is natural to think that the OO technologies will be increasingly used at the client as well as server sides of applications (see for example [Shan 1995], and [Rymer 1993]).

Figure 2.9 The Basic Distributed Objects Model

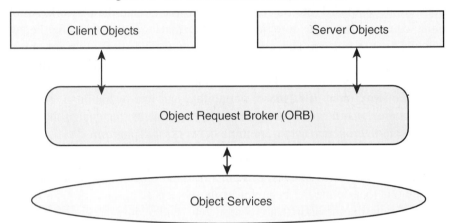

2.4.3   CORBA and ActiveX—Middleware for Distributed Objects

Support of distributed object applications requires special purpose middleware that allows remotely located objects to communicate with each other. Examples of middleware for distributed objects include Object Management Group's (OMG's) CORBA (Common Object Request Broker Architecture), and Microsoft's ActiveX. Both of these middleware packages use the distributed object model based on the object request broker (ORB) that receives an object invocation and delivers the message to an appropriate remote object (see Figure 2.9).

CORBA was introduced in 1991 by OMG to specify the technology for interoperable distributed OO systems. CORBA specifications represent the ORB technology adopted by OMG and are published as OMG documents. The key concepts of CORBA are (see Figure 2.10):

- CORBA essentially specifies the middleware services that will be used by the application objects.

- Any object (application) can be a client, server or both. For purpose of description, CORBA uses the C/S model where clients issue requests to objects (service providers).

- Any interaction between objects is through requests. The information associated with a request is an operation to be performed, a target object, zero or more parameters, etc.

- CORBA supports *static* as well as *dynamic binding*. Static binding is used to identify objects at compile time while dynamic binding between objects uses run time identification of objects and parameters.

- An *interface* represents contracts between client and server applications. A typical interface definition shows the parameters being passed and a unique interface identifier. An *Interface Definition Language (IDL)* has been defined specifically for CORBA. Program stubs and skeletons are produced as part of the IDL compiling.

- CORBA objects do not know the underlying implementation details—an *object adapter* maps generic model to implementation and is the primary way that an object implementation accesses services provided by the ORB.

Figure 2.10 CORBA Conceptual View

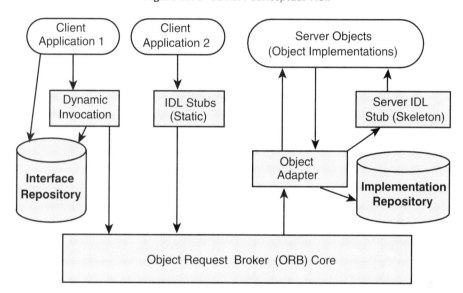

Note: Shaded areas represent middleware

ActiveX was introduced by Microsoft in March 1996 as its main strategy for distributed objects and Web. Microsoft is positioning ActiveX as a complete environment for components and distributed objects. Almost everything coming out of Microsoft at the time of this writing is based on ActiveX. Although ActiveX provides many capabilities, from a distributed objects point of view, the following features are significant (see Figure 2.11):

- All ActiveX components communicate with each other by using DCOM. So a Java applet (an ActiveX component) can call a remotely located Microsoft Word document (another ActiveX component) over DCOM. DCOM is the ORB in the ActiveX environment.

- The Web browser can behave as a container. For example, the Microsoft Internet Explorer can contain components such as Word documents, Java applets, C code, and Excel spreadsheets.

- Web technologies (browsers, HTML pages, Java applets) can be intermixed with desktop tools (spreadsheets, word processors) for distributed applications.

- Server facilities such as SQL servers and legacy access gateways can be invoked from ActiveX clients.

Figure 2.11 ActiveX Conceptual View

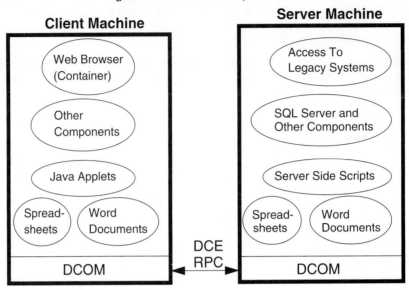

CORBA and ActiveX are reviewed in Umar [1997, Chapter 7]. Additional information can be found in Orfali [1996], Chappell [1996], Mowbray [1995], Linthicum [1997].

2.5   Object-Oriented Client/Server Internet Environments

Object-oriented client/server Internet (OCSI) environments combine the object-orientation, client/server, and Internet concepts to deliver business functionality. In particular, several attempts are underway to combine distributed objects with Web (see the sidebar "Combining Web with Distributed Objects"). Figure 2.12 shows the main building blocks of OCSI environments. Let us discuss the main components of this environment.

2.5.1   Client/Server Processes—The Applications

Client processes perform the application functions on the client side. Client processes can range from simple user interfaces and spreadsheets to complete application systems. Increasingly, the client processes are becoming Internet-based (i.e., they utilize Web browsers to interact with end users). *Server processes* perform the application functions on the server side. A server process, commonly referred to as a server, provides a service to the client. Server processes can be very simple functions such as time of day (TOD), or sophisticated applications such as order processing, electronic funds transfer, or CAD/CAM services. Other examples of server processes are print services, database services, object servers, and mail services.

The World Wide Web is introducing a new dimension to the application architectures. The main impact, from an application point of view is that the end user interfaces are being replaced with Web browsers. The Web users can directly access HTML documents from the Web servers or access corporate databases by using Web gateways. In addition, Java has popularized the notion of downloadable code where the Java applets are brought to the Web browser and executed there.

Figure 2.12 Middleware in Object-Oriented Client/Server Internet Environment

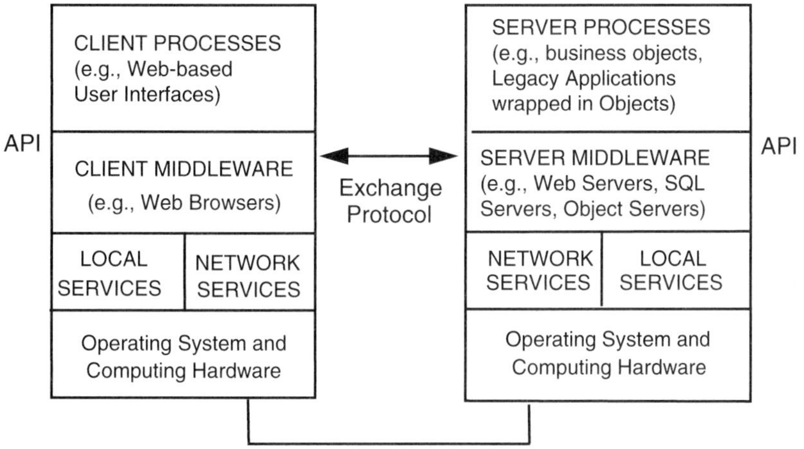

Combining Web With Distributed Objects
Netscape's IIOP and Microsoft's Active Platform

Web browsers are very suitable for human to computer communications, and distributed objects fit well for computer to computer communications. Pioneer work in combining these two technologies was done at the ANSA Consortium (http://www.ansa.co.uk) by developing the ANSAWEB prototype that allowed Web users to invoke CORBA applications. At present, this concept is being adopted by many industry products. Netscape's IIOP support and Microsoft's Active Platform are examples.

Netscape's IIOP (Internet Inter-ORB Protocol) provides CORBA support directly from Netscape browsers. IIOP is the core protocol of the CORBA distributed object model. This support allows Netscape browsers to directly interact with CORBA objects, in addition to accessing HTML documents and Web gateways through HTTP. Visit the Netscape site (http://www.netscape.cm) for more details.

Microsoft's Active Platform is a platform for developing Web-based distributed object applications and to integrate PC-based tools with Web tools. The Active Platform consists of three components (visit http://www.microsoft.com/webden/ for a white paper on Active Platform):

- Active Desktop that provides scripting, dynamic HTML, and component.
- Active Server to aid in Web server applications
- ActiveX to allow software components to communicate across a machine or a network.

Figure 2.13 shows a few OCSI architectures that allow Web users to access remote databases through a combination of distributed object and "classical" client/server technologies (e.g., RPC, remote SQL). Ideally, the clients and servers are viewed as objects from Web browsers that communicate through remote OO calls. We will discuss such architectures in great detail in Chapter 6.

Figure 2.13 OCSI Application Sample Architectures

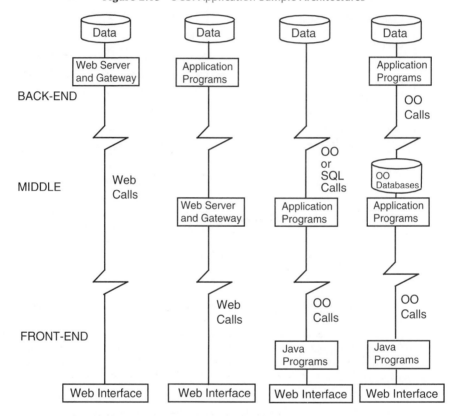

2.5.2   Middleware for OCSI Environments

The middleware enables applications and provides a wide range of functionality such as establishment of sessions between client and server processes, security, compression/ decompression, and failure handling. Detailed discussion about middleware can be found in the companion book [Umar 1997].

The middleware itself can be viewed in terms of client middleware that resides on every client machine and server middleware that resides on the server platforms. Let us look at the client and server side of middleware. ***Client middleware*** provides the interfaces between client processes and remote server processes. *Client middleware is essentially a set of software* *modules which can be invoked by the client processes through an application programming interface (API).* For example, many SQL servers provide API/SQL software that a client process can use to send SQL statements to the SQL servers. Examples of client middleware are Web browsers, Open Database Connect (ODBC) drivers, and CORBA client middleware. ***Server middleware*** monitors the client requests and invokes appropriate server processes. Server middleware receives a client request from the network services and parses the request. In order to parse, the server middleware must be able to understand the format in which the message was sent by the client middleware. This exchange protocol between the client/server middleware is a key to C/S interoperability (in many cases this exchange protocol is proprietary and thus requires clients from vendor X to interoperate with servers from vendor X only).

The middleware services have evolved, and continue to evolve, since the mid-1980s. Figure 2.14 shows this evolution in terms of middleware layers. Each layer has added more functionality and made it easier to develop and deploy distributed applications.The services provided by each layer are made available to the application programs through APIs. Examples of middleware layers are:

Network programming services that are used to invoke network services through APIs[5]. Examples of this low-level middleware are TCP/IP sockets, SNA Logical Unit 6.2 (LU6.2), IBM's NetBIOS for LANs, and AT&T's Transport Layer Interface (TLI). This middleware, also known as the first generation C/S middleware, is difficult to use (it is similar to writing assembly language code).

Basic C/S middleware that includes Remote Procedure Call (RPC), Remote Data Access (RDA), and Message Oriented Middleware (MOM). This middleware is typically built on top of the network transport services (e.g., RPC uses TCP/IP sockets; RDA uses TCP/IP sockets as well as LU6.2).

Distributed data and transaction management middleware that is responsible for access, manipulation, and update of distributed as well as replicated data. We categorize this middleware in the following two broad categories: distributed data access middleware that allows users to primarily retrieve data dispersed around a network, and client/server transaction processing middleware that handles the knotty issue of updating related data in distributed environments.

Object-oriented services that send messages to objects in the network. Examples of these services and standards are the Object Management Group's Common Object Request Broker Architecture (OMG CORBA) and Microsoft's ActiveX. Some of these services are built on top of the Basic C/S middleware (e.g., ActiveX is developed on top of RPCs).

World Wide Web middleware that includes Hypertext Transfer Protocol (HTTP), Hypertext Markup Language (HTML), Java, Web browsers, and Web gateways to access non-Web applications.

---

5. It can be argued that these services are so low level that they should not be included in middleware.

Figure 2.14 Layered View of Middleware

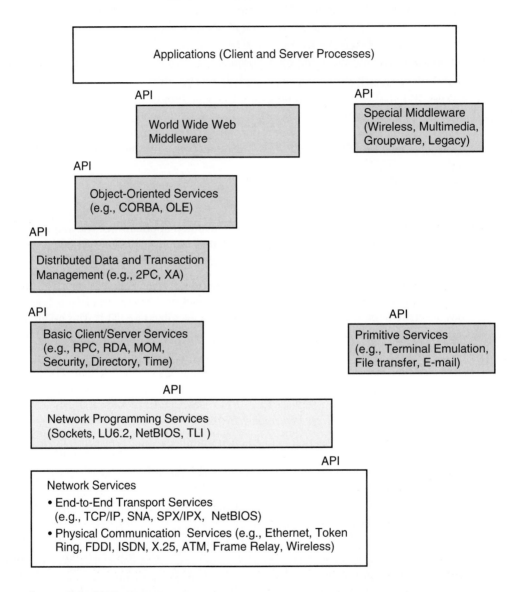

> **Special purpose middleware** that is being developed for emerging applications. Examples of this middleware are the wireless middleware for mobile computing applications, middleware for distributed multimedia applications, middleware for groupware (e.g., Lotus Notes), and middleware legacy system access/integration.

In addition to these layers, the middleware also provides a variety of management and support services such as security services, directory services, time services and management services. Although these services can span several layers, it is best to view them as part of the basic C/S middleware layer.

OCSI applications can use any of these middleware services. In general, there is a trade-off between the complexity of application and the complexity of the middleware. If the services provided by the middleware are simple and do not meet the application requirements, then this complexity shifts to the application developers.

Once again, these middleware layers are discussed in Chapters 3 through 9 in Umar [1997].

2.5.3   Network Services

Communication networks, or just networks, provide the lowest level of service (i.e., information transport) in distributed computing and C/S environments. In this context, a communication network is a collection of equipment and physical media, viewed as one autonomous whole that interconnects two or more computers. A wide variety of network configurations exists in enterprises. For example, a network may consist of three desktops connected through a cable, or it may serve an international airlines reservation system that employs global communication satellites, large processors, and thousands of terminals and workstations.

A network can be configured as a wide area network (WAN), which utilizes common carrier facilities for communications; a local area network (LAN), which utilizes vendor supplied cables for connecting computers within a building; a metropolitan area network (MAN) within a region, which may use the communication facilities of Cable TV, or a combination of LANs, MANs, and WANs. In addition, the communication between computing devices on a network can use analog or digital data transmission facilities over copper, wireless, or fiber optic communication media. The state-of-the-art advancement in network transmission technologies is the development of high-speed local and wide area transmissions, typically in the range of 100 million bits per second (Mbps) or higher. Another area of advancement is the integration of voice, data, and video images for multimedia applications such as teleconferencing and group problem solving, among others. Examples of the evolving network communication technologies are Asynchronous Transfer Mode (ATM), Frame Relay, Fiber Distributed Data Interface (FDDI), and wireless networks. In general, networks are becoming faster, ubiquitous, and more reliable.

A *network architecture* describes the physical components, the functions performed by the components, and the interfaces between the components of a network. Network architecture standards are needed to interconnect different networks from different vendors with different capabilities. For example, a Chicago bank that uses a Sun-supported network needs to communicate with a New York bank that uses an IBM supplied network. The *Open System Interconnection (OSI) Reference Model* specifies standards for networks from different vendors to exchange information freely. The OSI Model casts the functions needed to exchange information between interconnected computers in terms of seven layers (see Figure 2.15). Many network architectures have evolved in the last 20 years. Examples of the state of the market/practice network architectures are the *Transmission Control Protocol/Internet Protocol (called TCP/IP)* stack, IBM's *System Network Architecture (SNA)*, Novell's *Netware LAN*, and the Open System Interconnection (OSI) Model. See Umar [1997, Chapter 11] for a brief overview of these network architectures.

Figure 2.15 The OSI Reference Model

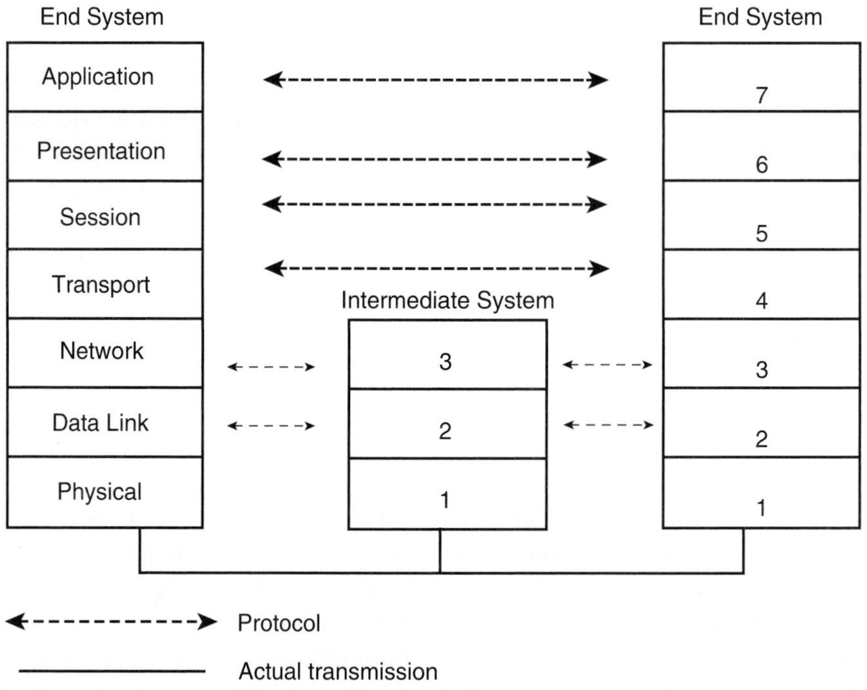

Network services provide the basic addressing and transport mechanisms across a network. These services communicate with the server and client middleware. Network services are provided typically by TCP/IP, SNA, and LAN protocols such as NetBIOS and Novell Netware SPX/IPX. *Network interconnectivity* is the key issue addressed by network services in enterprisewide networks to provide interfaces and transport of messages between remotely located client and server processes. The principal network interconnectivity devices are:

> *Bridges* connect two LANs to form a larger LAN. Bridges are simple devices that do not deal with the issues of routing and session control needed in enterprisewide networks.

> *Routers* find a path for a message in larger networks and then send the message over the selected path. A router is more sophisticated than a bridge because it knows alternate routes for a message and uses the alternate routes if needed. In most cases, enterprises have replaced bridges with routers. Over the years, routers have accumulated additional functionality such as security checking ("the fire walls")[6].

> *Gateways* translate one type of protocol to another. In most large networks, protocols of some subnetworks need to be converted to protocols of other subnetworks for end- to-end communications. A gateway connects two dissimilar network architectures and is essentially a protocol converter. A gateway may be a special purpose computer, a workstation with associated software (e.g., a PS2 with gateway software), or a software module that runs as a task in a mainframe. Examples of gateways for network interconnectivity are TCP/IP to SNA gateway and Novell Netware to mainframe gateway.

Routers and gateways are used commonly in enterprisewide networks. For example, if a client spreadsheet on a UNIX TCP/IP network in Chicago needs to access a database server on an MVS SNA network in New York, then a series of routers would be needed to find the path between the client and server process. In addition, a TCP/IP to SNA gateway will be needed for translating messages from TCP/IP to SNA protocols.

Figure 2.16 shows a realistic enterprise network that uses TCP/IP very heavily, except for the SNA network at the mainframe. The routers are used between all TCP/IP network segments and a gateway is used to convert the TCP/IP messages to SNA.

Detailed discussion of network issues are beyond the scope of this book.

2.5.4 Local Software

The local software in an OCSI environment provides access and manipulation of data and processes located on the machines in a C/S environment. Examples of the local software are:

- Database managers
- Transaction managers
- File managers
- Print managers

---

6. Some commercially available routers also convert lower-level protocol (e.g., Ethernet to Token Ring).

Figure 2.16 Network Interconnectivity in Client/Server Environment

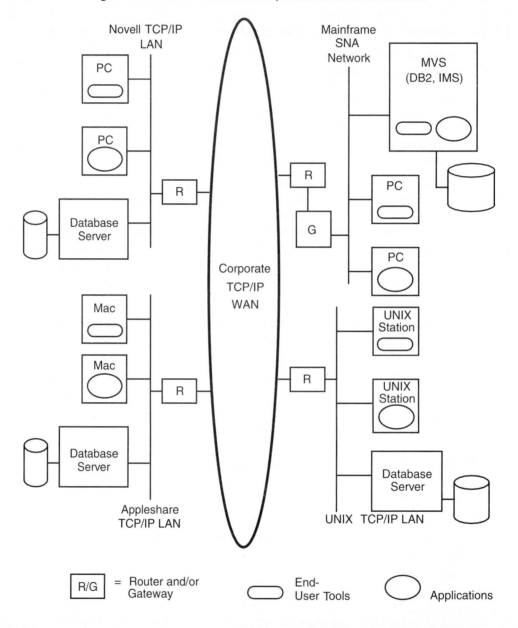

Database managers, also known as database management systems (DBMSs) provide access to databases for on-line and batch users. In a typical database environment, different users can view, access and manipulate the data in a database. A DBMS is designed to (a) manage logical views of data so that different users can access and manipulate the data without having to know the physical representation of data, (b) manage concurrent access to data by multiple users, enforcing logical isolation of transactions, (c) enforce security to allow access to authorized users only, and provide integrity controls and backup/recovery of a database. Relational database managers such as DB2, Oracle, Sybase, and/or Informix are typically used in many contemporary applications. Older systems use hierarchical database managers such as IMS. Object-oriented databases are still in their infancy (see Appendix A). The key issue in C/S environments is to access remotely located databases from a variety of client processes. This issue is discussed in detail in Umar [1997, Chapter 4].

Transaction managers (TMs), also known as transaction processing monitor (TP monitor), monitor the execution of transactions (sequence of statements that must be executed as a unit). TMs specialize in managing transactions from their point of origin to their termination (planned or unplanned). Some TM facilities are integrated with the DBMS facilities to allow database queries from different transactions to access/update to one or several data items (IBM's IMS DB/DC is an example). However, some TMs only specialize in handling transactions (CICS, Tuxedo, and Encina are examples). The key issue in C/S environments is how to extend the scope of local transaction management to managing the execution of transactions across multiple sites. See Umar [1997, Chapter 5] for a detailed discussion of this topic.

File managers are responsible for providing access and manipulation of text documents, diagrams, charts, images, and indexed files. A very wide range of file managers have been developed since the 1960s. An important issue in C/S environments is to provide access to files that are dispersed around a network. This issue has been addressed by middleware such as the SUN Network File Server (NFS).

Print managers are responsible for printing operations. Obviously, different types of print managers are available for different type of print devices. Almost all LANs, at present, provide access to print managers on the LAN.

2.6   State of the Practice: Typical Examples

Many organizations developed and deployed terminal-mainframe applications over private corporate networks in the 1970s and 1980s. In the 1990s, many new applications have been developed by using the C/S paradigm over the same networks. More recently, a few applications have started using distributed objects. Now, the Internet has taken off and has introduced Web browsers and servers all around us. Figure 2.17 shows the result of this evolution. Let us go through some details of this environment in terms of networks, clients, and servers.

The current corporate networks consist of private TCP/IP (Intranet) and non-TCP/IP (e.g., SNA) networks. The non-TCP/IP networks typically support the mainframes and Novell local area networks. The private TCP/IP networks are seeing most of the activities in client/server computing and support many client/server applications. These networks are now also supporting the corporate WWW activities and have thus been relabeled as the Intranets (i.e., private Internets). The private networks are connected to each other and to the public Internet through the gateways that provide protocol conversions between different networks. We are not showing security firewalls between these networks (firewalls, briefly, check the traffic between networks to make sure that only the authorized users are accessing the network).

Figure 2.17 Global View of Typical Environments

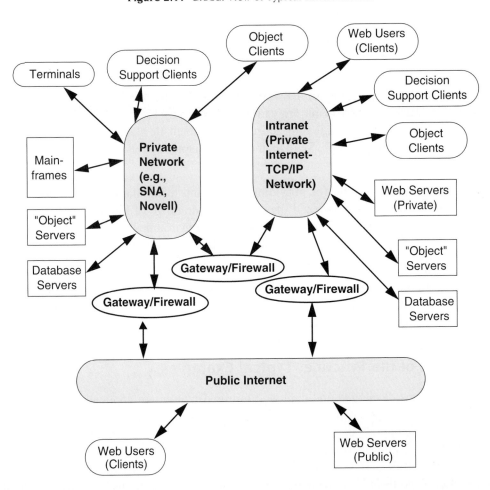

Client processes, or just clients, typically reside on desktop computers. However, a client may reside on a mainframe. For example, a client program on a mainframe may need to access a database server on a LAN. Here are some examples of clients, (only a few of these clients are shown in Figure 2.17):

- **Web browsers (clients)** that allow Internet users to access information over the Internet through GUIs. Common Web browsers, at present, are the Netscape browser and the Mosaic browser.

- **Decision support tools** that are preprogrammed to access remote servers. These tools do not require API level programming. Examples are the SQL query processors such as Clear Access, spreadsheets such as Lotus Data Lens, fourth generation languages such as PC/Focus, executive information systems such as Lightship, and graphical query generators such as Object-View.

- **Purchased and/or developed client applications**, which access remote data when needed. For example, an order processing application on a workstation may behave as a client and access customer information from a remotely located database server.

- **Object clients** that issue messages to remotely located objects. Examples of these clients are the CORBA and ActiveX clients. The object clients use the distributed object paradigm and view the servers as a collection of objects that can be invoked seamlessly.

- **Client application development tools**, which allow development of client applications on workstations. For example, PowerBuilder from PowerSoft is a popular C/S application development environment.

A variety of servers, dispersed across a network, can be accessed from clients that may reside at different computers. Examples of some of the commonly known servers are as follows (Figure 2.17 shows a few of these examples):

- **LAN servers** (e.g., Novell Netware) which are used in LANs so that many users (clients) can share the same printers and files. See Johnson 1995] for a review of the various LAN "network operating systems" (NOSs).

- **Window servers** (e.g., XWindow) which manage user windows (screens) on a workstation (see [Johnson 1990, Scheife 1990]).

- **Web servers** that receive requests from Web clients to provide Internet services. Examples of Web servers are advertising databases and commercially available Web servers such as the Publishing and Commerce server from Netscape.

- **Name/directory servers** that show the location of a named object (e.g., file, program)

- **Authentication server** that checks to see if a particular user is authorized to access particular resources

- **Distributed file servers** that provide transparent access to files allocated to different computers. Network File System (NFS) and Andrew File Server (AFS) are examples.

- **Database servers** (e.g., SQL servers) which take an SQL query and return the desired information (note that the SQL server may in fact access a nonrelational database).

- **Object servers** that present an OO interface to the clients. These servers may in fact be a legacy application that has been "wrapped" with an OO interface so that the clients can view and invoke these services remotely. These servers may use the facilities of CORBA or OLE to define these interfaces (i.e., use Interface Definition Language supplied by CORBA or OLE).

- **Transaction servers** that receive a transaction (e.g., update a bank account) and respond appropriately. A transaction server is responsible for assuring that the transaction either completes successfully ("commits") or is completely rolled out.

- **Application servers** that provide a complete application (e.g., credit checking) in response to a request from a client.

- **Groupware servers** (e.g., Lotus Notes) which manage semistructured information such as text, image, mail, bulletin boards, and work flow.

These functional servers can run on a variety of hardware boxes ranging from laptops to mainframes. These hardware boxes, also called "servers," (unfortunately) must have the hardware capability and the associated operating system support to schedule and execute multiple requests.

2.7   State of the Market: Commercial Products

State of the market for the OCSI environments (e.g., middleware, networks, database managers, transaction managers, operating systems, and computing hardware) is cluttered with hundreds of off-the-shelf products that are discussed regularly in trade magazines such as *Web Week, Client/Server Today, Client/Server Computing, Object Magazine, Datamation, Database Programming and Design,* and *Data Communications.* In addition, analysis of products are published regularly by consulting organizations such as the Gartner Group, Forrester Research, Seybold Group, and the Yankee Group. Let us quickly scan the state of the market for the key building blocks for application engineering/reengineering (middleware, networks, databases, and operating systems).

The middleware services have evolved, and continue to evolve, since the early 1990s. Each evolution has added more functionality and made it easier to engineer/reengineer the applications.

The growing number of commercially available middleware products should be seriously considered before undertaking in-house development. In most cases, it is better to develop applications that utilize the commercially available middleware. It is generally better to use the high level protocols and services, if available, to reduce the application complexity. The exceptions to these general guidelines are lightweight desktop applications. For these applications, it may not make sense to incorporate a heavyweight middleware that may more than double the cost of the application and impose platform restrictions (e.g., if the middleware runs on PCs only, then the application is restricted to PCs). In such cases, it may be better to use the network calls (e.g, TCP/IP sockets) for remote interactions.

In networks, TCP/IP and SNA have been state of the practice for a number of years. TCP/IP is a natural winner at present due to the popularity of Internet. Gateways and other interconnectivity devices between different networks are also commercially available from a multitude of vendors (Data Communications Magazine publishes information about these products regularly). Detailed discussion of networking issues is strongly beyond the scope of this book.

Database management systems have been state of the market since the 1970s. IMS, introduced in 1969, is still marketed and supported by IBM. However, most of the current database activity is centered around relational databases. Database vendors such as Oracle, Sybase, Informix, and IBM market and support relational database management systems for almost all platforms. OO databases, although very popular with the academic community since the mid-1980s, are not fully state of the market at the time of this writing. It is expected that the popularity of OO paradigm and distributed objects will push the OODBMSs into the main stream. We will just have to wait and see.

Operating systems, needless to say, are state of the market. MVS, introduced by IBM in the mid-1970s, is still being marketed and supported heavily by IBM. UNIX has become almost a de facto choice for mid-range computers. However, Microsoft's Windows NT is currently competing with UNIX.

2.8   State of the Art: Standards and Trends

Standards are needed for portability and interoperability of distributed applications. Many standards are important in an OCSI environment (e.g., middleware standards, network standards, database standards, etc.). However, from an application engineering/reengineering point of view, middleware standards are of vital importance (middleware shields the applications from networks and operating systems). In particular:

- Application Programming Interfaces (APIs) provided by the middleware impact the portability of distributed applications. For example, a client application that uses the Sybase API to issue remote SQL calls has to be reprogrammed if the middleware changes from Sybase to Informix.

- Exchange protocols used between the middleware components impact the interoperability of distributed applications. For example, Oracle client middleware encodes the remote SQL in a proprietary format so that only Oracle server can decode it. Thus an Oracle client cannot interoperate with an Informix server, and vice versa, without "gateways" that convert the exchange protocols.

Ideally, the APIs as well as exchange protocols should be open and based on standards. Unfortunately, many middleware APIs as well as the exchange protocols are proprietary.

A major area of growth is the object frameworks and component software to work in distributed environments. For example, frameworks at different machines can communicate with each other through the object request brokers (ORBs). In this context, we are using ORB as a generic feature which may be satisfied by CORBA or Microsoft DCOM. The melding of Web with distributed objects through object frameworks is also a natural area of growth. In essence, components can be integrated into frameworks and new components can be added to frameworks to build Web-based distributed applications. Microsoft's ActiveX Platform, especially with the popularity of Visual Basic components, is a good example of these developments. The key point is that components, frameworks, ORBs, and Web complement each other to deliver business value—the main theme of this book.

2.9   Summary

An object-oriented client/server Internet (OCSI) environment provides the infrastructure (i.e., middleware, networks, operating systems, hardware) that supports the modern distributed applications. We have reviewed the key concepts and building blocks of this enabling infrastructure. In summary:

- The client/server model is the most popular model for distributed applications at the time of this writing. Typically, this allows a user program at a workstation to act as a client issuing requests to programs and databases that may be located at many remote computing sites.

- The distributed object model extends the scope of the client/server model to include interactions between remotely located objects.

- The Web allows access to a multitude of information sources through Web browsers.

- Object-oriented client/server Internet (OCSI) environments combine the object-orientation, client/server and Internet concepts to deliver business functionality.

- OCSI applications represent the business logic as objects that may reside on different machines and can be invoked through Web services.

- Middleware supports and enables the OCSI applications. The middleware services have evolved and continue to evolve since the early 1990s.

- Network services transport the information between remote computers. Networks are largely moving towards TCP/IP.

Application engineering/reengineering in OCSI environments is not trivial and requires detailed architectural analysis of various applications as well as platform issues. Examples of the issues are performance trade-offs, security, flexibility, access/integration of legacy systems, and the interoperability and portability of client side software with server side software supplied by different vendors. We will discuss these issues in Parts II and III of this book.

2.10   Case Study: XYZCorp Review of IT Infrastructure Architecture

XYZCorp wants to review the IT infrastructure architecture that should serve as the platform for all the services and applications to be provided by XYZCorp. In particular, it should show how the networking services, the middleware components, and other services will support the growing number of Web-based OO applications that will also utilize mobile computing and groupware. This architecture should allow different applications and users at different sites to communicate with each other ("any data from any application anywhere in the company"). The current platforms consist of a variety of devices. The regional offices house minicomputers (mainly UNIX) which are connected to the corporate mainframe (MVS). The regional computers maintain regional inventory, customer information, and prices of items sold in the region. Some regions (e.g., Atlanta and San Francisco) are very UNIX-oriented; other regions have Novell LANs. The corporate headquarters is IBM mainframe-oriented (MVS, DB2, IMS, SNA, Token Ring). PCs are used commonly throughout the organization.

Hints about the Case Study

A high level view of the XYZCorp architecture is shown in Figure 2.18. There are two broad levels of interconnectivity:

- Network-to-network interconnectivity (bridges, routers)
- Applications-to-application interconnectivity (middleware)

Figure 2.18 XYZCorp IT Infrastructure High-Level View

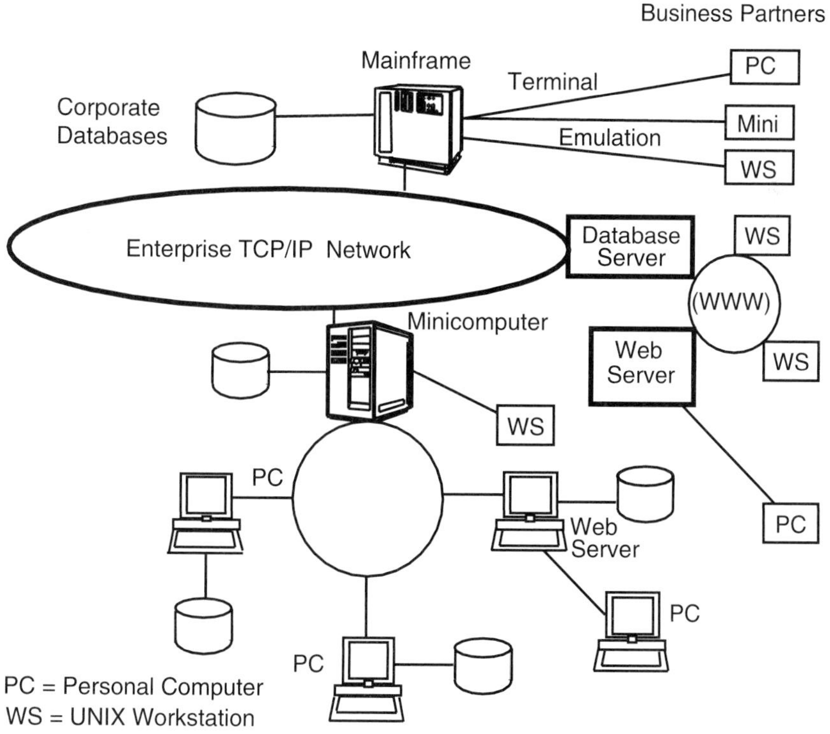

Figure 2.19 shows the middleware components of this architecture. We have shown a few components for the purpose of illustration. The sites where the servers (Web servers, group servers, database servers, etc.) will be housed and the protocols to be used by each of these servers are suggested. The protocol "stack" at each client is also shown.

2.11   Problems and Exercises

1. Present a different view of how client/server systems interrelate with distributed computing systems.

2. Give an example of a distributed application that does not use the client/server model.

3. Describe at least three different ways that you can invoke distributed object services from Web browsers, including applets.

4. Draw a conceptual diagram of IT infrastructure in an environment of your choice (e.g., business, finance, engineering, manufacturing).

5. List the factors you will use to evaluate off-the-shelf middleware to support OCSI applications.

2.12   APPENDIX 2A: Object-Oriented Concepts

2.12.1   Key Concepts

The purpose of this short tutorial is to give you the basic OO concepts that are of relevance to object-oriented client/server Internet environments. The basic object concepts are comprised of object, message, class, and inheritance.

Objects. *Objects are data guarded by a protective layer of code.* Figure 2.20 shows the conceptual view of a customer object. The data represent the **attributes** of the object and the code that surrounds the data represents the **methods** of the object. Methods are the only way any outsider can interact with the object (you cannot directly view or update customer balance without invoking the "Get-Balance-Due" or "Adjust-Balance" methods). Basically, an object is represented by at least two properties: attributes and methods. Attributes uniquely identify an object and a method shows the object behavior (what it can do or what can be done to it). A method hides the implementation details from the users of an object. A method typically receives a message, performs some operations, and sends the response back. An object essentially is a collection of attributes and the valid methods that manipulate the data elements.

Figure 2.19 XYZCorp IT Middleware Architecture

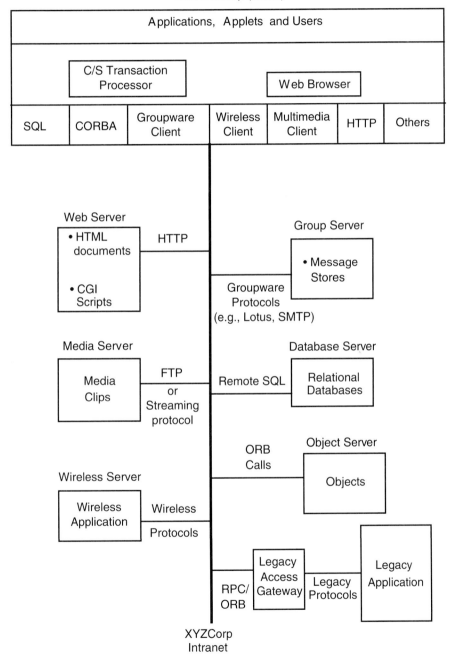

Figure 2.20 Conceptual View of a Customer Object

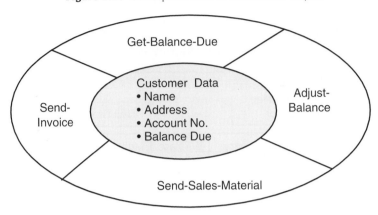

Customer object is customer data surrounded by code (methods)
- The attributes of the customer object are name, address, account no., balance due
- The methods associated with the customer object are Get-Balance-Due,
  Send-Invoice, etc.

Messages. Objects interact with each other by sending *messages*. These messages invoke particular methods. A message is simply the name of an object followed by the name of an appropriate method. In addition, the message may contain a set of parameters that the invoked method needs. Figure 2.21 illustrates two messages sent to the customer object, one with parameters the other without. Each method of an object knows the list of messages to which it can respond and how it will respond to each. The object that receives the message is responsible for providing the code that is needed for the invoked object. The receiver should also advertise its methods and the parameters to be invoked for each method so that the outside world can take full advantage of objects.

Figure 2.21 Messages to Customer Object

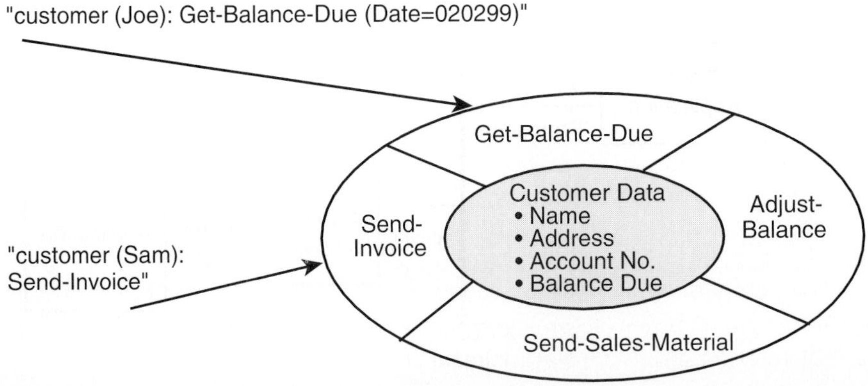

"customer (Joe): Get-Balance-Due (Date=020299)"

"customer (Sam):
Send-Invoice"

Get-Balance-Due

Send-
Invoice

Customer Data
• Name
• Address
• Account No.
• Balance Due

Adjust-
Balance

Send-Sales-Material

Classes. A *class* is a template that represents the properties that are common among similar objects. The basic purpose of class is to define a particular type of object. For example, the class employee can be used to represent the common properties of all company employees. The common properties include attributes such as name, address, employee id, grade, pay scale, et cetera and methods such as view, update, terminate, and the like. So, if in a programming system you have identified object types such as employees, customers, and products, then you will define three classes to correspond to these object types. Each class will define the properties of each object type. The objects belonging to a particular class are known as *instances* of that class. For example, the objects Joe Smith, Harry Kline, and Pat Hemsath are instances of the class employee. Once you have created a class, you can create any number of instances of each class (object-oriented programming languages provide statements to create instances). The instances contain the information that makes them unique. For example, the object instance of Joe Smith will have information unique to Joe Smith.

Inheritance. Classes can be defined independently of each other. For example, the employee, customer, and product classes can be defined independently of each other. However, classes can *inherit* common properties from other classes. The properties to be inherited can be attributes as well as methods. A class hierarchy can be constructed where lower level classes (*subclasses*) inherit the properties from higher level classes (*superclass*). Figure 2.22 illustrates a class hierarchy. We can set up a class hierarchy for our employee class with subclasses such as managers, technical support, administrative support, consultants, visiting residents, and part-time staff.

2.12.2 Object-Based Versus Object-Orientation

The basic object concepts can be used to represent powerful programming systems. An object-based system is defined as follows [Chin 1991, Taylor 1994]:

>   *object-based* = objects + classes

For example, an object-based programming language supports objects and classes as a language feature but does not support the concept of inheritance. ADA and Modula-2 are examples. Object-based concepts are quite general and can be found in application programs that existed before objects became fashionable.

Our interest is in *object-oriented* systems that go beyond object-based systems. The following widely accepted definition of object orientation is given by [Wegner 1987]:

>   *object oriented* = objects + classes + inheritance

OOPLs support classes, objects, methods, messages, and inheritance (note that methods and messages are implicit in this definition). A more generalized definition, more suitable for distributed systems, is given by [Nicol 1993]:

>   *object oriented* = encapsulation + abstraction + polymorphism

Figure 2.22 Class Hierarchies (*Source:* [Umar 1993])

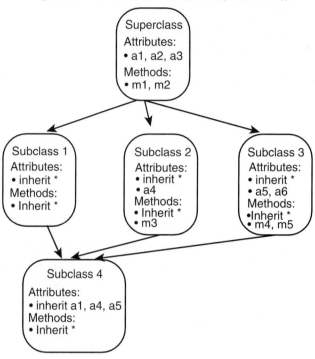

Notes:

1. The superclass defines the attributes a1, a2, a3 and the methods m1, m2 which are inherited by all immediate subclasses (and objects) in this system. "Inherit*" means that all properties of a superclass are inherited. If these properties are changed in the super-class, then all other classes inherit these changes.
2. The subclass 1 inherits all properties (methods and attributes) from the superclass. It does not define any of its own properties.
3. The subclass 2 inherits all properties (methods and attributes) from the superclass. In addition, it defines its own properties (attribute a4 and method m3).
4. The subclass 3 inherits all properties (methods and attributes) from the superclass. In addition, it defines its own properties (attributes a5, a6 and methods m4, m5).
5. The subclass 4 inherits attributes and methods from different subclasses. This is an example of multiple inheritance.

Let us review the three ingredients of this definition of OO. As we will see, this definition is quite similar to Wegner's definition, albeit more general.

Abstraction. Abstraction focuses on the outside view of an object, that is, how it will appear to the outside world. The following definition of abstraction has been given by Booch [1994, page 39]:

> An abstraction denotes the essential characteristics of an object that distinguish it from all other kinds of objects and thus provides crisply defined conceptual bound-aries, relative to the perspective of the viewer.

Thus abstraction allows us to group associated entities according to common properties, for example, the set of instances belonging to a class. Abstraction represents the object properties without attention to implementation details. Methods as well as messages support abstraction by focusing on the outside view of an object.

Encapsulation (Information Hiding). Encapsulation, also known as information hiding, prevents the clients from seeing the internals of an object. Encapsulation complements abstraction—encapsulation focuses on hiding the internals while abstraction focuses on presenting an external view. Encapsulation has been defined by Booch [1994, page 46] as following:

> Encapsulation is the process of hiding all of the details of an object that do not contribute to its essential characteristics.

Encapsulation as well as abstraction are important to the design of an OO system, especially when the objects can be at different sites. In particular, each object must have two parts: an interface and an implementation. The *interface* of an object only captures its external view (i.e., the object name, the method to be invoked, the parameters to be passed). The *implementation* of an object contains the mechanisms that achieve the desired behavior (i.e., the code for each method). The interface is also known as the *public part* of an object and the implementation is known as the *private part* of an object.

Polymorphism. Polymorphism is a Greek term meaning "many forms." Polymorphism allows you to hide alternative procedures behind a common interface. Basically, you can use the same method name in more than one class. A popular form of polymorphism is inclusion polymorphism in which operations on a given type are also applicable to its subtype (for example, a printer will start all types of printers). Inclusion polymorphism is often implemented via an inheritance mechanism. Polymorphism is defined as the quality or state of being able to assume different forms [Taylor 1994]. Polymorphism can be displayed in messages and/or objects. An example is send the same message, "delete," to different objects that respond to it differently. For example, some objects may completely erase the information while the others may just flag it for erasure at a later stage. Polymorphism is considered to be one of the defining characteristics of object-oriented technology. It distinguishes object-oriented programming languages from more traditional programming. By allowing the same method name in different classes, you can use the same message (e.g., delete, print, draw) to get different results by simply pointing to a different class at run time. Thus polymorphism takes advantage of inheritance and "dynamic binding" (i.e., deciding at run time what object you want to communicate with).

2.13   Additional Information

Literature on IT infrastructure is growing steadily. This chapter has quickly scanned the topics that are discussed in great detail in Umar [1997]. Additional information can be found in the books by Berson [1993], Khanna [1993], Orfali [1994], Stevens [1990], Umar [1993], and Vaskevitz [1993]. State-of-the-market and state-of-the-practice articles on IT infrastructure appear regularly in trade journals such as *Client/Server Today, Datamation, Database Programming and Design,* and *Data Communications.* Analysis of IT infrastructure directions can be found in the reports published by the Gartner Group, Forrester Research, and the Yankee Group.

Adler, R., "Distributed Coordination Models for Client/Server Computing," *IEEE Computer Magazine,* April 1995, pp. 14–22.

Amaru, C., "Building Distributed Applications with MOM," *Client/Server Today,* November 1994, pp. 83–93.

Andrews, G. R., "Paradigms for Process Interaction in Distributed Programs," *ACM Computing Surveys,* March 1991, pp. 49–90.

Andrews, G., and Schneider, F., "Concepts and Notations for Concurrent Programming," *ACM Computing Survey,* Vol. 15, No. 1, March 1983, pp. 3–44.

Appley, G., and Gallagher, M., "A Framework for Manufacturing-Process Simulation Software," *Object Magazine,* May 1996, pp. 33-41.

Bell, T., Adam, J., and Lowe, S., "Communications," *IEEE Spectrum 1996,* January 1996, pp. 30–41.

Berners-Lee, T., "WWW: Present, Past, and Future," *IEEE Computer Magazine,* October 1996, pp. 69–77.

Berners-Lee, T., Cailliau, R., Pellow, N., Secret, A., "The World Wide Web Initiative" *Proc. INET '93,* Internet Society, San Francisco, 1993.

Berson, A., *Client/Server Architectures,* McGraw-Hill, 1993.

Birrel, A. D., and Nelson, B. J., "Implementing Remote Procedure Call," *ACM Transactions on Computer Systems,* Vol. 2, pp. 39–59.

Booch, G., *Object-Oriented Design with Applications,* Benjamin Cummings, 2nd ed., 1994.

Burr, T., "Framework Technology for Web Pages and Web Servers," *Object Magazine,* May 1996, pp. 46-49.

Chappell, D., *Understanding OLE and ActiveX,* Microsoft Press, 1996.

Chin, R., and Chanson, S., "Distributed Object-Based Programming Systems," *ACM Computing Surveys,* March 1991, pp. 91–124.

Comeau, Greg, "Networking with UNIX," *BYTE,* February 1989, pp. 265–267.

Comerford, R., "Computers," *IEEE Software,* January 1996, pp. 42–25.

Comport, J., "Packaged Applications: Buy an Application, Inherit an Architecture," Gartner Group Briefing, San Diego, February 1995.

Corbin, J. R., *The Art of Distributed Applications: Programming Techniques for Remote Procedure Calls,* Springer-Verlag, 1991.

Coulouris, G., and Dollimore, J., *Distributed Systems: Concepts and Design,* Addison Wesley, 1988.

Davis, R., "A Logical Choice," *BYTE,* January 1989, pp. 309–315.

Davis, J., "Object-Relational Databases," *Distributed Computing Monitor,* Patricia Seybold Group, February 1995.

Eckerson, W., "Searching for the Middleground," *Business Communications Review,* September 1995, pp. 46–50.

Edelstein, H., "Mining Data Warehouses," *Information Week,* January 8, 1996, pp. 48–51.

Fingar, P., "The Blueprint for Business Objects," *SIGS Book and Multimedia,* 1996.

Finkelstein, R., "A Client for Your Server," *Database Programming and Design,* March 1992, pp. 31–45.

Foley, J., "High Speed Processors," *Information Week,* January 1, 1996, pp. 39–41.

Frye, C., "N-Tier at Your Own Risk," *Software Magazine,* December 1996, pp. 80–89.

Gallagher, S., "Constructing Better Visual," *Information Week,* January 1, 1996, pp. 50–53.

Gantz, J., "Cooperative Processing and the Enterprise Network," *Networking Management,* January 1991, pp. 25–40.

Garlan, D., and Perry, D., "Introduction to the Special Issue on Software Architecture: Guest Editorial," *IEEE Transactions on Software Engineering,* April 1995, pp. 269–274.

Gibson, W., *Neuromancer,"* Ace Books, New York, 1984.

Gillooly, B., "Multiprocessor Systems," *Information Week,* January 1, 1996, pp. 35–37.

Glass, B., "Relying on Netware NLMs," *Infoworld,* October 12, 1992, p. S80.

Gould, M., "Tomorrow's Microkernal-Based UNIX Operating Systems," *Patricia Seybold's Group Report,* Open Information Systems, August 1993.

Griswold, Charles, "LU6.2: A View from the Database," *Database Programming and Design,* May 1988, pp. 34–39.

Hackathoran, R., and Schlacvk, M., "How to Pick Client/Server Middleware," *Datamation,* July 15, 1994, pp. 52–56.

Hines, J., "Software Engineering," *IEEE Spectrum,* January 1996, pp. 60–64.

Hirsch, D., "Terminal Servers: Here to Stay," *Data Communications,* April 1990, pp. 105–114.

Hurwicz, M., "Connectivity Pathways: APPC or NETBIOS," *PC Tech Journal,* Vol. 5, No. 11, Nov. 1987, pp. 156–170.

IBM (International Business Machines), "Advanced Program-to-Program Communication for the IBM Personal Computer," *Programming Guide,* February 1986.

ISO/DP 9072/1 report, "Remote Operations Model—Notation and Service Definition," Geneva, Switzerland, October 1986.

Johnson and Reichard, *Advanced XWindow Applications Programming,* MIT Press, 1990.

Johnson, J., "Enterprise NOSs: Now is the Time," *Data Communications,* May 15, 1995.

Kernighan, B. W., and Pike, R., *The UNIX Programming Environment,* Prentice Hall, Englewood Cliffs, N.J., 1984.

Khanna, R., *Distributed Computing: Implementation and Management Strategies,* Prentice Hall, 1993.

Kim, W., *Introduction to Object Databases,* MIT Press, 1990.

Lewis, T., "Where is Client/Server Software Headed," *IEEE Computer Magazine,* April 1995, pp. 49–55.

Linthicum, D., "Reevaluating Distributed Objects," *DBMS,* January 1997, pp. 44–52.

Livingston, D., "Software Links Multivendor Networks," *Micro-Mini Systems,* March 1988.

Loomis, M., *Object Databases: The Essentials,* Addison Wesley, 1995.

Meade, D., "Object Lessons," *Beyond Computing,* July/August 1995, pp. 41–42.

Moad, J., "Double Impact," *Datamation,* August 1, 1992, pp. 28–33.

Mowbray, T., and Zahavi, R., *The Essential CORBA,* John Wiley, 1995.

Naylor, A., and Volz, R., "Design of Integrated Manufacturing System Control Software," *IEEE Transactions on Systems, Man and Cybernetics,* Vol. SMC-17, No. 6, November/December 1987.

Nehmer, J., and Mattern, F., "Framework for the Organization of Cooperative Services in Distributed Client/Server Systems," *Computer Communications,* Vol. 15, No. 4, May 1992, pp. 261–269.

Nesset, D., and Lee, G., "Terminal Services in Heterogeneous Distributed Systems," *Journal of Computer Networks and ISDN Systems,* 19 (1990), pp. 105–128.

Neuman, B., and Ts'o, T., "Kerberos; An Authentication Service for Computer Networks," *IEEE Communications Magazine,* pp. 33–37.

Nicol, J., et al., "Object Orientation in Heterogeneous Distributed Computing Systems," *IEEE Computer,* June 1993, pp. 57–67.

Nitzberg, B., and Lo, V., "Distributed Shared Memory: A Survey of Issues and Approaches," *IEEE Computer,* August 1991, pp. 52–60.

Nutt, G., *Centralized and Distributed Operating Systems,* Prentice Hall, 1992.

Orfali, R., Harkey, D., and Edwards, J., *Client/Server Survival Guide,* Van Nostrand Reinholt, 1994.

Orfali, R., Harkey, D., and Edwards, J., *The Essential Distributed Objects Survival Guide,* John Wiley, 1996.

Ozsu, M., and Valdurez, P., "Distributed Database Systems: Where Are We Now?" *IEEE Computer,* August 1991, pp. 68–78.

Pancake, C., "The Promise and the Cost of Object Technology: A Five-Year Forecast," *Communications of the ACM,* October 1995, pp. 32–49.

Pountain, D., "The X Window System," *BYTE,* January 1989, pp. 353–360.

Pree, W., "Frameworks—Past, Present, Future," *Object Magazine,* May 1996, pp. 24–27.

Ricciuti, M., "Universal Data Access," *Datamation,* November 1, 1991.

Ricciuti, M., "Here Come The HR Client/Server Systems," *Datamation,* July 1, 1992.

Rosenberry, W., et al., *Understanding DCE,* O'Reilly & Associates, 1993

Rumbaugh, J., et al., *Object-Oriented Modeling and Design,* Prentice Hall, 2d ed., 1994.

Rymer, J., "Business Objects," *Distributed Computing Monitor,* Patricia Seybold Group, January 1995.

Saunders, J., "A Survey of Object Oriented Programming Languages," *Journal of Object Oriented Programming Languages,* March/April 1989.

Scheife, R., *X Protocol Reference Manual,* O'Reilly and Associates, 1990

Schiller, J., "Secure Distributed Computing," *Scientific American,* November 1994, pp. 72–76.

Schlack, M., "The Key to Client/Server OLTP," *Datamation,* April 1, 1995, pp. 53–56.

Schulte, R., "Distributed Software Architecture in Full Bloom," *Gartner Group Briefing,* San Diego, February 1995

Sechrest, S., "An Introductory 4.3BSD Interprocess Communications Tutorial," *Computer Science Research Division,* Department of Electrical Engineering and Computer Science, University of California, Berkeley, 1986.

Shan, Y., "Introduction (Smalltalk on the Rise)," *Communications of the ACM,* October 1995, pp. 102–105.

Shatz, S. M, and Wang, J. P., "Introduction to Distributed Software Engineering," *IEEE Computer,* October 1987.

Sinha, A., "Client/Server Computing: Current Technology Review," *Communications of the ACM,* July 1992, pp. 77–96.

Snell, N., "The New MVS: Tuned to Serve?" *Datamation,* July 15, 1992, pp. 76–77.

Spooner, D., "An Object Oriented Data Management System for Mechnical CAD," *IEEE,* 1986 Conference on Graphics.

Stevens, W., *UNIX Network Programming,* Prentice Hall, 1990.

Svobodova, L., "File Servers for Network-Based Distributed Systems," *ACM Computing Surveys,* December 1984, pp. 353–398.

Tannenbaum, A., *Computer Networks,* 2d ed., Prentice Hall, 1988.

Tannenbaum, A., *Modern Operating Systems,* Prentice Hall, 1992.

Taylor, D., *Object-Oriented Technology: A Manager's Guide,* Addison Wesley, 1994.

Trllica, C. "Software Applications," *IEEE Spectrum,* January 1996, pp. 56–59.

Umar, A., *Distributed Computing and Client/server Systems*, Prentice Hall, rev. ed., 1993.

Umar, A., *Object-Oriented Client/Server Internet Environments,* Prentice Hall, 1997.

Vaskevitz, D., *Client/Server Strategies: A Survival Guide for Corporate Reengineers,* IDG Books, 1993.

Vaughan-Nichols, S., "Object-Futures: The Top Ten Trends of 1997," *Object Magazine,* January 1997, pp. 54–55.

Vinzant, D., "SQL Database Servers," *Data Communications,* January 1990, pp. 72–86.

Wegner, P., "Dimensions of Object-Based Language Design," *SIGPLAN Notices,* Vol. 22, No. 12, Dec. 1987, pp. 168–182.

White, D., "SQL Database Servers: Networking Meets Data Management," *Data Communications,* September 1990, pp. 31–39.

Whiting, R.(a), "Getting on the Middleware Express," *Client/Server Today,* November 1994, pp. 70–75.

Whiting, R.(b), "Turning to MOM for the Answers," *Client/Server Today,* November 1994, pp. 76–81.

Wilbur, S. and Bacarisse, B., "Building Distributed Systems with Remote Procedure Calls," *Software Engineering Journal,* September 1987, pp. 148–159.

Wood, A., "Predicting Client/Server Availability," *IEEE Computer Magazine,* April 1995, pp. 41–48.

Wooding, T., "Business Frameworks," *Object Magazine,* January 1997, pp. 50–53.

Zuck, J., "Front-end Tools," *PC Magazine,* September 1992, pp. 295–332.

3

Methodology Overview: Planning and Modeling

3.1   Introduction

This chapter presents a methodology "pattern" that can be customized to engineer new applications and reengineer existing (mostly legacy) applications in the object-oriented client/server Internet environments. There is no "one size fits all" approach but there are certain generic activities that take place whether you are developing a data warehouse, an electronic commerce application, a Web-based work flow system, a Web-based object wrapper for legacy applications, or a gateway for migrating legacy applications. In particular, you should not have to rethink the entire process for the aforementioned situations. Our goal is to present a set of generic activities and answer the following questions:

- What are the key customizable activities of a generalized application engineering/reengineering methodology (see Section 3.2)?

- How does planning fit into this methodology (see Section 3.3)?

- Can an object-oriented framework be used to model the wide range of applications being engineered and/or the legacy applications being reengineered (see Section 3.4)?

Key Points

- An application engineering/reengineering methodology pattern consists of successive iterations, refinements, and expansions of four broad activities: analysis, solution architectures, implementations, and deployment/support activities.

- Overall planning should always be the first iteration of the process and should concentrate on business opportunity analysis and risk analysis to determine the best strategy.

- The object model can be used as a foundation for almost all application engineering/reengineering issues.

3.2   Application (Re)Engineering Methodology[1]

A methodology is needed to direct the application engineering/reengineering activities. Before proceeding with details, we should acknowledge that formal methodologies have had

---

1. Throughout this book, we will use application (re)engineering to indicate application engineering/reengineering.

mixed results [Inmon 1993], and [Mowbray 1995]. The appeal of a methodology is that it directs the developers down a reasonable path with pointers for what to do, in what order to do it, what to produce, and what to expect as inputs. However, many methodologies fail because of their linear flow of activities, rigidity in a prescribed set of activities, and emphasis on diagramming tools. For example, more than two dozen methodologies based on object-orientation have been documented [Hutt 1994]. To ameliorate some of the concerns, work in standardizing software life-cycle activities has been initiated [Singh 1995].

Figure 3.1 shows a "methodology pattern" for application engineering/reengineering. This pattern represents a template that can be customized for specific cases. The key points of this methodology pattern are:

- Application engineering/reengineering is an intensely iterative process.
- All iterations are based on the refinement and expansion of the following core activities:
  - Analysis,
  - Solution architectures,
  - Implementations, and
  - Deployment/support
- Planning, prototyping/experimentation, first release, and subsequent releases are in fact iterations (not separate phases) in which each one of these activities is performed at different levels of detail.
- Some activities are more extensive than others in each iteration (represented by the width of activity triangle traversed in each iteration in Figure 3.1). For example, the first iteration requires extensive analysis and architecture but minimal implementation and deployment/support activities. This is because the first iteration emphasizes business opportunity analysis and assessment of technical feasibility through architectural evaluations. However, later iterations successively reduce the time spent in analysis and architecture activities but increase the implementation and deployment/support activities. Naturally, later releases of a system are heavily implementation and deployment/support centric.
- For a major release or enhancement of an application, you may restart the entire process with the first iteration.

Let us briefly review these iterations before getting into details (Figure 3.2 maps this methodology to the organization of this book).

> **Planning.** The first iteration, discussed in Section 3.3, essentially concentrates on overall planning. It identifies the business drivers; key stakeholders/funding sources; high-level requirements; and costs/benefits based on a quick review of proposed solution architectures, implementation considerations, and deployment/support issues raised. The main purpose of this iteration, in our case, is to answer the following application (re)engineering question: *Given the high level requirements and business drivers, should new application(s) be built (i.e., engineered) from scratch, should existing application(s) be reengineered, or should a mixture of engineering/reengineering approaches (e.g., build a small portion and interface it with existing) be used?*

Figure 3.1 A General Methodology Pattern

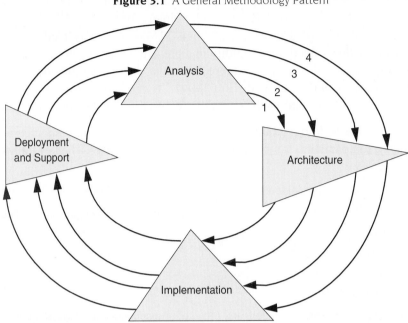

Notes:
The methodology template shows four broad iterative activities (stages). In each
iteration, each activity is performed, however, some activities are more extensive than others
in each iteration. The proportion of effort spent in each activity is represented
by the distance covered in each triangle. For example, the first iteration involves
extensive analysis and architecture, but very little implementation and deployment
activities. Later iterations successively reduce the analysis and architecture but
increase the implementation and deployment activities. The following iterations
are shown (more can be added):
   1 = First Iteration = Planning
   2 = Second Iteration = Prototyping and Experimentation
   3 = Third Iteration = First Release
   4 = Fourth Iteration = Second Release

Modeling and Prototyping. In the second iteration, discussed in Section 3.4, we typically
build prototypes and experiment with the architectures, implementations, and deployment/
support aspects of an application to gain insights into feasibility and effort sizing. In particular, the application (re)engineering decision made in planning is revised, if needed.
Although the specific steps and tools in this iteration depend on the type of applications, we
suggest that an object-oriented approach is quite useful as an overall framework. In particular, we show that development of an object model by using an object-oriented analysis
approach can be a good starting point for almost all application engineering/reengineering
activities (see Section 3.4).

Production Iterations. In the next iterations, the first and future releases of the application are built and deployed. The specific steps and tools in these iterations depend on the type of applications and on the type of application engineering/reengineering approaches. Part II and Part III of this book will explore these iterations in more detail.

Figure 3.2 Application (Re)Engineering Methodology—Another View

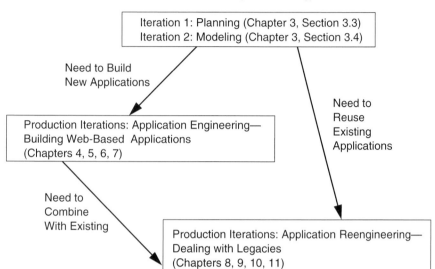

This general methodology pattern is based on my own experience in three different areas: (a) more than ten years of real life detailed participation in a wide range of application engineering/reengineering projects,[2] (b) development and teaching of numerous information system analysis and design courses, and (c) extensive examination of the extant literature in methodologies such as the following:

- IS planning methodologies [Blokdijk 1987], [Zachman 1982], [IBM 1978], [Rockart 1982], [Keen 1991], and [Luftman 1993].
- Object-oriented analysis and design methodologies [Booch 1994], [Rumbaugh 1994], [Jacobson 1992], and [Nerson 1995].
- Special design methodologies for application areas such as data warehouses [Inmon 1994] and [Inmon 1993], real-time systems [Fuhrt 1995], and [Gemmel 1995], hypermedia applications [Isakowitz 1995], and rapid prototyping [Gordon 1995].
- Methodologies for reengineering of legacy systems [Brodie 1995], [Sneed 1995], and [Desfrey 1996].
- Rapid prototyping approaches, such as the ones reported by Gordon [1995] that are based on review of almost 40 case studies.

---

2. Since the early 1980s, I have had several development, architecture, and project management assignments in different industry segments: manufacturing, government, and telecommunications. These assignments have spanned different underlying platforms (MVS, Unix, PC, SNA, TCP/IP, IMS, DB2, Informix, Oracle, etc.).

How to Succeed by Trying

1. Be clear about what you are trying to accomplish and what are the business drivers.

2. Involve business and IT groups early (planning stage) in the process.

3. Take every opportunity to improve the business processes and keep technology innovation as a lower level objective.

4. Keep projects short so that you can measure success/failure.

5. Base transition strategies on investments that are already necessary.

6. Get sponsorship/buy-in from senior management.

7. Do not forget/underestimate the people issues.

8. Overinvest in end-user support.

9. Use information technologies as enablers and not as drivers of change.

10. Pay special attention to reuse of existing resources including legacy.

Sources:

Adhikari, R., "Taking Care of Business," *Software Magazine,* June 1996, pp. 57–62.

Candler, J., et al., "The ORION Project: Staged Business Process Reengineering at FedEx," *Communications of the ACM,* February 1996, pp. 99–107.

Davenport, T., and Short, J., "The New Industrial Engineering: Information Technology and Business Process Redesign," *Sloan Management Review,* Summer 1990, pp. 11–27.

Schulman, J., "Transition to the New Computing Environment," *Gartner Briefing,* February 1995.

3.3 Application Planning—The First Iteration

3.3.1 Overview

The purpose of application planning is to align the application (re)engineering with business goals. Several methodologies have been developed for this planning process initiated with the "classical" information systems planning methodologies such as the following:

- IBM's Business Systems Planning [IBM 1978], and [Zachman 1982]
- Rockart's Critical Success Factors [Rockart 1982]
- Nolan's Stage Model [Nolan 1973]

Extensions of these methodologies have been reported such as the BSP extensions by Blokdijk and Blokdijk [Blokdijk 1987], and homegrown methodologies [Meyer 1996], [Highsmith 1987], [Hulfnagel 1987], and [Mushet 1985].

Of particular interest are the business process reengineering (BPR) approaches that align IT with business [Boar 1994], [Henderson 1990], [Keen 1993], [Luftman 1996], and [Venkatraman 1984] and the Internet related strategies [Cronin 1996]. Extensive discussion of BPR and planning methodologies is beyond the scope of this book (the aforementioned references should be reviewed for details). However, the following key BPR principle will guide our discussion: *You should use information technology to improve the performance of a business and cut costs by redesigning work and business processes from the ground up instead of simply automating existing tasks.*

This principle should be the driver as you go through the activities of the planning iteration (i.e., analysis, architectural trade-offs, implementation issues, and deployment/support considerations). Table 3.1 casts these activities into planning steps and Figure 3.3 ties these generic planning steps into a procedure. We will discuss these steps in the following subsections.

TABLE 3.1 APPLICATION PLANNING CHECKLIST

Activities	Steps
Analysis	**Step 1.** (a) Establish business drivers (b) Solicit high-level requirements (c) Analyze business opportunity
Architecture	**Step 2.** (a) Investigate application architecture approaches (b) Choose the most appropriate application engineering/reengineering strategy **Step 3.** (a) Assess IT infrastructure needed (b) Choose the most appropriate IT infrastructure
Implementation	**Step 4.** Investigate implementation issues (i.e., skill, resources, time, and money needed to implement)
Deployment and support	**Step 4.** (continued) • Estimate effort needed to deploy and support • Outline costs (pitfalls) and benefits (promises) • Evaluate if costs are worth the benefits

Based on the results of the planning iteration, and any other relevant information, an initial important decision is made: *given a business opportunity, should a new application be developed (application engineering), should existing applications be reengineered, or should a mixture of engineering/reengineering be used?*[3] This decision may be revised in later iterations as we develop a better understanding of the problem and the various trade-offs. However, this decision will help us to outline a rough project plan that specifies:

- Goals and objectives of (re)engineering
- Expected benefits and risks
- Main steps, the deliverables, and time lines
- Key staff assignments, i.e., the roles and responsibilities of internal IS staff as well as external consultants and systems integrators

This plan is used to define the next iterations and to decide how much effort will be spent in engineering versus reengineering. Keep in mind that planning does not need to take a long time, it just needs to be done. In my own experience, I have found that preparation of a response to each RFQ (request for quotation) essentially goes through the planning steps.

Figure 3.3 Overall Planning Procedure

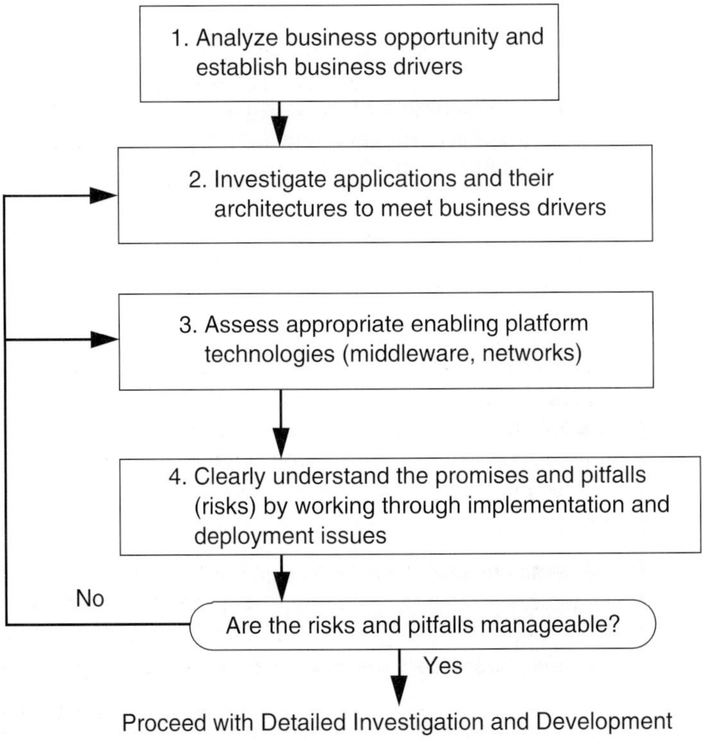

1. Analyze business opportunity and establish business drivers

2. Investigate applications and their architectures to meet business drivers

3. Assess appropriate enabling platform technologies (middleware, networks)

4. Clearly understand the promises and pitfalls (risks) by working through implementation and deployment issues

No

Are the risks and pitfalls manageable?

Yes

Proceed with Detailed Investigation and Development

---

3. In most practical cases, a mixture of engineering and reengineering is needed. For example, many new Web-based applications are being engineered that also require reengineering of existing applications.

3.3.2 Step 1: Identify Business Drivers and Establish High-Level Requirements

Application (re)engineering is an expensive and risky undertaking. The purpose of this step is to understand and analyze the basis and business motivation for this effort before fully launching it. Although different business drivers motivate application (re)engineering the following broad categories represent many business drivers:

- Business process reengineering (for example, BPR of healthcare industries has initiated many new applications to be developed and many legacy applications to be reengineered [Gambon 1996]).

- New services or business opportunities (for example, a large number of companies are building new Web-based applications to take advantage of the new opportunities created due to the explosion of Internet) [Cronin 1996].

- To gain and maintain competitive edge (for example, many companies are investigating electronic commerce to gain competitive edge in this rapidly growing area [Adam 1996].

- To align IT with business (for example, many companies are reevaluating their IT services and aligning them with the business [Luftman 1996]).

In addition to business drivers, you need to develop an understanding of the business requirements that drive the technical requirements (Figure 3.4). In particular, you need to identify the organization and the processes that will be served by the applications and develop an "end-user" profile that shows the characteristics of the user community (e.g., decision support versus operational support users, novices versus "power users"). You also need to identify the main customers and stakeholders who will benefit from the proposed applications. In addition, these requirements should capture:

- Business goals in terms of short-term and long-term goals of the FMO (Future Mode of Operation)
- The main stakeholders who will benefit from the effort
- The business problems with PMO (Present Mode of Operation)
- Funding sources and limits
- Time frame

Keep in mind that these requirements are very high level (also known as "thin" requirements) and are meant to help you assess readiness for (re)engineering. These requirements should be between 20 to 30 statements and must not include screen layouts and other programming details (all that comes later).

After identifying and clearly understanding the business drivers and high-level requirements, you should analyze the opportunity by posing questions such as the following:

- Are we doing the right things? (For instance, can the information technologies help us to reshape our future? Are our information services providing us competitive edge? Will they help us to administer our business objectives? Will they enable us to adapt to unexpected changes?)

- Are we doing things right? (Are we minimizing the unit costs for each information service? Is the value of information service worth the cost?)

- Are we heading in the right direction? (Are we listening to our customers and paying attention to their information services needs? Are we aware of the changing market and government conditions?)

- What are the services we are good at and what are the services we need to improve/ discontinue? (Are we sinking too much money into older technologies? How confident are we about the new technologies?)

As a result of these questions, an overall strategy can be established that defines a short and long range vision for the applications and services under consideration. It is the responsibility of management to develop and present a clearly defined and doable vision. Unfounded visions and too many visions ("vision of the day") cause serious problems. Announcing a vision is not enough; continued and visible support from management is essential for the success of a strategy [Henderson 1990], and [Luftman 1996]. One possible approach to achieve these objectives is to get the information technology experts involved early in the planning process. These experts can help in making the vision realistic and then work as agents and supporters during the implementation stages.

Figure 3.4 Business Requirements Drive the Technical Requirements

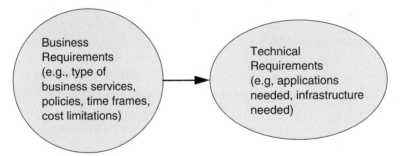

3.3.3   Step 2: Investigate Application Architecture Approaches

Given an understanding of the business drivers and high-level requirements that conform to an overall business strategy, the next challenge is to architect a solution approach that could satisfy these requirements. Specifically, you need to answer questions such as the following:

- Should an off-the-shelf package be used to satisfy the requirements?

- Should a new application software be developed from scratch and use existing databases?

- Should a new database be developed that is accessed from existing application software?

- Should a new user interface (Web interface) be developed while utilizing the existing databases and application software?

- Should the entire application be developed from scratch (i.e., new user interfaces, new application code, new databases)?

The answer depends on how new is the business undertaking, what already exists in your organization, what is available as a commercial off-the-shelf package, and how flexible is the existing system. In general, we can analyze these decisions based on the following three factors:

- **Databases.** Are new databases needed or can the existing databases do the job? For example, several existing databases of legacy systems contain valuable information (customer information) that is needed by new applications.

- **Business functions**. Are new business functions needed or can the existing business be invoked and used to satisfy the requirements? For example, many existing applications have code that performs regularly used business functions such as generating bills, checking inventory levels and crediting/debiting accounts. The question is: Can this code be reused?

- **User interfaces**. Are new user interfaces needed or can the existing user interfaces do the job? The user interfaces is an area of considerable activity at present due to the popularity of Web browsers. In many cases, Web interfaces are being developed for existing applications even if the current user interfaces are quite good. This is motivated by the desire of organizations to use Web browsers as the primary source for accessing *all* information.

Figure 3.5 shows how these three factors can be used to systematically generate application engineering/reengineering choices. Evaluation of these choices is a time-consuming, yet an essential, aspect of contemporary application engineering/reengineering practice. Broadly speaking, the choices are a mixture of purchasing off-the-shelf packages, developing new application components from scratch, and interfacing of new components with the existing, in many cases, legacy systems.

Purchasing off-the-shelf applications is a viable solution when new databases and new functions are needed. This strategy, if feasible, is by far the most attractive. Consequently, it must be considered as the first choice. For example, if a human resource (HR) application is needed and the requirements seem to be satisfied by an off-the-shelf HR system from a vendor, then this package should be evaluated seriously. The key evaluation criteria are:

- Will this package satisfy the current as well as future requirements?
- Will this package scale well?
- What is the current user experience base?
- Does it conform to the infrastructure standards?

In many cases, some or all portions of an application (databases, application code, user interfaces) need to be developed. For example, it is possible that the requirements can be satisfied by engineering (designing, developing, and deploying) a new database that is accessed by off-the shelf packages or end-user tools such as spreadsheets, data browsers, and report writers (e.g., data warehousing applications). If new application code needs to be developed, then we can assume that the new application code will be developed as an object-oriented C/S application. In a few cases, all components of new applications need to be developed. Part II of this book (Chapters 4 through 7) discuss these issues in detail.

Figure 3.5 Application Engineering/Reengineering Approaches

Database Needed	Business Functions Needed	User Interface Needed	Potential Application Engineering/Reengineering Choice
New	New	New	Buy a new system
New	New	New	Develop a new system from Scratch
Existing	New	New	Develop new application code and user interface (e.g., Web)
New	Existing	New	Develop a new user interface that invokes existing code
New	New	Existing	Develop new databases and application code
Existing	Existing	New	Develop new user interface (e.g. Web) to access existing (legacy) applications
Existing	New	Existing	Invoke new application functions from existing user interface
New	Existing	Existing	Develop a new database that is accessed from existing application code and user interfaces
Existing	Existing	Existing	Use existing application. May require some reengineering if the existing application is too old.

Legend:
- Unshaded rows: need entirely new application (application engineering)
- Lightly shaded rows: need a combination of new and existing (application reengineering)
- Dark shaded row: need to reuse existing application only
  Note that most real-life situations require a combination of engineering/reengineering.

Reengineering (redesign, migration, interfacing) of existing, in many cases legacy, applications is an important aspect of IT practice at present. For example, it may be possible to satisfy the requirements by reengineering (i.e., interfacing and migrating) the existing databases. Access to enterprise data, especially legacy data, from a diverse array of tools and applications residing on a variety of platforms and interconnected through different network technologies is of key importance in most enterprises. In particular, many Web-based tools need to access enterprise data. In several cases, the requirements can only be satisfied by re-architecting and migrating the existing legacy applications that are old, unstructured, and monolithic. Choice of an appropriate approach depends on several factors such as business value of the legacy system and its technical value (see Figure 3.6). We will discuss the legacy application reengineering issues in Part III of this book (Chapters 8 through 11).

Figure 3.6 Legacy Application Analysis (*Source*: [Sneed 1995])

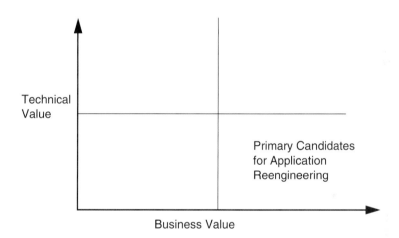

3.3.4   Step 3: Assess and Plan Infrastructure Architectures

IT infrastructure (platform) planning is concerned with determining the most appropriate technology needed to develop and deploy the application systems. Examples of such infrastructures are the Intranets that provide Web services in corporate private networks; factory networks that connect many manufacturing devices to cell and area controllers, and "Extranets" that connect many businesses (healthcare industry participants). IT infrastructure planning is a much more challenging and crucial task than network planning. This is because the diverse applications in business, engineering, and manufacturing written in different software/database formats that reside on heterogeneous computing devices need to be interconnected through different communication media by using a variety of communication software packages.

Specifically, the main infrastructure capabilities (middleware, network services, local computing services) needed to support applications that must be carefully examined in the planning iteration. (See Figure 3.7.) The IT infrastructure becomes increasingly important as you iterate through the system life cycle (i.e., planning iteration only concentrates on high level issues that could be "show stoppers" while the first release must go through detailed considerations such as the exact version of middleware needed). The details depend on the type of applications being engineered/reengineered. For example, legacy data access requires a different type of infrastructure than a Web-based distributed object application.

Basically, the entire IT infrastructure should appear as a tightly integrated environment that provides a range of networking, database, transaction management, remote messaging, naming, directory, security, and other services needed by the applications. The key question is: How can we put all these pieces together into a functioning IT infrastructure that can support the variety of services and applications needed by the modern enterprises? The following iterative steps are suggested as a starting point:

- Analyze the requirements for infrastructure
- Architect the infrastructure services
- Implement the infrastructure services
- Deploy and support the infrastructure services

Table 3.2 summarizes the main activities in each stage of the methodology introduced in Section 3.2 for the infrastructure services. The rows of this table show the four generic activities (i.e., analysis, architecture, implementation, deployment) and the columns represent the three classes of infrastructure services (i.e., middleware, network, local).

As discussed previously, infrastructure issues are beyond the scope of this book and were briefly introduced in Chapter 2. A detailed procedure for selection and evaluation of OCSI infrastructure can be found in the companion book [Umar 1997, Chapter 9].

Figure 3.7 Conceptual View of Infrastructure Role

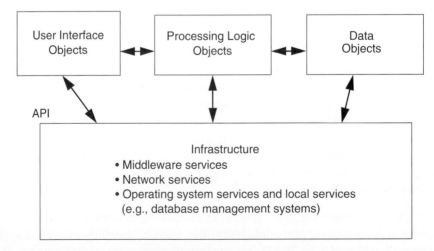

TABLE 3.2 SUMMARY OF INFRASTRUCTURE CONSIDERATIONS

Stage	Middleware	Network Services	Local Computing Services
Analysis	Specification and analysis of requirements for middleware services	Specification and analysis of requirements for network services	Specification and analysis of requirements for local computing services
Architecture	Select proper middleware (e.g., Web services, distributed objects, distributed data middleware)	Select proper network products (e.g., communication technologies, interconnectivity devices)	Select proper local computing products (e.g., database managers, operating systems)
Implementation	Select new vendor products and/or upgrade existing ones	Select new vendor products and/or upgrade existing ones	Select new vendor products and/or upgrade existing ones
Deployment and support	Examine and investigate deployment and support considerations	Examine and investigate deployment and support considerations	Examine and investigate deployment and support considerations

3.3.5   Step 4: Cost/Benefit Analysis

3.3.5.1   Overview

The main purpose of cost/benefit analysis is to compare the business benefits with the estimated time, money, computing, and human resources needed for the proposed application engineering/reengineering. The key idea is to determine if the proposed engineering/reengineering is cost-beneficial and if the risks are manageable. You must clearly understand the risks and payoffs before launching an effort, because engineering of new and reengineering of existing applications is not risk free. Although it is fashionable to jump on the latest technology bandwagon, many new technologies need to prove themselves in large scale mission critical situations and demonstrate business payoffs. Object-oriented, client/server, Internet-based technologies are no exception.

Costs and benefits of emerging technologies such as object-oriented, client/server, Internet (OCSI) environments is tricky. In general, most new technologies are accompanied by euphoric claims of benefits/promises with a deaf ear (typically for two to four years) to costs/pitfalls. To some extent, this "positive wave" is natural because the real costs and pit-falls are revealed only after some hands-on experiences have been accumulated. In recent years, this happened with client/server (C/S) systems. We do not know the real costs and benefits of OCSI at the time of this writing due to its newness. However, we can review the results of C/S computing and extrapolate some results to learn some lessons. Towards this goal, the costs and benefits of C/S computing are reviewed in Sections 3.3.5.2 and 3.3.5.3.

The client/server technology wave hit us all around 1992 as a cure for all the evils of the old mainframe-based systems. Many C/S success stories have been reported in the trade journal since 1992. However, there have been numerous failures, albeit not well documented (see the sidebar in Chapter 1 "Failures—Lessons from the Client/Server Wave"). Here is the main lesson: There will be successes as well as failures in OCSI implementations, but fail-ures will rarely be publicized and will come to surface a few years after the initial wave (usually at the beginning of the next wave).

Cost/benefit analysis of IT, in general, is fuzzy and subjective. The main idea is to be realis-tic in your expectations about benefits and costs. Since costs (and risks) are facts of life, you need to determine the strategies that maximize business benefits and minimize/manage costs and risks. Survey of a large number of case studies has indicated that successful application engineering/reengineering efforts exploit the promises of new technologies but carefully understand and manage the risks while the others do not (see Figure 3.8).[4] What precisely are the promises and pitfalls of OCSI applications from what we know at this point? See the sidebar in Chapter 1 "Why Object-Oriented Client/Server Internet-based Applications: Promises and Pitfalls." We will visit these issues in more detail in Chapter 4.

3.3.5.2 Estimating Costs of Client/Server

A few surveys for the costs/benefits of C/S computing have been published (see the sidebar "Sources of Information for Client/Server Costs/Benefits"). For example, a Gartner Group [Dec 1995] report analyzed costs for C/S computing (see Table 3.3). The main findings of this analysis are:

- Hardware/software costs represent only 15 to 20 percent of total cost
- Labor costs represent the largest expense (70 to 75 percent of the total costs are labor)
- Total cost per client is about $50K for five years

Dec [1995] also includes a report card on C/S computing. Basically, the report card gives C/S computing failing grades on lowering costs (costs go up), higher availability (C/S systems tend to fail more often), and serviceability (too many components to service). However, the grades for rapid deployment and better scalability are better (B and C, respectively).

---

4. More than 40 case studies were reviewed in preparation of this book. The case studies indicated successes as well as failures. We will discuss many of these case studies in subsequent chapters.

Figure 3.8 Recipes for Success and Failure

(a) Recipe for Success

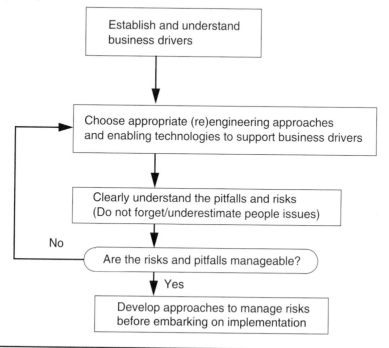

(b) Recipe for Disaster

TABLE 3.3 HOW MUCH DO CLIENT/SERVER SYSTEMS COST? (SOURCE: [DEC 1995])

	Small Organization	**Large Organization**
Configuration	Single site 20 clients One PC-based server One LAN administrator	250 remote sites with servers 5,000 clients Legacy and new enterprise servers 83 end-user support staff 55 application developers Centralized management
Total Costs	Total five-year C/S cost: $1,016,000 Cost per client = $50,000	Total five-year cost: $241,800,000 Cost per client: $48,400
Cost Break-down:	72% of the cost is labor 41%: End-user labor 15%: End-user support	72% of the cost is labor 41%: End-user labor 15%: End-user support

Many costs are hidden and are not apparent initially in C/S projects. For example, middleware costs per mainframe is about $200K, and per PC cost is about $500K. Installation of a large scale C/S system involving, for example, 1000 desktops could easily cost 0.5 million dollars. Distributed applications also require many software licenses at many computers, thus potentially increasing the software costs.

The initial axiom of one server machine per application has not resonated very well. According to a study conducted by the University of California at Berkeley's School of Business, every $1,000 spent on server hardware/software needs to be matched with $9,000 of management and maintenance costs [Jenkins 1995]. Owing to this, many organizations have started using powerful servers that can house many applications (i.e., more centralization).

While estimating costs, intangibles need to be considered. Examples of these intangibles are increases in interdependencies and points of failure, concerns for security and integrity control, and many management/support issues. We will visit these issues in Chapter 4.

Costs of migration to OCSI should be evaluated very carefully (we will visit this issue in Part III of this book). Basically, the potential of big savings for application migration to OCSI is there, but keep in mind that the mainframe costs are dropping.[5] In addition, many hidden costs are hard to control/quantify, because significant costs shift to consulting and training. Full cost savings can only be realized if the mainframes are retired completely and the expected payoffs do not happen right away (many efforts take three to four years with

---

5. A study by International Technology Group indicates that its average cost per mainframe user is $5K per year versus $88K per year for UNIX users [Simpson 1997].

payoffs in the last year). In addition, many people issues arise, because traditional IS staff and users may resist (new skills are usually needed) and responsibilities shift to end users. The bottom line: *hardware cost savings alone are not enough for transitions and should not be used as the key business drivers.*

In summary, it has been found that C/S *increases* total costs due to the following reasons:

- End-user effort in learning and operating desktops is higher
- End-user help desks require more support
- Many hidden costs at end-user sites (e.g., middleware) emerge
- Distributed applications are more complex

Guidelines for Cost Estimation

Over the last 20 years, many cost estimation techniques for information systems have been suggested. Despite a great deal of work, most cost estimates in information systems are based on heuristics and guidelines. Lederer and Prasad [Lederer 1992] suggest the following nine guidelines for better cost estimation, with numerous examples:

- Assign the initial estimating task to the final developers.
- Delay finalizing the initial estimate until the end of a thorough study.
- Anticipate and control user changes.
- Monitor the progress of the proposed project.
- Evaluate proposed project progress by using independent auditors.
- Use the estimate to evaluate project personnel.
- Computing management should carefully study and approve the cost estimate.
- Rely on documented facts, standards, and simple arithmetic formulas rather than guessing, intuition, personal memory, and complex formulas.
- Do not rely on cost estimating software for an accurate estimate.

3.3.5.3   Estimating Benefits of Client/Server

Most benefit surveys are not quantitative. Benefits typically occur in the end-user departments and not in the corporate IT departments (thus they are difficult to understand and quantify). Frequently mentioned benefits of C/S technology will be discussed in Chapter 4 and include:

- Better organizational fit (decentralization and local autonomy)
- Improves competitiveness (e.g., presence in new markets)
- Improves customer service quality, and responsiveness
- Supports business restructuring

- Allows faster development of new applications
- Improves flexibility of services
- Easier access to corporate data
- Improves end-user productivity
- Reduces training time due to GUI
- Allows exploitation of new technology

The introduction of C/S technologies has in general strengthened the position of IT departments because some of the functionality and budget dollars have shifted to the IT departments away from the central MIS departments. (A Gartner Group 1996 report indicates that the annual revenue for decentralized functions will jump from 2.3 percent to 6.8 percent between 1994 to 1999 and will reduce from 2.0 percent to 1.6 percent for the centralized functions in the same time period.) However, the central MIS departments are not extinct—their role has changed to more enterprisewide consultation, integration, and management [Grygo 1996].

Sources of Information for Client/Server Costs/Benefits

- *Datamation* supplement "Client/Server: The Business Advantage," June 15, 1994.

- Dec, K., "Client/Server—Reality Sets in," *Gartner Group Briefing,* San Diego, February 22–24, 1995.

- DePompa, B., "Corporate Migration: Harder Than It Looks," *Information Week,* December 4, 1995, pp. 60–68.

- "Dirty Downsizing," *Computerworld,* Special Report, August 10, 1992.

- "Enterprise Client/Server: Can We Get There from Here?" *Gartner Group Briefing,* July/August 1994.

- Grygo, E., "Upper Hand," *Client/Server Computing,* August 1996, pp. 34–42.

- Jenkins, A., "Centralization Strikes Again," *Computerworld Client/Server Journal,* August 1995, pp. 28–31.

- Liana, A., "Controlling Costs for Downsizing," *IBM Internet Journal,* June 1994, pp. 34–39.

- Moad, J., "Client/Server Costs: Don't Get Taken for a Ride," *Datamation,* February 15, 1994, pp. 34–38.

- Simpson, D., "Are Mainframes Cool Again?" *Datamation*, April 1997, pp. 46–53.

- Standish Group Conference on Client/Server Failures.
  See http://www.standish.com.

- "Where Do Client/Server Apps Go Wrong?" *Datamation,* January 21, 1994, p. 30.

In general, C/S benefits are scattered outside the IS department such as:

- Flexibility in handling business changes
- End-user control increases

3.4   Object Modeling and Prototyping— Second Iteration

3.4.1   Overview

The iteration after overall planning is concerned with demonstrating feasibility through prototypes and experiments. In particular, the application (re)engineering decision made in planning (i.e., what needs to be built from scratch and what needs to be reused/restructured) is revised, if needed, based on the additional insights. In this iteration, the four generic activities of analysis, architectures, implementation, and deployment/support are repeated with particular emphasis on hands-on discovery instead of endless paper and pencil analysis. Although the details of this iteration depend on what is being engineered or reengineered, we adopt an OO view as an overall framework for discussion. In particular, the object life cycle shown in Table 3.4 serves as a general approach that we will customize as we go along. The basic idea is to develop and use an object model in this iteration and then refine and expand it in later iterations as production systems are built.

Why the emphasis on OO so early in life cycle? The main reason is that an early adoption of OO concepts leads to increased reuse, which in turn results in improved productivity and rapid deployment/re-deployment of applications as the business changes. Extensive data on productivity have been gathered by Capers Jones of Software Productivity Research, Inc. Analysis of over 5,000 products by Capers indicates the following [Sutherland 1994]:

- Reusability of C code is 15 percent (this reusability factor is the same for other 3GLs and 4GLs).
- OO languages like Smalltalk can achieve 50 percent reuse in the second year
- Reuse of OO languages increases to 80 percent in third year

This section assumes that the reader has a very basic understanding of OO concepts. The short tutorial on OO concepts at the end of Chapter 2 (Appendix 2A) will get you started. The discussion here is intentionally brief since a large body of literature is readily available on this topic [Booch 1994], [Rumbaugh 1994], [Jacobson 1992], and [Nerson 1995]. The focus is on the underlying principles and not on diagramming techniques (e.g., Booch's diagrams). Once the principles are established, the reader may employ any diagramming technique and associated tools.

TABLE 3.4 OBJECT LIFE-CYCLE CHECKLIST

Activities	Steps
Analysis (Object Modeling)	• Capture key requirements • Develop an object class model • Develop a system dynamic model
Architecture (Apply the Object Model to Design Application)	• Translate object and system dynamics model into modules • Allocate modules to processors • Develop interprocess communications • Develop pseudo-code and database design
Implementation (Build Application)	• Implement the user interfaces, databases, and program code • Test the system
Deployment and support	• Install and support the system • Enhance and maintain the system

The generic object life cycle shown in Table 3.4 is a good starting point.

The objective of OO analysis is to capture the key requirements and then translate these requirements into an object class model and a system dynamic model. Development of the object class model, discussed in Section 3.4.2.2, is at the core of the OO analysis and design approaches and is vital to application (re)engineering. The system dynamic model, reviewed in Section 3.4.2.3, is useful in most types of applications (see Section 3.4.3.1).

Object-oriented architecture/design casts the results of the OO analysis into a specification that can be implemented. This activity consists of translating object and system dynamics models into modules, allocation of modules to processors, specification of interprocess communications, and pseudo-code and database design. You exit this activity when you have enough details for implementations. Most of the current OO approaches assume development of software for a single machine (i.e., distributed objects are not considered). Due to this reason, we will need to extend and modify this activity considerably for distributed applications (see Sections 3.4.3.1 and 3.4.3.2).

Object-oriented implementation involves developing and testing user interfaces, programming logic, and databases. Typically, OO programming languages are used to implement features such as classes, inheritance, polymorphism, methods, and messages. The implemented system may use OO user interfaces (i.e., view systems as objects, present operations on objects) and OO databases (i.e., store objects in databases, perform operations on objects in databases).

Figure 3.9 shows how the OO analysis interrelates with overall planning and architecture/implementation. We discuss the shaded blocks in the next two sections within the context of second iteration (i.e., prototyping/experimentation).

Figure 3.9 OO Analysis

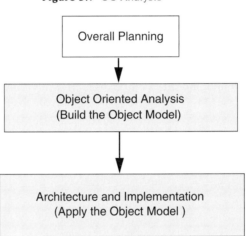

Note: Shaded areas are discussed in this section

3.4.2   Object-Oriented Analysis—Building the Object Model

3.4.2.1   Capture the Key Requirements

Capturing of key requirements is obviously important, independent of any methodology. In practice, the requirements are defined, refined, expanded, and modified based on additional insights gained through each iteration of the system. The requirements can be broadly viewed in terms of:

- Functional requirements that capture the capabilities to be provided by the application.

- Operational requirements represent a wide range of performance, security, and interconnectivity information.

- Management/organizational requirements establish the budgetary, time, and policy limits within which the application will be engineered/reengineered.

Specification of these requirements somewhat depends on the nature of applications being engineered/reengineered. We will discuss this topic in Part II and Part III of this book.

3.4.2.2 Develop an Object Model—The Core Activity

An *object model* represents the functional requirements of a system in terms of objects and classes in a tool and implementation independent fashion. The object model is developed by using the following activities:

1. Identify object classes

2. Specify relationships between object classes

3. Define the attributes and operations of object classes

4. Specify interfaces of objects

Consistent and complete notation is needed for representation of knowledge and communication of knowledge gained about the object model. Many CASE (computer aided software engineering) tools are based on notations to generate code. Notations should allow different views to be represented such as logical models, physical models, static semantics, and dynamic semantics. Common notations used in OO analysis and design are due to Booch and Rumbaugh, among others. Although we do not recommend any specific notation (you can choose a notation of your choice), we will use Booch's notation for illustration (see Figure 3.10).

Figure 3.10 Notation Used in OO Analysis (Booch)

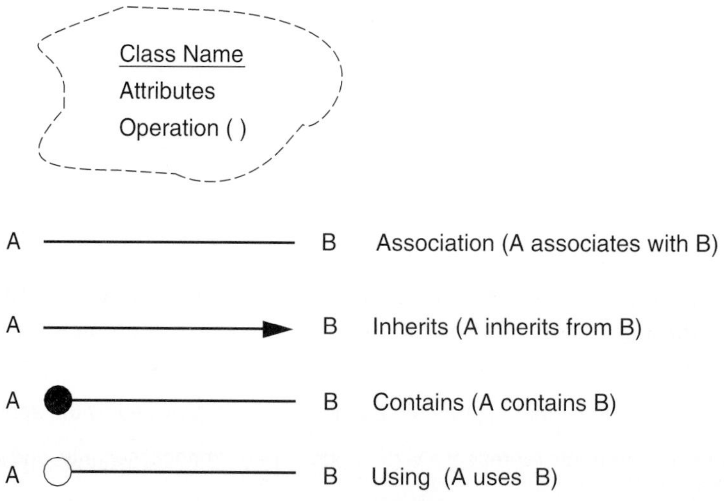

Class Name
Attributes
Operation ( )

A ———————— B Association (A associates with B)

A ————————▶ B Inherits (A inherits from B)

A ●———————— B Contains (A contains B)

A ○———————— B Using (A uses B)

Step 1: Identify Object Classes

Development of object classes, commonly known as classes, is at the core of OO analysis and design. Basically, a *class* is a template that represents the properties that are common among similar objects. For example, the class customer can be used to represent the common properties of all customers. The common properties include attributes such as name, address, customer id, et cetera and methods such as add, update, query, and the like. The relationship between an object and a class is straightforward—an object is an instance of a class. For example, if Buick is a class then all Buick cars can be viewed as objects (i.e., instances) of the class Buick. Due to this relationship, many people do not differentiate between objects and classes in this stage of analysis, because either way you are specifying the core components of the object model. To avoid confusion, the term object class is used sometimes to represent an object or a class (we will use the term class, because it is more commonly used).

How do you identify classes? Classes can represent real-world things such as a person, a building, a laptop computer, or a text editor. It can also represent concepts such as schedules, pay scales, or algorithms. *We strongly recommend to start with objects that represent business entities and not with programming objects such as GUI interfaces, stacks, queues, buttons, and the like* (see the sidebar "Business Objects: The Key to Reuse"). Here are some guidelines (see Fingar [1996], Baster [1997], and Gale [1997]):

- In the early iterations, concentrate on **business objects** (customers, orders) which represent business things and do not get bogged down with programming objects (stacks, queues) in developing an object model.

- Develop the model of your business processes as business objects (business entities with policies as methods). For example, you can represent different business units as objects (purchasing department, shipping/receiving department).

- Identify objects within the context of an application (the **application objects**) which can be used by other applications. This helps in reuse.

A wide range of techniques to assist in the intuitive task of identifying classes have been discussed [Booch 1994], [Rumbaugh 1994], [Rymer 1995], and [Vasudeva 1997]. Here are the key ideas:

- Start with reviewing the problem description and listing the nouns you encounter (classes often correspond to nouns).

- First focus on the nouns that represent physical objects (people, things, places, devices, machines). It is easier to think of real objects first and postpone abstract things for later iterations.

- Eliminate spurious classes by getting rid of redundancies (e.g., workers, employees and hired hands mean the same thing), irrelevant classes (e.g., classes that may not have anything to do with the application domain), attributes (e.g., names and addresses are attributes not classes), et cetera.

Business Objects: The Key to Reuse

The main business motivation for OO is increased reuse. The best way to achieve high reuse is to build objects that represent business entities (i.e., business objects). The basic idea of business objects is that the users can construct objects that represent the real-world concepts of the business. Examples of business objects are customer, order, product, and regional office. If software could be structured around such objects and other business concepts, then organizations would be able to build software that simulates current business strategy. Moreover, businesses could reuse these objects to build new applications by using the OO paradigm.

You can represent business processes as objects (business things with policies as methods). For example, you can represent different business units as objects (i.e., purchasing department, shipping/receiving department). Since these objects represent business processes, these objects can change as businesses change. By using the OO concepts of encapsulation and abstraction, you can hide the internal details of business processes and build new business processes from these objects. After the business processes have been modeled as business objects, you can build applications by implementing business objects into lower level technical objects (e.g., GUIs, databases, etc.).

Business objects started appearing in the marketplace around the introduction of OLE 2.0, OpenDoc, and CORBA-based products in 1994. Since then, OO tools designed to support creation of business objects have emerged from vendors such as Easel and applications that employ business objects have appeared from vendors such as SAP and IMRS. The Object Management Group (OMG) has found the Business Object Management Special Interest Group (BOMSIG) to help the industry understand and utilize this technology effectively. System integrators such as Anderson Consulting are also committing to deliver software environments that can be used to build custom applications based on business objects.

Business objects are at the core of "Class-Based Reengineering (CBR)" that integrates business process reengineering with object technologies [Newman 1996]. This approach starts out by building a business model in terms of object classes and then uses these classes to architect and build systems. The object classes can represent different business entities such as customers, loans, accounts, and the like. These classes can change to reflect business changes and tie into technology, because these classes can be implemented by using OO technologies.

Sources:

Fingar, P., "The Blueprint for Business Objects," *SIGS Book and Multimedia,* 1996.

Newman, D., "Class-Based Reengineering," *Object Magazine,* March 1996, pp. 68–74.

Object Magazine, January 1997, Special Issue on Business Objects.

Rymer, J., "Business Objects," *Distributed Computing Monitor,* Patricia Seybold Group, January 1995.

Sims, O., *Business Objects,* McGraw-Hill, 1994.

Sheldon, R., "Business Objects and BPR," *Data Management Review,* November 1994, pp. 6–20.

- Now extend the classes by adding Information sources/sinks (e.g., databases, files), concepts and events as potential classes if they are relevant to the application domain.

- It may also be advisable to identify the things used by the customers as objects.

- Go through several iterations and refinements by working through the design stage. In many cases, new object classes are discovered and existing classes are eliminated during the design stage.

For database designers, the process of identifying classes is very similar to identifying the entities in an entity-relationship data model.

Figure 3.11 shows the classes identified in a customer information system in which customers buy a variety of products such as TVs, radios, and their parts. We will expand this example as we go along.

Figure 3.11 Customer Information Object Model—Classes

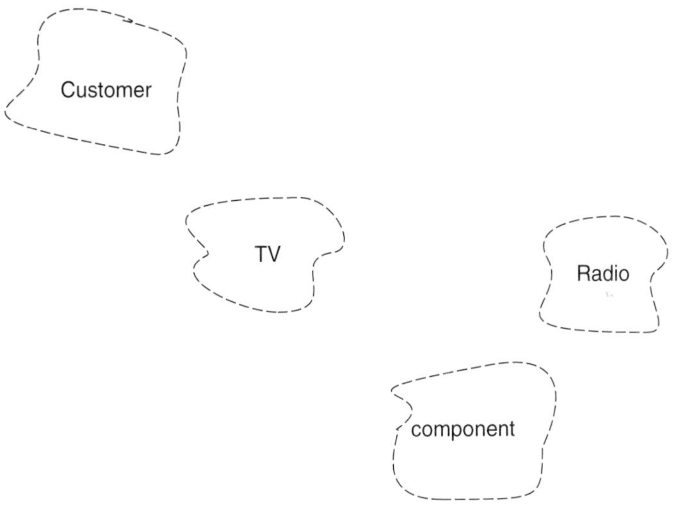

Identification of classes in large scale problems is an extensive undertaking (you can easily come up with hundreds of classes). Most methodologies for identifying object classes utilize English descriptions (nouns are classes/objects) and "use-cases" that exercise various scenarios. Many start with domain analysis, that is, rely on domain experts to help in identifying the classes and their behaviors. The domain analysis procedure for identifying classes starts with abstracting the things that are used in the domain and proceeds to representations of real-world objects such as an employee, machine, product, facility, or an organizational unit (e.g., a department). In addition, groups of users can be modeled as an object class. You may use the following guidelines:

- Develop a strawman general model of the domain by consulting with domain experts.

- Examine existing systems within the domain before concentrating on the new system.

- Note the similarities and differences between the existing and new systems.

- Keep the classes as close to the notion of "business objects" as possible. Make sure that the classes you are defining can be used by other applications.

- Keep the following "implementation" issues in mind: First, calls should not be modeled as objects because they are specific to implementations. Second, "size" of objects (in terms of the number of interactions) should be considered carefully. If objects are too small and involve too many interactions then too much intersystem communication can result. However, if objects are defined too broadly, then the memory requirements to handle such objects can be very large.

Classes at a Glance

Classes

- Class: set of objects with common properties (structure + behavior)
- Object: instance of a class
- Interface defines external view (i.e., what operations can be performed)
- Interface can consist of:

    Public: available to all classes

    Protected: available to class, subclass, and friends

    Private: available to class and friends only

Class Relationships

- Association: Links between classes.

    One to one

    One to many

    Many to many

- Aggregation: Part of (Containment relationships)
- Inheritance: inherit properties (data plus methods)

    Single inheritance

    Single polymorphism

    Multiple inheritance

- Using: Refinement of association

    Single direction (Client/server relationship)

- Metaclass: A class of classes

    Instances are classes

The output produced by this step is a list of classes that may be stored in a dictionary for later use. Additional details to these classes will be added later. We will see later that once you have identified a class, then you can easily translate it into code and can create any number of instances (objects) of each class (object-oriented programming languages provide statements to define classes and create objects).

Step 2: Specify Relationships (Associations) between Object Classes

Relationships, also known as associations, between object classes show how the objects of an application collaborate with each other to satisfy user needs. Interacting objects collectively describes behavior of a system. Basically, any dependency between two or more object classes is an association. For example, the dependency between an employee and a company is an association (the works-for association) and the dependency between a customer and a product is also an association (the purchasing association). Associations between objects can be one-to-one, one-to-many, and many-to-many.

As we will see in a moment, associations can be of different types. In the first iteration of building an object model, it is enough to identify associations without categorizing the association types. However, in later stages of an object model, the following types of associations (relationships) play a key role:

- Use relationships
- Container relationships
- Inheritance relationships

A **use relationship** between two object classes indicates that the two classes collaborate by sending messages to each other. For example, the statement "sales clerk updates a customer account" shown in Figure 3.12, indicates three pieces of information: (1) the salesclerk class uses the customer account class, (2) an "update" operation is supported by the customer class, and (3) an "update" message is sent from the salesclerk class to the customer account class. Notice the use of notation in this example.

Use relationships focus on the dynamic behavior of classes and objects. By collecting all the use relations to and from an object, you will have a good idea about behavior of the object and the system requirements. Given a collection of objects involved in use relationships, each object may play one of three roles:

- **Actor**—an object that can operate upon other objects, but that is never operated upon by other objects.
- **Server**—an object that never operates upon other objects; it is only operated upon by other objects.
- **Agent**—an object that can operate on other objects and can be operated on by other objects.

Figure 3.12 A Simple Using Relationship

The ***container relationship***, also known as parent/child relationship, represents subparts of an object class. For example, container relationships exist between a car and the car engine, wheels, seats, and the like. Container relationships are very useful in reducing the number of objects that are visible in a system. For example, if an application does not need it, all parts of a car can be contained in a car class. Thus, the details of car parts are encapsulated in the car class. However, container relationships do lead, if needed, to coupling between objects that cannot be distributed among machines.

The ***inheritance relationships***, an important part of an object model, represent the common properties (attributes, operations) between classes. For example, all cars have some common properties. The notion of inheritance is borrowed from an artificial intelligence "ISA" relationship. For example, "Sun ISA computer" represents that the common properties of a computer are inherited by a Sun workstation. In some cases, only a subset of properties is inherited. This can be represented through "a kind of (AKO)" relationship. For example, "computer is a kind of electronic machine" shows that computer only inherits a small number of electronic machine properties. A class hierarchy can be constructed where lower level classes (***subclasses***) inherit the properties from higher-level classes (***superclasses***). For example, we can set up a class hierarchy for an employee class with subclasses such as managers, technical support, administrative support, consultants, visiting residents, and part-time staff.

Figure 3.13 shows a refinement of the customer information object model we introduced earlier. We have basically added use and container relationships between the classes and also have added a class "product" from which the TV and radio classes can inherit properties.

The main activities involved in developing the associations are as follows:

- Choose a family of classes that appear to be related

- Identify dependencies between classes (each dependency is an association)

- Associations between classes are typically represented by verbs in a statement (e.g., "customer buys products" identifies an association "buys" between the two classes of customers and products)

- Walk through various scenarios to make sure that all associations are identified

- Refine associations into inheritance, container and use relationships

- Exit when most relationships have been identified

Figure 3.13 Customer Information Object Model—Relationships

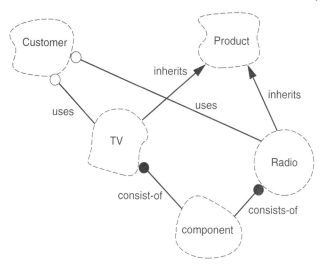

Step 3: Identify Attributes and Operations

Attributes are properties of individual objects, such as name, age, weight, height, or color. Attributes should not be used for associations (e.g., do not use product-purchased as an attribute of a customer; use it as an association between a customer class and a product class). It is important to identify only those attributes that are important for the problem domain (i.e., use abstraction principles). For example, if you are designing an airline reservation system, then you only need to define a very few attributes of each city (e.g., number of airports, distance to the main city, etc.). However, if you are designing a travel guide, then many more attributes of each city are needed.

An operation is an activity performed by or on an object. The operations performed on each object are listed as a starting point. In addition, the information associated with each operation (inputs needed, outputs generated, preceding and/or subsequent activities, sequence restrictions) is specified. You should also list security restrictions associated with the operations being defined. The following guidelines can be used:

- You do not need to represent *all* operations on an object. You should primarily identify those operations that are needed by the users of the application at hand.

- Relationships between objects are a good starting point to specify the operations that can be performed, and the results that can be expected. For example, a "purchase-product" relationship between a customer and a product indicates that "purchase-product" operation should be supported by the product class.

- The operations external to the current application should only be considered if the external operations change the state of the object. If they do, you must synchronize the activities in order to ensure integrity of object data.

Figure 3.14 illustrates the results of identifying attributes and operations for the simple customer information system we have been reviewing. We have shown an object (customer), four operations performed on this object, and the input/output of each operation. We have not specified any pre- and postconditions and any other sequencing information that could have been identified here. A ***method*** is a set of software instructions that is invoked when an operation is invoked. Thus the customer object must provide four methods (software instructions) that are invoked when operations such as add a customer, view a customer, update customer information, and delete a customer are invoked. The information produced as a result of this step can be represented by any of your favorite representation tools (text, formal languages, graphical tools, Booch diagrams, etc.).

Figure 3.14 An Example of Object Operations

Object	Operations	Inputs	Outputs
Customer	Add a customer	Customer Information	Status
	View customer information	Account number	Customer information
	Update customer information	Account no., new information	Status
	Delete a customer	Account number	Status

Figure 3.15 shows the customer information object model with attributes and operations identified. Recall that the notation we are using identifies class names with underlines, operations with "()" and attributes just as items. We have only identified a few key attributes and operations.

Figure 3.15 represents a complete object model—it shows the classes, the relationships between classes, the attributes, and the operations. This object model can be easily translated to code by using OO programming languages (we will see this later).

Step 4: Define Interfaces

Interface of an object is the collection of operations and their ***signatures*** (signature of an operation defines the operation's name, its arguments, and argument types). For example, the following statements could be used to specify the interface for a customer object that supports two operations: create customer and view customer (the language is illustrative):

```
interface customer /* interface name is customer */
Operation create_cust (/*The operation is create_cust */
[in] char customer_info; /* input parameter */
[out] integer status ) /* output parameter */
Operation view-cust ( /*The operation is view_cust */
[in] char cust-id; /* input parameter is cust-id */
[out] char customer_info; /* output parameter 1 */
[out] integer status ) /* output parameter 2 */
```

The interface specification at first attempt can be at a high level by omitting some of the information about argument types.

One or more interfaces may be defined for an object. Interfaces are essentially declarations of how an object can be used by other objects. Although interfaces are defined for most object models, interface definitions have become an essential aspect of distributed object applications. This is because distributed objects can reside on different machines with different character and numeric representations. Interface definition languages (IDLs) are provided by middleware (e.g., OSF DCE IDL and CORBA IDL) for defining interfaces formally. The interface definitions are compiled by using vendor-provided IDL compilers and can be stored in an Interface Repository for other objects to utilize. We will discuss IDLs in more detail in Chapter 7. In addition, modern OO languages such as Java provide constructs for interface specifications.

Figure 3.15 Customer Information Object Model—Attributes and Operations

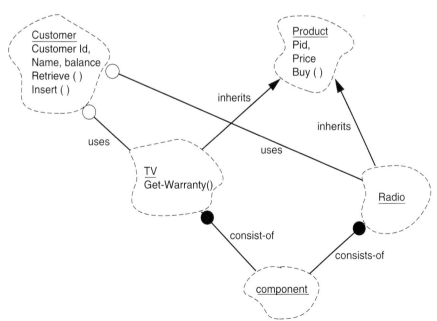

We should note that interface specifications are not typically considered as part of developing an object model at the time of this writing. However, as distributed objects become more popular, the notion of interface specification will become an important aspect of developing the object model. In essence, interface specification formally describes certain aspects of the requirements of a system and should be considered as part of formal requirement specification—an area of considerable research activity in software engineering [Finkelstein 1996], [Ramamoorthy 1996], [Ng 1990], [Nicol 1993], and [Pankaj 1991].

3.4.2.3 Develop Dynamic Model

Dynamic behavior of objects deals with issues such as synchronization of messages and event notification. The objects involved in using relationships must synchronize the messages. Synchronization is essential for the server object that may need to manage multiple threads of control. In general, objects can interact with each other in two manners:

- **Synchronous**—the sending object is blocked (suspended) until a response is received.

- **Asynchronous**—the sending object is not blocked and continues processing. The sending object typically checks for an event that indicates that the initiated interaction has been completed.

Synchronous communication may be sufficient for many real-life systems. In addition, many middleware packages only support synchronous communications (e.g., DCE RPC is strictly synchronous). However, it may be desirable to exploit asynchronous interactions for some applications. Asynchronous communications require more effort by programmer's because code must be provided to handle unscheduled events. Asynchronous interactions can be achieved by generating (local) concurrent synchronous interactions. For example, a client can initiate three "threads" for three synchronous interactions and thus achieve desirable parallelism.

Event handling is a crucial aspect of object-oriented applications. Most GUI applications are event-driven, that is, they must respond to a large number of mouse clicks, window activations, function keys, key strokes, timers, and various other scheduled as well as unscheduled events. In particular, multimedia applications are intensely event-driven with events from remote control, voice input, and mouse [Rosenberg 1995]. It is essential that a comprehensive event model be specified. A wide variety of techniques can be used to specify and analyze events (e.g., directed graphs, message sequence charts, timing diagrams, Petri nets, discrete event simulations). Details about these techniques can be found elsewhere [Booch 1994], [Rumbaugh 1994], and [Rosenberg 1995].

3.4.3 Architecture and Prototyping—Applying The Object Model

The object model and other information gathered during OO analysis is used to develop architectures and build prototypes of new applications and experiment with restructuring of existing applications. The knowledge and experience gained is used to refine the object model and build production systems.

3.4.3.1   Build Prototypes of New Applications

There is no "one-size-fits-all" approach for prototyping all new applications in the modern environments. For example, decision support applications mainly require a database design with almost no software development. These applications rely heavily on off-the-shelf query and browse tools and use the object model to design the database. (We will see later that the object model is very similar to the data model that is typically developed by the database designers.) There is virtually no reason to develop a system dynamics model for decision support applications (most activities are queries). On the other hand, enterprisewide mission- critical operational support applications may require extensive software development and may require, in addition to the object model, a great deal of information about the system dynamics and flow. The real-time applications rely, for obvious reasons, on a very extensive system dynamics model.

Figure 3.16 suggests the main activities in prototyping different classes of applications. The rows of this table show the four generic activities (analysis, architecture, implementation, deployment) and the columns represent the three broad application categories (i.e., decision support, operational support, and real time). We introduced these application categories in Chapter 1 and discussed them in terms of span (i.e., departmental, enterprisewide, interenterprise).

You can extend this discussion to other cases that require mixtures of the cases discussed here (e.g., applications that are operational support at corporate level but provide decision support capabilities at the departmental/group level) for these classes of applications. We will explain the entries in this table in Chapter 4.

3.4.3.2   Experiment with (Re)engineering of Existing Applications

The object model and other information gathered during OO analysis can be used to experiment with (re)engineering of a wide range of existing applications, including legacy. The exact activities depend on the type of reengineering strategy chosen. For example, access and integration of legacy applications requires selection of appropriate surround technologies that "wrap" the legacy functions and data ("object wrappers" are increasingly being used for this purpose at present). In this case, the object model can be used to represent various legacy functions and data as object classes. Data warehouses, a popular approach to deal with legacy systems, are decision support applications that require database design and data warehouse tools. Design of data warehouses uses the object model to represent the database design as discussed previously in decision support applications. For migration, the object model can be used to encapsulate the application components that will be transitioned, thus making the migration transparent to the users (see [Desfrey 1996] for a case study).

Figure 3.16 New Application Prototyping Activities

	Decision Support Applications	Operational Support Applications	Real-Time Applications
Analysis Stage (Refine the Object Model)	• Gather information requirements iteratively • Develop the object model for database design • No dynamic model (or lightweight)	• Gather and analyze detailed requirements • Develop the object model • Develop the dynamic model	• Gather the "hard" requirements • Develop the object model • Develop the dynamic model in great detail
Architecture Stage (Build architecture for prototyping)	Mainly data architecture (iteratively)	Data + application software architecture	IT infrastructure is of great interest because it can determine success/failure
Implementation Stage (Build the prototype)	Selection and testing of tools; population of databases	Application software development and testing (if cannot be purchased)	May involve middleware development
Deployment and support (Run pilots, if possible)	Installation of tools at user sites and quick response to changing needs	Installation of software at user sites and technical support/help desks	Installation of specialized hardware and software at user sites and technical support/help desks

Figure 3.17 suggests the main activities for different application reengineering "experiments." The rows of this table show the four generic activities (analysis, architecture, implementation, deployment) and the columns represent the three main application reengineering strategies (access/integration, data warehouses, migration). We will explain the entries in this table in Part III of the book in the chapters on access and integration, data warehouses, and migration, respectively.

Figure 3.17 Application Reengineering Activities

	Access and Integration	Data Warehouses	Migration
Analysis (Refine the Object Model)	• Detailed requirement specification and analysis for accessing and integrating legacy system (e.g., types of legacy systems, types of access needed) • Use of object model to wrap the legacy system components	• Detailed requirement specification and analysis for data warehouses (e.g., informational requirements, data mining needs, interconnectivity requirements). • Use of object model to design data model	• Detailed requirement specification and analysis for migration (e.g., time allowed, level of migration, budget and policy restrictions) • Use of object model to encapsulate functions to be migrated
Architecture (Evaluate solution approaches)	Evaluate access/ integration strategies, choose middleware for access/ integration	Data warehouse architecture (e.g., what data are in the warehouse, synchronization policy)	Evaluate and determine a migration strategy (e.g., user interface migration, data migration)
Implementation (Install and Test the experiment)	Choose needed middleware and underlying networking technologies	Design the data warehouse data and select tools	Choose the most appropriate migration gateway
Deployment and support (use as a pilot)	Determine cost, time, and staffing considerations	Assess training and support considerations	Gradual migration support considerations

3.5 State of the Practice, Market, and Art

Popular methodologies at present fall into the following broad categories:

- Building new applications by using OO concepts [Booch 1994], and [Rumbaugh 1994]).
- Building decision support systems such as data warehouses [Inmon 1994].

- Platform specific methodologies such as for CORBA [Mowbray 1995], [Otte 1996] and OSF DCE [Rosenberry 1993].

- Migration methodologies for transitioning of legacy applications to new platforms [Brodie 1995], [Sneed 1995], and [Desfrey 1996].

- Business process reengineering (BPR) methodologies that tie BPR to IT architecture [Henderson 1990], [Keen 1993], and [Luftman 1993].

However, no methodology at present attempts to tie all these methodologies into an overall framework that can be used for building new applications and dealing with legacy applications in OCSI environments. We have attempted to accomplish this in this chapter. Naturally, the current state of the practice and market for such methodologies is sparse. However, this is an area of potential research. The key research question is: Can a systematic sequence of steps be defined that takes into account the wide range of new and existing application issues in the evolving IT infrastructure? There is some recognition of this work in the marketplace (see the sidebar "An Expert System for Generating Methodologies").

3.6   Summary

An application engineering/reengineering methodology pattern is presented that will be customized for a wide range of application engineering/reengineering situations. The pattern consists of successive iterations, refinements, and expansions of four broad activities: analysis, solution architectures, implementations, and deployment/support activities.

Overall planning should always be the first iteration of the process and should concentrate on business opportunity analysis and risk analysis to determine the best strategy.

The object model can be used as a foundation for almost all application engineering/reengineering issues. We have shown how an object model can be used as a starting point for decision support applications, operational support applications, data warehouses, legacy data access, and application migration.

The IT infrastructure issues need to be considered in a systematic manner with iterative analysis, architectures, implementation, and deployment/support.The infrastructure evaluation should be considered throughout the system life cycle.

3.7   Case Study: XYZCorp Embarks on Application (Re)Engineering

In the next few years, several new applications will be developed and many of the existing applications will be reengineered at XYZCorp. At present each application engineering/reengineering is considered as a unique case. It is felt that an overall methodology is needed for engineering of new applications and reengineering of existing (mostly legacy) applications. In other words, how should the corporation approach the issues involved in building new Web-based applications and establish suitable strategies for dealing with its embedded base of mainframe-based legacy applications.

XYZCorp has embarked on a major initiative to extend and integrate the applications that support the business processes (payroll, accounts receivable/accounts payable, order processing, marketing information systems, and computerized checkout systems), engineering processes (computer-aided design, computer-aided engineering, computer-aided process planning), and manufacturing processes (material requirement planning, production scheduling, and flexible manufacturing systems). The company is primarily interested in integrating and automating the order processing, inventory control, CAD/CAM (computer-aided design/computer-aided manufacturing) and the "manufacturing" processes of the company products (IBM PC desktops, laptops, network computers, personal digital assistants). This system, referred to as the XYZAICS (Advanced Integrated Control System), will receive a customer order and assemble and pack a product for shipping within half an hour of order reception.

An Expert System For Generating Methodologies

Methodologies depend on the type of architectures being used. For example, methodologies for developing client/server systems differ from the conventional mainframe development methodologies. In particular, project planning steps are dependent on the underlying application architecture being deployed. Is it possible to use expert systems in developing project plans based on a few questions?

C/S10,000 from Client/Server Connection is an expert system tool for generating customizable methodologies that are driven by technical architectures. This tool guides the user through a series of questions aimed at identifying a few (one or two) application architectures from an inventory of 125 application architectures. After the user selects an architecture (this may require some iterations), the expert system prompts the user through additional questions for selecting a suitable network architecture from an inventory of 85 network architectures. After this, the tool generates a work breakdown structure (WBS), project estimate and supporting materials for a project plan. The tool also includes an inventory of products that can be used to implement selected architectures.

Source:

    Hunter, R., and Conway, B., "C/S 10,000: Methodology Gain Without Pain?" *Gartner Group Research Note,* August 29, 1996.

The company is in a time crunch and has authorized a two week initial planning project. The management has been talking to a consultant (a good guy who writes very good books!) and has agreed to design XYZAICS by using the methodology template discussed in this chapter.

Hints about the Case Study

The first two iterations of the methodology described in Sections 3.3 through 3.5 should be completed as much as possible within the two-week time constraint. In the planning iteration, an understanding of IMCS is developed and very initial choices are made about what portion of XYZAICS should be built, what should be purchased, and what should be based on a reuse of existing systems. A high level object model is built in the second iteration to gain further insight and to scope out the work in more detail.

Figure 3.18 shows a very high-level view of XYZAICS—a result of the planning process. The first stage in this system is an order processing system that processes orders for a product. If the specified product is in stock and the customer credit is acceptable, the product is shipped to the customer from the finished product inventory that is adjusted to show products shipped. For an out of stock product, a CAD/CAE system produces the design based on the customer's specifications. The design is then downloaded to a Computer Aided Process Planning (CAPP) system where the manufacturing program is automatically created that shows how the product will be assembled. The CAPP system uses the information about available assembly equipment to generate the process plans. An MRP (Material Requirement Planning) system determines the materials needed for the product. MRP systems use sophisticated algorithms to take into account quantity discounts, vendor preferences, various capacity constraints, and factory status. The manufacturing program is downloaded to a flexible manufacturing system (FMS) which consists of an area controller, two cells, and several manufacturing devices. FMS also receives a production schedule (how many products to manufacture) and needed raw materials. Because FMS is a real-time system, it must conform to the constraints of real-time control on factory floors.

As can be seen, this system has a combination of application types such as operational support (e.g., inventory manager, order processing), decision support (MRP), and real-time (FMS). At present, the MRP and order-processing systems with associated databases exist (shaded areas in Figure 3.18). Other components either need to be built and/or purchased. This observation is enough for the time being. We will consider the details later as different parts of XYZAICS in the case studies in later chapters.

In the second iteration, a very high-level object model is developed due to the time constraints. The object model developed in Section 3.4 and shown in Figure 3.13 is a good starting point. Other object classes in the XYZAICS system (order, robots, invoice, et cetera) can be added to this object class diagram. This object model is at a business object level (i.e., represent business entities). The overall IT infrastructure of the XYZCorp should also be reviewed very briefly in this iteration. The review of the XYZCorp IT infrastructure at the end of Chapter 2 should do the job.

Figure 3.18 Advanced Integrated Control System (AICS)

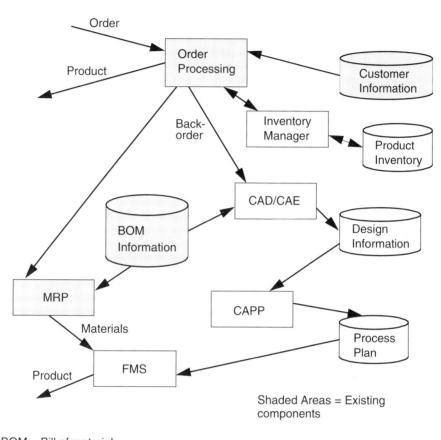

BOM = Bill of material
CAD/CAE = Computer-aided design/computer-aided engineering
CAPP = Computer aided process planning
FMS = Flexible manufacturing system
MRP = Materials requirement planning

3.8 Problems and Exercises

1. There is a common saying that "It seems there is never enough time to do a job right the first time, but there is always time to do it over." Does the methodology presented in this chapter address this tendency? How?

2. Show how this methodology can be used to develop applications such as electronic commerce, expert systems, and videoconferencing.

3. Compare and contrast this methodology with the OO methodologies [Booch 1994], and [Rumbaugh 1994] and the RMM methodology for hypermedia applications [Isakowitz 1995].

3.9   Additional Information

Adam, N., *Electronic Commerce,* Springer Verlag, 1996.

Baster, G., "Business Components for End-User Assembly," *Object Magazine,* January 1997, pp. 38–45.

Blokdijk, A. and Blokdijk, P., *Planning and Design of Information Systems,* Academic Press, 1987

Boar, B., *Practical Steps for Aligning Information Technology with Business Strategies,* John Wiley, 1994.

Booch, G., *Object Oriented Design with Applications,* Benjamin Cummings, 2d ed., 1994.

Brodie, M.L., and Stonebraker, M., *Migrating Legacy Systems: Gateways, Interfaces & the Incremental Approach,* Morgan Kauffman, 1995.

Cronin, M., "The Internet Strategy Handbook," *Harvard Business School Press,* 1996.

Davidson, W., "Beyond Reengineering: The Three Phases of Business Transformation," *IBM Systems Journal,* Vol. 32, No. 1, 1993, pp. 65–79.

Dec, K., "Client/Server—Reality Sets in," *Gartner Group Briefing,* San Diego, February 22–24, 1995.

DePompa, B., "Corporate Migration: Harder Than It Looks," *Information Week,* December 4, 1995, pp. 60–68.

Desfrey, P., "Automated Object Design: The Client-Server Case," *IEEE Computer,* February 1996, pp. 62–66.

Dewire, D., "Client/Server 101: Business Process (Re)Engineering," *Client/Server Computing,* March 1986, pp. 102–103.

Fillon, M., "What's Ahead for 1997," *Client/Server Computing,* December 1996, pp. 32–43.

Fingar, P., *The Blueprint for Business Objects,* SIGS Book and Multimedia, 1996.

Finkelstein, A., "Requirements Engineering Research: Coordination and Infrastructure," *Requirements Engineering Journal,* Vol. 1, No. 1, 1996, pp. 63–69.

Fuhrt, B., et al., "Design Issues for Interactive Television Systems," *IEEE Computer,* May 1995, pp. 40–51.

Gale, T., and Eldred, J., "The Abstract Business Process," *Object Magazine,* January 1997, pp. 32–37.

Gambon, J., "Healthcare Gets Technology Transfusion," *Information Week,* July 1, 1996, pp. 14–19.

Gemmel, D., et al., "Multimedia Storage Servers: A Tutorial," *IEEE Computer,* May 1995, pp. 40–51.

Gordon, V., and Bieman, J., "Rapid Prototyping: Lessons Learned," *IEEE Software,* January 1995, pp. 85–95.

Grygo, E., "Upper Hand," *Client/Server Computing,* August 1996, pp. 34–42.

Henderson, J., "Plugging into Strategic Partnership: The Critical IS Connection," *MIT Sloan Management Review,* Vol. 31, No. 3, 1990, pp. 7–18.

Henderson, J., and Venkatraman, "Strategic Alignment: Leveraging Information Technology for Transforming Organizations," *IBM Systems Journal,* Vol. 32, No. 1, 1993, pp. 4–16.

Highsmith, J., "Structured Systems Planning," *Information Systems Management,* Vol. 4, No. 2, Spring 1987.

Hulfnagel, E.M., "Information Systems Planning: Lessons from Strategic Planning," *Information and Management,* Vol. 12, No. 5, 1987, pp. 263–270

Hutt, A., ed., *Object-Oriented Analysis and Design,* John Wiley, 1994.

IBM Corporation, "Business Systems Planning," 1978, GE20-0527

Inmon, W.H., *Developing Client/Server Applications,* QED Publishing Group, rev. ed., 1993.

Inmon, W., *Using Data Warehouses,* John Wiley, 1994.

Isakowitz, T., et al., "RMM: A Methodology for Structured Hypermedia Design," *Communications of the ACM,* August 1995, pp. 34–44.

Jacobson, I., et al., *Object-Oriented Software Engineering,* Addison Wesley, Reading, MA, 1992.

Jenkins, A., "Centralization Strikes Again," *Computerworld Client/Server Journal,* August 1995, pp. 28–31.

Keen, P., "Shaping the Future," *Harvard Business School Press,* Boston, 1991.

Keen, P., "Information Technology and the Management Difference: A Fusion Map," *IBM Systems Journal,* Vol. 32, No. 1, 1993, pp. 17–39.

Lederer, A., and Prasad, J., "Nine Management Guidelines for Better Cost Estimation," *Communications of the ACM,* February 1992, pp. 34–49.

Linthicum, D., "Distributed Objects Get New Plumbing," *Internet Systems,* January 1997, pp. 4–5.

Luftman, J., *Competing in the Information Age: Strategic Alignment in Practice,* Oxford University Press, 1996.

Luftman, J., Lewis, P., and Oldach, S., "Transforming the Enterprise: The Alignment of Business and Information Technology Strategies," *IBM Systems Journal,* Vol. 32, No. 1, 1993, pp. 198–221.

Meyer, M., and Zack, M., "The Design and Development of Information Products," *Sloan Management Review,* Spring 1996, pp. 43–59.

Mowbray, T., and Zahavi, R., *The Essential CORBA: Systems Integration Using Distributed Objects,* John Wiley, 1995.

Mushet, M., "Application Systems Planning," *Information Systems Management,* Winter 1985.

Nerson, J. M., and Walden, K., *Seamless Object-Oriented Software Architecture: Analysis and Design of Reliable Systems,* Prentice Hall, 1995.

Newman, D., "Class-Based Reengineering," *Object Magazine,* March 1996, pp. 68–74.

Ng, P., and Yeh, R., editors, *Modern Software Engineering: Foundations and Current Perspectives,* Van Nostrand Reinhold, 1990.

Nicol, J., et al., "Object Orientation in Heterogeneous Distributed Computing Systems, *IEEE Computer,* June 1993, pp. 57–67.

Nolan, R., "Managing the Computer Resource: A Stage Hypothesis," *Communications of the ACM,* Vol. 16, No. 7, July 1973, pp. 399–405.

Otte, R., Patrick, P., and Roy, M., *Understanding CORBA,* Prentice Hall, 1996.

Pankaj, J., *An Integrated Approach to Software Engineering,* Springer-Verlag, 1991.

Ramamoorthy, C.V., et al., "Advances in Software Engineering," *IEEE Computer Magazine,* October 1996, pp. 47–57.

Rockart, J., "The Changing Role of the Information Systems Executive: A Critical Success Factors Perspective," *Sloan Management Review,* Vol. 24, No. 1, 1982, pp. 3–13.

Rosenberg, D., "Applying Object-Oriented Methods to Interactive Multimedia Projects," *Object Magazine,* June 1995, pp. 40–49.

Rosenberry, W., et al., *Understanding DCE,* O'Reilly & Associates, 1993.

Rumbaugh, J., et al, *Object-Oriented Modeling and Design,* Prentice Hall, 2nd ed., 1994.

Rymer, J., "Business Objects," *Distributed Computing Monitor,* Patricia Seybold Group, January 1995.

Sheldon, R., "Business Objects and BPR," *Data Management Review,* November 1994, pp. 6–20.

Sims, O., *Business Objects,* McGraw-Hill, 1994.

Simpson, D., "Are Mainframes Cool Again?" *Datamation,* April 1997, pp. 46–53.

Singh, R., "The Software Life-Cycle Processes Standard," *IEEE Computer,* November 1995, pp. 89–90.

Sneed, H., "Planning the Reengineering of Legacy Systems," *IEEE Software,* January 1995, pp. 24–34.

Sutherland, J., "Business Objects Architecture: Key to Client/Server Development," *Data Management Review,* November 1994, pp. 46–50.

Varney, S., "IS Takes Charge of Customer Service," *Datamation*, August 1996, pp. 46–51.

Vasudeva, R., "Reusing Business Objects," *Object Magazine,* January 1997, pp. 32–37.

Venkatraman, N., and Camillus, J., "Exploring the Concept of "Fit" in Strategic Management," *Academy of Management Review,* Vol. 9, 1984, pp. 513–525.

Zachman, J.A., "Business Systems Planning and Business Information Control Study," *IBM Systems Journal,* Vol. 21, No. 1, 1982, pp. 31–53.

PART II

APPLICATION ENGINEERING: BUILDING WEB-BASED APPLICATIONS

This part of the book concentrates on issues related to building new, primarily Web-based applications. The need for developing new applications, it is assumed, has been determined in the initial planning iterations described in Chapter 3. These applications, or their subparts, may need to be interfaced/integrated with the existing applications, including legacy, for enterprisewide services (Part III).

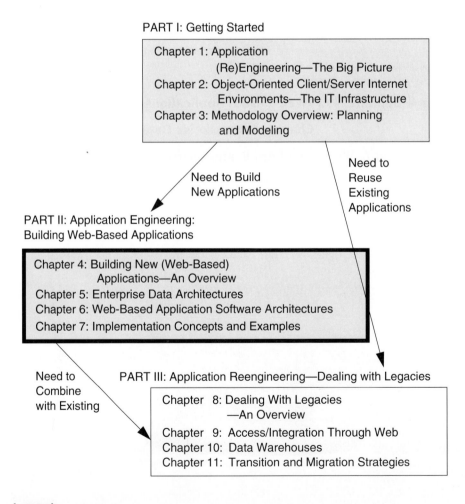

PART I: Getting Started

Chapter 1: Application
                (Re)Engineering—The Big Picture
Chapter 2: Object-Oriented Client/Server Internet
                Environments—The IT Infrastructure
Chapter 3: Methodology Overview: Planning
                and Modeling

Need to Build
New Applications

Need to
Reuse
Existing
Applications

PART II: Application Engineering:
Building Web-Based Applications

Chapter 4: Building New (Web-Based)
                Applications—An Overview
Chapter 5: Enterprise Data Architectures
Chapter 6: Web-Based Application Software Architectures
Chapter 7: Implementation Concepts and Examples

Need to
Combine
with Existing

PART III: Application Reengineering—Dealing with Legacies

Chapter 8: Dealing With Legacies
                —An Overview
Chapter 9: Access/Integration Through Web
Chapter 10: Data Warehouses
Chapter 11: Transition and Migration Strategies

Legend:
• Shaded areas indicate topics covered, dark border indicates current topics
• Arrows indicate interdependencies

4

Building New (Web-Based) Applications—An Overview

4.1   Introduction

Most of the new Web-based applications are being, and will be, developed by using a combination of object-orientation, client/server, and Internet technologies—the ***object-oriented client/server Internet (OCSI) applications***. Engineering (i.e., building) of this new breed of Web-based applications is a daunting task owing to the large number of infrastructure options (e.g., Web servers, Web gateways, Java versus CGI-based development, distributed object middleware, data access technologies, network configurations), a multitude of vendor products (e.g., the suite of tools from different suppliers), an almost unlimited number of off-the-shelf applications, and a handful of configuration choices (see Figure 4.1). Add to this the potential risks and pitfalls associated with any new technology, and you get the picture. This chapter presents an overview of OCSI application engineering issues and introduces a development methodology that will be expanded and explained in later chapters of this part of the book. The discussion in this chapter is guided by the following questions:

- What are the various classes of Web-based applications and how do the OCSI applications fit into this picture? See Section 4.2.

- What are the promises and pitfalls of OCSI applications? See Section 4.3.

- What approach can be used to systematically build the OCSI applications, deal with various trade-offs, and make judicious decisions in architecture and implementation? See Section 4.4.

- How can the approach be customized for different classes of OCSI applications (e.g., Web-based decision support, operational support, and real-time applications? See Section 4.5.

- What type of development tools are needed to develop OCSI applications? See Section 4.6.

- What is the state of the art, state of the market (e.g., CASE tools) and state of the practice in building OCSI applications? See Section 4.7 through 4.9.

Figure 4.1 The Application Engineering Challenge

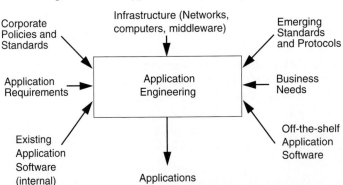

Figure 4.2 shows a general framework for applications that shows how our view of applications compares and contrasts with the OSI Reference Model. We focus only on the business-aware aspects of application and view the business-unaware aspects as part of the middleware (recall that we have defined middleware to be the software that resides between the network services and the business-aware applications). The Application Layer of the OSI Reference Model includes business-unaware services such as e-mail, file transfer, terminal emulation, and the like (these are part of middleware in our model). Basically, our view of applications is the upper part of OSI Application Layer.

Figure 4.2 Application Framework

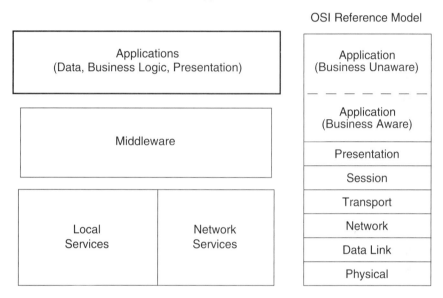

Key Points

• OCSI applications are the special breed of Web-based applications that are both powerful and complex. They offer many promises, but you should not ignore the risks and the pitfalls.

• Many considerations about developing OCSI applications can be separated in terms of application type: operational, decision support, real time.

• Application architecture = data architecture + software architecture + IT infrastructure.

• KISS (Keep It Simple "Sir") principle is very important to get started. If possible, stay with a single vendor middleware, limit mix-and-matching, do not over-distribute, and get the system up and running to gain your own insights (there is no substitute for experience).

4.2   Modern Web-Based Applications

Web-based applications employ Web technologies (i.e., Web browsers, Web servers, HTML, HTTP) to provide business value. These applications can be simple HTML applications that retrieve and display HTML pages or sophisticated corporate applications that integrate Web with corporate resources. For the purpose of analysis, we will categorize these applications into the following classes:

- Static HTML-based applications
- Server-side (CGI-based) applications
- Client-side (Java-based) applications
- Object-oriented client/server (OCSI) applications

Although we are primarily interested in OCSI applications, we briefly scan the other classes of Web-based applications for completeness.

4.2.1   Static HTML-Based Applications

These applications, shown in Figure 4.3, basically retrieve and display the HTML documents that reside on the Web server site. The designers of these applications create HTML pages and determine how the documents are interlinked and navigated through hypertext links. A large number of Web sites at present use this application model. The sidebar "Building Static HTML-Based Applications: A Checklist" shows the main steps needed to develop such applications. For a more formal approach, see the methodology, called RMM (Relationship Management Methodology), that has been proposed for structured hypermedia application design [Isakowitz 1995].

Figure 4.3 Static HTML-Based Applications

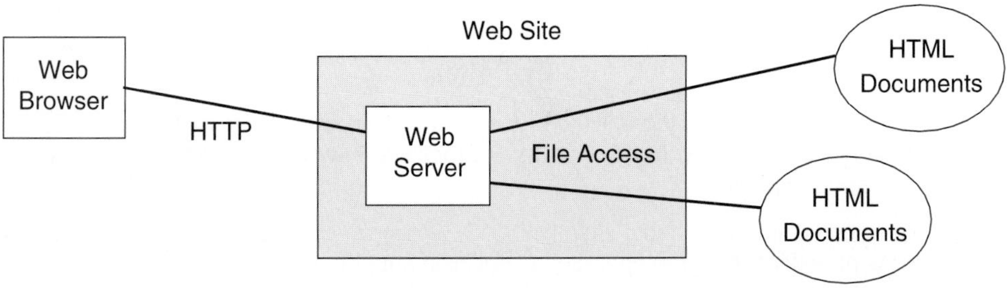

Let us review HTML briefly. HTML prepares the media type that the Web browsers understand. HTML is a cross-platform documentation language—any computer equipped with a Web browser can read and display HTML documents. You create an HTML document as an ASCII text file by using HTML markup tags (see the sidebar on HTML example) or by using HTML filters that convert word processing documents such as Microsoft

---

Building Static HTML-Based Applications: A Checklist

Analysis:

- Establish end-user requirements, that is, determine what pieces of information are needed by whom, when

- Develop an information model that shows how the information will be organized in pages and how it will be navigated

Architecture:

- Translate the information model into a physical "page" model that shows the URL for each page

- Design the layout of the home page and other pages in the hierarchy

- Determine the server where the home page will reside and establish any security/access mechanisms

Implementation and Deployment:

- Build the HTML pages by coding HTML or using filters that generate HTML from other data sources

- Install the pages on the appropriate servers

Word into HTML. HTML tags are used to indicate headings, italics, bolds, ordered lists, and places where graphics, sound bytes, and other pieces of information can be located in the document.

Hypertext and hypermedia are at the core of HTML and WWW. A *hypertext* is a series of documents, each of which displays at least one visible link on the screen, called a *hypertext link*, to another document in the set. *Hypermedia* extends hypertext in two ways: it incorporates multimedia into hypertext documents, and it allows graphic, audio, and video elements to become links to other documents or multimedia elements. In other words, hypermedia allows you to link multimedia elements by providing multimedia links (i.e., you can click on a graphic instead of just a text link).

For our purpose we need to concentrate on the "*hotlinks*" that are the main distinguishing feature of hypertext, hypermedia and HTML. These hotlinks[1] are hyperlinks (i.e., hypertext or hypermedia links) that provide a path from one document to another. HTML provides tags so that you can create these hyperlinks anywhere in your document. The hyperlinks are highlighted (usually in color and underlined) when displayed by the Web browsers. Use of HTML allows you to browse through Web documents in a manner similar to, but more pow-

---

1. In this book, we will use the term hyperlink to indicate the family of hotlinks such as hypertext link and hypermedia links.

erful than, browsing through a library—you click on the hotlink and get access to the needed page/document that may be located anywhere on the Web. For example, suppose that you are browsing an "HTML-ized" book catalog that lists various books, and each book listed has a hyperlink to the publisher page. Then, you can directly access additional information about chosen books by simply pointing and clicking. By using hyperlinks, you can start with the catalog that is stored in Atlanta and the next page you read is the publisher in New York City and the next from Singapore. Each click to a hyperlink initiates an HTTP session (connect, request, response, close).

HTML capabilities include basic features as well as "fill-in forms" for sending search arguments, comments and other pieces of information (credit card numbers, telephones, and addresses) to the Web servers. The basic features describe how to use the HTML tags to define titles, lists, paragraphs, image placements, and the like. The simple HTML example shown in the sidebar illustrates many of these features. The fill-in form capabilities are provided by the FORM statement. FORM is an HTML construct that has been used for developing Web gateways to corporate information systems and relational databases. Basically a FORM contains some fields where the user enters data in a structured way, a button to submit the form (which simulates submitting a form similar to the real world), and a button to clear the user's input so that the form can be used again.The browser uses the FORM statement to construct a URL and data that are sent to the Web server. The Web server passes this information to a script that performs the needed operations and returns the results back to the client.

4.2.2 Server-Side (CGI-Based) Applications

The CGI (Common Gateway Interface) is a program that resides on the Web server. This program, usually known as a CGI gateway, can be a script (e.g., a UNIX shell script or a Perl script) or an executable program (C or C++ code). After this program has been written it is readied for execution by the Web server (this step typically involves placing of the CGI program in the /cgi.bin/ directory or another designated library of the server). Hyperlinks to this program can then be included in HTML documents in the same way as hyperlinks to any other resource. For example, if the CGI program is called "inventory.pl," the URL for this program is

>   http://www.myserver.com/cgi.bin/inventory.pl

This URL is included in the HTML page at an appropriate place. For example, we can write the following HTML statement to invoke *inventory.pl* (Href is used to indicate a hypertext link):

>   <A Href="http://www.myserver.com/cgi.bin/inventory.pl">

When the user clicks on this hyperlink, the CGI program URL is passed to the Web server. The Web server locates the CGI program in the /cgi.bin/ directory and executes it. The output produced by this program is sent back to the Web browser.

A Simple HTML Example

Suppose you wanted to create a simple home page that looks like the following:

The Flat-Footed Zombie Resort

Welcome to our resort. By using this home page, you can do the following:

- Read about our services
- Access home pages of cooperating resorts

Now choose the connections by pointing and clicking to the following hotlinks:
    Our services
    Cooperating Resorts

The following HTML statements can be used to design this home page (we have inserted appropriate URLs for the hotlinks):

```
<TITLE>The Flat-Footed Zombie Resort</TITLE>
<H1>The Flat-Footed Zombie Resort </H1>
<P> Welcome to our resort. By using this home page, you can
do the following:
<UL>
<LI> Read about our services
<LI> Access home pages of cooperating resorts
</UL>
<P> Now choose the connections by pointing and clicking to
the following hotlinks.
<a href="http://www.zombies.com/services.html"> Our
services</a>
<a href="http://www.resorts.org"> Cooperating Resorts</a>
```

The fundamental difference between a user accessing a regular HTML file and accessing a CGI program is that the CGI program is executed on the server to perform some specialized functions (including creation of HTML pages, if needed) instead of just fetching and displaying an existing HTML page.

What type of CGI gateways can be developed? Virtually anything. Examples range from simple time and date retrievals to sophisticated database applications. In general, CGI gateways fall into two categories (see Figure 4.4):

- Single-Step CGI Gateway—An application program is executed as a CGI executable itself, thereby forking the application process for every request. In this case, the CGI executable contains the application logic invoked by the Web client.

- Two-Step CGI Gateway—An application program runs as a daemon process. A CGI executable just dispatches the request rather than performing any application functions. In this case, the CGI gateway has no business logic and is just used as a dispatcher.

Figure 4.4 CGI Gateways

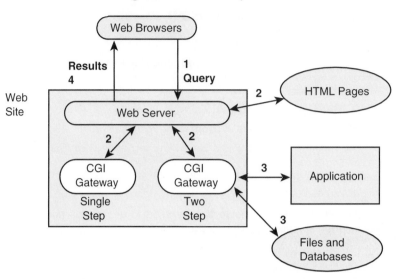

1. A Web browser sends a query (usually in FORM) to Web server.
2. The Web server interacts with CGI scripts and/or HTML pages.
3. CGI scripts access applications and data sources and construct answers in HTML.
4. The results, in HTML format, are sent back to the browser.

Single-step CGI gateways are typically used for quick and relatively simple functions. The two-step CGI gateways are more useful for large, and in many cases, legacy applications. Two-step CGI gateways are commonly used for connecting existing applications with the Web (it is easier to invoke existing programs from CGI scripts than to rewrite them completely as CGI scripts). You may also use a combination, that is, perform some functions in the CGI executable and then dispatch existing applications where needed. Figure 4.5 shows a CGI-based application.

Figure 4.5 CGI-Based Applications

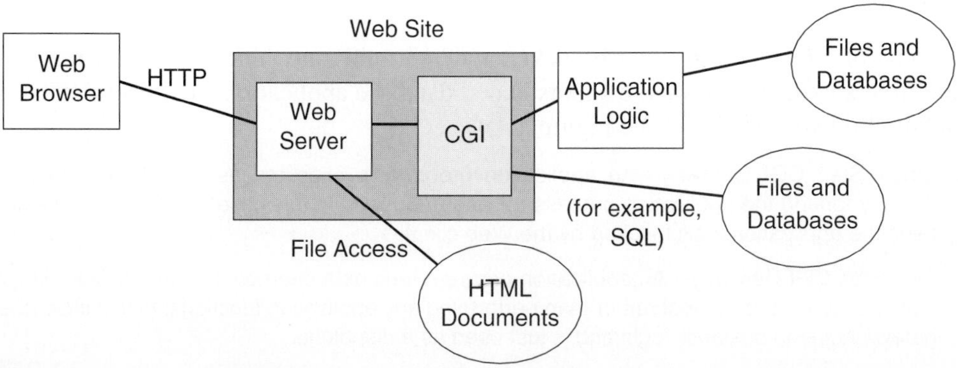

Building CGI-Based Applications: A Checklist

Analysis:

- Establish end-user requirements, that is, determine what pieces of information are needed by whom, when

- Develop an information (preferably an object) model that shows conceptually how the information will be organized, accessed, manipulated, and presented

Architecture:

- Data architecture: determine what data sources (HTML, files, databases) will be needed, where they will be located, and how they will be accessed

- Software architecture: determine what will be written as CGI code, what will be written as modules called by CGI, where the various modules will reside, and how they will be invoked

- Infrastructure architecture: determine the server where the home page and the CGI code will reside, the type of gateways that will be employed, the type of middleware that will be needed to invoke remote services from the CGI code, and the type of computing platforms (Unix, Windows NT) used.

Implementation and Deployment:

- Build the HTML pages by coding HTML or using filters that generate HTML from other data sources (word documents)

- Develop and test the CGI code and the CGI-called modules

- Purchase and install the appropriate infrastructure components

- Test, install, and deploy the system

4.2.3 Client-Side (Java-Based) Applications

Java is an object-oriented programming language that is playing a unique role in WWW. Java has gained a unique status for supporting a very diverse array of Web applications and can be used for distributed applications across the Internet. Java was introduced by Sun Microsystems and is similar to C++ but draws heavily from other object-oriented languages such as Eiffel and Smalltalk.

Small Java programs, called *Java applets*, can be embedded in Web pages (these are called *Java powered pages*). Java powered Web pages can be downloaded to the Web client side where they run. Java is the foundation of client-side applications, because Java applets can run on Java-enabled browsers. Basically, the Java applets are downloaded to the Web browser site when the user clicks on the Java powered pages, where they run doing whatever they were programmed to do. There are several implications of this:

- Java applets exemplify "downloadable code" that is developed at one site and is migrated to another site on demand. This introduces several security issues but also creates many interesting research opportunities.

- Java applets make Web applications really client/server, because the Java code can run business logic on the Web client site (i.e., the Web browser houses the first tier).

- The Web screen layout can be changed dynamically based on the user type. A Java program can determine the user type and modify the screen layout.

- Different advertisements can be shown and highlighted to the user depending on the user characteristics (age, job type, education level, credit history, salary level).

- You can produce graphs and charts dynamically at your browser instead of fetching predefined graphs and images from the Web server (transferring images takes a very long time over the Internet).[2]

- You can run animations, invoke business transactions, and run spreadsheets at your browser site.

By using Java applets, access to remote applications and databases can be invoked directly from the browser. This does depend on whether your Web browser allows Java applets to establish remote interactions for security purposes. In fact, many Web browsers are configured to disallow remote connections from Java applets because this increases security risks. In these cases, the Java applets can only access the resources located on the Web server from where the Java applets were loaded. A "Proxy Server" is built on the Web server site that acts as a server to the browsers and as a client to the target application resources (proxy servers are commonly built for security purposes to mediate between "outside" users and the corporate resources).

You can, however, configure your browser to allow Java applets to invoke remote operations if you have taken care of security concerns. If allowed, the Java applet can ask the user to issue a query and then send this query directly to a remote application or database (Figure 4.6). This is especially interesting for database gateways where the database gateway functionality could run on the client side. A standard called JDBC has been developed to allow Java programs to issue calls to relational databases (at present, JDBC uses Web server site for proxy services). In addition, Java applets can use CORBA or Sun Microsystem's Remote Method Invocation (RMI) to invoke remote interactions. If restricted, then Java applets can issue remote resources through the Web server.

Keep in mind that large-scale applications are difficult to convert into Java applets. However, some aspects of an application, perhaps the user interface processing, can be re-coded as Java applets and thus used to integrate the applications with WWW.

---

2. I once tried to access a home page from Germany. The home page had some image files that were somewhat complicated. I could simply not get the page even after hours of trying (the session timed out repeatedly).

Figure 4.6 Java-Based Application

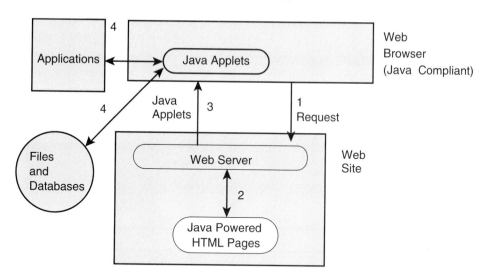

1. User asks for a Java powered HTML page
2. The Java powered page is accessed by the Web server
3. The Java applets are sent to the browser along with the HTML page
4. The Java applets are invoked by the browser and access remote databases and applications, if not restricted by the browser.

Note: This assumes that browser allows remote interactions from Java applets

---

Building Java-Based Applications: A Checklist

This checklist is very similar to the CGI-based applications. The main differences are in the architecture and implementation. Here are the main differences:

- Architecture: What will be coded as Java applets, what type of Java-based middleware will be needed, and what Java-based gateways will be used to invoke remote programs and databases?

- Implementation: Develop Java code, prepare Java powered HTML pages, and test Java-based applications from different Java enabled browsers.

We will integrate these steps into the general OCSI application development checklist.

4.2.4   Object-Oriented Client/Server (OCSI) Applications

Object-oriented client/server (OCSI) applications, as previously stated, combine Web technologies with object-orientation and client/server to deliver business functionality. These applications are of primary interest to us, because they combine many powerful technologies to provide the flexibility and reusability needed in modern enterprises (see the sidebar "Object-Oriented Client/Server Internet (OCSI)—Happy Together"). Figure 4.7 shows a conceptual view of OCSI applications. Specific properties of these Web-based applications are:

- Web technologies are used by the end users to access any of the business logic and/or data sources. In particular, Web technology is used to access programs and data sources that may be located anywhere in the network through a variety of gateways.

Figure 4.7 Object-Oriented Client/Server Internet Applications

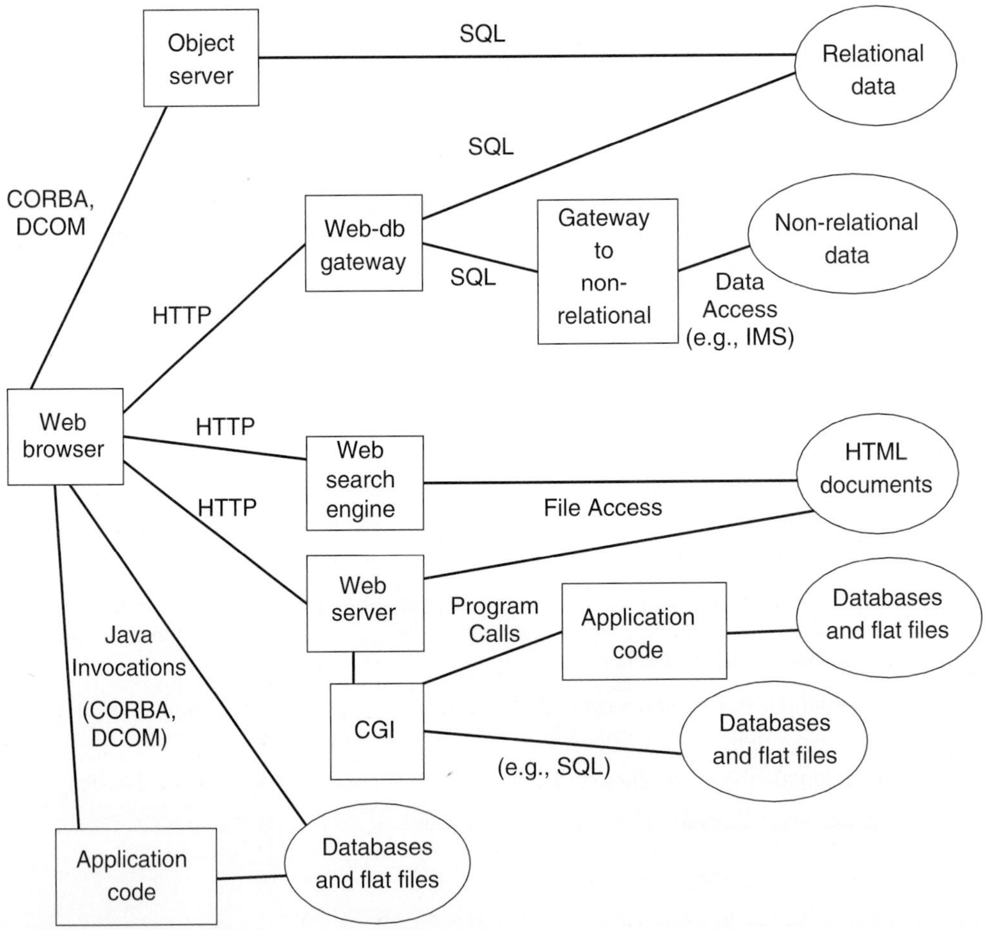

- Object-orientation is used in at least one component of the application. At present, most of the OO concepts are utilized in developing graphical user interfaces. The application programs are becoming increasingly OO with the popularity of OO programming languages such as C++ and Smalltalk. The application databases, however, are largely non-OO (very few OO databases are being used for very few corporate data applications).

- The business aware functionality is decomposed into servers (service providers) and clients (service consumers). Clients and servers have well-defined interfaces (i.e., they hide internal information). Typically, servers are applications database servers, and clients are front-ends (e.g., spreadsheets, GUIs). The application logic can be at server, client, or both. Once again, most of the OO concepts are being used more on the client side of business logic because OO technology is very useful for GUI programming. There is no reason why OO technology cannot be equally useful on the server side due to the advances in distributed object computing and OO databases.

- The databases are largely non-OO. The databases are accessed typically through SQL or other data access technologies.

OCSI applications are event-driven. The events can be due to intensive GUI programming (e.g., handling the points and clicks) and/or due to the messages exchanged between clients and servers over the network.

Object-Oriented Client/Server Internet (OCSI)—Happy Together

The OCSI applications take full advantage of the synergy between the three technologies.

World Wide Web over the Internet allows access to resources located around the world. For all practical purposes, the Web provides a GUI interface, the browser, which can access information by pointing and clicking through hypertext linkages that chase unique resource identifiers, called *Uniform Resource Locators (URLs)*. However, the Web has some limitations—it is limited in application execution and requires Web gateways to access corporate databases and applications through Web browsers. For example, a Web-based application that requires access to customers at 10 different systems can create a messy situation with 10 different gateways activated through 10 different CGI scripts.

Object-oriented technology steps in very well, because it can be used to develop reusable software and to reduce complexity through inheritance and encapsulation. For example, you can now group and view the 10 systems as a customer object that hides all the internal details between different types of customers, where they are located, what technologies can be used to access them, and the like.

Client/server technology also plays an important role in this equation. It provides the middleware needed for communications between computing processes at different machines, (for example, a Web server machine and a remotely located database). The exact C/S technology used may be remote SQL, RPCs, or remote object interactions. In fact, Web browsers and Web servers use a C/S paradigm and employ HTTP, a simplified version of RPC.

This synergy is the foundation of interest in consolidating these technologies [Robicheaux 1996], and [Dick 1996] and is the foundation of CORBA support for Netscape browsers and the ActiveX Platform from Microsoft.

Figure 4.8 shows a short-term as well as long-term view of OCSI applications. Basically, the current new applications are heavily using Web and OO technologies in user interfaces (e.g., GUIs). The application logic itself is increasingly becoming OO due to the popularity of OO programming languages and due to the commercial availability of class libraries. The long-term trend appears to rely on increased use of OO technologies at all levels (it is not clear if OO databases will ever replace the large embedded base of relational databases). It is also expected that the middleware will increasingly support the OO paradigm and the distributed object model. The OCSI applications are a transition stage between the "first generation" C/S applications (they basically replaced local SQL calls with remote SQL calls) and the fully distributed object computing systems (these will use OO databases extensively).

Figure 4.8 Stages of Object-Oriented Client/Server Internet Applications

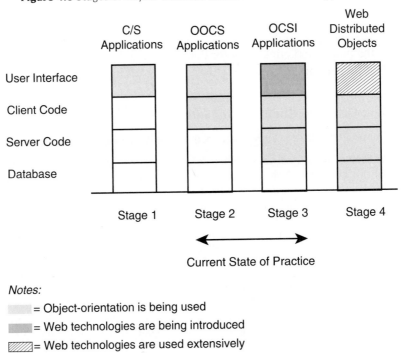

4.3   Promises and Pitfalls of OCSI Applications

Market trends are indicating an explosion of OCSI applications that integrate Web-based technologies with client/server and distributed objects. According to a 1996 Sentry Market Research survey report, almost 50 percent of the respondents are integrating Web into their client/server applications; the other 50 percent are planning to do so in the next 18 months [Fillon 1996]. In addition, distributed objects are moving into mainstream client/server applications with Web interfaces. For example, Netscape has reportedly shipped 20 million copies of CORBA-enabled browsers in 1996 [Linthicum 1997], and Microsoft has made ActiveX (a Web-distributed object technology) its main product direction. Consequently, numerous approaches to integrate Web with objects are currently viable and more are on the way. (See the sidebar "Combining Distributed Objects with the Web.") Why? Here are some potential promises.

Flexibility. The various resources (e.g., databases, programs, HTML pages, video clips, sound bytes) can be dispersed across a network to maximize flexibility and availability. From Web browsers, users can access resources that can be balanced among mixtures of mainframes, microcomputers, and minicomputers to meet different requirements and to respond to competitive pressures quickly.

Strategic factors. Customers, suppliers, and companies do not exist at one site. Thus OCSI applications, which tie these entities together through Web can improve services and provide competitive edge. For example, Boeing's IT managers reportedly reach 20 times more customers with their new Web-based parts sales system [Varney 1996].

User interfaces. The desktops are well suited for sophisticated graphical user interfaces (GUIs) with speech and multimedia capabilities. These desktops are becoming powerful tools due to the ubiquitous Web browsers and Java applets that can support attractive display features.

Configurability. OCSI applications can improve performance and reliability through redundant data and processing. For example, OCSI applications distribute workload among computing platforms.

Equipment costs. The average cost per MIP (million instructions per second) on a mainframe is several times more than on a workstation. OCSI applications allow more economical use of computer equipment.

Development costs. The cost and time needed to develop Web and OO-based software on desktop is generally lower due to potential of reuse, the availability of OO class libraries in several areas, and an upsurge of Web-based development tools from vendors such as Netscape, Microsoft, and Oracle. For example, Web-based packages for OO development, GUIs, spreadsheets, graphics, fourth generation languages and executive information systems make it very easy to develop OO applications on desktop computers.

User knowhow and control. The users of computing services are becoming increasingly computer literate and "Webby" and want to control their own applications. Distributed applications put data and processing close to the user.

Exploitation of special hardware. Desktop computer software can use the hardware features of these platforms. For example, Java applets can be used for a variety of sophisticated applications. In addition, each computer can be used as a dedicated server to satisfy requests from clients.

Combining Distributed Objects with the Web
Let Me Count the Ways

There are several ways to combine distributed objects with Web. Here are the principal ones that use CORBA, OLE/ActiveX, and others.

The CORBA route:

- Invoke CORBA calls from a CGI procedure (a script or a subroutine written in C or in any other language) that resides on the Web server. In this case, the CGI procedure is the CORBA client. This is the oldest and the best known method.

- Invoke CORBA directly from the Web browser. Netscape browsers are beginning to support the CORBA IIOP calls directly. Thus, the Web browser sites behave as CORBA clients.

- Use CORBA to interact between Java applets across machines. This option is currently supported by a few vendors (especially Sun).

The OLE/ActiveX route:

- Invoke DCOM calls from a CGI procedure (a script or a subroutine written in C or in any other language) that resides on the Web server.

- Invoke DCOM calls directly from the components contained in the Web browser (e.g., the Microsoft Internet Explorer). These components may be written in C, C++, Visual Basic, Java, or other programming languages behaving as ActiveX Controls and contained inside the browser.

- Invoke DCOM calls from the ActiveX components such as spreadsheets that may invoke Java applets or other components residing on Web servers.

Other routes:

- Use the Sun Remote Method Invocation (RMI) between remotely located Java applets. This technology is very well supported by SunSoft tools but is restricted, at the time of this writing, to interactions between Java applets only.

- Use HTTP to invoke remote objects. A few small companies have implemented this option by using HTTP between ORBs. This option should be used rarely, if at all. We are mentioning it for completeness.

However, no new technology is risk free—OCSI applications are no exception. Unfortunately, many pitfalls of new technologies are discovered after the fact and are usually not paid attention to in the initial euphoric technology introduction stages. OCSI applications present many potential dilemmas and pitfalls such as the following:

> **Hidden costs.** Many costs are hidden and are not apparent initially. For example, middleware license costs at each site can gradually add up (middleware cost can range from $200 per

desktop to $250K per mainframe). In addition, management and maintenance costs can be very high (up to nine times) compared to server machine cost [Jenkins 1995]. Many costs are human related. The cost studies in C/S computing have shown that C/S *increases* total costs due to reasons such as the following: end-user effort in learning and operating desktops is higher; end-user help desks require more support; many hidden costs at end-user sites (e.g., middleware,) emerge; and distributed applications require more programming support due to their complexity [Simpson 1997], [Dec 1995], [DePompa 1995], and [Moad 1994]. Hidden costs are hard to control/quantify because significant costs shift to consulting and training.

Concerns for security and integrity control. Interactions between data and programs on multiple computers across Internet introduce many security and integrity control issues that are not easy to address. For example, Internet has introduced a very wide range of security exposures in authentication and authorization. In addition, failure handling and backup/ recovery of data across networks such as Internet is not easy.

Increase in complexity. OCSI applications introduce complex issues and interdependencies that are not well understood. For example, one misbehaving application at one site may inflict misery on many innocent applications residing at remote sites. In addition, many points of failure are introduced that make application recovery difficult.

Interoperability, integration, and portability issues. OCSI applications raise these serious issues because of different applications, many layers of middleware and networking options. These issues require many standards that depend on agreements between vendors and international/national organizations.

Difficulties in large application design. Breaking applications into pieces, where each piece can reside on a separate computer is nontrivial. In addition, many application configurations and interconnectivity options need to be carefully evaluated.

Lack of support and management approaches. At present, many of the management and support issues have not been understood and addressed. Many management and support challenges emerge when applications cross multiple operating systems, hardware platforms, databases, and networks. For example, changing management in such environments is a nightmare. Issues of staffing and organizing also need attention.

Too many options and confusion. It takes a long time for the developers to understand all options and make the best decisions. Developers need more training to develop efficient distributed applications that employ Web and distributed objects. It is also difficult to differentiate between state-of-the-art, state-of-the-market, and state-of-the-practice issues.

In other words, while there are many promises of OCSI, it does have some potential pitfalls. So what should be done? The best approach is to clearly specify the business drivers and application requirements. Based on this, a judgment needs to be made about how well the OCSI approach enables these drivers and requirements. If chosen, then the potential pitfalls need to be managed as risks. In the next section, we will suggest such an approach.

Building OCSI Applications: A Checklist

This checklist is an abstraction of the approach that will be presented in Section 4.4 and explained in great detail in the next three chapters.

Analysis:

- Establish requirements, that is, functional (determine what pieces of information are needed by whom, when), performance, security, operability, and management

- Develop an object model that shows conceptually how the information will be organized, accessed, manipulated, and presented in terms of objects

Architecture:

- Data architecture: determine what data sources (HTML, files, databases) will be needed, where they will be located, and how they will be accessed

- Software architecture: Determine what will be written as CGI/Java code, what will be written as modules called by CGI/Java, where will the various objects/ modules reside, and how will they be invoked (CORBA, RPC, etc.)

- Infrastructure architecture: determine the servers where the home page and the objects/modules will reside, the type of gateways that will be employed, the type of middleware that will be needed to invoke remote services and objects (CORBA, ActiveX, RPC, SQL), and the type of computing platforms (PC Windows, Unix, Windows NT, mainframes) used.

Implementation and Deployment:

- Build the HTML pages (including Java powered pages) by coding HTML or using filters that generate HTML from other data sources (e.g., word documents)

- Develop and test the software modules and objects

- Purchase and install the appropriate infrastructure components

- Test, install, and deploy the system

4.4   An Approach to Building OCSI Applications

4.4.1   Overview

Development of an OCSI application is like development of a series of mini applications, that are closely tied together to solve a business problem. Different parts of this application may support different classes of users (decision support, operational support), utilize different programming languages, run at different sites, utilize different computing platforms, employ different database technologies, and be interconnected through a diverse array of

---

Will Web Kill Client/Server?

In 1996, many opinions about Web killing the client/server have been voiced. This discussion is flawed at a very fundamental level—it confuses the concept of client/server with the implementation of client/server. The concept of client/server, as explained in Chapter 2, is at the core of the World Wide Web (Web browsers are clients to the Web servers). The client/server concept has been implemented in a variety of ways. A popular implementation of the C/S concept in the early 1990s was the remote SQL model that housed the application and presentation logic at the client machine while the server was a SQL server. This model, also known as the "Fat Client Model," has unfortunately been used to exemplify the C/S applications. Web uses a "Thin Client Model" where the client has only limited logic (this is changing with Java, however).

While reviewing the industry reports about Web versus C/S, keep in mind the distinction between the concept and the implementation of C/S. The concept of C/S is alive and well in Web. The debate is centered around which implementation is most suitable for modern enterprises.

---

network communication devices and software. A systematic methodology is needed to develop OCSI applications that maximize the benefits to the enterprise and minimize the risks. The methodology must be able to answer the following questions:

- What type of requirements need to be captured early to clearly understand the business drivers and to minimize surprises and risks?

- How can an effective overall solution approach be established quickly to take into account the buy versus reuse versus develop considerations?

- How can an architecture be developed that, when implemented, will satisfy the functional as well as operational requirements of the application and conform to the infrastructure and management budgetary as well as policy issues?

- How should an OCSI application be implemented (coded, tested, deployed) given different types of middleware?

- How can the applications be properly managed and supported after deployment?

Figure 4.9 shows the "methodology pattern" for developing new applications. This pattern, introduced in Chapter 3, consists of successive iterations, refinements, and expansions between analysis, architectures, implementations, and deployment/support activities. The sidebar checklists for building different types of Web-based applications have already used this methodology pattern. The first two iterations, discussed in Chapter 3, determine if a new application needs to be built (application engineering) from scratch, should existing applications be reengineered, or should a mixture of engineering/reengineering be used. This part of the book concentrates on the later iterations in which new applications are developed and deployed (i.e., we zero in on application engineering activities). Sections 4.4.2 through 4.4.5 discuss the details of analysis (requirement specification, logical modeling), architecture (data, software, and infrastructure architectures), implementation, and deployment/support activities for building new OCSI applications. Section 4.5 shows how these broad activities can be customized for different classes of applications such as decision support, operational support and real time.

Figure 4.9 Application Engineering Methodology Patterns

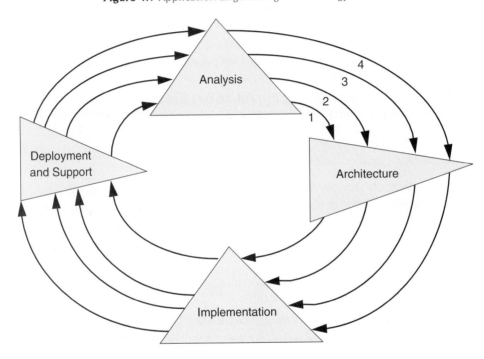

Notes:
The methodology template shows four broad iterative (stages). In each iteration, each activity is performed. Some activities are more extensive than others in each iteration. The proportion of effort spent in each activity is represented by the distance covered in each triangle. For example, the first iteration involves extensive analysis and architecture, but very little implementation and deployment activities. Later iterations successively reduce the analysis and architecture but increase the implementation and deployment activities. The following iterations are shown (more can be added):

    1 = First Iteration = Planning
    2 = Second Iteration = Prototyping and Experimentation
    3 = Third Iteration = First Release
    4 = Fourth Iteration = Second Release

The methodology for engineering new applications, introduced here and expanded in the next three chapters, is based on a synthesis of concepts from a variety of sources. Specifically, the Henderson-Venkatraman model [Henderson 1993] is used to align IT with business. The OO analysis and design approach is used to understand all aspects of a system (i.e., decompose a system into objects and classes). In particular, we use the object-oriented design methodologies presented by Booch [1994] and Rumbaugh [1994] (see Chapter 3 for a quick review of OO design approach). In the architecture activities, the ANSA principles proposed by the ANSA Consortium are used. ANSA is a Cambridge, England-based collaborative industry effort to advance distributed systems technology with focus on architectures for distributed applications, vendor neutrality, contribution to standards, and advanced technology prototypes [Herbert 1994]. In addition, we use the OSCA Architecture principles where possible. OSCA Architecture is a set of guidelines, proposed by Bellcore, which have been used widely in the telecommunications industry to develop large-scale portable and interoperable applications in heterogeneous distributed environments [Umar 1993, Chapter 9]. For implementation, we use the platform-specific guidelines and tools. For example, PowerBuilder and OSF DCE documents describe how to translate designs into specific implementations. In addition, the concepts presented in general literature on developing distributed applications are used where appropriate [Adler 1995], [Nicol 1993], [Ng 1990], [Pankaj 1991], and [Papelis 1992].

To avoid the "camel" disease, the methodology is presented as a set of guidelines instead of rigid steps requiring mandatory diagramming tools and techniques. These guidelines, shown in the sidebar "Top 10 Guidelines and Practical Hints," can be extended, modified, and customized for different projects and any techniques for representing information can be used.

4.4.2 Analysis

The purpose of this iterative activity is to completely understand the problem by defining the requirements and analyzing/evaluating these requirements that will drive the application engineering project. We are assuming that high-level requirements and a rough project plan have been completed in the planning iteration discussed in Chapter 3. Analysis activity involves

- Requirement specification
- Logical modeling

Requirement Specification. Requirements can be defined at different levels of detail. As you progress through different iterations, you refine, expand, and modify the requirements based on additional insights gained through each iteration. The requirements can be broadly viewed in terms of:

- Functional requirements
- Operational requirements
- Management/organizational requirements

Top 10 Guidelines and Practical Hints

1. Always keep the business drivers and customer needs in mind. Avoid overengineering (i.e., do not build things that nobody needs). See the sidebar "Rolls Royce—A Lesson in Overengineering."

2. The best approach is to clearly specify the business drivers and application requirements that meet the customers' needs (see the sidebar "Keeping Customers Happy"). Based on this, a judgment needs to be made about how well the new technologies enable these drivers and requirements. If chosen, then the potential pitfalls need to be managed as risks.

3. The life cycle of the reason for undertaking an application engineering effort should be longer than the life cycle of the undertaking itself. In other words, if you undertake a three-year application engineering effort for a business process that may disappear in a year, then you may be looking at a very tough two years.

4. While choosing the infrastructure, keep in mind that the goal here is to build cost-effective applications for the business—not to be in the system integration business. Infrastructure selection (especially middleware) should be a separate organizational activity that feeds into application development.

5. It is better to buy than to develop. This is especially true in case of Web-based software. However, you should be careful about the "free-ware."

6. Do your best to utilize a common API (application programming interface) throughout your application. However, do not develop your own API, unless absolutely essential, that sits on top of other APIs. This may stop you from quickly buying and using off-the-shelf software.

7. It is important to maximize reuse. In particular, the class libraries and object frameworks, commonly available for OO software, should be utilized as much as possible to increase reuse.

8. Do not overdistribute. In some cases, replacing a powerful machine with 10 interconnected machines is like replacing a horse with 10 chickens to pull a buggy —you have the same type of coordination problems. If two processes interact with each other frequently, then put them on the same machine. It has been found that the cost of maintaining and managing a server machine can be up to nine times the hardware purchase costs [Jenkins 1995].

9. Specify systems using good OO concepts (i.e., abstractions and encapsulation). In other words, use objects to define a high-level model for distributed applications (see Chapter 3, Section 3.4).

10. Use tools, as much as possible, to automatically generate the engineering details needed for implementation (e.g., adequate libraries, bindings, stub generator) and hide the underlying middleware APIs (application programming interfaces) from programs (i.e., API calls should be produced by the tools).

The functional requirements focus on the capabilities to be provided by the new application. Examples of the main functional requirements are:

- User commands (inputs) and responses (outputs)

- Tasks performed by the application

- The organization and the business processes that will be served by the new system

- An application "profile" that shows the characteristics of the application such as decision support versus operational support, span of use, novices versus "power users"

The operational requirements represent a wide range of performance, security, and interconnectivity information. Examples of operational requirements are:

- Size information (number of users who will access the system, frequency of transaction arrival at different sites, database size)

- Response time (average, worst case) requirements of the users

- Scaling and growth requirements (growth in end users, growth in work of end users)

- Security requirements (encryption, secure ID)

- Availability restrictions (7 days a week, 24 hours a day)

- Conformance to existing industry middleware standards (e.g., CORBA, HTTP, CGI, SMTP)

- Connectivity needed from user sites (e.g., from PCs, Macs, and UNIX users connected on a TCP/IP LAN, packet-switching network, or dial-up lines)

- Interoperability and interfaces with other (existing/proposed) systems (e.g., are these data closely related to other databases on the mainframe)

- Backup/recovery needs and disaster handling (e.g., will the migrated data be harder to recover in and operate in a disaster situation)

The management/organizational requirements establish the limits within which the new system will be developed. Examples of these requirements, also viewed as management restrictions, are:

- Budgeted money for this project (how much money can be spent?)

- Budgeted time for this project (when is the system expected to be available?)

- Corporate Infrastructure standards and standard operating environments (SOE) that must be adhered to (e.g., Macintosh cannot be used, only Oracle RDBMS must be used, Iona's ORBIX must be used for CORBA, etc.)

- Policy restrictions (e.g., organizational standards and policies to be followed, application control and auditing restrictions)

It is important to capture these requirements as quickly as possible (first or second iteration). However, for large-scale systems, capturing all these requirements can be a very time-consuming undertaking. In these cases, it is prudent to focus on those requirements that are of key importance in establishing a solution approach. For example, we should concentrate on application type (OLTP or decision support) and span (e.g., small group level or large enterprisewide) of the proposed application. As we will see later, this information can be used to quickly establish a solution strategy.

In my own experience, I have found that an early and quick understanding of the management and operational requirements is just as important as the functional requirements, especially in new areas such as OCSI. Otherwise, too much time and effort is wasted in pursuing "exciting" new technologies that may be too expensive, immature, or not part of the corporate standards and policies.

Rolls-Royce—A Lesson in Overengineering

In the 1980s, the prestigious and well established British car company Rolls-Royce went out of business because of overengineering. Basically, Rolls-Royce kept on adding features that the customers really did not need. The end result was that the price of the car went far beyond what the customers were willing to pay.

There is a lesson for application engineers in this. It is very easy to get carried away and introduce a lot of new features that exploit new technologies but do not add any value to the customers. This typically happens in the requirement definition stage in the form of "feature creep." Over the years, I have seen new features find their way into requirements several times without any customer explicitly asking for them. A simple, but effective tool is to evaluate requirements in terms of value to the customers before embarking on expensive development efforts.

Source:

> English, L., "Data Quality; Meeting Customer Needs," *Data Management Review*, November 1996, pp. 44–51.

Keeping Customers Happy

It is obviously important to build systems that keep the customers happy. Here are some pieces of information to highlight the stakes:

- By some estimates, it costs five times more to obtain a new customer than to keep an old one.
  Source: Fisher, S., "How To Be a Market Leader? Cozy Up to Your Customers," *Datamation*, August 1996, p. 49.

- Twenty-five percent of customers generate 85 percent of profits.
  Source: Kirk Strwsee, Ernst and Young.

- It is not enough to just take orders from customers (anybody can do that). It is important to work intimately with the customers to explore new needs.
  Source: Wiersema, F., and Treacy, M., "How To Be a Market Leader?"

Despite a great deal of technology, requirement gathering remains an intensely human activity. It involves interviewing the customer, apprenticing with the customer, and participating with the customer as essential ingredients. Requirement specification and analysis tools should be viewed as aids in these human activities and not as substitutes.[3] *The Communications of the ACM,* May 1995, is a special issue on human aspects of requirements gathering and contains excellent articles on the subject matter.

Logical Modeling. Once the core requirements have been defined, different models of the application are developed to understand the static as well as dynamic behavior of the application. We advocate an OO modeling approach based on an ***object model*** that shows:

- The object classes that represent the real as well as conceptual objects within the scope of an application

- The relationships (associations) between object classes

- A class hierarchy that shows how different object classes inherit properties from other objects (a class is, as stated previously, a collection of similar objects)

- The operations supported by the object classes

- The interfaces of each object (i.e., the methods supported by each object).

In addition to the object model, a ***dynamic model*** is constructed to capture the dynamic semantics of the objects (e.g., timing, flow, and synchronization information). A large body of literature is readily available on object and dynamic modeling [Booch 1994], [Rumbaugh 1994], and [Jacobson 1992]. A brief overview of building the object and dynamic models was presented in Chapter 3.

A variety of tools can be used to document, represent, examine and analyze the requirements and the logical model. Approaches include simple examinations, diagramming tools such as Booch's diagrams, formal specification languages, and knowledge-based requirement analyzers. We do not spend any time on diagramming techniques, because our focus is on principles and not on diagramming techniques. The reader may employ any diagramming technique and associated tools that are becoming commercially available.

Numerous requirement specification and analysis techniques have been introduced since the early 1980s [Meyer 1989], [Ng 1990], [Pankaj 1991], [Pressman 1987], [Rubenstein 1991], [Yeh 1984], and [Zave 1984]. Issues specific to distributed systems such as timing, parallelism, and deadlocks are discussed by [Papelis 1992], and [Chen 1983]. Once the requirements have been documented, they are circulated to and analyzed by the end users, the managers, the developers, marketing representatives, et cetera. *IEEE Software,* March 1996, and *Communications of the ACM,* May 1995, are special issues on requirement engineering and should be consulted for additional details.

---

3. In my own experience, I have found several analysts and developers shy away from customer contacts and take solace in tools and gadgets. This is similar to assuming the problem away and solving the residue rigorously.

4.4.3 Application Architectures

Architectures play a vital role in distributed systems, because they show how the "mini-systems" tie together to satisfy the requirements stated previously. The ***architecture*** of any system describes:

- the components (what are the pieces of a system?)
- the functions of components (what do they do?)
- the interfaces/interactions between the components of a system (how do they interoperate with each other?)

Development of an application architecture is a complex task that consists of (see Figure 4.10):

- Data architecture
- Application software architecture
- Platform architecture

Data architecture, discussed in detail in Chapter 5, is concerned with the crucial issues of definition of data (what they are, who owns them, who generates them, who uses them, etc.), placement of data in an enterprise (what data are located where in the enterprise network, how many copies of data exist, where do they exist, which copy is primary), mechanisms for accessing the data (who needs to accesses the data, on what platforms do they reside, will the users employ Web or other technologies to access the database), and administration of data (who is responsible for the integrity, security and quality of data[4]). Data architecture, in some form, is always needed for new applications. Even when an off-the-shelf application is being installed, you have to decide where the database will be installed, who will access it, are duplicated copies needed, and the like. For new applications such as decision support that only require a new database, data architecture is the primary, and most expensive activity. For new applications that need to be developed from scratch, data architectures are typically established in parallel with the application software architecture (in some cases, data architectures are established first, and application architectures are built around the data architectures).

Application software architectures, discussed in detail in Chapter 6, show the application components, the interrelationships between these components, their allocations, and their coordination paradigms. Application software architectures in distributed environments raise several portability and interoperabilty issues, because they tie several mini applications together to satisfy business and technical requirements. Specifically, application architectures for OCSI applications include the following steps: (a) refine the object model, (b) extend it to a distributed object model by dividing the application logic between client and server objects and evaluate issues such as two- versus three-tiered configurations, (c) evaluate/choose infrastructure, especially the middleware, and (d) evaluate the allocation strategies. A complete application architecture includes the data architecture and gives enough information to the implementers.

---

4. Data quality has become a major area of concern in corporate databases and must be included in enterprise data architectures.

Figure 4.10 Application Architecture Components

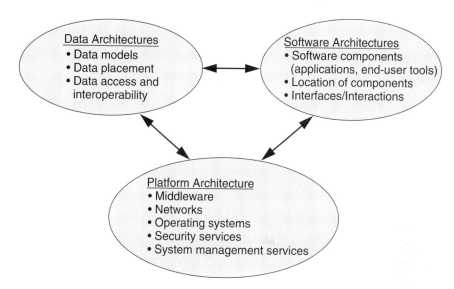

<hr>

Client-Side versus Server-Side Development— Fat Clients versus Fat Servers

Web-based applications can use a "Fat Client" or a "Fat Server" architecture. The Web tools support either of these two architectures.

The Fat Client Web applications typically use Java applets that run on the Web browser. This model is useful if you have a powerful desktop. At present, Netscape and Sun heavily support this model with the CORBA-enabled browsers and Java development tools.

The Fat Server Web applications use the traditional CGI and server APIs to run application logic on the Web server sites. This model is useful if you want central control (i.e., one Web server). The Microsoft ODBC and ActiveX support this model.

Source:
Reichard, K., "Inner Workings: Server-Side Development Decisions," *Internet Systems,* January 1997, pp. 6–10.

<hr>

Platform (infrastructure) architectures provide the set of technologies (middleware, networks, operating systems, hardware, etc.) that glues together the application pieces across an enterprise. For example, the OCSI applications may use a combination of middleware such as Web technologies (Web browsers, Web servers, HTML, and HTTP), distributed object technologies (CORBA and Distributed OLE), and SQL middleware (ODBC drivers, database gateways) that operate over TCP/IP networks across PC Windows, Windows NT, UNIX, and MVS platforms. We have briefly discussed these technologies in Chapter 2. A detailed discussion of these issues is beyond the scope of this book (see Umar [1997] for details).

Individual applications must exist within an ***enterprise information architecture*** (see Figure 4.11). Enterprise information architectures are a considerable industrial activity at present [Melling 1995], and [Comport 1995]. We will use the following definition:

> **Definition**: An ***enterprise information architecture (EIA)*** specifies the IT-based solution approach that will satisfy the information requirements of an enterprise.

Figure 4.11 Levels of Architecture

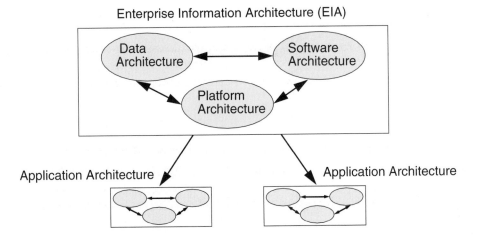

For example, enterprise information architecture for a bookstore chain would show what pieces of information will be stored where and in what format, how the employees can locate the books, order them, ship them, and the like. In addition, what type of enterprise platform architecture would be needed (e.g., where should Web technologies be used? should CORBA be used anywhere? how should the enterprisewide network service be provided?). It should be remembered that EIA is a high level activity and should be as much machine independent as possible. Thus, questions such as what version of UNIX to use, should an HP machine be used instead of Prime, how much memory should I get on my PC are irrelevant to information architecture. As a matter of fact, *a good test of an enterprise information architecture is its survivability through hardware and infrastructure changes (ideally for about 5 years)*. See the sidebar on "Attributes of a Good Enterprise Information Architecture."

The goal of the enterprise information architecture is to specify those pieces of information (platforms, enterprise data, applications) which maximize benefits and minimize costs and risks. Cost/benefit analysis, discussed in Chapter 3, can play an important role in establishing information architectures. Cost/benefit analysis produces cost categories (end-user labor, support labor, hardware/software), benefit categories (end-user benefits, corporate benefits), and choice of an approach that maximizes the cost/benefit ratio.

Development of EIAs is similar to establishing design of a city for an ever-changing and ever-evolving industrial and residential population. You have to worry more about how the individual parts of the city will be known to the city dwellers and how will they be interconnected (the infrastructure needed), instead of how the individual buildings will be designed internally (you basically establish policy, rules and guidelines for the buildings). In a similar vein, EIA specifies the common facilities needed by individual applications and end-user tools needed to make them portable and interoperable in the enterprise.

4.4.4   Implementation

Implementation is concerned with building, testing, and deploying the new application. Specifically, this activity includes detailed design of each application component (user interface, programs, databases), construction (write programs, populate database), and test the application code, user interfaces, and databases. Implementation is largely dependent on the architectural choices and the middleware used. For example, a Web-based application that uses Web gateways (CGI gateways) and remote SQL to access corporate databases differs significantly from an RPC-based application implemented entirely by using the OSF/DCE middleware. We will discuss implementation issues in Chapter 7. In particular, we will show the similarities and differences between application implementations by using Web, ActiveX, CORBA, PowerBuilder, OSF/DCE, and Encina environments. The topics discussed in Chapter 7 also include:

- Concepts in building OCSI applications

- Testing of OCSI applications

- Examples of application development in Web, CORBA, PowerBuilder, OSF/DCE, and Encina environments

Ideally, new applications should be implemented by using the OO paradigm and middleware. However, many new applications need to access existing resources such as legacy databases that do not support object-orientation. How can a "pure" OO application be implemented in situations where operations on remote objects, inheritance, encapsulation, and polymorphism are not supported. The key trick is to develop a ***wrapper*** on the client side that receives object invocations and issues and appropriate calls (RPCs) to one or more back-end servers (see Figure 4.12). The wrapper is developed as a class with methods that construct and issue RPCs, SQL, or any other "non-OO" interactions. The client application code invokes methods provided by this wrapper (the wrapper basically creates an object view of the server functionality). An object wrapper may be thin (just issue an RPC) or thick (serve as a gateway to legacy systems by providing protocol conversion, security checking, logging, etc.). The wrappers may be invoked by Web browsers (Java applets), Web servers (CGI scripts) or any other piece of code. We will discuss object wrappers in more detail in Chapter 9.

Figure 4.12 Object Wrappers for OCSI

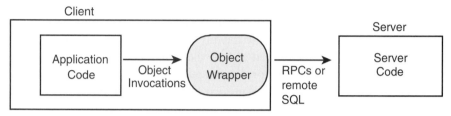

Attributes of a Good Enterprise Information Architecture

Ideally, a good enterprise information architecture should minimize the impact of platform and vendor selection/modification on applications. In particular, this architecture should promote use of tools that hide the underlying middleware APIs (application programming interfaces) from programs (i.e., API calls should be produced by the tools). The sequence of activities for new applications in a well architected environment would be as follows:

● Define and analyze application requirements

● Develop an application architecture (data + software) which conforms to the enterprise information architecture

● Choose the target platforms and vendors that conform to the enterprise information architecture

● Implement the application on the chosen platform

● Deploy and operate the application

● Move the application components between computers, if needed

● Change platform and vendors if needed

The most significant aspect of this life cycle is that once an overall enterprise information architecture is chosen, the selection and modification of the platforms does not affect the implemented application. Thus, an investment in implemented applications is protected despite platform and vendor changes.

An important issue in implementing OO applications is to encapsulate the relational databases as objects. Although an OO program written in languages such as C++ can issue a SQL statement, it becomes cumbersome to translate an object view in C++ to a relational model for queries (this is called "impedance" mismatch between programming code and data manipulation languages). Figure 4.13 shows different approaches to "objectifying" RDBMSs. Basically, an OO client can issue SQL calls or use a wrapper that translates OO calls to SQL. At present, off-the-shelf wrappers for relational databases are commercially available. DBTools.h++ from Roguewave and the wrappers provided by Persistence Software are examples.

Figure 4.13 Wrappers for Relational Databases

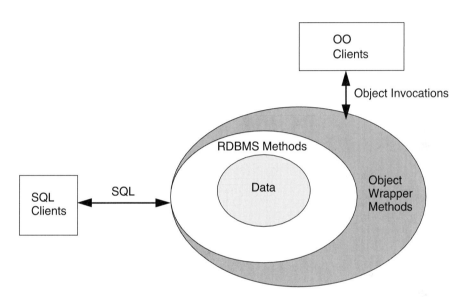

4.4.5   Deployment and Support

After an application has been implemented, it is deployed and managed/supported. The best architected and implemented systems fall apart without proper management and support platforms, policies, and procedures. Effective management and support must address three issues. First, the functions to be supported such as fault management (detecting, diagnosing and recovering from faults), performance management (monitoring, controlling, and predicting performance), configuration management (defining, changing, monitoring, and controlling), accounting (recording usage of resources and generating billing information), security (ensuring authorized access to resources), and operational support (help desks, backup and recovery, and automated operations). Second, the type of components monitored and controlled such as network hardware devices, middleware, and application objects. Finally, the level of support to be provided such as consulting support in which a user is advised on how to monitor and control the resources, and "hands-on" support in which the service center actually monitors and controls the resources for a user.

Pilot Projects and Prototypes

Well-designed and controlled pilot projects and prototypes are essential to the success of enterprisewide applications (imagine putting an airplane into production without well-designed pilot and prototype projects). In addition, rapid prototyping is a viable approach for reducing time to market [Andriole 1992], and [Dollas 1995]. Pilot projects and prototypes are an essential aspect of any methodology and should be designed to accomplish the following:

- Gain end-user acceptance and buy-in by getting them involved in the project

- Develop feedback from users

- Use the experience to reduce time to market

- Gain real insights into the infrastructure needed to support the applications

- Develop an understanding of vendor support

- Study the trade-offs in application architectures

- Estimate the effort needed to deploy and support the application

- Gain insights for policies, procedures, and roles/responsibilities

- Train key staff members for production

For most enterprisewide applications, pilot projects and prototypes may last between three to six months. The objective should be to focus on the aforementioned, and other clearly stated, results. Pilot projects and prototypes have been used widely in most of the successful C/S applications. For example, the Hewlett-Packard transition of legacy systems to C/S architectures involved a team of six people to experiment with the new technology and to develop a structured pilot for six months before the corporate commitment for large scale migration was made [Ross 1994].

4.5   Customizing the Methodology

4.5.1   Overview

There is no "one size fits all" methodology for developing all applications in the modern environments. For example, a departmental decision support application will not require some of the activities needed for an enterprisewide mission-critical operational support application. Let us customize the methodology presented in Section 4.4 for a few sample application development situations. The application situations we will discuss are based on three broad application categories: decision support, operational support, and real time. Table 4.1 summarizes the main activities in each stage of the methodology for these classes of applications (we will explain these activities in the following subsections). We introduced these application categories in Chapter 1. The discussion in this section admittedly only considers a few cases. You can extend this discussion to other cases that require mixtures of the cases discussed here (e.g., applications that are operational support at corporate level but provide decision support capabilities at the departmental/group level).

TABLE 4.1 Sample Methodologies

	Decision Support Applications	Operational Support Applications	Real-Time Applications
Analysis Stage	• Gather information requirements iteratively • Develop the object model for database design • No dynamic model (or light-weight)	• Gather and analyze detailed requirements • Develop the object model • Develop the dynamic model	• Gather detailed requirements with focus on hard performance requirements. • Develop the object model • Develop an extensive dynamic model
Architecture Stage	Mainly data architecture (iteratively)	Data + application software architecture	Main focus is on hardware platforms to satisfy performance requirements
Implementation Stage	Selection and testing of tools; population of databases	Application software development and testing (if they cannot be purchased)	Application software development and testing (may involve middleware development)
Deployment and support	Installation of tools at user sites and quick response to changing needs	Installation of software at user sites and technical support/help desks	Installation of software at user sites and quick technical support/help desks

4.5.2 Building Web-Based Decision Support Systems (DSSs)

Decision support applications are primarily intended for "knowledge" workers and managers and focus on informational data to drive the business. The DSS applications are intensely data query and data browsing processes that help the decision analysts to discover information as they go along.

The development methodology for DSS leans heavily towards building a database quickly that is increasingly made available to the users over the Web browsers. This database and the access facilities are extended and improved as more feedback from the users is received. DSS applications are not developed one application at a time, instead they are developed around corporate data that are shared across different applications and users.

The analysis stage for decision support concentrates on defining the scope of data being used and the target users. The users are interviewed to gather the information require-ments.These applications rely heavily on off-the-shelf query and browser tools and use the object model to design the database. There is virtually no reason to develop a system dynamics model because most activities are queries.

The architecture stage concentrates heavily on the data architecture activity (i.e., data mod-eling, logical database design, data partitioning, data allocation, and data access). See Chap-ter 5. There is virtually no need for software architectures, because most of the decision support needs can be satisfied by off-the-shelf DSS tools (data browsers, report writers, spreadsheets, data mining tools) that can be installed on the analyst workstations. Most of these tools are becoming Web browser-based at the time of this writing. The architecture must be very flexible to support rapidly changing users needs.

The implementation activity does not require programming. Instead, it concentrates on pur-chasing and installing the decision support tools and the infrastructure needed to provide access from the tools to the database (database gateways).

The deployment and support stage is, in effect, a stepwise refinement activity that responds to the analysts through their needs and discovery processes. The main purpose is to learn quickly about the changing user needs and expand the database and the tools accordingly.

The amount of time spent in these stages depends on the span of the applications. For a departmental/group DSS application, the analysis stage can be considerably shortened by giving the analysts a database that they can start experimenting with. For enterprisewide DSS applications, more time should be spent on developing information requirements. The data architecture, discussed in the next chapter in detail, in this case is a considerable activ-ity because many issues in data modeling and data allocation need to be addressed.

An example of decision support application is data warehouses (see Chapter 10). Many DSS applications are currently desktop-based and are increasingly becoming Web-based due to the popularity of Web browsers.

4.5.3   Building Web-Based Operational Support Applications

Operational support applications provide the day-to-day operational activities of an orga-nization and typically use OLTP (on-line transaction processing) capabilities. Operational support applications are very requirement-driven (you need to understand the core requirements completely before making major architectural choices). These applications are typically designed one application at a time.

Electronic commerce is an interesting and rapidly advancing area of Web-based transaction processing. In particular, the Web-based purchasing systems are becoming commercially available to allow customers to search catalogs through Web browsers, build an "electronic shopping cart" in which the chosen items are placed, and then make payments through credit cards, and electronic checks. Examples of Web-based purchasing systems are the Netscape Merchant Server and Microsoft Commerce Server.

The analysis stage for operational support applications typically involves detailed requirement definition which specifies the functional, operational, and management requirements. The effort spent in this stage depends on the scope of the application. Naturally, enterprise-wide mission-critical applications demand much more analysis as compared to departmental applications to be used by a dozen users. Large-scale applications require a detailed object model and a system dynamics model (e.g., state transition diagrams).

The application architecture for OSS applications may include data as well as software architectures that are discussed in the next two chapters. The effort needed in developing the application architecture depends on the following options:

- Purchase the entire application
- Develop the database only and purchase or reuse existing programs and user interfaces
- Develop the entire application

Purchasing off-the-shelf systems, if it satisfies the requirements, is by far the most attractive approach from a cost/benefit point of view. Consequently, it must be considered as the first choice. In particular, a large number of Web-based applications are becoming available commercially. For example, if an order processing application is needed and the requirements seem to be satisfied by an off-the-shelf order-processing system from a vendor, then this package should be evaluated seriously. The key evaluation criteria, as stated previously, are:

- Will this package satisfy the current as well as future requirements?
- Will this package scale well?
- What is the current user experience base?
- Does it conform to the infrastructure standards?

The next best thing is to find that the requirements can be satisfied by developing one or more new databases. This approach assumes that the application logic and user interface processing can be provided by off-the-shelf packages, existing programs, or end-user tools such as spreadsheets, data browsers, and report writers. This strategy is typically useful for applications where information stored in a database is accessed by desktop tools. This strategy is especially useful for OO applications because availability of class libraries and Object Frameworks is making it easier to reuse software code.

If an entire new application needs to be developed, then we can assume that the new application will be developed as an OCSI application. As stated previously, most new applications are heavily using Web technologies in user interfaces with the application logic increasingly becoming OO (C++, Java and Smalltalk code) and OO databases rarely being used. The "object wrappers," introduced later in Section 4.4.4 in this chapter, may be needed to provide a layer that makes the non-OO services appear as OO. The architectural issues discussed in Chapters 5 and 6 are of value to this type of application development.

The implementation and deployment/support stages depend heavily on how much software is developed from scratch or purchased/reused. For heavily purchased/reused software, these two stages are dominated by software purchasing, testing, and installation activities; for applications that require considerable software development, these two stages are coding, testing, and maintenance intensive.

4.5.4   Real-Time Application Development

Real-time applications are embedded in real-life activities and are part of a real-life process (a telephone switching system, a manufacturing process). Many new applications (desktop videoconferencing) are becoming real-time because they use distributed multimedia and moving videos.

Real-time applications must satisfy hard performance and availability requirements. The analysis stage for real-time applications concentrates on clearly specifying the hard performance and availability requirements. The real-time applications rely, for obvious reasons, on very extensive system dynamics models.

The main activity in the architecture stage is to determine a combination of hardware and software capabilities that will meet the performance and availability requirements. Unlike many corporate operational and decision support applications, the real-time applications may not share a common IT platform. Instead, many real-time applications are deeply hard-wired to the underlying platforms for performance reasons (e.g., multimedia over ATM networks, real-time control systems used in manufacturing environments). Thus, the IT platform for real-time applications is of key importance.

The implementation stage of real-time applications is also very hardware dependent with frequent utilization of hardware interrupt facilities and scheduling [Stankovic 1995], and [Walker 1995]. In many cases, this stage may involve development of middleware services for the specialized needs of real-time applications (this activity is almost unjustifiable for decision support and operational support applications at the time of this writing).

Basically, all stages need to be customized to emphasize the stringent performance and fault tolerance requirements and may require development of specialized infrastructure capabilities. It should be noted that specialized services for popular real-time applications such as distributed multimedia systems are being developed and standardized at present [Gemmel

1995], and [Furht 1995]. Also, OMG (Object Management Group) has several Special Interest Groups (SIGs) in the emerging areas (e.g., The OMG SIG in Multimedia Systems). An early example of real-time streaming applications for Java can be found in [Swanson 1996].

4.6   Application Development Environments

Most new applications are being written in programming languages such as C and C++ with Smalltalk gaining ground gradually (see the October 1995 issue of *Communications of the ACM*). For Web-based applications, Java is very popular for client-side software, and Perl (a scripting language) is used heavily for CGI-based development. Microsoft's ActiveX is tying desktop development tools to Web development by allowing Web browsers to serve as containers of spreadsheets, Word documents, and Visual Basic applications, among others (i.e., you can run a spreadsheet from a Web browser and invoke a Web browser from a spreadsheet [Chappell 1996]). Computer-aided software engineering (CASE) tools are needed to support these applications throughout their life cycle. The main objective of the CASE tools is to encapsulate the infrastructure details (middleware, networks) and thus make it easier to develop, deploy, and manage the new breed of applications that use a combination of OO, C/S, and Web technologies. CASE tools are needed that will, ideally, allow us to describe what needs to be done and then generate all infrastructure related components and interfaces (API calls, stubs).

It is desirable to have CASE tools that support the entire life cycle of scalable, portable and robust distributed applications. The current CASE tools for OCSI applications fall into the following broad categories, in increasing levels of complexity:

- Class libraries that enable programmers to reuse standard routines and encapsulate lower-level functions. Tools.h++ is an example.

- Simple GUI client development tools such as Visual Basic and Microsoft Access.

- Two-tiered remote SQL-based tools such as PowerBuilder and Oracle CASE.

- Three-tiered DCE or Encina-based tools such as ParcPlace Visual Works.

- Distributed object-based tools such as Forte.

- Web-based tools from Microsoft, Netscape, and Oracle. In addition, many aforementioned CASE tools are being extended to include Web facilities such as HTML and Java.

A review of the CASE tools for traditional C/S applications can be found in Linthicum [1995], and Darling [1995]. The rapidly evolving Web development tools are reviewed, and tools such as Sybase's Internet-Enabled Powerbuilder, Borland's Web Tools, Microsoft's Web Tools, SunSoft's JavaScript, Next's WebObjects, Iband's Backspace and others are analyzed in Linthicum [1996] and Salim [1997]. Current information about state-of-the-market tools can be found from the Web sites of key players (e.g., http://www.microsoft.com, http://www.oracle.com, http://www.sybase.com, http://www.netscape.com, http://www.forte.com). See the sidebar "Synopsis of Web-Based Development Environments."

Synopsis of Web-Based Development Environments

Microsoft's ActiveX Platform (http://www.microsoft.com). Microsoft is positioning ActiveX as an environment for Web and distributed objects. The Web browser can behave as a container for components such as Word documents, Java applets, C code, and Excel spreadsheets. All ActiveX components communicate with each other by using DCOM. Most of the development tools and environments from Microsoft are being based on ActiveX at the time of this writing.

Oracle's NCA—Network Computing Architecture (http://www.oracle.com). Oracle is pushing its NCA as the ultimate environment for building and operating Web-based applications. Based on NCA, a *Web Developer Suite* has been announced by Oracle for building distributed object, Web-based applications that utilize Oracle 7 Server, CORBA, a workgroup server, and many Oracle development tools. At the core of NCA is the notion of IDL-defined pluggable components, known as *cartridges*, that can be built for clients, database servers, or application logic. In particular, Datacartridges for database servers can be developed in PL/SQL, C/C++ or Java. Cartridges are similar to ActiveX components.

Netscape's One (http://www.netscape.com). Netscape is also rolling out a suite of tools for Web-based applications under the umbrella of Netscape One. These tools are based on open industry accepted standards such as HTTP to support Web browsers and servers, IIOP to support CORBA interactions over the Internet, LDAP for directory access, and SMTP for e-mail. In addition, a set of Internet Foundation Classes (IFCs) are included in Netscape One to provide common building blocks for rapid application development. You guessed it—IFCs are similar to ActiveX components and Oracle Cartridges.

Besides these big players, other development environments are worth noting.

Forte's Development Environment (http://www.forte.com) provides a set of OO tools for large scale (thousands of users) client/server applications. The main feature of Forte is that the application developers define the business functionality at a high level, as if it were to run on a single machine. Forte generates the client and server code for different middleware (e.g., OSF DCE and CORBA), thus hiding the middleware APIs from application developers. A Forte Web SDK (Software Developers Toolkit) is available to include Web browsers as clients.

BlueStone's Saphire/Web (http://www.bluestone.com) is a database development tool for Web applications. It supports Java, ActiveX, stored procedures, dynamic SQL, and HTML authoring tools.

NetDynamics' Studio (http://www.netdynamics.com) is a point-and-click Web-development environment that automatically generates Java code, provides "Wizards" for generating displays, and includes interfaces to PeopleSoft applications.

How can the existing and evolving CASE tools be compared, evaluated, and selected? Table 4.2 suggests a list of factors that can be used to evaluate support provided by potential CASE tools in terms of life-cycle activities, programming languages, type of middleware used, computing platforms, scalability, vendor information, et cetera.

TABLE 4.2 CASE TOOLS FOR OCSI APPLICATIONS

Evaluation Factors	Tool 1	Tool 2
Life-cycle support (requirements, architectures, design, coding, testing, maintenance)		
Scope (client only, server only, client and server)		
Programming Languages Supported (C, C++, Java, Smalltalk, Object Cobol, 4GLs, etc.)		
Type of underlying middleware being used (HTTP, remote SQL, RPCs, TRPCs, MOM, CORBA, transparency to underlying middleware)		
Web support (CGI support, Java support, Internet security support, access to Web resources)		
OO Support (Dynamic object-oriented programming, distributed objects)		
Platform support (UNIX, PC, Windows NT, MVS, cross platform)		
Cost factors (initial, maintenance, site licenses)		
Scale (small/departmental or large scale)		
Vendor information (size, partnerships, staying power, type of support provided)		
Current customer base/customer experiences		
Learning curve/ease of use		

4.7   State of the Practice: Examples and Case Studies

Many new applications at present are using corporate Intranets to provide access to documents, marketing information, Web-based billing systems, and other corporate resources (see, for example, Grygo [1996] for several specific examples). However, numerous new applications are beginning to combine object-orientation, client/server, and Internet technologies. Most OCSI applications only provide an OO view to the end user and access information from different remotely located servers (see Figure 4.14). Examples of the common OCSI applications are as follows (of course, many existing applications at present are beginning to use Web interfaces):

Figure 4.14 Conceptual View of OCSI Applications

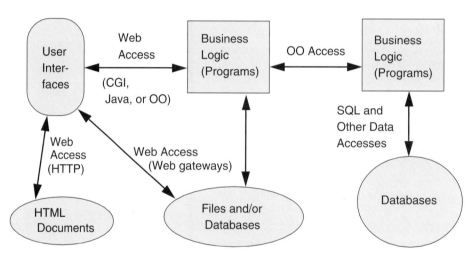

Notes:
HTML (Hypertext Markup Language) is used to prepare Web documents.
HTTP (Hypertext Transfer Protocol) is used in Web to access HTML documents.
Web Gateways are used to access non-HTML documents.
CGI (Common Gateway Interface) is used to invoke scripts or programs.

General World Wide Web (WWW) applications that allow users to access a very wide variety of information over the network in a client/server fashion. WWW applications utilize the Web browsers and are breaking new ground by including new technologies such as Java to make applications more "alive" and entertaining through multimedia presentations. Here are some examples:

- The U.S. Senate Web site that provides information to the staffers (e.g., staff directory, dining menus, meetings, health promotion programs), allows them to purchase items from an authorized stationery store, and potentially invokes security procedures by authorized users [Murphy 1996].

- Federal Express uses Web browsers to allow customers to see when a package arrived at its destination and who signed for it [Bickell 1996].

- Fidelity Investment employs Web technologies to enhance object reuse. The company developed an internal Web page that lists all the objects that have been incorporated in the existing applications. Attributes and other necessary information about each object can be found by using the various Web search tools. Programmers at the start of an application development project browse through this Web page to find objects that can be reused. *Source:* "Fidelity Finds a Way to Reuse Objects," *Application Development Trends,* June 1996, pp. 18–19.

Decision support applications that utilize many modeling, analysis, and evaluation tools residing on workstations that access remotely located information from many sites. The tools usually present an OO view to the users. In particular, data warehouses have become a multibillion dollar industry for decision support. An area of particular growth is data mining that employs AI and statistical analysis techniques to recognize patterns. The decision support applications are also becoming very "Webby" (i.e., they use Web interfaces). See Chapter 10 for details on data warehouses and several case studies.

Electronic commerce applications that allow business to conduct commercial activities (e.g., ordering materials, invoice processing, document exchanges) over the networks. These applications are increasingly using the Internet to transfer e-mail, EDI (Electronic Document Exchange), and enhanced Fax. An interesting example of Internet-based electronic commerce is the Internet Shopping Network (ISN), a totally Web-based company, that sells about 35,000 computer hardware and software products (*Source: Datamation*, April 1, 1996, p. 40). Additional information about ISN can be found from the company Web site (http://www.isn.com). Numerous other examples of electronic commerce can be found in the automotive industries (the Automotive Network eXchange between Caterpillar, Chrysler, Ford, GM, John Deere), telecommunications industries (Bell Atlantic's evaluated receipt and billing system linking Bell Atlantic to its suppliers), and others (real estate, military, local governments, financial, insurance, etc.).

Real-time applications in telecommunications, manufacturing, and aerospace industries, among others, which require exchange of information between geographically distributed processors. Here are some examples:

- **Videoconferencing systems and groupware systems** that allow remotely located workers to hold meetings, work on joint projects, collaborate on solving problems, and review and critique each other's work. Through text, video, and voice, these systems attempt to create an atmosphere in which remotely located workers interact with each other as if they were located at one site.

- **Multimedia applications** that combine data, voice, and moving videos on the same workstation. In most cases, the text, the pictures, and the moving video/voice appear on different windows of the same workstation as objects. The information being displayed can be extracted from sources located anywhere in the network.

- **Manufacturing control systems** in which the processes, the data, and the user interfaces are distributed to cell controllers, program logic controllers, robots, and shop floor monitoring devices. All devices in this system are viewed as objects.

- **Voice over the Internet (talking applications)** that employ middleware that converts voice into data packets that are shuffled across the Internet like other data packets (e.g., e-mail messages, hypertext pages, database queries). These talking applications are providing interesting opportunities (see [Gareiss 1996]).

These newer applications are characterized by a high volume of data that needs to be transmitted interactively across networks. Many applications require 100 million bits per second (Mbps) data transfer rates with sessions that can last for several hours. These characteristics impose demands on the networks, computing hardware and the application software. Basically, the data rate of 100 Mbps and higher are needed at LAN as well as WAN level. This is one of the reasons for the popularity of FDDI and Fast Ethernet LANs (both operate at 100 Mbps) and Frame Relay and ATM WANs (see Umar [1997] for details).

4.8   State of the Market: Products and Standards

Many products and tools are emerging in the marketplace to accelerate the introduction of OCSI applications. Examples of such products and tools can be found in areas such as object frameworks, business objects, and OCSI CASE tools.

An example of commercial object frameworks is IBM's object frameworks strategy that is beginning to materialize as products. The objective of this strategy is to create "seas of objects" with object frameworks as the glue to tie these objects into applications. The IBM object framework consists of two major components: application frameworks and middleware frameworks. The application frameworks, also known as desktop frameworks, provide programmer productivity tools for compound documents, multimedia, groupware, mail, 3D graphics, and decision support applications. The middleware framework covers an extensive set of C/S middleware services such as transaction processing, database access, directory services, telephony, authentication, and systems management. This strategy relies heavily on the IBM SOM/DSOM products for interactions between objects. The *Object Magazine,* May 1996 issue, is devoted to object frameworks and provides a good state-of-the-market discussion in this area.

Business objects have been talked about since the introduction of OLE 2.0, OpenDoc, and CORBA-based products in 1994. The tools designed to support creation of business objects have appeared from vendors such as Easel, and applications that employ business objects have appeared from vendors such as SAP and IMRS. The Object Management Group (OMG) and Business Object Management Special Interest Group (BOMSIG) are trying to help the industry understand and utilize this technology effectively. System integrators such as Anderson Consulting are also committing to delivering software environments that can be used to build custom applications based on business objects.

Many CASE tools for OCSI application development are becoming available from Internet companies such as Netscape. Examples of some of these tools are PowerBuilder from PowerSoft, Oracle CASE from Oracle, SQL Windows from Gupta, Neuron Data from Neuron Data, VisualAge from IBM, Forte from DEC, and VisualWorks from ParcPlace. In addition, Microsoft is introducing a family of tools around its ActiveX platform. These and other tools are improving in sophistication, cross platform support, scalability, and other factors shown in Table 4.2.

Standards that will benefit the overall OCSI applications effort are being developed by ISO as well as many other standardizing bodies and industry consortia. For example, ISO has been working on the Open Data Processing (ODP) Reference Model [Schurmann 1995]. ODP standards are aiming towards support for interworking between ODP systems, portability of applications, and distributed transparencies. OSI is positioning ODP for a future framework for activities concerned with OSF-DCE and OMG CORBA. At the time of this writing, the European Object Interest Group (OIG) is working on deployment of reusable components in large scale organizations (see Wooding [1997] for a discussion of OIG's work).

4.9   State of the Art: Research Notes

The research topics in OCSI applications span several areas such as distributed object computing, electronic commerce, intelligent agents, and others. Let us review a few for the purpose of illustration.

Ideally, object-oriented distributed programming should be the same as centralized programming. An OO distributed program can be written in programming languages such as C/C++, Smalltalk, or Object Cobol. However, several specialized programming languages like DPL, MML and LYNX [Silberschaatz 1980], [Castelli 1986], [Birman 1990], and [Scott 1987] have been developed specifically for distributed programming. An extensive survey of the "classical" programming languages for distributed systems is presented by [Bal 1989]. This paper discusses 15 distributed programming languages and contains an extensive bibliography that lists over 100 programming languages. These languages were developed to maximize parallelism, provide coordination through communication messages, and deal with partial failures. A more recent survey can be found in [Blelloch 1996].

Distributed object-based programming systems is an area of considerable academic research for distributed application support environments. Simply stated, an object-based programming language supports objects as a language feature but does not support the concept of inheritance. (The languages that support inheritance are referred to as object-oriented.) Thus languages such as C++ and Smalltalk are object-oriented, whereas ADA and Modula-2 are object-based [Chin 1991]. A distributed object-based programming system (DOBPS) is an amalgamation of object-based programming languages with distributed operating systems.

This is due to the decreasing distinction between an operating system and the programming languages it supports. A DOBPS typically provides

- A distributed operating system that allows a collection of computers (possibly heterogeneous) to be viewed as a single entity. A distributed operating system provides a wide range of location transparency, fault tolerance, workload migration, recovery and integrity services, and resource management (memory management, processor management, disk management) across loosely coupled heterogeneous computers.

- Object-based programming languages that allow object creation (structure definition and relationship definition), object management (performance, security, reliability, synchronization), and object interaction management (object location, message passing, failure handling).

It can be seen that a combination of these two facilities can provide an extensive and efficient support environment for distributed programming. Chin and Chanson [Chin 1991] give an extensive survey of the work in this interesting area with numerous examples about how DOBPS are being developed in distributed operating systems like Amoeba, Argus, CHORUS, Clouds, Eden, Emerald, and TABS/Camelot. Additional information about using distributed objects in customizing operating systems can be found in Islam [1995]. *The IEEE Computer,* November 1995, is a special issue on parallel and distributed processing tools and has several interesting articles in this subject area.

Another relevant area of research is formal specifications of distributed systems. The importance of formal specifications is well recognized by the International Standards Organization (ISO) because the distributed systems standards could be jeopardized by misinterpretations and imprecise notations. Due to this reason, ISO has introduced a formal specification language called LOTOS [Bolognesi 1988]. LOTOS has been used to describe various aspects of distributed systems such as distributed multimedia systems [Blair 1995]. Due to the diverse requirements of distributed systems standards such as the Open Data Processing (ODP) Reference Model, attention is being paid to development of general frameworks for formal specifications of ODP components.

Turning to electronic commerce, the inadequacy of EDI for end-to-end automation is being realized and research is needed to integrate EDI with work flows and distributed transaction processing [Adam 1996]. The basic idea is to conduct transactions across businesses that include EDI transactions that tie work flows and transaction processing capabilities between multiple businesses. For example, the HOST (Healthcare Open Systems and Trials) project is attempting to establish work flows among multiple doctors, hospitals, and insurance companies for conducting business. The Web site, http://www.eitech.edu, is a good source of information in this growing area.

Intelligent agents (IAs), also known as Virtual Agents and Knowbots, provide many interesting areas of research because they combine AI with WWW. IAs are intelligent software entities that simulate the behavior of "capable" human agents such as an experienced insurance agent. Examples of IAs are a software entity that extracts, organizes, and presents information on a given topic (e.g., ancient history); a travel agent that makes travel arrangements (e.g., makes reservations, purchases tickets) for a trip within time and money constraints; and a buyer agent that might travel across the Internet to find the seller agent offering the best possible deal for a given commodity. There are a very large number of potential research topics in Web-based IAs such as dynamic collaboration systems, mobile intelligent agents, digital proxies, Intelligent middleware for Web, training and advising software, peer-to-peer protocols for IAs, and intelligent executive information systems. *The IEEE Expert,* December 1996, is a special issue on IAs and contains several articles on these and other research topics.

4.10 Summary

The focus of this part of the book is on developing new applications in OCSI environments (the shaded area in Figure 4.15). In general, application engineering requires development of new databases and, in many cases, development of new application software. Currently, most of the new applications are being developed by using object-orientation and the client/server paradigm. We have established a framework for discussion and introduced a methodology for developing new applications. Development of new OCSI applications requires several iterations of planning/analysis, architecture, implementation, and support activities. We have introduced these activities in this chapter and discussed how these activities can be modified for different classes of applications. These activities will be expanded and explained in later chapters of this part of the book.

Figure 4.15 The Application Challenge

	New Database(s)	**Existing Database(s)**
New Application Software	Application Engineering	Reengineer existing database(s)
Existing Application software	Reengineer existing application software	Reengineer application software plus database(s)

4.11 Case Study: XYZCorp Builds New Applications

A wide range of new applications have been identified as part of the XYZAICS (Advanced Integrated Control System) initiative (we introduced this initiative at the end of Chapter 3).

In particular, the following three "high-tech" applications that utilize OO, C/S, and Web technologies are planned:

- A new "advanced" inventory management system for integrated order processing/inventory management has been proposed that will utilize the latest in OO, C/S and Web technologies for entering, reviewing, processing, and tracking orders/inventory levels. This system will use several major databases (customers, inventory, products, prices).

- A management planning system that allows the management to review and analyze the market trends, the sales of the existing products, the most profitable stores, and other vital business information. This is a decision support system that will allow access to various pieces of information that may be located anywhere in the corporation.

- A flexible manufacturing system (FMS) that builds (assembles and packages) the various electronic products in real time. This system uses multimedia (text, graphics, voice) to monitor and control the activities of various machines during the manufacturing process.

Three interrelated projects have been "fired up" to establish the requirements and an overall plan for these applications. What are the benefits and risks to develop these systems and what is the strategy to manage these risks?

Hints about the Case Study

The generic application approach described in Section 4.4 can be used in these projects. The discussion in Section 4.5 shows how the generic approach can be customized for different types of applications. Let us highlight the key points.

For the inventory management system, an operational support system, you need to:

- Gather and analyze detailed requirements
- Develop the object model
- Develop the dynamic model
- Develop the data + application software architecture
- If the application cannot be purchased, then implement the application software + databases and test it
- Install software at user sites and provide technical support/help desks

For the planning system, a decision support application, you need to:

- Gather information requirements iteratively
- Develop the object model for database design (dynamic model is lightweight)
- Focus on data architecture and expand it iteratively
- Populate the databases and select the tools to access and analyze the data
- Install tools at user sites and be prepared to quickly respond to changing needs

For the FMS, a real-time multimedia system, you need to:

- Gather detailed requirements with focus on hard performance requirements

- Develop the object model

- Develop an extensive dynamic model

- Focus on hardware platforms to satisfy performance requirements

- Develop and test application software (may involve middleware development)

- Install software at user sites and provide quick technical support/help

4.12   Problems and Exercises

1. Expand Table 4.1 to include more classes of applications and scope of applications. Give examples of each.

2. Obtain information about the Software Life Cycle Processes Standard (ISO/IEC 12207) which has been approved by the ISO JTC1 [Singh 1995]. Map this standard to the methodology template presented in this chapter.

3. Your company has asked you to propose a requirement definition standard for specifying distributed applications. List the outline of the standard.

4. Choose a case study of OCSI development from the extant literature and analyze it in terms of intended use, the approach used, the benefits, and the pitfalls. Hint: Many case studies are published regularly in magazines such as *Client/Server Today, Client/Server Computing, Object Magazine,* and *Datamation.*

5. Convert the sidebar "Combining Distributed Objects with the Web" (page 160) into a diagram.

4.13   Additional Information

Development considerations for distributed applications in object-oriented client/server environments are discussed in several books [Hutt 1994], [Inmon 1993], [Mullender 1993], [Ng 1990], [Orfali 1994], [Shatz 1993], and [Sims 1994]. A great deal of practical information in this general area is published regularly in trade journals such as Client/Server Computing, *Client/Server Today, Datamation;* and from consulting group reports such as *Gartner Group reports*, and Patricia Seybold's *Distributed Computing Monitor.*

Adam, N., and Yesha, Y., editors, *Electronic Commerce,* Springer, 1996.

Adler, R., "Distributed Coordination Models for Client/Server Computing," *IEEE Computer,* April 1995, pp. 14–22.

Andriole, S., *Rapid Application Prototyping,* QED Publishing Group, 1992.

Bal, H., Steiner, J., and Tannenbaum, A., "Programming Languages for Distributed Computing Systems," *ACM Computing Surveys,* September 1989, pp. 261–322.

Bickell, R., "Building Intranets," *Internet World,* March 1996, pp. 72–75.

Birman, K.P., et al., *Isis—A Distributed Programming Environment: Users Guide and Reference Manual,* Department of Computer Science, Cornell University, N.Y., September 1990.

Blair, L., et al., "Formal Specification and Verification of Multimedia Systems in Open Distributed Processing," *Computer Standards and Interfaces,* 17, 1995, pp. 413–436.

Blelloch, G., "Programming Parallel Algorithms," *Communications of the ACM,* March 1996, pp. 85–97.

Bolognesi, T., and Brinksma, E., "Introduction to the ISO Specification Language LOTOS," *Computer Networks and ISDN Systems,* Vol. 14, No. 1, 1988, pp. 25–59.

Booch, G., *Object-Oriented Design with Applications,* Benjamin Cummings, 2d ed., 1994.

Castelli, G., and Simone, R., "An Experimental Distributed Programming Language: Design and Implementation," *IEEE Phoenix Conference on Computers and Communications,* March 1986, pp. 406–411.

Chappell, D., *Understanding OLE and ActiveX,* Microsoft Press, 1996.

Chen, B., and Yeh, R., "Formal Specification and Verification of Distributed Systems," *IEEE Transactions on Software Engineering,* November 1983, pp. 710–722.

Chin, R., and Chanson, S., "Distributed Object-Based Programming Systems," *ACM Computing Surveys,* March 1991, pp. 91–124.

Comport, J., "Packaged Applications: Buy an Application, Inherit an Architecture," *Gartner Group Conference,* February 22–24, 1995.

Darling, C., "Immortalize Your Apps," *Datamation,* August 1, 1995.

Davis, M., *Applied Decision Support,* Prentice Hall, 1988.

Dec, K., "Client/Server—Reality Sets in," *Gartner Group Briefing,* San Diego, February 22–24, 1995.

DePompa, B., "Corporate Migration: Harder Than It Looks," *Information Week,* December 4, 1995, pp. 60–68.

Dick, K., "Objects and the Web," *Object Magazine,* May 1996, pp. 34–35.

Dollas, A., and Kanopoulos, N., "Reducing Time to Market Through Rapid Prototyping," Guest Editor's Introduction, *IEEE Computer Special Issue on Reducing Time to Market Through Rapid Prototyping,* February 1995, pp. 14–15.

Fillon, M., "What's Ahead for 1997," *Client/Server Computing,* December 1996, pp. 32–43.

Fuhrt, B., et al., "Design Issues for Interactive Television Systems," *IEEE Computer,* May 1995, pp. 40–51.

Gareiss, R., "Voice Over the Internet," *Data Communications,* September 1996, pp. 93–100.

Garlan, D., and Shaw, M., "An Introduction to Software Architecture," in *Advances in Software Engineering and Knowledge Engineering,* New York, *World Scientific,* Vol. I, 1993.

Gemmel, D., et al., "Multimedia Storage Servers: A Tutorial," *IEEE Computer,* May 1995, pp. 40–51.

Goglia, P., *Testing Client/Server Applications,* QED Publishing Group, 1993, pp. 65–74.

Grygo, E., "Intranet Reality Check," *Client/Server Computing,* May 1996, pp. 22–32.

Henderson, J., and Venkatraman, "Strategic Alignment: Leveraging Information Technology for Transforming Organizations," *IBM Systems Journal,* Vol. 32, No. 1, 1993, pp. 4–16.

Herbert, A., "An ANSA Overview," *IEEE Network,* January/February, 1994, pp. 18–23.

Hutt, A., ed., *Object Oriented Analysis and Design,* John Wiley, 1994.

Inmon, W., *Developing Client/Server Applications,* QED Publishing, 1993.

Isakowitz, T., "RMM: A Methodology for Structured Hypermedia Design," *Communications of the ACM,* August 1995.

Islam, N., "Distributed Objects: Methodologies for Customizing Operating Systems," *IEEE Computer Society Press,* 1995.

Jacobson, I., et al, *Object-Oriented Software Engineering,* Addison Wesley, Reading, MA, 1992.

Jenkins, A., "Centralization Strikes Again," *Computerworld Client/Server Journal,* August 1995, pp. 28–31.

Leff, A., and Pu, C., "A Classification of Transaction Processing Systems," *IEEE Computer,* June 1991, pp. 63–65.

Linthicum, D., "The Rugged Road to Totally Transportable Apps," *Datamation,* May 1, 1995, pp. 51–55.

Linthicum, D., "WWW Development Tools," *Distributed Computing Monitor,* Special Issue, Vol. 11, No. 4, 1996.

Linthicum, D., "Distributed Objects Get New Plumbing," *Internet Systems,* January 1997, pp. 4–5.

Melling, W., "Authoring an Enterprise Information Architecture: A Pragmatist's Approach to a Process," *Gartner Group Conference,* February 22-24, 1995.

Meyer, B., "On Formalism in Specifications," *IEEE Software,* January, 1989.

Moad, J., "Client/Server Costs: Don't Get Taken For a Ride," *Datamation,* February 15, 1994, pp. 34–38.

Mowbray, T., and Zahavi, R., *The Essential CORBA: Systems Integration Using Distributed Objects,* John Wiley, 1995.

Mullender, S., editor, *Distributed Systems, 2d ed.,* Addison Wesley, 1993.

Murphy, K., "Bean Soups to Bombs: Senate Web Has It All," *Web Week,* June 17, 1996, p. 17.

Ng, P., and Yeh, R., editors, *Modern Software Engineering: Foundations and Current Perspectives,* Van Nostrand Reinhold, 1990.

Nicol, J., et al., "Object Orientation in Heterogeneous Distributed Computing Systems," *IEEE Computer,* June 1993, pp. 57–67.

Orfali, R., Harkey, D., and Edwards, J., *Client/Server Survival Guide,* Van Nostrand Reinholt, 1994.

Pankaj, J., *An Integrated Approach to Software Engineering,* Springer-Verlag, 1991.

Papelis, Y.E., and Casavant, T.L., "Specification and Analysis of Parallel/Distributed Software and Systems by Petri Nets with Transition Enabling," *IEEE Transactions on Software Engineering,* March 1992, pp. 252–261.

Pressman, R., *Software Engineering—A Practitioner's Approach,* 2d ed., McGraw-Hill, 1987.

Robicheaux, M., "Client/Server Web: Extending Your Reach," *Object Magazine,* May 1996, pp. 50–53,

Ross, W., "Hewlett Packard's Migration to Client/Server Architecture," published in *Distributed Computing: Implementation and Management Strategies,* ed. by Khanna, Prentice Hall, 1994.

Rubenstein, H., and Waters, R., "The Requirements Apprentice: Automated Assistance for Requirement Acquisition," *IEEE Transactions on Software Engineering,* March 1991, pp. 226–240.

Rumbaugh, J., et al., *Object-Oriented Modeling and Design,* Prentice Hall, 2d ed., 1994.

Salim, J., "Application Development in the Internet Age," *Data Management Review,* January 1997, pp. 68–72.

Schurmann, G., "The Evolution from Open System Interconnection (OSI) to Open Distributed Processing (ODP)," *Computer Standards and Interfaces,* 17, 1995, pp. 107–113.

Scott, M. L. , "Language Support for Loosely Coupled Distributed Programs," *IEEE Transactions on Software Engineering,* Vol. SE-13, No. 1, January 1987, pp. 88–103.

Shan, Y., Earle, R., and McGaughey, S., "Rounding Out the Picture: Objects Across the Client/Server Spectrum," *IEEE Computer,* October 1995, p. 60.

Shatz, S., *Development of Distributed Software: Concepts and Tools,* Macmillan, 1993.

Silberschaatz, A. "A Survey Note on Programming Languages for Distributed Computing," *Proc. IEEE Conference on Distributed Computing,* September 1980, pp. 719–722.

Sims, O., *Business Objects,* McGraw Hill, 1994.

Singh, R., "The Software Life Cycle Processes Standard," *IEEE Computer,* November 1995, pp. 89–90.

Simpson, D., "Are Mainframes Cool Again?" *Datamation,* April 1997, pp. 46–53.

Stankovic, J., et al., "Implications of Classical Scheduling Results for Real-Time Systems," *IEEE Computer,* June 1995, pp. 16–25.

Swanson, S., and Travis, G., "Real-Time Streaming and Java," *Object Magazine,* May 1996, pp. 36–39,

Turban, E., *Decision Support and Expert Systems,* 2d ed., Macmillan, 1993.

Umar, A., *Distributed Computing: A Practical Synthesis,* Prentice Hall, 1993.

Umar, A., *Object-Oriented Client/Server Internet Environments,* Prentice Hall, 1997.

Varney, S., "IS Takes Charge of Customer Service," *Datamation,* August 1996, pp. 46–51.

Walker, W., "Interrupt Processing in Concurrent Processors," *IEEE Computer,* June 1995, pp. 36–46.

Wooding, T., "Business Frameworks: The (European) Object Interest Group Confirms Underlying Need," *Object Magazine,* January 1997, pp. 50–53.

Yeh, R., Zave, P., Conn, A., and Cole, G., "Software Requirements: New Directions and Perspectives," *Handbook of Software Engineering,* Van Nostrand, 1984.

Zave, P. "The Operational versus the Conventional Approach to Software Development," *Communications of the ACM,* February 1984, pp. 104–118.

5

Enterprise Data Architectures

197

5.1   Introduction

Enterprise data, the data that are shared by different business processes, are a cornerstone of many applications and services in contemporary environments. An example of enterprise data, also known as corporate data, is customer information that is used in different applications such as order processing, billing, accounts receivable/payable, and marketing information systems. From a new application development perspective, *the needed data must be "architected" (i.e., modeled, designed, allocated, interconnected) and managed carefully, even though the application functionality could be satisfied by an off-the-shelf package.* Although it is possible to discuss the enterprise data issues from a single application's point of view, it is essential to discourage this view. Why? Because the enterprise data are shared by multiple applications and end-user tools over a very long time frame. The enterprise data thus must not be viewed as serving one application—enterprise data is an enterprise asset and not a single application captive property. This view, particularly true for decision support applications, suggests that you establish an enterprise data architecture before diving into the individual application architectures. In many practical situations, however, software and data architectures are developed in parallel. Depending on your situation, you may want to read this chapter after Chapter 6, or vice versa.

This chapter is devoted to the issues of data architectures with special attention to enterprise data in modern distributed environments (see Figure 5.1). In particular, the following questions guide the discussion in this chapter:

- What framework should be used to systematically manage enterprise data throughout its life cycle in modern distributed environments (Section 5.2)?

- What information should be gathered from the end users, system administrators, and corporate management to minimize the risks and maximize the benefits (Section 5.3)?

- How should the data be modeled and how should a logical database design be constructed (Sections 5.4 and 5.5)?

- How should the data be partitioned and segmented so that different classes of users/applications (e.g., decision support or operational support users and applications) access needed data most of the time (see Section 5.6)?

- Where should the data be placed (allocated) in the network, should the data be duplicated between sites, and how will the duplicated data be synchronized (Section 5.7)?

- How will the databases be accessed by client applications and end-user tools and how will they interoperate with each other (Section 5.8)?

The chapter concentrates on the issues and approaches that are unique to the modern distributed systems with particular attention to the OCSI (object-oriented client/server Internet) environments. The issues of data allocation, duplication, and access are discussed in some detail. We basically discourage the notion that availability of Web and OO technologies eliminates the need for careful data allocation and duplication. In fact, Web and OO technologies only give the *appearance* that the location of data is unimportant to the end users and programmers; however, the data still has to be allocated, synchronized, and managed properly in an OCSI environment. The chapter concludes with a detailed example that shows how the principles discussed in this chapter can be used to design a database in OCSI environments.

This chapter assumes a certain know-how of database technologies. Interested readers should review adequate material (see the book by Chris Date [1995]) before proceeding.

Figure 5.1 Data Architecture as a Component of Application Architecture

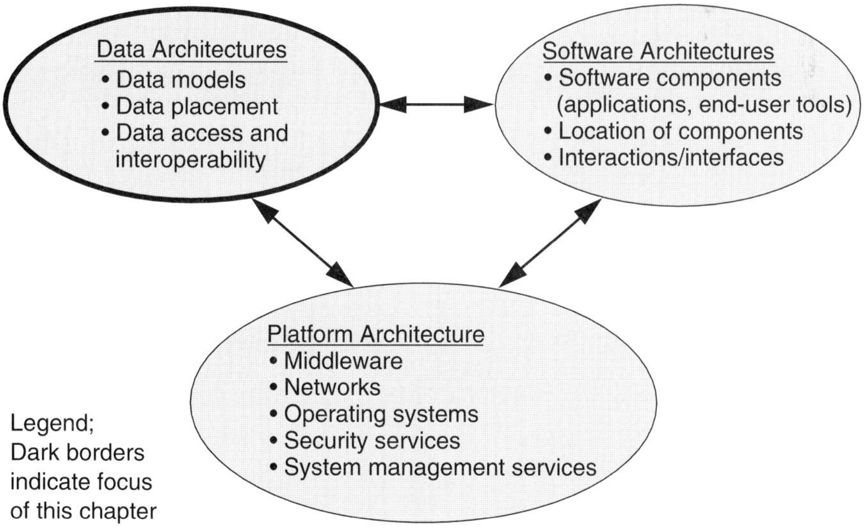

Key Points

● Data architecture issues need to be considered even when an off-the-shelf application is being purchased and installed.

● Enterprise data issues are much more complex in distributed environments due to the creation of duplicated copies, data synchronization issues, heterogeneity of data sources, and the wide range of interconnectivity options.

● Enterprise data life cycle is a good framework for discussing data architecture issues in distributed environments.

● Most new applications use relational database technologies for enterprise data. Due to this, it is best to design the databases in terms of relational tables that can be viewed as objects. Object-oriented databases, when and if they become widely used for corporate data, will allow the data to be stored, viewed, and accessed as objects.

5.2   Concepts and Definitions

5.2.1   Enterprise (Corporate) Data

Enterprise Data (also known as Corporate Data) is the information that is used or created by a corporation in conducting business and is shared across the business processes of the corporation. Enterprise data issues are, of course, much more complex in distributed environments—especially heterogeneous ones. And we are moving in this direction. Although a large proportion of enterprise data is stored in mainframe databases, these data are increasingly being migrated to SQL database servers (the new applications are predominantly using relational database technology) that are available from many DBMS vendors (object-oriented databases are still struggling in this arena). The data are accessed by end-user tools (e.g., spreadsheets, 4GLs, data browsers, report writers, object-oriented viewers) from different suppliers and/or applications written in C, C++, Cobol and other programming languages. The database access is enabled through a variety of middleware (SQL middleware for remote data access and Web gateways) that is purchased from different suppliers.

Figure 5.2 illustrates the good news (flexibility) and the bad news (complexity) associated with typical corporate environments. In these environments, databases are located on MVS, UNIX database servers (Oracle, Sybase, Informix), PC LAN database servers (Microsoft SQL Servers, Gupta SQLBase) and Appleshare database servers. These databases can be accessed from Web browsers, end-user tools, and/or applications that reside on PCs, Macs, and UNIX workstations. The data may be partially or fully duplicated across machines to improve response time (this data will need to be synchronized). A remote interaction may be restricted to a LAN (a spreadsheet on a PC accessing a database server on the same Novell

LAN), or it may cross a corporate WAN (the PC spreadsheet accessing an MVS-DB2 database or a UNIX database). In some cases, a client may involve joins between databases located on two different database servers (DB2 on MVS and Oracle on UNIX). A variety of gateways may be needed in such an environment. The gateways may convert network protocols (Novell IPX/SPX to TCP/IP) or database protocols (Web gateways that convert HTTP to remote SQL).

Figure 5.2 Databases in Client/Server Environments

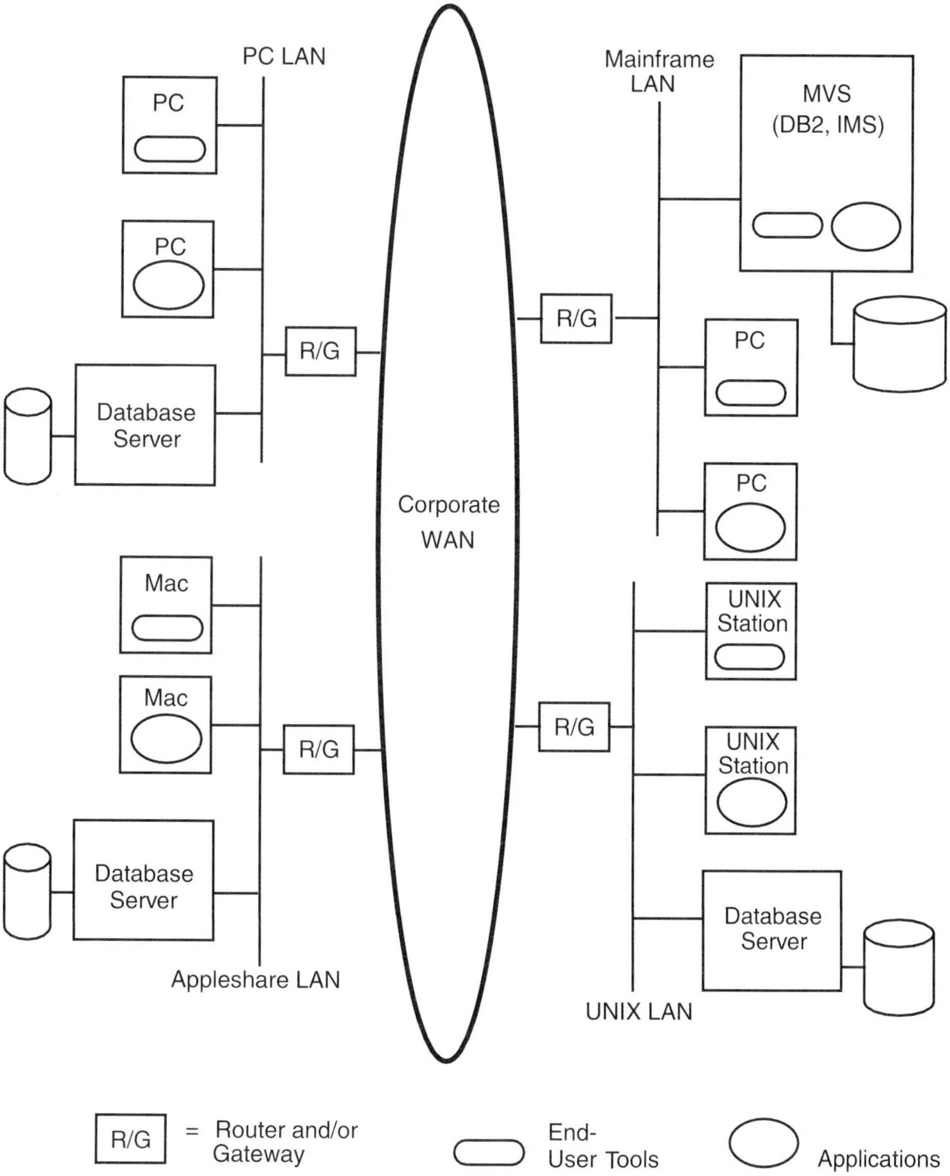

5.2.2   Data Life Cycle

Data, enterprise or not, go through a *"Data Life Cycle"* that consists of the following activities (these activities are usually overlapping and are performed concurrently for several business processes):

- **Data Requirements.** This concentrates on understanding the data requirements of business processes and creation of the Enterprise Logical Data Model (ELDM) with appropriate entities, relationships, and attributes. Data modelers usually create and maintain ELDM.

- **Data Architecture.** This converts the ELDM to physical datasets that can be used by business processes. This activity provides (see later discussion of data architecture also):
    - Refinement of ELDM (further definition of data, who owns it, who generates it, who uses it, etc.).
    - "Global" activities of data partitioning and allocation to different sites. This involves segmentation of data for different user communities (e.g., decision support versus operational support) and evaluating the trade-offs between data redundancy, mainframe versus midrange allocation, and performance/availability trade-offs.
    - Data access strategies, that is, the tools and techniques needed to access and manipulate enterprise data from Web browsers, client applications and end-user tools. Specifically, this includes data access middleware selection and deployment (e.g., choice between the vendor provided gateway products, data access standards and protocols such as ISO RDA, ODBC, DRDA). For legacy databases, data access may involve evaluation of data migration and data warehousing strategies (see Part III of this book).
    - Enterprisewide database interoperabilty in terms of information exchange between different databases, network transports, and operating systems.

- Implementation and Deployment. This involves issues such as:
    - Choice of appropriate database technologies (relational, object-oriented, knowledge bases) for enterprise data.
    - Local database design and implementation activities such as database normalization/denormalization, physical structure design, indexing, and data population (loading the databases with business values).

- Enterprise Data Administration. This involves the following issues throughout the operation and use of enterprise data:
    - Data integrity management (security, backup/recovery, integrity controls, auditing).
    - Data quality assurance (data cleanup and data redundancy management).
    - Data change management (physical versioning of enterprise data).
    - Data use management (performance monitoring, bottleneck analysis, diagnostics).

5.2.3   Data Architecture

Data architecture, as viewed from enterprise data life-cycle point of view, concentrates on establishing how the data will be defined, where they will be located, and how they will be accessed/shared by enterprise users. In practice, *data architects*, the people who are responsible for enterprise data architectures, must be responsible for the enterprise data throughout their life cycle (they may not do everything, but they must lead and influence the activities in all enterprise data life-cycle activities). Data architects of the 1990s and beyond are the visionaries of the "information paradigm" [Inmon 1989]. They are responsible for the following:

- Definition of data—what is it, who owns it, who generates it, who uses it, et cetera.

- Partitioning of data—what data are needed by what users; what data need to be summarized; what data are read only (i.e., used for decision support), and the like.

- Location of data in an enterprise—what data are located where in the enterprise network; how many copies of data exist; where do they exist; how will the replicated data be synchronized.

- Mechanisms for accessing the data—who needs to access the data; on what platforms do they reside; how will the users be connected to the database (the middleware puzzle).

- Database interoperability—how will different corporate databases interact and interrelate to each other and with the applications and end users as well.

- Administration of data—who is responsible for the quality, integrity, and security of data.

The following steps, explained in detail in the balance of this chapter, are used *iteratively* to develop a data architecture (these steps are illustrated through a simple example in Figure 5.3):

Analysis steps:

1. Gather information requirements
2. Build a data model

Why Separate Data Architecture from Application Software Architecture?

It can be argued that enterprise data architecture should not be separated from application software architecture. However, we are separating enterprise data architecture for the following reasons:

- Enterprise data do not belong to a single application and/or user group. Enterprise data are shared between a multitude of applications and end-user tools. It should not be architected from one application's point of view.

- Due to an increase in shrink-wrapped and off-the-shelf software, many new applications can be deployed by just architecting the data needed by these applications and then buying off-the-shelf packages where appropriate.

- Data quality has become an area of interest in itself. The quality must be built into the product by proper data architecture. See the sidebar "Data Quality Becomes a Big Issue."

Who comes first? In reality, data and application software architectures are parallel activities and should be treated as such.

Figure 5.3 Data Architecture

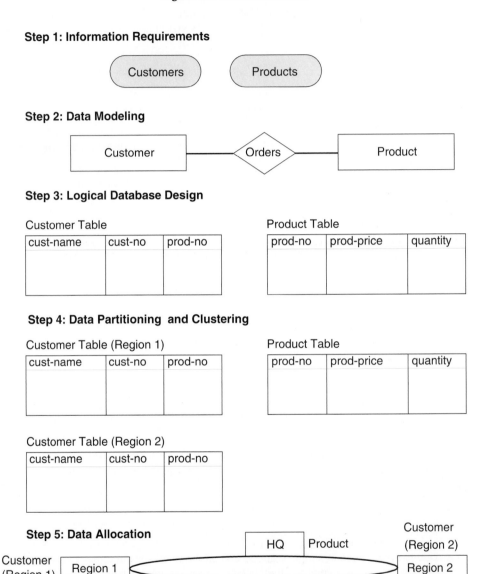

Step 1: Information Requirements

Customers　　Products

Step 2: Data Modeling

Customer ── Orders ── Product

Step 3: Logical Database Design

Customer Table

cust-name	cust-no	prod-no

Product Table

prod-no	prod-price	quantity

Step 4: Data Partitioning and Clustering

Customer Table (Region 1)

cust-name	cust-no	prod-no

Product Table

prod-no	prod-price	quantity

Customer Table (Region 2)

cust-name	cust-no	prod-no

Step 5: Data Allocation

Customer (Region 1) — Region 1 — HQ Product — Region 2 — Customer (Region 2)

Step 6: Data Access and Interoperability

- Choose database access paradigm and technologies (e.g., Web gateways)
- Select data interoperability strategy (e.g., how will data flow between systems)

Data architecture steps:

3. Develop a logical database design
4. Partition and cluster the data
5. Allocate the data to suitable sites
6. Provide data access and data interoperability

The information requirements and data modeling steps concentrate on understanding and representing the information that is stored in the database. The result of these steps is a logical data model that is typically translated into relational tables in the logical database design step. The first three steps have been discussed extensively in a large number of database design books since the late 1970s [Teorey 1982], [Teorey 1994], [Elmasri 1989], [Date 1995], and [Abiteboul 1995]. Consequently, our coverage of these steps is somewhat brief. However, the later steps are unique to distributed environments and are the primary focus of this chapter.

The data partitioning and clustering step first attempts to decompose the data for user/application specific (among other) processing. For example, as shown in Figure 5.3, the customer table is partitioned by regions, because different customers reside in different regions of a company. However, partitioning can lead to a very large number of tables. It may be necessary to cluster the partitioned data into *datasets* that can be allocated as one allocation unit. For example, in Figure 5.3 if the products were also region specific, then product and customer information for each region could be clustered together. Data partitioning and clustering is discussed in Section 5.6.

The datasets created in the partitioning and clustering step are allocated to one or more computers in the data allocation step. The datasets D1, D2,...,Dn can be allocated to one central computer, or distributed among different database server machines in a distributed environment. The dataset can be allocated uniquely (i.e., no duplicate data) or duplicate copies can be kept for increased performance and availability. The cost/benefit of these allocations can be estimated in terms of storage cost, communication costs (cost to read, cost to update), response time and data availability. In addition, some of these allocations may not be feasible due to the software and/or hardware restrictions. In general, the problem of determining "best" data allocation is complex and may require considerable analysis. The decision can be based on intuitive/educated guesswork, paper and pencil calculations, and/or use of formal optimization techniques. The discussion in Section 5.7 concentrates on intuitive analysis. Appendix 5A (Section 5.15) presents an analytical treatment of data allocation.

After data allocation, the issue of data access and interoperability is addressed. For example, how will the users at HQ access the customer information allocated to region 1 and region 2. In particular, the tools and applications residing on desktops may generate SQL statements that are routed to the appropriate database servers. The users increasingly rely on Web browsers that use Web middleware (e.g., CGI gateways) that connects/sends requests to the

Data Quality Becomes a Big Issue

Data quality has emerged as a major issue recently due to its potential severe impact on the effectiveness of an organization. For example, a leading computer industry information service indicated that it expects most business process reengineering initiatives to fail through lack of data quality [Wand 1996]. In addition, wrong price data in retail databases may cost American industry as much as $2.5 billion in overcharges annually [English 1996]. However, state of the practice in data architectures typically does not include data quality issues. The data architecture work should explicitly include the following two data quality considerations:

- How to measure data quality (i.e., metrics), and

- How to improve data quality

There are different views and definitions of data quality (see English [1996], Wand [1996], and Moriarity [1996]). We will use the following operational definition of data quality [Redman 1992]:

> *"A product, service, or datum X is of higher quality than product, service, or datum Y if X meets customer needs better than Y."*

This definition needs further refinement and elaboration. In particular, we need to focus on the following quality attributes of data:

- Accuracy: reflects correctness to real life

- Consistency: two or more things do not conflict with each other

- Currency: how recent is the information

- Completeness: degree to which values are present in a data collection

These attributes provide the core data quality metrics. Measurement of these metrics and improvements in data quality by using these metrics as a yardstick is the main challenge of data quality work at present. The data architects should use these metrics to improve the quality of data with concomitant improvement in business processes that rely on data.

The approaches to obtain data quality fall into the following broad categories:

- Data cleanup

- Process cleanup

Data cleanup involves use of a tool to identify "bad data" (i.e., not accurate/consistent/current/complete) and then elimination of bad data through automated and/or manual processes. A wide variety of "data scrubbers" are commercially available from vendors such as Vality to perform this task. However, data cleanup needs to be a periodic effort that must be repeated several times over the life cycle of data. It is better to establish a process that cleans the data and keeps it clean. This process must be built into the data architecture steps.

database server by using SQL middleware such as ODBC (Open Database Connectivity). In addition to access, the interoperability of data between different systems (i.e., how the data will flow between different participating systems) needs to be decided. Section 5.8 describes data access and interoperability in more detail.

These steps generate a data architecture that can be used by many applications and end-user tools for business processes. Data architectures from different business domains of an enterprise can be combined together to develop an enterprisewide data architecture.

After establishing a data architecture, the individual databases are designed for each computer, populated, and deployed. These activities include physical database design, indexing techniques, database programming, and database administration. These topics are beyond the scope of this book.

Throughout this chapter, we assume that datasets are assigned statically (i.e., the assigned data and programs are not moved around dynamically during application execution).

Data Quality: Sources for Information

Azuma, M., "Software Products Evaluation System: Quality Models, Metrics and Processes—International Standards and Japanese Practice," *Information and Software Technology,* Vol. 38, Issue 3, 1996.

"Data Quality—A Critical Information Systems Consideration," *Data Management Review,* July/August 1996.

English, L., "Data Quality; Meeting Customer Needs," *Data Management Review,* November 1996, pp. 44–51.

Moriarity, T., "Barriers to Data Quality Part I, Better Business Practices," *Database Programming and Design,* July 1996, pp. 59–61.

Moriarity, T., "Barriers to Data Quality Part II; Business Practices," *Database Programming and Design,* May 1996, pp. 61–63.

Redman, T., *Data Quality,* Bantam Books, 1992.

Wand, Y., and Wang, R., "Anchoring Data Quality Dimensions in Ontological Foundations," *Communications of the ACM,* November 1996, pp. 86–95.

5.3   Step 1: Information Requirement Definitions

This is the first, and in many ways the most important, step in the data life cycle. The information requirements are specified after interviewing the producers as well as users of data. These requirements specify the data, the natural relationships between data, the transactions to access and manipulate the data, and software platform for database implementation. Many of the information requirements discussed here should have been specified during the general requirements definition activity (we are repeating them here to emphasize that you need to collect this information *somehow*). The process used in this labor intensive step involves three steps. First, understand the business organization and the business processes that will be served by the database. Second, document the transactions that will be executed by the users of the database. In this context, a transaction can provide any of the CRUD (Create, Read, Update, Delete) operations. Finally, identify the information needed for the transactions.

In addition to these functional requirements, it is important to develop an understanding of the following operational requirements before proceeding (these requirements are used in the later steps of data life cycles such as partitioning/clustering, data allocation decisions, and database connectivity and interoperability):

- Size information (number of users who will access the database, database size)

- Response time (average, worst case) requirements

- Scaling and growth requirements

- Data security requirements

- Data availability restrictions

- Data synchronization requirements (i.e., how frequently duplicate data should be synchronized: immediately, hourly, daily, etc.)

- Connectivity needed from user sites (e.g. from PCs, Macs, UNIX)

- Interoperability and interfaces with other (existing/proposed) systems

- Portability between computing platforms (data portability, processing portability, user interface portability)

- Backup/recovery needs and disaster handling

- Policy restrictions (e.g., standards and policies to be followed, application control, and auditing restrictions)

5.4   Step 2: Data Modeling

After requirements, data modeling is the next step in developing data architecture. A data model essentially gives the analyst a conceptual understanding of the data entities to be stored in a database. It represents the view of data at several levels of detail. It is extremely important to capture a comprehensive view of data for business operations (see the sidebar "Importance of Customer Information: An Example").

The high level data models are represented by the entity-relationship-attribute (ERA) diagrams. Figure 5.4 shows a simple ERA diagram. The data modeling activity is primarily concerned with identifying and representing the business entities that are needed in the database terms of an ERA diagram.

Figure 5.4 A Sample Entity Relation Attribute (ERA) Model

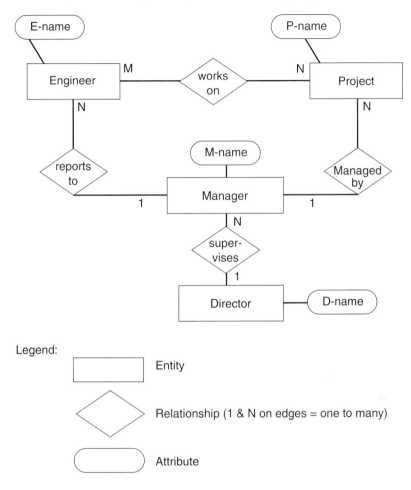

Legend:

Entity

Relationship (1 & N on edges = one to many)

Attribute

Note: Only one attribute is shown per entity for simplicity

Basically, development of an ERA-based data model involves the following steps:

1. Define entities (the principal data objects about which information is to be collected)

2. Identify relationships (the real-world associations) between entities. Relationships between entities can be one to one, one to many, and many to many

3. Identify and develop attributes (characteristics of entities)

4. Represent this information by using an ERA diagram

Importance of Customer Information: An Example

An airline was flying a customer to Europe on a business trip. The customer was not happy because he had lost his luggage a few times and the flights were typically late. So the customer stopped using the airline.

The airline did a lifetime profitability analysis of this customer and found that the airline had lost a potential $400,000 over the life of the customer (had he stayed with the airline). The airline also found out that there were several clues about his unhappiness (he had called the lost luggage department several times and had written complaint letters to the chairman).

Instead of developing a composite and complete profile of the customer history, each incident was treated separately and the customer was sent two free-drink coupons every time he complained.

Source:
    "Cultivating An Information Culture: An Interview with Thomas Davenport," *CIO,* January 1995.

Although the principles of data modeling are straightforward, the practice of building a business data model for large database applications is nontrivial. This is primarily due to the coordination and agreements needed between different information owners. In practice, development of a large data model may need to be completed in several steps and may need top management support or involvement of some dedicated people who are devoted to the notion of a business data model. The modeling process must include users as an essential part of the loop. It is important to review the model with the users, resolve definition issues, and challenge old misconceptions (data models may reveal aspects and practices of business that some users are not aware of). Due to the difficulties in building logical data models from scratch, some tools have started appearing that contain generic data models for different industries (aerospace, hospitals) and different functions (order processing). Inmon Data Models is an example of such a tool.

Data modeling involves other issues such as view integration and object-oriented data modeling. In essence, view integration is concerned with building ERA models from different views (e.g., end-user view, management view, support staff view) and then integrating these views into a unified single data model. Object-oriented (OO) modeling identifies the objects, the properties (attributes) of objects, the behavior (operations) of the objects and the interrelationships (interactions) between the objects. The following statements show the similarities/dissimilarities between OO data models and ERA diagrams:

- Each object is similar to an entity

- The properties of an object are the same as entity attributes

- The interrelationships between objects can be represented through ERA relationships

---

What is the Difference Between Data Model and an Object Model

How does an object model, the foundation of OO analysis and design advocated in this book, relate to a data model. An object model presents the view of a system in terms of objects, their interrelationships, and the operations supported by the objects. An object model includes the information needed for a data model. Basically:

Object model = Data model + Inheritance + Operations

Thus you can develop an object model by adding inheritance and operations to the data model. Pragmatically, you can build a data model first for data architectures and then add the inheritance and operations for application software architectures.

If an object-oriented database is used, then the objects can be directly stored in the database, and the reason for differentiating between object models and data models essentially disappears.

- The object behavior (operations) do not directly correspond to anything in ERA diagrams. Extensions of the ERA model would be needed to represent object behavior

Detailed discussion of ERA modeling is beyond the scope of this book. Interested readers should review [Reingruber 1994], [Teorey 1994], and [Elmasri 1989].

5.5   Step 3: Logical Database Design

Logical database design transforms the ERA model into relational tables. Figure 5.5 shows a possible transformation of the ERA diagram shown in Figure 5.4 into relational tables. The following simple procedure has been used for this transformation:

- Transform each entity in the ERA model into a relational table. The attributes of each entity become the attributes of the table. This principle leads to the four tables shown in Figure 5.5.

- If the relationship between two entities is one to one, then the two tables can be combined into one. This principle does not apply to Figure 5.5, because no one-to-one relationships have been identified.

- If the relationships between two entities are one to many, then make sure that a common attribute ("a foreign key") exists on which the two tables can be joined. For example, manager name is a foreign key in the director table and project name, engineer name are foreign keys in the manager table (see Figure 5.5).

- If the relationships between two entities are many to many, then create another table ("intersection table") that cross-references the two entities. The assignment table in Figure 5.5 is created for this purpose.

This simple procedure needs to be extended for more complex ERA diagrams. In addition, the tables generated by this procedure should be further refined for performance, integrity, and maintainability. For example, when the entire database is represented by one large table, it can result in lengthy searches, large amounts of redundant data, expensive updates, and unwanted elimination of useful data due to deletions. A database design process called "normalization" is used to remove these anomalies. Database normalization is covered extensively in almost all contemporary database design books [Date 1995], [Elmasri 1989], [O'Neil 1994], and [Teorey 1994]. A discussion of this topic is beyond the scope of this book.

Figure 5.5 Transformation of ERA Model to Relational Tables

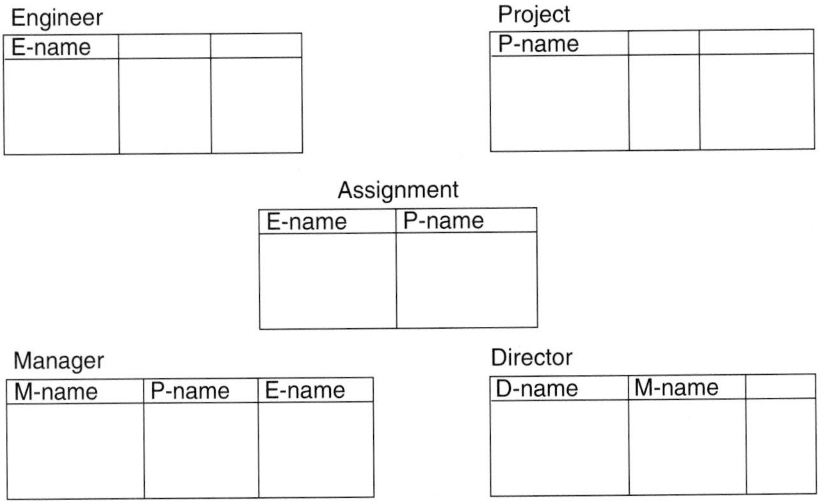

Engineer

E-name		

Project

P-name		

Assignment

E-name	P-name

Manager

M-name	P-name	E-name

Director

D-name	M-name	

5.6   Step 4: Data Partitioning and Clustering

5.6.1   Overview

Logical database design leads to a set of relational tables. In distributed environments, these tables may be allocated to computers (database servers) that are dispersed throughout an organization. Allocation of data in computing networks is a complex decision which raises several questions such as where should the data be placed, should there be a duplicate copy, how frequently the duplicated copy should be synchronized, et cetera. These questions, if not addressed correctly, can cause major discomforts and misery later on in the life cycle.

The data partitioning and clustering step is a preparatory step for data allocation and, in some cases, can be included in the allocation step (see Section 5.7). Before allocating the tables generated in the logical database design step, you should try to *partition* the tables to improve the availability and performance of data access to different user communities. Data

---

Example of Partitioning and Clustering

Consider the tables generated in Figure 5.5:

> Engineer table
>
> Project table
>
> Assignment table
>
> Manager table
>
> Director table

These tables can be allocated to any of the 10 regions of a company. Each region has a designated database server where these tables can be allocated. Let us assume that projects, employees, and managers are region specific (e.g., Washington region has government projects; Detroit region has manufacturing projects). Then we can partition (fragment) these tables as follows (the number in parentheses indicates a region number):

> Engineer (1), Engineer (2),,,,,,,, Engineer (10)
>
> Project (1), Project (2),,,,,,,,,, Project (10)
>
> Assignment (1), Assignment (2),,,,,, Assignment (10)
>
> Manager (1), Manager (2), ,,,,,,,, Manager (10)
>
> Director (not partitioned because directors reside at HQ)

Partitioning has increased the number of tables from 5 to 41. However, we can cluster these fragments to form the following datasets (each dataset will be allocated to a region):

> Region 1 dataset has Engineer (1), Project (1), Assignment (1), Manager (1)
>
> Region 2 dataset has Engineer (2), Project (2), Assignment (2), Manager (2) and the like.

This partitioning and clustering simplifies the allocation problem.

---

partitioning can lead to a large number of *fragments* (subsets of tables). It may be necessary to group *(cluster)* some of these fragments into **datasets**, where a dataset is a unit of data that can be allocated as a unit.[1] The sidebar shows a simple example in which tables are partitioned by regions and then all fragments belonging to one region are clustered together.

5.6.2   Data Partitioning (Fragmentation)

Typically, large tables (tables with a large number of rows and/or columns) are partitioned into disjoint subtables (fragments). The *fragments* r1, r2,....rn of a table *r* contain sufficient

---

1. We will use the term "dataset" to indicate a collection of data that can be allocated to a computer as a unit. A dataset may consist of a collection of tables, a single table, a subset (fragment) of a table, or a collection of subsets from different tables.

information to reconstruct the original table r. The fragments can be managed independently and can be allocated to a dedicated database server machine. The partitioning of data into fragments can be based on criteria such as the following:

- by product type
- by numbers (e.g., first 200 items in fragment 1, second 200 items in fragment 2, etc.)
- by organizational unit
- by geography
- by date, or
- a mixture of the above

Basically, a table can be partitioned horizontally or vertically. Horizontal fragmentation partitions a large table by rows while vertical fragmentation partitions the table by columns. The following rules should be considered for fragmentation. First, fragments must be disjoint and their unions must become the whole table. Second, fragmentation must maintain a balance between extreme cases (the largest fragment is the whole table and the smallest fragment is a single record). Large segments disallow the efficiency of allocating data to local computers by usage. However, small fragments that are spread over a network can cause serious performance problems due to joins across networks.

5.6.3   Clustering

Partitioning can lead to a large number of fragments. For example, an inventory control and purchasing system in a medium-sized organization may consist of 20 data fragments that may need to be allocated to 100 computers (mainframes, minicomputers and workstations). This produces 20×2^{100} possible allocations. Evaluation of all these allocations is too large for even supercomputers. In general, allocation of K datasets to N computers requires $K \times 2^N$ allocations (see side bar "Estimation of Number of Allocations" for an explanation). Clustering attempts to reduce K as well as N by using the techniques described in Sections 5.6.3.1 and 5.6.3.2. In most practical cases, clustering should be a quick procedure for minimizing the allocation effort. If a large mathematical programming algorithm is needed for clustering, then it is better to include clustering as a step in the allocation activity discussed later. This approach is used by Mariani and Palmer [1979], [1984]. It is also important to verify and refine the results of the partitioning/fragmentation steps before proceeding. In fact, some researchers include the entire partitioning process in clustering [Ozsu 1991].

5.6.3.1   Clustering to Minimize Datasets to be Allocated

Some data is location specific—it must exist at a given location. For example, some sensitive information must be kept at the corporate office; manufacturing device status information needs to be kept on the plant floor, and the like. The first step of clustering attempts to identify the location-specific data so that they can be eliminated from the allocation step. A table or a fragment of a table can be location-specific due to several reasons. First, user requirements restrict some operations and data to be performed at certain computers. Second, security and management restrictions require some data to be restricted to certain computers such as corporate office. Third, there is a similarity and natural affinity of certain data items to certain computers (e.g., most manufacturing operations are performed at the plant floor). Finally, Financial considerations (an animation must be performed on the machines that have software licenses for the animation packages).

Estimation of Number of Allocations

One dataset can be allocated to 3 computers as shown in the following assignment matrix (1 indicates that the dataset is assigned, 0 indicates not assigned):

0	0	0	(dataset not allocated anywhere)
0	0	1	(dataset allocated to computer 1)
0	1	0	(dataset allocated to computer 2)
1	0	0	(dataset allocated to computer 3)
1	0	1	(dataset allocated to computer 1 and 3)
1	1	0	(and so on)
0	1	1	
1	1	1	

The total number of assignments in this table are 2^3

The total number of assignments for allocating 1 dataset to N computers is 2^N

The total number of assignments for allocating K dataset to N computers is $K2^N$

Similar data items are clustered together to form "datasets." A dataset is essentially a collection of tables and fragments that cannot be subdivided among computers. For example, all information about a product can be clustered into a dataset, because this information is almost always accessed together. In addition, all information accessed by a group of users who reside on specific computers can be clustered together. *A good rule of thumb is to cluster the tables that are joined frequently.* This minimizes the network traffic due to remote joins.

Instead of trial and error, clustering can utilize formal techniques such as the following:

- Standard statistical clustering procedures [Everret 1974] that consist of choosing and computing an appropriate similarity or dissimilarity (distance) function and then utilizing hierarchical and mathematical programming techniques to minimize the distance function. For example, a distance function could indicate the amount of common data between processes. Buckles and Harding [Buckles 1979] give several analytical examples of distance functions and describe a clustering procedure. A distance function can be defined for remote joins; a clustering procedure can then be devised to minimize remote joins.

- Fuzzy logic, mode-seeking, or clumping techniques for "fusing" similar objects. These techniques have been used in artificial intelligence and group technology in manufacturing [Negoita 1985].

5.6.3.2 Clustering to Minimize Number of Allocation Computers

To minimize the number of candidate computers, two approaches can be used:

- Clustering of candidate computers into "allocation sites"
- Clustering of similar computers into computer "families"

The candidate computers where the data can be allocated are clustered into "*allocation sites*" where each allocation site has a designated database server machine. For example, consider a medium-sized corporate network consisting of 1,000 computers (mainframes, minicomputers, and desktops). Allocation of one dataset to this network would generate 2^{1000} allocation possibilities. A simple observation can significantly reduce the size of this problem—the corporate network may be organized as 10 subnets where each subnet, may consist of 100 computers. For example, the corporation may have 10 branch offices, each supporting a LAN. In this case, the datasets can be initially allocated to the 10 LANs and then the best place within each LAN can be found as a separate problem. In many cases, each LAN may have a designated database server with appropriate licenses and backup/recovery procedures. Thus we can assume 10 allocation sites, and the size of the problem is reduced from 2^{1000} to 2^{10}.

The candidate computers can also be clustered into computer "families" to reduce the size of the allocation problem. For example, most distributed data allocation problems can be categorized as the following: data on MVS only (access data through clients at UNIX, PC, Macs); data on UNIX only (access through clients at UNIX, PC, Macs); data on a PS2 server, such as Novell; (access through clients at UNIX, PC, Macs); and mixture of the above. Thus an allocation problem in an organization with one MVS system, dozens of UNIX systems, and hundreds of PS2 machines can be analyzed in terms of the aforementioned categories.

5.6.4   Example of Partitioning (Fragmentation) and Clustering

Let us work through a simple example to illustrate the key points. In a medium-sized manufacturing organization, 20 relational tables (d1, d2,...,d20) needed to be allocated to a 300 computer network.[2] The following steps were used in the partitioning/clustering procedure:

- d1,...,d10 were location-specific due to security and/or other corporate restrictions. For example, d1–d4 were restricted to one computer due to security restrictions, d5–d6 had to be allocated to

---

2. This example is roughly based on an actual consulting assignment of this author.

a central site for management control, and the other files were location-specific because of the application area (factory floor, payroll, etc.). These files were allocated to the desired computers and eliminated from further processing.

- d11, d12, d13 were part of a purchased CAD/CAM package that only accessed local data. These were clustered into one dataset D1.

- The remaining 7 tables (d14,..,d20) were clustered into 3 datasets to minimize intercomputer communication. In particular, the focus was to eliminate the remote joins. Thus the tables that were joined frequently were clustered together.

- The 300-computer network was reduced into a 4-site network because the overall network consists of 4 subnets.

- The size of the problem was reduced to allocating 4 datasets to 4 computers. The final allocation was determined by using simple paper and pencil calculations.

5.7   Step 5: Data Allocation Strategies

5.7.1   Overview

In this stage, the datasets are allocated to one or more computers. The data allocation decision significantly affects the query/transaction processing performance, security, concurrency control and availability of a database in a distributed environment. Datasets D1, D2,.., Dn can be allocated by using one of the following strategies:

1. All datasets are allocated to a mainframe or a centralized database server machine.

2. Datasets are uniquely allocated to database server machines where they are most frequently accessed. No data is duplicated (e.g., D1 is allocated to computer C1; D2 and D3 are allocated to computer C2; D4 is allocated to computer C3, etc.).

3. Datasets are allocated as described in strategy 2; however, one or more duplicate copies are kept at other computers for read-only purposes. The read-only copies are synchronized periodically (once a day, once a week).

4. Datasets are allocated as described in strategy 3; however, the duplicate copies are updated simultaneously (i.e., if a transaction updates D1 at one computer, then all copies of D1 at other computers must also be updated before the transaction completes).

The cost/benefit of these allocations can be estimated in terms of storage cost, communication costs (cost to read, cost to update), response time and data availability. In addition, some of these allocations may not be feasible due to the software and/or hardware restrictions (for example, an Informix database may not be allocated to IBM mainframes because Informix databases are not supported on MVS at the time of this writing).

We first describe trade-offs in data duplication and then describe a general data allocation problem. The approaches to solve this problem are then described.

5.7.2   Trade-offs in Data Duplication

Basically, duplicated data improves the availability and read performance but increases the storage and update synchronization costs. Figure 5.6 shows the impact of data duplication (increasing number of copies as *x* axis) on "costs" of storage, read communication, update communication, local I/O, and the like. It can be seen from Figure 5.6 that:

- The storage cost increases as the number of copies increases.

- The communication traffic (cost) is shown in terms of read and update communication costs. The read communication cost decreases as the number of copies increases, because most data can be found at local computers thus eliminating need for communication calls. The update communication cost increases with the number of copies, because duplicated data will need to be updated.

- The local I/O processing at each computer increases with data duplication. The increase is due to the locking/unlocking and logging activities to synchronize duplicate data and to prepare for failure handling.

- The availability of data increases with the number of copies in the system. The costs due to "lack of availability" drop in a manner similar to the read communication costs (we have not shown the lack of availability costs explicitly).

Figure 5.6 Data Duplication Trade-offs

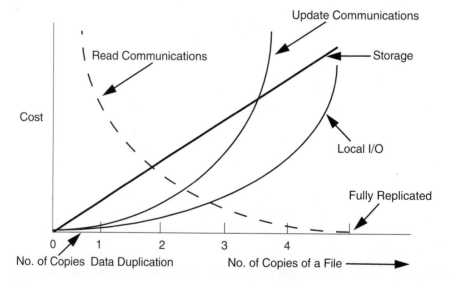

In extreme cases, you can keep only one copy of dataset D (no duplication) or duplicate D at every computer (fully duplicated). The main challenge is to determine a strategy that minimizes the overhead of synchronizing the updates and failure handling of duplicate data while still maximizing the benefits of increasing the availability and read performance. We have discussed the issues of data duplication extensively in Umar [1997, Chapter 6] where we introduced the concepts of Distributed Transaction Processing and Data Replication Servers. We will highlight the main results here for completeness. You should review Umar [1997] for more details.

Update synchronization, also known as ***update propagation,*** refers to making all copies of data reflect the same values (i.e., if one copy is updated, then the others must be also updated). At the highest level, the solutions fall into two categories:

- Transaction level synchronization schemes
- Periodic synchronization schemes

Transaction level synchronization schemes are based on the assumption that if one copy of data is updated, then all other copies must be updated *before* the transaction terminates. If this cannot be accomplished, then the transaction must be aborted. These schemes, used by the contemporary distributed transaction managers, use two-phase commit (2PC). The 2PC-based distributed transaction managers are known as "***TP-Heavy.***"

The periodic synchronization schemes allow the primary copy to be updated and then terminate the transaction. Other copies are updated through data replication servers (an off-line process) periodically (based on time and/or events). Many data replication servers are becoming commercially available. The data are updated typically by employing database procedures to update the primary copy and then use a data replication server to send the updated data to secondary sites. The data replication server-database procedure approach is commonly known as "***TP-Lite.***"

TP-Lite as well as TP-Heavy have certain pluses and minuses in distributed environments. The following questions should be asked by a data architect before deciding on TP-Lite versus TP-Heavy (also see the sidebar "Synchronization Interval—When to Synchronize Updates"):

- What is the requirement for data synchronization? If the data synchronization interval is periodic, then a TP-Lite solution may be useful to handle updates against replicated data.

- In what format is the data stored (databases, flat files)? If the data is stored in multiple databases and flat files then TP-Lite is not suitable (database procedures only work in RDBMS environments).

- How many SQL servers do the data reside on? If the application needs to update and commit data within a transaction that is stored on multiple servers then TP-Heavy should be used (database procedures cannot participate with other database procedures in a distributed transaction).

- What are the requirements for performance and load balancing? TP-Lite solutions are much faster on the surface than the TP-Heavy solutions that require synchronization between sites. But TP-Heavy solutions provide many sophisticated procedures for dynamic load balancing, priority scheduling, process restarts, and pre-started servers that are especially useful for large-scale production environment. These features are the main strength of TP-Heavy products, because many of these products have been used over the years to handle thousands of transactions in production OLTP (on-line transaction processing) environments.

Synchronization Interval—When to Synchronize Updates

Data synchronization interval is the time period for which two copies of data can be out of synchronization from a business point of view. For example, a business may tolerate an employee's phone number in two files to be different for a day (data synchronization interval is one day) but may not tolerate critical inventory items to be out of synchronization for more than a second. The synchronization interval can be specified as one of the following:

- Transaction synchronization—data must be synchronized within the duration of a transaction. This implies that if the said data are not synchronized then the transaction aborts.

- Periodic synchronization—data must be synchronized within a specified period (once an hour). This implies that a separate transaction can go around and synchronize data periodically.

Depending on the data synchronization interval, we can use different strategies to duplicate and synchronize duplicated data. For example, transaction synchronization requires TP Heavy while periodic synchronization requires TP Lite.

The following guidelines are suggested to designers of databases in distributed environments (see Umar [1997], Chapter 6 for more details):

- Keep data replication as minimal as possible. Large numbers of replicates can cause serious problems in 2PC as well as Replication Servers.

- If data must be synchronized as a transaction, then keep the number of copies small (experience shows not more than three) and use 2PC.

- If concurrency requirements outweigh "subsecond" data integrity requirements (i.e., data can be synchronized periodically) then use Replication Servers.

- If the network and nodes are unreliable, then use Replication Servers.

For detailed discussion of TP Heavy, TP Lite, replication servers and other client/server transaction processing considerations, see Umar [1997, Chapter 6].

5.7.3   Intuitive Data Allocation Analysis

The objective of intuitive analysis is to systematically study and evaluate various data allocation strategies and eliminate unacceptable options as quickly as possible. For example, let us review the following data allocation strategies:

Centralized: All dataset are allocated to a mainframe or a centralized database server machine.

Uniquely Distributed: Datasets are uniquely allocated to database server machines where they are most frequently accessed. No data is duplicated (e.g., D1 is allocated to computer C1; D2 and D3 are allocated to computer C2; D4 is allocated to computer C3, etc.).

Primary Copy: Each dataset is assigned a primary copy that is updated in real time. The primary copy datasets are distributed uniquely. One or more duplicate copies (secondaries) are kept at other computers for read-only purposes.The secondary copies are synchronized periodically.

Multiple Copies. Datasets are allocated redundantly where the duplicate copies can also be updated simultaneously (i.e., if a transaction updates D1 at one computer, then all copies of D1 at other computers must also be updated before the transaction completes).

Factors used in evaluating these strategies should include application and business requirements such as size information (number of users who will access the database, database size), response time (average, worst-case) requirements, scaling and growth requirements, security and control requirements, connectivity needed from user sites (from PCs, Macs, UNIX), backup/recovery needs and disaster handling, user independence needs and user/staff training level. These needs should be specified during the information requirement definition stage (Section 5.3).

Table 5.1 shows results of intuitive analysis of the four allocation strategies(columns) in terms of the information requirements (rows). The four allocation strategies are evaluated against typical information requirements by using some criteria (e.g., +3 to indicate a highly effective solution, and –3 may mean highly ineffective as shown in Table 5.1). It is not necessary to discuss the entries in this table, because the purpose of this analysis is to suggest a framework for evaluating the allocation decisions. The actual requirements and the values assigned will depend on the particular databases being designed.

How does this analysis help? Let us work through an example in which a database is to be designed with the following key requirements (in most business cases, a few key requirements drive the decisions):

Performance

Availability

Cost

A quick scan of Table 5.1 shows that unique distribution allocation is the best strategy for this example. Now, the analyst can proceed with determining what is the best allocation within this strategy (see next section).

The analysis shown in Table 5.1 is an extremely useful tool in understanding the qualitative impact of data allocations before proceeding with an analytical optimal allocation algorithm. An analyst can assign different weights to the different requirements for additional insights. In many cases, this exercise may provide enough information for data allocation without further analysis.

TABLE 5.1 INTUITIVE ANALYSIS OF DATA ALLOCATION STRATEGIES

Data Allocation Strategies Evaluation Factors (Information Requirements)	Centralized: All Data Centralized on One Computer	Unique Distribution: Distributed Uniquely to More Than One Computer	Primary Copy: Data Distributed Redundantly (Updates Restricted to a Primary Copy)	Multiple Copies: Data Distributed Redundantly (Any Copy Can Be Updated)
Flexibility and Growth	−2	+3	+3	+3
Performance	−3	+3	+3	+3
Availability	−3	−1	+3	+3
Cost	+3	−1	−1	−3
Manageability and Control	+3	0	−1	−3
Security	+3	+1	−1	−3
Data Consis-tency	+3	+3	−1	−3
Total Points	+4	+8	+5	−3

Legend: Evaluation factors (−3 to +3) indicate how well the configurations satisfy the requirements:

    −3 = does not satisfy at all

    +3 = very well satisfied

    0 = no impact

5.7.4 Analytical Data Allocation

In some cases, intuitive data allocation is not enough. In those cases, you may want to pursue analytical approaches to data allocation. This step can replace or follow the intuitive data allocation step, if needed.

An optimal data allocation can be theoretically determined that minimizes the total cost (storage + communication + local I/O) subject to response time, availability, and hardware/software constraints. This problem, traditionally referred to as the File Allocation Problem (FAP), in computing networks was first addressed by Wesley Chu in 1969 [Chu 1969]. Since then over 20 different file allocation algorithms have appeared in the literature in the 1970s and 1980s [Buckles 1979], [Casey 1972], [Chandy 1976], [Chang 1981], [Chu 1969], [Coffman 1980], [Doty 1982], [Eswaran 1974], [Finckenscher 1984], [Fisher 1980], [Irani 1981], [Koh 1985], [Levin 1975], and [Mahmood 1976]. Earlier allocation problems were simple, while later methods are actual design methodologies that utilize the allocation techniques as one of the decisions [Brahmadathan 1992], [Ceri 1984], [Jain 1987], and [Umar 1984]. A common FAP is formulated as follows:

Given:

>   Files $f1, f2, f3,,,$
>   Nodes $n1, n2, n3,,,,, $.

Determine: $A(f,n) = 1$ if f is allocated to n, 0 otherwise.

To minimize: storage cost + communication cost + local processing cost.

Subject to:

>   response time constraints
>   availability constraints
>   network topology
>   security restrictions

Variants of this problem have been cast into a mathematical programming problem and are solved by using nonlinear, integer and/or dynamic programming methods by the aforementioned researchers. However, many of the available techniques are academic and cannot be used in practical situations due to several reasons. First, the number of options in real-life situations is very large. Second, the interrelationships between distributed configurations and assignment trade-offs are not adequately represented in these algorithms. Third, many of the management and security restrictions are not included. Fourth, it is very difficult to translate real-life large-scale problems to mathematical programming and then solve them rigorously. Consequently, many simplifying assumptions are needed that limit the scope of the problem. Finally, most of the available research does not take into account the impact of emerging high-speed and reliable WANs, LANs and MANs operating at over 100 million bits per second. For example, most of the available work assumes slow and unreliable wide area networks of the 1970s.

Application of the existing FAP problems depends on the nature of the problem, the availability of information needed to reach an exact solution and the need to determine optimal versus approximate solutions in real life. For several real-life situations, sophisticated FAPs are rarely needed. In most cases, data allocation decisions can be made by exercising judgment and using real-life constraints of security and management. It is preferable to use a combination of tools and techniques and focus on simple analytical models to support the decisions and improve insights. Appendix 5A (Section 5.15) at the end of this chapter presents two allocation methods that can be used in quick paper and pencil analysis.

"Universal Databases"—Integrating Objects with Legacy Data

Many applications at present need to combine legacy data (data managed by old DBMSs such as IMS), with relational data and objects that may represent multimedia data such as sound, images, documents, HTML pages, and video clips. For example, the Internet Shopping Network (http://www.isn.com) would like such a database to store all information about 35,000 items it sells to its Web users. While the object databases are still trying to find their place for corporate use, the database vendors are working on "universal databases" that go beyond object databases to meet this demand. Universal databases are expected to facilitate storage, retrieval, manipulation, and management of legacy data, relational data, and multimedia objects. To be commercially successful, these databases need to provide the performance, flexibility, and scalability currently provided by the relational databases. This is not turning out to be an easy task due to different approaches and philosophies.

Source:
  Foley, J., "Open The Gates To Objects," *Information Week,* May 13, 1996, pp. 44–50.

We assume here that datasets are assigned statically (i.e., the assigned data and programs are not moved around dynamically during application execution). The dynamic resource allocation will perhaps be available through the distributed operating systems of the future. At that point, this whole step may need to be eliminated.

5.8 Step 6: Database Connectivity and Interoperability

After a database has been allocated, two practical issues arise:

- Connectivity: How will the database be accessed from remotely located end-user tools and applications?

- Interoperability: How will the new database interoperate with other new and/or existing databases in the system?

These two issues are explored in this section. Additional information about database connectivity and interoperability can be found in the books by Umar [1997], Hackathorn [1993], and Salami [1993]. Additional papers such as Sayles [1996], Rymer [1995], Chadda [1995], and Jessup [1996] should also be reviewed.

5.8.1 Data Connectivity Strategies

Data connectivity is of vital importance for end-user tools and/or application programs in distributed environments. In particular, access to databases from Web browsers is of great interest at present. See, for example, the January 1997 issue of *Database Programming and*

Design. Figure 5.7 shows an example of Web access to heterogeneous relational databases through a CGI (Common Gateway Interface) gateway. The CGI gateway can invoke a variety of middleware to access the remotely located databases. We are showing the CGI gateway that invokes ODBC (Open Database Connectivity) drivers to access Informix, Oracle, and Sybase databases. The main advantage of using ODBC in this case is that you can use one gateway to access these three types of databases. Otherwise, you will need one gateway for Oracle, one for Informix, and one for Sybase. In this case, the CGI gateway behaves as a client to the back-end database servers.

Figure 5.7 Web Access to Heterogeneous Relational Database

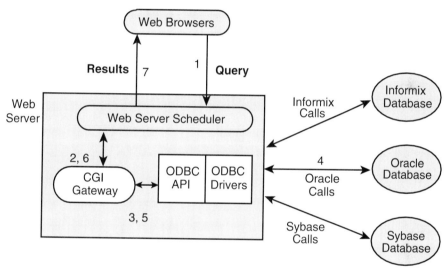

Note: The numbers indicate the sequence of activities

Let us go through some details. Many decision support systems assume widely distributed database servers that are accessed from remotely located applications, end-user tools, and Web middleware (e.g., CGI gateways). These tools and applications typically reside on computers that are connected to the database servers over LANs and/or WANs. The SQL statements generated by these clients are packaged and sent to the appropriate database servers by the client/server middleware by using the RDA (remote data access) protocols. Middleware for remote database access needs the following capabilities:

- Client middleware that receives the client call, converts it to an appropriate format, connects to the database server, and the like.

- Database server middleware that handles client tool calls, submits them to the database engine, builds the response, and routes them back to the client.

Object-Relational Databases
Accessing Relational Databases from Objects

Relational database management systems (RDBMSs) are used heavily in corporations at present. However, relational databases are not well suited for storage and retrieval of complex objects (e.g., cars, computing networks). Relational databases currently provide BLOB (binary large object) support for storage and retrieval of pictures and texts as relational table columns. But this is not enough for complex object manipulations. Object-oriented database management systems (OODBMSs) are intended to address this limitation of RDBMSs. However, OODBMSs do not directly support SQL—a major problem. The solution is the object-relational database management systems (ORDBMSs) that merge RDBMS with OO technologies.

Although implementations of ORDBMSs differ between vendors, the following figure shows a common architecture. In essence, the object manager serves as the OO wrappers around RDBMS. This approach has the advantage that the investment in relational databases is protected. Another approach is to provide a SQL interface to OODBMS, but this approach is not widely implemented.

Many vendors such as Hewlett Packard, Informix, UniSQL, and Oracle access these databases. For an initial state of the market analysis of ORDBMSs, see Davis [1995]. More recent information can be found from vendor Web sites.

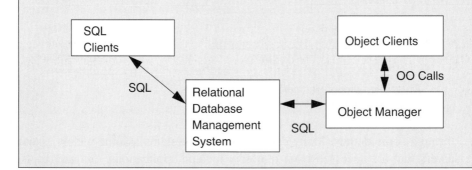

This middleware is discussed extensively in Umar [1997, Chapter 5]. For most end-user "plug and play" tools, remote data access (RDA) is the most frequently used client/server interaction paradigm. In some cases, database RPCs may be useful in databases to invoke canned reports. Many application programs employ the RPC paradigm where a remotely located program on a database server is invoked by a client program. The choice of the appropriate middleware software and protocols depends on the target database and the client working environment.

Figure 5.8 shows a general heterogeneous environment in which DB2, Oracle, and Informix databases exist. The Web browsers access these databases through the Web server that may invoke SQL middleware. The Informix clients in the TCP/IP LAN can access Informix databases or DB2 databases (the access to DB2 is provided by an Informix-DRDA gateway developed by Informix). The Informix DRDA gateway is installed on a TCP/IP LAN and is connected to the mainframe through an SNA WAN. The ODBC client can also access the Informix and DB2 databases by using the ODBC drivers. For extensive discussion of the data access middleware, see Umar [1997, Chapter 5].

Figure 5.8 Example of Heterogeneous Database Access

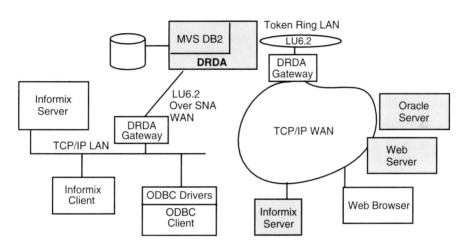

Many Web gateways, at present, operate on the Web server (CGI gateways are an example). Java applets allow these gateways to reside on Web browsers, because Java applets can be imbedded in HTML pages and sent to the Web browsers where they execute. By using this approach, access to remote applications and databases can be invoked directly from the browser if the browser allows it. The Java applet can receive a query and then send this query to a remote application or database (Figure 5.9). This is especially interesting for database gateways where the database gateway functionality runs on the client side. A standard called JDBC (Java Database Connectivity) has been developed to allow Java programs to issue calls to relational databases. JDBC is roughly similar to ODBC.

5.8.2 Data Interoperability

Data interoperability is concerned with two key issues: (a) what strategy to use to exchange data between different systems, and (b) what type of infrastructure to use to carry out the said exchanges.

Data can be exchanged between systems by using one of the following paradigms:

- Synchronous exchanges
- Asynchronous exchanges
- Bulk data transfers

Figure 5.9 Access to Databases from Java

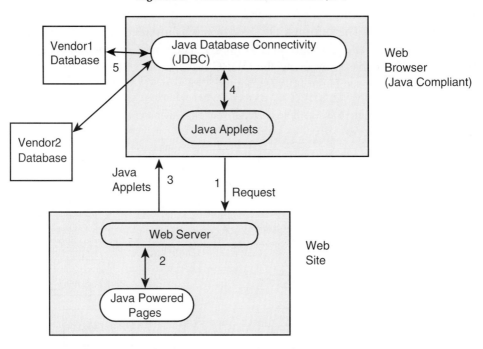

Note: The numbers indicate sequence of activities

Synchronous exchanges use the send-reply-send paradigm in which the sender is blocked from any further processing unless it receives a response. This paradigm, used commonly in remote procedure call (RPC) and remote data access (RDA) systems, is primarily appropriate between closely interacting partners. Asynchronous exchanges use the send-send-reply-reply paradigm in which the sender continues to send data without being blocked from further processing. This paradigm, supported by the extant message-oriented middleware (MOM), can be used between largely independent systems (the senders keep putting messages on a queue and the receivers keep picking them up from the queue). Bulk data transfers employ the send-send-send paradigm in which the needed data are extracted and sent to destinations periodically (no one waits for a response). This paradigm is useful for very loosely coupled systems (e.g., data from mainframes are extracted and sent to different sites periodically). You need to decide the most appropriate data exchange strategy between different systems (many systems at present use bulk data transfer).

The infrastructure needed for data exchanges depends largely on the paradigm being used. Naturally, bulk data transfer is easier to handle. Let us concentrate on the synchronous/asynchronous data exchanges. Data interoperability in these paradigms is greatly influenced by the exchange protocol (i.e., the format of the data and the rules of exchange) that is used between clients and servers. Let us ask the following question: Can a database stored in vendor X database exchange information with vendor Y tools? In general, the answer to this question is no, because the exchange protocols are largely proprietary at the time of this writing (i.e., clients from vendor X can only access vendor X database). This mismatch has led to "database gateways" that convert vendor X protocols into vendor Y protocol. DRDA (Distributed Relational Database Architecture) Gateways are an example of such gateways (DRDA Gateways from Informix, Oracle, and other vendors convert the Informix and Oracle protocols to DB2 protocols). Table 5.2 shows the various exchange protocols that can be used between various senders and receivers. Additional information about the middleware that supports the exchange protocols can be found in Umar [1997].

TABLE 5.2 MIDDLEWARE FOR DATA ACCESS

Data Exchange Paradigm	Exchange Protocol Examples	Comments
Remote Procedure Call (RPC)	OSF DCE RPC exchange protocol is a de facto standard	Sender and receiver has to use DCE facilities to be able to communicate
Remote Data Access (RDA), i.e., remote SQL	1. DRDA for exchange Protocol 2. OSI RDA	1. Senders from different suppliers can exchange information with DB2 by using DRDA 2. Senders from any suppliers can exchange information with any database by using ISO RDA (if commercially available)
Message-Oriented Middleware (MOM)	1. IBM's MQ protocols 2. DEC Message Q	No standards (de facto or otherwise) at the time of this writing
Distributed Object Access	1. CORBA 2. Microsoft DCOM	Sender and receiver must use the CORBA or DCOM facilities (bridges between CORBA and DCOM are commercially available)
Bulk Data Transfer	FTP is a widely accepted standard	Need to extract before sending over FTP. Numerous extractors and replication servers becoming commercially available.

5.9 State of the Practice: Case Studies and Examples

Many case studies about enterprise data architectures are published regularly in trade journals such as *Database Programming and Design, Client/Server Computing,* and *DBMS.* A few short case studies give a small sample. Due to the differences in detail provided by different case studies published in the literature, we explore one case study in detail to illustrate the enterprise data architecture approach presented in this chapter.

5.9.1 Short Case Studies ("Snippets")

Customer Information Architecture. Griffin [1995] describes in detail a blueprint for building a customer information architecture that integrates customer information across all products and services of an enterprise. This architecture, applied at the First Union Bank (Charlotte, North Carolina) includes intelligent front ends, a metamodel that holds data descriptions, a data warehouse that holds the customer data, legacy systems that hold the source data, and a data collection and loading facility that extracts data from the legacy systems and loads into the data warehouse.

Internet Shopping Network (ISN). ISN is a totally Web-based company that sells about 35,000 computer hardware and software products (*Source: Datamation,* April 1, 1996, p. 40). Information about these products is kept in two Sun machines using the Informix database servers. These servers handle about 5 million transactions per day. Once an order is placed, a message is sent that establishes automatic EDI links to the suppliers. The credit card transaction is handled by a separate server for security purposes. ISN, like many other similar companies, is looking for a "universal database" that can integrate sound, images, text, and other complex data types with relational data. Additional information about ISN can be found from the company Web site (http://www.isn.com).

Web-Based Data Services. Haynes [1996] describes how Windermere Real Estate architected data services for its 150 individually owned and operated offices. After analysis, a central database was designed that could be accessed by remote Web users through a Web database gateway (WebDBC from Nomad). The database contains 8,000 home listings and 4,000 agent records. By using WebDBC, the authorized remote offices can input agent personnel information, customer and client information, and property listing information directly into the database. The input screens are created by WebDBC and the output screens are also generated by WebDBC.

Data Architectures for Healthcare. Valigra [1996] describes how five healthcare providers use client/server technologies to stay competitive. Data architectures for access and management of enterprise data is a key concern for these organizations. Examples include help to outside physicians by the Medical Center of Delaware, getting medical records off paper and putting them online by the VA Medical Center (West Palm Beach, Florida), improving services to attract and keep corporate customers by Kaiser Permanente (Portland, Oregon), improving Human Resource services by the Saint Joseph Hospital (Orange, California), and generating new revenue streams by Boulder Community Hospital (Boulder, Colorado).

AT&T General Purpose Data Collector. This system uses object database technology to collect, process and reconcile all internal voice service records. AT&T chose Versant ODBMS to store the information. The database and the needed application software resides on the Web server. The users access this application through Web browsers within the AT&T's Intranet. *Source:* 1996 *Computerworld,* Object Application Awards, Best Distributed Applications Using Object Technology Category.

Product Data Management System at Hughes. Garner [1995] describes the product data management system at Hughes. The company first established a data architecture that divided its data into three distinct categories: product, operational, and management. This architecture has resulted in a data warehouse for ad hoc queries, a decision support system, and a number of applications for human resources, scheduling, and financial purposes. The data are collected in Oracle databases and are accessed by a potpourri of applications and tools residing on user desktops.

5.9.2   A Detailed Example

A database needs to be developed for an order processing system of a corporation with one headquarter (HQ) and 3 regional sales offices in different parts of the United States (see Figure 5.10). The database is used by the HQ as well as regional users. The HQ has an MVS mainframe and each regional site has at least one UNIX computer that can be used as a database server. The sites are connected through a 56,000 Kbps packet-switching network.

Figure 5.10 : Network Topology for Order Processing

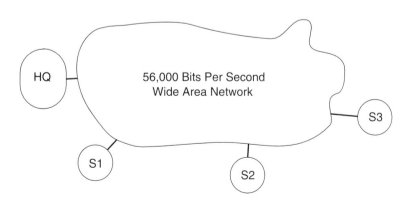

5.9.2.1   Step 1: Information Requirements

The primary business driver is to develop a corporatewide order processing database that will be used by all regions of a corporation. The following information describes the requirements to be satisfied by the database:

- The database will keep information about customers, products ordered by the customers, salespersons who place the order, and the order itself.

- Each regional site has its own sales staff and customers. However, all sites offer the same type of products.

- The database will be used to track orders, customers, and salespersons to maximize customer service. The database will also be used for management decisions such as marketing and sales planning. Many transactions (queries plus updates) are issued in this order-processing system. However, the system needs to be optimized for the following critical (dominant) database transactions:

    T1: Which salesperson placed a particular order (issued once per hour at each region and three times per hour at HQ)?

    T2: What is the activity for a given order—the customer, the products ordered, and the salesperson involved (issued three times per hour at each region and 10 times per hour at HQ)?

    T3: Place a new order (issued 100 times per hour at each region and 10 times per hour at HQ).

- The database will be accessed by 30 users (salespersons plus administrators) who reside at HQ and at the regional sites.

- The following size(cardinality) information is provided:

    Regions = 4 (1 HQ, 3 regions)
    Salespersons = 24
    Customers = 100,000
    Orders = 1,000,000
    Products = 10,000

- Response time (average, worst case) requirements are to minimize the response time for the three dominant transactions.

- Scaling and growth should be provided for 10 percent growth per year in the number of products and customers.

- Security requirements dictate that the database will be accessed only by the users (salespersons plus administrators) who reside at HQ and at the regional sites.

- Availability for the three transactions must be 100 percent between the normal business hours.

- Data synchronization interval for product information must not exceed an hour. Other pieces of information can be synchronized once a day.

- Connectivity needs to be provided from PCs to the databases (all users have access to PCs). In addition, access from Web browsers is important.

- Interoperability and interfaces with an MVS-DB2-based materials requirement planning (MRP) system is necessary.

- Portability between computing platforms (data portability, processing portability, user interface portability.

- Backup/recovery and disaster handling is required for all databases.

- Audit controls are required.

5.9.2.2 Step 2: Data Modeling

Figure 5.11 shows the data model of the order-processing system as an ERA diagram. This diagram shows the four major entities (salesperson, customer, order, and product) and the relationships between these entities.

Figure 5.11 Data Model for Order Processing

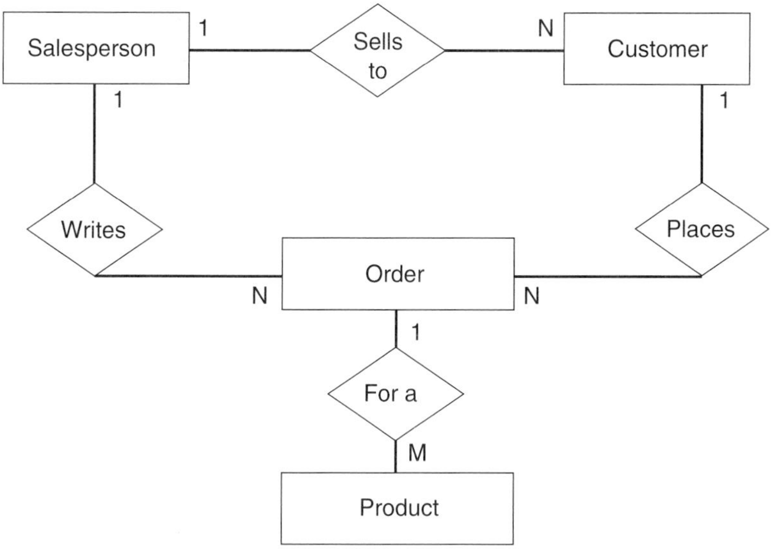

5.9.2.3 Step 3: Logical Database Design

The first step in logical database design is to transform the ERA model to relational tables. In our ERA diagram, all relationships between data entities are one to many. Thus, each data entity can be transformed into a relational table leading to the following tables:

> Customer
>
> Product
>
> Order
>
> Salesman

However, these tables need to be normalized. Figure 5.12 shows the result of normalization. Basically, the order table has been split.

Figure 5.12 Logical Database Design for Order Processing (Normalized)

Customer

cust-no	cust-name	. . . .

Product

prod-no	prod-name	qty

Order

order-no	sales-name	cust-no

Order-line

order-no	prod-no

Salesperson

sales-name	addr	dept	job-level

5.9.2.4   Step 4: Fragmentation and Clustering

For fragmentation, the relational tables (products, customers, orders, salespersons, etc.) and the transactions T1, T2, and T3 are analyzed. The results of this analysis are shown in Table 5.3 and Table 5.4. Table 5.3 shows the size and access information about the products, customers, orders, and salespersons' relational tables. Table 5.4 shows the results of transaction analysis. For example, Table 5.4 shows that T1 accesses the order table 24 times per invocation of T1 (24 reads, 0 writes). In addition, T1 is issued once per hour from the regional sites and 3 times from HQ. As shown in Table 5.4, all regional sites have similar transaction arrival patterns but the HQ has different arrival rates. Note that the same transaction T1 is issued from HQ or from S1, S2, and S3. The information about T2 and T3 is self-evident in Table 5.4. It should also be recalled that, other than HQ, the transactions issued from each regional site are region-specific (e.g., Chicago region issues queries about customers and salespersons in the Chicago region).

Based on this analysis, the following fragmentation and clustering decisions are made:

- No tables are partitioned vertically because this requires modification of the relational schema.
- Most tables are small in size, so the need for fragmentation due to size is not urgent.
- Customer and salesperson tables are partitioned per region to satisfy the regional queries for customers and salespersons.
- Order and order-line tables are clustered together into an order dataset for the purpose of allocation. This clustering will assure that order and order-line tables are always assigned to the same computer thus eliminating remote joins between these two tables (it is assumed that these two tables are referenced frequently together). Please keep in mind that the order and order-line tables will exist as separate tables on the destination computer; the clustering only helps in the allocation step.

- All region-specific fragments are clustered into "regional datasets" that can be allocated to the respective regions. For example, the customer and salesperson fragments for the Chicago customers and salespersons are clustered into a "Chicago" dataset. In the allocation step, the Chicago dataset can be allocated to the Chicago site, and so on.

- The allocation sites can be clustered based on similarity. For example, all regional sites have similar behavior in terms of transaction arrival rates and have similar hardware configuration in terms of UNIX platforms. This leads to two candidate allocations: HQ and regional site (i.e., solve for one regional site).

TABLE 5.3 RELATIONAL TABLE ANALYSIS

Table	Size	Average Local Query (Update) Time in Milliseconds	Average Remote Query (Update) Time in Milliseconds
Customer	500 KB	100 (120)	400(500)
Product	1.0 MB	200 (250)	1,000(1,200)
Order	2.0 MB	300 (400)	2,000 (2,500)
Salesperson	100 KB	100 (120)	400 (500)

TABLE 5.4 TRANSACTION ANALYSIS

Transaction	Originating Sites	Frequency of Arrival per hour	Customer Table Accesses (Reads, Writes)	Product Table Accesses (Reads, Writes)	Order Table Accesses (Reads, Writes)	Salesperson Table Accesses (Reads, Writes)
T1	S1, S2, S3 HQ	1 3	(0, 0)	(0, 0)	(24, 0)	(0, 0)
T2	S1, S2, S3 HQ	3 10	(1, 0)	(10, 1)	(1, 0)	(1, 0)
T3	S1, S2, S3 HQ	100 100	(1, 0)	(10,10)	(1, 1)	(0, 0)

5.9.2.5 Step 5: Data Allocation

The main data allocation questions are:

- Should the region-specific customer and salesperson datasets be allocated to each region or should they be kept at the HQ?
- Should a read-only copy of the regional information be kept at the HQ?
- Where to put the product and order datasets? These datasets are not region-specific.

Table 5.5 shows an intuitive high level analysis of the allocation decisions that helps us to

TABLE 5.5 HIGH LEVEL ANALYSIS OF ALLOCATION STRATEGIES

Requirements with Weights (0-5)	Data on HQ Mainframe Only	Data Partitioned across Sites, Nothing on HQ	Data Partitioned across Sites, Secondary on HQ	Data Allocated Redundantly
Flexibility and Growth (3)	−2	+3	+3	+3
Performance (3)	−3	+3	+3	+3
Availability (5)	−3	−1	+3	+3
Cost (3)	+3	−1	−2	−3
Manageability and Control (2)	+3	0	−2	−3
Security (2)	+3	+1	−2	−3
Data Consistency (1)	+3	+3	−1	−3
Total Weights	−6	15	18 (max.)	9

Legend: Evaluation factors (−3 to +3) indicate how well the configurations satisfy the requirements:

  −3 = does not satisfy at all

  +3 = very well satisfied

   0 = no impact

answer some of these questions. The requirements in Table 5.5 are shown with weights to indicate their relative importance. Note that data availability is the key driving requirement. The last row in Table 5.5 shows a total weight for each data allocation strategy. Based on this analysis, we can make the following decisions:

- Allocate the region-specific customer and salesperson information to the regional sites
- A copy of product and customer information is kept at HQ
- A replication server for synchronizing updates between the regional databases and the HQ database will be used
- Allocation of the product and order information requires more analysis, because these tables can be allocated to HQ, S1, S2, or S3

It should be emphasized that Table 5.5 is a very effective tool in understanding the interrelationships between various allocation strategies and information/operational requirements of a database. In practice, an analyst would work through this exercise a few times before making a decision. Based on first-hand experience, this exercise leads to a better understanding, refinement, and expansion of the requirements.

At this point, we have eliminated customer and salesperson datasets from further analysis. However, we need to allocate product and order datasets. We will use the Best Fit Method described in Section 5.15 to determine the optimal allocation for product and order datasets. Table 5.6 shows the computations of the local references for different data allocations. Based on the calculations shown in Table 5.6, the product and order datasets should be allocated to the HQ mainframe.

TABLE 5.6 LOCAL REFERENCES FOR EACH TABLE AT EACH SITE

Table	Allocated to Site	Transactions T1 (frequency)	Transactions T2 (frequency)	Transactions T3 (frequency)	Total References Per Hour
Product	S1, S2, S3	0 reads, 0 writes (1)	10 reads, 1 write (3)	10 reads, 10 writes (100)	2,033
	HQ	0 reads, 0 writes (3)	10 reads, 1 write (10)	10 reads, 10 writes (100)	2,110 (max.)
Order	S1, S2, S3	24 reads, 0 writes (1)	1 read, 0 writes (3)	1 read, 1 write (100)	227
	HQ	24 reads, 0 writes (3)	1 read, 0 writes (10)	1 read, 1 write (100)	282 (max.)

The main data architecture after this analysis is:

- Allocate the customer and salesperson information at the regions. Keep a secondary copy at HQ that is updated periodically through a Replication Server

- Allocate the products and orders at the HQ mainframe

5.9.2.6 Step 6: Database Connectivity and Interoperability

Figure 5.13 shows the data architecture of the order processing system. To illustrate the various connectivity and interoperability issues, the data architecture is mapped on the physical corporate network. As shown in Figure 5.13, each regional site has an Ethernet LAN (10 Mbps) and all regional sites are connected to the HQ mainframe through a 56 Kbps WAN packet-switching system. The corporate WAN uses TCP/IP and all sites are UNIX-TCP/IP environments. Thus routers are used extensively for network connectivity. Note that the customer and salesperson information is partitioned and allocated to each region for region-specific processing. Secondary copy of customer and salesperson information is kept at HQ for backup (this information is updated once a day). However, the product and order information is centralized at the HQ mainframe.

We can make the following observations from this configuration:

- Each site can access the local information (customer, salesperson) very quickly because the LAN access data rate is at 10 Mbps.

- Web browsers use HTML pages that invoke the CGI scripts at the Web servers. The CGI scripts provide the Web gateway functionality for accessing remote databases.

- Remote interactions between sites and with mainframe require the use of a corporate WAN. The data rate of WAN is more than 10 times slower than the site LANs. Thus these interactions will be much slower.

- Remote interactions between local sites and mainframe to access the product and order information will be especially slow (keep in mind that remote interactions are real time).

- Since all sites use UNIX, any of the available vendor-provided middleware would provide database connectivity. However, the interoperability between sites when different vendor products are at different sites needs to be carefully examined.

- The UNIX users at the regional sites can access the mainframe database by using DRDA or other appropriate database connectivity gateways.

- The clients in the network can use a combination of OLTP programs and end-user tools to access the order processing data. The SQL statements generated by these tools are routed to the appropriate database server by the client/server middleware.

The main bottleneck in the data architecture proposed in Figure 5.13 appears to be the corporate WAN. The following two choices should be reviewed to eliminate this bottleneck:

- Replicate the product and order information at each site so that each site can access information locally. However, this data is updated frequently and the impact of synchronization should be carefully reviewed.

Figure 5.13 Databases in Client/Server Environments

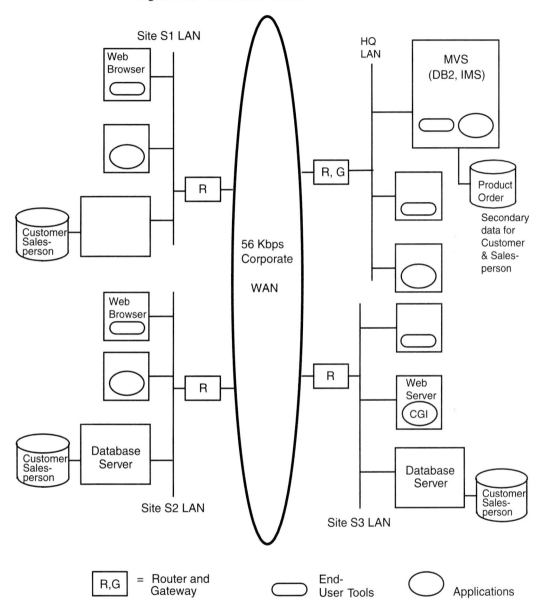

- Change over to a faster WAN. For example, fast Frame Relay and Asynchronous Transfer Mode (ATM) packet-switching systems exceed the Ethernet LAN data rates (the data rates of fast packet-switching systems exceed 100 Mbps).

5.10   State of the Market: Standards and Products

The extant C/S databases are currently dominated by SQL servers (Microsoft SQL Server, Sybase Server, Oracle Server, etc.). Even nonrelational databases use SQL as an exchange protocol between clients and database servers (EDA/SQL from Information Builders is an example). In such cases, the clients send an SQL request to a database server that uses a "driver" to convert the SQL request to a native (e.g., IMS) database call. It seems that SQL and relational databases will continue to dominate the C/S state of the market and state of the practice. This is due to the following reasons:

- Continued improvements in price/performance of relational databases

- Increased availability of powerful yet inexpensive SQL servers on desktops

- Continued growth of SQL-based end-user tools that employ the C/S paradigm

- Continued growth of knowledge in SQL

The natural question is: What is the role of object-oriented (OO) technologies in C/S databases? Many contemporary tools present an OO view of relational data—end users see objects and invoke operations on objects while these operations generate SQL calls. However, widespread use of OO databases in enterprisewide C/S applications still remains to be seen.

Many standards impact the data architecture issues in distributed environments. Due to the heavy usage of SQL, the ISO SQL3 standard that includes Object SQL features, stored procedures, triggers, and user-defined functions is of interest [Melton 1996]. For database access, the embedded SQL standards and the wide range of command-level interfaces (CLIs) such as the SAG CLI and the X/Open CLI are evolving. In industry-based CLIs, the Microsoft ODBC CLI is very popular, but other CLIs such as the Borland/IBM/Novell/WordPerfect, Integrated Database Application Programming Interface (IDAPI), and the Oracle Glue are worth mentioning. For exchange protocols, the ISO/Xopen RDA standard is evolving while IBM's DRDA (Distributed Relational Database Architecture) is being used heavily in the industry. We have reviewed many of these standards in the chapter on SQL middleware [Umar 1997, Chapter 5]. Another standard activity that needs to be watched is the evolution and collaboration of standards in SQL and object-oriented databases. For example, the Object Database Management Group (ODBMG) and ISO are attempting to merge the ISO SQL3 standards with the ODBMG Object Query Language (OQL) [Barry 1995].

Another area of considerable market activity at present is the "Web gateways" that are appearing commonly as CGI gateways or dedicated gateways. In particular, the interest in client/side (Java) gateways is high because they allow access to SQL databases directly from the Web browser. The Java applet receives the user query and sends it to a remote database. In this case, the database gateway functionality runs on the client side. Special attention needs to be paid to JDBC (Java Database Connectivity) that allows Java programs to issue calls to relational databases. Products that combine object databases with Web are beginning to appear [Black 1997], [Dick 1996], and [Attwood 1996].

5.11 State of the Art: Research Notes

An interesting area of research is the automatic workload migration algorithms that move the data automatically across a network based on access patterns. This work would have great impact on the data allocation algorithms discussed in this chapter.

Another area of interesting research is the use of object-oriented databases, active databases, intelligent databases, and knowledge bases for enterprisewide applications. Detailed analysis is needed to determine what database technology should be used for what class of applications and under what type of performance and operational requirements.

A potential area of work includes use of semistructured data (memos, spreadsheets, graphs, and multimedia information) in enterprisewide applications. This is especially true for decision support applications, because much of the decision support information may exist in memos, meeting notes, spreadsheets, and other semistructured formats.

An interesting area of work is the "universal database" technology that combines legacy data (i.e., data managed by old DBMSs such as IMS), with relational data and objects to represent sound, images, documents, HTML pages, video clips, and other multimedia objects. Development of universal databases that provide the performance, flexibility, and scalability currently provided by the relational databases is turning out to be a difficult task.

Of course, the issues related to data access through the Internet are intriguing to many people. In particular, how the data can be partitioned, allocated, accessed, and managed to support interenterprise applications is of great importance, because this data may be stored in a variety of sources that are accessible through the World Wide Web.

Quality of enterprise data has emerged as a major research area recently. Of particular interest are the two fundamental questions: how to measure data quality (i.e., metrics), and how to improve data quality of widely distributed data sources (including Web sites). In addition, how data quality can be integrated into data architectures needs further investigation. The research initiated in the Data Quality Project at the MIT Sloan school of Management [Wand 1996] is of particular importance.

The importance of data synchronization and consistency in the increasing mobile world of tomorrow also needs special attention. The problem of data consistency in the mobile world is complicated due to the multiple levels of heterogeneity (operating systems, coding schemes, DBMS vendors) and timing issues. The critical problem is to synchronize the mobile devices with current data and to update the master database with the results of transactions that have occurred offline. The Gartner Group is investigating this issue in detail (see Scherberger [1997], and Percy [1996]).

In general, many new challenges and issues of data quality, data access, data allocation, and data operability in the large scale global networks are surfacing. These large scale data management issues need investigations. See Gray [1996] for an evolution of data management.

5.12   Summary

Databases in distributed environments are mostly relational databases that are installed on SQL database servers available from many DBMS vendors. These databases are accessed remotely by end-user tools (spreadsheets, 4GLs, data browsers, report writers, object-oriented viewers) and/or applications written in C, C++, Cobol, and the like, located on computers throughout an enterprise. Architecture of data in distributed environments involve a combination of issues such as the following:

- Classical relational database design issues such as data modeling and logical database design (i.e., database normalization)

- Distributed database design issues such as data partitioning and data allocation

- Middleware issues such as choice of appropriate C/S paradigms and protocols (RDA, RPC) and database gateways

A database life cycle ties these issues and approaches into a consistent framework. We have discussed this framework in this chapter and have illustrated it through a detailed example. The main steps of this life cycle are information requirements, data modeling, logical database design, data partitioning and clustering, data allocation, and database connectivity, and interoperability issues. Our coverage of the first three steps in this chapter has been somewhat brief because this information can be found in almost any contemporary database design book. However, steps related to data allocation and database connectivity/interconnectivity are unique to client/server and distributed environments and have been the primary focus of this chapter. A detailed example has attempted to illustrate the key points about designing databases in modern distributed environments.

5.13   Case Study: Data Architecture for XYZCorp

Data architecture is the next step after initial analysis. XYZCorp management has authorized data architecture work for the following three applications that were identified in the XYZAICS initiative:

- A new "advanced" inventory management system for integrated order processing/inventory management

- A management planning system that will support the management decisions in marketing and product planning

- A flexible manufacturing system to automate the manufacturing of electronic products. Application engineering projects that have been initiated are below:

The enterprise data architectures for the three applications should show the data allocation strategies and the data access/sharing mechanisms across the XYZCorp network.

Hints about the Case Study

The six-step data architecture procedure described in Sections 5.3 through 5.8 can be used to establish data architectures for these three applications.

The data architecture for the inventory management system can be generalized from the detailed case study presented in Section 5.9.

The data architecture for the management planning system (MPS) is of key importance. The data needed for this system is currently spread at different sites of the XYZCorp. A typical approach for decision support systems such as MPS is to extract information from various sources and store it in a data warehouse for analysis. We will discuss data warehouses in detail in Chapter 10.

The flexible manufacturing system does not require an extensive data architecture study because it is a real-time system. In systems of this nature, most of the data exist in flat files and main memory for performance reasons, and there is no need to support ad hoc queries and reports (robots are not very good at issuing ad hoc queries!). It is educational to go through the six steps to understand the unique data architecture problems of real-time systems.

5.14   Problems and Exercises

1. How does data architecture differ from database design? Explain through examples.

2. Consider an application of your choice. Develop the data architecture of this system by using the six-step data architecture procedure described in Sections 5.3 through 5.8. For each step, list the major decisions, the techniques/tools employed and the final choices made by you.

3. How will the data architecture steps be modified if all data were stored in object-oriented databases? Give specific examples.

4. How will the data architecture steps be modified if data quality measurement and improvement were explicitly included in data architectures? Hint: Look at the data quality literature shown in sidebar "Data Quality: Sources for Information" before proceeding.

5. Investigate and analyze the "best in class" commercially available middleware for accessing remote databases from Web-based object-oriented tools.

6. Investigate a data allocation algorithm that we have not discussed in this chapter and compare/contrast it with the two algorithms discussed in Appendix 5A.

7. Review, expand, and improve Table 5.1 to make it general for any data allocation evaluation.

8. Complete Table 5.2 to evaluate some of the IT infrastructure products for data access.

5.15   Appendix 5A: Two Analytical Data Allocation Methods

5.15.1   Non-Redundant Best Fit Data Allocation Method

The "Non-Redundant Best Fit Data Allocation Method" is simple enough to be useful for hand calculations for small problems (or large problems that have been reduced significantly through clustering and intuitive analysis). If needed, program can be written easily to automate the calculations. This method, first introduced by Ceri and Pelagatti [Ceri 1984], determines the single site to maximize the benefit of data allocation. Benefit is defined as the total number of update and retrieval references. The basic idea is to minimize the intercomputer communication by maximizing local references. In other words, this algorithm determines the site S^* where a dataset R is allocated uniquely to maximize the total number of local updates and query references. The main procedure is:

- Allocate dataset R_i to a site S_j.

- For each transaction T_k, compute the number of local references to R_i when it is allocated to S_j.

- Choose the site S^* with maximum number of local references

This method is illustrated through an example in which three datasets $R1$, $R2$, and $R3$ need to be allocated to four sites $S1$, $S2$, $S3$, and $S4$. The three datasets are accessed by two transactions T1 and T2 that are issued by users who reside at $S1,,,S4$. Table 5.7 shows the transaction activity. The calculations for determining the local references for $R1$, $R2$, and $R3$ when these datasets are allocated to sites $S1$, $S2$, $S3$, and $S4$ are shown in Table 5.8. As a result of this analysis, $R1$ and $R3$ can be assigned to site $S1$ because this allocation will maximize the local references. The dataset $R2$ could be assigned to $S1$ or $S2$ because both sites maximize the local references as shown in Table 5.8. Let us assign $R2$ to $S2$ because $S1$ is getting somewhat loaded and could thus become a performance and availability bottleneck (2 datasets are assigned to it already).

Let us explain the entries in Table 5.8 by working through the calculations for dataset $R1$.

- $R1$ is allocated to site $S1$. Transaction T1 issues 4 local reads and 1 local write at $S1$. The frequency of these reads/writes is 1 per hour as indicated in Table 5.7. Transaction T2 issues 3 local reads and 2 local writes at $S1$ (the frequency of this occurrence is 3 times per hour as shown in Table 5.7). The total number of local references when $R1$ is assigned to $S1$ is 20 $[(5 \times 1) + (5 \times 3) = 20)]$.

TABLE 5.7 TRANSACTION ACTIVITY

Transaction	Originating Sites	Frequency of Occurrence per hour	Table R1 Access (Reads, Writes)	Table R2 Access (Reads, Writes)	Table R3 Access (Reads, Writes)
T1	S1, S2 S3, S4	1 0	(4, 1)	(10, 1)	(0,0)
T2	S1 S2 S3, S4	3 0 2	(3, 2)	(0, 0)	(6,0)

TABLE 5.8 LOCAL REFERENCES FOR EACH TABLE AT EACH SITE

Dataset	Allocated to Site	Local References from Transaction T1 (frequency)	Local References from Transaction T2 (frequency)	Total Local References for a Dataset
R1	S1	4 reads, 1 write (1)	3 reads, 2 writes (3)	20 (max.)
	S2	4 reads, 1 write (1)	3 reads, 2 writes (0)	5
	S3	4 reads, 1 write (0)	3 reads, 2 writes (2)	10
	S4	4 reads, 1 write (0)	3 reads, 2 writes (2)	10
R2	S1	10 reads, 1 write (1)	0 reads, 0 writes (3)	11 (max.)
	S2	10 reads, 1 write (1)	0 reads, 0 writes (0)	11 (max.)
	S3	10 reads, 1 write (0)	0 reads, 0 writes (2)	0
	S4	10 reads, 1 write (0)	0 reads, 0 writes (2)	0
R3	S1	0 reads, 0 writes (1)	6 reads, 0 writes (3)	18 (max.)
	S2	0 reads, 0 writes (1)	6 reads, 0 writes (0)	0
	S3	0 reads, 0 writes (0)	6 reads, 0 writes (2)	12
	S4	0 reads, 0 writes (0)	6 reads, 0 writes (2)	12

- R1 is allocated to site S2. Transaction T1 issues 4 local reads and 1 local write at S2. The frequency of these reads/writes is 1 per hour as indicated in Table 5.7. Transaction T2 issues 3 local reads and 2 local writes at S2. However, the frequency of this occurrence is 0 per hour as shown in Table 5.7. The total number of local references when R1 is assigned to S2 is 5 (5x1+0=5).

- R1 is allocated to site S3. Transaction T1 issues 4 local reads and 1 local write at S3. The frequency of these reads/writes is 0 per hour as indicated in Table 5.7. Transaction T2 issues 3 local reads and 2 local writes at S3. The frequency of this occurrence is 2 times per hour as shown in Table 5.7. The total number of local references when R1 is assigned to S3 is 10 (5x0+5x2=10).

- R1 is allocated to site S4. Transaction T1 issues 4 local reads and 1 local write at S4. The frequency of these reads/writes is 0 per hour as indicated in Table 5.7. Transaction T2 issues 3 local reads and 2 local writes at S4. The frequency of this occurrence is 2 times per hour as shown in Table 5.7. The total number of local references when R1 is assigned to S4 is 10 (5x0+5x2=10).

- The local references are maximized if R1 is assigned to S1. Thus R1 should be assigned to S1.

The Best Fit method, as can be seen, is simple and intuitive. However, it does have a few limitations. For example, it does not accurately take into account response time and disk service time. In addition, it does not help in data replication (this method, however, can be used to allocate primary copies while secondary read-only copies can be allocated based on intuition and inspection). We describe a better allocation method as a special topic at the end of this chapter (Section 5.15).

5.15.2 The Redundant Data Allocation Method

The Redundant "All Beneficial Sites" allocation method can be used for either the redundant or non-redundant case. This method starts with no copy or one copy of a dataset. Additional copies are assigned and the cost as well as benefit of each additional copy is estimated. The algorithm stops when the cost of allocating an additional copy is greater than the benefit.

The benefit of allocating an additional copy is that it eliminates the need for a remote read, —the benefit is the reduction of time in accessing data multiplied by the frequency of data accessed. In particular, the benefit B_{ds} of an additional copy of a dataset d at the site s is given by the following formula:

$$B_{ds} = F_{ds} * (R-L)$$

where F_{ds} = Frequency of queries (reads) to dataset d from site s

R = time elapsed due to a remote query (i.e., d not available locally)

L = time elapsed due to a local query (i.e., d available locally)

The cost of allocating an additional copy is that it increases the write time due to update synchronization—the cost is measured in terms of local write time plus the remote write times multiplied by the frequency of writes.[3] In particular, the cost C_{ds} of an additional copy of a dataset d at site s is given by the following formula:

---

3. In this discussion, "write" is used to indicate database operations that modify the database (create, update, delete), and "query" is used to indicate the database operations that do not modify the database (read).

$$C_{ds} = W_{ds} * L' + W'_{ds'} * R'$$

where W_{ds} = Total frequency of local writes to dataset d from site s

$W'_{ds'}$ = Total frequency of remote writes to dataset d from all other sites s' where s' is not the same as s

R' = time elapsed due to a remote write (i.e., d not available locally)

L' = time elapsed due to a local write (i.e., d available locally)

Let us illustrate this method by reworking the example used to illustrate the Non-Redundant Allocation Method discussed earlier in this chapter (Section 5.9). Table 5.9 and Table 5.10 show the transaction activity and read/write times we will use. Table 5.11 and Table 5.12 show the benefit and cost estimates, respectively, for allocating dataset $R1$ to sites $S1$, $S2$, $S3$, and $S4$. Let us explain a few entries in these Tables.

The benefit estimates for allocating $R1$ to $S1$ (first entry in Table 5.11) are based on the following calculations. The queries are issued to $R1$ from $S1$ from transactions T1 and T2 as shown in Table 5.9; each T1 arrives at $S1$ 10 times per hour and each arrival issues 4 reads to $R1$, thus 40 queries are issued from T1 to $R1$ at $S1$ per hour; and each T2 arrives at $S1$ 30 times per hour and each arrival issues 3 reads to $R1$, thus 90 queries are issued from T1 to $R1$ at $S1$ per hour. The allocation of $R1$ to $S1$ for each query has the benefit, according to the formula for B_{ds}, of reducing the query time from remote query to local query (i.e., 600–100 milliseconds according to Table 5.10). Thus the benefit as shown in Table 5.11 is (40+90)x 500 = 65,000 milliseconds.

The cost calculations for allocating $R1$ to $S1$ (first entry in Table 5.12) are based on the following calculations.

- Local writes to $R1$ are issued from $S1$ from transactions T1 and T2 as shown in Table 5.9. Each T1 arrives at $S1$ 10 times per hour and each arrival issues 1 write to $R1$, thus 10 writes are issued from T1 to $R1$ at $S1$ per hour. Each T2 arrives at $S1$ 30 times per hour and each arrival issues 2 writes to $R1$. Thus 70 (i.e., 10 + 2 * 30) writes are issued from T1 to $R1$ at $S1$ per hour. Since the time per local write is 200 millisecond (Table 5.10), the total time for local updates to R1 when it is allocated to $S1$ is 70 * 200 = 14,000 milliseconds.

- Remote writes to $R1$ are issued from transaction T1 at $S2$ and T2 at $S3$ and $S4$ as shown in Table 5.9 (note that the frequency of T1 at $S3$ and $S4$ is zero and the frequency of T2 at $S2$ is zero). Each T1 arrives at $S2$ 10 times per hour and each arrival issues 1 write to $R1$, thus 10 remote writes are issued from T1 to $R1$ per hour. Each T2 arrives at $S3$ and $S4$ 20 times per hour and each arrival issues 2 writes to $R1$. Thus 90 (i.e., 10 + 20 * 2 + 20 * 2) remote writes are issued per hour from T1 to $R1$ when $R1$ is assigned to $S1$. Since each remote query time is 500 milliseconds (Table 5.10), the total remote write time is 90 * 500 = 45,000 milliseconds.

- The total cost of assigning $R1$ to $S1$ = local write time + remote write time = 14,000 + 45,000 = 59,000 milliseconds.

TABLE 5.9 TRANSACTION ACTIVITY

Transaction	Originating Sites	Frequency of Occurrence Per Hour	Table R1 Access (Reads, Writes)	Table R2 Access (Reads, Writes)	Table R3 Access (Reads, Writes)
T1	S1, S2 S3, S4	10 0	(4, 1)	(10, 1)	(0,0)
T2	S1 S2 S3, S4	30 0 20	(3, 2)	(0, 0)	(6,0)

TABLE 5.10 SIZE AND QUERY/UPDATE TIME

Table	Size	Average Local Query (Update) Time in Milliseconds	Average Remote Query (Update) Time in Milliseconds
R1	500 KB	100 (200)	600(500)
R2	1.0 MB	200 (250)	1,000(1,200)
R3	2.0 MB	300 (400)	2,000 (2,500)

TABLE 5.11 BENEFIT ESTIMATES

Dataset	Allocated to Site	Query Transactions from S	Frequency*Reads*(remote query time -local query time)	Total Time (Benefit)
R1	S1	Queries from S1: T1 from S1, T2 from S1	10*4*(600–100) + 30*3*(600–100)	65,000
	S2	Queries from S2: T1 from S2	10*4*(600–100)	20,000
	S3	Queries from S3: T2 from S3	20*3*(600–100)	30,000
	S4	Queries from S4: T2 from S3	20*3*(600–100)	30,000

TABLE 5.12 COST ESTIMATES

Dataset	Allocated to Site	Local Write and Remote Write Transactions	Frequency * no. of writes * write time	Total Time (cost)
R1	S1	Local writes: T1 from S1, T2 from S1 + Remote writes: T1 from S2, T2 from S3 and S4	10*1*200 + 30*2*200 + 10*1*500 + 20*2*500 + 20*2*500	59,000
	S2	Local writes: T1 from S2, T2 from S2 Remote writes: T1 from S1, T2 from S1, S3, S4.	10*1*200 + 0*20*200 + 10*1*500 + 30*2*500 + 20*2*500 +20*2*500	77,000
	S3	Local writes: T1 from S3, T2 from S3 Remote writes: T1 from S1 and S2, T2 from S1, S2, and S4.	0*1*200 + 20*2*200 + 10*1*500 + 10*1*500 +30*2*500 + 0*2*500 + 20*2*500	68,000
	S4	Local writes: T1 from S4, T2 from S4 Remote writes: T1 from S1 and S2, T2 from S1, S2, and S3.	0*1*200 + 20*2*200 + 10*1*500 + 10*1*500+ 30*2*500 +0*2*500 + 20*2*500	68,000

A review of Table 5.11 and Table 5.12 indicates that *R*1 should be allocated to *S*1 because this allocation yields more benefits than costs (the total cost for allocating *R*1 to *S*1 is 59,000 milliseconds while the total benefit is 65,000 milliseconds).

This method can be extended to include queuing delays by including the average queuing delays for local and remote queries and writes in the measurements shown in Table 5.10.

5.16 Additional Information

The data architecture book by Inmon [1989] gives a good, conceptual framework. The principles of designing databases have been covered in textbooks such as Date [1995], Elmasri [1989], and O'Neil [1994]. The books by Teorey [1994], Martin [1995], Ozsu [1991], and Burleson [1994] cover the distributed database design and client/server databases quite well. The issues of database connectivity and interoperability are discussed in the books by Hackathorn [1993], and Salami [1993].

State-of-the-market and state-of-the-practice information appears regularly in magazines such as *Database Programming and Design, Datamation, Database Adviser,* and *Data Access.* For state-of-the-art discussion of this subject area, the reader should keep abreast of publications such as *IEEE Conferences on Data Engineering, ACM Annual Conference on Very Large Databases,* and *ACM Special Interest Group on Data Management (SIGMOD)* publications.

Abiteboul, S., et al., *Foundations of Databases,* Addison Wesley, 1995.

Andrews, G.R., *Concurrent Programming: Principles and Practice,* Benjamin Cummings Publishing Co., 1992.

Attwood, T., "Object Databases Come of Age," *Object Magazine,* July 1996, pp. 60–63.

Barry, D., "Databases: On the Road to Standards," *Object Magazine,* October 1995, pp. 84–86.

Bhatia, S., and Ally, A., "Performance Advisor: An Analysis Tool for Computer Communication Systems," *IEEE International Communications Conference '86,* Toronto, June 1986, pp. 206–211.

Black, B., "Database and the Web: Giant Steps," *Database Programming and Design,* January 1997, pp. 34–43.

Blaha, M., et al., "Converting OO Models into RDBMS Schema," *IEEE Software,* May 1994, pp. 28–39.

Brahmadathan, K., and Ramarao, K., "On the Design of Replicated Databases," *Information Sciences,* Vol. 65, No. 1 and 2, 1992, pp. 173–200.

Buckles, B.P., and Harding, D.M., "Partitioning and Allocation of Logical Resources in a Distributed Computing Environment," *General Research Corporation Report,* Huntsville, Alabama, 1979.

Burleson, D., *Managing Distributed Databases,* John Wiley, 1994.

Casey, R.G., "Allocation of Copies of a File in an Information Network," *SJCC 1972,* AFIPS Press, Vol. 40, 1972.

Ceri, S., and Pelagatti, G., *Distributed Databases: Principles and Systems,* McGraw Hill, 1984.

Chadda, P., "Dancing with Data: Check Your Choreography," *Datamation,* 1995, pp. 59–64.

Chandy, D.M., and Hewes, J.E., "File Allocation in Distributed Systems," *Proc. of the Intl. Symp. on Computer Performance Modeling, Measurement and Evaluation,* March 1976, pp. 10–13.

Chang, S.K., and Liu, A.C., "A Database File Allocation Problem," *COMPSAC,* 1981, pp. 18–22.

Chu, W.W., "Optimal File Allocation in a Multiple Computer System," *IEEE Transactions on Computers,* October 1969, pp. 885–889.

Coffman, E.G., Gelenbe, E., et al, "Optimization of the Number of Copies in Distributed Data-bases," *Proc. of the 7th IFIP Symposium on Computer Performance Modeling, Measurement and Evaluation,* May 1980, pp. 257–263.

Coulouris, G., and Dollimore, J., *Distributed Systems: Concepts and Design,* Addison Wesley, 1989.

Date, C., *An Introduction to Database Systems,* 6th ed., Vol. 1 and 2., Addison Wesley, 1995.

Davis, J., "Object-Relational Databases," *Distributed Computing Monitor,* Patricia Seybold Group, February 1995.

Dick, K., "Object Databases and the Web," *Object Magazine,* July 1996, p. 59.

Doty, K. W., McEntyre, P. L., and O'Reilly, J. G., "Task Allocation in a Distributed Computer System," *Proceedings of IEEE INFOCOM,* 1982, pp. 33–38.

Elmasri, R., and Navathe, S., *Fundamentals of Database Systems,* Benjamin Cummings, 1989.

English, L., "Data Quality; Meeting Customer Needs," *Data Management Review,* November 1996, pp. 44–51.

Eswaran, K.P., "Allocation of Records to Files and Files to Computer Networks," *IFIP,* 1974, pp. 304–307.

Everret, B., *Cluster Analysis,* Heinemann Educational Books LTD., London, 1974.

Finckenscher, G. "Automatic Distribution of Programs in MASCOT and ADA Environments," *Royal Signal and Radar Establishment,* London, 1984.

Fisher, M. L., and Hochbaum, D. sp., "Database Location in Computer Networks," *ACM Journal,* Vol. 27, No. 4, October 1980.

Foley, J., "Open the Gates to Objects," *Information Week,* May 13, 1996, pp. 44–51.

Garner, R., "Of CIOS and Rocket Scientists," *Client/Server Journal,* Computerworld Special Issue, June 1995, p. 13.

Gray, J., "An Approach to Decentralized Computer Systems," *IEEE Transactions on Software Engineering,* June 1986, pp. 684–692.

Gray, J., "Evolution of Data Management," *IEEE Computer Magazine,* October 1996, pp. 38–46.

Griffin, J., "Customer Information Architecture," *DBMS,* July 1995, pp. 58–63.

Hackathorn, R., *Enterprise Database Connectivity,* John Wiley, 1993.

Haynes, P., "Web DBC Enables Top Real Estate Company," *Internet Advisor,* Premiere Issue, 1996, pp. 30–31.

Inmon, W., "Data Architectures: The Information Paradigm," *QED,* 1989.

Irani, K.B., and Khabbaz, N.G., "A Combined Communication Network Design and File Allocation for Distributed Databases," *2d Intl Conference on Distributed Systems,* Paris, April 1981.

Jain, H., "A Comprehensive Model for the Design of Distributed Computer Systems," *IEEE Transactions on Software Engineering,* October 1987, pp. 1092–1104.

Jessup, T., "WAN Design with Client-Server in Mind," *Data Communications Magazine,* August 1996, pp. 52–60.

Katz, R., Scachi, W., and Subrahmanyam, P., "Environments for VLSI and Software Engineering," *The Journal of Systems and Software 4*, 1984, pp. 13-26.

Kleinrock, L., *Queuing Systems,* Vol. 2, John Wiley, 1976.

Kleinrock, L., "Distributed Systems," *Communications of the ACM,* November 1985, Vol. 18, No. 11, pp. 1200–1213.

Koh, K., and Eom, Y.I "A File Allocation Scheme for Minimizing the Storage Cost in Distributed Computing Systems," *First Pacific Computer Communication Symposium,* Seoul, Korea, October 1985, pp. 310–317.

Larson, R. E., et al., "Distributed Control: Tutorial," *IEEE Catalog No. EHO 199-O,* October 1982.

Levin, K. D., and Morgan, K. H., "Optimizing Distributed Databases–A Framework for Research," *Proc. NCC,* 1975, Vol. 44, pp. 473–478.

Mahmood, S., and Riordan, J. S., "Optimal Allocation of Resources in Distributed Information Networks," *ACM Transaction on Database Systems,* Vol. 1, No. 1, March 1976, pp. 66–78.

Mariani, M. P., and Palmer, D. F. (eds.), "Tutorial: Distributed System Design," *EHO 151-1, IEEE Computer Society,* 1979.

Mariani, M. P., and Palmer, D. F., "Software Development for Distributed Computing Systems," *Handbook of Software Engineering,* ed. by C. V. Ramamoorthy and C. R. Vick, Van Nostrand, 1984, pp. 656–674.

Martin, J., and Leben, J., *Client/Server Databases,* Prentice Hall, 1995.

Melton, J., "Assessing SQL3's New Object Direction," *Database Programming and Design,* August 1996, pp. 51–56.

Negoita, C., *Expert Systems and Fuzzy Sets,* Benjamin Cummings, 1985.

Nitzberg, B., and Lo, V., "Distributed Shared Memory: A Survey of Issues and Approaches," *IEEE Computer,* August 1991, pp. 52–60.

O'Neil, P., *Database: Principles, Programming, Performance,* Morgan Kaufman, 1994.

Ozsu, M., and Valduriez, P., "Distributed Database Systems: Where Are We Now?" *IEEE Computer,* August 1991, pp. 68–78.

Ozsu, M., and Valduriez, P., *Principles of Distributed Database Systems,* Prentice Hall, 1991.

Patrick, R.L., *Application Design Handbook for Distributed Systems,* CBI Publishing Co., 1980.

Percy, A., "Data Consistency in the Mobile World," *Gartner Group Research Note,* December 23, 1996.

Ramamoorthy, C. V., and Vick, C. R., *Handbook of Software Engineering,* Van Nostrand, 1984.

Ramamoorthy, C. V., Garg, V., and Prakash, A., "Programming in the Large," *IEEE Transactions on Software Engineering,* Vol. SE-12, No. 7, July 1986, pp. 769–783.

Redman, T., *Data Quality,* Bantam Books, 1992.

Reingruber, M., and Gregory, W., *The Data Modeling Handbook,* John Wiley, 1994.

Ricciuti, M., "Universal Data Access!" *Datamation,* November 1, 1991.

Ricciuti, M., "Here Come The HR Client/Server Systems," *Datamation,* July 1, 1992.

Rymer, J., "Business Intelligence: The Third Tier," *Distributed Computing Monitor,* June 1995.

Salami, J., *PC Magazine Guide to Client/Server Databases,* Ziff-Davis, 1993.

Sayles, J., "Enterprise Client-Server Database Design and Tuning: Parts 1, 2, and 3," *Database Adviser,* April-June, 1996.

Scherberger, K., and Smith, C., "Data Synchronization Model: Part 1 and Part 2," *Gartner Group Research Note,* February 5, 1997.

Teorey, T.J., and Fry, J.P., *Design of Database Structures,* Prentice Hall, 1982.

Teorey, T.J., *Database Modeling and Design,* 2d ed., Morgan Kaufmann, 1994.

Teorey, T. J., and Umar, A., "Distributed Database Design Strategies," *Database Design and Programming,* April 1989.

Umar, A., "The Allocation of Data and Programs in Distributed Data Processing Environments," Ph. D. Dissertation, University of Michigan, 1984.

Umar, A., *Distributed Computing and Client/Server Systems,* Prentice Hall, 1993.

Umar, A., *Object-Oriented Client/Server Internet Environments,* Prentice Hall, 1997.

Umar, A., and Teorey, T. J., "A Generalized Approach to Program and Data Allocation in Distributed Systems," *First Pacific Computer Communication Symposium,* Seoul, Korea, October 1985, pp. 462–472.

Umar, A., and Teichroew, D., "Computer-Aided Software Engineering for Distributed Systems," *Proceedings of IEEE Conference on Computer Communications,* Seoul, Korea, August, 1987.

Umar, A., and Teichroew, D., "Pragmatic Issues in Conversions of Database Applications," *Information and Management Journal,* 19 (1990), pp. 149–166.

Valigra, L., "Good Medicine for Big Hospitals," *Client/Server Computing,* April 1996, pp. 32–38.

Wand, Y., and Wang, R., "Anchoring Data Quality Dimensions in Ontological Foundations," *Communications of the ACM,* November 1996, pp. 86–95.

White, S., "A Pragmatic Formal Method for Specifications and Analysis of Embedded Computer Systems," Ph. D. Dissertation, Polytechnic Institute of New York, May, 1987.

Wohl, Amy, "Is Downsizing Right for You?" *Beyond Computing,* IBM Publication, August/September 1992, pp.10–11.

Woodside, C. M., and Tripathi, S.K., "Optimal Allocation of File Servers in a Local Area Network Environment," *IEEE Transactions on Software Engineering,* August 1986, Vol. SE-12, No. 8, pp. 844–848.

Wreden, N., "The Ups and Downs of Downsizing," *Beyond Computing,* IBM Publication, August/September 1992, pp. 12–15.

Yau, S. S., Jia, X., and Bae, D. H., "Software Design for Distributed Computer Systems," *Computer Communications,* Vol. 15, No. 4, May 1992, pp. 213–224.

6

Web-Based Application Software Architectures

6.1   Introduction

This chapter deals with developing software architectures for flexible, portable, and interoperable Web-based applications to satisfy growing enterprise needs. An application software architecture when combined with the data architecture produces an application architecture because (see Figure 6.1):[1]

> Application architecture = data architecture + application software architectures + IT infrastructure

Software architecture, as you will see when you go through this chapter, is an extensive activity that involves analysis and evaluation of a very large number of alternatives. Is it always needed so rigorously? Well, not always. Basically, software architecture should be a lightweight activity if you are buying an off-the shelf application. In addition, this activity may not be necessary if you are developing a decision support application (for DSS, you build a database and typically use off-the-shelf-packages for queries). The primary focus of this chapter is on software architectures for enterprisewide operational support applications. This class of applications raises fundamental questions such as the following:

- How can an application model (an object model) be developed to faithfully represent the application functional requirements?
- How can the application be decomposed into clients and servers to provide maximum flexibility and suitability?

---

1. Should data architecture be completed before software architecture, or vice versa? It depends. In database intensive applications, such as decision support systems, the data architectures should be completed before software architectures. The reverse is true in business processing intensive applications, such as operational support systems, In many practical situations, software and data architectures are developed in parallel as an iterative process. Depending on your situation, you may want to read this chapter before Chapter 5, or vice versa.

- Which tiering approach (i.e., two versus three tiers) will be most suitable for this application?
- What are the most appropriate infrastructure services needed by the application to provide maximum portability and interoperability? In particular, how can the applications take advantage of existing and evolving open standards and architectures?
- Where will the application components (e.g., databases, programs, user interfaces) be allocated to maximize performance and availability?
- What is the state of the art, state of the market, and state of the practice in software architectures?

The approach presented in this chapter attempts to answer these questions systematically and provides a road map to proceed with this venture. Our objective is to provide you with a checklist of issues and suggested courses of actions which you can modify, extend, and trim depending on the size of the project (spending a year on establishing software architecture for a small application to be used by 10 people is absurd). How about software architectures for DSS applications? DSS applications are data intensive and thus the enterprise data architecture and design activities described in the previous chapter are essential for DSS. The software architecture activity, as stated previously, is lightweight or even nonexistent because most DSS work can be done through off-the-shelf query and analysis tools. We will discuss the DSS specific architecture issues in a later chapter on data warehouses. The discussion of software architectures in this chapter when combined with the data architectures and data warehouses provides strategies for decision support as well as operational applications.

Figure 6.1 Application Architecture Components

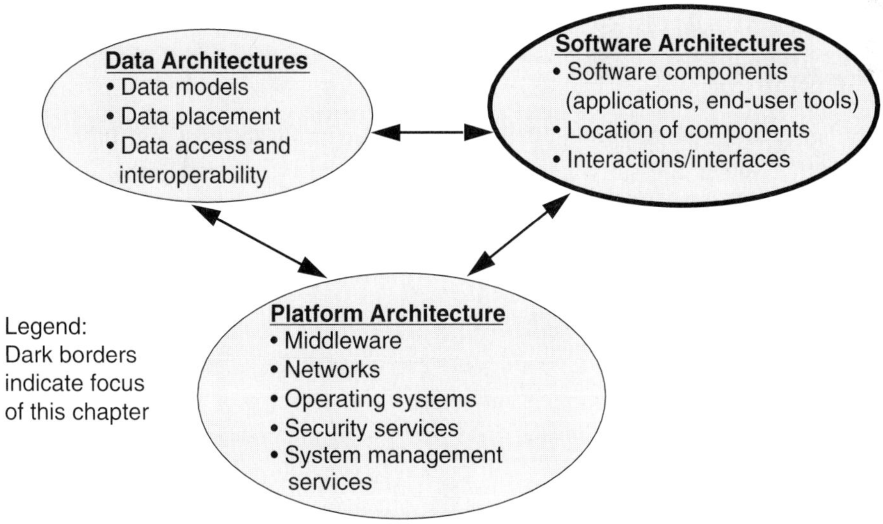

Key Points

- A good test of software architectures is their longevity—a well-architected application should last for a long time (five years or more) despite changes in user requirements, workloads, computing hardware, network configurations, and middleware.
- Communication between architects and developers is crucial and should be planned for through frequent walkthroughs and other communication tools (e.g., e-mail, meetings, etc.).
- Software architecture should be a lightweight activity for applications that will use off-the-shelf software (many decisions are made by the suppliers) and are heavyweight for applications that require large-scale new software development.
- Importance of architectures increases with size—the larger the application, the more attention needs to be paid to architectures.
- Separation of issues between presentation, application logic, and data management is important for application maintainability and portability.
- Develop application objects to keep reuse in mind, that is, objects developed for one application should be reusable in other applications.
- Choose standards-based (open, de facto, de jour) architectures to minimize the impact of platform and hardware selection/modification on distributed applications.
- The application architecture should be flexible and open enough so that the selection and modification of the platforms do not affect the architecture and the implemented application. Thus, an investment in implemented applications is protected despite platform and vendor changes.

6.2   Software Architecture Concepts

6.2.1   Definition

The term "software architecture" is being used increasingly to represent high-level design information that shows the software components and the interactions among these components [Garlan 1993], [Perry 1992], [Shaw 1995], [Mowbray 1995], and [Salim 1997]. We will use the following definition of *software architecture* that was developed in a software architecture discussion at the Software Engineering Institute [Garlan 1995]:

> The structure of the components of a program/system, their interrelationships, and principles and guidelines governing their design and evolution over time.

The basic purpose of the software architecture is to develop a formal specification that enables implementors to build applications and system integrators to interface applications with other applications and/or off-the-shelf packages. The output produced by an application architecture is a document that specifies (a) the physical components of the application, (b) the functions performed by these components, and (c) their interrelationships and interfaces.

As stated in a previous chapter, development of architectures for enterprisewide Object-oriented Client/Server Internet (OCSI) applications is similar to establishing design of a city for an ever-changing and ever-evolving industrial and residential population. You have to worry more about how the individual parts of the city will be known to the city dwellers and how will they be interconnected (i.e., the infrastructure needed), instead of how the individual buildings will be designed internally (you basically establish policy, rules and guidelines for the buildings). In a similar vein, designing architectures of OCSI applications is like designing many mini-applications that need to interact with each other for corporate business goals. The emphasis is on identifying the individual components (i.e., objects) of the application, and the infrastructure needed to make this application operable as an enterprisewide application.

It may be argued that the notion of developing software architecture is outdated because the work in business objects, object frameworks, and component-based software will make it possible for us to assemble the applications "on the fly." While this is an interesting notion and should be pursued diligently, we should be careful not to develop the generic wheel that can fit everything that moves (bicycles, cars, trains, and airplanes). This difficulty has been recognized in the industry [Rymer 1995]. In the meantime, we are focusing on developing application pieces that can be reused and or customized for other applications.

6.2.2   A Software Architecture Approach

Development of software architecture for OCSI applications is quite complex. The architects must take into account the data architectures, the application requirements (functional, operational, organizational), existing applications that may need to be interfaced with, off-the- shelf products, and the ever-evolving infrastructures and standards. An approach is needed which decomposes the architecture activity into smaller and simpler steps. Figure 6.2 shows such an approach, consisting of the following major steps:

Step 1. Refine and extend the object model to represent the abstract components of the application and abstract messages between these objects. Granularity of objects (i.e., small objects that represent program routines versus large "business object" that represent business entities) is a major concern. This step uses the commonly used OO analysis and design techniques, introduced in Chapter 3, to build an abstract model that captures the functional requirements of the system in a tool and implementation-independent fashion. None of the infrastructure-related information is relevant in this step. See Section 6.3 for details.

Step 2. Separate the concerns by grouping the objects into three layers: presentation, application logic, and data management. This separation of concerns promotes the notions of interoperability, reuse, and manageability of applications in distributed environments because different modules can be designed and deployed on different machines for different presentation styles, user groups, and data management software. Section 6.4 gives details of this step.

Figure 6.2 Software Architecture Steps

Step 1: Develop/Extend an Object Model

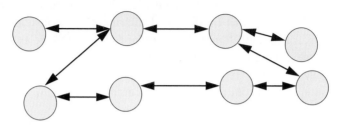

Step 2: Separate Concerns (Logical Tiers)

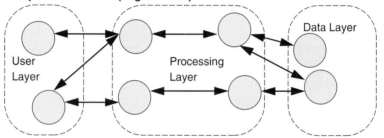

Step 3: Decompose Application into Client and Server Programs

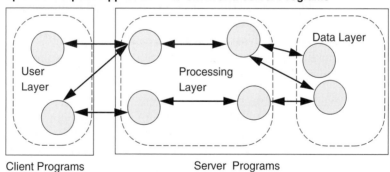

Client Programs   Server Programs

Step 4: Evaluate and Choose Infrastructure

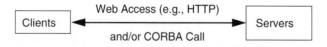

Step 5: Analyze Performance and Allocation Trade-offs

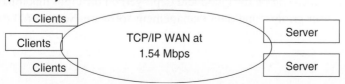

Step 3. Cast the logical architecture into a first-cut client/server configuration which identifies the *physical tiers* (i.e., physical levels of distribution) of the application. A single-tiered system represents the classical terminal host model in which all application objects (user, processing, and data) are restricted to one computing machine. Details about this step with a discussion of trade-offs between different tiering strategies, especially between two- versus three-tiered systems, can be found in Section 6.5.

Step 4. Evaluate and select the appropriate infrastructure needed to support the application. This step requires examination of a wide range of issues such as APIs, exchange protocols, data management software, object request brokers, directory services, network services, and so on. This is a challenging step, especially when numerous distributed applications span multivendor environments. See Section 6.6 for more details.

Step 5. Allocate the objects to various computers and analyze performance trade-offs. Other factors may include security, administrative support, availability, business pressures, and so on. The main decision is to determine the best sites for allocation of data, processes, and user interface handling. The performance can be improved by locating data at the sites where they are most frequently used and the availability can be improved by replicating programs and data to more than one site. However, this increases the complexity and security exposure of the application systems. This step is discussed in detail in Section 6.7.

These steps may need to be performed iteratively before an acceptable architecture is reached. The decisions made in these steps accept a large number of inputs such as application system requirements (functional, performance, interconnectivity, etc.), the underlying infrastructure needed (network architecture and design, computer systems, middleware available), and the emerging standards.

6.2.3 Organizational Notes

Development of an application architecture is an intensely iterative and stepwise refinement process that requires experimentation, discovery, and communication between different groups. How can the architecture activity be organized? Here are some thoughts:

- Use a single (chief) architect
- Use a team of architects
- Establish a corporate architecture group

The chief architect approach usually provides a coherent and elegant architecture. This depends, of course, on the background of the chief architect and the size of the project. A team of architects may be needed in large projects when different contingencies from different technology and user groups need to be considered. The risk of architecture teams is that it can lead to complex architectures because it is often easier to include additional complexity due to compromise than to engage in bitter battles [Mowbray 1995]. For this reason, it may be advisable for large organizations to establish a corporate architecture group to provide overall guidance to the various development groups in an organization. This group can help in choosing an enterprisewide infrastructure and participate in application development projects as architects (see Figure 6.3). This group can effectively provide interoperability, portability, and integration of applications by imbedding appropriate choices in the enterprise information architectures and guidelines. Although the guidelines can vary widely between organizations, a set of sample guidelines based on the ANSA Consortium are suggested in the sidebar "Sample Guidelines for Application Architectures." Several organizations have adopted this approach.[2]

Figure 6.3 Application Architecture Organizational Approaches

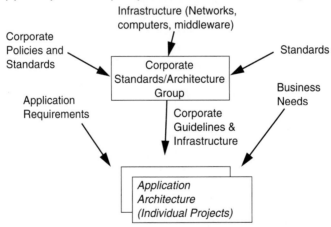

(a) Each Group Defines Individual Architecture

(b) A Corporate Group Helps Individual Architecture Groups

Notes:
• The corporate group can monitor the developments in industry standards, infrastructure technology evolution, and corporate policies, thus freeing the individual groups from this burden (good news).
• The corporate groups can hinder quick application deployments (bad news).

---

2. The Bellcore OSCA Architecture provides a set of guidelines that have been used for this purpose in the telecommunications industry.

SAMPLE GUIDELINES FOR APPLICATION ARCHITECTURES
Source: ANSA Consortium [Herbert 1994]

- Define services in terms of function, quality of delivery, and ownership.
- Exploit distribution and federation as much as possible by reversing centralized, single-processor, single-manager assumptions.
- Hide irrelevant detail to reduce complexity and expose necessary details to obtain control.
- All components should be assumed to be physically or logically remote from one another.
- The architecture must tolerate all types of failures, including partial ones.
- It must not be assumed that some inherent system characteristics will synchronize processes.
- Do not assume the existence of a universal data pool that can be accessed directly from everywhere.
- Architectural components must be efficient in small systems and sufficiently functional to fit large systems.
- Federation (i.e., loosely coupled autonomous components) should be utilized as much as possible.
- Architects should indicate where parallelism is possible or required but should abstain from *how* it is to be achieved.
- Late binding of clients to servers is essential, that is, the clients should not know the exact location of the server before run time.

6.3 Step 1: Refine/Extend the Object Model

An ***object model*** is an abstract model that captures the functional requirements of the system in a tool and implementation-independent fashion. We discussed development of an object model in the feasibility/prototyping iteration of the general methodology (Chapter 3). Establishing an information model, discussed in the previous chapter, concentrates on the data aspects of the object model (i.e., objects, attributes to represent the objects, and interrelationships between objects). We now need to proceed further and refine/extend the object model by using the following activities:

- Determine operations on the objects
- Establish the interfaces of each object. Each object has one or more interfaces.
- Refine the model through iterations

We have already discussed these activities in Chapter 3. Let us quickly recap them before proceeding.

The primary objective of this step is to describe and formalize the operations that will be supported by the objects identified in earlier iterations. The operations supported by each object are listed as a starting point and refined by using the following guidelines [Rumbaugh 1994]:

- You do not need to represent *all* operations on an object. You should primarily identify those operations that are needed by the users of the application at hand.

- The operations external to the current application should only be considered if the external operations change the state of the object. If they do, you must synchronize the activities in order to ensure integrity of object data.

Figure 6.4 illustrates the results of identifying objects and their operations for a simple customer information system. The customer object must provide four ***methods*** (i.e., software instructions) that are invoked when operations such as add a customer, view a customer, update customer information, and delete a customer are invoked.

The ***Interface*** of an object is the collection of the operations and their ***signatures*** (signature of an operation defines the operation's name, its arguments, and argument types). For example, the following statements could be used to specify the interface for a customer object that supports two operations: create customer and view customer (the language is illustrative):

```
interface customer /* interface name is customer */
 Operation add_cust (/*The operation is add_cust */
   [in] char customer_info;   /* input parameter */
   [out] integer status ) /* output parameter */
 Operation view-cust ( /*The operation is view_cust */
   [in] char cust-id; /* input parameter is cust-id */
   [out] char customer_info; /* output parameter 1*/
   [out] integer status ) /* output parameter 2 */
```

Interface Definition Languages (IDLs) are provided by middleware (e.g., OSF DCE IDL and CORBA IDL) for defining interfaces formally. The interface definitions are compiled by using vendor-provided IDL compilers and can be stored in an interface repository for other objects to utilize. We will discuss IDLs in more detail in the next chapter. Interfaces can be, at least, of the following kinds:

- Operational interfaces,

- Stream interfaces, and

- Management interfaces.

Figure 6.4 An Example of Object Operations

Object	Operations	Inputs	Outputs
Customer	1. Add a customer	Customer Information	Status
	2. View customer information	Account number	Customer information
	3. Update customer information	Account number, new information	Status
	4. Delete a customer	Account number	Status

Operational interfaces contain a set of named operations (i.e., methods or procedures) needed for applications. Stream interfaces use a set of linked information flows for unstructured communications needed for multimedia applications. Management interfaces are used for diagnosing and controlling distributed objects. The example of the interface definition (Figure 6.4) is an operational interface. Operational interfaces have the typical remote procedure call style of interactions. Stream interfaces, on the other hand, are used to describe unstructured communications such as video, voice streams, multimedia information, and e-mail. Management interfaces are used for network management applications. Available middleware may or may not support different types of interfaces. We will discuss IDL and these interfaces in the next chapter.

In large-scale distributed systems, additional information about the semantics and pragmatics (e.g., performance and security) is needed for a complete service to be provided by an object. This information can be documented as a *service specification* which refers to an interface that actually provides this service. Keep in mind that we are only describing the pieces of information that should be collected and *somehow* documented. This, and other information, will serve to evaluate and choose the most appropriate infrastructure support (e.g., development and run-time environment) needed by an application. We will briefly review the development environments in the next chapter.

Interfaces and service specifications are the major mechanism for applications to interoperate with each other. For example, different objects may reside on different computers, interconnected through different networks, under different operating systems, and use different database managers. A description of an object's inputs, outputs, syntax, semantics and pragmatics (e.g., performance and security) unambiguously defines the functions it provides to other objects. For an object to be interoperable, all of its interfaces (and therefore all of its functions) must be documented and fully supported. Other than these interfaces, no object needs to know the internal logistics of any other object. Thus an object can be substituted by another object with the same interfaces. The functions performed within each object must show high cohesion with each other and low coupling with the functions of other objects.

6.4   Step 2: Separate Concerns (Layers)

A key trend in current applications is the separation of business rules (i.e., the functional logic unique to the user organization) from the presentation (user interface) and data management functions of applications. This separation of concerns leads to a three-layered application architecture: presentation services, data services, and processing services. This separation promotes the notions of interoperability, reuse, and manageability of applications in distributed environments (see, for example, the Hyatt case study [Grygo 1995]). For example, different modules can be designed and deployed on different machines for different presentation styles, user groups, and data management software by using layered concepts. Although the C/S community seems to have "discovered" the glory of layered architectures (see the sidebar "What Are Tiers?"), this concept has been formalized and used in the telecommunications industry through the Bellcore OSCA Architecture[3] since the late 1980s. For purpose of illustration, we will briefly discuss how the OSCA Architecture concepts can be applied to the object model developed in Step 1. You can, of course, use any other guidelines.

The OSCA Architecture is a set of well-known guidelines in the telecommunications industry. These guidelines allow the combination of software products from many suppliers and promote interoperability of products that span mainframes, minicomputers, and desktops. Objectives of the OSCA architecture are to (a) provide an implementation-independent framework to give the business enterprise the needed flexibility, (b) combine software products in ways which best satisfy their business needs, and (c) provide access to corporate data by all authorized users. Basically, OSCA categorizes the objects into three logical layers (see Figure 6.5):

- **Data layer**, which shows the corporate data management functionality.
- **Processing layer**, which shows the business aware operations and control functions (e.g., business rules).
- **User layer**, which reflects human interaction functionality.

---

3. Bellcore OSCA Architecture, a trademark of Bell Communications Research, is described in "The Bellcore OSCA Architecture," Technical Advisory, TA-STS-000915, Issue 3, 1992. Additional information can be found in Mills [1991], and Umar [1993].

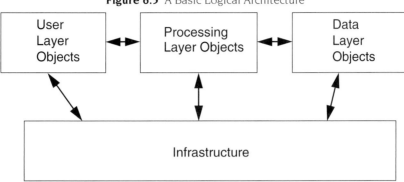

Figure 6.5 A Basic Logical Architecture

Figure 6.6 presents different applications, ranging from simple to complex, in terms of the layers.

Corporate data, a key element of OSCA Architecture, are viewed as data that are shared across the business processes of a corporation and are partitioned into portions, each of which is *stewarded* by a data layer object. In addition to the corporate data, each object may have private data which are not shared and are not visible to other objects. Private data may be redundant, permanently stored, or may be working data. The following OSCA guidelines to promote interoperability and portability should be of value (we have "objectified" some of the OSCA terms here to avoid another set of terms—we have enough terms the way it is):[4]

- Release independence: Each instance of an object must be able to be installed and updated without concurrently installing other instances of itself and other objects.

Figure 6.6 Views of Application Layers

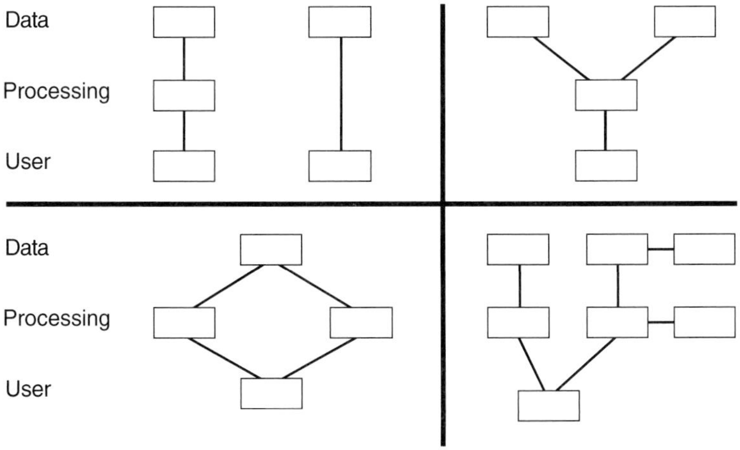

Data			
Processing			
User			

---

4. The term "object" in these guidelines should be viewed as a building block of the application (i.e., a large object) that can be installed and maintained independently of other objects.

- Infrastructure and resource independence: Objects can share infrastructure and resources as long as no violation of portability occurs.

- Unavailability semantics: Each object communicating with another object must be able to respond to the unavailability of the target object and not itself become unavailable in the process.

- One recoverable domain: Each object is deployed in a single recoverable domain which represents the span of control of a single transaction manager (the transaction manager may be distributed among many computers).

- Location independence: Addressable units, such as objects, are identified by logical addresses that are network location independent.

- Contract independence: All interactions among objects are defined by contracts (i.e., interfaces) to attain interoperability. Thus contracts must be defined for general use, must employ widely used syntax encoding, and infrastructure services used must be based on standards.

- Secure environment: An object must provide a secure environment with full support for authentication and journaling/logging.

These guidelines can be, and should be, added to the sample guidelines suggested in the sidebar "Sample Guidelines for Application Architectures."

6.5   Step 3: Decompose Application into Tiers

As a result of the previous steps, application objects are clustered into layers and the abstract messages between these objects are specified. The next step is to structure and cast these objects into a physical client/server configuration. Figure 6.7 shows how the object model represented in terms of user, processing, and data layer objects can be cast into levels of distribution (*hardware tiers*). See the sidebar "What Are Tiers?" An application can be physically configured as following (see Figure 6.7):

> **Single Tiered (one level of distribution)**: In this case, all application layers (user, processing, and data objects) are assigned to one computer (typically a mainframe or a mid-range computer). This configuration represents the traditional terminal-host model.
>
> **Two Tiered (two levels of distribution)**: The application layers are split between "front-end" and "back-end" computers. The front-end computer provides the user interface objects (a client machine) and the back-end computer provides the database support. The processing logic is assigned to the client machine in typical two-tiered C/S applications (e.g., Power-Builder), but may reside on the back end.
>
> **Three Tiered (three levels of distribution):** The application layers are split across three types of machines: a front-end machine (usually a desktop), a middle machine (usually a LAN server or a minicomputer) and a back-end machine (usually a mainframe).

What Are Tiers?

The term "tiers" is used commonly in the C/S literature. However, there is no general agreement about what a tier is. In the literature, tiers are used to indicate two different things [Porter 1997], [Shulte 1996], [Frye 1996], [Schulte 1995], [Dickman 1995], and [Comport 1995]:

Software tiers: treat each *layer* of application (user, processing, data) as a tier.

Hardware tiers: treat each *level* of machine (client machine, server machine, intermediate machine) as a tier.

Although seldom stated explicitly, most discussions about tiers assume hardware tiers. For example, two-tiered architectures commonly refer to the traditional C/S applications that use remote SQL to access database servers (tier 2 machines) from programs and user interfaces residing at desktops (tier 1 machines); and three-tiered architecture introduces a middle machine dedicated to application logic [Dickman 1995]. However, in some cases, the term tier is implicitly used to indicate software tiers [Frye 1996].

We recognize the need for separating software tiers (the three layers) from the hardware tiers. For example, an application may have three software tiers but one, two, three, or even four hardware tiers (see Figure 6.7).

To avoid confusion, we will use the term **application layer** to indicate software tier and the term **tier** to indicate hardware tiers. For example, when we say two tiers, it means two levels of machines (client machine and a server machine) and does not say anything about number of application layers (some applications may have only data and user layers).

Naturally the notion of hardware tiers is of importance in distributed systems because it indicates levels of distribution. A single-tier application indicates a centralized application and a two-tier application means that the application layers are distributed over two levels of machines connected over a network.

Determination of an appropriate level of distribution (hardware tiers) is of fundamental importance in application architectures. This decision impacts the choice of infrastructure, especially middleware, performance results, and implementation considerations. We discuss these issues in the following subsections.

In addition to identifying the tiers, you also need to determine how the processes in different tiers will communicate with each other. The communications may use paradigms such as Remote Procedure Calls (RPCs), Remote Data Access (RDAs), Message-Oriented Middleware (MOM), Object Request Brokers (ORBs), and even file transfers and e-mail. This amounts to translating the abstract messages between objects to communication messages.

The major issues to be considered are: How many hardware tiers to use (the primary concern is two- versus three-tiered applications), how much functionality (application objects) should be treated as clients versus servers (fat clients versus fat servers), and what type of interaction paradigms will be used (remote procedure calls, remote data access, queued messages, object brokers, and file transfer). These issues are discussed next. Before getting into detailed trade-offs, we should remember that the choice does depend on the type of application (see, for example, Table 6.1, that shows the typical choices made for On-Line Transaction Processing (OLTP) and decision support applications).

Figure 6.7 Software to Hardware Tiers (Typical Configurations)

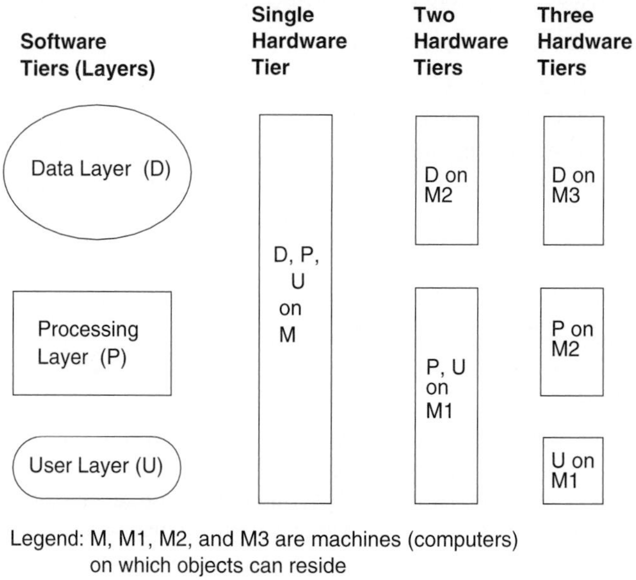

Legend: M, M1, M2, and M3 are machines (computers) on which objects can reside

TABLE 6.1 TYPICAL CHOICES FOR TYPICAL APPLICATIONS

Application Types Configuration Choices	Decision Support Applications	On-line Transaction Processing (OLTP) Applications
Software Tiers (Layers)	Two layers because most work requires ad hoc queries	Three layers (typically many business rules)
Hardware tiers	Two tiered works well (i.e., use a remote database server)	Three tiered may be needed
Fat client versus fat server	Fat client	Fat server
Access paradigms	RDA	RPC, MOM, ORB

6.5.1 Single-Tiered Application Architectures

The single-tiered (terminal-host) application architectures typically do not get any respect because they represent the "old mainframe model." However, this model is still quite suitable for mission-critical OLTP applications. Since the early 1970s, the CICS- and IMS-based OLTP systems have gradually improved in performance, reliability, and administrative control features. The C/S transaction processing middleware, on the other hand, is still evolving (see C/S transaction processing discussion in Umar [1997], Chapter 6). Availability of industrial strength C/S transaction processors is a crucial issue for enterprisewide C/S applications [Natis 1996] and [Johnson 1995]. In the meantime, single-tiered architectures may still be a viable choice for enterprisewide mission-critical applications that require strong central control and high transactions per second for thousands of users.

Some observers feel that the "network computers," introduced by Oracle, operate roughly around a single-tiered application architecture [Porter 1997]. A network computer is essentially an appliance with a very simple operating system and no disk. It downloads whatever functions are needed from powerful back-end servers. In addition, Web-server based applications are close to the single-tiered applications.

6.5.2 Two-Tiered Application Architectures

Figure 6.8 shows two-tiered application architectures that represent how the user interfaces, processing programs, and databases can be distributed at two levels (tiers)—the client and server machines. These architectural configurations were first introduced by the Gartner Group. We have extended this model to indicate the typical exchange protocols used in the Web-based application architectures such as HTTP, IIOP, DCOM, RPCs, MOM, and RDA (see the sidebar "Common Exchange Protocols between Remote Processes" for a quick synopsis).

The architecture shown in Figure 6.8 (a) shows the simplest architecture where the presentation (user interface) is assigned to the client machine, usually a desktop computer. This architecture, used in many presentation-intensive applications, has the benefit that the user interface processing is parcelled out to the end-user sites. It especially fits very well for situations where different user interfaces for the same application are needed. For example, user interfaces in different languages (e.g., Chinese, Japanese, French) and/or different graphical symbols and toolbars can be easily supported by the remote presentation architecture.This architecture is commonly used in the Web-based applications where the client is the Web browser and everything else (HTML documents, CGI programs, and databases) reside on the Web server site. The protocols used can be HTTP (to access HTML documents and invoke CGI programs), CORBA IIOP (to invoke CORBA objects from the Netscape-IIOP enabled browsers), and/or DCOM (to invoke remotely located spreadsheets, Java applets, and other ActiveX components).

The distributed presentation architecture shown in Figure 6.8 (b) is employed in many cases to provide a "face lift" to legacy applications by building a Web interface that invokes the older text-based user interfaces of legacy applications. A set of tools, commonly referred to as ***screen*** *scrapers*, have emerged for this face lifting (see Chapter 9 for details). For Web-based applications, this configuration may be used to provide Web interfaces to an existing application. Typical exchange protocols used in this configuration are HTTP, CORBA IIOP, and DCOM.

Figure 6.8 (c) represents the distributed application program architecture in which the processing programs are split between the client and server machines. This architecture, implemented in the very popular Remote Procedure Call (RPC) systems, is based on message exchange between two remote programs. This architecture is especially appealing for the situations where it is not advisable to parcel the entire processing logic to the client machines. In particular, many enterprises have common application logic that is better kept at the corporate center to enforce corporatewide rules. A typical exchange protocol used between the client and server program modules is RPC, although CORBA and queued message MOM-based solutions are gaining popularity. This architecture also suits the situations where a small amount of message exchange is needed between clients and servers and a great deal of processing time is used on both sites (e.g., enterprisewide applications that need to use the relatively slow WAN lines). For Web-based applications, this application supports Java applets on the client side that may invoke programs on the Web server or other servers through RPCs, DCOM, and CORBA.

Figure 6.8 Two-Tiered Application Architectures

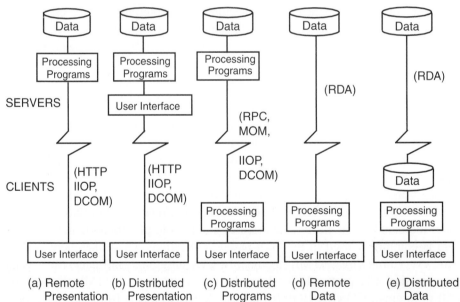

(a) Remote Presentation   (b) Distributed Presentation   (c) Distributed Programs   (d) Remote Data   (e) Distributed Data

Note 1: The application software on client side may be implemented as Java applets.
Note 2: The application components can be separated by a firewall so that some (or all) components can reside inside a secure corporate Intranet while others can reside in the public Internet. For example, the database and application logic can be inside the firewall but the user interfaces may be outside the firewalls.

Fat Clients versus Fat Servers

A client or a server is considered "fat" if it provides many functions (i.e., has many objects). The trade-offs between fat clients versus fat servers need to be considered when the application objects are assigned to two or three tiers. The following guidelines and rules of thumb can be used to decide between fat clients versus fat servers:

OLTP versus decision support applications: OLTP applications generally require fat servers because more functionality is needed at the database site (commits, logging, rollbacks, etc.). On the other hand, decision support applications generally require fat clients because each user can run his/her own tools (e.g., spreadsheets, data browsers, report writers) that access a back-end database.

Cost, security, and performance considerations: Fat clients can be more expensive to support because more powerful client machines and associated software are needed. Fat servers can be used to enforce corporatewide business rules and security requirements. However, fat servers can become performance bottlenecks.

Location specificity: Some application objects are location specific—they must exist at a given specific location. For example, company financial information must be kept at the corporate office, manufacturing device status information needs to be kept on the plant floor, and so forth. Thus location-specific knowledge can be used to assign application objects to clients or servers. An object can be location specific due to

- User requirements for some operations and data to be performed at certain sites
- Security and management restrictions which require some components to be restricted to certain sites such as a corporate office
- Similarity and natural affinity of certain processes to certain sites (e.g., most manufacturing operations are performed on the plant floor)
- Architecture matching the functionality (e.g., workstations for user interfaces and minicomputers for database servers)
- Financial considerations (e.g., an animation must be performed on the machines which have software licenses for the animation packages)

Impact of purchased software: A readily available business software package may automatically cluster many objects together and may also determine whether these objects will behave as clients or servers. Thus a buy versus build decision can make the client or the sever fat. While it is a good idea to buy rather than to build, you should not buy 20 client application software packages which require 20 different servers and 20 different middleware packages to access the same corporate data. It is better to acquire one server which can support multiple clients from multiple suppliers (this requires open APIs and/or may require some software development).

Clustering: Objects can be grouped together to form "clusters." A cluster is essentially a collection of objects which cannot be subdivided among computers. For example, a purchased product can be considered a cluster because most purchased products cannot be subdivided into independent modules.

Common Exchange Protocols between Remote Processes

Remote Procedure Call (RPC). The client process invokes a remotely located procedure (a server process), the remote procedure executes, and sends the response back to the client. RPCs are supported widely at present.

Remote Data Access (RDA). The client programs and/or end-user tools issue ad hoc queries, usually SQL, against remotely located databases. RDA is heavily supported by database vendors.

Message-Oriented Middleware (MOM). The client message is stored in a queue and the server works on it when free. MOM support is becoming commonly available.

Hypertext Transfer Protocol (HTTP). An extremely simple request/response model that establishes a connection with the Web server from the Web browser, retrieves the needed document or invokes the CGI script, and closes the connection. HTTP is the core protocol between Web browsers and Web servers.

CORBA IIOP (Internet Inter-ORB Protocol). CORBA IIOP support provides CORBA message exchanges over the Internet. Netscape browsers support IIOP and all CORBA vendors support IIOP.

DCOM (Distributed Component Object Model). DCOM is the ORB in the Microsoft ActiveX environment—all ActiveX components communicate with each other by using DCOM.

For an extensive discussion of these, and other protocols, see the companion book [Umar 1997].

Figure 6.8 (d) represents the remote data architecture[5] in which the processing programs, in addition to the user interfaces, are fully assigned to the client machines. The remote data are typically stored in a "SQL server" and are accessed through ad hoc SQL statements sent over the network (i.e., the RDA protocol). This "fat client" architecture, used in many management decision support applications (spreadsheets, projections, simulations, etc.), is especially suitable for departmental/group C/S applications (ad hoc SQL over a slow corporate WAN causes "minor discomforts"). This architecture is very popular with the ever-increasing SQL Server vendors' CASE tools (e.g., PowerBuilder and Gupta SQL Windows) and is especially appealing for end users who need to perform different application processing on the same shared data (e.g., different users of a subject database need to perform different processing). This architecture also suits the situations where a small amount of remote data are accessed and a great deal of processing time is used in analyzing and presenting the data. However, this architecture can generate unpredictable traffic on the network because ad hoc SQL can result in a large amount of data that are selected and sent back to the client machine. Fast networks (e.g., LANs or broadband WANs) are a prerequisite for this architecture. In Web-based applications, this architecture supports Java programs and other programs (components in ActiveX) to access remotely located databases through ODBC (Open Database Connectivity) or JDBC (Java Database Connectivity).

---

5. This architecture is the most commonly used example of two-tiered architectures.

Figure 6.8 (e) represents the case where data, processing programs as well as user interfaces are distributed to many sites. In particular, the data exist at client as well as server machines (distributed data architecture). This architecture has many advantages (e.g., access to local data quickly), but it presents challenges of distributed data and transaction management (e.g., integrity of distributed and replicated data). Typical C/S protocols used for this architecture are the RDA and DTP (Distributed Transaction Processing) protocols such as two-phase commit and replication servers. Other variations include periodic bulk data transfer to update the client database and usage of "cache data" at the client side instead of a permanent database. A performance study based on detailed simulations has indicated that a cache-based C/S architecture shows superior performance to other popular configurations [Dale 1993]. In Web-based applications, this configuration is supported by ActiveX where the ActiveX components and SQL servers can reside on a platform such as Windows NT.

In essence, these five architectural configurations represent the continuum between completely centralized (all data, processing programs and user interfaces at one computer) and completely decentralized applications (no common data, application programs and user interfaces). These architectures provide the basis for a transition strategy from centralized to distributed applications in which the user interfaces are distributed first, followed by distribution of application programs and data. Table 6.2 shows trade-offs between these five archi-

TABLE 6.2 TRADE-OFFS BETWEEN SINGLE- AND TWO-TIERED ARCHITECTURES

	Terminal Host (Single Tiered)	Remote Presentation	Distributed Presentation	Distributed Programs	Remote Data	Distributed Data
Transaction needs	+3	+2	+2	+1	−2	−2
End-user flexibility and growth	−3	−2	−2	+2	+2	+3
Performance	−3	−2	−2	+2	+2	+3
Availability	−3	−2	−2	+2	+2	+3
Cost	+3	+2	+2	+1	−1	−3
Manageability and Control	+3	+3	+3	−2	−2	−3
Security	+3	+3	+3	−2	−2	−3

Legend: Evaluation factors (−3 to +3) indicate how well the configurations satisfy the requirements:
    −3 = does not satisfy at all
    +3 = very well satisfied
    0 = no impact

tectures and the single-tiered terminal host system in terms of transaction processing needs, flexibility, performance, availability, cost, manageability, and security. For example, Table 6.2 shows that more decentralization leads to improved flexibility, performance, and availability but raises some issues in manageability and security. It should be kept in mind that this table is suggested as a framework for analysis (the factors and the values can be modified if needed).

6.5.3 Three-Tiered Application Architectures

The configurations shown in Figure 6.9 show sample three-tiered application architectures with three levels of distribution (three tiers). In a three-tiered application model, the application layers are split across three machines: a front-end machine (usually a desktop equipped with a browser), a middle machine (usually a Web server or a LAN server on UNIX or Windows NT) and a back-end machine (usually a mainframe). The following two fundamental points need to be kept in mind:

- The interactions between every tier use a C/S model (e.g., real-time message exchange) for three-tiered C/S application architectures. Several case studies claim to have a three-tier C/S application architecture while in fact the exchange between the back end and middle machine is batch file transfer (the exchanges between the front end and middle machine are C/S). Such configurations should be referred to as **hybrid application** architectures instead of three-tiered C/S application architectures.

- Some business-aware functionality must exist at each of the tiers for a three-tiered application. In many real-life situations, the middle machines serve as gateways that essentially convert one type of protocol to another (e.g., network gateways that convert one type of network protocol to another and database gateways that convert one type of database call to another). Business-unaware gateways can make a C/S environment a three-tiered computing platform but not a three-tiered C/S application (recall from the definitions that C/S application implies business-aware functionality to be split across machines and uses C/S model for message exchange).

The three-tiered model allows more flexibility than a two-tiered model and is a natural fit for the common three-tiered corporate computing environments (desktops, LAN servers/mid-range computers, mainframes). It is particularly suited for large-scale (thousands of users), mission-critical, enterprisewide applications because you can dedicate different machines for different tasks and exploit different scalability, performance and reliability options. It also allows use of different protocols at different levels to provide tremendous flexibility (see the different C/S protocols that can be used between tiers in Figure 6.9). However, it can introduce several unnecessary points of failure and does require more design effort. In addition, performance can degrade due to many hops over the network (middle machine can introduce networking and processing delays).

Web-based applications fit naturally into a three-tiered model because the Web browser machine behaves as tier 1, the Web server machine operates as tier 2, and the back-end corporate resources are treated as tier 3 (see Figure 6.10). This view of a Web server as the middle tier is the cornerstone of corporate Intranets [Bickell 1996], and [Frye 1996] and is at the core of Oracle's Network Computing Architecture and Microsoft's ActiveX strategy.

Figure 6.9 Sample Three-Tiered Application Architectures

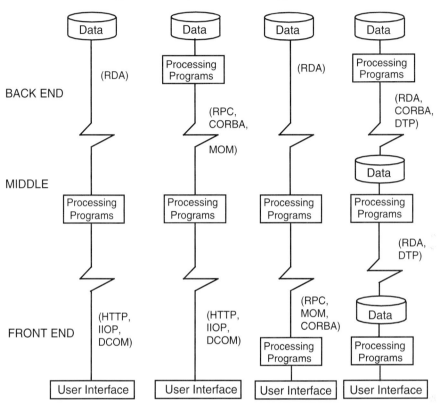

Note 1: For Web-based applications, the middle tier application programs are typically CGI programs, and the front-end application programs may be coded as Java applets.

Note 2: The application components can be separated by a firewall so that some (or all) components can reside inside a secure corporate Intranet while others can reside in the public Internet. For example, the database can be inside the firewall but the application logic may be outside the firewalls.

Another natural application of the three-tiered architecture is in the area of legacy system reengineering. In such cases, the middle machine behaves as a "legacy system gateway" between the back-end machine on which the legacy system resides and the front-end machine on which the new C/S applications reside. The legacy gateway receives calls from the front-end machines in a C/S protocol (e.g., a remote procedure call) and translates it into a format suitable for the back-end legacy system (e.g., a 3270 data stream). These gateways, also known as *mediators* and *surround technologies*, do have some business-aware functionality. These gateways are discussed in Chapter 9.

Figure 6.10 Web-Based Applications as Three Tiers

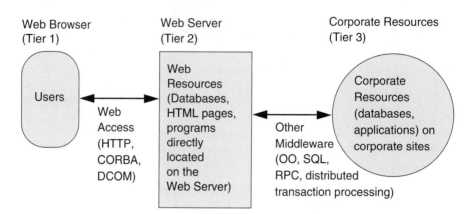

Main trade-offs between two- and three-tiered architecture are (see Schulte [1996], Percy [1996], Dickman [1995], Schulte [1995], and Comport [1995]):

- Support for two-tiered architectures is widely available from numerous DBMS vendors (e.g., buy the DBMS, programming tools, and middleware from one vendor). On the other hand, support for three-tiered architectures usually requires support across vendors. This situation is changing rapidly, because most architectures for Intranets are based on three-tiered architecture with the Web server being the middle tier.

- Two-tiered architectures have been implemented widely at LAN levels due to the availability of tools and the relatively fast data rates of LANs. Implementations of three-tiered architectures at the enterprise level are growing rapidly, especially in corporate Intranets.

- Three-tiered architectures provide more flexibility and conform easily to typical three-tiered organizational topologies (i.e., corporate office, regional offices, local offices). In addition, three-tiered architectures play a key role in the reengineering of legacy systems. However, these systems do require more careful planning and control.

6.5.4   Mixed Architectures (Hybrids)

Applications in distributed environments can be configured as a mixture of single-tiered, two-tiered, or three-tiered. In many cases, these hybrids are used to interface with transition legacy applications and databases. Some of the popular mixed architectures shown in Figure 6.11 are

(a) C/S interactions between the first two tiers but bulk data transfer or e-mail between the second and third tiered machines. This configuration is used widely as "departmental computing" where the PCs access a LAN SQL server that is periodically updated from a mainframe database. This configuration is very common in implementing data warehouses (see Chapter 10).

(b) C/S interactions between the first two tiers but terminal emulation between the second and third tiered machines. This configuration is used commonly to interface with legacy systems through screen scraping. The middle tier essentially accepts a C/S call and converts it into a terminal emulation session (see Chapter 9).

(c) Terminal emulations in the first two tiers but C/S interactions between the second and third tier machines. This configuration may be used as a "migration gateway" that allows the back-end legacy systems to be transitioned gradually to the new middle system while not affecting the current users (see Chapter 11).

Figure 6.11 Sample Mixed Architectures

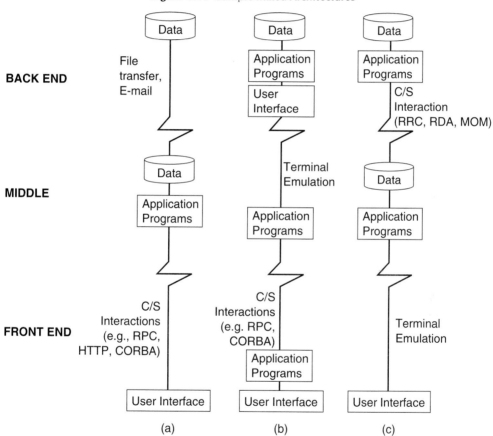

6.5.5 Choosing Number of Tiers—The "Tiering Debate"

An application can be configured as a single-, two-, three-, N-, or mixed-tiered architecture. The main debate seems to hover around the two-tiered versus three-tiered architectures [Schulte 1996]. Typical questions being asked are: Is three-tiered architecture always better than two tiers? Should the single-tiered architecture be used anywhere? Are the same type of architectures useful for OLTP and decision support applications? What appear to be the market trends, and can some guidelines be developed for making decisions? See, for example, Malik [1996], and Smith [1996] for additional questions.

Table 6.3 attempts to put this debate in perspective and shows trade-offs between the different tiered configurations in terms of application types, flexibility, end-user independence, performance, availability, initial cost, upgrade cost, manageability, and security. Only a few factors have been chosen for illustration. Other factors can be added based on application requirements. Based on the discussion in the previous sections, we recognize that different configurations within two- and three-tiered architectures can exist. However, the objective here is to give a broad discussion of trade-offs.

Table 6.3 suggests the following:

- More tiers lead to improved flexibility, end-user independence, and availability but raise some issues in manageability and security.
- The three-tiered model is very flexible and is a natural fit for the burgeoning corporate Intranets. However, it lacks, at the time of this writing, the extensive OLTP capabilities of mainframe-based systems. This situation could change quickly in a few years.
- More tiers can introduce several unnecessary points of failure, performance bottlenecks, and the need for more design effort.
- Performance, if not analyzed carefully, can be a problem in any configuration.

In general, three-tiered architectures seem to be winning over due to the popularity of the World Wide Web and the rate at which software vendors are improving three-tier tools. In addition, many packaged applications are using three-tiered architectures. Moreover, three-tiered architectures play an important role in reengineering of legacy applications because the middle tier "mediates" between the legacy back end and the new front end (see Chapter 8). But two-tiered applications also have some advantages. For example, two tiers are very easy to implement and are natural for data centric applications such as data warehouses.

So what should you do? The answer depends on the fundamental question: *What are the key business drivers?* If flexibility and end-user independence are the key drivers then more tiers are better (the potential negative impacts have to be considered as business risks). Another important question is: What type of application is being developed? In general, data centric applications for decision support are natural for two tiers while function centric applications for operational support do well as three tiered.

Newer technologies such as component software and distributed objects do not fundamentally change this debate. Instead, these technologies enable the two- or three-tiered architectures. You still have to decide what components will reside on the client side, on the server side, or in between. At present, many OLE-based applications use two-tier models where the OLE components reside on client side instead of the server side. However, this situation is changing with the Oracle Network Computing Architecture that advocates thin client three-tiered models and introduces "data cartridges" as components to be stored on the database server. See Schulte [1997] for discussion.

This discussion and Table 6.3 are intended to provide a framework for analysis (the factors and the values can be modified if needed). See the sidebar "Choosing Architectures: The Bottom Line" for a general approach. Many other discussions of trade-offs between different C/S architectures can be found in the literature. For example, Schulte [1996] discusses two-tier vs. three-tier trade-offs in detail and Shedletsky and Rofrano [Shedletsky 1993] present detailed analysis of eight different configurations and their trade-offs. More information about the trade-offs can be found in Porter [1997], Schulte [1997], Schulte [1996], Percy [1996], Frye [1996], Dickman [1995], Comport [1995], and Schulte [1995]. For continued discussion and analysis, the Gartner Group System Software (SSA) Research Reports are a good source of information.

TABLE 6.3 TRADE-OFFS BETWEEN TIERED ARCHITECTURES

Application Characteristics	Single Hardware Tier (Terminal Host)	Two Hardware Tiers	Three Hardware Tiers
Application type suitability	Mission-critical OLTP	Departmental decision support	Enterprisewide applications
Flexibility and growth	Not good	Good	Very good
Scope	Enterprise	Departmental	Enterprise
Number of users	Large (thousands)	Small (less than 100)	Large (thousands)
User independence	Not good	Good	Very good
Performance	Congestion at host	Congestion at network	Many choices
Availability	Not good	Good	Very good
Initial cost	Low	Medium	High
Upgrade cost	High	Medium	Low
Manageability and control	Very good	Good	Not good
Security	Very good	Good	Not good

Choosing Architectures: The Bottom Line

Here is the bottom line: adopt an architecture that minimizes the risks of failure by reducing technology shock. In other words, do not load the architecture with unnecessary technologies that you are not experienced with. Start with a flexible architecture that satisfies your application and business needs (you can use Table 6.3 for this purpose). Then use proven middleware and evolve it gradually.

6.6   Step 4: Evaluate/Choose an Infrastructure

Application programmers are, and should be, mainly concerned with APIs to get their job done. But systems architects must supply the infrastructure that, in addition to the APIs, must support interoperability, facilitate different interaction paradigms, enable system management (e.g., security, naming/directory, failure handling, performance management), and ensure needed network services for connectivity between remotely located client and server processes. We have discussed the infrastructure issues briefly in Chapter 3. Table 6.4 shows a checklist of the issues that must be considered to select new and/or to evaluate existing infrastructure. The following subsections quickly review the pertinent infrastructure.

TABLE 6.4 A CHECKLIST FOR EVALUATING INFRASTRUCTURE

Evaluating Factors	Vendor 1	Vendor 2
Core Application Support • Distributed Object Support (CORBA, ActiveX) • Internet Support (CGI, Web gateways) • C/S Protocol Support (RDA, RPC, MOM)		
Enterprise Data Support • Distributed File Services • Distributed Database Support • Distributed Transaction Processing • Replication Servers		
Special Services Support • Groupware Support (e.g., E-mail, work flow) • Wireless and Multimedia Support • EDI support		

Evaluating Factors	Vendor 1	Vendor 2
Management and Support Services • Security Services • Directory Services • Performance and Fault Management Services		
Network Support • Network Architectures Needed (TCP/IP, SNA, Novell IPX/SPX, OSI, NetBIOS) • Network Interconnectivity (routers, gateways)		
Operating Systems Support • PC Windows, Windows NT, Windows 95 • Macintosh • UNIX • MVS		
Vendor Information • Company Size and Staying Power • Current Installed Base • License and Pricing Arrangements Available • Level of Support		

6.6.1   General Considerations

6.6.1.1   Selecting a Middleware Layer

Figure 6.12 shows the different levels of middleware we have briefly discussed in Chapter 2. Application objects (user layer, processing layer, and data layer) at different machines communicate with each other through messages which may use several middleware layers. A given application system should use an appropriate layer of middleware. For example, consider an application object that needs to send a message to a remote object for synchronizing a database. The application developer has the following choices shown in Figure 6.12:

1. Use an object-oriented interface such as CORBA which directly supports interactions between remote objects. CORBA implementation may activate lower layers to actually perform the database synchronization.

2. Use the distributed data management services to access and synchronize the remotely located data. In this case, the developer may have to develop his/her own "wrapper," say in C++, which receives the method invocation and issues the call needed by the distributed data management services.

3. Use the basic services such as RPCs and do update synchronization yourself, in addition to a wrapper that receives an object message and invokes the needed RPCs.

4. Use the primitive services (e.g., sockets) and do whatever programming needs to be done to wrap, access, and update duplicated data.

Figure 6.12 Layered View of C/S Middleware

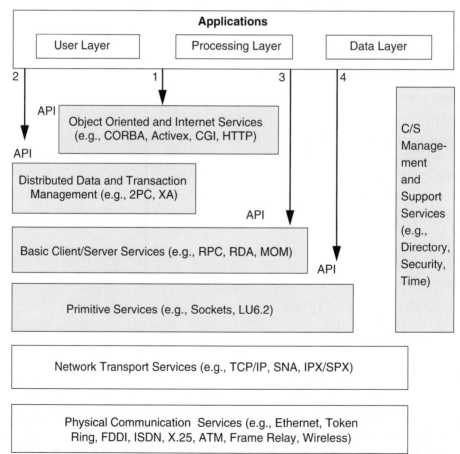

Note: Shaded Area = C/S Middleware
          C/S Middleware is shown at 4 layers

Naturally, it is desirable to use high-level middleware layers to reduce application development costs (the higher the layer, the less code application developers have to write). Application architects must be aware of the interplays between middleware and applications. In particular, it must be kept in mind that middleware stacks (layers) impact the performance as well as cost of an application (see, for example, [Rolia 1995] for a formal performance analysis of layered systems). Higher-level middleware makes it easier and cheaper to develop complex distributed applications, but too many stacks can impede the performance of an application and introduce the administrative overhead of installing, interfacing, maintaining, and supporting the middleware software from different suppliers. In addition, too many layers of middleware may impede the enterprisewide deployment of an application. Consider the following examples.

- If an application requires CORBA, then *all* participating sites as well as purchasers of the application must support CORBA.
- For a cheap (say about $200) application package, the organization may choose to use TCP/IP socket calls and ignore the middleware stacks altogether.
- If an enterprisewide application needs to be developed that crosses several underlying platforms, then a development environment such as Forte should be used to support RPCs, CORBA, and other middleware layers.

The issues of portability and interoperability also play a key role. Application Programming Interfaces (APIs) provided by the middleware impact the portability of applications. For example, a client program that uses an RDA API cannot be ported to an RPC environment without some reengineering. Exchange protocols used between the C/S middleware impact the interoperability of C/S applications. For example, if a server uses RPCs, then the clients must adhere to the specific RPC implementation used by the server. We discuss these issues in the next two subsections.

6.6.1.2 Application Programming Interfaces (APIs): The Portability Issues

The client process should be portable from one vendor C/S environment to another. Similarly, a server process should be portable from one vendor C/S environment to another. The mechanism needed for portability of client and server processes is a uniform and consistent API that can be used across different C/S environments. However, life is not that simple. Here is why.

- APIs for different levels of middleware are different due to the type and scope of service being provided (see Figure 6.12 for different levels/layers of C/S middleware). For example, APIs for distributed transaction processing differ from the APIs for network-level services.
- APIs at the same level but for different paradigms are different. For example, APIs for RPC differ from the API for RDA.
- APIs at the same level and for the same paradigm are also typically different between vendors. For example, the APIs provided by DBMS vendors for remote data access differ significantly between vendors. Thus a client process that issues remote data access calls for Informix has to be recoded if it needs to access Sybase data.

It seems hopeless but there are several encouraging signs. First, Microsoft's ODBC has become a de facto API standard for RDA client processes. The clients issue the same ODBC calls no matter what the target database is. The ODBC calls are converted by ODBC drivers to access different vendor databases. Second, Open Software Foundation's DCE RPC has become a de facto standard for RPC clients. Third, the Internet-based protocols (HTTP, CGI) are supported on all Web platforms. Fourth, the CORBA and DCOM facilities are gaining popularity and will help a little (unfortunately, CORBA and DCOM are not interoperable, but bridges between CORBA and DCOM are commercially available). Finally, object-oriented technologies help because a "wrapper" can be developed which gives one uniform API to the end users. The wrapper internally issues whatever actual API calls are needed. CORBA is expected to facilitate the object wrapper approach. We will discuss these issues in the next chapter.

6.6.1.3 Exchange Protocols: The Interoperability Issues

Clients and servers must use the same or similar protocols and/or services in order to inter-operate (work together). Basically, clients and servers must understand each other. For example, if a server uses RPCs, then the clients must adhere to the specific RPC implementation used by the server. Unfortunately, different implementations of RPCs are available (e.g., SUN RPC, Netwise RPC, OSF RPC) which do not interoperate with each other. In another case, RDA protocols between different DBMS vendors also do not interoperate. At a lower level, if TCP/IP Sockets are used by the clients and not by the server, then they will not interoperate. Similar to the API discussion, we must be aware of the following interoperability issues:

- Clients and servers must operate at same level of middleware (see Figure 6.12 for different levels/layers of C/S middleware).

- Clients and servers must use the same paradigm (i.e., client cannot use RDA if the server uses RPCs).

- Within each paradigm, clients and servers must use the implementations that interoperate with each other (e.g., SUN RPC and OSF DCE RPC do not interoperate; similarly, remote object invocations through CORBA and DCOM do not interoperate).

Interoperability in large distributed environments becomes a serious problem if clients and servers from different vendors are intermixed. Better standards are needed in this area. IBM's DRDA and OSF DCE are good examples of interoperability standards. The standards being developed for interoperability of distributed objects (e.g., CORBA 2.0) and the bridges between CORBA and DCOM are encouraging signs. In general, developments in broker architectures should help in this area (see the sidebar "Broker Architectures").

Broker Architectures

Distributed applications should employ broker architectures as brokers mature. A broker mediates between clients and servers (that is, instead of a client directly connecting to a server, it first connects to a broker that in turn finds a suitable server). The concept of a broker is independent of the implementation of the broker. For example, the best known implementation of the broker architecture is the Object Request Broker (ORB) as presented in the OMG CORBA specification. In CORBA, the ORB mediates the interactions between remote objects. Other brokers, such as message and Web brokers, are emerging.

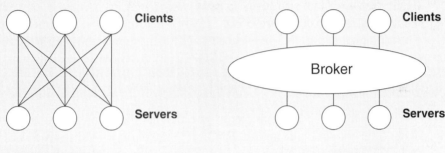

(a) Point-to-Point Architecture   **(b) A Broker Architecture**

Message Brokers. A message broker is not restricted to objects. Instead, it delivers messages between disparate applications, including legacy applications. The underlying technologies used by the message broker may consist of RPCs or MOMs, although MOM does appear to fit this model quite well. The basic idea of a message broker is that it can provide brokerage services asynchronously and, if needed, support a "publish/subscribe" model. The message broker can also be rule-based, that is, you specify the rules to be used by the middleware to perform certain actions. See, for example, NEONet (http://www.neonsoft.com). Message brokers can be very effective in a wide range of distributed applications including group communications, integration of existing applications, and large-scale work flow. See Bort [1996] for details.

Web Request Brokers. These brokers take requests from Web browsers and then pass them along to the back-end resources. You can think of Web request brokers as large Web gateways with intelligence (e.g., directory and naming services) to locate and dispatch the most appropriate services such as purchasing services, payment services, and other transactional services. An example of such a request broker is the Oracle Web Request Broker that is being positioned for the electronic commerce market [Burton 1996].

6.6.2   Evaluate Middleware for Remote Message Support (RPC, RDA, MOM, CORBA, DCOM)

At a basic level, clients and servers of most C/S applications interact with each other by using one or more of the following well-known services: remote data access (also known as data passing), remote procedure calls, and message-oriented middleware (see Chapter 2 for an overview and Umar [1997] for details). These services may be invoked directly by applications through appropriate APIs (e.g., DCE RPC) or indirectly through a "higher-level" service (e.g., CORBA or DCOM). For example, IBM's implementation of CORBA, known as DSOM, is expected to invoke basic services such as DCE RPCs or message queues through the IBM MQI interface, and primitive services such as TCP/IP Sockets or LU6.2. The DSOM system installers can configure DSOM to use whatever services are most appropriate (i.e., DSOM ORB may use LU6.2 between two MVS machines and may use DCE RPCs between two DCE machines). Microsoft's DCOM is built on top of DCE RPC (i.e., messages exchanged between two DCOMs use DCE RPC). See the sidebar "RPC versus Remote Invocation: An Example."

It is best, especially for OCSI applications, to use the distributed object model for middleware services—this model will invoke RPC, MOM, or any other services. However, CORBA and DCOM are contenders for distributed object model middleware. Basically, CORBA is more suitable for heterogeneous (PCs, UNIX, MVS) environments, and DCOM is powerful in the PC environments (Windows, Windows NT). We will have to see how this issue is settled. By the way, appropriate support for the lower-level services needed by the application, directly or indirectly, must be supplied by the infrastructure. For example, if your transaction processor requires a lower-level service (e.g., Encina is based on DCE), then the middleware needed to support the lower-level service must be acquired, installed, and maintained.

6.6.3   Choose Enterprise Data Management Middleware (TP-Lite or TP-Heavy)

As stated previously, enterprise data (also known as corporate data) is the information that is used or created by a corporation in conducting business and is shared across the business processes of the corporation. In a distributed environment, the enterprise data can exist on various platforms with varying degrees of replication, in different formats, under the control of different DBMSs, and accessed by a variety of client applications and end-user tools. A sound enterprise data architecture, discussed in the previous chapter, is essential for mission-critical applications. This data architecture, along with the middleware needed for enterprise data management, must be integrated with the application architecture. In particular, the decisions about appropriate database (usually SQL) gateways and C/S transaction processing middleware discussed in Umar [1997, Chapters 5 and 6] must be reviewed in this step.

RPC versus Remote Object Invocation: An Example

Suppose you want to invoke a remote procedure "query-balance" to check your bank balance in two different banks (bank1 and bank2). How will you implement this by using an RPC (e.g., DCE RPC) versus a remote object invocation (e.g., CORBA call).

Using RPC:

You will issue the following call:

> query-balance (bankid, accountno, return)

You have to pass the bankid as a parameter. The query-balance procedure will process the request, identify which bank is being queried by parsing the bankid parameter and then invoke the appropriate procedure.

Using Object Invocation:

You will issue the following calls:

> query-balance.bank1 (accountno, return)
>
> query-balance.bank2 (accountno, return)

Notice that the bankid does not need to be a parameter. In an OO system, the two bank instances are created and identified as bank1 and bank2. The same operation on the two different bank objects will get different results due to the magic of polymorphism.

Discussion

So what are the trade-offs? Mainly in RPC, the procedure query-balance will have to have more code to determine the bank type and then invoke internal procedures for the different banks. In the case of object invocation, the appropriate procedure for the different banks is invoked by using polymorphism (i.e., the same method on different objects can produce different results).

In both cases, you need to develop an IDL (Interface Definition Language). In the case of RPC, your IDL will define an operation with three parameters but in CORBA, your IDL will define the object (bank) which supports the operation query-balance with two parameters.

It is best not to approach enterprise data management from a single application's point of view. The best approach is to analyze the enterprise data issues at an enterprise level because the same enterprise data may be shared by multiple applications and end users. Due to this, we devoted a complete chapter (Chapter 10) to enterprise data architecture to present a more global view than a single-application captive activity.

6.6.4   Evaluate Internet and Special Application Support

Internet support is maturing quickly due to the very large number of Web-based applications that are being developed to operate on the Internet ranging from entertainment to electronic commerce. Example of the middleware needed ranges from core Web middleware such as HTTP and HTML to Web gateways and servers from numerous vendors.

In addition to Internet, many new applications are emerging. These applications require specialized middleware. For example, new applications may use groupware products such as Lotus Notes to allow people in different parts of an organization to work together by collecting and sharing information such as documents, graphs, spreadsheets, and e-mail. More applications are also using wireless communications and utilizing distributed multimedia technologies. Electronic commerce applications need Electronic Data Interchange (EDI) capabilities. In addition, compound document support, for example, is needed for applications that serve as containers for objects such as text paragraphs, spreadsheets, graphs, and sound bites.

6.6.5   Evaluate Management and Support Services

The following management and support services must be evaluated carefully.

Security: Security in distributed systems, including OCSI applications, is a major challenge because more points of contact (files and programs accessible from the network) exist and each host cannot remember all the users. Infrastructure services must be able to support authentication, authorization, and audit. At present, individual approaches exist (e.g., Kerberos in UNIX and RACF in MVS); thus security within one vendor environment is easier to deal with than security between systems that cross many vendor environments (e.g., MVS, UNIX, OSF DCE, Novell).

Threat analysis is typically the first step in dealing with security issues. Threats to Web-based applications can be broken down into the following groups:

> **Confidentiality threats.** Users of OCSI applications must be assured that their data are only being viewed by those for whom they are intended, and not by other individuals, be they legitimate users of the application, or unauthorized parties.

> **Integrity threats.** Users of OCSI applications must also be assured that the data that they obtain from the application are legitimate, and in the same form as created by the originator.

> **Authenticity threats.** Users must be assured that they are communicating with exactly whom they believe they are communicating.

> **Authorization Threats.** Certain portions of the application services may be restricted to authorized users.

Based on the level of threat, technologies are assessed and evaluated. The sidebar "Security for Web-Based Applications" gives an overview of security technologies. The issues of firewalls and proxy servers are discussed in the sidebars "Where to Put the Firewalls?" and "What are Proxy Servers?"

Security for Web-Based Applications

The technologies to address security threats operate at the network level (e.g., firewalls that filter unwanted traffic and proxy servers that rewrite packets to hide their original source) and application-level security (authentication and authorization).

Authentication. Many applications use one-time passwords. However, the use of such one-time passwords often requires the deployment of expensive token cards and software. For this reason, many applications choose to make use of cryptographic applications such as the following, which allow incorporating public-key cryptography to provide encryption and digital signatures:

- Kerberos, a cryptographic authentication scheme using a third-party authentication server to grant cryptographic "tokens" that authenticate users to a given service
- Entrust, a product from Northern Telecom that uses public-key cryptography to generate "certificates" that authenticate one party to another party
- PGP (Pretty Good Privacy), a popular program available on the Internet that uses public-key cryptography to authenticate users to each other without the use of certificates
- A number of public-key based cryptographic infrastructure tools, such as the Microsoft and Netscape Certificate Servers, which allow for the inclusion of public-key certificates in various applications

Authorization. While public-key certificates provide strong authentication, integrity, and confidentiality for data while in transit, they do very little to provide any form of authorization or access control to individual parts of a system. For this reason, many applications must provide this sort of access control on their own.

Application-specific access control and authorization provide the finest level of granularity but also require a great deal of administration. Whereas services such as Kerberos and Entrust allow for global administration of certificates, application-specific authorization requires separate administration for individual applications, which can become somewhat cumbersome. However, this is often a necessity, as it is not always possible to provide intraapplication access control using Kerberos or public-key schemes. See the book by Bhimini, et al., *Internet Security for Business,* John Wiley, 1996.

Directory Services. Applications and users need to know the names and locations of the objects being managed. The ANSI/OSI Directory Standard (X.500) is a standard for global naming and directory services. For enterprisewide applications, it is important to have global naming services so that objects located anywhere in the enterprise can be used. Different middleware packages such as OSF DCE and CORBA use X.500 services for this purpose. At present, LDAP (Light Weight Directory Access Protocol), a version of X.500 on the Internet, is very popular and is heavily being supported by Netscape, Microsoft, Novell, and others.

Failure Handling. Failure handling in distributed systems, especially when data at multiple sites are updated, is nontrivial. Failure handling becomes especially difficult when your server communicates with other servers to satisfy a request. An analyst must evaluate the trade-offs between C/S transaction processors which use two-phase commit or replication servers that perform periodic updates. The reader should differentiate between network failure management versus application failure management. For network failure management, many tools (e.g., NetView 6000, HP OpenView) are commercially available. However, application failure management is done primarily by transaction processors.

Performance management. The infrastructure must provide appropriate tools for performance management of distributed applications as well as network. For example, performance management tools must be able to detect, diagnose, and predict network delays as well as the node processing delays for distributed applications. In addition performance modeling tools should be considered (see Section 6.7).

6.6.6   Analyze Network Support

Middleware provides the application-to-application connectivity by using network services for the basic addressing and transport mechanisms across a network. From the OSI reference model point of view, network services are the responsibility of layers 1 to 4 and the application-to-application connectivity is the responsibility of layers 5 to 7. It is important to analyze the physical media, network configurations, and interconnectivity devices for enterprisewide applications. Specifically, the following issues must be addressed:

- What will be the network data rates needed to support the new applications (for example, a distributed multimedia application may require between 10 to 15 million bits per second (Mbps) for a single user.)?

- What type of LANs (Ethernet, Token Ring, Fast Ethernet), MANs (FDDI, SMDS), and WANs (X.25, ISDN, ATM, Frame Relay) will be needed to support the new applications and databases? For example, many existing LANs (e.g., Ethernet and Token Ring) provide between 10- to 16-Mbps data rates and many existing WANs operate at 56 Kbps. However, the state-of-the-art advancement in network transmission technologies is the development of high-speed local and wide area transmissions, typically in the range of 100 (Mbps) or higher.

- Has interconnectivity between the necessary LANs, MANs, and WANs been established through appropriate bridges, routers, and switches? In addition, have network gateways been established to convert network protocols between TCP/IP, SNA, and LAN protocols such as Net-BIOS and Novell Netware SPX/IPX (e.g., TCP/IP to SNA gateways and Novell Netware to mainframe gateways)?

- Have potential performance bottlenecks in the network due to the added traffic generated by the new application been considered? The bottlenecks can occur due to the congestion on interconnectivity devices (routers and gateways are well-known potential bottlenecks) or due to the over-utilization of physical media (for example, Ethernet LANs start having problems with a utilization of 0.3). We will discuss performance analysis in the next section.

Some people may consider discussion of network support issues to be too "low level" for the application architecture phase. Our objective here is to simply include this activity as part of a checklist so that these issues are not overlooked (see the sidebar "Do Not Overlook Network Issues—A Personal Experience").

Where To Put The Firewall?

Firewalls separate the private ("Intranet") corporate resources from the publicly accessible (Public Internet) resources. It is important to decide where to put the firewall while architecting Web-based applications. The following diagram shows how the data, application programs and user interfaces can be placed on either side of the firewall [Natis 1996].

The private applications (configuration a) are completely within the corporate Intranets and are within the company firewalls. The public applications (configuration e) are on the other extreme and completely reside on the Public Internet. In between, there are several configurations where the data as well as programs can be placed behind the corporate firewall. The factors to be considered while making these decisions naturally include the security, privacy, and reliability requirements.

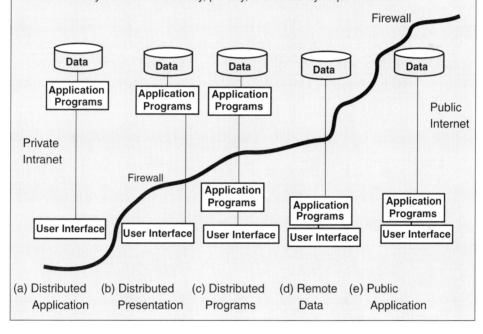

6.6.7   Understand Operating System Support

From an application perspective, the main role of operating systems is to schedule server processes that need access to resources such as main memory, files, databases, printers, and so forth. The operating system facilities needed to develop clients and servers must be carefully evaluated (UNIX, MVS, OS/2, Windows and Windows NT all provide different capabilities for developing client as well as servers). In addition, middleware vendor support for a given operating system must be reviewed. For example, if an enterprisewide C/S application is expected to use UNIX in the mid-tier, then it would be very nice if the vendor middleware on UNIX were robust. You should also consider network operating system (NOS) support for remote printing and remote file access (see Umar [1997], Chapter 3).

What are Proxy Servers?

A proxy server is essentially an intermediate program that behaves as a server but in fact passes the requests to real server(s). In effect, it is a fake server. In most practical cases, the proxy server receives the client calls, does some processing (typically security checking) and then itself becomes a client to other servers. Why would anyone want to use proxy servers? Here are some scenarios:

a) A proxy server sits outside the firewall to receive the Public Internet calls, authenticates the clients, and then invokes services inside the firewall for authorized users. In many cases, these proxy servers rewrite packets to hide unneeded information. .

b) A proxy server, residing on an HTTP server machine, receives Java applet calls (recall that many browsers restrict Java applets to communicate with the HTTP server from where they were loaded) and then establishes connections with remote databases and programs on behalf of the Java applets.

c) A proxy server behaves as an application gateway by receiving calls from different clients for different applications and then invoking needed applications.

The following example shows how a proxy server is used between two businesses. We are assuming here, for simplicity, that business 1 resides entirely on the Public Internet. A second firewall and proxy server can be introduced for generality.

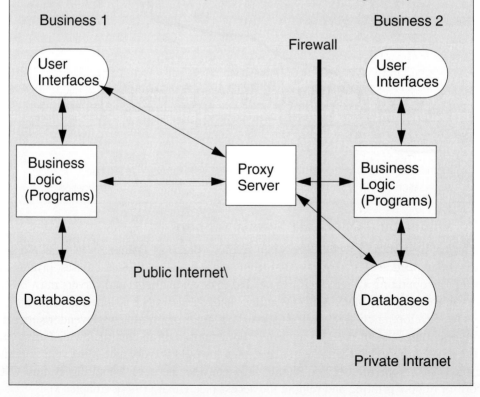

Do Not Overlook Network Issues—A Personal Experience

Once upon a time (around 1993), in a large organization, a group of people in a department developed a beautifully architected C/S application on a vendor middleware that utilized NetBIOS protocol (NetBIOS is used heavily in IBM PC LANs). After running a local successful test, the group proposed to make this application enterprisewide by moving the data to a mainframe DB2 database while keeping the clients at the local offices. The users were told about this prospect and they were excited. There was only one problem: The network routers that had been installed for the enterprise network did not support NetBIOS. Thus the NetBIOS clients (this application) could not access the mainframe database. This caused, to use a "medical" term, minor discomfort to all concerned.

The best approach is to involve networking folks in the system architecture activities so that they can review and comment on the architecture and minimize surprises like this.

6.6.8   Keep Business Reality in Mind

Finally, before adopting an infrastructure, the architects must evaluate the business aspects of the infrastructure providers. Specifically, the following questions should be asked:

- What are the size and staying power of the supplier?
- What is the current installed base of the infrastructure service?
- Is the cost range within budget limit?
- Are adequate documentation, training, and support available?
- Does the supplier's long-range strategy correspond with your long-range strategy?
- Are there user conferences, and other channels, to gauge user experiences?

6.7   Step 5: Performance and Allocation Analysis

6.7.1   Overview

Allocation (placement) of application components to computers profoundly impacts the performance of distributed applications. A well-architected application can easily self-destruct if its components are assigned to slow or congested computers that are interconnected through slow communication links. It is important to optimize the performance of applications by placing application components (databases and programs) at the most appropriate sites. Although exact placement of data and application programs can be changed at run time, it is best to minimize surprises by studying the trade-offs during the architecture stage. Most of the existing middleware (e.g., CORBA, OSF DCE) hide the physical location of servers by providing directories that are accessed at run time to determine the location of servers.

It can be argued that C/S performance is a nonissue: If the performance is not acceptable, then you can move the data/programs to faster machines, get bigger/faster server machines, or get faster network links. However, we need to be careful about it. For example, some users may be restricted to certain wide area communication lines (e.g., the Hyatt Sales Support System had to share 56-Kbps lines with other users [Grygo 1995]). Also, even though databases and programs can move easily at run time, in reality movement of mission-critical application components is a serious issue that must consider *all* users. (Imagine your logging on to your favorite machine to query your favorite database and finding out that the database has been moved to another machine to which you do not have access authority. This could easily ruin your entire day!)

Our objective is to present broad allocation/performance principles that will help us to determine any bottlenecks which may require a rearchitecture or new hardware/software (e.g., transition from X.25 to ATM or Frame Relay, new computers for housing databases, etc.). We introduced the main concepts and approaches of data allocation in the previous chapter. We now expand this discussion to include the following approaches that can be used to study performance impacts due to allocations:

> **Intuitive Analysis:** In this approach, the application components are allocated to the computers based on intuition and rules of thumb. This approach is appropriate if the number of candidate computers is small and also if the need for accuracy is low.

> **Trial and Error**: In this approach, an initial allocation choice is made based on intuition and then the performance and other objective functions are measured through experiments. If the desirable results are not obtained, then the components are moved to other sites and the experiments are repeated.

> **Predictive Models:** This approach is conceptually similar to the trial and error approach. The main difference is that analytical and/or simulation models are used instead of the actual allocating and experimentation with the database. The analytical model discussed in Section 6.7.3 can be used in this approach.

> **Optimization Algorithms:** These algorithms can be used to automatically determine the allocations that will minimize given objective functions. This approach is typically useful for large numbers of computers where there is a need for some degree of accuracy (see Section 6.7.4).

> **Mixtures:** The above approaches can be mixed in a variety of ways to solve data allocation problems.

Table 6.5 shows how these approaches can be used based on two problem parameters: number of candidate computers and the needed accuracy of results. As shown in Table 6.5, common-sense approaches can be used for small problems which do not require very accurate results. However as the size of the problem as well as the accuracy requirements grow, the need for more formal approaches increases. As stated previously, however, a mixture of approaches can be, and should be, used in real life. The sidebar "A Realistic Procedure for Performance and Allocation Analysis" suggests such an approach. The key point is that the judgment of the analyst plays a pivotal role. This hierarchical approach allows the analyst to gradually use more sophisticated tools for more complicated problems. Based on his/her judgment, an analyst may decide to terminate this procedure at any step if enough information has been gained to make a good decision. This procedure can be used at the core of a knowledge-based decision support system for distributed resource allocations.

In the previous chapter, the intuitive and paper/pencil techniques for quick analysis were explored. In this chapter we expand the tools and techniques that may be needed for enterprisewide applications. In particular, the focus is on performance prediction and optimization (normative) tools, discussed in Sections 6.7.3 and 6.7.4. Our objective is to highlight the key C/S performance issues and approaches that are important to establish the architecture. Many detailed "tuning" issues are dealt with in the implementation phase.

TABLE 6.5 Suggested Approaches for Problem Types

	Small Number of Candidate Computers	Large Number of Candidate Computers
Low Accuracy Requirements	Use Intuitive Analysis	Use Trial and Error Method
High Accuracy Requirements	Use Predictive Model	Use Optimal Allocation Algorithms

---

A Realistic Procedure for Performance and Allocation Analysis

Step 1: Use intuitive analysis, described in the previous chapter, to narrow down choices and to eliminate unsuitable solutions. A qualitative decision table helps the user to make major high-level decisions.

Step 2: If a candidate solution is found, then go to Step 4; else proceed.

Step 3: Use a simple allocation algorithm to determine a candidate solution. Depending on the need, any of the allocation methods described in this chapter and/or the previous chapter can be used here.

Step 4: Do a quick paper and pencil analysis of the candidate solution to estimate the response time by using the response time estimation method described in Section 6.7.3.

Step 5: Based on this analysis, allocate the datasets to the computer(s) and perform actual measurements and experiments.

Step 6: If the results are satisfactory, then stop; else go back to Step 1. If the problem is too large, then a detailed optimization algorithm may be employed, if needed.

6.7.2   Client/Server Performance: Issues and Guidelines

The performance of a C/S application must take into account the network performance, the volume of computational processing, and the volume of database operations [Hamilton 1994], and [Inmon 1993]. Examples of considerations are minimization of the network delays between clients and servers, examining the trade-off of firing up a new server for every client request versus a single reentrant server which is called repetitively, and the performance penalty due to remote joins. The C/S performance problems are unique due to several reasons.

- The interactions between clients and servers are in real time. Thus if any delay occurs, then the users see the direct impact (i.e., yawn while sitting in front of the frozen screen).
- A large number of choices exist in C/S application architectures. These architectural choices can have a profound impact on the performance of C/S applications.
- The network traffic patterns are not predictable, primarily due to the message traffic and remote joins between distributed databases. This presents challenges in estimating the bandwidth and the best/worst cases for a given network.
- The network response time is hard to predict because a given message can be routed through several potential delay points.
- The problems of scaling are not well understood. It is not clear, for example, how the current protocols and algorithms will perform on very large networks that may span many countries [Ozsu 1991].

In the next section, we will present a paper and pencil procedure for estimating C/S application performance. Before getting into the mathematics, you should review the sidebar "Practical Guidelines for Client/Server Performance."

Many simulation studies for C/S architectures have been published. For example, Dale [1993] described a detailed simulation study that compares and contrasts the performance characteristics of three C/S architectures. Other simulation examples can be found in Bhide [1988]. Few modeling tools for C/S applications are currently available. An example is the Bachman/Wind-Tunnel from Bachman Associates. The *IEEE Computer Magazine,* September 1995, is a special issue on performance evaluation tools for parallel and distributed processing and contains survey articles on visual display of performance data, performance visualization, performance measurement tools, and use of virtual reality for system performance.

6.7.3   Estimating Response Time Performance

Let us introduce a simple procedure for estimating the performance of a C/S application. Simply stated, response time of an application is the elapsed time between application submission, and completion. In the simplest case, the total Response Time (RT) of an application is given by the sum of all processing and queuing delays. Without queuing, RT, the response time, is given by

$$RT = \sum_i N(i)S(i) \qquad (6\text{-}1)$$

where $S(i)$ = time needed for completion of service i, $N(i)$ = number of times service i is needed, and service i represents any activity needed to complete an application (e.g., transmission of the messages between clients and servers over networks, processing of the message to produce the results, and transmission of the results back to the user. $S(i)$ and $N(i)$ can be easily measured through prototyping. The example shown in Table 6.6 illustrates the usefulness of this simple formula. As illustrated in Table 6.6, this formula can be used to calculate lower bounds (best case) of response time estimates. Given two sites M and N where a database server D can be allocated, the analyst can compute the Response Times (RTs) for the two allocations and choose the site with minimal response time.

TABLE 6.6 A SIMPLE EXAMPLE OF RESPONSE TIME ESTIMATION

PROBLEM:

The client of a two-tiered C/S application sends a 20-byte customer account number to the server. The server searches a customer database for the account number and then sends the customer information (2,000 bytes) to the client. The server can be allocated to the following two computers:

- Computer M, mainframe, which is connected to users through 5,600-bps WAN lines. M can complete 20 customer retrievals per second on the average

- Computer N which is connected to users through 10-Mbps LAN (e.g., Ethernet). N can complete 10 customer retrievals per second on the average

Should the server be allocated to M or N? We can assume that each byte occupies 10 bits in the network (8-bit data, 2 start/stop bits).

SOLUTION:

Three services are needed to complete this application: For M, we get

   S(1) = transmit time (transaction input) = 20 x 10/5600 = 0.03 secs
   S(2) = transmit time (transaction output) = 2000 x 10/5600 = 3 secs
   S(3) = time per service = 1/20 = 0.05 secs
   Total Response Time (RT) for M = S(1) + S(2) + S(3) = 0.03 + 3 +.05 = 3.1 secs

In this case, the bottleneck (the service where most time is consumed) is the communication line.

Now, let us calculate S(1), S(2) for N:

   S(1) = 20x10/10,000,000 = 0.00002 secs
   S(2) = 2000x10/10,000,000 = 0.002 secs
   S(3) = 1/10 =0.1 secs
   Total Response Time (RT) for N = S(1) + S(2) + S(3) = 0.1 sec (approximately)

In this case, the computer disk is the bottleneck.

Comparing the response times for the two computers, it seems that N is a better choice.

Practical Guidelines for Client/Server Performance

- Build performance into each application component by analysis, experimentation, and prototyping. Make sure that each component is well designed (this is nothing new, but we get surprises).

- Optimize performance between application components by considering co-location. For example, application components that are tightly connected (e.g., programs that communicate with each other frequently, tables that are joined frequently) should not be split between machines (network operations are much slower than local operations).

- Play it close by clustering clients and servers in a fast LAN, if they cannot/should not be co-located. In other words, try to cluster closely interacting clients and servers within LANs, keeping WAN use for exceptions as much as possible.

- Do not overdistribute, especially across WANs. Sharing of heavily distributed data among thousands of users does become more difficult and the performance may not improve because the network instead of the computers becomes the congestion points. This is especially true for WANs, unless fast packet switching networks such as ATM are used (ATM is preferable to frame relay because it has less latency [Jessup 1996]).

- Try to determine the bottlenecks before throwing hardware at the problem. The procedure described in the next section can help in determining bottlenecks. Use modeling tools or measurement tools to determine bottlenecks.

- Use software with performance enhancements, as much as possible. The latest network operating systems and packages include many performance enhancements like caching to minimize network traffic.

- Closely review, estimate, and monitor the network traffic due to ad hoc SQL over the network. I have seen, for example, marketing folks join remotely located huge tables with 5 million rows each. Due to this "SQL threat," some organizations have restricted the use of such queries to LANs only.

- Overinvest in network bandwidth because network congestion, especially due to ad hoc SQL, can be unpredictable.

- Nothing beats experience. After careful analysis, experimentation, and prototyping, run a pilot instead of infinite paper and pencil analysis. After implementation, perform measurements and tuning.

- Monitor, monitor, monitor. It is important to keep monitoring the performance to understand response time patterns and bottlenecks. This allows you to pro-actively respond to performance nightmares.

  Sources of additional information on this topic are Jessup [1996], Rolia [1995], Hamilton [1994], and Dale [1993].

Although the best case estimates are a good starting point, they ignore the impact of queuing on response time calculations. Queues are formed due to two reasons: The device providing the service may be busy or it may be locked by another activity. The first condition is an indication of workload (too many services requested) and the second condition is a result of resources being reserved (e.g., a file being updated) by one activity. In this section, our primary focus is on queuing due to workload.

We need to introduce another parameter, $A(i)$, to handle queuing. $A(i)$ = arrival rate of requests for service i. For example, if 10 workstations send 5 queries per hour to a database server, then $A(i) = 50$ per hour for the database server.

The following formula[6] shows utilization $U(i)$ of a database server i:

$$U(i) = \text{server } i \text{ utilization} = A(i) * S(i) \qquad (6\text{-}2)$$

A rule of thumb used in queuing calculations is that $U(i)$ should be kept below 0.7 to avoid queuing. The theoretical foundation for this rule of thumb is the following well-known M/M/1 (Markovian arrival, Markovian service time, 1 server) formula [Kleinrock 1976]:

$$\text{Queue length at server } i = Q(i) = U(i)/1{-}U(i) \qquad (6\text{-}3)$$

where $Q(i)$ shows the number of customers in the system, including the one being served. Thus $Q(i)=1$, if $U(i)=0.5$; $Q(i)$ reaches infinity if $U(i)=1$. The basic assumptions of the M/M/1 queuing formula are

- Arrivals at the server are independent of each other.
- Service times are independent of each other.

It is not necessary for the users to know that these two assumptions are based on stochastic processes and queuing theory. For example, these arrival and service time patterns are called Poisson and exponential distributions, respectively, in stochastic processes. Poisson arrival rates and exponential server times are referred to as Markovian behavior in queuing systems.

The net effect of queuing is that the service time increases due to queuing. The service time $S(i)$ is replaced with $S'(i)$:

$$S'(i) = \text{service time at server } i \text{ after queuing} = S(i) + S(i)^* Q(i) \quad (6\text{-}4)$$

The example shown in Table 6.7 illustrates the impact of server utilization on queue length and response time. This example essentially reworks the example shown in Table 6.6 by adding queuing calculations.

So far we have focused on queuing for a single server. In most practical situations, a queuing network is formed where output of one server becomes an input to another server. Jackson's theorem [Kleinrock 1976] shows that the following very useful results apply as long as Pois-

---

6. In most of the formulas in this section, "*" is used to indicate multiplication.

son arrival and exponential server assumptions hold at each server in the queuing network:

- Each server can be treated independently.
- Arrival rate at a server is the sum of all arrivals from all sources.

Jackson's theorem is used heavily because it applies to stochastic routing also, that is, if a message is routed to server i with probability $p(i)$. In fact, even when the Poisson arrival and exponential service time assumptions are not satisfied, this formula is used because there is no other straightforward method for the analytical calculations of response times in queuing networks. Table 6.7 gives another example to illustrate queuing calculations in a network.

The following procedure may be utilized to estimate the performance of an application component allocation (see the sidebar "Response Time Estimation" for key points).

- Perform best case analysis by ignoring queuing. In this case, only S and N are needed for computations (see Equation (6-1). These calculations can be used as a starting point.
- Determine if performance constraints are satisfied. If not, then there is no need for queuing analysis because if a system does not satisfy the best case calculations, then it will not satisfy conditions with the workload.
- Study the effect of queuing and workload by estimating arrival rates A. The estimate A may be at peak time or average time. Estimate total time including queuing by using Equations (6-2) through (6-4).
- Try to reduce U to less than 0.7 for most devices in the network. In addition, determine the bottleneck device (devices with largest U). Try to reduce U by decreasing A and S. For example, if U of a database server is too high, then the following steps can be taken:
  - Reduce arrival rates A by adding another server that may contain the entire database or most queried data items.
  - Reduce service time S by getting a faster machine or by eliminating other work being done on the server.
- If detailed analysis of a configuration is needed, then you may need to simulate.

Response Time Estimation: The Key Points

- Response time can be roughly estimated in terms of three easily observable parameters :

  S = Service time of a device

  A = Arrival rate at the device

  N = the number of devices in the network

- Utilization U, simply given by $A*S$, is a good indicator of server congestion. U should be kept less than 70 percent to avoid excessive queuing.

- In a network of devices, the device with the largest U is the bottleneck.

- U can be reduced by decreasing the arrival rate A, decreasing the service time S, or both.

The examples shown in Table 6.6 and Table 6.7 illustrate this procedure.

TABLE 6.7 IMPACT OF QUEUING ON RESPONSE TIME

Consider the same customer database example in Table 6.6. We want to consider the impact of queuing on computers M and N. We assume that 60 clients will use this application and each client will generate the customer retrieval message 11 times per minute. This gives us an arrival rate A(3) at the server machine = 60x11/60 = 11 per second.

Let us compute new service time at M and N. The following table shows the utilization, the average queue length, the average wait time, and the total service time at the I/O server (computers M and N). We have dropped the index in this table for simplicity.

Computer	Arrival Rate A at server	Service Time S	Utilization $U = A*S$	Queue Length $Q = U/1-U$	Wait Time $= S*Q$	New (Total) Service Time $S' = S + S*Q$
M	11 per Sec	0.05 Sec	0.55	1.2	0.06 Sec	0.11 Sec
N	11 per Sec	0.1 Sec	1.1	Infinite	Infinite	Infinite

It can be seen that although N was favored in the simple analysis shown in Table 6.6, the queuing at N causes serious congestion and thus N should not be used for storing the customer database. Note that N is not a good choice even though it is connected through a fast network.

To make N a candidate for data allocation, the utilization U must be reduced to less than 0.5. In other words, $A.S < 0.5$. Assuming that the service time of N is fixed (i.e., 10 requests per second), then we can compute the desirable value of A from the following equation:

$A(0.1) < 0.5$

Thus we should keep the arrival rate at N at less than 5 per second. This could be achieved by reducing the number of clients that query N by creating a copy of the customer database on another computer. Otherwise, a faster machine must replace N to reduce U.

6.7.4 Optimal Allocation Algorithms

Performance analysis does not show exactly what application system components should be allocated where. Instead, it shows the *impact* of allocations. In a C/S application, the following three allocation decisions need to be made:

- Where to allocate the user interfaces
- Where to allocate the application programs
- Where to allocate the data.

User interfaces can be allocated to any computer which has the necessary client-interface software to connect to the data servers. For example, if a user interface requires sophisticated multimedia presentations, then an appropriately equipped workstation should be used. In Web environments, the user interfaces are handled by the Web browsers that are available on almost all hardware platforms.

The application programs can also be allocated for similar reasons. A special consideration for program allocation to a particular computer is the availability of specialized software needed (e.g., fourth-generation languages, simulation software, etc.) on the user computer. In Web environments, the application software can be allocated to the Web server site, to the Web client site (i.e., as Java applets or ActiveX components), or on a back-end (third tiered) machine.

Data allocation, however, is a different story. The allocations can be based on several factors such as amount of storage, read communication (cost, time), update communication (cost, time), local I/O at each computer, and response time. For example, a unique allocation (assign one data object to one computer) yields a small amount of storage, high read communication traffic, small update communication, and small local I/O at each computer. Duplicate allocation (more than one copy) yields a large amount of storage, small read communication traffic, high update communication, and local I/O at each computer. We introduced the following two data allocation strategies in the previous chapter:

> Nonredundant Best Fit Method

> Redundant All Benefit Site Method

Optimal allocation algorithms attempt to automatically assign the application objects (e.g., data, processing logic) to locations so that a "cost" function is minimized. As stated in the previous chapter, more than 30 optimal allocation algorithms, mostly focusing on data allocations, have been published in the literature. Figure 6.13 gives you a flavor of these algorithms by showing a simplified version of a data allocation algorithm for a three-computer network which minimizes a cost function.[7] Many data allocation algorithms use an N-cube for an N computer network in which each vertex of the cube shows an allocation. The allocation is represented as 1 and no allocation is represented as 0 on the vertices of the cube (see Figure 6.13). For example, the vertex 001 shows that a file (a server or a task) is allocated to computer 3 and not to computers 1 and 2. Thus as we move from vor-

---

7. A three-computer network here means that there are three candidate sites where data can be allocated. For example, even if an enterprise network consists of many desktops, mid-range computers, and mainframes, only a handful of sites may be candidates for large database allocations.

Figure 6.13 A Simple Optimal Allocation Algorithm

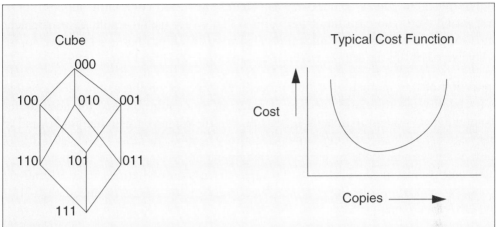

Legend:

- Vertex (100) means that the file is allocated to computer 1 only.

- Vertex (101) means that the file is allocated to computers 1 and 3 only.

A Simple Optimal Allocation Algorithm to Minimize Cost C:

1. Pick an allocation A with single object allocation (e.g., 001, 010, 100).

2. Calculate the constraints for A.

3. If constraints violated, then reject this allocation, pick the next allocation A on the same level of the vertex, and go to step 8.

4. Store A in a feasible set FS.

5. Calculate the cost function C for A.

6. Set $A^*=A$, where A^* is the optimal allocation and set $C^* = C$ where C^* is the minimum cost.

7. Pick another A by adding one more copy on the cube (e.g., 101 110, 011).

8. Calculate the constraints for A.

9. If constraints violated, then reject this allocation, pick the next allocation A on the same level of the vertex, and go to step 8. If no more allocations left, then stop.

10. Store A in the feasible set FS.

11. Calculate the cost function C for A.

12. Compare C with C^*. If $C < C^*$, then set $A^*=A$ and $C^*=C$. If not, then ignore all allocations with additional copies.

13. Pick another A if available and go to step 8. Otherwise stop.

tex 000 to 111, more copies of files exist. In addition, as shown in Figure 6.13 the cost (sum of storage, communication, and local traffic) usually first drops and then increases rapidly with more copies of data. We can search down the cube until the cost starts to increase and then ignore all the lower vertices. This very useful result, first indicated by [Chu 1969], is included in the allocation algorithm listed in Figure 6.13. More sophisticated versions of this algorithm can be found in Jain [1987], and Umar [1985].

Application of the optimal allocation procedures depends on the nature of the problem, the availability of information needed to reach an exact solution, and the need to determine optimal versus approximate solutions in real life We have found that for several real-life situations, sophisticated algorithms are rarely needed. In most cases, several allocation decisions can be made by exercising judgment and using real-life technology, application, and management constraints. Detailed discussion of optimal data allocations is beyond the scope of this book. The interested reader should review Brahmadathan [1992], Jain [1987], and Umar [1984].

Our experience has shown that the intuitive data allocation approach, coupled with the two analytical data allocation methods discussed in the previous chapter, are quite effective in many real-life situations. The additional considerations listed in the sidebar "General Allocation Considerations" should be used for overall guidance. The best approach is to start with a single data allocation on a fast server (many fast SMP servers are becoming commercially available, see for example The [1995]. Then ask the question: What constraints are being violated by using this approach? If needed, then spread data to multiple sites with no duplicates, and consider duplicate copies for read-only or read-mostly data.

6.8   State of the Practice: Examples and Case Studies

A variety of applications have been architected in distributed C/S environments. These applications utilize a combination of single-tiered, two-tiered, three-tiered architectures, and hybrid application architectures. A large number of case studies that describe different application architectures are appearing in the Gartner reports (see, for example Melling [1995]), and in trade journals such as *Client/Server Computing*, *Client/Server Today*, *Datamation*, *Information Week*, and *Computerworld*. However, very few real-life examples of Web-based applications are published as we go to press due to the relative newness of the subject area. We describe a few examples to highlight different approaches in Web-based as well as the traditional C/S application architectures. Also see the sidebar "Internet Transaction Processing: Backbone of Electronic Commerce."

General Allocation Considerations

- Flexibility and growth needs are better served by distributing data as well as programs.

- Downsizing initiatives that require moving applications away from the mainframe are best served by distributing data as well as programs.

- Availability needs are better satisfied by allowing data duplication.

- Development costs generally decrease by distribution because end-user computing increases productivity.

- Performance may or may not improve with distributed applications (these configurations reduce the central site congestion but increase network communications).

- Data sharing among thousands of users does become more difficult as data are more decentralized.

- Applications which are tightly connected to other applications on the same computer should not be separated (this generates extra traffic).

- Large databases are generally better handled at centralized mainframes.

- Control and security needs, at present, are better satisfied by centralized systems, because distributed applications introduce many security issues.

- More training is needed to operate and manage distributed applications.

- Maintenance and operation costs may increase due to multiple licenses and the need for expensive middleware.

- Backup and recovery procedures are easier with centralized applications.

- Management and support are harder in distributed applications due to a lack of good tools (at the time of this writing).

Corporate Intranet Applications utilize Web browsers as the first tier, the Web server as the second tier, and the back-end applications and databases as the third tier. Bickell [1996] gives several examples of how this "three-tiered" architecture is being used in organizations. Examples include a large engineering firm that implemented a Web-based time-sheet submission and reporting system across a network of 900 Macs, 900 PCs, and 300 UNIX workstations. The system uses a back-end Sybase database. The company was able to develop this system in two weeks because there was no need to implement a different user interface for different platforms. A similar example is given of a medium-sized (10,000 employees) chemical research company that implemented a Web-based application across multiple platforms (Web browsers were used as the first tier). Robinson [1996] describes how the Web-based architectures with thin clients (i.e., Web browsers only display information) and thick servers (i.e., Web servers house the HTML pages plus the databases and application code) are used in several organizations. Additional examples of Web-based application architectures can be found in Grygo [1996].

Internet Transaction Processing: Backbone of Electronic Commerce

Transaction processing (TP) in Internet is the backbone of electronic commerce because all buying/selling activities involve transactions. However, Internet (unsupervised and free access) is contrary to the notion of commercial transactions (highly controlled and supervised). In particular, TP requires the following:

- Guaranteed message delivery, i.e., once you have sent a message the middleware will be responsible for delivering the message. If the message is not delivered, the middleware will try to deliver it again.

- Guaranteed message processing, i.e., once the message is delivered, it is processed correctly (committed). If a message processing error occurs, the results of processing are rolled back.

- Improved security and privacy i.e., the transactions are protected from unauthorized users. The transaction activities are also logged for audit trails.

How will these requirements be satisfied in the Internet? First, increased use of message-oriented-middleware (MOM) will provide guaranteed message delivery. Second, Internet TP will typically use the fat server model in the Internet world because most of the TP processing will continue to take place in the back-end systems with proven TP technology for guaranteed message processing. The client side may include Java applets that do minimal processing. Third, the servers will reside inside the corporate firewalls for security and the public clients will reside outside the firewalls. The clients and the servers will use improved security services such as public/private keys and Secure Socket Layer (SSL) in the Internet world. These factors, plus consortia such as CommerceNet, will be vital for electronic commerce.

It is interesting to note the transaction processing strategies of key players in the context of the Internet. IBM has dominated the mainframe-based TP market since the 1970s due to its CICS and IMS product lines. At present, IBM is repositioning its products through its Distributed Computing Blueprint [Umar 1997, Chapter 9] and BOSS strategy that ties desktops, distributed objects, Web, OSF DCE, and IMS/CICS (consult http://www.IBM.com for details). Microsoft is also gradually arming the PC application developers with TP capabilities through extensions to Visual Basic, Windows NT, and Windows95. In addition, the ActiveX support is beginning to tie desktops to the back-end TP systems through DCOM (see, "Microsoft's Transaction Processing Strategy", Gartner Group Research Note, September 18, 1996). The Object Management Group (OMG) is also working diligently to specify "object transactions" that could exist in the Internet world (see http://www.omg.org for details).

A Real-Life Corporate Intranet System. A large corporation is developing a variety of new applications on the existing infrastructure shown in Figure 6.14 and transitioning to an Intranet. The infrastructure consists of an IBM SNA mainframe, many Ethernet LANs (UNIX TCP/IP LANs, a Novell LAN, and an Appleshare LAN), all interconnected through a TCP/IP corporatewide Intranet. The routers are used to find the appropriate paths between various computers in this network. A gateway is used to convert the TCP/IP network protocols to Token Ring and SNA. All computers on the existing network can access other computer resources through terminal emulation and file transfer. The Novell and Appleshare servers are used in this network for file and print services. The two databases (MVS DB2 and UNIX) are accessed by the client processes (applications and end-user tools) on various PCs in Figure 6.14. The client processes can access the DB2 and UNIX databases by using a two-tiered architecture. However, some specialized application processes (e.g., forecasting applications) reside on the UNIX application server that also need the data located in the UNIX database server. In this case, the PC client processes access the application server which in turn issues the SQL statements against the UNIX database server by using a three-tiered architecture. The FDDI ring is used to provide fast access to the UNIX database server (FDDI is a 100 million bits per second LAN as compared to the Ethernet LANs that operate at 10 million bits per second). Web browsers (not shown in the diagram) at desktops (PCs, Apples) will access the corporate resources through Web servers that are being added to this network.

Distributed Objects at Boeing [Horn 1996]. This example, described in a presentation, showed how Boeing Aerospace uses distributed object technology for a materials information system. This system uses a three-tiered architecture that employs distributed object technology at all levels. Microsoft OLE is used at client side and CORBA at the back end. This is an interesting example of integrating OLE and CORBA for distributed applications.

Figure 6.14 A Sample Corporate Configuration

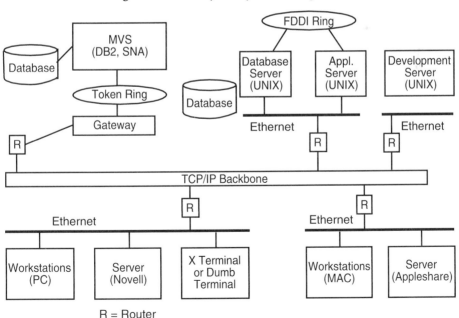

Distributed Object-Based Military Patient Care System. TRAC2ES is a logistics and tracking system that plans and monitors the movement and care of U.S. military patients around the globe. This application analyzes mission data and hospital availability data for planners so that they can, for example, provide an injured soldier in Europe with a trip to a suitable hospital in the United States. The system responds to problems such as missed flights, airport closings, and hospital bed availability fluctuations. The data are stored in distributed object databases that are spread around the world. These data are accessed from clients around the globe. *Source:* 1996 *Computerworld* Object Application Awards, Best Distributed Applications Using Object Technology Category.

United Behavioral Systems [Ricciuti 1994]. United Behavioral Systems (UBS), a mental health care provider, developed two major C/S applications. These applications allow the managers to monitor patient progress in detail, pinpoint how much business is generated by each of the more than 14,000 doctors in 32 clinics, quickly verify insurance coverage for each new patient, and provide centralized on-line reporting capabilities. Figure 6.15 shows the architecture used at UBS. Basically, the new applications are developed by using PCs for presentation services, an RS/6000 for business logic (application server), and another RS/6000 for databases (data server). Both C/S applications can access the Unisys mainframe health care data to verify that the claimants are eligible for mental health coverage. The connection with the mainframe allows C/S applications to grow to meet business pressures while still leveraging the investment in the mainframe data.

Figure 6.15 United Behavioral Systems

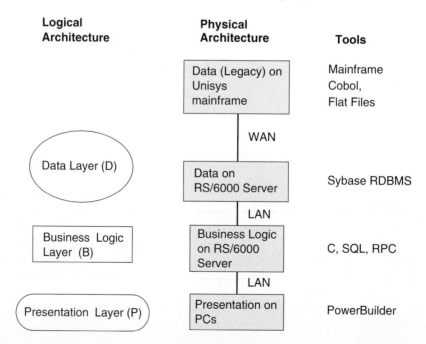

Hyatt's Three-Tiered Sales System [Grygo 1995]. Hyatt Corporation realized in 1992 that its sales managers could do a much better job of selling hotel space for groups if they could quickly access reservation information about the 87 Hyatt hotels and 16 resorts. The new sales system, titled Envision, was officially initiated in 1994 to mimic the way sales people function and swap out components at will. To accomplish this, the Envision team insisted on a three-tiered application architecture that encapsulates the business logic in a single set of modules—thus separating presentation and data management services from the ever-changing business logic. The presentation layer uses PowerBuilder and the data management is based on Informix database engine. After some debate, it was decided not to use remote SQL due to its possibility of clogging the WAN lines (Hyatt used 56-Kbps lines; this was the most constrained resource). RPC middleware was used instead due to its effectiveness in minimizing network load, separation of concerns, load balancing, and security. The system, being used by 100 users and expected to be ramped up to 600 users, has already resulted in an effective change in the roles and responsibilities of the sales force.

Distributed Objects for Motorola's Iridium [Rymer 1995(b)]. Motorola is developing a new "network in space," called Iridium, to support a worldwide, on-demand voice and data communications system. The Iridium satellites move at more than 20,000 miles per hour; thus the mobile users appear to be stationary to these satellites. This is quite different from the stationary cells that are used in the current cellular networks. These satellites make up a dynamic network that routes traffic among themselves and manage up and down links. The Systems Control Segment (SCS) project is building the management and control software for Iridium. The SCS software is based on distributed objects that are dispersed over several Windows PCs and UNIX machines. Specifically, the project will use CORBA, C++ class libraries, object databases, and an object-oriented expert system. This software will be installed around the world in tracking stations, satellite control facilities, and gateways connecting different equipment, and operations centers. The distributed object architecture addresses the challenges of managing a virtual environment, handling of large amounts of data, and unique user requirements.

Bank of Boston Three-Tier Customer Information System [Wilson 1995]. The Bank of Boston, a 210-year-old bank, has developed a comprehensive customer information system that allows the authorized bank employees to tap into extensive historical information about its customers. This application also ranks customers according to actual and potential profitability and measures sales increases by customer, product, and market segment. The application employs a three-tiered architecture where the IBM 3090 serves as a third tier that feeds financial and customer data to a second tier SQL server. The client software written in C++, Visual Basic, and PowerBuilder runs on PC Windows platforms.

CorpTech Repository [Meyer 1996]. Corporate Technology Information Systems (CorpTech) provides business, management, product, and employment information to 40,000 U.S. companies operating in technology-intensive industries. The data are stored in a relational database and are updated by a team of trained telephone surveyors who regularly

contact the information providers to verify or update the repository. The repository information is used to develop a variety of special reports and publications. The system uses a two-
physical-tiered architecture by using a thin client and a fat server model.

6.9   State of the Market: Standards and Products

Special standards for application architectures are not needed. However, standardized APIs
are essential for portable and interoperable applications. The previously discussed API
developments for remote SQL (e.g., ODBC, DRDA), RPCs (e.g., OSF DCE RPC), and distributed object services (e.g., CORBA, OLE, and OpenDoc) should be carefully watched.

Tools are needed to help the architects in examining and evaluating the various architectural
choices. Ideally, these tools should allow an analyst to specify requirements, develop object
models to satisfy the functional requirements, specify existing or proposed infrastructure,
evaluate the C/S configurations (e.g., two versus three tiers, fat clients versus fat servers),
and examine performance/allocation trade-offs. Comprehensive tools in this area are virtually nonexistent at this point.

6.10   State of the Art: Research Notes

Development of software architecture for modern distributed applications is quite complex
and requires synthesis of results from several rapidly advancing disciplines. Examples of the
disciplines are distributed and parallel software engineering [Blelloch 1996], [Shatz 1993],
and [Shatz 1987], distributed objects [Linthicum 1997], [Orfali 1996], and [Rymer 1995],
distributed database design [Teorey 1994], program and database fragmentation and allocation problems [Jain 1987], and [Umar 1985], middleware and IT infrastructure issues [Umar
1997], and the evolving standards in network and software architectures.

Many interesting areas of research need attention because client/server applications at
present are a transitional phase to fully distributed object-based applications [Vaughan-
Nichols 1997], and [Lewis 1995]. The main area of research involves the trade-offs between
different distributed object models such as object frameworks and componentware for large-
scale systems. Additional work is needed to understand the impact of intelligent agents and
the coordination models needed between different application components [Hendler 1996],
and [Adler 1995]. Other areas of research include a systematic theory of software architectures and architecture refinements/evaluations [Tsai 1997], and [Moriconi 1995], specification and analysis of system architectures by using tools [Brinkley 1997], [Pancake 1995],
and [Luckham 1995], design patterns [Hellenack 1997], and [Schmidt 1995], and abstractions for software architectures [Shaw 1995]. Another area of potential research is the use of

physical product development methodologies for information product architectures [Meyer 1996]. *The Information Systems Journal*, Vol 21, No. 2, 1996, is a Special Issue on Advanced Information Systems Engineering and contains five thoroughly researched papers on different aspects of software engineering.

There are interesting developments in architectures where service-oriented architectures are evolving instead of application by application architectures (see the sidebar "Service-Oriented Architectures; Going Beyond Application Architectures"). In addition, research is needed to develop expert systems that generate project plans based on chosen architectures (see the sidebar "Generate Project Plans By Using Application Architectures")

Service Oriented Architectures: Beyond Application Architectures

While many applications are architected on application by application basis, the notion of architecting services is quite appealing in real-life situations. The basic idea is that business logic and data are shared among different applications to provide a set of services. For example, customer services span many application areas such as marketing, purchasing, and billing. Instead of designing these applications individually, the customer services should be architected to maximize sharing of data and logic between the marketing, purchasing and billing applications. Service-oriented architectures are essentially multi-tiered applications with the following software tiers:

- Shared corporate data needed for the services (e.g., customer data)

- Shared business logic that is common to multiple applications (e.g., integrity checks, steps to enter an order)

- Application logic specific to each application area

- User interfaces for users residing at different types of devices (desktops, Web browsers, wireless devices)

The notion of service-oriented architecture has been around for several years under different names. For example, the Bellcore OSCA, discussed earlier in this chapter, is based on a similar notion. These architectures use familiar forms of middleware but separate application program functions into application-specific and application-common modules. Earlier versions used RPCs between service modules but now distributed-object middleware such as CORBA, component software, and message brokers are potential candidates.

The Gartner Group published a series of research notes on service oriented architectures in April 1996 and discussed a case study about the obstacles encountered by a company in delivering such architectures in a December 23, 1996, research note. For additional information, contact the Gartner Group at http://www.gartner.com.

6.11   Summary

Modern object-oriented, client/server Internet technology offers many promises such as flexibility and end-user control but also introduces the risks of increased complexity and manageability. The applications must be architected to maximize the benefits and minimize the risks. In particular, the goals must be clearly defined and adhered to, and hardware cost savings should not be overemphasized. As the needed middleware becomes increasingly state of the market, the application architects need an understanding of the interrelationships between business drivers, modern middleware, and costs and benefits of various strategies. The systematic procedure presented in this chapter starts with construction of an object model that is refined and expanded through various steps of logical decompositions, config-uration analysis, infrastructure evaluation, and performance/allocation evaluations. This methodology takes into account the various interrelationships and can be used for large-scale as well as small-scale departmental applications.

6.12   Case Study: Application Software Architectures for XYZCorp

The application software architecture is progressing in parallel with the data architecture for the following three new Web-based applications:

- A new "advanced" inventory management system for integrated order processing/inventory management
- A management planning system that will support the management decisions in marketing and product planning
- A flexible manufacturing system to automate the manufacturing of electronic products.

Recall that these three applications were identified in the XYZAICS initiative. You have been asked to develop the application software architecture for the three applications and answer questions such as the following: What are the logical components of these applica-tions? How many tiers will be used? What will each tier do? What type of middleware com-ponents will you use?

Hints about the Case Study

The five-step application software architecture procedure described in Sections 6.3 through 6.7 should be used to establish the software architectures for these three applications.

The effort to develop the application software architecture for the management planning system (MPS) should be very lightweight. As mentioned in the previous chapter, a typical approach for decision support systems such as MPS is to extract information from various sources and store it in a data warehouse for analysis (see Chapter 10). For most data ware-houses, a two-tiered architecture works well because you can run most analysis tools at the user desktops and use remote SQL middleware to access the data warehouse database.

Generate Project Plans by Using Application Architectures

Project planning steps are dependent on the underlying application architecture being deployed. Thus it is possible to use expert systems in developing project plans based on architectural choices. C/S10,000 from Client/Server Connection is an expert system tool that exploits this principle. It generates project plans that are driven by technical architectures. This tool guides the user through a series of questions aimed at identifying a few (one or two) application architectures from an inventory of 125 application architectures. After the user selects an architecture (this may require some iterations), the expert system prompts the user through additional questions for selecting a suitable network architecture from an inventory of 85 network architectures. After this, the tool generates a work breakdown structure (WBS), project estimate and supporting materials for a project plan. The tool also includes an inventory of products that can be used to implement selected architectures.

Source: Hunter, R. and Conway, B., "C/S 10,000: Methodology Gain Without Pain?" *Gartner Group Research Note*, August 29, 1996.

The application software architecture for the inventory management system can be an extensive effort. A three-tiered architecture would do the job in this case. The first tier can be a Web browser, the second tier can perform the application logic that can be invoked from a CGI gateway, and the third tier can be the database that was allocated as part of the data architecture effort.

The flexible manufacturing system does not require an extensive software architecture study because it is a real-time system. In systems of this nature, most of the data and processing programs reside on the same machines for performance reasons. It is educational to go through the five steps to understand the unique software architecture problems of real-time systems by working through this exercise.

6.13   Problems and Exercises

1. Describe a distributed application system of your choice in detail. What are the advantages and disadvantages of this application?

2. Point out the major differences between conventional and distributed software architectures.

3. Consider a Web-based order processing application. Develop the architecture of this system by using the five-step application software architecture procedure described in Sections 6.3 through 6.7. For each step, list the major decisions, the techniques/tools employed, and the final choices made by you.

4. Review, expand, and improve Table 6.3 to make it general for any tiering decision evaluation.

5. Complete Table 6.4 to evaluate some of the IT infrastructure products.

6. Discuss how the methodologies, tools, and techniques outlined in this chapter would change for real-time embedded control systems and for newer applications such as multimedia applications.

7. Convert the procedure described in this chapter to a checklist that can be used to guide an application architecture process.

8. Suppose that you have been asked to architect an electronic commerce application. Can you use CORBA in this application? Be specific where you can use CORBA and where you cannot (and why not).

6.14   Additional Information

The literature on different aspects of application architectures is growing gradually. The book by Shatz [1993] contains a good technical overview. The paper by Shedletsky and Rofrano [Shedletsky 1993] describe the various architectural choices in detail. Additional papers by Adler [1995], Herbert [1994], Lewis [1995], Schneiderwind [1989], Shatz [1987], and Schulte [1995] establish the basic concepts in distributed application design. The *IEEE Transactions on Software Engineering* special issue on distributed systems, January 1987, contains many original ideas. The *IEEE Transactions on Software Engineering*, April 1995, is a special issue on software architecture and contains seven interesting articles on emerging research areas in software architectures. The Gartner Group Research Notes on System Software Architecture are a rich source of practical analysis and insights into the subject matter.

Adler, R., "Distributed Coordination Models for Client/Server Computing," *IEEE Computer,* April 1995, pp. 14–22.

Andersen, J., "The Dynamic Model," *Object Magazines,* July/August 1995, pp. 45–47.

Andrews, G. R., "Paradigms for Process Interaction in Distributed Programs," *ACM Computing Surveys,* March 1991, pp. 49–90.

Andrews, G. R., *Concurrent Programming: Principles and Practice,* Benjamin Cummings Publishing Co., 1992.

Andriole, S., *Rapid Application Prototyping,* QED Publishing Group, 1992.

Bhide, A., and Stonebraker, M., "A Performance Comparison of Two Architectures for Fast Transaction Processing," 4th International Conference on Data Eng., February, 1988, pp. 32-40.

Bickell, R., "Building Intranets," *Internet World,* March 1996, pp. 72–75.

Blelloch, G., "Programming Parallel Algorithms," *Communications of the ACM,* March 1996, pp. 85–97.

Booch, G., *Object Oriented Design with Applications,* Benjamin Cummings, 2d ed., 1994.

Bort, J., "Can Message Brokers Deliver?" *Applications Software Magazine,* June 1996, pp.70–76.

Brahmadathan, K., and Ramarao, K., "On the Design of Replicated Databases," *Information Sciences,* Vol. 65, Nos. 1 and 2, 1992, pp. 173–200.

Brinkley, J. F., and Prothero, J. S., "Slisp: A Flexible Software Toolkit for Hybrid, Embedded and Distributed Applications," *Software–Practice and Experience,* Vol. 27, No. 1, 1997, pp. 33–48.

Bruno, G., and Balsamo, A., "Petri Net-Based Object-Oriented Modeling of Distributed Systems," *OOPSLA'86 Proceedings,* pp. 284–293, September 1986.

Burton, B., "The Evolution of Oracle's Web Request Broker," *Gartner Group Research Note,* December 30, 1996.

Casey, R. G., "Allocation of Copies of a File in an Information Network," Summer Joint Computer Conference (SJJC) 1972, AFIPS Press, Vol. 40, 1972

Chandy, D. M. and Hewes, J. E., "File Allocation in Distributed Systems," *Proc. of the International Symposium on Computer Performance Modeling, Measurement, and Evaluation,* March 1976, pp. 10–13.

Chang, S. K., and Liu, A. C., "A Database File Allocation Problem," COMPSAC, 1981, pp. 18–22.

Chen, B., and Yeh, R., "Formal Specification and Verification of Distributed Systems," *IEEE Transactions on Software Engineering,* November 1983, pp. 710–722.

Chin, R., and Chanson, S., "Distributed Object-Based Programming Systems," *ACM Computing Surveys,* March 1991, pp. 91–124.

Chu, W. W., "Optimal File Allocation in a Multiple Computer System," *IEEE Transactions on Computers,* October 1969, pp. 885–889.

Coffman, E. G., Gelenbe, E, et al., "Optimization of the Number of Copies in Distributed Databases," *Proc. of the 7th IFIP Symposium on Computer Performance Modeling, Measurement, and Evaluation,* May 1980, pp. 257–263.

Comport, J., "Packaged Applications: Buy an Application, Inherit an Architecture," *Gartner Group Report,* February, 1995.

Corbin, J. R., *The Art of Distributed Applications: Programming Techniques for Remote Procedure Calls,* Springer-Verlag, 1991.

Coulouris, G., and Dollimore, J., *Distributed Systems: Concepts and Design,* Addison Wesley, 1989.

Dale, A., and Roussopoulos, N., "Performance Comparison of Three Modern DBMS Architectures," *IEEE Transactions on Software Engineering,* February 1993, pp. 120–138.

Dhumne, A., "Multitier Application Benefits," *Application Development Trends,* June 1996, pp. 52–56.

Dickman, A., "Two-Tier versus Three-Tier Apps," *Information Week,* Nov. 13, 1995, pp. 74–80.

Dollas, A., and Kanopoulos, N., "Reducing Time to Market through Rapid Prototyping," guest editor's introduction, *IEEE Computer,* special issue on reducing time to market through rapid prototyping, February 1995, pp. 14–15.

Edelstein, H., "Lions, Tigers, and Downsizing," *Database Programming and Design,* March 1992, pp. 39–45.

Estrin, G., Fenchel, R.S., Razouk, R.R., and Vernon, M.K., "SARA (Systems Architecture Apprentice): Modeling, Analysis, and Simulation Support for Design of Concurrent Systems," *IEEE Transactions on Software Engineering,* February 1986, pp. 293–311.

Eswaran, K. P., "Allocation of Records to Files and Files to Computer Networks," IFIP, 1974, pp. 304–307.

Everret, B. *Cluster Analysis,* Heinemann Educ. Books Ltd., London, 1974.

Frye, C., "N-Tier at Your Own Risk," *Software Magazine,* December 1996, pp. 80–89.

Garlan, D., and Perry, D., "Introduction to the Special Issue on Software Architecture: Guest Editorial," *IEEE Transactions on Software Engineering,* April 1995, pp. 269–274.

Garlan, D., and Shaw, M., "An Introduction to Software Architecture," in *Advances in Software Engineering and Knowledge Engineering,* Vol. I, World Scientific, 1993.

Gray, J., "An Approach to Decentralized Computer Systems," *IEEE Transactions on Software Engineering,* June 1986, pp. 684–692.

Grygo, E., "Regency Systems Solutions: Hyatt Fill Group Reservations With Three-Tiered Sales System," *Client/Server Computing,* October 1995, pp. 28–38.

Grygo, E., "Intranet Reality Check," *Client/Server Computing,* May 1996, pp. 22–32.

Hamilton, D., "Don't Let Client/Server Performance Gotchas Getcha," *Datamation,* November 1, 1994, pp. 39–40.

Hellenack, L., "Object-Oriented Business Patterns," *Object Magazine,* January 1997, pp. 21–22.

Hendler, J., "Intelligent Agents: Where AI Meets Information Technology," *IEEE Expert,* December 1996, pp. 20–23.

Herbert, A., "An ANSA Overview," *IEEE Network,* January/February, 1994, pp. 18-23.

Hill, J., et al., "The Multibackend Database System (MDBS): A Performance Study," Intern. Conf. on DBs, Parallel Architectures, and their Applications, March, 1990, pp. 139–143.

Horn, C., and O'Toole, A., "Distributed Object Oriented Approach," International Conference on Distributed Platforms, Dresden, Germany, Feb. 1996.

Inmon, W. H., *Developing Client/Server Applications,* QED Publishing Group, rev. ed., 1993.

Jacobson, I., et al., *Object-Oriented Software Engineering,* Addison Wesley, 1992.

Jain, H., "A Comprehensive Model for the Design of Distributed Computer Systems," *IEEE Transactions on Software Engineering,* October 1987, pp. 1092–1104.

Jessup, T., "WAN Design with Client-Server in Mind," *Data Communications,* August 1996, pp. 52–60.

Johnson, J., "Client-Server's Magic Bullet," *Data Communications,* August 1995, pp. 44–54.

Kleinrock, L., "Distributed Systems," *Communications of the ACM,* November 1985, Vol. 18, No. 11, pp. 1200–1213.

Kleinrock, L., *Queuing Systems,* Vol. 2, John Wiley, 1976.

Lewis, T., "Where is Client/Server Software Headed?" *IEEE Computer,* 1995, pp. 49–55.

Linthicum, D., "Reevaluating Distributed Objects," *DBMS,* January 1997, pp. 44–52.

Luckham, D., et al., "Specification and Analysis of Systems Architecture Using Rapide," *IEEE Transactions on Software Engineering,* April 1995, pp. 336–355.

Malik, W., "Fundamental IS Architecture Questions and Answers," *Gartner Group Research Note,* July 30, 1996.

Martin, R. "The Standards Test for Portability," *Datamation,* May 15, 1989.

Melling, W., "Putting it All Together: Case Studies in Architecture," and "Case Studies in Architecture," *Gartner Group Reports,* February 1995.

Meyer, B., "On Formalism in Specifications," *IEEE Software,* January, 1989.

Meyer, M., and Zack, M., "The Design and Development of Information Products," *Sloan Management Review,* Vol. 37, No. 3, 1996, pp. 43–59.

Mills, J., "An OSCA Architecture Characterization of Network Functionality and Data," *Journal of System Integration,* July 1991.

Moad, J., "The New Agenda for Open Systems," *Datamation,* April 1, 1990.

Moriconi, M., "Correct Architecture Refinement," *IEEE Transactions on Software Engineering,* April 1995, pp. 356–372.

Mowbray, T., and Zahavi, R., *The Essential CORBA: Systems Integration Using Distributed Objects,* John Wiley, 1995.

Natis, Y., "Internet Transaction Processing: Q&A," *Gartner Group Research Note,* March 8, 1996.

Negoita, C., *Expert Systems and Fuzzy Sets,* Benjamin Cummings, 1985.

Nitzberg, B., and Lo, V., "Distributed Shared Memory: A Survey of Issues and Approaches," *IEEE Computer,* August 1991, pp. 52–60.

Nutt, G., *Open Systems,* Prentice Hall, 1992.

Orfali, R., Harkey, D., and Edwards, J., *Essential Distributed Objects Survival Guide,* John Wiley, 1996.

Ozsu, M., and Valduriez, P., "Distributed Database Systems: Where Are We Now?" *IEEE Computer,* August 1991, pp. 68–78.

Pancake, C., et al., "Performance Evaluation Tools for Parallel and Distributed Systems," *IEEE Computer,* November 1995, pp. 16–19.

Pankaj, J., *An Integrated Approach to Software Engineering,* Springer-Verlag, 1991.

Papelis, Y. E., and Casavant, T. L., "Specification and Analysis of Parallel/Distributed Software and Systems by Petri Nets with Transition Enabling," *IEEE Transactions on Software Engineering,* March 1992, pp. 252–261.

Paulson, D., and Wand, Y., "An Automated Approach to Information System Decomposition," *IEEE Transactions on Software Engineering,* March 1992, pp. 174–189.

Percy, A., "The Real Architectural Destination," *Gartner Group Research Note,* July 30, 1996.

Perry, D. and Wolf, A., "Foundations for the Study of Software Architecture," in *ACM SIGSOFT Software Eng. Notes,* Vol. 17, No. 4, 1992.

Porter, P., "Net Offensive," *Software Magazine,* January 1997, pp. 26–34.

Radding, A., "Dirty Downsizing," *Computerworld,* August 10, 1992, pp. 65–68.

Ramamoorthy, C. V., Garg, V. and Prakash, A., "Programming in the Large," *IEEE Transactions on Software Engineering,* Vol. SE-12, No. 7, pp. 769–783, July 1986.

Ramamoorthy, C. V., and Vick, C. R., *Handbook of Software Engineering,* Van Nostrand, 1984.

Ricciuti, M., "Universal Data Access!" *Datamation,* November 1, 1991.

Ricciuti, M., "Here Come the HR Client/Server Systems," *Datamation,* July 1, 1992.

Ricciuti, M., "The Best in Client/Server Computing," *Datamation,* March 24, 1994, pp. 26–35.

Robinson, T., "Road Warriors Charge the Gates," *Client/Server Computing,* December 1996, pp. S13–S15.

Rolia, J., and Sevcik, K., "The Method of Layers," *IEEE Transactions on Software Engineering,* August 1995, pp. 689–700.

Rosenberg, D., "Applying Object-Oriented Methods to Interactive Multimedia Projects," *Object Magazine,* June 1995, pp. 40–49.

Rubenstein, H., and Waters, R., "The Requirements Apprentice: Automated Assistance for Requirement Acquisition," *IEEE Transactions on Software Engineering,* March 1991, pp. 226–240.

Rumbaugh, J., et al., *Object-Oriented Modeling and Design,* Prentice Hall, 2d ed., 1994.

Rymer, J., "Business Objects," *Distributed Computing Monitor,* Patricia Seybold Group, January 1995 (a).

Rymer, J., "How Distributed Objects Will Manage a Network in Space," *Distributed Computing Monitor,* Vol. 10, No. 4, 1995 (b), pp. 31–35.

Salim, J., "Application Development in the Internet Age," *Data Management Review,* January 1997, pp. 68–72.

Schmidt, D., "Using Design Patterns to Develop Reusable Object-Oriented Communications Software," *Communications of the ACM,* October 1995, pp. 65–74.

Schneiderwind, N., "Distributed System Software Design Paradigm with Application to Computer Networks," *IEEE Transactions on Software Engineering,* April 1989, pp. 402–412.

Schulte, R., "Distributed Software Architectures in Full Bloom," *Gartner Group Report,* February, 1995.

Schulte, R., "The Impact of Component Software on Three-Tier Designs," *Gartner Group Research Note,* January 15, 1997.

Schulte, R., "Two-Tier vs. Three-Tier Trade-offs" Part 1 and Part 2, *Gartner Group Research Note,* December 23, 1996.

Shatz, S., *Development of Distributed Software: Concepts and Tools,* Macmillan, 1993.

Shatz, S. M., and Wang, J., "Introduction to Distributed Software Engineering," *IEEE Software,* October 1987.

Shatz, S. M., and Wang, J., "Tutorial: Distributed Software Engineering," *IEEE Computer Society,* No. 856, 1988.

Shaw, M., et al., "Abstractions for Software Architecture and Tools to Support Them," *IEEE Transactions on Software Engineering,* April 1995, pp. 314–335.

Shedletsky, J., and Rofrano, J., "Application Reference Designs for Distributed Systems," *IBM Systems Journal,* Vol. 32, No. 4, 1993, pp. 625–646.

Smith, D., "Common Questions about Cross Platform and Thin Clients," *Gartner Group Research Note,* December 23, 1996.

Teorey, T. J., *Database Modeling and Design,* 2d ed., Morgan Kaufmann, 1994.

Teorey, T. J., and Fry, J. P., *Design of Database Structures,* Prentice Hall, 1982.

Teorey, T. J., and Umar, A., "Distributed Database Design Strategies," *Database Design and Programming,* April 1989.

The, L., "SMP Servers for DSS: Go for the Package Buy," *Datamation,* October 15, 1995, pp. 91–98.

Tsai, J., et al., "Parallel Evaluation of Software Architecture Specification," *Communications of the ACM,* January 1997, pp. 83–86.

Umar, A., "The Allocation of Data and Programs in Distributed Data Processing Environments," Ph.D. Dissertation, Univ. of Michigan, 1984.

Umar, A., *Distributed Computing: A Practical Synthesis,* Prentice Hall, 1993.

Umar, A., *Object-Oriented Client/Server Internet Environments,* Prentice Hall, 1997.

Umar, A., and Teichrow, D., "Computer Aided Software Engineering for Distributed Systems," *Proceedings of IEEE Region 10 Conference on Computer Communications,* Seoul, Korea, August, 1987.

Umar, A., and Teorey, T. J., "A Generalized Approach to Program and Data Allocation in Distributed Systems," *First Pacific Computer Communication Symposium,* Seoul, Korea, October 1985, pp. 462–472.

Umar, A., Chase, T., and Teichrow, D., "A Knowledge-Based Simulator for Distributed Systems," CASE Conference, Ann Arbor, MI, May, 1987.

Ural, H., "Logic Specifications for Communication Systems," IEEE Phoenix Conf. on Computers and Communications, March 1986, pp. 121–128.

Vaughn-Nichols, S., "What's New for 1997?" *Object Magazine,* January 1997, pp. 54–55.

Wilson, L., "A Beautiful Relationship," *Client/Server Journal, Computerworld* special issue, June 1995, p. 13.

Wohl, Amy, "Is Downsizing Right for You?" *Beyond Computing,* IBM Publication, August/September 1992, pp.10–11.

Woods, E., "Application Construction: Architecting Applications for Change," *Client/Server Computing,* October 15, 1995, pp. 80–83.

Woodside, C. M., and Tripathi, S. K., "Optimal Allocation of File Servers in a Local Area Network Environment," *IEEE Transactions on Software Engineering,* August 1986, Vol. SE-12, No. 8, pp. 844–848.

Wreden, N., "The Ups and Downs of Downsizing," *Beyond Computing,* IBM Publication, August/September 1992, pp. 12–15.

Yau, S. S., Jia, X., and Bae, D. H., "Software Design for Distributed Computer Systems," *Computer Communications,* Vol. 15, No. 4, May 1992, pp. 213–224.

7

Implementation Concepts and Examples

(Web, CORBA, ActiveX, DCE, Encina, PowerBuilder)

7.1   Introduction

This chapter shows how the architectures developed in the previous chapters can be implemented (i.e., designed in detail, coded, and tested). Our particular interest is in the class of distributed applications that use object-oriented, client/server, and Internet (OCSI) technologies to deliver business value. Most of the implementation activities are middleware dependent—implementation of a Web-based application that accesses relational databases differs significantly from implementation of a CORBA or DCE application. However, there are a few general concepts that are common to development of all distributed applications. Our objective is to answer the following questions:

- What are the basic implementation concepts for object-oriented client/server Internet (OCSI) applications?

- What are the conceptual issues in defining interfaces, building clients, building servers, and testing OCSI applications?

- What are the specific issues involved in implementing OCSI applications that combine the World Wide Web with technologies such as CORBA, ActiveX, OSF DCE, PowerBuilder, and Encina?

After discussing the general concepts in Section 7.2, we present a sample example in Section 7.3 that is used to illustrate how applications are developed by using Web, CORBA, ActiveX, PowerBuilder, OSF DCE, and Encina. These middleware products were chosen to highlight different aspects of modern Web-based application implementations. We view Web-based applications in terms of the three-tiered architectural components:

- Front ends that involve interactions between tier 1 (e.g., Web browser) and tier 2 (e.g., Web server)
- Back ends that are invoked from the second tier

The front ends consist of Web technologies (e.g., HTML pages, Web servers, CGI, Java applets) and the back ends can consist of a variety of technologies such as CORBA, ActiveX, OSF DCE, SQL middleware, transaction processing middleware, and messaging middleware on an as-needed basis. To give a broad perspective, the Web is used to show how Web-based front ends can be developed, CORBA is used to show how distributed object-based applications can be implemented, OSF DCE is discussed to point out the implementation issues in an open RPC-based environment, Encina is used to highlight implementation issues related to distributed transaction processing, and PowerBuilder is discussed to illustrate remote SQL-based implementations. It is not our objective to describe *every* implementation detail. Instead, the key attributes and comparative analysis are emphasized.

The wide range of issues discussed in this chapter should be of interest to a majority of IT professionals. The first few sections of this chapter should be of interest to the managers and the developers alike. However, the later sections have some coding examples that are intended for developers and technically savvy managers (we use pseudocode that resembles C language).[1] Due to the reliance on middleware, it is expected that the readers have some basic understanding of the modern middleware technologies (the needed information can be obtained from Umar [1997]).

Key Points

- Implementation of client/server applications is like implementing a series of mini- applications that are tied together.

- In general, development of server code is much harder (and expensive) than development of client code. This is not strictly true in the Web world (many tools are making it very easy to develop Web server-based applications).

- Off-the-shelf servers and reuse of existing servers significantly reduces software development costs.

- Complexity, and cost, of testing increase significantly with application architectures that are too inclusive and too ambitious (i.e., are overly distributed).

- When implementing an application, try to use "late binding" between clients and servers (i.e., determine the exact location of the server at run time).

---

1. The pseudocode in this chapter contains several simplifications. It should not be implemented without consulting the vendor-provided programming manuals.

7.2   Implementation Issues: General Concepts

7.2.1   Overview

Implementation of distributed applications is heavily dependent on architectural choices and the middleware selected. For example, in a remote SQL-based environment (e.g., Oracle and PowerBuilder), you only need to write code for client programs that issue SQL calls to access remotely located data sources. In remote SQL environments, coding of client programs is very similar to writing stand-alone programs (yes, we have to issue connects to the remote databases and handle additional return codes, but the activity is not *fundamentally* different). However, for CORBA and OSF DCE environments, you need to code the client programs, code the server programs, and create interface definitions. Conceptually, implementors of distributed applications have the following choices:

- Use off-the shelf applications and customize them where necessary and possible.

- Use off-the shelf servers (typically SQL servers or directory servers) and use CASE tools (e.g., PowerSoft's PowerBuilder) to develop C/S applications (typically client programs only).

- Develop applications by using the "open" middleware (e.g., OSF DCE, OMG CORBA). In this case, you build the clients, the servers, and the interface definitions.

- Write everything on your own, including the middleware. In this case, you build the clients, the servers, the interface definitions, and some middleware (e.g., a layer that resides on top of the existing middleware layers, specialized security and directory services, special error handling such as needed for wireless applications, etc.).

The first choice, if it satisfies stated requirements, is naturally most desirable because suitable off-the-shelf systems can save a great deal of time and money (see Table 7.1). The last choice should be considered only if the first three choices do not satisfy the application requirements (this may happen in the case of specialized real-time applications such as distributed multimedia applications and C/S over wireless). In most real-life situations, the second and third choices are used frequently. These cases are the focus of this chapter.

7.2.2   Implementation Approach

Assuming that we have already gone through the architecture exercise (i.e., developed an object model, decomposed the application into client and server components, and selected the enabling infrastructure), OCSI application implementation involves the following major activities (see Figure 7.1):

1. **Develop a detailed design.** The application architecture developed in the previous stages is refined and a detailed application design is created (see Section 7.2.3).

2. **Create interface definitions.** These definitions are used to advertise the external interfaces (services) that are available to prospective clients. These definitions, described in Section 7.2.4, are not needed if off-the-shelf or existing servers are used.

These definitions are also not needed if you are developing a remote SQL application because the SQL server interfaces are advertised by the vendors as remote SQL APIs.

3. **Build server programs**. The server programs that provide the advertised services are coded (see Section 7.2.5). This activity is also not needed if off-the-shelf or existing servers (e.g., SQL servers) are used.

4. **Build client programs**. The client programs that invoke the servers are coded (see Section7.2.6). This activity is always performed, unless an off-the-shelf tool can be used to provide the client functionality.

5. **Test the application**. All components of the application are constructed, tested, documented, and put into operation (see Section 7.2.7).

TABLE 7.1 IMPLEMENTATION EFFORT NEEDED FOR DIFFERENT CHOICES

Choices / Effort	Use off-the-shelf application	Use off-the-shelf server (e.g., SQL server)	Use off-the-shelf middleware (e.g., OSF DCE, CORBA)	Develop everything on your own
Develop client code	Not needed	Needed	Needed	Needed
Develop server	Not needed	Not needed	Needed	Needed
Create interface definitions	Not needed	Not needed	Needed	Needed
Build or modify middleware	Not needed	Not needed	Not needed	Needed
Testing	Needed	Needed	Needed	Needed

Figure 7.1 Client/Server Application Development

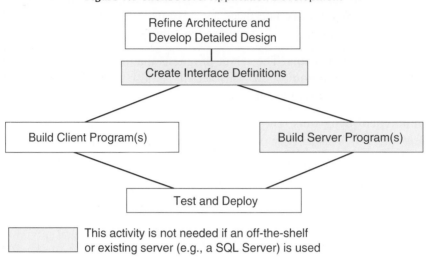

This activity is not needed if an off-the-shelf
or existing server (e.g., a SQL Server) is used

7.2.3   Step 1: Detailed Design

The results of the architecture activities are refined to produce a detailed design that can be
used to build the applications. Detailed design basically shows

- Objects used by the application

- Operations to be performed on these objects and the methods that will execute each operation
  requested on an object

- Decomposition of objects into clients and servers

- Interaction paradigms to be used (i.e., RDA, RPC, MOM)

- Coordinating the execution of clients and servers (e.g., synchronous versus asynchronous processing)

- Security restrictions that limit remote accesses

- Detecting and recovering from failures in the network and the critical resources

We have discussed these topics in the previous chapter and will not repeat them here. This is
just a reminder that a complete specification with these pieces of information is needed
before proceeding with the implementation activities. If for some reason, any of these pieces
of information is not available at sufficient detail, this is a good place to complete it.

In addition to the aforementioned information about the external interfaces between different components of an application, it may be necessary to complete an internal component
design at this stage (e.g., the internal structure of the modules) by using the typical software
engineering principles. In many cases, this internal design is left to the implementors who
actually build the components.

It is recommended that a "design review" be held at this stage involving the architects, the implementors, and the end-users. The purpose of this review is to make sure that the system to be built will indeed satisfy the end-user needs and minimize the risks and maximize the benefits to all concerned.

7.2.4   Step 2: Create Interface Definitions

Simply stated, an **interface** specifies the API that the clients can use to invoke remote operations. In particular, an interface describes (a) the set of operations that can be performed on an object and (b) the parameters needed to perform the operations. For OCSI applications, interface definitions are used to advertise the set of operations that a server can provide to prospective clients. Thus the server's data are accessible only through the server interface. Consequently, the server is encapsulated by its interface and can be viewed as an object [Mowbray 1995], and [Nicol 1993].

When do you need to create interface definitions and when do you not? Basically, you do not need to go through this trouble if you are using a server program that already exists. In particular, you do not need to create interface definitions if

- You are using a SQL server to develop remote SQL applications. For example, Powerbuilder applications, data warehouses, and many other decision support applications do not need interface definitions.
- You are invoking server programs that are commercially available (e.g., application servers from SAP and Peoplesoft).
- You are invoking OSF DCE and/or CORBA server programs that have been developed by other programmers.
- You are using existing servers such as the X.500 directory servers or the Internet mail servers.

You do need to create these definitions when you are developing your own server programs. Figure 7.2 shows an interface of a simple inventory server that supports two operations: query inventory and update price (a definition of this interface is given in Table 7.2). These operations can be invoked by client programs.

Figure 7.2 Example of an Interface

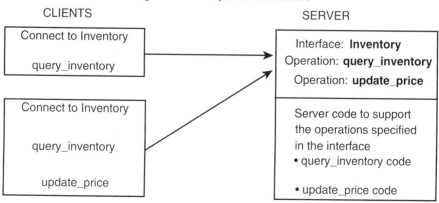

One or more interfaces may be defined for an object. An interface definition includes some or all of the following:

- The interface header that shows an interface name and interface header attributes that uniquely identify the interface. Examples of such attributes are UUIDs (Universal Unique Identifiers) and version numbers of the interfaces.

- Constant and data type definitions that are used to specify data properties (e.g., size) so that clients and servers can exchange data conveniently between different machines.

- A set of operations (procedures) and the signatures for each operation. A signature specifies the operation's name, its arguments, and argument types.

The interfaces are defined by using an **Interface Definition Language (IDL)**. Different middleware products provide IDL compilers with utilities and commands to store and retrieve IDLs from repositories. Client application developers can browse through these repositories to learn about the available server objects and determine the type of operations that can be invoked on an object. IDLs are basically declarative languages—they do not specify any executable code. IDL declarations (e.g., syntax, character types allowed, argument coding, etc.) must conform to the vendor-provided IDL compilers. After you create the interface definition using IDL, you compile the IDL file to create header files and "stubs" that are used in building clients and servers. Table 7.2 shows the IDL of a simple inventory system that supports query inventory and update price operations. The syntax used in this example is abstract. We will see actual IDL specifications for OMG CORBA, OSF DCE, and Encina later on in this chapter.

TABLE 7.2 A SAMPLE ABSTRACT IDL

```
uuid 008B3C84-11c7-8580), version (1.0) /* Header */
interface inventory /* interface name is inventory */
{
        query_inventory (/*The operation to query inventory */
    in char item_id; /* input is item id */
    out integer on_hand; /* output is on hand */
    out integer status ) /* output status */
        update_price ( /*The operation is to update price */
    in char item_id; /* input parameter is item -id */
    in integer new_price; /* input: new price */
    out integer status ) /*output parameter */
}
```

An IDL is a very powerful tool for communication between teams of programmers. Once an IDL has been created, then development of the application pieces can proceed almost asynchronously (i.e., different programmers can write client and server code that uses the IDL). The following issues are concerned with IDLs:

- Why and when should an interface be defined?
- What is the impact of IDL data types?
- How are objects represented through IDLs?
- What are the open areas of work in IDLs (i.e., IDLs for multimedia applications)?
- How do interfaces impact client and server designs?

Interface definitions need to be created only when a *new* service (operation) will be available to the clients. The new service may be provided by a new server or it may be a consolidation of existing services. Interface definitions are not needed if you are planning to use an off-the-shelf SQL Server.[2]

Data types can map to different sizes on different systems. For example, a long data type in C may be 16, 32, or 64 bits, depending on the system. IDL data types ensure that the same size is generated on all systems of a distributed application. IDLs specify data properties (e.g., size) so that clients and servers can exchange data conveniently and efficiently between different machines. Most IDLs allow a wide array of data types (simple and complex), and some support OO concepts such as inheritance. If a variable is not defined by IDL, then it cannot be used by the calling clients. Extra code is needed to be written on the client as well as server side for data that cannot be represented by IDLs.

Representation of objects in IDLs is an important issue for distributed applications. For example, if a complex object (i.e., an object that contains other objects) needs to be sent from a client to a server, then client code needs to "flatten" the complex object into a simpler structure and the server needs to unflatten this object (see the sidebar "Object Flattening/Unflattening").

Interfaces and interface definitions are of two major kinds: **operational interfaces** which contain a set of named operations (i.e., procedures or methods) and **stream interfaces**, in which communication is organized as a set of linked directional flows. We have discussed operational interfaces so far. Let us now briefly review stream interfaces.

Stream interfaces are used to support distributed multimedia systems. Basically, stream interfaces are used to describe unstructured communications such as voice and video streams in multimedia systems. Stream interfaces can also be used for electronic mail. The basic characteristic of stream interfaces is that they must support *continuous data transfers* over relatively long periods of time, for example, real-time playout of video from a remote surveillance camera. In addition, the timeliness of such transmissions must be maintained for the duration of the media presentation. Distributed multimedia systems must also support real-time synchronization between voice and video (e.g., maintaining lip synchronization

---

2. This could be different if an object wrapper is available on the SQL Server. The operations supported by the wrapper need to be defined by IDL.

between an audio and video channel) [Blair 1995]. Development of stream interfaces to support distributed multimedia systems is an area of considerable research and standardization activity (including the ISO standards for open data processing for distributed multimedia).

Interfaces significantly impact the design of client and server programs. First, the server is expected to provide at least the operations required by the client, and the client is required to accept at least the set of results generated by the server. This implies that the server will never respond with a "method/procedure not supported" message to a prospected client. Second, the clients may not use some of the operations provided by the interface. This implies that the server interfaces can be extended to include more operations without requiring any change to the client. Finally, and most importantly, the "size" of the interface needs to be carefully examined. For example, it is not a good idea to specify an interface that supports 100 operations. In such a case, if one operation needs to be changed, then a new IDL will have to be compiled and the server as well as *all* client programs will have to be recompiled (this could be quite irritating). It is best to design a separate interface for each group of users (e.g., one interface for end users, one for the system administrators, etc.).

Interfaces and IDL provide the basic glue for distributed object computing. IDL is used not only to define new services provided by objects, but also to "wrap" existing and legacy systems so that they behave externally as objects. For example, a legacy application written in COBOL could behave as a server object as long as it has an IDL and it provides the operations defined by the IDL. Thus the "IDL-ized" programs run on top of an ORB (Object Request Broker) without revealing their internal details (see Figure 7.3).

Figure 7.3 Interface Definition Language in Action

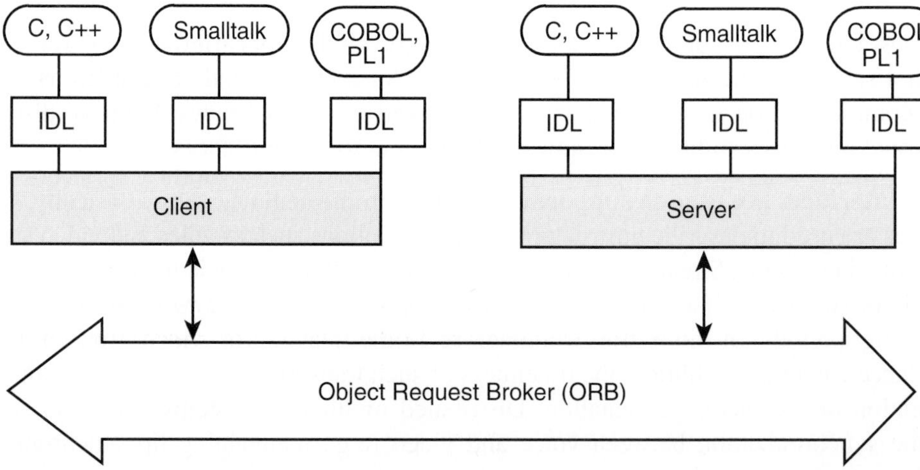

Object Flattening/Unflattening

In some cases, the objects exchanged between clients and servers need to be "flattened." This is especially important if method parameters involve complex objects which point to other objects. The main issue is that complex objects involve pointers to other objects. But these pointers are storage pointers (i.e., show the main memory locations). How can this information be transmitted over the network? The basic idea is to convert these pointers and include the information contained within a complex object as an array (typically). This is called *flattening*. The flattened object is then sent to the other side, with some information for the receiver to reconstruct (*unflatten*) the object back into its original format.

Flattening/unflattening is the responsibility of the middleware. For example, if a particular data structure can be represented by the DCE IDL, then it is the responsibility of DCE middleware to perform flattening and unflattening. When do application programmers need to worry about flattening/unflattening? This happens when some objects being exchanged are too complex to be represented by the middleware IDL, In these cases, objects must be flattened into the IDL parameters before issuing the remote invocation and unflattenend on the other side. This, unfortunately, is the responsibility of application developers. However, as IDLs become more sophisticated (e.g., the CORBA IDL), this need should diminish with time.

7.2.5   Step 3: Build Server Programs

Each server needs code to initialize (i.e., make itself available for use), enter a main loop to receive requests, and exit after releasing resources. Within this general framework, servers can be quite complex because they have to handle many remote interactions, support different options for initialization, and may invoke other application processes (e.g., one for each remote interaction). Due to their complexity, an effort should be made to use an existing and/or off-the-shelf server (server code re-use has big payoffs). Building a server requires knowledge of the interface definition and the middleware run-time routines. The following steps are used to build a server:

- Develop server initialization code
- Design a scheduler that listens to the incoming requests and invokes needed processes
- Develop code for each remote process
- Write special event and error handling code

Server initialization performs a variety of housekeeping functions such as initializing variables, and so forth. The most important aspect of server initialization is to **register** the server interface so that the clients can find the server. A **binding relationship** is established between a client and a server when a client finds an appropriate server and establishes a remote interaction (e.g., an RPC). **Binding information** is network communication and location information for a particular server. The binding information is usually stored in a directory, also known as a repository, by the servers at startup. Clients retrieve this information when they issue a remote interaction. Thus a server can be moved from one host to another without impacting client code.

The server scheduling code basically listens to the communication channel and invokes an appropriate process. The schedulers can be built by using operating system facilities, transaction managers, or specialized middleware routines (e.g., OBB_BOA_main_loop in CORBA and rpc_server_listen in OSF DCE). In UNIX networks, for example, a daemon process usually "listens" to a socket and then forks a server process. In IBM MVS, transaction managers such as IMS/DC and CICS usually schedule the server processes.

The major activity in building a server is to write the code for the remote operations supported by the server (e.g., update a customer information). This code can include calls to other processes, to legacy applications, and/or database accesses. Servers can be categorized as single- or multistep servers. In **single-step servers**, the scheduler itself performs the service. An example is the Date server in which a separate server process is not activated—the scheduler finds the date and returns it. In single-step servers, the server process is usually very small and must be very efficient. In a **multistep server**, there are many choices, such as the following:

- Provide a centralized server process which is invoked by many clients
- Schedule each process separately (i.e., no process sharing)
- Provide conversational server support
- Share tasks between replicated processes

Multistep servers typically use multithreading to support multiple processes concurrently. **Threads** run in parallel, so each RPC can be handled by a separate thread. Threads share the same address space; thus they make it easy to share information and variables among processes. However, thread safety is an issue because threads can overwrite each other's data. Thread safety is handled differently by different middleware products. For example, DCE handles thread safety through **mutexes** (mutual exclusions). A mutex is basically a flag, also known as a semaphore, that is used by an application to gain exclusive control of data (i.e., the data cannot be modified by anyone as long as the mutex flag is on).

Requirements for special events and error handling can significantly complicate the task of server development. Some applications may require sophisticated security checking, audit trails, and error handling. Large-scale enterprisewide applications typically require support for deadlock detection and resolution, sequence checking, synchronization of resources with locking/unlocking for access control, rollback of changes due to failures, and interrupts/ shutdowns if needed. Naturally, it is extremely desirable to use off-the shelf middleware to provide these capabilities. However, in large-scale heterogeneous systems, some of this code may have to be developed, especially when you cross technology umbrellas. For example, even if a Distributed Transaction Processor (DTP) handles failures quite well, what do you do when parts of an application are not within the control of this DTP (e.g., some part of applications are under control of Encina while others are under the control of IMS)? Failure detection and resolution in such cases are extremely complicated tasks and should be carefully planned and thought through.

7.2.6   Step 4: Build Client Program(s)

Client code invokes the IDL defined operations on the remotely located objects. This code consists of the following components:

- User interface processing
- "Local" business logic
- Connecting (binding) to the appropriate server
- Invoking remote operations
- Providing any wrapping and object/flattening/unflattening services, if needed
- Handling special conditions and events

The user interface processing provides the "look and feel" for the services provided by an application. The user interface processing can be of three types: *GUI* (Graphical User Interface), *OOUI* (Object-Oriented User Interface), and non-GUI/OOUI. GUI provides graphic dialogs, menu bars, color, scroll boxes, and pull-down and pop-up windows. GUI dialogs use the object/action model where users can select objects and then choose the actions to be performed on the selected objects. Most GUI dialogs at present are serial in nature (i.e., perform one operation at a time). GUIs are currently very popular and are used in Microsoft Windows 3.X and OSF Motif applications. OOUIs are highly iconic, object-oriented user interfaces to support multiple, variable tasks whose sequence cannot be predicted. Examples include multimedia-based training systems, executive and decision support systems, and stockbroker workstations. Examples of OOUIs are NextStep, OS/2 Workplace Shell, and Macintosh. Although GUIs and OOUIs are very fashionable at present, we should not forget the non-GUI/OOUI clients that generate server requests with a minimal amount of human interaction. Examples of such clients are daemon programs, barcode readers, robots, automatic teller machines, cellular phones, fax machines, intelligent metering equipment, and automated testers.

The business logic code provides the business-aware functionality needed on the client side. For OCSI, this code should be written in object-oriented programming languages such as C++ or Smalltalk. This code may need to access databases or any other data sources. Many client applications use synchronous calls (i.e., the client is blocked while the server is processing the request). For asynchronous processing, a client application code may use a paradigm such as message queuing or employ multiple threads to invoke multiple methods.

Our main interest is in the client code that first connects (i.e., **binds**) to a server and then invokes the remote operations. Clients typically bind to a server by using an **explicit binding** (i.e., the client gives the explicit address of a server) or **implicit binding** (i.e., the system selects an appropriate server by searching a directory). The binding information is stored in a directory by the server initialization routines at server startup. The exact statements for establishing the connection are middleware dependent and will be discussed later.

After establishing a connection, the client invokes the remote operations. The client code that invokes remote operations depends on the type of Remote Interaction Paradigm. For example, SQL statements are sent to the database server for remote database access (RDA). In this case, the client code prepares a SQL statement, sends it over the network, receives the responses, and processes them. The RPCs are invoked for the remote procedure call paradigm (naturally!). In this case, the client code invokes one or more operations defined by the IDL. Operations on remote objects are invoked by using the CORBA facilities. In this case, clients invoke CORBA-IDL-defined operations directly by using CORBA run-time libraries.

For a "pure" OCSI application, it is best to utilize OO middleware such as CORBA and ActiveX to perform remote operations. However, how can a "pure" OCSI application be implemented by using middleware such as DCE? The main idea is to develop an **object wrapper**, commonly known just as a wrapper, on the client side that receives object invocations and issues appropriate calls to one or more servers (see Figure 7.4). Object wrapping is the practice of providing OO views, given pre-existing components, many times from old and obsolete systems. A wrapper is typically developed as a class with methods which construct and issue "non-OO" interactions such as RPCs, and remote SQL. As shown in Figure 7.4, the client application code invokes methods provided by this wrapper (the wrapper basically creates an object view of the server functionality). The encapsulation provided by the wrapper exposes only those attributes and operation definitions desired by the software architects. We will show examples of wrappers for DCE and Encina later on in this chapter.

An object wrapper may be thin (e.g., just issue an RPC) or thick (provide a great deal of security checking, logging, etc.). A wrapper, for example, may perform the following functions (we will discuss the role of wrappers in integrating legacy systems in Chapter 9):

- Check security at client site before issuing a remote call
- Perform logging if logging is needed (e.g., for performance monitoring and debugging traces)
- Flatten the parameter objects, if needed (see the discussion on object flattening previously)
- Construct and issue the appropriate remote invocation such as an RPC
- Get the response back from network transport and prepare the response for the client application code

Figure 7.4 Object Wrappers for Distributed Applications

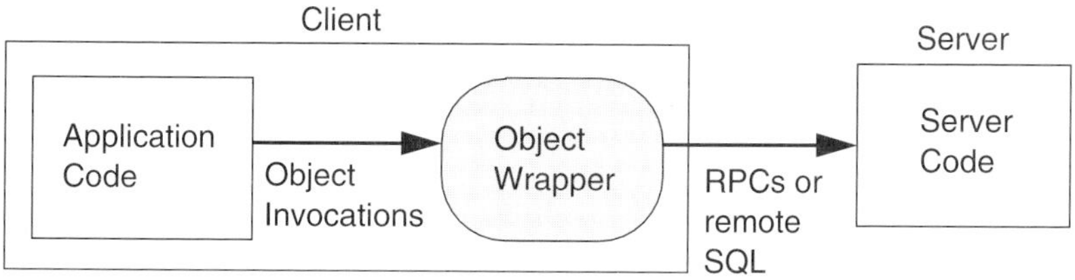

The client code must provide support for special events and failure handling. In general, remote interactions can generate many error conditions and status codes. The client program must be able to properly deal with these error conditions. Examples of these conditions are timeouts, security violations, network failures, and so forth.

7.2.7   Step 5: Testing

Testing of distributed applications such as OCSIs, in general, is a far more challenging and expensive task than mainframe-based applications. Why? Here are the main reasons. First, these applications are inherently more complex and "shaky" because they employ many new technologies that must work together. Second, distributed applications introduce many points of failures, partial failures, and congestions that require thorough testing. Third, the selected infrastructure components (middleware, networks, databases), their interrelationships and their impact on the distributed application must be thoroughly tested. Fourth, the application developers, at the time of this writing, are not experienced in this field. Fifth, large-scale distributed applications routinely employ multiple vendor components and cross-technology boundaries (e.g., part of the application is under a distributed transaction monitor on UNIX while the other parts use a "TP-less" approach on PCs). Finally, the operational support (managing the physical sites, change management, disaster handling, backup and recovery, software distribution, help desk) procedures must be tested before deployment.

The key idea is that the complexity of testing should be thought of as a consequence of developing application architectures that are too inclusive and too ambitious. In addition, even though many GUI tools hide the underlying complexity and help in generating code, the resultant applications *are* complex and do require extensive testing.

Let us discuss how we can take into account these considerations during the following typical testing activities:

- Unit testing
- System (integration) testing
- Acceptance testing
- Operational procedure testing

Unit testing verifies that each client and server component works according to the specifications. To test the individual components, test drivers are needed and "stubs" are built (a stub, in this context, is a dummy program that can operate as a server to test the clients and vice versa). Unit testing is usually the responsibility of developers who have developed the unit (client or server).

System testing, also known as integration testing, verifies that the entire distributed application performs the business functions while meeting the specified operational requirements. This activity is by far the most crucial, and most difficult, for these applications. The following general approach can be used Goglia [1993], and Hetzel [1988]:

- A total system test environment needs to be set up, preferably as a test laboratory, where *all* components (clients, servers, networks, print/fax services, database services, directory services) can be tested rigorously.

- The application and the underlying infrastructure should be logically decomposed into small units which can be tested in relationship to the interfacing components. For example, application component interfaces need to be tested with appropriate middleware and middleware component interfaces need to be tested with networks, and so forth.

- A baseline should be established to indicate which components do not need to change between different test streams. For example, if two applications need to be deployed on a Novell LAN, then the Novell LAN can be used for baselining.

- Interoperability and coexistence between interacting components must be tested. This may involve application to application, application to infrastructure, and infrastructure to infrastructure testing.

- Failure handling and scalability issues must be tested by simulating failures and increasing workloads. This should shake out the failure recovery procedures and the flexibility of the architecture to meet increased workloads.

System testing is typically performed by a team of testers. Tools and techniques may include dynamic and/or static testing methods. In a ***dynamic testing*** environment, the system is tested by executing (running) the various programs. ***Static testing***, on the other hand, relies on analysis and debugging of a system without having to run it. Dynamic testing and debugging are more reliable but are very expensive in distributed systems. For example, it is difficult to create many error conditions in large distributed software systems due to a large number of potential global conditions. Another problem in dynamic testing is reproducing the error conditions. Static testing mainly examines the control flow of programs, through techniques such as Petri Nets, and is not as accurate as dynamic testing. The main advantage of static testing is that expensive distributed testbeds are not needed. Moreover, this testing can be done while the system is not completely developed yet because static testing does not require a platform. However, it is not possible to determine all system faults through static testing. In practice, some combination of static and dynamic testing is needed for system testing of C/S applications.

Acceptance testing provides the users with assurance that the application is ready for production use. This activity is performed by the users with close collaboration with the developers. The foundation of this activity is the system requirement document and the end-user documentation that is tested against the actual system.

Operational procedure testing assures the management that the application will be properly supported. The procedures to be tested include help desk, change management, disaster handling, backup and recovery, software distribution, and site management. This activity is best performed in the pilot phase of a new application where the users and the support staff work through the procedural details and logistics.

A great deal of work is needed in developing testing procedures and automated testers for distributed software. This issue has been discussed by Devanbu [1996], [Conway 1996], and Shatz [1993]. The books on client/server testing by Patricia Goglia [Goglia 1993] and Daniel Mosley [Mosley 1997] contain a rich set of practical and administrative information about C/S testing. Automated testing tools for distributed applications are beginning to appear in the marketplace. See Conway [1996], Whiting [1995], and Sylvester [1995] for a state-of-the-market examination of C/S automated testing tools. Additional practical information about this topic can be found in Ryan [1997].

7.3   A Sample Application

Let us now turn our attention from general concepts to specific cases. We will use a simple Customer Information System as an example to illustrate the similarities and differences between OCSI implementation in Web, CORBA/ActiveX, OSF DCE, PowerBuilder, and Encina environments. We have chosen these environments for the following reasons:

- Web browsers are becoming the primary vehicle for ubiquitous access to almost all resources such as documents, databases, and programs.

- CORBA environments are based on the OMG CORBA specification and are ideal for developing distributed object applications. We will use CORBA to illustrate the implementation considerations for OCSI applications.

- OSF DCE environments are based on the RPC paradigm and are available on a wide array of computing platforms. DCE does use certain object-oriented principles (e.g., encapsulate the server by requiring an interface definition). We will use OSF DCE to illustrate the implementation considerations for distributed applications by using an RPC paradigm.

- Encina is a distributed transaction processing (DTP) system that operates on top of OSF DCE. We will use Encina to illustrate how a distributed application can be developed in a DTP environment.

- PowerBuilder is a popular C/S development environment that is used to build SQL database applications. We will use PowerBuilder to illustrate the implementation considerations for the applications that utilize off-the-shelf SQL servers.

The Customer Information System consists of a relational table that contains customer information (e.g., customer name, address, and balance). This table is managed by a "customer object" that responds to requests from clients to add, view, update, and delete a customer. For example, a client invokes a customer view operation by passing a customer ID. The customer object receives the request and invokes a method that reads the customer information and sends it back to the client. Table 7.3 shows the object model for the customer object. In the sections that follow, we will use this model as a starting point for defining the interface, building a server, and building clients in PowerBuilder, CORBA, OSF DCE, and Encina environments. Other than PowerBuilder, we have discussed these environments in the companion book. You should review the relevant chapters before proceeding.

TABLE 7.3 THE CUSTOMER OBJECT

Object	Operations	Inputs	Outputs
Customer	1. Add a customer	Customer Information	Status
	2. View customer information	Account number	Customer information
	3. Update customer information	Account number, new information	Status
	4. Delete a customer	Account number	Status

7.4   Developing Web-Based Applications

7.4.1   Overview

Web-based applications, as stated in Chapter 4, come in the following flavors:

- Static HTML-based applications that retrieve, display, and browse HTML pages by using the core Web facilities such as HTML and HTTP.

- CGI-based applications that retrieve, display, and browse remote database information and/or invoke remote programs from Web browsers through CGI scripts

- Java-based applications that invoke Java applets that run on the Java-enabled browsers.

- Object-Oriented Client/Server Internet (OCSI) applications that combine Web technologies with distributed objects and client/server middleware. These applications invoke CGI scripts or Java applets that trigger other middleware products such as CORBA, ActiveX, message-oriented middleware, SQL gateways, and/or OSF DCE.

For the Customer Information System example, the static HTML-based applications are not suitable because you will have to create HTML pages that contain all the customer information. Let us illustrate the other three approaches.

7.4.2   CGI-Based Application

For this type of Web-based application, you invoke a Web gateway that accesses the Customer Information. You basically develop four HTML forms that ask the user to invoke operations such as "add a customer," "view customer information," "update customer information," and "delete a customer," respectively. In addition, an initial HTML "home page" for this application needs to be designed.

These HTML forms invoke a relational database gateway that receives the form statements, constructs SQL queries from these statements, and then sends these queries to the database servers. The results of the queries are received by the gateway and converted to HTML before being sent back to the Web browsers.

Let us go through some details.

The following HTML page illustrates a simple form that allows a user to type in a 30-byte-long query to view a customer and push a submit button after typing the statement (the statements are processed by a gateway process `"/cgi.bin/viewquery"`):

```
<TITLE> View Customer Query </TITLE>
<HI> View Customer Query </HI>
Please enter your query specifying the customer name:
<FORM METHOD=POST ACTION="/cgi.bin/viewquery"
Enter your query: <INPUT TYPE = 'TEXT' NAME="query" SIZE "30" <P>
<INPUT TYPE="SUBMIT" VALUE="Submit your form"> <P>
</FORM>
```

The CGI program `/cgi.bin/viewquery` resides on the Web server. This program can be a script (e.g., a UNIX shell script or a Perl script) or an executable program (e.g., C or C++ code). For our purpose, this program will have the following pseudocode (see the sidebar "Writing CGI Programs: An Extremely Short Tutorial" for additional information):

```
/* prepare the following SQL query. Assume that
the name is passed in parameter &name */
select * from customer where cust-name = &name;
/* construct the response as an HTML page */
```

After this program has been written, it is readied for execution by the Web server (this step typically involves placing the CGI program in the /cgi.bin/ directory or other designated library of the server). When the user pushes the submit button in the HTML page shown previously, the Web server locates the CGI program in the /cgi.bin/ directory and executes it. The output produced by this program is sent back to the Web browser. Figure 7.5 shows how this CGI program is invoked.

Figure 7.5 CGI-Based Application

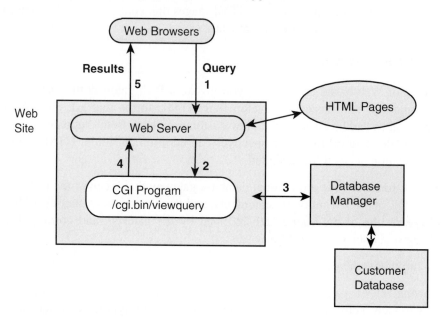

Note: The numbers show the sequence of events

7.4.3 Java-Based Applications

For a Java-based Customer Information application, you develop four Java powered pages that ask the user to invoke operations such as "add a customer," "view customer information," "update customer information," and "delete a customer," respectively. These operations are provided by four Java applets (notice that instead of the CGI programs, we are now invoking Java applets). The Java applets receive user queries, construct SQL queries from these statements, and then send these queries to the customer database servers. The results of the queries are received by the applets and displayed on the Web browsers. Let us go through some details.

By using Java applets, access to remote applications and databases can be invoked directly from the browser. The Java applet can ask the user to issue a query and then send this query to a remote application or database (Figure 7.6). This is especially interesting for database gateways where the database gateway functionality runs on the client side. A standard called JDBC (Java Database Connectivity) is being developed to allow Java programs to issue calls to relational databases.

Writing CGI Programs: An Extremely Short Tutorial

CGI programs should be written in programming languages such as C/C++. However, Perl, a scripting language is very popular and is used here for illustration. The CGI programs are written to respond to two types of queries:

- Form-based queries

- Document-based queries

The Form-based queries are used most commonly (this type of query is used in Section 7.4.3). In this type of query, especially by using the "POST" method shown in Section 7.4.3. the name/value pairs of the query are passed directly to the gateway script through standard input. Your CGI program receives the parameters, parses them and acts on them. Many tools are commercially available for parsing the CGI inputs. The following CGI psuedo Perl code will do the job for the /cgi.bin/viewquery program example in Section 7.4.3:

```
1 echo '<HTML> <HEAD>'
2 echo '<TITLE> Customer Name  </TITLE>  </HEAD>'
3 echo '<BODY>'
4 $FORM_ query = &name
5 select * from customer where cust-name =&name
6 /* code to display results in HTML format  */
7 echo '</BODY> </HTML>'
```

An echo statement indicates an output in Perl. The first 3 lines of this code set up HTML tags to be sent to the browser. Line 4 captures the input sent to this program and stores it in a variable &name. Line 5 uses this variable to query the database. Line 6 in practice will be several lines for displaying the results to the browser in HTML. Line 7 ends this program by generating the proper HTML tags.

The document-based queries operate differently. This type of query works in two passes. In the first pass, the browser invokes the CGI program that sends an HTML page with a special tag. The said tag is <ISINDEX> in the HTML head section. (i..e., HTML document head has statements: <HEAD> <ISINDEX></HEAD>). When the browser detects this tag, it presents the user with a box for input. The user enters a string in this box and then presses enter. The browser sends the same URL (i.e., invokes the same gateway but sends the string entered by the user as a parameter, preceded by ?). Now the CGI program is in the second pass. It now detects the input parameters and processes the query.

The CGI code for document-based queries first tests if any parameters have been passed. If none, then it assumes pass 1 and returns. If not, it retrieves the parameter preceded by ? (e.g., ?joe) and acts on it. This technique is used to pass any string to the CGI program in a quick and dirty way.

Figure 7.6 Java-Based Application

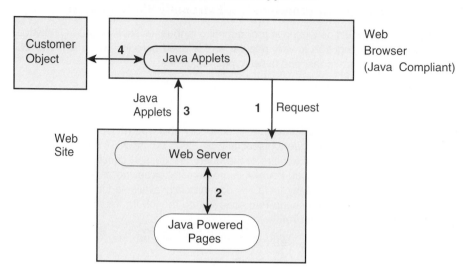

Note: The numbers indicate the sequence of events.

Java applets are not stand-alone applications and they run as part of a Java-enabled browser.[3] A Java applet contains methods (subroutines) to initialize itself, draw itself, respond to clicks, and so forth. These methods are invoked by the Java-enabled browser. A Java-powered HTML page contains a tag (the APPLET Tag) that indicates the location of a Java applet. When the browser encounters this tag, it downloads it and runs it. Java applets are indicated by an APPLET tag. For example, the following tag indicates the Java applet called "viewapplet.class" that is run in a window size of 110 by 100:

```
<APPLET CODE=viewapplet.class WIDTH =110 HEIGHT=100>
</APPLET>
```

The applet code is assumed to be on the same site where the HTML page resides. The browser loads the indicated class and other needed classes (Java-"enabled" browsers also keep local classes that may be used by the applets). After the applet has been loaded, the browser asks it to initialize itself (init( ) method) and draw a display area that is used for input/output. Java applets have access to a wide range of libraries that allow Java applets to perform many operations such as graphics, image downloading, playing audio files, and user interface creation (i.e., buttons, scrollbars, windows, etc.) See the sidebar "Simple Java Programming Examples" for sample Java code.

---

3. Programming Note: From a programming point of view, a Java application is Java code ("Java Class") that has the main ( ) method. The Java interpreter looks for main ( ) and executes it. Java applets do not contain main ( ). Instead, Java applets contain methods that are invoked by the Java-enabled browsers.

Simple Java Programming Examples

Note: These examples are intended for people who know C++ and want to know what simple Java code looks like. These people will recognize the similarities between C++ and Java code.

Example 1: Hello World Application in Java

```
/*   a Java simple application    */
public class Helloworld {
    public static void main (String args []) {
        System.out..println ("Hello, World");
    // comment:  System.out..println = output
        }
}
```

To compile and run this application:

- Put the source statements in Helloworld.java
- Compile by typing: javac Helloworld.java
- This creates a file: Helloworld.class   (in bytecode)
- To run, type; Java helloworld

Example 2: A Simple Java Applet That Draws a Line

```
/* File LineApplet.java */
import java.awt.*; // include the java tool classes and
import java.applet.*; // include applet classes (i.e., imports
necessary classes)
public class LineApplet extends Applet { // LineApplet is a
subset of Applet
public void paint (Graphics g) { // paint method is overridden
Dimension r = size(); // find out how big the applet window is
g.setColor (Color.green); // set color  to green
g.drawLine(0,0, r.width, r.height); // draw the line from cor-
ner to corner
    }
}
```

If you need to write a Java application where a Java applet on your Web browser invokes another Java applet on another machine, then you can use distributed object middleware such as CORBA. Sun has developed a new feature of Java that allows Java applets to talk to each other across machines without needing any middleware such as ORBs. This feature, known as Remote Method Invocation (RMI) allows Java applets to communicate with each other over the Internet. In addition, Sun has added a capability that allows Java applets to work across a firewall.

Keep in mind that many Web browsers are configured to disallow remote connections from Java applets because this increases security risks. In these cases, the Java applets can only access the resources located on the Web server from where the Java applets were loaded. A "Proxy Server" is built on the Web server site that acts as a server to the browsers and as a client to the target application resources (we discussed proxy servers in the previous chapter).

Java is quite popular at present and its popularity keeps growing steadily. However, some security concerns have been raised mainly because Java is a downloadable application (i.e., it is downloaded from a Web server site). Java is not alone in this area. ActiveX also supports downloadable components. Different approaches to deal with the security of downloadable software such as Java and ActiveX controls are being pursued at present (see the sidebar "Handling Security of Downloadable Software").

7.4.4   Object-Oriented Client/Server Internet (OCSI) Applications

These applications are of primary interest to us because they leverage Web technologies with object orientation and client/server leverage. These applications can be viewed in terms of (see Figure 7.7):

- Front ends that are invoked directly from the Web browser
- Back ends that are invoked from the front ends

We have discussed the front ends so far (HTML pages, Web servers, CGI, Java applets, etc.). The back ends can consist of a variety of technologies such as CORBA, OSF DCE, SQL middleware, transaction processing middleware, and messaging middleware on an as-needed basis. We will discuss the implementation issues related to many of these technologies in the balance of this chapter. The main power of the OCSI applications is that a diverse array of existing technologies can be integrated by viewing the Web as the front end of a three-tiered architecture (see Figure 7.7). Let us not forget that as the Web technologies evolve, more and more resources can be directly called from the Web browser, thus moving into the front-end arena.

Handling Security of Downloadable Software
Java and ActiveX Controls Issues

Java applets are downloaded from the Web server and run at the Web browser site. This raises several concerns about Java. There are three different approaches to security for Java applets.

- Trusted servers

- Sandboxes

- Digital signatures

Trusting the server is a viable choice within the secure corporate intranet (files are downloaded regularly from corporate file servers). The corporate servers can be trusted not to deliver components that contain viruses or damage the system on which they're loaded and executed.

Sandboxing constrains the components themselves, making it impossible for them to execute unwanted functions. Sandboxing can guarantee security by dictating that the downloaded components be obligated to play only in their own sandbox. The disadvantage of this approach is that sandboxed components are prohibited from doing things that can sometimes be useful, like writing to a file on the client machine's local disk.

Digitally signing each downloaded component is an attractive approach. The digital signature can be checked by the browser that receives the component. If it is correct, the browser can be certain that the component was created by a specific trusted entity and that it has not been modified.

Java applets currently support the first two methods. Digital signatures on downloadable Java components are areas of active work.

A related issue is how the downloaded ActiveX controls can be made secure. ActiveX downloading currently supports only the first of these three methods, that is, downloading from a trusted server. This is because they are shipped to the client as binaries; thus it is hard to sandbox them. Naturally, digital signatures are an interesting area of work for ActiveX controls.

Digital signatures offer the most general solution to the problem, one that would work well with Java as well as ActiveX controls. Let us hope that a single standard will be created that will be usable with both.

Figure 7.7 Object-Oriented Client/Server Internet Applications

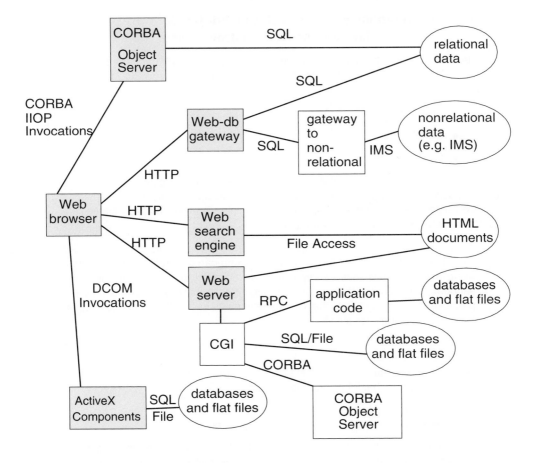

Legend: Shaded areas are part of the front end (can be invoked directly from Web browers).

7.5   CORBA for Developing OCSI Applications

7.5.1   Overview

CORBA was introduced by OMG to specify the technology for interoperable distributed OO systems. CORBA specifications represent the ORB technology based on a distributed object model. CORBA objects can be application code, stored in OO databases, or OO programming language objects. CORBA objects do not know the underlying implementation details —an *object adapter* maps the generic model to implementation and is the primary way that an object implementation accesses services provided by the ORB. You should review the CORBA discussion in [Umar 1997, Chapter 7] before proceeding.

OCSI application development in CORBA is a very natural path at present because you can issue CORBA calls from the Netscape IIOP-enabled browsers. In this case, the browser becomes a CORBA client. But there are other ways of combining CORBA with the Web. In essence, you can take any one of the following paths for developing an OCSI application in CORBA:

- Invoke CORBA calls from a CGI procedure (a script or a subroutine written in C or in any other language) that resides on the Web server. In this case, the CGI procedure is the CORBA client. This is the oldest and the best-known method.

- Invoke CORBA directly from the Web browser. Netscape browsers support the CORBA IIOP calls directly. Thus, the Web browser sites behave as CORBA clients.

- Use CORBA to interact between Java applets across machines. This option is currently supported by a few vendors (especially Sun).

Let us now focus on developing applications with CORBA. The activities involved in developing applications in CORBA environments involve the following major activities (see Figure 7.8):

- Create CORBA definitions by using OMG IDL
- Build the server
- Build the client
- Deploy the application

Figure 7.8 CORBA Application Development

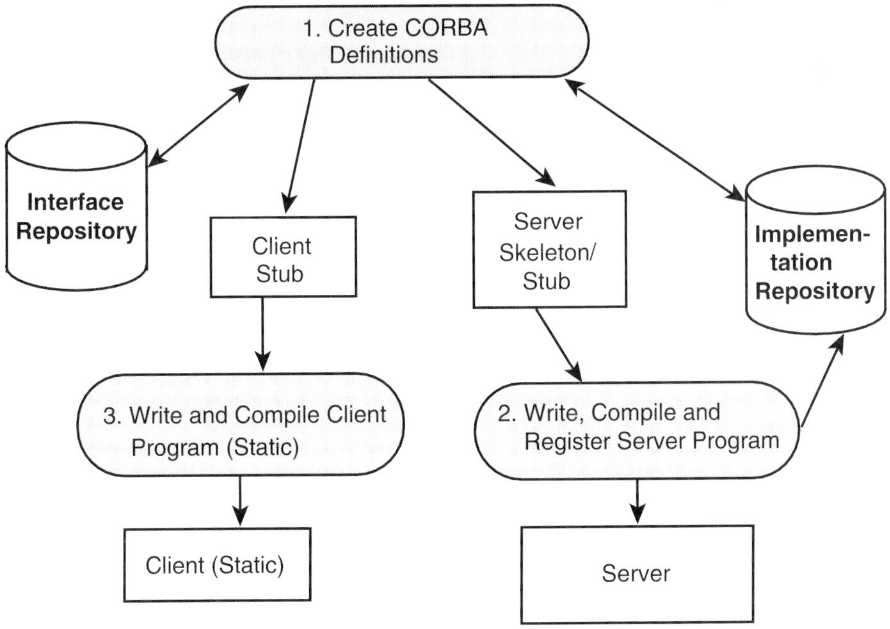

7.5.2   Create CORBA Definitions

The following CORBA definitions are created as the first step in CORBA application development:

- Define the interface
- Define the implementation
- Define the method map

The interface is defined by using a text editor in the CORBA IDL format. The IDL statements are compiled by using an IDL compiler. The IDL definitions can be kept in text files or be stored in an interface repository. The implementations are specified by using CORBA IML (Implementation Mapping Language). IML is used to describe the implementation details of each interface, including the operating-system-specific information used for invocation, the attributes used for method selection, and the methods that make up the implementation. You can use CORBA commands to generate a default implementation description from the interface definition.These implementations are loaded into the implementation repository.

Let us go through some of the details.

As stated previously, the interface of an object is used to declare the behavior of an object. Interface definitions, after being processed through an IDL compiler, can be stored in a CORBA **interface repository** so that the clients can learn about the server objects and determine what type of operations can be invoked on an object. An object interface consists of a collection of the operations and their signatures, that is, the operation's name, its arguments, and argument types. For example, the following statements specify the interface for the customer object in CORBA IDL (we have simplified it somewhat for illustrative purposes):

```
module CUST_PACKAGE {
    interface customer_interf /* interface name is customer */
    create_cust (/*The operation is create_cust */
in object customer_obj; /* input is customer object */
out integer status ) /* output parameter */
    view_cust ( /*The operation is view_cust */
in char cust-id; /* input parameter is cust-id */
out object customer_obj; /* output: customer object */
out integer status ) /*output parameter 2 */
}
```

The module statement is used to name a group of interfaces that relate to each other and can be used to represent a **package** (i.e., a group of objects). The module name becomes part of the name that the client and server use to reference an interface. The interface statement shows what operations can be performed on the customer object (we have only shown two operations; others can be filled in by the reader). Each interface statement defines an interface and contains the descriptions of the operations (operation signatures). The complete name of an operation includes the module and the interface name. For example, "CUST_PACKAGE::customer_interf::create_cust" is the fully qualified name of the operation that creates a customer account.

CORBA IDL has C++ type syntax, allows a wide array of data types (simple and complex), and supports OO concepts such as inheritance. For example, CORBA allows definition of complex objects (objects which have references to other objects). In addition, interfaces can be defined as **base interfaces** or **derived interfaces.** A derived interface inherits properties from a base interface**.** One or more interfaces may be defined for an object. The interface definitions are compiled by using vendor-provided IDL compilers and can be stored in an interface repository for other objects to utilize. The interfaces can be displayed by CORBA compliant commands or the **repository manager**. IDLs are basically declarative languages—they do not specify any executable code. IDL declarations (e.g., syntax, character types allowed, argument coding, etc.) must conform to the CORBA compliant vendor-provided IDL compilers.

After you create the interface definition using IDL, you compile the IDL file to create two very important components for building your application: the **client stub** and the **server skeleton.** The client stub and server skeleton are the code templates for building CORBA client and server programs (see Figure 7.8). The client stub is used only to build client programs that use static binding, that is, the client code is linked with the client stub to form the client application (see Section 7.5.4). The client stub is not used to build client programs that use dynamic invocation (see Section 7.5.5). The server skeleton is always used as the framework for building the server application, regardless of the invocation type used by the client (see Section 7.5.3).

Operations on objects are accomplished by executable code called **methods.** For example, the customer object must contain the code ("create-customer" method) that will be executed to actually create a new customer when an operation "create-customer" is invoked by a client. The collection of methods that accomplishes the set of operations required for an object is called an **implementation**. Some CORBA environments offer a mapping language for describing implementations called the **Implementation Mapping Language (IML)**. The implementation descriptions can be stored in an **implementation repository** which can be displayed by CORBA-compliant commands or the **repository manager**. The following IML statements show the implementation of customer methods (once again, we have simplified this somewhat):

```
implementation CustomerImpl
  (
  activation_type (program);
  implementation _identifier ("676873.0c.03.00.00.00.00");
  Create_customer ( )
implements (CUST_PACKAGE::customer_interf::create_cust);
invoke_builtin ("Create_customer_code)
;
);
```

The `implementation` statement is used to specify the name of the implementation. The first few, in our case the first two, statements in an implementation specification are used at startup time. The `activation_type()` statement specifies the manner in which the implementation is started once it is selected. For example, (program) indicates that a program will be started; other options indicate dynamic load and script executions. The `implementation _identifier()` clause is used to assign a unique identifier to an implementation. The unique identifier is automatically generated in response to the CORBA command "`orbgen`." For each method in the implementation, you define the method name, the operation it supports, and how to run it. In our example, we have defined only one method (Create_customer) that implements the create_cust operation defined in the IDL and invokes a built-in module. Method specifications allow invocation options for dynamic and script executions.

In addition to IML, you may need to define **method maps.** These maps are used by the ORB to locate the best server method for the object operation requested when there is more than one active implementation of an interface. For example, when a client invokes the "create_customer" operation, then the ORB looks at the method maps to determine the most appropriate method to invoke. Some CORBA environments offer a mapping language, called the **Method Mapping Language (MML)**, which enables developers to define criteria for selecting a method to perform an operation on an object. The method map can be stored in the interface repository along with the interface definitions. You can use CORBA commands to generate a default method map from the interface definitions.

7.5.3   Build the Server

CORBA servers can be quite complex and diverse. These servers fall into two broad categories: (a) **program servers** that use executable images, dynamic libraries, or built-in executable methods and (b) **script servers** that use operating system commands in a script (e.g., Bourne shell in UNIX), or command procedures. Let us first focus on the program servers. Building program servers requires the following steps:

- Generate the server skeleton
- Develop server initialization code
- Develop code for each method
- Compile, link, and test the server components
- Register the server

The first step is to specify the IDL statements and then compile these statements to generate a server skeleton. This compilation also uses the information contained in the IML files. The server skeleton contains method templates that show entry points for all of the implementation methods. The server skeleton also contains the server dispatcher code that makes the implementations and the methods known to the ORB (the dispatcher is called by the *Basic*

Object Adapter).[4] A registration routine is also generated as part of the server code (this routine is called at server startup).

Each server initialization needs code to register the implementation (e.g., make itself available for use), activate the server's implementation, enter a main loop to receive requests, and exit after unregistering and releasing resources. In addition, the server needs routines for creating objects and managing references to these objects. The server skeleton is used to develop this code. The initialization code uses CORBA run-time routines (these routines are identified as CORBA_ or ORB_). An example of the server C-type pseudocode for the customer example is listed below (we have simplified this code by ignoring the error checking and by using a generic "parameter" for the CORBA provided functions):

```
#include <stdio.h>
#include <orb.h>
#include customer.h /* the IDL generated header */
main ( )
{
printf ("Customer server starting \n");

/* Register the implementation */
status = RegisterImpls (parameters);

/* Create object and its reference */
status = CreateObjRefs(parameters);

/*Make server ready */
CORBA_BOA_impl_is_ready (parameters); /* indicate server ready */

/* main loop to listen to client messages */
OBB_BOA_main_loop (parameters); /* enter the main loop */

/* exit code */
CORBA_BOA_dispose(parameters); /* Frees object references */
OBB_BOA_imp_unregister (parameters); /* Unregister */

/* Methods code templates */
        void create_cust (customer_obj, status);
        /* .... insert code for create_cust method ...*/
        void view_cust ( cust-id, customer_info, status);
        /* .... insert code for view_cust method ...*/
}
```

---

4. Basic Object Adapter (BOA) can be used for most ORB objects with conventional implementations. CORBA requires that a BOA be available in every ORB.

The major activity in building a CORBA server is to write the code for the methods that execute the operations. For each method template, you must create the code for the methods. Methods can be implemented as executable code, calls to legacy applications, or scripts to integrate command-line interfaces with existing applications. Methods can be written to invoke OLE (Object Linking and Embedding), DDE (Dynamic Data Exchange), and SQL database accesses. For example, the following pseudocode to access the customer relational table can be added to the create_cust and view_cust methods:

```
void create_cust (customer_obj, status);
/* code for converting customer_obj object into
SQL table attributes such as cname, caddress, balance */
exec sql;
insert cname, caddress, balance into customer_table;
end sql;
/* .. include other code */

void view_cust (cust-id, customer_obj, status);
exec sql;
select cname, caddress, balance from cust_table where
c_id=:cust_id;
end sql;
/* code for storing cname, caddress, balance into an object */
}
```

The final step in building a server is to compile and link the methods, server initialization code, the generated server dispatcher and the generated registration routine. The server code can be tested and debugged by using CORBA tracing facilities.

Steps discussed so far pertain to building program servers. Building script servers requires somewhat different steps. First, the IML must indicate the "activation_type (script)" parameter. In addition, special techniques for handling input-output are needed because scripts are not interactive. Passing information from clients to the scripts also requires calls to special routines. Script servers also have several limitations such as data types, performance restrictions, and object creation. Despite several limitations, script servers are handy tools for quickly developing CORBA applications.

After a CORBA server has been built, its implementation must be registered by using CORBA commands or implementation manager utilities. Registering the implementation allows the ORB to know which services are offered by the server. This registration is accomplished by placing an entry in the implementation repository. The task of server registration may be incorporated into the installation procedure of the server. The details of this step vary between CORBA environments. For example, there are three types of registrations:

- Place entry in interface repository. This registers a service, not the server that provides the service.

- Place an entry in the implementation repository (this entry can be also placed in a name server or a trader). This registers the server and allows the clients to obtain object references to the server.

- Tell ORB that the server is ready via Impl-is-ready(). This allows ORB to route interactions to server processes.

7.5.4 Build Client (Static Invocation)

After a server has been built and registered, clients can be built to invoke the servers. As stated previously, CORBA clients can use static invocations (i.e., clients know at compile time the objects and the operations on these objects) or dynamic invocation (i.e., the clients determine at run time the objects and the operations on these objects). We will focus on static invocation in this section and review dynamic invocation in the next section.

Static invocation has several advantages over dynamic invocations. First, it is easier to program—you call the remote method by simply invoking it by name and passing it the parameters. Second, it provides more robust type checking because the compiler enforces type checking at build time. Finally, it performs well and it is self-documenting. The steps involved in building a static invocation CORBA client are

- Generate client stub

- Define the context object

- Build the client code

- Compile and link the client

The client stub can be generated from IDL, IML, and MML source files or from the interface repository. The generated stub consists of a header file that contains definitions, and the C language stub routines.

A **context object** shows a set of properties providing information about the client, the environment, or characteristics of the request. The context object is used by ORB during method resolution to identify user preferences for server selection. Basically, it provides a means of maintaining information between requests for conversational applications. The context information is difficult to pass as parameters in a distributed application. The IDL is used to specify whether the ORB should also retrieve information regarding the request from the context object (the "context" clause in IDL). If no context object is specified, the ORB uses the default context object definition. Context objects can be specified at user level (e.g., user preferences), group level (e.g., data restricted to a group of users), or system level (e.g., display types for an application).

The client code includes a header file generated by IDL, "local" client code (e.g., communicate with the user), invoking object operations defined in IDL, and handling errors/exceptions.

To invoke the object operations, a client needs to first get an object reference (object references can be stored by the server at startup in an external file or registery), and then invoke a method on the object. The following client pseudocode illustrates the key points of a client that invokes the create_cust and view_cust methods:

```
#include <stdio.h>
#include cust.h /. the IDL generated header ./
/* define variables, etc. */
main ()
{
 /* code to obtain object reference. This code depends on where the server
stored the reference. If object reference is in a file, then use fget, for
example, to read the object reference */

customer-interf *pptr; /* *pptr is the object reference */

/* Now invoke the create_cust and view_cust methods */

            /* put information in customer_obj */
            pptr->create_cust (customer_obj, status); /* invoke the object
            method */
            printf ("customer added");
            cust_id = "1111";
            pptr->view_cust ( cust-id, customer_obj, status); /* invoke the
            object method */
            printf ("customer information", customer_info);
/* Other client code, e.g., free resources, error processing, etc. */
```

After coding the client, it is compiled, linked, and debugged by using the CORBA environment compilers and tracing facilities.

7.5.5   Building a Client (Dynamic Invocation)

CORBA's Dynamic Invocation APIs allow a client program to build and invoke requests on objects at run time. These APIs provide maximum flexibility by allowing new objects to be added at run time. The client specifies, at run time, the object to be invoked, the method to be performed, and the set of parameters through a call or a sequence of calls. The client code typically obtains this information from the interface repository. To invoke a dynamic method on an object, the client must perform the following steps:

- Obtain the method description from the interface repository
- Create the argument list
- Create the request
- Invoke the request

CORBA specifies about 10 API calls for locating and obtaining objects from the repository. An example of such an API call is *lookup_name( )*. A *describe* call is issued, after an object is located, to obtain its full IDL definition. To create an argument list, CORBA specifies a *NameValue list* as a self-defining data structure for passing parameters. The list is created by using the *create_list operation*. After this, the request is created using the CORBA *create_request* call. Eventually, the client can invoke the request by using either an *invoke* call (send the request and obtain the results, i.e., a synchronous call), or a *send* call (an asynchronous call). The following pseudocode shows a sample dynamic invocation:

```
/* Create method description */
lookup_name()
describe ()
/* Create argument list */
create_list ()
add_arg(),,, add_arg(),,,, add_arg()
/* create the request */
create_request(Object Reference, Methods,
Argument List)
/* Invoke the remote method synchronously, i.e.,
as an RPC */
invoke()
/* Now process the results */
```

7.5.6   Deploy and Run the Application

CORBA applications can be packaged and shipped as server only, client only, or a collection of clients and servers. In most cases, you need to send your IDL, IML, and MML files, in addition to the executables. The application is installed and used in a CORBA run-time environment (see Figure 7.9). The IDLs and IML are loaded into the interface and implementation repositories first. Then the server is installed. At server startup, it registers itself so that the invoking clients can locate it. The dynamic invocation interface allows dynamic construction of object invocation. The interface details are filled in by consulting with the interface repository and or other run-time sources. The Client IDL stubs make calls to the ORB using interfaces and make it easier for the clients to issue static requests to objects across a network. Object adapters allow an object implementation to access the ORB services. CORBA specifies that each ORB must support a standard adapter called the Basic Object Adapter (BOA). Server Skeletons (server IDL stubs) provide the static interfaces to each service supported by the server.

7.6   ActiveX for Developing OCSI Applications

Application development in ActiveX and CORBA are similar, in principle, because both are based on the distributed object model. ActiveX uses DCOM to provide communications between remote ActiveX components. In this sense, DCOM is the ORB for ActiveX and provides the basic brokerage services for ActiveX. It supports APIs for static as well as dynamic invocation of objects. DCOM uses DCE RPC for interactions between COM objects. It also supports an IDL and rudimentary object services such as a basic licensing mechanism and a local directory service. See the sidebar "DCOM versus CORBA" for additional discussion.

Figure 7.9 CORBA Run-time Environment

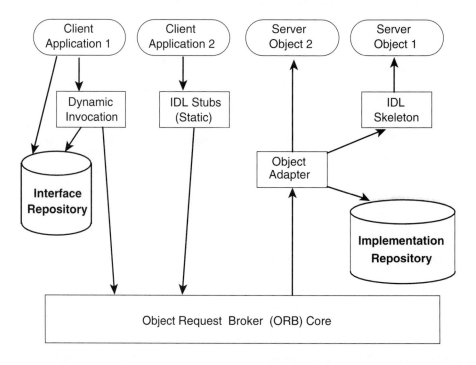

An ActiveX component is the basic unit of ActiveX applications. Examples of components are Visual Basic applications, Excel spreadsheets, Java applets, C/C++ code, and Word documents. Components execute in *containers* which provide an environment for components. For example, the Microsoft Internet Explorer (version 3.0 or higher) browser can be used as an ActiveX container. Thus the Web browser can now contain spreadsheets, Word documents, and code written in C++, C, Java, or other programming languages. You can build powerful applications that may, for example, supply specialized viewers with the data to be viewed (the viewer and the data are loaded as needed from the network and run inside the Web browser as a container).

This merging of Web browsers with the wide range of components makes ActiveX a natural tool for OCSI applications. You can combine ActiveX applications with the Web by using any one of the following routes:

- Invoke DCOM calls to remotely located components directly from the components contained in the Web browser (e.g., the Microsoft Internet Explorer). These components may be written in C, C++, Visual Basic, Java, or other programming languages behaving as ActiveX components and contained inside the browser.

- Invoke DCOM calls from a CGI procedure (a script or a subroutine written in C or in any other language) that resides on the Web server.

- Invoke DCOM calls from the ActiveX components such as spreadsheets that may invoke Java applets or other components residing on Web servers.

From an implementation point of view, you basically use the same steps as CORBA because CORBA objects can also be invoked from Web browsers. Thus development of ActiveX for the customer information system example would require the following CORBA-type steps:

1. **Create interface definitions.** The definitions for the customer object are used to advertise the external interfaces (services) that are available to prospective clients. We can assume that the customer object is an ActiveX component. The definitions of COM IDL are similar to the CORBA IDL definitions.

2. **Build server programs**. The server programs that provide the advertised services for the customer object are coded. For ActiveX, this code can be written in C, C++, Java, or Visual Basic. The code is very similar to the one discussed in the CORBA example.

3. **Build client programs**. The client programs that invoke the customer component are coded. ActiveX supports clients that may be Excel spreadsheets, Visual Basic programs or Java applets. For the customer information example, we will assume that the clients are Java applets that run under the control of the Microsoft Internet Explorer browser (version 3.0 or higher).

4. **Test the application**. All components of the application are constructed, tested, documented, and put into operation. In this case, the application will be delivered as an ActiveX application that will be invoked from the Internet Explorer browser.

Due to the conceptual similarity to CORBA, we will not give ActiveX code samples here. For more details, see the book *Understanding ActiveX and OLE* by David Chappell, Microsoft Press, 1996.

7.7   OSF DCE for Developing OCSI Applications

7.7.1   Overview

OSF DCE, commonly referred to as DCE, provides an open environment for C/S applications. DCE provides a set of services such as security, directory and timing, built around remote procedure calls. C/S applications developed in DCE are portable to many computers because DCE is available on many different computers from different vendors. DCE applications can interface with Web through CGI. The reader should review the OSF DCE facilities discussed in Umar [1997, Chapter 3] before proceeding.

DCE supports encapsulation but not polymorphism. In addition, RPC is similar to a function call and not the same as OO method invocation. Although DCE does not use the distributed object model used by CORBA, OCSI applications in DCE can be developed by using object wrappers (see, for example, Yasrebi [1995]). As discussed in Section 7.2.6, you can develop OCSI applications on a non-OO middleware by developing a wrapper on the client side. The client code issues object interactions to this wrapper and the wrapper issues the DCE RPCs.

DCOM versus CORBA: Similarities and Differences

At a high level, there are several similarities between CORBA and DCOM. However, several differences appear when you look closely.

Similarities:

- Both are based on the object model.

- Both utilize the interface concept and utilize an Interface Definition Language (IDL).

- Both use static and dynamic calls from clients to servers.

- Both use a repository to locate objects and invoke them (CORBA calls it the Interface Repository and DCOM calls it a Type Library).

Dissimilarities:

- DCOM uses, in addition to IDL, Object Definition Language (ODL), for defining metadata. CORBA uses a single IDL for everything.

- DCOM uses the universal unique ID (UUID), based on OSF DCE, to locate and invoke objects. CORBA does not use UUIDs. It uses object references and a repository to locate and invoke objects.

- DCOM uses the OSF DCE RPC as the basic transport mechanism between remote objects. CORBA uses several options such as IIOP (Internet Inter-ORB Protocol) that uses TCP/IP sockets and ESIOP (Environment Specific Inter-ORB Protocol) that runs on top of DCE.

- CORBA only uses connection-based (i.e. TCP) services while DCOM favors connectionless (i.e., UDP) services. DCOM does support TCP connections, but it favors UDP for the purpose of scaling (do not have to keep track of large number of open sessions).

- CORBA2.0 has specified a very extensive set of services that include transaction management, security, concurrency control, life cycle, query, and so forth. In comparison, DCOM services at present are somewhat limited (these are being added through the ActiveX Platform).

However, both technologies are evolving at the time of this writing and consequently the similarities/dissimilarities will also change with time.

OSF DCE can interface with Web through CGI. From that point of view, OSF DCE can be viewed as a back end of an OCSI application where the DCE client is a CGI script or program. We should mention the role of ActiveX and DCOM here. As stated previously, DCOM uses DCE RPC as a means of exchanging messages between remotely located ActiveX components. However, DCOM does not support the "full blown" version of DCE— the focus of this discussion.

Assuming that you have already designed the application as a distributed C/S application, then the steps in developing DCE applications are (see Figure 7.10):

- Develop the interface (IDL)
- Build the server(s)
- Build the clients(s)
- Deploy the application

These steps are briefly reviewed here. Additional details can be found in Shirley [1993], and [Rosenberry 1993].

Figure 7.10 Implementing DCE Applications

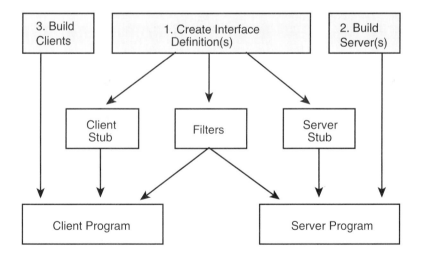

7.7.2   Create Interface Definitions

The C/S application model generated as a result of the application architecture is refined and represented as **objects** used by the application, and **operations** to be performed on these objects. This model is used to define the **interfaces** for each object. An object interface consists of a collection of the operations and their signatures, that is, the operation's name, its arguments, and argument types. In DCE, an interface is an externally known entry point of a

DCE server. For example, the following statements specify the interface for the customer object in DCE IDL (notice the similarities between CORBA and DCE IDLs):

```
uuid (C38950-0000-2122)
interface customer_interf /* interface name is customer */
void create (/*The operation is create cust */
     [in] struct customer_info; /* input parameter */
     [out] integer status ) /* output parameter */
void view ( /*The operation is view cust */
     [in] char cust-id; /* input parameter is cust-id */
     [out] struct customer_info; /* output parameter 1*/
     [out] integer status ) /*output parameter 2 */
```

The interface statement shows what operations can be performed on the customer object. The DCE interface definition contains a unique identifier (universal unique identifier), definition of one or more remote procedures, procedure name, parameters passed (input, output), and data types.

OSF DCE IDL has C type syntax and it does not support OO concepts such as objects and inheritance. Note that we have used a structure variable to represent the customer information in this IDL as compared to the object definition in CORBA IDL. You compile the IDL file to create the **client stub** and the **server stub.** The client stub and server stub are the code templates for building DCE client and server programs (see Figure 7.10). You store these IDL statements in a file; let us call it the customer.idl file. You compile this file by typing:

```
idl cutomer.idl
```

This compile generates the following files:

```
customer_cstub.o (client stub)
customer_sstub.o (server stub)
customer.h  (header file)
```

7.7.3　Build a DCE Server

Building a DCE server requires knowledge of the interface definition and RPC run-time routines. The following steps are used to build a server:

- Develop server initialization code

- Establish security procedures, if needed

- Develop code for each remote procedure

- Compile, link, and test the server components

Each server needs code to initialize (i.e., make itself available for use), enter a main loop to receive requests, and exit after releasing resources. Server initialization uses calls to RPC run-time routines to register the interface with the run-time libraries and creates binding information so that the clients can find the server. **Binding information** is network communication and location information for a particular server. A binding relationship is established between a client and a server when a client issues an RPC. Binding information shows

- Server host that specifies the network address of the computer where the server resides (e.g., Internet Protocol address of host where server resides)

- End point that represents the specific server process running on a host (e.g., a TCP port number)

- Protocol sequence that describes network communication used between a client and a server (e.g., TCP or UDP)

The binding information is stored in the DCE directory by the servers (i.e., servers "export" to the Directory). Clients retrieve this information (e.g., import) when they issue an RPC. A server can be moved from one host to another without impacting client code—the server initialization exports the server address at startup, and the client imports the server address from the directory before it binds with the server.

DCE can include different levels of security. By default, security is turned off. To include security, you must call the **rpc_binding_set_auth_info** routine in the DCE server initialization routine; each client must also issue a similar call to communicate with this server. An argument in this call sets the security level to be used. Thus, if the security level sent by a client does not match the security level set by the server, then the client request is rejected. The security level information includes encryption, mutual authentication, checksums, and so forth. It should be kept in mind that these features are included automatically in RPCs by DCE as a result of the **rpc_binding_set_auth_info** call (you do not need to provide any code yourself). The RPCs that include authentication are called **authenticated RPCs**. Additional information about DCE security can be found in Rosenberry [1993].

An example of the server skeleton code for the Customer Information System example is listed below (this code shows many calls to the RPC run-time libraries; these calls start with rpc_).

```
#include <stdio.h>
#include customer.h /* the IDL generated header */
main ()
{
printf ("Customer server starting \n");
/* This server handles two RPCs: create and view */

/* Register interface with the RPC runtime */
rpc_server_register_if(parameters);

/* Create and obtain binding information */
rpc_server_use_all_protseqs(parameters);
rpc_server_inq_bindings (parameters);
/* Export entry to Name Directory and register endpoints */
```

```
rpc_binding_binding_export (parameters);
rpc_ep_register (parameters):

/* Main loop to listen to client messages */
rpc_server_listen (parameters); /* enter the main loop */

/* exit code */
rpc_binding-vector_free (parameters) /* Free binding handles */
```

The major activity in building a DCE server is to write the code for the remote procedures. These procedures can include calls to other processes, to legacy applications, and/or database accesses. For example, the following pseudocode to access the customer relational table can be added to process the create and view RPCs:

```
void create (customer_info, status);
            /* code for converting customer_info structure into
            SQL table attributes such as cname, caddress, balance */
            exec sql;
            insert cname, caddress, balance into customer_table;
            end sql;
            /* .. include other code */

void view (cust-id, customer_info, status);
            exec sql;
            select cname, caddress, balance from cust_table where c_id=:cust_id;
            end sql;
            /* code for storing cname, caddress, balance into the customer_info
            structure */
}
```

The final step in building a server is to compile and link the server initialization code, the remote procedures, and the server stub generated as part of IDL compilation (e.g., customer_sstub.o, the server stub generated due to the compilation of customer.idl). The server code can be tested and debugged by using DCE facilities.

DCE servers can be quite complex because they have to handle many RPCs, support different options for initialization and binding, and may invoke other application processes (e.g., one for each RPC). The servers may use multithreading to support multiple processes concurrently. **Threads** run in parallel, so each RPC can be handled by a separate thread. Threads share the same address space; thus they make it easy to share information and variables among processes. However, thread safety is an issue because threads can overwrite each other's data. Thread safety in DCE is handled through **mutexes** (mutual exclusions). A mutex is basically a flag, also known as a semaphore, that is used by an application to gain exclusive control of data (i.e., the data cannot be modified by anyone as long as the mutex flag is on). More information about using threads in DCE can be found in Peterson [1995], Shirley [1993], Rosenberry [1993].

7.7.4   Build a DCE Client

DCE client code, written in languages such as C, C++, or any other language, invokes an RPC to a DCE server. Client code includes a header file generated by IDL, "local" client code (e.g., communicate with the user), RPCs defined in IDL, and client logic to handle different conditions. Recall that DCE only supports static invocation of servers by clients. DCE applications can use a **context handle** that is, in principle, similar to the CORBA context object, that is, it provides a means of specifying information between RPCs. When the RPC is issued, the client stub code finds the appropriate server with the interface definition and "binds" to it. Binding can be explicit or implicit (binding to a server is similar to CORBA's object references). Implicit binding uses the DCE name/directory service to locate an appropriate server. Explicit binding asks for a specific server on a specific machine by passing a binding handle as the first parameter of the RPC.

How can an OCSI application be implemented by using DCE? The key idea is to develop a wrapper on the DCE client side that receives object invocations and issues appropriate RPCs to one or more DCE servers (see Figure 7.11).

Figure 7.11 Object Orientation in OSF DCE

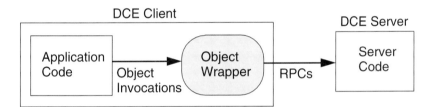

The wrapper is developed as a class with methods which construct and issue DCE RPCs. DCE client application code invokes methods provided by this wrapper (the wrapper basically creates an object view of the server functionality). For example, the following client application pseudocode could be used to create a customer object and then to view it:

```
#include <stdio.h>
#include customer.h /. the IDL generated header ./
/* define variables, etc. */
 main ()
{
/* Now invoke the create and view methods */

        c1.create_cust(&customer_obj, status);

        c1. view_cust ( cust_id, &customer_obj);
/* Other client code, e.g., free resources, error processing, etc. */
```

where `create_cust` and `view_cust` are the methods defined on the customer class (the customer wrapper) and `c1` is a customer object. The code in the `create_cust` and `view_cust` methods will have details which are hidden from the client application developers. Each method issues one or more RPCs. Recall that RPCs are synchronous calls (i.e., the client is blocked while the server is processing the request). For asynchronous processing, a client application code may use multiple threads to invoke multiple methods.

Basically, the object wrapper prepares the RPCs that will be sent to the server. It may perform additional functions such as security, logging/audit trails, and object/flattening. For example, the following pseudocode illustrates the `create_cust` and `view_cust` methods that were invoked from the client application:

```
create_cust (customer_id, customer_obj);
            /* variable definitions */
            /* code to flatten customer_obj and store
            information
            in customer_info structure to be used in RPC */
            create (customer_info, status); /* invoke the RPC
            */

create_cust (customer_id, customer_obj);
            /* variable definitions */
            view ( cust-id, customer_info, status); /* invoke
            the view RPC */
            /* code to convert customer_inf to customer_obj */
/* Other client code, e.g., free resources, error processing, etc. */
```

The DCE client code is compiled, linked, and debugged by using the DCE environment compilers and tracing facilities.

7.7.5   Deploy Application

To deploy and run a DCE application, you need to package and send the IDL, the server code, the client code, and any other routines/files to the destination sites. Assuming that the destination site already has a DCE environment setup (this is a nontrivial task), then the installation of a new DCE application is relatively straightforward. Figure 7.12 shows a conceptual view of OSF DCE and shows the normal processing sequence of clients and servers.

DCE can be used to develop OCSI applications because DCE does support several OO properties such as encapsulation. However, DCE IDL does not support inheritance and complex objects (these properties exist in CORBA IDL). As compared to CORBA, it is difficult to implement polymorphism in DCE. DCE also does not support dynamic invocations supported in CORBA.

Figure 7.12 DCE Run-Time Environment

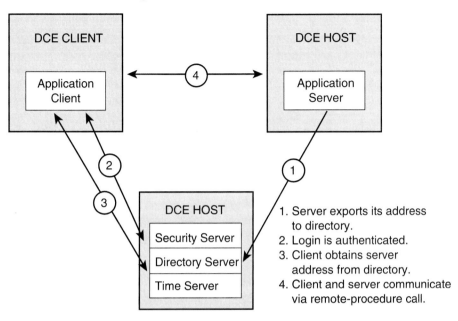

7.8   Encina for Developing OCSI Applications

7.8.1   Overview

Encina is a distributed transaction processor, built over DCE. OSF DCE is used as a transport for Encina. Encina makes extensive use of DCE facilities and provides database support over DCE. In addition, Encina follows XOpen standards such as TX and XA. Basically,

Encina = DCE + Transactional RPC + Application recovery

+ Monitor functions + Database support

Encina can interface with the Web through CGI. From this point of view, OCSI applications in Encina are similar to DCE, that is, Encina can be viewed as a back end of an OCSI application where the Encina client is a CGI script or program. The reader should review discussion of distributed transaction processing and Encina in Umar [1997, Chapter 6] before proceeding.

Assuming that you have already designed your application, the following steps are involved in implementing an OCSI applications using Encina:

- Construct a transaction model
- Develop the transaction interface (transactional IDL)
- Build the server(s)
- Build the client(s)
- Deploy the application

7.8.2   Construct a Transaction Model

An application can be converted to a transaction model by deciding what portions of the application need Transaction Processing (TP) capabilities. In C/S environments, TP capabilities can be included at three levels:

- Servers only
- Clients only
- Clients and servers

For server-only TP capabilities, the servers treat their internal operations as a unit of consistency. For example, any database updates within a server RPC processing are committed at the end of RPC processing. This option is chosen primarily when transactions between servers are not needed (i.e., all data that need to be committed reside on one server machine). In this case, clients are not involved in transaction processing (they just send requests and receive responses from remote transactions).

The client-only transaction processing capabilities are used when a transaction processor needs additional information from an external source, without involving the external source in the transaction processing. For example, a transaction that is updating inventory information may need to retrieve information about product managers from remote sites. However, this information may not be crucial enough to abort the inventory update. In this case, a transaction behaves as a client that issues a nontransactional request from a remote server.

The full DTP capabilities are utilized when clients as well as servers are included within the scope of a transaction. In this case, *all* operations performed within a client and invoked on behalf of the client are considered as a unit of consistency. This topic is discussed extensively in Umar [1997, Chapter 6].

7.8.3   Create Interface Definitions

An interface in Encina, as expected, is an externally known entry point of an Encina server. Encina interface definition is similar to DCE and is defined by using TIDL (Transaction Interface Definition Language). The main difference is that a **transactional** parameter can be specified to indicate transactional RPC. For example, in the Customer Information System example, we can assume that create is a transactional RPC, but view is just a simple RPC. Then the following TIDL represents the interface definition for the CIS application:

uuid (C38950-0000-2122)

```
interface customer_interf /* interface name is customer */
[transactional] void create (/*The operation is create customer. It is
treated as a transaction. */
    [in] struct customer_info; /* input parameter */
    [out] integer status ) /* output parameter */
void view ( /*The operation is view cust */
    [in] char cust-id; /* input parameter is cust-id */
    [out] struct customer_info; /* output parameter 1*/
    [out] integer status ) /*output parameter 2 */
```

These TIDL statements are stored in customer.tidl file. You compile this file by typing

```
tidl simple.tidl
```

This compile generates the following files:

customer_cstub.o (client stub)
customer_sstub.o (server stub)
customer.h (header file)

A transactional attribute configuration file (TACF) is created to show which interfaces are exported.[5]

7.8.4 Build an Encina Server

Building an Encina server is similar to building a DCE server, with the major difference in developing transaction processing servers in response to (T)RPCs (this may involve two-phase commit between sites and interoperability of Encina with different databases by using the XA interface standard). The following steps are used to build an Encina server:

- Develop server initialization code

- Develop code for each remote procedure

- Develop code for each transactional remote procedure

- Compile, link, and test the server components

Encina server initialization is very similar to DCE (this should be no surprise because Encina is based on DCE). An example of the skeleton server pseudocode for the Customer Information System example is listed below:

```
#include <stdio.h>
#include <customer.h> /. TIDL generated code/header ./
```

---

5. The exact file names may be installation dependent.

```
 inModule ("application server")
 main ()
{ Transaction
{/. initialization code ./
/. listen to TRPC calls ./
/. TRPC code ./
{
printf ("Customer server starting \n");
/* This server handles two RPCs: create and view */

/* Register interface with the RPC runtine */
rpc_server_register_if(parameters);

/* Create and obtain binding information */
rpc_server_use_all_protseqs(parameters);
rpc_server_inq_bindings (parameters);

/* Export entry to Name Directory and register endpoints */
rpc_binding_binding_export (parameters);
rpc_ep_register (parameters):

/* Main loop to listen to client messages */
rpc_server_listen (parameters); /* enter the main loop */

/* exit code */
rpc_binding-vector_free (parameters) /* Free binding handles */
```

As expected, the major activity in building an Encina server is to write the code for the trans-action remote procedures. These procedures can include calls to other transaction processes that may be dispersed on different machines. In our case, we have to write the code for two procedures: the create transaction procedure and view procedure (nontransactional).

For the create transaction, let us use the XA interface of Encina.XA. As discussed in Umar [1997, Chapter 6], it is a standard interface between a transaction manager and resource (database) manager. XA, if used, must be initialized during the Encina server initialization routines. XA transactions are logically divided into three parts:

- Beginning a transaction. This is done through the "transaction" keyword.
- Working on behalf of a transaction. This is typically a sequence of SQL statements. In particular these statements must conform to an XA compliant database manager (e.g., Informix, Oracle, Sybase).
- Ending a transaction. This is done through the "on commit" and "on abort" commands.

The following skeleton code represents the create transaction:

```
void create (customer_info, status)
transaction { /* start database transaction */
              /* code for converting customer_info structure into
              SQL table attributes such as cname, caddress, balance */
              exec sql;
              insert cname, caddress, balance into customer_table;
              end sql;
              /* .. include other code */
/* end db transaction */
              onCommit printf ("completed")
              onAbort ("aborted")
```

The code for the nontransactional RPC is straightforward and the same as we showed for DCE (we do not need the `transaction, oncommit, and onabort` commands):

```
void view (cust-id, customer_info, status);
              exec sql;
              select cname, caddress, balance from cust_table where
              c_id=:cust_id;
              end sql;
              /* code for storing cname, caddress, balance into the
              customer_info structure */
}
```

The final step in building a server is to compile and link the server initialization code, the remote procedures, and the server stub generated as part of the IDL compilation (e.g., customer_sstub.o, the server stub generated due to the compilation of customer.idl). The server code can be tested and debugged by using Encina facilities.

Encina servers may use multithreading to support multiple processes concurrently. Thread safety in Encina can be handled through DCE provided **mutexes** (mutual exclusions). However, threads may use Encina-provided locks for read, write, and intent.

7.8.5   Build an Encina Client

Encina client code, written in languages such as C, C++, or any other language, invokes a (T)RPC[6] to an Encina server. As usual, client code includes a header file generated by TIDL, "local" client code, (T)RPCs defined in TIDL, and client logic to handle different error conditions and exceptions. Encina applications can also use a DCE type **context handle.** When the (T)RPC is issued, the client stub code finds the appropriate server with the interface definition and "binds" to it. To develop OO applications, you develop a wrapper on the Encina client side that receives object invocations and issues appropriate (T)RPCs to one or more

---

6. (T)RPC means transactional RPC or just a DCE RPC. An Encina client can issue either. RPC is used when commit processing is not needed and (T)RPC is used when commit processing is needed.

Encina servers (see Figure 7.13). Specifications for Object-Oriented Transaction Management (OTM), such as being considered for CORBA, are expected to eliminate the need for these customized wrappers.

Figure 7.13 Object Orientation in Encina

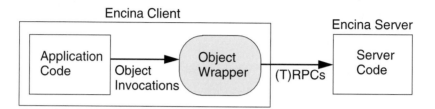

The wrapper is developed as a class with methods which construct and issue (T)RPCs. The discussion of the client code is very similar to the DCE client. We give the main code and discuss the differences briefly:

```
#include <stdio.h>
#include customer.h /. the IDL generated header ./
/* define variables, etc. */
 main ()
{
/* Now invoke the create and view methods */

        c1.create_cust(&customer_obj, status);

        c1. view_cust ( cust_id, &customer_obj);
/* Other client code, e.g., free resources, error processing, etc. */
```

The following pseudocode illustrates the `create_cust` and `view_cust` methods that are invoked from the client application (note that `create_cust` includes commit processing logic because it is a transaction):

```
Transaction
create_cust (customer_id, customer_obj);
        /* variable definitions */
        /* code to flatten customer_obj and store information
        in customer_info structure to be used in RPC */
        create (customer_info, status); /* invoke the RPC */
onCommit
      printf ("transaction committed. Customer added" )
on Abort
      printf ("transaction aborted. Customer not added")

create_cust (customer_id, customer_obj);
```

```
                  /* variable definitions */
                  view ( cust-id, customer_info, status); /* invoke
                  the view RPC */
                  /* code to convert customer_inf to customer_obj */
/* Other client code, e.g., free resources, error processing, etc. */
```

The Encina instructions such as `transaction`, `on commit`, and `on abort` perform obvious transaction processing capabilities such as start of a transaction and event handling. Note that these instructions are only used in the `create_cust` transaction. Encina supports many different ways of initializing transactions. Discussion of these topics is beyond the scope of this book.

7.8.6   Deploy Application

To deploy and run an Encina application, you need to package and send the TIDL, the server code, the client code, and any other routines/files to the destination sites. Installation of Encina programs is similar to OSF DCE; however Encina administration is quite different from DCE administration.

In an Encina environment, an application server is the server portion of an Encina application. It runs on a secure node, handles the Encina client calls, and may communicate with resource managers (e.g., database managers) to process the client calls. Encina assigns a monitor daemon (***Mond***) to each application server. In addition, each application server is configured with a predefined set of ***Processing Agents*** (PAs). When an Encina client issues an RPC or (T)RPC call for the application server, the Mond assigns a PA to handle this call as a transaction. For the duration of this transaction execution, the PA is assigned to do this work. Each PA is a separate process. In addition, multiple application threads can execute within each PA. When a transaction is completed, the PA is freed. The specific steps used in establishing a connection with an application server are (this is an example of Encina explicit binding):

- Before use, each application server is configured by using the Encina Monitor command ("Monadmin Create Server"). This command specifies the number of PAs to be assigned to each application server. This command also specifies the maximum time limit for a transaction to be executed by this application server.

- At run time, the application server is brought up and initialized (e.g., it makes known, i.e. "exports," its address and location).

- The client first obtains a Mond handle for the application server in question.

- From the Mond, the client obtains the binding handle of a free PA which can process the (T)RPC.

- The client issues (T)RPCs with this binding handle.

- The PA executes the (T)RPC for each client in a separate thread.

- After the (T)RPC has been executed, the PA is freed so that the next client call can be assigned to it.

Encina provides a variety of facilities (e.g., reserving and sharing PAs) for load balancing.

Discussion of these facilities is beyond the scope of this book. Visit the Transarc Web site (http://www.transarc.com) for the latest information and details about Encina.

7.9   PowerBuilder for Developing OCSI Applications

7.9.1   Overview

PowerBuilder from Powersoft, currently owned by Sybase, is a popular PC-based application development environment. Although heavily used at present in PC-Windows environments, PowerBuilder is also commercially available on UNIX workstations and supports Web interfaces (known as Web.works). Using PowerBuilder, you can develop object-based window database applications without coding C or C++. PowerBuilder uses a remote data access paradigm and supports a wide array of SQL Servers from vendors such as Oracle, Sybase, and Informix. In addition to supporting many remote databases, PowerBuilder also supports a local database (Watcom SQL).

The PowerBuilder development environment consists of a series of integrated graphical *painters* that enables application development and testing through a series of point-and-click operations. These painters are used to construct the various application components such as menus, windows, queries, reports, databases, and user-defined objects. These painters appear as icons on the PowerBuilder toolbar. Specifically, PowerBuilder provides the following main painters, discussed alphabetically:

Application painter. This painter defines the application in terms of application name and icon, scripts for application events, default colors and fonts, and the libraries to be searched for the application objects. Whenever you develop a PowerBuilder application, the Application painter is the first painter used. The Application painter allows an entire application to be viewed graphically and creates an executable (.EXE) file to deliver the completed application to the end user.

Database painter. This painter provides interactive facilities for creating and maintaining SQL databases. Developers use the Database painter to create tables and views, assign primary and foreign keys, edit data in the database, and perform database administration tasks such as security. As stated previously, PowerBuilder is installed with a single-user Watcom SQL database. In addition, PowerBuilder allows access to remotely located databases such as Oracle, Informix, Sybase, and DB2. The Database painter can be used to define Watcom or other databases. The Database painter also allows storage of extended column information such as labels, headings, display formats, and validation rules.

DataWindow painter. This painter creates a data object for viewing, manipulating, and updating relational databases without any SQL code. DataWindow objects are a very useful and powerful feature because they allow users to connect to a database, retrieve rows, display the rows in various styles, and update the database. The DataWindow painter includes several point-and-click options for designing the DataWindow layout.For example, the

DataWindow painter allows creation of business graphics, automatic summaries, and computed columns without writing any code.

Help painter. This painter provides the typical on-line help capabilities with searches for key words, browsing, adding notes, and copying/printing help information.

Function painter. This painter allows developers to create and maintain functions which are used repetitively in applications.

Library painter. This painter allows the application objects (e.g., menus, windows, DataWindows) to be stored in one or more libraries either locally or on a network. Once created, these objects can be shared/reused by other applications. A check-in/check-out facility maintains the integrity of the shared objects by preventing multiple developers from updating a single object at the same time.

Menu painter. This painter creates menus and toolbars that can be attached to a window created by the Window painter. The Menu painter allows developers to create sophisticated menus and toolbars through a few point-and-click operations.

Query painter. This painter provides graphical means for creating a database query and saving it as an object. The Query painter user points-and-clicks to create database queries by using graphic SQL (e.g., graphic joins between tables and views). Access to the SQL SELECT statement is provided for SQL literate folks. Query objects can be used in the DataWindow object and reports (results produced by query objects can be used in DataWindows and reports).

Window painter. This painter builds the user interfaces (windows) for applications. Windows can display information, request information from a user, and respond to mouse or keyboard actions. To support these operations, the Window painter creates controls (e.g., command buttons, list boxes, scroll bars, check boxes, and DataWindow controls) needed for window-based applications.

In addition to these painters, PowerBuilder provides point-and-click abilities to debug and run applications.

Building an application by using PowerBuilder involves the following steps:

- Create an application object
- Prepare a server for use
- Build the client application code, menus, screens, and so forth
- Deploy the application

7.9.2   Create an Application Object

The first step in building a PowerBuilder application is to create an application object. Your application is always developed within the scope of an application object. The Application painter is used to create and name an application object. For the Customer Information System (CIS) application, we create an application object CIS and store it in the PowerBuilder library CIS.pbl (all PowerBuilder libraries have the extension .pbl, pronounced "pibble"). The process of creating an application is very intuitive and requires about 10 minutes of pointing and clicking. After the application object has been created, you can specify an icon for the application and also control the type of toolbars to be used.

7.9.3   Prepare the Server for Use

In PowerBuilder, you do not need to build a server because the database server used by PowerBuilder acts as a generalized server. The clients send SQL requests to this server; it processes them and sends the response back. As we have discussed earlier, development of a server is a challenging task. You have to write code for server initialization, registration, and binding. In fact, the major advantage of remote data access-based middleware such as PowerBuilder is that you do not need to write a server (it is available to you as a SQL server). All you need to do is create your databases and tables and then populate them. These operations are performed by using the Database painter. For our CIS example, we use the Database painter to define and populate the customer database and table.

7.9.4   Build Client Application

The major effort in building a PowerBuilder application concentrates around building the client applications. This includes developing windows for user screens, DataWindow objects for manipulating the database, and a user interface with appropriate menus and icons. In addition, scripts are developed for processing where needed. Once again, PowerBuilder painters are used to develop these client components. For the CIS application, we develop the following client components:

- Build windows, user interface screens, that will allow a user to enter customer information, customer ID; and other relevant information. The user can use these screens to create a new customer, view existing customers, update customer information, and delete a customer. We also add an exit button on the screen to quit the application.

- Build and add four DataWindow objects to the application. These DataWindow objects are used to create a new customer, view existing customers, update customer information, and delete a customer. These DataWindow objects also display the needed information with correct headings, and so forth.

7.9.5   Deploy the Application

After an application has been built, you can create an EXE file for an executable version of it for distribution to the users. The users can run this executable version from the Windows Program Manager like any other Windows application (such as Word or Excel). We created a CIS.EXE file for the Customer Information System.

Information about PowerBuilder can be found in the vendor documentation (see the site http://www.powersoft.com) and in several books on PowerBuilder (see, for example, Deyhimi [1996], Mahler [1995]).

7.10   State of the Practice: Case Studies

Several implementation examples and case studies utilizing the middleware discussed above have been discussed in the literature. Many implementation examples so far have concentrated on smaller applications utilizing PowerBuilder. Some examples of using OSF DCE in enterprisewide applications have also been reported. An example of using OSF DCE in large-scale systems is the Adapt/X TraxWay system developed at Bellcore. Adapt/X TraxWay serves as a gateway between OSF DCE clients and mainframe-based legacy systems. The clients issue DCE RPCs that are converted by Adapt/X TraxWay to initiate screen scraping, queued messaging, and other mainframe-based sessions.

Examples of using CORBA are sparse at the time of this writing due to the relative newness of CORBA, although experience in this area is growing rapidly. For example, a detailed case study of utilizing CORBA to develop DISCUS (Data Interchange and Synergistic Collateral Usage Study) has been described by Mowbray and Zahavi [Mowbray 1995, Chapter 7]. DISCUS represents the U.S. government's first CORBA-based application system. The project is a relatively small project with only 150 lines of OMG IDL definitions. These definitions describe interfaces for data interchange, access to data sources, and access to application functions. The ANSA User Conferences are a good source of case studies for CORBA and distributed object applications.

We should keep in mind that most of the published case studies and examples do not provide implementation details. Implementation details are usually proprietary and are typically mitigated from open publications.

7.11   State of the Market: Standards and Products

The implementation of OCSI applications will be significantly impacted by the advances and growth in CORBA, OLE, and Web technologies. In particular, the CORBA 2.0 specifications are of significance. CORBA 2.0 includes ORB-to-ORB interoperability specifications, client and server initialization specifications, programming language bindings for additional languages such as C++ and Smalltalk, and interface repository specifications. Future work in object transaction management specifications from OMG will also play a significant role. In the meantime, the popularity of Microsoft's OLE/COM and OpenDoc is growing. The key problem at present is the incompatibility between the object models among CORBA, OLE, and OpenDoc [Rymer 1995].

Many commercially available products are becoming available for OSF DCE, CORBA, and distributed transaction processing. For example, OSF DCE products are available from IBM, Hewlett-Packard, and Sun Microsystems. CORBA products are available from IBM

(SOM/DSOM), Digital (ObjectBroker), ICL (DAIS), Iona (ORBIX), and Sun (DOE). Distributed transaction processing capabilities, in addition to Encina, are being provided by Tuxedo System 5, among others.

7.12   State of the Art: Research Notes

Research is needed in efficient, detailed design, programming, and testing techniques for OCSI applications. Examples of the research areas are distributed programming languages and operating systems for distributed objects [Islam 1995], and [Chin 1991], distributed coordination models [Adler 1995], and distributed software engineering [Shatz 1993]. In particular, theoretical work in efficient design of distributed and parallel programs is applicable here. The *IEEE Parallel & Distributed Technology* magazine and the *IEEE Transactions on Parallel & Distributed Systems* regularly report advances in this field.

An area of considerable interest is the study of the application-level performance characteristics of OCSI applications, in particular, performance models for distributed applications that utilize the RPC technology. Mehrad Yasrebi [Yasrebi 1995] describes a detailed performance model for a LAN/WAN gateway that utilizes object-oriented RPCs. Rolia and Sevcik [Rolia 1995] present a Method of Layers [MOL] model that can be used to provide performance estimates of layered systems.

Yet another area of research is the implication of using OODBMS for implementing OCSI applications. As the object technology becomes more pervasive, the push toward using OODBMS in the middleware (e.g., for implementing CORBA) as well as application databases will increase. This will raise many integration issues at the implementation level.

7.13   Summary

The architectures developed in the previous chapters can be implemented by using appropriate middleware such as Web, CORBA, PowerBuilder, OSF DCE, and Encina. Although most of the implementation activities are middleware dependent, the following generic steps are commonly used:

1. Develop a detailed design

2. Create interface definitions

3. Build server programs

4. Build client programs

5. Test and deploy

We have presented an example that is used to illustrate how applications are developed by using CORBA, PowerBuilder, OSF DCE, and Encina. CORBA is ideal for OCSI; however,

DCE can be used to develop OCSI applications because DCE does support several OO properties such as encapsulation. However, DCE IDL does not support inheritance and complex objects (these properties exist in CORBA IDL). As compared to CORBA, it is difficult to implement polymorphism in DCE. DCE also does not support dynamic invocations supported in CORBA. Although Encina can be used to develop OO transaction management applications, facilities like OOTM support from CORBA should help alleviate a lot.

7.14   Case Study: XYZCorp Implements Web-Based Systems

XYZCorp has approved the application architecture determined in the previous chapters. The next undertaking is to work through the detailed design, implementation, and testing steps of the following new applications:

- A new "advanced" inventory management system for integrated order processing/inventory management

- A management planning system that will support the management decisions in marketing and product planning

- A flexible manufacturing system to automate the manufacturing of electronic products.

Specifically, you have been asked to implement these applications by using the chosen middleware components and to develop detailed architecture diagrams that map the system to the underlying platform. These diagrams should show the pieces of the systems, where they reside, and how they interact with each other (i.e., middleware). For the implementation and testing steps, you should produce the needed code and documentation.

Hints about the Case Study

The five-step implementation and testing procedure introduced in Section 7.2 and refined/customized in later sections can be used to implement and test these three applications.

The effort to implement the Management Planning System (MPS) should be very lightweight because you can purchase and install the software tools needed for most decision support applications. For example, you need to worry only about installing and testing the tools (most of the five steps are bypassed).

The implementation for the inventory management system can be an extensive effort. We recommended a three-tiered architecture for this application. The first tier can be a Web browser, the second tier can perform the application logic that can be invoked from a CGI gateway, and the third tier can be the database that was allocated as part of the data architecture effort. You can use CORBA and Web technologies to implement this application (see Sections 7.4 and 7.5).

The flexible manufacturing system will require an extensive software implementation effort because it is a real-time system. In systems of this nature, it is difficult to find off-the-shelf packages and middleware at present (you may have to implement the middleware yourself). It is educational to go through the five implementation steps to understand the unique software implementation problems of real-time systems by working through this exercise.

7.15   Problems and Exercises

1. Convert the pseudocode discussed in this chapter into an actual running system by using C++ and/or Java.

2. Show how you will implement a groupware application by using the approach used in this chapter.

3. Show how you will implement a mobile computing application by using the approach used in this chapter.

4. Show specifically how you will use a particular Web gateway (e.g., WebSQL) to implement the Customer Information application.

5. Show how you will develop a Web front end to the CORBA application developed in this chapter.

7.16   Additional Information

Most of the implementation-level information is available in the vendor-provided products discussed in this chapter. The books by Mahler [1995], Mowbray [1995], and Shirley [1993] give good overviews of developing PowerBuilder, CORBA, and DCE applications, respectively.

Adler, R., "Distributed Coordination Models for Client/Server Computing," *IEEE Computer,* April 1995, pp. 14–22.

Blair, L., et al., "Formal Specification and Verification of Multimedia Systems in Open Distributed Processing," *Computer Standards and Interfaces,* Vol. 17, 1995, pp. 413–436.

Chin, R., and Chanson, S., "Distributed Object-Based Programming Systems," *ACM Computing Surveys,* March 1991, pp. 91–124.

Conway, B., Loureiro, K., "The C/S Automated-Testing Tools Market: Hotter than Hot," *Gartner Group Research Note,* August 28, 1996.

Devanbu, P., et al., "Generating Testing and Analysis Tools with Aria," *ACM Transactions on Software Engineering and Methodology,* January 1996, pp. 42–62.

Deyhimi, P., *Advanced PowerBuilder 5.0 Techniques,* John Wiley, 1996.

Goglia, P., *Testing Client/Server Applications,* QED Publishing Group, 1993.

Hetzel, B., *The Complete Guide to Software Testing,* John Wiley, 1988.

Hu, W., "DCE Security Programming," O'Reilly & Associates, Inc., 1995.

Islam, N., *Distributed Objects: Methodologies for Customizing Operating Systems,* IEEE Computer Society Press, 1995.

Mahler, P., *PowerBuilder: Building Client/Server Applications,* Prentice Hall, 1995.

Mosley, D., *Real-World Issues in Client-Server Software Testing,* Prentice Hall, Target Summer, 1997.

Mowbray, T., and Zahavi, R., *The Essential CORBA: Systems Integration Using Distributed Objects,* John Wiley, 1995.

Nicol, J., et al., "Object Orientation in Heterogeneous Distributed Computing Systems, *IEEE Computer,"* June 1993, pp. 57–67.

Peterson, W., *DCE: A Guide to Developing Portable Applications,* McGraw-Hill, 1995.

Rolia, J., and Sevcik, K., "The Method of Layers," *IEEE Transactions on Software Engineering,* August 1995, pp. 689–700.

Rosenberry, W., et al., *Understanding DCE,* O'Reilly & Associates, 1993.

Ryan, H., et al., *Practical Guide to Client/Server Computing,* Auerbach, 1997.

Rymer, J., "Distributed Object Interoperability," *Distributed Computing Monitor,* March 1995.

Shatz, S., *Development of Distributed Software: Concepts and Tools,* Macmillan, 1993.

Shirley, J., *Guide to Writing DCE Applications,* O'Reilly & Associates, 1993.

Sylvester, T., "Automated Testing Tools–Client/Server Today Labs," *Client/Server Today,* February 1995, pp. 75–82.

Umar, A., *Object-Oriented Client/Server Internet Environments,* Prentice Hall, 1997.

Whiting, R., "Technology Briefing: Automated Testing Tools," *Client/Server Today,* February 1995, pp. 54–59.

Yasrebi, M., "Experience with Distributed Objects in a Portable and Multithreaded Library for a LAN/WAN Gateway Application," *IEEE 20th Local Computer Network Conference,* Minneapolis, MN, Oct. 15–18, 1995.

P A R T

APPLICATION REENGINEERING: DEALING WITH LEGACIES

III

This part of the book concentrates on issues related to reengineering of existing, mostly legacy, applications. The need for reengineering, it is assumed, has been determined in the initial planning iteration described in Chapter 3.

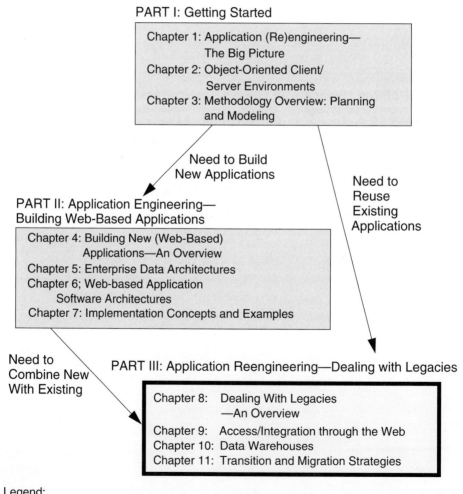

PART I: Getting Started

Chapter 1: Application (Re)engineering—
The Big Picture
Chapter 2: Object-Oriented Client/
Server Environments
Chapter 3: Methodology Overview: Planning
and Modeling

Need to Build
New Applications

Need to
Reuse
Existing
Applications

PART II: Application Engineering—
Building Web-Based Applications

Chapter 4: Building New (Web-Based)
Applications—An Overview
Chapter 5: Enterprise Data Architectures
Chapter 6; Web-based Application
Software Architectures
Chapter 7: Implementation Concepts and Examples

Need to
Combine New
With Existing

PART III: Application Reengineering—Dealing with Legacies

Chapter 8:   Dealing With Legacies
—An Overview
Chapter 9:   Access/Integration through the Web
Chapter 10: Data Warehouses
Chapter 11: Transition and Migration Strategies

Legend:
• Shaded areas indicate topics covered; dark border indicates current topics.
• Arrows indicate interdependencies.

8

Dealing with Legacy Applications: An Overview

8.1   Introduction

Simply stated, a legacy application is an *application of value* that has been passed on to the next generation. Many of these applications are old (many were developed in the late 1960s and early 1970s) that are showing signs of age and years of patching and fixing. These systems are vital to the survival of several organizations; however, they are becoming increasingly expensive to maintain and operate (some systems take several months for a simple enhancement such as a new calculation). As the business pressures to provide flexible and timely information for management decisions and operational support grow, the inadequacy of legacy applications is highlighted. In addition, off-the-shelf software and flexible C/S architectures are showing the weaknesses of legacy applications. However, legacy applications are the workhorses for most organizations and cannot be thrown away (it is difficult to throw away applications that support critical services such as billing, inventory control, payables/receivables, and purchasing). This presents a serious dilemma: You cannot live with them or without them.

This chapter introduces the main concepts of legacy applications, identifies the main issues, and establishes a framework for dealing with legacy applications. This framework is the foundation of the next three chapters which explore the details of accessing/integrating legacy applications, developing data warehouses, and transitioning (migration). The issues and approaches related to dealing with legacy applications are complex and multidimensional, involving a mixture of technical and organizational factors. The following questions will guide the discussion:

- What are the main characteristics of legacy applications and what are the challenges associated with legacy applications?

- What approaches should be used to deal with legacy applications? In particular which one of the following main strategies should be used:

- Disregard them for all future developments **(ignore)**
- Rewrite them from scratch **(cold turkey)**
- Consolidate them into the current and future activities by providing access in place **(integrate)**
- Build a "shadow" system **(data warehousing)**
- Rearchitect and transition them gradually **(gradual migration)**

- How can the reengineering of legacy applications be planned, that is, what type of business factors, architectural solutions, implementation issues, and cost/benefits analysis are needed?

- What is the state of the practice, state of the market, and state of the art in this field?

Section 8.2 introduces the core concepts and discusses the challenges of dealing with legacy applications. Section 8.3 discusses the pros and cons of the five basic approaches to deal with legacy applications (i.e., ignore, cold turkey, integrate, data warehousing, and gradual migration) and presents a framework for analysis. It is argued that the first two approaches are not viable in most situations. In most practical situations, organizations concentrate on integration, data warehousing, and gradual migration. These three strategies are discussed in detail in the next three chapters. Section 8.4 presents a planning methodology that systematically combines the business factors, architectural solutions, implementation issues, and cost/benefit analysis into a systematic procedure. The chapter concludes with state-of-the-practice, state-of-the-market, and state-of-the-art observations (Sections 8.5, 8.6, and 8.7).

Key Points

- Clearly understand the business reasons that drive the legacy application reengineering effort.

- Legacy applications are critical to the survival of many organizations and should not be dealt with lightly.

- Legacy application reengineering means a combination of approaches such as access, integration, rearchitecture, and migration strategies.

- Migration is not the only reengineering option. Other options are integration, data warehousing, and, of course, doing nothing.

- The life cycle for undertaking a reengineering effort should be longer than the life cycle of the undertaking itself.

- Success in legacy application reengineering requires a mixture of the right people, skill set, tools, and methodologies (it is not a technical issue only).

- Many application reengineering efforts do not succeed due to lack of training (users and technical staff) and lack of project management.

- When migrating an application to distributed architectures, use the application engineering principles discussed in Part II of this book to build new components.

8.2   Legacy Application Concepts

8.2.1   What Is a Legacy Application?

According to Webster, legacy is "something of value received from an ancestor or predecessor or from the past." The term legacy is being used in several contexts such as "legacy LANs" (e.g., Ethernet LANs), "legacy operating systems" (e.g., PC DOS), and "legacy management styles" (e.g. "Taylorism"—the Scientific Management Movement by Frederick Taylor [Taylor 1911]). Some people use the term legacy to indicate anything that is not fashionable. For example, labeling anything that is not Java as legacy (see the sidebar "What Is Legacy—An Anecdote" in Chapter 1). We will use the following definition:

> **Definition.** A *legacy application* is an application of value inherited from the past.

The keywords in this definition are *of value* (critical to the business) and *inherited from the past* (typically five years or beyond). Legacy applications have also been defined as "large software systems that we don't know how to cope with but that are vital to our organization" [Bennet 1995], "any application in production" [Schick 1995], and "any information system that significantly resists modification and evolution to meet new and constantly changing business requirements" [Brodie 1995]. Many legacy applications are mainframe-based IMS applications (according to a 1993 Forrester Research Survey conducted for IBM, 80 percent of enterprise data are stored in IMS databases). Specifically, legacy applications are a class of applications that are (Brodie [1993], Bennet [1995], Gotlieb [1993], and Mayers [1994]):

- Crucial to the day-to-day operation of corporations

- Heavily invested over the years and cannot be simply "wheeled out to the parking lot"

- Large (e.g., millions of lines of code, thousands of programs)

- Old (e.g., 5 to 20 years old, some are older)

- Used heavily (e.g., thousands of transactions per day)

- Not well documented and difficult to understand (documentation changes have not kept up with code changes)

- Inflexible, costly, time-consuming, and risky to maintain and change

- Based on older database technology (e.g., IMS databases) or no database technology at all (e.g., VSAM/ISAM files)

- Written in older programming languages (e.g., COBOL, PL1, and assembler)

- Based on text-based user interfaces (e.g., 3270 screens) instead of GUI (e.g., windows)

- Vertically integrated and "monolithic" (e.g., tightly coupled user, process, and data management)

- Repositories of years of corporate experience and practices (e.g., many business rules are embedded in the legacy code)

Billing Systems—Example of a Legacy Application

Many companies started using computers in the late 1960s for billing purposes. The billing applications in that time period were written in assembler language due to the severe storage shortage (some of us dinosaurs remember working on machines with 5K of main memory). Later, these programs, or parts of them, were converted to "state-of-the-art" technologies such as COBOL programs and indexed files. Many smaller companies included other functions such as order processing as part of billing (why have two applications if one can do the job!). As time went on, the companies grew and the billing systems also grew. "Young" programmers in the 1970s insisted on modern languages such as PLI and data management technologies such as IMS databases. So by the end of 1970s, many billing systems were using a mixture of assembler, COBOL, and PLI code with IMS databases and ISAM files.

You can imagine what happened in the 1980s. Of course, more expansions were needed and they were introduced by using the DB2 database technology. By the 1990s, many billing systems have become a hodgepodge of badly documented and badly structured functions, programming languages, and data management technologies. These systems are crucial to the survival of companies (not many companies can survive without billing their customers) but are becoming extremely expensive to maintain and operate. Many legacy applications have gone through similar growing pains and consequently have similar characteristics.

Many business applications that were developed in the 1970s and early 1980s are good examples of legacy applications. A common example is the billing systems (see the sidebar "Billing Systems: Example of a Legacy Application"). Other common examples are order processing, accounts receivables/payables, medical claim processing, and materials handling systems. But legacy applications are not necessarily very old (during my work assignments, I have heard statements such as "non-Java applications are legacies," "anything not OO is legacy," and "anything not using the Web are legacies." In fact, legacy applications will always be with us (some of the new OCSI applications will be legacy in a few years, if they survive). Due to this reason, we will emphasize the key principles in this chapter that can be used to reengineer any existing application.

8.2.2 Legacy Application Reengineering Dilemma

Legacy applications are a dominant concern of IT management at present. If possible, the IT management would like to keep the legacy systems as they are for several reasons. First, they provide vital services that are very risky to disrupt. Second, many users and support staff are trained on how to operate these systems and are used to them. Third, many legacy systems are very reliable and perform very well, contrary to the common belief (for example, many IMS-based applications at present handle hundreds of on-line transactions per second—a goal many new C/S applications are still struggling with). Fourth, the administrative support of mainframe-based legacy applications (e.g., backup/

recovery, disaster handling, change management, security) has matured over the years. Finally, there is some emotional attachment to legacy applications among senior staff because these systems have survived through years of fundamental changes in business practices and technologies. For example, the constraints of machine storage and speed have been replaced with business constraints of flexibility and adaptiveness. You cannot blame a system for satisfying the requirements when it was built (e.g., minimize machine resource utilization) just because the requirements have changed (no one seems to care if a program saves 1K of memory).

However, something must be done about these systems. First, legacy applications are becoming increasingly expensive to maintain and operate (it takes months to introduce a change). Second, these applications do not satisfy the flexibility and growth requirements of modern enterprises. Third, many off-the-shelf C/S packages with nice GUIs are becoming available, especially for small- and medium-sized organizations, that are highlighting weaknesses of legacy applications. Finally, new employees do not want to work on systems that were created before the employees were created!

So we are left with a serious dilemma: What to do with legacy applications? The approach presented in Section 8.3 will attempt to help you. Let us first present a high-level analysis of the problem and define the key terms. Let us assume that an information service is needed to support a business process. The high-level choices are represented by the following two key application-related questions (see Figure 8.1):

- Should a *new* application be developed from scratch (i.e, develop a new database and application software)? We call it the ***application engineering*** challenge.

- Should the existing/legacy databases and/or application software be used to provide the information service? We call it the ***application reengineering*** challenge.

Figure 8.1 shows these dilemmas in terms of databases and software. For example, application engineering requires new databases and new software (the shaded area). Application reengineering, however, can occur due to the need to utilize existing databases and/or software. The focus of this part of the book is on reengineering, so let us define the main terms.

Figure 8.1 The Engineering/Reengineering Dilemma

	New Database(s)	**Existing Database(s)**
New Application Software	Application engineering	Reengineer existing database(s)
Existing Application Software	Reengineer existing application software	Reengineer application software plus database(s)

Reengineering means different things to different people. We will use the following definitions of reengineering:

- **Business process reengineering** is concerned with the conversion of business processes, and not of computer processes [Hammer 1993].

- **Software reengineering** is concerned with conversion of the form and not of the functionality of the software [Chikofsky 1990].

- **Data reengineering** is concerned with conversion of data format and not its content [Aiken 1994].

- **Application reengineering** means that the application functionality does not change but its form changes. Application reengineering can involve data and/or software reengineering.

- **Legacy application reengineering** means a combination of approaches such as access, integration, rearchitecture, and migration strategies.

8.2.3   Categories of Legacy Applications

Legacy applications consist of the legacy data, the functionality (application logic), and the user presentation. From an application reengineering perspective, legacy applications can be classified into the following categories depicted in Figure 8.2 (these are extension of the categories introduced by Brodie and Stonebraker [Brodie 1993, Brodie 1995]):

- Highly decomposable applications
- Data decomposable applications
- Program decomposable applications
- Monolithic applications

Highly decomposable applications are very well structured applications that have the following characteristics. First, application components are separable into user interface processing, application processing logic, and data access services. In other words, these are the three logical tiered applications. In particular, data access services have well-defined interfaces so that the application data can be accessed remotely without having to invoke application functionality. Second, application modules are independent of each other (no hierarchical interdependencies exist). Finally, application modules have well-defined interfaces with database services, user interfaces, and with other applications. Many applications may be highly decomposable if they are developed by using structured design techniques; or the object-oriented techniques where each object has a well-defined interface. These application architectures are the friendliest toward transitioning and external access. For example, each component of the legacy application can be accessed directly and components can be replaced gradually during the transition process.

Figure 8.2 Architectural Categories of Legacy Applications

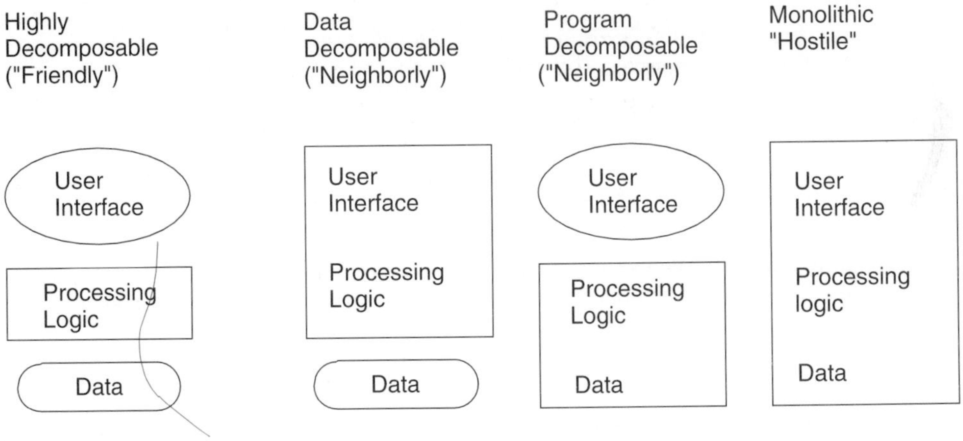

Note: More decomposable applications are "friendlier" towards reengineering than less decomposable ones.

Data decomposable applications are semistructured (semidecomposable) applications that have two characteristics. First, application components are separable into two units: data access services, and user interface processing/application processing logic intermixed as one unit. In other words, these are the two logical tiered applications where data are one tier and the program/user interface is the other. Second, interfaces to other applications are well defined. In this category of applications, the data can be directly accessed, but the application logic cannot. For example, the data services can be rearchitected or accessed from remotely located programs or tools due to the well-defined interfaces of data services. Ideally, the data services interfaces should be so well defined to enable replacement of one DBMS package with another (e.g., Informix with Oracle) without impacting the application. Unfortunately, the application logic of this category of applications is intertwined with the user interface processing and thus cannot be remotely invoked. But these applications are still somewhat friendly, perhaps neighborly, from an application reengineering point of view.

Program decomposable applications are also semistructured (semidecomposable) applications but with the following distinguishing characteristic: Application components are separable into two units—user interface processing units, and application processing logic/database processing intermixed as one unit (see Figure 8.2). The interfaces to other applications are well defined just as the previous category. In other words, these are the two logical tiered applications where user interface is one tier and the program/data services is the other. In this category of applications, the data cannot be directly accessed—they can be accessed only by invoking predefined functions on the data. Many existing legacy applications fall into this category. In these application architectures, the raw data may not be understood by the end users and/or the database administrators are unwilling to provide the subschema needed by the application programmers. In addition, the data schema of the legacy applications is considered proprietary in many cases and can be accessed only through the functionality provided by the application. These applications are also neighborly.

Unstructured (monolithic) applications have the following characteristics: (a) All application components appear as one inseparable component and (b) user interface, application, and data access logic are intermixed throughout. These single-tiered applications are usually old applications with no structure. In essence, the data from these applications can be accessed only through terminal invocations. In general, these applications are hostile toward reengineering and are the hardest to integrate and transition.

Many applications may have an architecture which is a combination of the four. These categories play a key role in deciding whether a given legacy application should be gradually rearchitected and migrated, integrated/interfaced with new applications, or rewritten from scratch. We will use these classification of legacy application architectures to analyze and determine the most appropriate strategies to deal with legacy applications.

8.3 Legacy Application Reengineering Strategies

8.3.1 Overview

The reengineering strategies needed to deal with legacy applications fall into the following categories [Bennet 1995], [Nassif 1993], and [Gotlieb 1993]:

- **Ignore**—discard them for all future developments
- **Cold turkey**—rewrite them from scratch
- **Integrate**—Consolidate them into the current and future applications by access in place
- **Data warehouse**—build a "shadow" system to house the frequently accessed data
- **Gradual migration**—rearchitect and transition them gradually

The exact mix and sequence of these approaches to form a strategy are based on a combination of business drivers, the technical status of the legacy application being considered, the flexibility and growth requirements, the corporate attitude toward IT reengineering, and several other business as well as technical issues. A high-level understanding of the strategies to be used can be gained by focusing on the following three key factors (these factors should be identified clearly in the analysis/planning stage):

> **Business value of the legacy application.** To justify any reengineering, the legacy applications must support significant current as well as future business processes. The business value can be

measured in terms of contribution to profit, type of business processes supported, and market value. If needed, business value can be measured in terms of a score between 0 to 10 to indicate the importance of this legacy application to the corporation.

Flexibility and growth requirements. If the application does not need to be modified extensively for flexibility and growth, then minimal effort to integrate with new applications may be appropriate. Flexibility and growth requirements can be measured in terms of the number of functional and performance enhancements needed in the next few years (typically two to three years).

Technical status ("friendliness") of the legacy application. If the legacy application is nondecomposable and written in assembler language with outdated indexed file systems, then it may be better to rewrite it at some point. Technical status represents the quality of the legacy application in terms of its modularity, error rates, flexibility and utilization of current technologies. Technical quality can be measured in terms of international quality standards such as ISO 9126. Informally, technical status can represent "hostility" of the legacy application to reengineering (monolithic applications are more hostile than completely decomposable ones).

Applications Can Be Hostile—An Anecdote

In a consultation assignment, a customer mentioned that some of the legacy applications they are trying to deal with are hostile. At that time, I had already characterized legacy applications in terms of decomposability as proposed by Mike Brodie [1995]. However, this notion of application hostility gave me an idea to rethink application reengineering issues in terms of application hostility/friendliness. It seems like a natural fit so I have started using this notion (I am sure that under serious scrutiny this analogy, like many other good ones, will fall apart, but it is worth a try). So here are the main ideas (see Figure 8.2):

Hostile applications are those applications that do not allow you to interface with them. You are basically forced to use the outside facilities (i.e., those commands that are available to the "general public").

Neighborly applications are the applications that allow authorized users to access a few of their internal resources (e.g., programs or databases).

Friendly applications are those applications that allow authorized users to access most of their internal resources (e.g., databases plus programs).

Figure 8.3 shows how these three factors contribute toward a first-cut understanding of what strategy may be most appropriate to reengineer legacy applications. In general, the applications that have low business value should not be considered for reengineering systems (these are represented by the plane AEFD in Figure 8.3). If needed, the operation and maintenance of these applications could be outsourced. At the other extreme, a great deal of the time and effort should be spent on applications with high business value (the plane

BCGH in Figure 8.3). The applications that have low technical value (the plane ABCD in Figure 8.3) are the hardest to deal with and are very expensive to reengineer. These applications are typically very old and monolithic. At the other extreme, the applications with high technical value (the EFGH plan) are relatively easy and inexpensive to reengineer and interface with newer applications. Legacy applications in this category are typically well structured RDBMS-based applications. Lastly, the flexibility dimension also plays a key role in this analysis. Legacy applications that do not need to grow dramatically (the AEHB plan) are good candidates for integration with new applications while the legacy applications with high flexibility and growth requirements (the CDFG plane) should be eventually rearchitected and migrated.

The cube shown in Figure 8.3 is an effective tool for "application portfolio" analysis to determine the status of the current applications. Naturally, other factors can be, and should be, added for further analysis. Table 8.1 includes additional factors such as corporate pressures toward application downsizing, data query requirements, data currency requirements, and integration requirements to suggest guidelines in choosing the appropriate approach (other factors can be added to this table). This table can be used as a decision table. For example, it shows that gradual migration could be chosen if flexibility and growth requirements are high and if corporate pressures for application/data downsizing are also high. Similarly, data warehousing may be appropriate if the data query requirements are very high and if data currency requirements are low (e.g., planning data); and access in place may be appropriate for the data for which data query requirements are low but the data accuracy requirements are high.

Figure 8.3 Framework for Analyzing Strategies

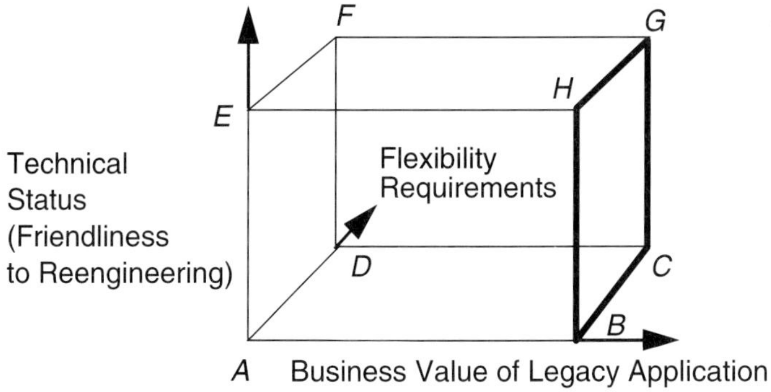

Note: The dark lines should be the main area of focus.
H = Ignore, B = Access in place, C = Migration (gradual or cold turkey), G = Data warehousing

TABLE 8.1 GENERAL GUIDELINES FOR DEALING WITH A LEGACY SYSTEM

Evaluation Factors	Ignore the Legacy System	Cold Turkey	Integrate (Access in Place)	Data Warehousing	Gradual Migration
Business value of legacy application	Low (short range/not critical)	High (very long range)	High	High	High
Flexibility and growth requirements	None to very low	Very high and immediate	Low	Medium	High
Technical status of legacy application	High (decomposable)	Very low	Low to medium	Medium	Medium to low
Corporate pressure toward downsizing and client/server systems	Low	High and immediate	Low	Medium	High and long range
Data query (ad hoc) requirements	Low	Medium	Low	High to very high	Medium
Data currency requirements			High	Low	Medium
Integration needs with other host applications	Low to very low	High to very high	Low	Low	High to very high
Number of host applications accessed by clients for needed data			Few	Large	

Note: Blank entries indicate "don't care," that is, the factor does not influence the choice.

8.3.2   Strategy 1: Ignore the Legacy Applications

This approach is not practically viable in most situations because many legacy applications cannot be ignored due to their embedded base and heavy use. In particular, the legacy data may be of value even when the business rules (the functionality) may be outdated. For example, many new telecommunications applications need access to the site and customer data used heavily by the legacy telecommunications applications. As shown in Table 8.1, this approach is advisable when the business functions supported by the legacy application are not needed and are being phased out, the technical status of the application is high enough to minimize maintenance costs, the requirements for growth and flexibility are none, and the need for integration with other applications is very low.

Some organizations are ignoring their legacy applications by outsourcing them to software houses that specialize in operating and maintaining legacy applications. These software houses maintain an array of older computing platforms and serve as "nursing homes" for retiring legacy applications.

8.3.3 Strategy 2: Rewrite from Scratch (Cold Turkey)

This approach is also not viable in many practical situations because it is not easy to rewrite legacy application systems from scratch due to the following reasons (see Brodie [1993] for a detailed discussion):

- A better system must be promised because management does not allow large investments just for the promise of flexibility.

- Business conditions do not stand still to allow for new developments (for some legacy applications, 5 to 10 requests for changes are received per month).

- Specifications for legacy systems rarely exist and undocumented dependencies frequently exist.

- Legacy application rewrite efforts can be too large to manage easily.

- Rewrite of large legacy applications may take a long enough time to make the rewrite itself legacy at completion (many of the new technologies may become legacy in three to five years).

As shown in Table 8.1, this approach should be considered for those applications with long expected life (to recover from the conversion cost), and with high demands for flexibility, downsizing, and integration with other applications. Outsourcing of legacy application rewrites is a viable option for many organizations. In particular, outsourcing of application rewrites to off-shore software houses can be cost-effective. Dedene and DeVreese [Dedene 1995] report two case studies that explain the advantages of off-shore reengineering. We will review these case studies in Section 8.5.

8.3.4 Strategy 3: Provide Access in Place (Access/Integration)

In many cases, access in place is the best approach to deal with legacy applications. This approach allows access to legacy data and integration of legacy applications with new applications and tools without any modification to the legacy applications. This merging old with new strategy is facilitated by surrounding the legacy applications with mediators such as gateways and object wrappers. Access in place is useful for the following situations (see Table 8.1):

- The business value of the data and/or the application logic is high.

- The access to needed data is urgent and cannot be postponed until after the completion of migration.

- The needed data can be accessed by client applications and end-user tools by employing off-the-shelf technologies.

- The data query requirements are low (most access in place solutions do not work well if a very large number of *new* queries start arriving at the legacy system).

- The data currency requirements are high, that is, users need to access the most recent copy of data (a shadow database or a data warehouse is not adequate).

Access in place is achieved through "surround" technologies (also known as "mediators") which hide the legacy application details from client applications and end-user tools (see Figure 8.4). Appropriate surround technologies, such as the World Wide Web (WWW), can considerably ease the task of integrating legacy applications with newer applications (users and programmers do not know whether the data were retrieved from an old IMS-based system or a more modern object-oriented system). It is naturally important to choose the most appropriate surround technologies for access in place. The chosen technologies can employ middleware such as Web, CORBA, and SQL gateways. It is essential to bind the solution approach by setting limits on what features will be included in the surround technology and when these features will be needed. Analysis of the organizational issues (staff estimates, training, roles, and responsibilities) and estimation of time and cost needed for implementation and deployment are also of key importance. We will discuss access in place and various integration approaches, especially through the Web, in the next chapter.

Figure 8.4 Surround Technologies for Access in Place

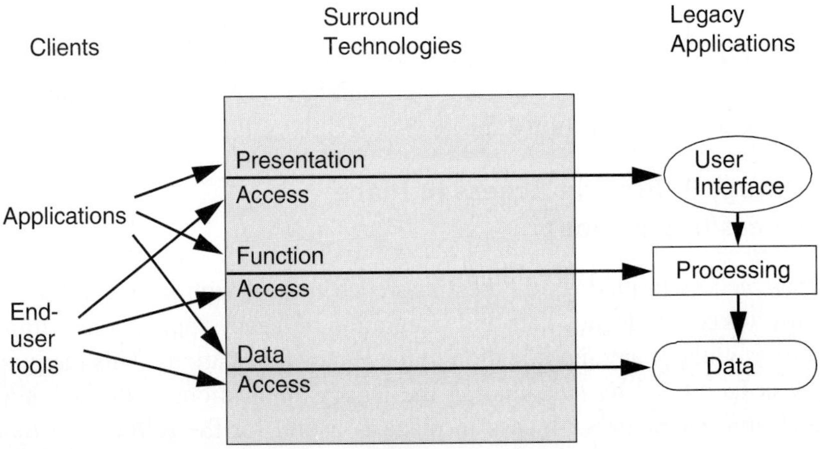

8.3.5   Strategy 4: Data Warehousing

Data (information) warehousing involves extraction of suitable data and storage of these data into a database which is devoted to meet the information needs of decision support personnel. Data warehouses do create some duplicate data but are, in many cases, the best approach to access legacy data for reporting and other types of applications with high ad hoc access requirements. The concept of a data warehouse is based on the notion that organizational data exist in two formats:

- Operational data which are used for day-to-day transaction processing. These data are updated frequently.

- Analysis (decision support) data which are used for business analysis and report generation. These data are extracted from operational data periodically and downloaded, usually, to another computer for report generation and analysis.

Data warehousing may be appropriate if the enterprise data are currently used by on-line transaction processing systems but are also needed for decision support applications for heavy ad hoc queries (see Table 8.1 for additional factors). In such cases, you may establish a data warehouse for decision support users instead of providing access in place to the legacy data. Data warehouses are quite popular at present and are being used widely to provide a uniform and consistent view of detailed and summarized data that are accessed by decision support tools such as report writers, data browsers, spreadsheets, 4GL, "drill-down" applications, on-line analytical processing (OLAP) tools, and other planning and modeling tools [Inmon 1993], and [Waterson 1994]. Many case studies of information warehousing have been reported in the literature since the early 1990s [Ferrent 1992], [Eberhard 1993], [Giordano 1993], [Appleton 1996], and [Radding 1996]. We will discuss data warehouses in detail in Chapter 10.

8.3.6 Strategy 5: Gradual Migration

This approach is used to gradually migrate the legacy applications to the more modern and well-structured client/server applications ("target applications"). This approach is important if access in place is not economical over a long period of time or if the enterprise does intend to phase out existing legacy applications (see Table 8.1). The gradual migration strategies for legacy applications are generally more effective than the rewrite from scratch (cold turkey) strategy. The gradual migration strategy involves several steps over a period of several years and uses "surround technology" to hide the transition from client applications and end users.

The legacy and target systems must coexist during the migration stage. The main challenge is to design a gateway to isolate the migration steps so that the end users do not know if the needed information is being retrieved from an old module/database or a new module/database. During the migration, the gateway should provide [Brodie 1993]:

- Access to legacy application functions or data from target user interfaces

- Access to target application functions or data from legacy user interfaces

- Hiding through encapsulation the details of the legacy and target system from the users (see Cerdingley [1993])

- Synchronization of target and legacy data

Development of gateways to facilitate migration is usually an expensive undertaking. The total costs, time lines, staffing, and organizational considerations needed for migration must be considered carefully. We will discuss gradual migration in Chapter 11.

8.4   Planning for Legacy Application Reengineering

8.4.1   Overview

Proper planning is vital to the success of legacy application reengineering projects. The potential risks (e.g., reengineered application not working properly, introducing new bugs), costs, benefits, and the most appropriate solution strategies must be clarified during the planning process. Planning is the first iteration of the "methodology template" that was first introduced in Chapter 3 and was later expanded in Chapter 4 for engineering of new applications (see Figure 8.5). The template consists of successive iterations, refinements, and expansions between a few broad activities (stages): analysis, solution architectures, implementations, and deployment/support. In this chapter, we revisit the planning iteration with special attention to legacy applications. The later chapters of this part of the book will go through the later iterations of this template by customizing it for integration, data warehousing, and gradual migration. We will discuss the following activities within the scope of planning:

- Opportunity analysis to establish goals and objectives of application reengineering

- Evaluating solution architectures to determine the most appropriate technical solution strategy

- Implementation considerations to determine how the strategy will be implemented (i.e., who will do what)

- Cost/benefit analysis and project scheduling to factor the management considerations

The result of the reengineering planning process is a project plan that recommends and justifies the chosen reengineering strategy. The project plan also specifies goals and objectives of reengineering; expected benefits and risks; main steps, the deliverables, and time lines; key staff assignments, the roles and responsibilities of internal IS staff as well as external consultants and systems integrators. Planning for legacy application reengineering has received attention relatively recently (see Sneed [1995]).

8.4.2   Opportunity Analysis

The purpose of opportunity analysis is to establish the business goals and objectives of the reengineering effort. The specific steps of this activity are the following:

(1) Identify, and obtain consensus on, the business drivers for reengineering. In many cases, the application reengineering is driven by the business process reengineering effort. Other reasons can be introduction of new services that need to be integrated with legacy systems, increases in flexibility needs, cost savings (e.g., maintenance costs may be getting out of control).

Figure 8.5 A Methodology Template

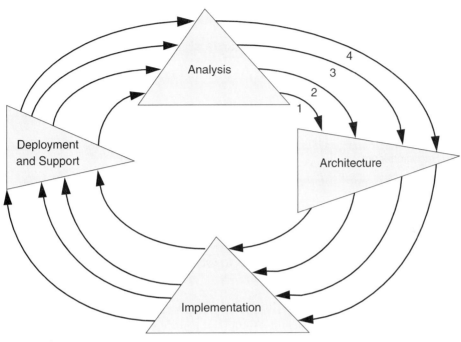

Legend:
1 = First Iteration = Planning
2 = Second Iteration = Prototyping and Experimentation
3 = Third Iteration = First Release
4 = Fourth Iteration = Second Release

(2) Identify the legacy applications and data sources which are candidates for reengineering. Analyze and categorize the legacy applications in terms of business value and technical value (see Figure 8.6). The applications with high business value and low technical value are the primary candidates for reengineering. Investment in reengineering these critical but older applications could have a high payback.

(3) Determine the flexibility and growth requirements that must be satisfied by the candidate applications. Once again, flexibility and growth requirements are driven by the business processes supported by these applications.

(4) Gather additional information about the applications and end-user tools that need the legacy applications (e.g., access the legacy information). It may also be necessary to collect information such as number of users, where located, and time frames when legacy information is needed.

(5) Understand and document management and policy issues such as cost and time limitations within which the reengineering has to occur.

Figure 8.6 Portfolio Analysis (*Source:* [Sneed 1995])

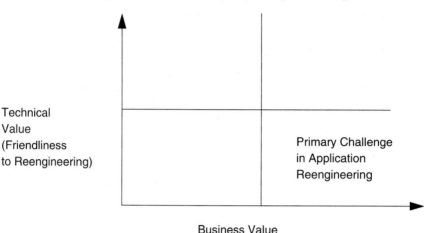

The purpose of this information collection is to ascertain if a business case exists for application reengineering.

Not all legacy system challenges are technical. Serious staffing and organizational issues play an important role in this arena. For example, it is difficult to attract and retain good staff for legacy application assignments, yet it is crucial to keep these systems running because they are mission critical. In essence, the legacy assets need to be managed just like any other asset. See the sidebar "Staffing and Organizational Approaches for Legacy Systems."

8.4.3   Choose a Solution Architecture

The objective of this activity is to determine which one of the following strategies, or a mixture thereof, will be *technically* best:

- Do nothing
- Rewrite from scratch (i.e., cold turkey)
- Provide access "in place" (i.e., do not move or convert the data and applications)
- Establish an information warehouse for decision support, if needed
- Rearchitect the host legacy applications with new technologies and architectures

The technically suitable strategy can be found by analyzing the following factors (these factors should be identified clearly in the opportunity analysis stage):

- Business value of legacy application
- Flexibility and growth requirements
- Technical status of legacy application
- Corporate pressure toward downsizing and client/server systems

---

Staffing and Organizational Approaches for Legacy Systems

Legacy systems introduce several staffing and organizational issues that need sound management approaches. Examples of key approaches are:

- Recognize that it is difficult to attract and retain good staff for legacy application assignments. Consequently, serious reexamination of who is and who should be staffing legacy systems should be of high priority to keep mission critical systems running and reduce turnover.

- Assign good staff on a rotation basis to legacy systems projects. Legacy access/integration and data warehouses are good assignments for this purpose because they both are "hot" areas but they require extensive exposure to legacy systems (a nice way to expose new staff to the legacy systems).

- Explore offsite and, if needed, off-shore software houses for migration of legacy systems.

- Identify the legacy systems that are in retirement stage (i.e., low business value) and explore the use of "legacy nursing homes" for such systems. Many software houses are beginning to provide these services. You can reassign your staff to the newer projects,

- Develop a legacy asset management plan that includes improving maintainability and increasing the value of these assets by merging legacies with new efforts.

A good source of additional information on this topic is the *Information Systems Management Journal,* Winter 1997, Vol. 14, No. 1, special issue on Leveraging Legacy Assets.

- Data query (ad hoc) requirements
- Data currency requirements
- Integration needs with other host applications
- Number of host applications accessed by clients for needed data

We have previously discussed high-level guidelines in choosing the appropriate approach in terms of these factors. Table 8.1 shows these guidelines (other factors can be added to this table). This table can be used as a decision table. For example, it shows that rearchitecture could be chosen if host application flexibility and growth requirements are high and if corporate pressures for application/data downsizing are also high. Similarly, data warehousing may be appropriate if the ad hoc query access requirements are very high and if data accuracy requirements are low (e.g., planning data); and access in place may be appropriate for the data for which ad hoc query requirements are low but the data accuracy requirements are high. In practice, a strategy should be chosen after review of factors such as shown in Table 8.1 and detailed analysis and iterations of the steps described below.

Application Reengineering: View from OO

Different views exist on the best approach for application (re)engineering based on experiences with OO technologies. Here is a quick sampling (we have integrated the key ideas in the methodology presented in this chapter).

Fayad et al. [Fayad 1996] relate their seven years of experience with transitioning large-scale software development to object-oriented software engineering. They present a detailed methodology that consists of three iterative stages:

- Planning and preproject stage that concentrates on business issues, business culture transformation, customer buy-in and team formation.

- Technology introduction stage that deals with the technical innovation, technology assessment, architecture selection, and training issues.

- Project management stage that focuses on prototyping, implementing, testing, project tracking, documentation, and quality measurement and control.

Newman [Newman 1996] describes "Class-Based Reengineering (CBR)" that integrates business process reengineering with object technologies. This approach starts out by building a business model in terms of object classes and then uses these classes to architect and build systems. The object classes can represent different business entities such as customers, loans, accounts, and so forth. These classes can change to reflect business changes and tie into technology because these classes can be implemented by using OO technologies.

Hinnant [Hinnant 1995] describes an approach to justify object technology. The basic idea is to consider business and market factors, staffing issues, technical issues, and combine them with a methodology that concentrates on reuse.

Sources:

Fayad, M., et al., "Transition to Object-Oriented Software Development," *Communications of the ACM,* February 1996, pp. 108–121.

Hinnant, D., "Justifying Object Technology," *Object Magazine,* June 1995, pp. 70–75.

Newman, D., "Class-Based Reengineering," *Object Magazine,* March 1996, pp. 68–74.

8.4.4   Implementation Considerations

Planning of reengineering must consider the risks associated with implementing the strategy chosen based on architectural analysis. For example, even if gradual migration may appear to be the most appropriate technical strategy, adequate tools and gateways to implement the strategy may not be commercially available. In addition, it is essential that adequately trained staff be available to reengineer and test the implementation. Keep in mind that many C/S migrations fail [DePompa 1995]. Implementation considerations may modify the technical decision made in architectural analysis. The following implementation-related questions should be considered:

- Are the enabling reengineering tools available commercially?

- Is the needed IT infrastructure in place to implement the strategy? For example, if a reengineering effort intended to allow users in Chicago to access legacy data in Los Angeles, then it would not be a bad idea to have a network ready with adequate protocols for users in Chicago to access Los Angeles. For example, DePompa [1995] describes failure of a C/S project in a utility company because the C/S implementation required the NetBIOS protocol but the company network did not support NetBIOS (this was found after the project had moved along considerably).

- What is the experience level of internal staff to implement the chosen strategy?

- Will enough technically qualified people be available for reengineering? For example, Dedene and DeVreese [Dedene 1995] describe the situation at Sidmar Steel where reengineering a large application was estimated at 145 staff years and the company's total technical staff was about 120 people.

- Are consulting and contracting resources available that can help expedite the chosen strategy?

- Will the users be properly trained to use the reengineered system adequately?

- Will the reengineered system be able to scale well, perform adequately and be reliable enough?

8.4.5   Cost/Benefit Analysis

Cost/Benefit analysis is an important aspect of determining an appropriate application reengineering strategy. The costs and benefits of all strategies, including doing nothing, should be analyzed before reaching a final decision.

Estimation of cost for reengineering is somewhat easier because the application already exists. This gives you a starting point to estimate reliably the lines of code, the number of modules, the complexity of the application, the database accesses, and the data volume. This information can be used to estimate cost of application rewrite (complete or partial) by using the well-known software cost estimation methods such as Cocomo [Boehm 1983]. It is important, however, to pay special attention to testing costs because testing in distributed environments is an expensive and lengthy undertaking. In addition, the technical staff/end-user training and infrastructure costs must be included.

The benefit analysis must include the benefits of the chosen strategy versus other strategies. For example, it may be beneficial to integrate an existing application instead of rewriting it from scratch. The benefits can be measured in terms of tangibles such as savings in maintenance and operation costs, and intangibles such as flexibility and scalability. The sidebar "Quantitative Cost/Benefit Analysis" shows 16 factors that can be used to quantify the costs/benefits for at least three strategies: do nothing, reengineering, and redevelopment. In addition to these factors, additional factors may be included to show the increase in "appeal" of the system to developers (many bright and young developers do not want to touch COBOL programs that were written before they were born!).

8.4.6   Justification and Scheduling

After all the analysis (opportunity analysis, architectural analysis, implementability analysis, and cost/benefit analysis), the chosen strategy needs to be justified and scheduled. Justification of reengineering is not easy because reengineering requires considerable time and money with many risks, potential pitfalls, and dubious payoffs. Many application reengineering efforts do not succeed (see the "Dirty Downsizing," *Computerworld,* Special Report, August 10, 1992; the Standish Group conference on client/server failures, "Where Do Client/Server Apps Go Wrong," *Datamation,* Jan. 21, 1994, p. 30). Justification should summarize the main results of the aforementioned analysis and clearly recommend a strategy to deal with legacy applications. Table 8.2 shows a sample summary where the results of the analysis are ranked between 0 to 10 (10 meaning highly desirable).

TABLE 8.2 SAMPLE PROJECT JUSTIFICATION SUMMARY FOR A HYPOTHETICAL PROJECT

	Ignore the Legacy System	Access/ Integrate in Place	Data Warehousing	Gradual Migration	Cold Turkey
Opportunity Analysis Ranking	3	5	6	5	5
Architectural Analysis Ranking	2	5	5	8	10
Implementability Analysis Ranking	10	10	8	3	2
Cost/Benefit Ranking	2	7	6	4	3
Total Ranking	17	27	25	20	20

Note 1: The rank (0 to 10) indicates the desirability (10 indicates highly desirable).

Note 2: This example illustrates that architecturally elegant solutions may not be desirable due to implementation and cost/benefit analysis.

Finally, the chosen strategy must be scheduled either as an in-house activity or contracted to a software house. Staff skills and availability are crucial factors in deciding this option. In-house development may overburden the already exasperated technical staff. Reengineering can be contracted to local, remote, or even overseas software houses depending on the typical cost and risk trade-offs. In a case study about off-shore reengineering reported by Dedene and DeVresse [Dedene 1995], the time difference is considered an interesting advantage. For example, the time difference of seven to eight hours between the contracting software house and the parent organization worked well because the contractors could be working on the system while the parent organization staff slept, and vice versa. Contracts are typically granted on time and material or turnkey (i.e., we pay you so much and you bring a functioning system). See Dedene [1995], and Sneed [1995] for contracting information. Detailed discussion of contracting arrangements is beyond the scope of this book.

The main idea is that strong project management is needed for a successful legacy application reengineering project. As we have mentioned previously, distributed systems are much more complex and require additional skills to operate and manage than the traditional terminal host systems. Management support is needed to avoid cost and schedule overruns and to ensure that the new system is not worse than the existing system

8.5   State of the Practice: Case Studies

A large number of case studies that describe different approaches to deal with legacy applications have been published in the literature. We give synopses of a few to illustrate the key points. Detailed case studies are described in the individual chapters.

8.5.1   Off-Shore Reengineering

Dedene and DeVreese [Dedene 1995] describe how two large-scale legacy applications from Sidmar Steel and Catholic University of Leuven, both from Belgium, were reengineered by using off-shore software houses. The results of this experience are positive. We describe the experience with Sidmar Steel. The interested reader should review the original source for additional information.

Sidmar Steel had a large-scale mainframe-based application consisting of more than 7,000 programs that managed everything from production to finance and sales. The application originated in 1965 and had evolved into a complex system that utilized IBM 370 assembler code, PLI programs, and IMS and DB2 databases. The developers estimated that it would require approximately 145 staff years to reengineer this application. The size of the effort eliminated the in-house conversion as a viable option (the company had only 120 qualified staff members who could perform the conversion). Outsourcing the job to a European, preferably Belgian, software house was eliminated due to prohibitive costs (these houses typi-cally use time and material-based contracts which are expensive and "open-ended"). A Philippine software house was selected after reviewing the bids from many off-shore soft-ware houses due to its cost, availability of skilled talent (the software house was associated with a nearby university computer science department), convenient time differences (Philip-pine staff could work on conversion while the Belgian staff slept and vice versa), and lan-guage (English).

Quantitative Cost/Benefit Analysis (*Source*: Sneed [1995])

The following parameters can be used to quantify cost/benefit analysis:

P1: Current annual maintenance cost

P2: Current annual operations cost

P3: Current annual business value

P4: Predicted annual maintenance cost after reengineering

P5: Predicted annual operation cost after reengineering

P6: Predicted annual business value after reengineering

P7: Estimated reengineering cost

P8: Estimated reengineering calendar time

P9: Reengineering risk factor

P10: Predicted annual maintenance cost after redevelopment

P11: Predicted annual operations cost after redevelopment

P12: Predicted annual business value after redevelopment

P13: Estimated redevelopment costs

P14: Estimated redevelopment calendar time

P15: Redevelopment risk factor

P16: Expected life of the system

The benefit of maintaining the status quo is given by

$$Benefit_M = [P3 - (P1+P2)] * P16$$

The benefit of redeveloping the system is given by

$$Benefit_D = [(P12 - (P10+P11)) * (P16 - P14) - (P13*P15)] - Benefit_M$$

The benefit of reengineering is similarly given by

$$Benefit_R = [(P6 - (P4+P5)) * (P16 - P8) - (P7*P9)] - Benefit_M$$

Note: The term reengineering used by Sneed represents form conversion only (i.e., no functionality improvements) and redevelopment includes functional improvement (i.e., a new system)

A satellite link was established between the Philippine software house and Sidmar. The Philippine software house's computers acted as terminals, thus eliminating the need for any additional computing resources on either side. This arrangement eliminated many logistic hurdles (e.g., the software was converted and tested on the machines and computing environments where it was intended to operate). The project ended on time and within budget; the working relationship was quite satisfactory; and the conversion quality was quite high. Mainly, the computer link was key to the project success and the Philippine software house saved Sidmar 35 percent compared with U.S. or European software houses.

8.5.2 University of Florida Reengineers via the World Wide Web

Roseen [1996] describes how the University of Florida changed its registration process by moving away from the old central registration system to a self-service system that uses voice response units and the World Wide Web. In the new system, the students do not have to wait in line at the start of each semester to register for courses, pay tuition, and buy books. Instead, they use the Web technology in a self-service mode by using their desktops.

The University of Florida (a 40,000-student and 20,000-employee university) was running all applications on an IBM4300 using COBOL. Students and administrators accessed the system through dumb, text-based terminals. The university decided to first adopt a client/server strategy and started developing applications in INTERSOLV's tools that ran on mainframes as well as on PCs. Student registration and many other administrative applications were developed by using C/S model.

The student registration system generates student ID cards by using a client/server model (the student data and business logic are kept at the mainframe and the student's digitized pictures reside in the workstations). The system currently uses the Web technology and voice response units (where needed) to allow students to register for courses and pay tuition without having to stand in line. The Web browsers especially eliminate the user interface problems for on- and off-campus registration. The university hands out free Netscape software to students for installation on their home PCs to promote the use of Web technology.

8.5.3 Hewlett-Packard's Migration to Client/Server Architecture

Ross [1996] illustrates many application reengineering concepts by reviewing Hewlett-Packard's migration to client/server architecture. Hewlett-Packard (HP) is an international corporation with more than 90,000 employees and annual revenues exceeding $16 billion. HP initiated an effort to move its terminal-host legacy information systems to client/server applications in 1989. This move was driven by the following business drivers:

- The rapidly changing business requirements required flexibility and end-user control which was not possible with the terminal-host information systems (host systems required lengthy procedures to produce new reports and/or to add new capabilities).

- HP management needed real-time access to operational data (e.g., information about the status of business). These data were embedded in "vertical" applications which made it very difficult to access cross application data.

- The global customers expected HP to act and look the same anywhere in the world, while the local customers in different countries needed different "local" views to support local legal and competition requirements. This two-level view is very difficult to maintain with terminal-host systems.

Figure 8.7 shows the application architecture proposed to satisfy the stated requirements. The architecture consists of user interfaces, user task logic, data services, and business transaction logic. The process/task clients contain the logic that performs the processes/tasks needed by the user. This client contains user task logic in addition to the user interface handlers. The data servers provide the clients with access to one or more databases. Ideally, a database contains a single data subject—a collection of closely related data such as customer, product, and order. Business transactions, defined in the business data model and managed in the data dictionary, are the means for communications between clients and servers. HP clients communicate with HP servers by using business transactions. The clients essentially invoke these business transactions through messages which are sent over the HP network.

Figure 8.7 Hewlett-Packard's Client/Server Architecture

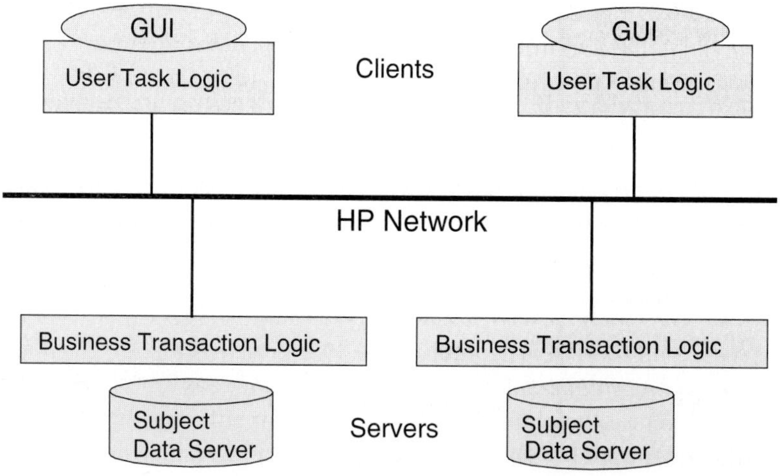

The migration from legacy terminal-host applications to this C/S application architecture took two forms: leverage and design from scratch. HP decided to leverage the operational applications and decided to redo the obsolete applications (the literature does not clarify the exact business decisions).

To leverage terminal-host applications, the application structure and logic were carefully analyzed. Typical applications consisted of several hundred thousand lines of COBOL code which incorporated program logic, screen handling, and database access calls in large monolithic applications. The leveraging activity consists of the following steps:

- The existing database is retained, but a server is put around it.

- The server logic is built by reviewing the legacy application code and translating the useful part of this code into business transactions. The useful portion of the code is "cut" from the monolithic application code and used to build the server. HP claims to reuse up to 60 percent of the old code by using this technique.

- The screen handling code is scratched and rebuilt for GUI client interfaces. The client code is typically 30 percent of the C/S application code. The clients take advantage of 4GLs, data browsers, and GUI tools.

The design from scratch decision was made for those applications which could not be leveraged. HP used the "information engineering" methodology for the new development. According to this framework, the following activities are performed in sequence: an information strategy is planned, a data model is constructed, a data flow diagram is developed, database schemas and software design are built, and the database as well as software modules are implemented. CASE tools and a repository were used to develop these applications. The following rules were used to cast this model into a C/S application architecture: (a) the client application logic automates the processes from the Data Flow Diagram (DFD), (b) the business transaction messages are the data flows in the data flow diagram, (c) the business transaction logic is built from the data relationships in the ERA diagrams, and (d) the data manager is constructed by using the database schema. This transition spanned three years (1989–1992). The main steps of this transition are:

- At the start of the project in early 1989, about six people were assigned for six weeks to experiment with and learn the C/S technology. No specific deliverables were assigned to them.

- After the experimentation, a task force was formed to develop a C/S application and platform architecture.

- A structured pilot was conducted to test the C/S architecture developed by the task force. Another team of six people was assigned to this task for six weeks. This team built three clients and three servers of different types (PC and UNIX workstations accessing relational and nonrelational data servers).

- In February 1990, a major terminal-host application was "leveraged" to C/S. This was accomplished in eight months through three teams: a client team, a server team, and a network team. After initial interactions needed to describe business transactions, the three teams worked somewhat independently and reportedly finished this conversion on time.

- In summer 1990, a C/S application was designed from scratch in six months.

- In spring 1991, the C/S architecture was standardized for companywide deployment after a few modifications.

- In May 1992, applications were developed to demonstrate the reusability of the client/server components to build new applications.

During this migration, HP invested in hardware, software, telecommunications, and staff training. New skills for developers as well as data center staff were needed. In addition, standards and guidelines were developed for development methodologies and platforms.

8.5.4   United Nations' Personnel Information System

The United Nations in New York both replaced its 30-year-old applications and automated hundreds of manual procedures to develop its IMIS (Integrated Management Information System). IMIS is among the four winners of *Datamation's* 1994 Client/Server Solutions contest [Ricciuti 1994]. IMIS is essentially a personnel information system that is supposed to provide around-the-clock service to about 1,800 users in locations such as Addis Ababa, Amman, Bangkok, Nairobi, and Geneva. The logical and physical architecture of IMIS is shown in Figure 8.8. Basically, the presentation services were divided between desktop PCs and LAN servers to allow maximum flexibility in presentation (different languages and styles), and the HP servers were used for business logic and data management services. IMIS is a "large" C/S system with a total worldwide budget of $47 million, 60 full-time developers working for more than two years, more than 500 database tables, 332 application screens, 1,600 help screens, several LANs and WANs around the world, and about 2,400 training courses.

8.5.5   Burlington Coat Factory Information System Reengineering

Source: "Rightsizing: Reengineering Information Systems through Client/Server Technology—Case Studies," *Sun Microsystems,* 1993.

Burlington Coat Factory (BCF) is a Burlington, New Jersey-based major retailer of apparel. Over the last 20 years, BCF has grown from $20 million to over $1 billion in annual revenues, adding 15 new outlets per year on the average. In addition, BCF has expanded its product line from large-ticket items such as outerwear to smaller items which result in more frequent sales transactions and changes in inventory levels. This growth and diversification have challenged the Information Services department.

Figure 8.8 United Nations' Integrated Management Information System (IMIS)

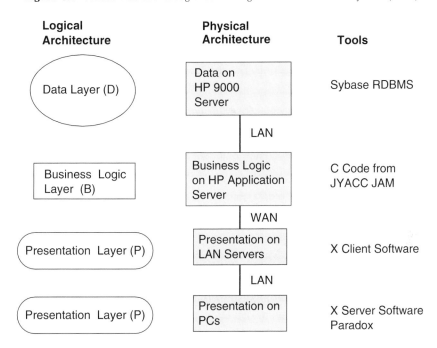

Logical Architecture	Physical Architecture	Tools
Data Layer (D)	Data on HP 9000 Server	Sybase RDBMS
	LAN	
Business Logic Layer (B)	Business Logic on HP Application Server	C Code from JYACC JAM
	WAN	
Presentation Layer (P)	Presentation on LAN Servers	X Client Software
	LAN	
Presentation Layer (P)	Presentation on PCs	X Server Software Paradox

BCF ran its operations on a Honeywell mainframe using the Dartmouth Time Sharing System (DTSS) operating environment. The mainframe ran a mixture of batch and on-line applications to support inventory, accounting, stock ledger, and shipping and receiving. Each local store, connected to the mainframe through X.25 lines, had an Altos computer to control cash registers for point-of-sale processing and to run local applications such as merchandising and reporting. The current configuration presented the following problems:

- DTTS, a non-Honeywell third-party operating system, lacked tools for application development and became a bottleneck in developing new applications.

- The mainframe was overloaded and did not provide the scalability needed to meet the business growth.

- The mainframe became a single point of failure with long downtimes.

- Transfer of information between stores and the mainframe was slow and unreliable (it took two to three days for the mainframe to process a store's daily activity).

- Long delays in authorizing credit cards and approving checks were causing loss of business (customers had to wait in long lines for credit card approvals) and bad check costs ($14 million per year).

To overcome these problems, BCF initiated a pilot project to investigate "open" technologies. As a result of this pilot, the following configuration was implemented:

- The data center consists of six database servers running a distributed Oracle database, a Sun NFS server, and many application servers which run the BCF applications. The BCF applications use the Oracle databases and utilize the Tuxedo transaction management system for load balancing and distributed transaction management.

- In each store, a Sun computer runs PC-NFS, controls the cash registers, and runs other local applications. PC-NFS allows the store applications to directly access the data center NFS services. The store applications are event driven—they send a message to the data center and spawn a transaction in the data center to update the central database whenever an event such as receiving occurs.

- The stores are connected to the data center through a TCP/IP-based wide area network.

- Application development is done in C language and Oracle tools such as SQL*Forms and SQL*ReportWriter.

This architecture gives a great deal of flexibility and scalability to BCF for its growing business needs. The cost of this architecture reportedly is one-eighth of the mainframe-based cost.[1] At the time of this writing, this system is reportedly being expanded. For example, cash register applications are not event driven at present (the cash register events queue up on the store computer and are sent to the data center after the cash register is closed). BCF is planning to make these applications event driven so that each cash register event triggers a message to the data center to run an update transaction.

Comments: Several interesting decisions are made in this case study. First, the mainframe is replaced with a data center consisting of several computers with distributed databases and several application servers. This improves availability and scalability but creates some challenges in managing such an environment. Second, the application processing is spread over several computers which access databases over several computers. This adds to the scalability and availability of the system. Finally, the store applications use message passing to invoke remotely located transactions. This is a widely used technique in distributed applications design.

8.5.6 Short Case Studies ("Snippets")

Arvin Industries, Inc., a Buffalo, NY manufacturer, initiated a three-year downsizing effort, moving away from IBM mainframes. The engineering-oriented users took off in every direction, accumulating a diverse array of computers, software packages, and LANs. Things went out of control because there was no overall design in mind. Much of the

---

1. It is not clear from the case study how much money was spent in staffing and training.

expected cost savings and advantages were eaten up by continual maintenance and cumbersome multistep conversions. *Source:* "Dirty Downsizing," *Computerworld,* special report, August 10, 1992.

Northern Telecom in Brampton, Ontario, developed a comprehensive Invoice Management (CIM) system that won the *Computerworld* 1996 award in the Best Use of Object Technology to Integrate Legacy Systems Category. CIM uses the Northern Telecom Customer Order Database (CODB) which consolidates all separate and distinct legacy systems data into one common database. From this database, CIM extracts data for the processing of orders and updates CODB where needed. The application reuses objects for its internal operations and hides many of the legacy system's interfaces by using object wrappers. *Source:* 1996 *Computerworld* Object Application awards.

Synchronized Supply Chains—A Road to Electronic Commerce [Francett 1996]. Many interesting examples of legacy system access and integration are appearing in manufacturing organizations. These organizations rely on a chain of consumer-supplier for their items. For example, an auto manufacturer has to rely on several suppliers who in turn rely on their suppliers. This "supply chain" needs to be synchronized to shorten the cost and the time involved in the supply chain. Technically, this involves interfaces and integration of numerous legacy systems that exist in the supply chain. Many of these systems are being integrated by using Web technologies.

Pacific Bell Leverages Legacy Applications. Pacific Bell leverages its investment in two large-scale legacy applications by combining them with the newer services. One application is the network management centers and the second is an expert-system-based work flow system for billing reconciliation. These two applications are accessed from a variety of new applications being developed on PC desktops and UNIX workstations that use Enterprise/ Access (a screen scraper) from Apertus for access in place. *Source:* http://www.apertus.com.

8.6   State of the Market: Reengineering Tools

A wide variety of tools for reengineering legacy applications are appearing in the marketplace. These tools range from simple code analyzers to large-scale gateways. It is best to describe these tools in terms of the strategy they support. For example, the tools for access/ integration in place include screen scrapers, object wrappers, and database gateways; the tools for data warehousing include data extractors, data propagators, and data repository managers; and the tools for migration include "migration gateways" and reverse engineering aids such as code analyzers and specification extractors. See the state-of-the-market sections in the next three chapters for more information.

8.7   State of The Art: Research Notes

To consider research trends, a few facts should be kept in mind. First, legacy applications will be with us always (some of the new Web-based applications will be legacy in a few years, if they survive). Second, being legacy is not necessarily bad (survivors become legacy). Finally, most legacy applications cannot be ignored. In the foreseeable future, the realistic approaches to deal with legacy applications will be a mixture of access in place, data warehousing, gradual migration, and cold turkey. These approaches will accommodate a very wide range of client applications and end-user tools which need to interact with a diverse array of legacy applications. Choice of appropriate access surround technology will be crucial to hide the different design choices, rearchitectures, and migrations from the client application developers and end users. We will review the specific research issues in the next three chapters. At this stage, we should note that more work is needed to extend the planning methodology presented by Harry Sneed [Sneed 1995] and the legacy- and reuse-based software life cycle proposed by Ahrens and Prywes [Ahrens 1995].

8.8   Summary

Approaches to deal with legacy systems are challenging tasks which require review of user needs, business pressures, evolving standards and protocols, and an ever-growing potpourri of products from numerous suppliers. Although legacy systems can be dealt with in a variety of ways (including ignoring them for future considerations or rewriting them from scratch), the following three approaches are viable for most practical situations and will be discussed in the next three chapters:

- Access/integration in place—integrate legacy systems by keeping the legacy data and applications intact and use "surround" technology to provide remote access.

- Data warehousing—create a shadow database from the legacy system which is easier to access.

- Gradual migration—transition and migrate the legacy applications and data to new architectures.

8.9   Case Study: XYZCorp Embarks
on Application Reengineering

The XYZAICS (Advanced Information Control System) initiative involves many legacy applications. Examples of the legacy applications are

- A financial information system that processes financial data (e.g., personnel costs, materials costs, etc.) stored on the IBM mainframe in a DB2 Relational database.

- A mainframe-based existing corporate Material Requirement Planning (MRP) system that contains bill of materials (raw materials) information in IMS databases and outside vendor information in DB2 databases. These two databases are also needed by PC-based decision support for long-range planning.

- A UNIX-based order processing system that was developed in the 1980s to receive orders, verify them, and send them to the mainframe for shipping/receiving and billing purposes.

The company wants to establish a reengineering strategy for all these applications. The management is especially worried about the financial system because the finance department has been getting many complaints about their financial report distribution system. The current financial information (personnel costs, materials costs, etc.) is stored on the IBM mainframe in a DB2 relational database. Currently, reports for each area manager (store managers, engineering department manager, other managers at the corporate office) are printed once a month on the mainframe printer. These reports are then mailed through office mail to the managers. The problems with this approach are

- The reports are usually too late for the managers to react.

- All reports are in a standardized format. Many managers do not like this format.

- The managers cannot get more details about their budgets easily.

Due to these reasons, the company's budgets are not managed as well as they could be. Many managers maintain their own DP staff who take the data from the printed reports, type the data into a spreadsheet, and produce their own reports. A task force has been established for a long-range architecture for financial information. The long-range architecture is driven by the following major functional requirements:

- Financial information should be available to authorized users to print customized reports, perform spreadsheet analysis, and exercise decision support software for greater insight.

- New applications and new approaches to existing applications should be easily facilitated.

- Different local processing (especially at overseas offices) must be provided.

A debate has erupted in the corporation about how to best deal with these requirements. The following four options are being discussed:

- Put printers in the regional offices for the reports (do nothing to the existing system).

- Keep the system on mainframe and develop Web-based clients in regions before accessing this system.

- Move some of the financial information into a data warehouse that can be accessed from the regional sites.

- Rearchitect and migrate the application to a UNIX platform and use an OCSI paradigm.

A task force has been established to produce an overall strategy and a plan to deal with the financial and other existing applications. In particular, which strategy will be selected and why.

Hints about the Case Study

The methodology presented in Section 8.4 can be used to establish the needed strategy. Let us highlight the key points for the finance system.

The requirements of the finance system have been stated above. The main activity in this methodology is the solution architecture selection step. In this step, the four solution options need to be evaluated in terms of cost of implementation, time needed for implementation, flexibility and growth, security, and so forth. Table 8.1 can be used directly to make this decision. For a cost/benefit analysis, Table 8.2 can be used.

8.10   Problems and Exercises

1. Collect other definitions of legacy systems and compare/contrast these definitions with the one suggested in this chapter.

2. Point out the major differences between legacy applications and the new Web-based applications. Show these differences as a table.

3. We have presented only a few options in dealing with legacy applications (e.g., ignore, access/integrate, data warehousing, migration). Are there other choices? Discuss in detail.

4. Review, expand, and improve Table 8.1 to make it general for any application reengineering decision evaluation.

5. Choose a legacy application of your choice and work through the application reengineering methodology described in Section 8.4. Describe the decisions made and tools/techniques used in each step.

8.11   Additional Information

Literature on legacy systems has grown steadily since 1992. Relevant literature appears under headings such as "legacy migration," "application/system downsizing," "software reengineering," and "reverse engineering." *IEEE Software,* January 1995, is a special issue on legacy systems and contains several informative papers. The book by Brodie and Stonebraker [Brodie 1995] contains detailed discussion of legacy systems with special attention to incremental migration of legacy applications. *Communications of the ACM,* May 1994, is a special issue on software reengineering and should be consulted. Periodicals such as *Datamation, Information Week,* and *Client/Server Today* regularly publish state-of-the-market and state-of-the-practice articles on legacy systems.

Ahrens, J., and Prywes, N., "Transitioning to a Legacy-and-Reuse-Based Software Life Cycle," *IEEE Computer,* October 1995, pp. 27–36.

Aiken, P., Muntz, A., and Richards, R., "DOD Legacy Systems—Reverse-Engineering Data Requirements," *Communications of the ACM,* May 1994.

Andrews, G., "Paradigms for Interprocess Interactions in Distributed Programs," *ACM Computing Surveys,* March 1991, pp. 49–90.

Appleton, E., "Use Your Data Warehouse to Compete," *Datamation,* May 15, 1996.

Bannister, D., "Trading Places (UNIX Connectivity)," *Connection,* June 16, 1993, pp. 14–15.

Bennet, K., "Legacy Systems: Coping with Success," *IEEE Software,* January 1995, pp. 19–23.

Bernstein, P., and Chu, D.W., "Using Semi-Joins to Solve Relational Queries," *JACM,* January 1981.

Boehm, B., *Software Engineering Economics,* Prentice Hall, 1983.

Brodie, M. L., "The Promise of Distributed Computing and the Challenge of Legacy Information Systems," in Hsiao, D., et al. (eds.), *Proc. IFIP TC2/WG2.6 Conference on Semantics of Interoperable Database Systems,* Lorne, Australia, November 1992.

Brodie, M. L., and Stonebraker, M., "DARWIN: On the Incremental Migration of Legacy Information Systems," Technical Memorandum, Electronics Research Laboratory, College of Engineering, University of California, Berkeley, March 1993.

Brodie, M. L., and Stonebraker, M., *Migrating Legacy Systems: Gateways, Interfaces & the Incremental Approach,* Morgan Kauffman, 1995.

Cerdingley, E., and Dai, H., "Encapsulation—An Issue for Legacy Systems," *BT Technology Journal,* July 1993, pp. 52–64

Chikofsky, E., and Cross, J., "Reverse Engineering and Design Recovery—A Taxonomy," *IEEE Software,* January 1990, p. 13.

Dedene, G., and DeVreese, J., "Realities of Off-Shore Rengineering," *IEEE Software,* January 1995, pp. 35–45.

Delligatta, A., and Umbaugh, R. E., "EUC Becomes Enterprise Computing," *Information Systems Management,* Vol. 10, No. 4, 1993, pp. 53–55.

DePompa, B., "Corporate Migration: Harder Than It Looks," *Information Week,* December 4, 1995, pp. 60–68.

Eberhard, E., "Information Warehouse: A User Experience," *Info DB,* Vol. 7, No. 2, 1993, pp. 6–12.

Ferrent, R., "BT's Information Warehouse," *Logistics Information Management,* Vol. 5, No. 4, 1992, pp. 42–43.

Francett, B., "The Synchronized Supply Chain: From Connectivity to Commerce," *Software Magazine,* December 1996, pp. 113–116.

Giordano, R., "The Information 'Where?' House," *Database Design and Programming,* September 1993.

Gotlieb, L., "Learning to Live with Legacy Systems," *CMA,* May 1993, pp. 10–11.

Hammer, M., and Champy, J., "Reengineering the Corporation: A Manifesto for Business Revolution," *Harper Business,* 1993.

Inmon, W., *Building Data Warehouses,* John Wiley, 1993.

Lindstrom, F., "Reengineering of Legacy Systems Using an Object-Oriented Technology," 4th International Workshop on Computer-Aided Software Engineering, Irvine, CA, December 1990, p. 26–30.

Mayers, C., "Legacy Data Access," ANSA User Group Meeting, Cambridge, England, April 1994.

Nadeau, M., "Remote Connections," *Datamation,* June 1994, pp. 195–198.

Nassif, R., and Mitchussen, D., "Issues and Approaches for Migration/Cohabitation between Legacy and New Systems," SIGMOD '93, International Conference on Management of Data, May 1993, pp. 471–474 .

Nassif, R., Zhu, J., Goyal, P., "Basic Issues for Developing Distributed Applications Interacting with Legacy Systems and Databases," *Proceedings RIDE-IMS '93,* Third International Workshop on Research Issues in Data Engineering: Interoperability in Multidatabase Systems, Vienna, Austria, April 1993.

Ozsu, M., and Valduriez, P., *Distributed Database Systems,* Prentice Hall, 1991.

Radding, A., "Monoliths Are Out," Sentry Market Research Report on Data Warehouse Directions, *Client/Server Computing,* December 1996, pp. S27–S28.

Ricciuti, M., "The Best in Client/Server Computing," *Datamation,* March 24, 1994, pp. 26–35.

Roseen, J., "University of Florida Reengineers via the World Wide Web," *Data Based Adviser,* June 1996.

Ross, W., "Hewlett-Packard's Migration to Client/Server Architectures," in *Distributed Computing,* ed. R. Kanna, Prentice Hall, 1994.

Schick, K., "The Key to Client/Server—Unlocking the Power Legacy Systems," *Gartner Group Conference,* February 1995.

Sheth, A., and Larson, J., " Federated Database Systems for Managing Distributed, Heterogeneous, and Autonomous Databases," *ACM Computing Surveys,* September 1990, pp. 183–236.

Sneed, H., "Planning the Reengineering of Legacy Systems," *IEEE Software,* January 1995, pp. 24–34.

Taylor, F., *The Principles of Scientific Management,* Harper & Bros., New York, 1911.

Thomas, G., "Remote Database Access Service Concepts," *Bellcore Special Report,* December 1993.

Thomas, G., "Databases in Distributed Systems," *ANSA User Group Meeting,* Cambridge, England, April 1994.

Umar, A., and Marchese, F., "Client/Server in Heterogeneous (MVS, UNIX, PCs, Macs) Environments: Initial Analysis Results," *Bellcore Memorandum*, October 1992.

Umar, A., and Thomas, G., "Open Enterprise Data Access and the Issues of Legacy Data Access," *Bellcore Technical Memorandum (Draft),* July 15, 1994.

Waterson, K., "The Changing World of EIS," *Byte,* June 1994, pp. 183–191.

9

Access and Integration of Legacy Applications through the Web

9.1   Introduction[1]

The focus of this chapter is on accessing legacy information (commonly known as legacy data access) and, where possible, integration of legacy applications with the newer applications/end-user tools (in particular, Web-based tools and applications). We concentrate on the "access/integration in place" approach where the legacy application itself is not modified; instead it is "surrounded" by technologies which mediate between the legacy systems and the new systems. Integration of legacy applications with new applications and end-user tools is a very effective strategy for many organizations in the 1990s and beyond. This strategy leverages the existing investment in legacy systems and minimizes the risks involved in migrating large-scale mission-critical legacy applications. Due to this reason, many consulting firms such as the Gartner Group are predicting very high success rates as reflected in the following statement:

> Through 1999, AD (application development) organizations that integrate new development and legacy systems will have a higher success rate, at optimal cost, in the implementation of client/server applications (0.8 probability). [Schick 1995, p. 3]

A tremendous growth in the remote-access market is expected due to the popularity of accessing existing remotely located resources. For example, a February 1997 Dataquest study predicts that the remote access market will more than triple by the year 2000 (i.e., rise from $4 billion in 1996 to $12.2 billion in the year 2000). In particular, Web access to legacy applications is an extremely active area of market at present. For example, there are dozens, perhaps even hundreds, of middleware suppliers vying to become the sole provider of Web to enterprise links [Tucker 1997].

---

1. Many ideas presented in this chapter are based on discussions and collaborative work with my colleague and mentor, Dr. Gomer Thomas, a principal engineer at Bellcore.

Key Points

- Integration of legacy applications with new applications and end-user tools is a very effective strategy because it leverages the existing investment in legacy systems and minimizes the risks involved in application conversions.

- The Web adds another layer to the multilayer surround technology needed to access and integrate legacy applications with any new applications.

- Legacy applications can be accessed at three broad levels: legacy data access, legacy function access, and legacy presentation access.

- It is best to view legacy information access as a class of enterprise information access problem; thus the concepts and tools to access an enterprise information source (e.g., DB2) can be used even when an organization cannot decide if DB2 is legacy or not.

- Object wrappers can play a vital role in integrating legacy applications. These wrappers can integrate the services provided by a single application or can be used as an integration gateway that integrates multiple resources from a diverse array of legacy applications.

But should the access/integration approach always be used? When should it be used and when not? In the previous chapter, we presented a framework to answer these questions and to help you decide when to use access/integration instead of other approaches such as ignore, cold turkey, data warehousing, and gradual migration. The framework introduced several evaluating factors such as the business value, technical value, and flexibility/growth requirements. See the sidebar "When to Access/Integrate and When Not To" for a summary.

Access and integration of legacy applications with a diverse array of tools and applications, including the Web, are quite complex. An organization undertaking this effort typically faces questions such as the following:

- What are the different approaches and issues in accessing and integrating legacy applications?

- How does the Web factor into these approaches?

- What are the classes of problems in accessing legacy information (i.e., legacy data access)? What type of access is needed to this information (i.e., do the users need access to legacy data, functionality, or both)?

- What are the extant surround technologies to access remotely located data sources, why do they differ so much in cost, and what problems do they solve?

- How does integration differ from access and what approaches should be used when integrating legacy applications?

- What are the surround technologies such as object wrappers and how do they address the legacy application integration problem?

When to Access/Integrate and When Not To

The access/integration approach works well when

- The new applications need access to the most recent legacy data.

- The access requirements for legacy data and any other resources (e.g., legacy business logic) are relatively infrequent and light.

- There is a need to migrate the legacy application gradually by hiding the migration details through surround technologies (see Chapter 11 for additional information).

Access/integration does not work well if:

- Data access requirements are very high. In this case, the surround technologies introduce a great deal of workload to an already overburdened existing system (in such cases, a data warehouse may be more useful).

- The target legacy applications are too inflexible and expensive to maintain (keep in mind that the access/integration approach only surrounds the old system, it does not replace it). A migration strategy is needed to improve flexibility and maintainability of legacy applications.

- Is it possible to develop a methodology that combines the various management and technical issues into a series of systematic steps?

- What is the state of the art, state of the market, and state of the practice in accessing/integrating legacy applications?

The main objective of this chapter is to answer these questions for an overall perspective on the complexity and multidimensionality of this problem. A framework is suggested in Section 9.2 that first focuses on access issues and then adds integration considerations and Web factors. This framework is used to survey and categorize the "surround" technologies that range from screen scrapers which primarily emulate terminal sessions to sophisticated "integration" gateways which support multiple-access mechanisms and coordinate results from multiple information sources (Sections 9.3 and 9.4). The appropriate Web technologies are explored in Section 9.5. A systematic procedure is suggested in Section 9.6 to tie the various business issues and technologies together and present guidelines on how to approach this problem. The chapter concludes by discussing several short case studies and by showing how this methodology can be used to access and integrate DB2 and IMS applications and by commenting on the state of the market and state of the practice.

9.2   Access and Integration Framework

Access is the first step toward integration. Within the context of legacy applications, **access** basically provides a connection, a path, between the new applications/end-user tools and the legacy application resources. **Integration** goes a step beyond by making the access more transparent and natural. Specifically, integration in the legacy application context implies combining information from different legacy applications and presenting it to the users in a natural manner (see Section 9.4 for discussion). Integration of legacy applications by "surrounding" them with technologies that hide their internal information leverages the existing investment in legacy systems and minimizes the risks and costs involved in application conversion.

Our discussion involves

- The core concepts that can apply to access/integration of legacy applications with new applications and tools (see Section 9.2.1).

- The Web factor that concentrates on the unique considerations for access/integration of legacy information through Web browsers (see Section 9.2.2).

9.2.1 The Basic Framework

The basic idea is that the legacy applications are not touched; instead they are surrounded by technologies such as object wrappers, screen scrapers, data gateways, and application gateways (we will discuss these technologies later in this chapter). Figure 9.1 shows a framework that we will use to illustrate the different aspects of access/integration of legacy applications. The framework consists of the following components:

- *Legacy applications* that are custodians of the needed information,

- *Clients*, the new applications and end-user tools, that are the consumers of the needed information,

- *Access paradigms* that are used to remotely access the legacy resources, and

- *Surround technologies* that attempt to hide the characteristics of the legacy applications from the clients.

Figure 9.1 Legacy Access/Integration Framework

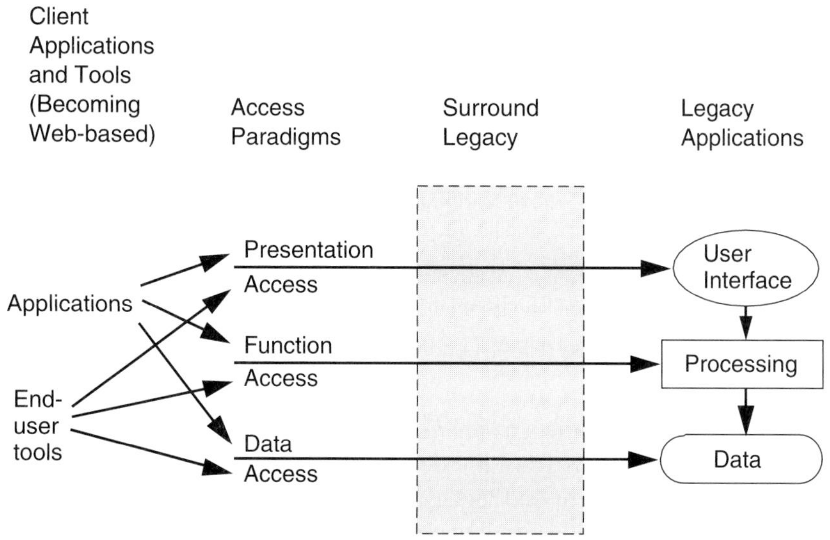

A legacy application, as defined in the previous chapter, is used to indicate an application of value inherited from the past (five years or beyond). These applications are typically crucial to the day-to-day operation of corporations and are thus very valuable from a business point of view. However, legacy applications are inflexible, costly, time-consuming, and risky to maintain and change. Legacy applications can be classified into the following categories (we discussed these categories in the previous chapter):

- **Friendly**. Completely decomposable (all components are well structured and separable) so that the components can be accessed easily from the outside.

- **Neighborly.** A few components can be accessed because the applications are data decomposable (data services are well structured and have well-defined interfaces) or program decomposable (program modules are well structured and have well-defined interfaces).

- **Hostile.** Monolithic (unstructured) application with intermixed data, program logic, and user interface processing so that you cannot access it other than with the user interfaces.

Clients are the applications and tools that need to access legacy applications. Client applications have the typical OCSI characteristics (e.g., increased utilization of Internet and Web technologies, written in C or C++, developed on UNIX or PC platforms, and heavy use of GUI technology, utilization of distributed and client/server paradigms). End-user tools which need access to legacy information are typically report writers such as the Informix ACE report writer, 4GL tools such as Focus, spreadsheets such as Lotus and Excel, object-oriented data browsers such as Business Objects and ObjectView, executive information system drill-down tools such as Forest & Trees from Trinzic Corp and Command Center from Pilot Software ("drill down" tools support query traversal from highly summarized data to more detailed information). Most of these tools are becoming Web-based and run on the PC, UNIX, and/or Macintosh platforms and have capabilities to access remote data by using ad hoc SQL.

Access paradigms are the methods used to access legacy application resources. Specifically, the client applications and end-user tools access the legacy information through a mixture of access paradigms such as the following (we will discuss these paradigms in detail in Section 9.3):

- **Remote Data Access** (RDA)—access of legacy information, typically through remote SQL, without invoking any enterprise functionality (e.g., business logic).

- **Remote Function Access** (RFA)—access of legacy information (e.g., a COBOL procedure that creates trouble tickets) through CORBA, RPC or other means of invocations.

- **Remote Presentation Access** (RPA)—access of legacy information through some presentation services by invoking terminal emulator sessions.

Surround technologies, also known as *mediation technologies*, are a group of technologies that shield the client applications from the details of the legacy applications. Depending on the differences between the client and legacy environments and the level of hiding needed, surround technologies can provide simple connection software to sophisticated coordination and integration of results from multiple systems by using varying levels of encapsulation. For the purpose of this chapter, we will categorize surround technologies capabilities at the following two levels (see Figure 9.2):

- Access technologies
- Integration technologies

Access technologies provide the software needed for remote connections. Gateways are an example of access technologies. A *gateway* is essentially a protocol converter. Gateways can operate at different levels depending on the level (e.g., OSI Layer) of protocols being converted. For example, network gateways exist for Ethernet to Token Ring protocol and for TCP/IP sockets to SNA LU6.2. Other examples of gateways are mail gateways and database gateways. We will discuss different access technologies later in this chapter (Section 9.3.6).

Integration technologies provide a layer above the access technologies and hide the access details to different resources of one or more applications. Object wrappers are a popular example of integration technologies because object wrappers can present an object-oriented view of many diverse systems. At a higher level, integration gateways can be devised for integrating data, functions, and presentation accesses from very heterogeneous legacy systems.

Figure 9.2 Legacy Access/Integration Framework: A Second Look

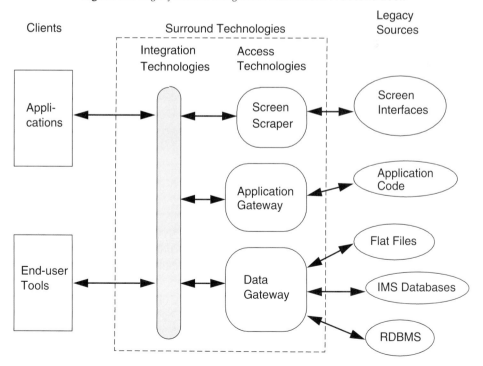

The framework first presented in Figure 9.1 and later refined in Figure 9.2 will be used throughout this chapter. We will first focus on the access aspects of legacy information and describe the remote data, remote function, and remote presentation paradigms in detail (Section 9.3). The main issues of integrating legacy applications are discussed in Section 9.4.

9.2.2   Web Factor—Access/ Integration through the Web

Now, let us add the Web considerations to access and integrate legacy information. Simply stated, Web browsers provide a front end because they can invoke, through appropriate Web gateways, the mediators that access legacy information. For example, a Web gateway program can invoke a screen scraper, data gateway, or procedure gateway. An example of such a gateway is shown in Figure 9.3.

Figure 9.3 Web Gateway for Legacy Data Access

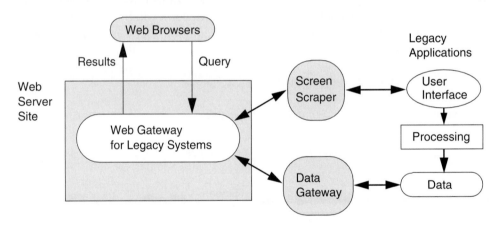

Conceptually, Web gateways can be used to integrate the corporate information that contains HTML documents, relational databases, and legacy information sources. A common technique is to use an object wrapper that can be invoked from a Web gateway (see Figure 9.4).

Many Web gateways at present use CGI (Common Gateway Interface) technology. However, as we will see in Section 9.5, many other options are available. For example, in addition to CGI gateways, the legacy surround technologies can also be invoked from the Java applets or Microsoft ActiveX components residing in the Web browser. In addition, the CORBA-enabled Web browsers can directly invoke the CORBA object wrappers. We will discuss the various Web gateways in Section 9.5. See [Tucker 1997] for a state-of-the-market review.

Figure 9.4 Integrated Access through the Web

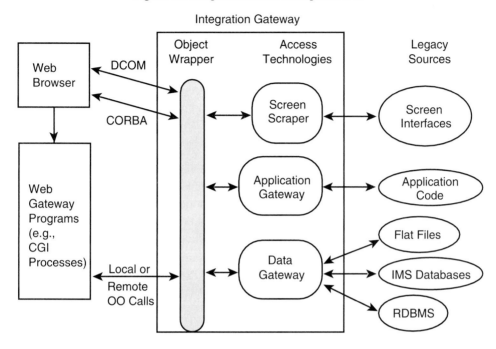

9.3   Legacy Information (Data) Access

9.3.1   Overview

Legacy applications contain very valuable information that is embedded in legacy databases/ flat files and application code. In many cases, legacy applications are the *only* source of years of business rules, historical data, and other valuable information. Access to this information is of vital importance to new and emerging tools and applications. These tools and applications reside on a variety of platforms (PCs, Macs, UNIX workstations) that access legacy applications through different network technologies (TCP/IP, SNA, Novell IPX/SPX, Appletalk). This problem has been discussed widely in the literature under the headings of "legacy data access," "universal data access," "corporate data access," "open data access," and so forth, and has been ranked among the top corporate problems in several surveys (e.g., the *Computerworld* survey, October 16, 1993; *Datamation,* October 1, 1992, special report; and *Distributed Computing Monitor,* P. Seybold Group, special report, "Database Interoperability," Oct. 1992). In general, many industries are experiencing rapid changes and new competitions to which enterprises must respond quickly and effectively. In order for enterprises to deploy services rapidly, they must be able to effectively access their existing information and invoke new functionality for new services. For example, many new services still need customer information that is typically stored in legacy systems.

Legacy information access spans a wide range of issues and approaches. The needed information is stored in diverse data sources (hierarchical, network, or relational databases, in addition to the flat files such as sequential, indexed, and direct files), program code, and command files. Most of the legacy information is at present stored in the hierarchical/network databases and/or flat files, with some examples of DB2 relational databases. We view legacy information access as a class of enterprise information access problems. Instead of dealing with legacy information access problems as unique and isolated problems, our view has the benefit that the concepts and tools to access an enterprise information source (e.g., DB2) can be used even when an organization cannot decide if DB2 is legacy or not.

What are the different approaches (paradigms) for accessing legacy information? We will use the framework shown in Figure 9.1 to examine the different information access paradigms (i.e., remote data access, remote function access, and remote presentation access). The framework is cast into a table (Table 9.1) to analyze the trade-offs between different approaches. Essentially, the rows of this table show the clients (applications and end-user tools) and the access paradigms to be used. The columns show the applications to be accessed. For example, the columns can show legacy applications and the rows can show the report writers and new desktop applications which need to access information from these legacy applications through ad hoc SQL (remote data access) and RPCs (remote function access).

TABLE 9.1 A FRAMEWORK FOR INFORMATION ACCESS

Clients	Access Paradigms	Legacy Application[1]	Legacy Application[2]	Legacy Application[3]
Application[1]	Remote Data Access			
Application[2]	Remote Function Access			
Application[3]	Remote Presentation Access			
End-user tool[1]	Remote Data Access			
End-user tool[2]	Remote Function Access			
End-user tool[3]	Remote Presentation Access			

9.3.2   Remote Data Access (RDA) Paradigm

The Remote Data Access (RDA) paradigm concentrates on accessing remotely located data sources, typically by using remote SQL (see Figure 9.5). For legacy information access, this paradigm is useful if the data can be separated (e.g., a decomposable application system) and/or if the business rules (the functionality) are of no value. This paradigm implies a certain level of application friendliness because the raw data must be exposed to external users and the database administrators must be willing to provide the subschema (e.g., names and structure of relational tables) needed by the external application programmers. As stated previously, in many cases the data of the legacy information systems are considered proprietary and can be accessed only through the functionality provided by applications (e.g., invoking an IMS transaction). In real life this paradigm can be used if the legacy data are stored in relational databases such as DB2, Informix, Oracle, and Sybase. Access to nonrelational databases such as IMS by using this paradigm usually requires translation of SQL to nonrelational access (e.g., IMS calls). EDA/SQL from Information Builders Incorporated provides such translators for many data sources.

The applications and end-user tools access the remotely located data by using data access statements (e.g., SQL statements which are sent to the legacy application host). Remote Data Access (RDA) protocols and products give end users and application developers access to remote data with location transparency. Accessing a remote database is similar, if not identical, to accessing a local database—the same tools and languages are used to access local as well as remote databases. At present, RDA technology is based on the relational database model and SQL. The clients typically send SQL queries to database servers by using an RDA protocol which is mutually agreed upon between the clients and servers. An RDA protocol is a layer 7 protocol in the OSI reference model. It basically defines what messages should go back and forth between data clients and data servers and what the format of the messages should be.

Figure 9.5 Remote Data Access Paradigm

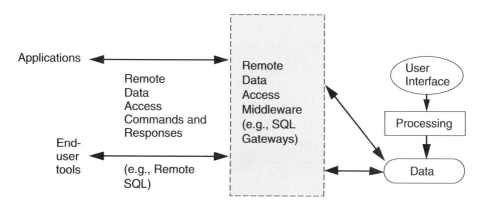

Bulk data transfer can be viewed as a special case of RDA because instead of accessing remote data in an ad hoc manner, a File Transfer Protocol (FTP) is used to extract and download remote data. Bulk data transfer is of importance in legacy data access in the following cases:

- Data warehousing: Data from legacy applications are extracted periodically and loaded into an information warehouse for decision support. Information warehouses are established around relational database technologies and are equipped with a variety of forecasting, planning, decision support, and executive information system tools. Information warehouses are not easy to establish by using the older legacy technologies.

- Data downsizing/transitioning: Data from legacy applications on mainframes are extracted and migrated to cheaper mid-range and desktop computers. Although this migration is usually permanent, in many real-life situations, the two systems operate in parallel for a while.

- Temporary storage: Data from legacy applications are extracted and stored temporarily in different formats on different computers for quick reports and spreadsheet analysis. After the analysis, the data are deleted.

9.3.3   Remote Function Access (RFA) Paradigm

Remote function access allows the client applications and end-user tools to access legacy information by invoking preexisting functions of the legacy application (see Figure 9.6). For example, a PC-based application can invoke an IMS or CICS transaction. In addition, a UNIX application can directly invoke an IMS Batch Message Processing (BMP) program to access IMS information. This paradigm is useful when the legacy application code can be decomposed (i.e., application code exists as modules with well-defined interfaces) and when the legacy application functionality is of value (e.g., business logic represented by a COBOL subroutine). The middleware for legacy function access requires a certain level of application friendliness and may provide a wide range of mechanisms for accessing the functions of legacy applications such as the following:

- Remote invocation of batch jobs and distributed programs

- Queued message processing

- Remote procedure calls

- CORBA invocations

Many IMS-based legacy applications have Batch Message Processing (BMP) programs that can be invoked remotely. In addition, MVS batch programs can be invoked remotely by using the MVS internal reader. The legacy code written as LU6.2 programs can be invoked remotely from other programs located on UNIX, PC, and MVS-based programs.

Figure 9.6 Remote Function Access Paradigm

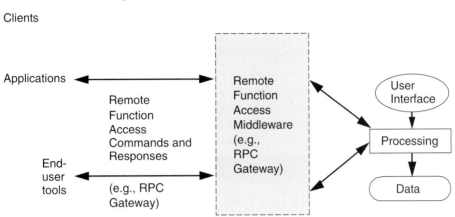

Queued message processing is another example of remote function access. In this paradigm, the receiver stores the incoming message in a queue and works on it when free. This model is used in many transaction processing systems including IBM's MQM system, It allows the senders to asynchronously send requests to the receiver. Once a request is queued, the request is processed even if the sender is disconnected (intentionally or due to a failure). In queued message processing, arriving messages are first queued and then scheduled for execution. Once execution begins, the sender does not interact with the execution process. Queued message processing and the Message-Oriented Middleware (MOM) are discussed in Umar [1997, Chapter 4].

The Remote Procedure Call (RPC) is a well-known example of a remote function access paradigm in which one process makes a request and the other process responds to the request. The request can be simple (e.g., retrieve time of day) or complex (e.g., provide a circuit of type X from location A to location B). Each request/response is treated as a separate unit of work; thus each request must carry enough information for a reply. RPC is currently used very heavily in C/S computing where a client issues requests to server processes located in the network. This paradigm can also be used by peers where process 1 sends a request to process 2, process 2 sends the response back, and later sends an independent request to process 1. The OSF DCE RPC is a widely accepted RPC standard. Use of DCE RPC for legacy applications requires reprogramming of legacy applications to behave as DCE servers—a nontrivial task. Gateways are usually needed to mediate between RPC clients and legacy applications (see the discussion on application gateways later in this chapter).

CORBA (Common Object Request Broker) is the Object Management Group (OMG) specification for distributed objects. CORBA has a great deal of potential for remote function access because the legacy code can be "wrapped" to look like objects. However, development of object wrappers is nontrivial (see Section 9.4.4 for discussion of object wrappers).

9.3.4   Remote Presentation Access (RPA) Paradigm

The applications and end-user tools access the needed legacy information by invoking the legacy presentation services (see Figure 9.7). For example, a Web browser or a C++ application can invoke a terminal emulator or screen scraper to simulate a 3270 terminal and thus access the legacy applications. This paradigm is used for legacy applications that are hostile to outside access because you cannot directly access the data or program code. For example, you will use this paradigm to access information about a customer account status from a system that does not allow you to directly access the customer data or to invoke programs that could generate the status information. You are forced to "fake" a logon session as a user would. This paradigm is very slow due to the extra overhead of emulating terminal sessions but is used very frequently because many legacy systems are hostile due to administrative choice or due to their lack of structure (a big blob of code with intermixed data, business logic, and interface processing). The following steps are used in this paradigm:

- A client application issues a request for data.
- The request is converted to a format which is, say, a 3270 data stream format.
- A terminal emulator is invoked to send this stream in a format so that it appears to the legacy application as if the legacy presentation service is being invoked.
- The legacy application processes the request and sends the response.
- The terminal emulator receives the call, "scrapes" the screen characters from the response, and sends a response back to the client application.

In a real-life situation, one method of invocation may invoke a series of calls to the legacy application to simulate multiple screen operations. A major limitation of this paradigm is that if a host application screen design changes, then all the client applications using the screens have to be modified. In addition, screen scraping is slow and tedious. However, this may be the only choice when the legacy applications are completely monolithic (i.e., neither the data nor the functionality can be accessed directly). Many terminal emulators and screen scrapers are commercially available. See the discussion in the next section.

9.3.5   Analysis of Paradigms for Legacy Information Access

Table 9.2 summarizes how the paradigms discussed so far can be used to access the different categories of legacy applications. It can be seen that the client applications can access the needed information by using any of the three paradigms depending on the legacy application architectures. Most end-user SQL-based tools primarily use the remote data access paradigm (embedded SQL or ODBC are common). However, this paradigm is not supported if the data are not decomposable (e.g., monolithic legacy applications). In addition, very few end-user tools support the remote function access paradigms (perhaps more end-user tools will start supporting OSF DCE RPCs). Many end-user tools do support remote presentation access through terminal emulators and screen scrapers.

Figure 9.7 Remote Presentation Access Paradigm

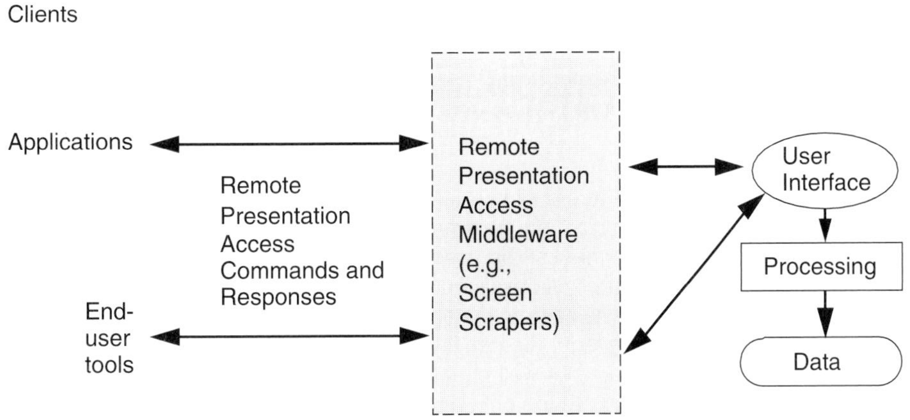

Clients

Table 9.2 Analysis of Paradigms

Clients	Access Paradigms	Decomposable Application	Data Decomposable	Program Decomposable	Monolithic
Application	RDA	Yes (used heavily)	Yes (used heavily)	No	No
Application	RFA	Yes	Yes	Yes (used heavily)	No
Application	RPA	Yes	Yes	Yes	Yes (used heavily)
End-user Tool	RDA	Yes (used heavily)	Yes (used heavily)	No	No
End-user Tool	RFA	Yes (rarely used)	Yes	Yes (rarely used)	No
End-user Tool	RPA	Yes	Yes	Yes	Yes

Legend: RDA = Remote Data Access, RFA = Remote Function Access, RPA = Remote Presentation Access.

9.3.6   Access Technologies

A wide range of surround technologies are becoming available to enable legacy information access. These access technologies can be purchased from a diverse array of vendors, with different capabilities and price ranges. The access technologies fall into the following broad categories:

- **Screen Scrapers.** Screen scrapers allow client applications to simulate the terminal keyboard/display features and thus act as programmable terminal emulators. Commercially available screen scrapers provide APIs that can be used by application programs to build screen images, send the screens to the host applications, simulate keyboard strokes, receive screen images from the host, and retrieve the new fields from the screen image by "scraping" the screen images (i.e., removing all screen formatting tags). Screen scrapers are inexpensive and are frequently used to access legacy systems that are not well structured (monolithic). In many old systems, terminal emulation and screen scraping are the only ways to access legacy data.

- **Bulk Data Transfer (File Transfer)**. File transfer is commonly used to extract a portion of a file or a database and send it to another site for off-line processing. A client application can invoke a file transfer package to download legacy data to a desktop and use the end-user tools (data browsers, spreadsheets, report writers) to analyze the data. Bulk data transfer works well if the data change infrequently (e.g., monthly), the file size is small, and if only approximate data are needed (i.e., if the changes between extracts are not significant for the applications using the data).

- **Database Gateways**. Most database gateways are based on the remote SQL paradigm. The main feature of these gateways is that the end-user tools and/or applications running on a desktop interactively retrieve data in an ad hoc manner. The gateway software makes a remote database look like a local database to the applications and tools running on a desktop. For relational databases, ODBC is a de facto standard. To provide access to legacy data that is stored in nonrelational databases such as IMS, some database gateways provide "SQL-to-IMS" converters which cast SQL calls to IMS data manipulation calls. Database gateways are discussed in detail in Umar [1997, Chapter 5].

- **Application Gateways.** These gateways allow invocation of remote functionality to access legacy information and typically include some host application-related information. The remote function can be any piece of code at the host. These gateways hide the host application environment information from the client applications (i.e., act as the surround technology). An API and additional software for remote calls are needed by the client applications. Off-the-shelf application gateways are not widely available. Most application gateways are "homegrown" at present.

These technologies can provide different levels of support for access to a single application, multiple applications on the same machine, applications across machines, read or update capabilities, distributed query processing support, and distributed transaction processing support. Each technology also has its strengths and weaknesses as shown in Table 9.3. Additional details about these technologies can be found in Umar [1997, Chapter 8].

TABLE 9.3 ANALYSIS OF ACCESS TECHNOLOGIES

	Strengths	**Weaknesses**
Screen Scrapers	1. Inexpensive. 2. Only choice for monolithic systems.	1. Slow and tedious. 2. Mainframe workload increases due to screen scraping.
File Transfers	1. Inexpensive. 2. Offload work to receivers. 3. Good for infrequently changing data. 4. Good for data that is not time critical. 5. Especially effective in situations where extensive analysis and report generation are needed (i.e., a user extracts the needed data, downloads it to a local computer, and then runs the analysis and reports by using the local computer tools).	1. Create duplicate data which must be synchronized periodically. 2. Not a good solution for applications which need recent data from large files which change frequently. 3. Can be very time-consuming when a large number of users need to access the same data (e.g., it is almost impossible to send the corporate data daily to hundreds of users). 4. The data must be in a flat file format before being transferred over the network.
Database Gateways	1. Flexibility. 2. End-user control. 3. Very suitable for legacy applications that use relational databases and are decomposable.	1. Raise many network and system performance issues (e.g., size of SQL results sent over the network is unpredictable). 2. Can be expensive (in the range of $200,000 for mainframe-based systems)
Application Gateways	1. Can be more efficient than database gateways. 2. Exploit reuse of legacy code.	1. Can only be used if host application is decomposable. 2. Mostly homegrown systems.

9.4 Integration of Legacy Applications

Let us shift our attention from accessing legacy information to integration of legacy applications. Before getting into the details, we should quickly note that integration, in general, is a desirable goal that can be quite expensive to obtain and sustain. It is essential to understand the different aspects of integration and carefully evaluate the business value and associated expenditures. Specifically, we should keep the following questions in mind:

- What is integration of legacy applications?
- Why is integration needed beyond access and what are the trade-offs?
- What are different approaches to integrate legacy applications?

9.4.1 What Is Legacy Application Integration?

Simply stated, *integration* refers to the ease with which systems can be used [Nutt 1992]. Integrated systems basically minimize the effort needed to use them. This implies that two systems, S1 and S2, are integrated if they

- Share and exchange information without external intervention,
- Are seamless in terms of operations, and
- Show consistency of behavior and presentation.

For example, a voice mail system S1 and an e-mail system S2 are integrated if the voice mail from S1 can easily be stored as e-mail for S2 (and vice versa) easily, and S1 and S2 provide the same "look and feel" (same type of commands, icons, and screen formats). Examples of such integrated message systems that seamlessly combine voice mail, fax, and e-mail are given by Rosenberg [1995]. In the same vein, a legacy application S1 is integrated with a new application S2 if S2 can exchange information with S1 seamlessly and if S1 has the same "look and feel" as S2. Obviously, this type of integration is quite challenging. This is why most applications focus only on integrating portions of legacy applications with new applications. For example, a new order processing system may be integrated with the data of a legacy billing system (i.e., the user accesses data from billing system and the order processing system by using the same type of commands). As we will discuss later, this is achieved through surround technologies such as object wrappers and integration gateways.

9.4.2 Access versus Integration Trade-Off—An Example

Let us illustrate integration through an example. Let us consider a new marketing application of a large organization that is expected to utilize customer information (of course!). Unfortunately, the customer information is scattered around 10 machines in different parts of the company. These systems have evolved over the years somewhat independently because they represent the new branches and business directions of the company, acquisition of new businesses, and mergers. Consequently, the customer information is stored in these

10 machines under different file/data formats and requires different access mechanisms, that is, different logon sequences and different database accesses. The company can follow two approaches (see Figure 9.8):

- The marketing application accesses the 10 systems by invoking different technologies and adhering to the different formats and protocols of the back-end systems (Figure 9.8a).

- The marketing application calls a customer object wrapper that integrates the information and presents it back to the application. The logic of accessing the back-end systems is embedded in the wrapping code (Figure 9.8b). Note that now other applications can also use this wrapper.

Figure 9.8 Access versus Integration Example

(a) Access. The marketing application accesses several systems.

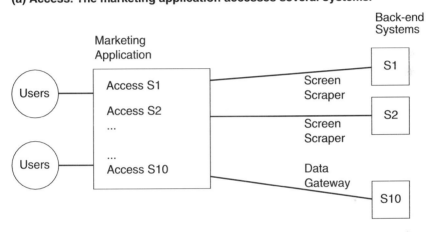

(b) Integration. The applications invoke an integrator that presents a uniform API.

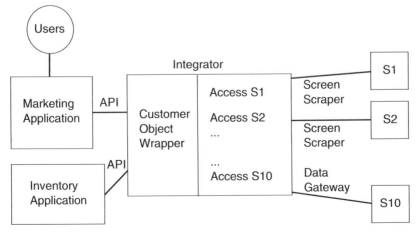

Note: The customer API may be a CORBA API
represented through CORBA IDL.

What are the trade-offs in these two approaches? Naturally, the integration is more elegant. It also allows other applications (e.g., inventory, order processing) to invoke appropriate methods on the customer object. Thus the customer information is available, through a uniform API such as provided by the CORBA IDL, to many new and existing applications and users. However, development of wrappers that integrate different sources is a time-consuming task and must be cost justifiable (see the sidebar "Why Integrate? Promises and Pitfalls").

How far can this integration be pushed realistically? Let us continue by assuming that some customer information is duplicated at more than one site (a typical scenario). You have two choices (life is full of choices, isn't it?): (a) use the integrator just to find the customer and do the merging/selection in the application, or (b) move the merging/selection logic to the integrator. What if the customer information needs to be validated against quality rules (e.g., missing phone number)? Where does the validation logic go? As we will see later on in this chapter, the integration gateways can be quite complex, operating in dedicated middle-tier machines.

A few rules of thumb should help. First, it is better to view the integrator as middleware (i.e., business unaware). Thus business aware functionality such as data quality rules should not be moved into this integrator. Second, the cost of developing an integrator that performs special common functions should be balanced against the need for the common functionality from different users and applications.

Why Integrate? Promises and Pitfalls

Integration goes a step beyond access by making the access more transparent and natural. What are the benefits and costs of this extra step? When and why should the extra layer of integration be built?

Promises. In general, integration of legacy applications with new applications and end-user tools is a very attractive strategy due to several reasons. First, it extends the useful life of the legacy systems by making them useful to new applications. Second, it hides the unnecessary legacy internals so that if the legacy application is transitioned gradually, the new applications are not impacted. Third, it leverages the existing investment in legacy systems by taking advantage of their capabilities. Finally, it minimizes the risks and costs involved in application conversion.

Pitfalls. Integration does have a few pitfalls. First, legacy application integration can be an expensive undertaking especially when it involves many legacy systems. Second, integration technologies are mostly homegrown at the time of this writing while most access technologies are becoming available as off-the-shelf middleware. Third, the addition of yet another layer can introduce performance delays. Finally, well-qualified staff is needed to develop/purchase, install, and maintain the integration technologies.

What should be done? The best approach seems to be

- Evaluate if suitable access technologies are available.

- Determine the costs and benefits of the extra effort needed in integration.

- If integration adds significant *business value*, then undertake integration; otherwise stay with access.

9.4.3   Approaches to Integrate Legacy Applications

We have discussed that the legacy information can be accessed by using a mixture of remote data access, remote function access, and remote presentation access paradigms. These three paradigms correspond to the typical approaches used in system integration:

- user view integration,
- process integration, and
- data integration.

User view integration, also known as end-user transparency, implies the following [Nutt 1992, p. 21]:

- Consistency of presentation. All presentations to the user should be the same so that the user does not have to relearn. For example, all windows should behave similarly (i.e., similar ways to start windows, close windows, redraw, etc.).
- Consistency of operations. There should be similar ways to perform similar tasks such as initiating print jobs, sending mail, establishing sessions, saving files, and so forth.

Process integration is normally achieved through seamless processes which share and exchange information without human intervention. For example, a computer integrated manufacturing environment is achieved through business processes, manufacturing processes, and engineering processes which automatically share and exchange information to automate production.

Data integration combines and interrelates data elements from different sources so that all users can view, access, and manipulate data in a consistent manner. Many systems are integrated around a common database because a database can provide consistency of presentation and operation.

Which one of these approaches is used to integrate legacy applications with the new applications and tools depends on the business drivers and the cost/benefits of each approach. A major factor is the integration technologies such as object wrappers and integration gateways. We will discuss these technologies in the next section. In most cases, user view integration is most commonly used.

9.4.4   Integration Technologies: Object Wrappers
and Integration Gateways

The integration technologies enable integration of legacy applications by providing a layer on top of the access technologies. Object wrappers and integration gateways are the main promising integration technologies. These technologies are discussed in Umar [1997, Chapter 8]. The following discussion highlights the key points.

9.4.4.1 Object Wrappers

An *object wrapper* is essentially a software layer between an OO system and a non-OO system—it receives object invocations and issues appropriate calls (e.g., 3270 data streams, remote procedure calls, SQL statements, IMS messages) to one or more non-OO applications. Object wrappers can be used as surround technologies for integrating legacy applications into the object-oriented client/server Internet world (see Figure 9.9). The object wrappers sit on top of the access technologies and encapsulate the access technologies as objects. For example, if your program invokes an operation on an object "customer," then an object wrapper can translate the object invocation to the database specific call (e.g., SQL). The wrapper basically creates an object view of the legacy system. An object wrapper may be thin (e.g., just issue SQL calls) or thick (integrate information from different legacy systems residing on different computing platforms of different vintages). We will discuss the thick object wrappers later as "integration gateways."

Figure 9.9 Object Wrapper

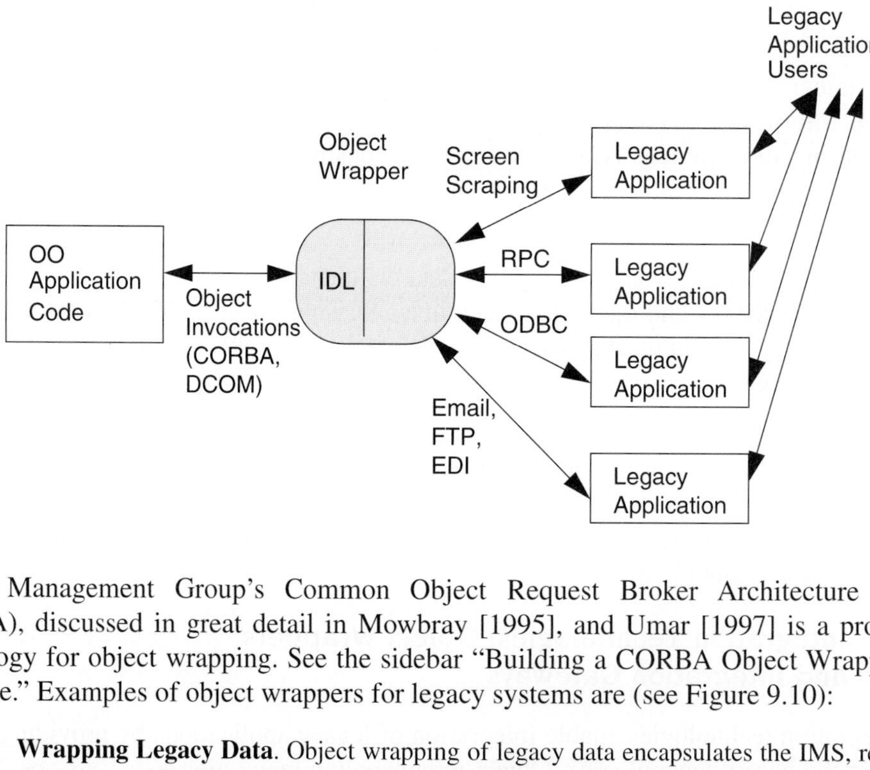

Object Management Group's Common Object Request Broker Architecture (OMG CORBA), discussed in great detail in Mowbray [1995], and Umar [1997] is a promising technology for object wrapping. See the sidebar "Building a CORBA Object Wrapper: An Example." Examples of object wrappers for legacy systems are (see Figure 9.10):

> **Wrapping Legacy Data.** Object wrapping of legacy data encapsulates the IMS, relational database, and flat file entities as objects. Although an OO program written in languages such as C++ can issue SQL, IMS, and flat file calls, it becomes cumbersome to translate an object view in C++ to a non-OO data model for queries (the "impedance" mismatch between programming code and data manipulation languages). In many practical cases, object wrappers provide an extra layer on top of legacy data access technologies.

Building a CORBA Object Wrapper: An Example

Let us work through the process of building an object wrapper based on CORBA for the customer information example introduced in Section 9.4.2. The following steps are needed to develop the front-end of the wrapper (see Chapter 7 for CORBA implementation details):

1. Build an object model of the customer information. In this case, it is natural to identify a customer object with three operations: add, modify, and query.

2. Map the object model to CORBA Interface Definition Language (IDL). CORBA IDL specifies the object (customer), the operations performed on the objects (add, modify, query), and the signature (the parameters) of the operations.

Most of the effort in building the wrapper is devoted to designing the methods to be invoked (i.e., the back end of the wrapper). Example of these steps is:

3. Identify the legacy applications that need to be accessed/integrated to provide the customer information. Let us assume that there are 10 such applications.

4. Analyze if the 10 applications are decomposable (i.e., can the customer information be accessed at the data, function, or user interface level). This analysis leads to an appropriate access/integration approach (i.e., legacy data access, legacy function access, or legacy presentation access).

5. Determine if you will be developing a thin or a thick wrapper. Let us assume that each one of the 10 applications fully contains customer information. In this case, a thin wrapper will do the job that will invoke the appropriate legacy access mechanism technology (e.g., screen scraper, database gateway). However, if you need to fetch pieces of customer information from different systems and then present a unified view, then you need to build a thick wrapper that includes a customer integration layer.

Now, you can complete the object wrapper by using the following steps:

6. Code the methods identified above. This code is at the heart of an object wrapper and implements all the mapping needed between CORBA objects to the legacy systems.

7. Build a CORBA object server that receives the object invocations specified by IDL and then invokes the appropriate methods. For thick object wrappers, the object server may invoke an intermediate layer for mapping between legacy and CORBA views.

8. Register the IDL in the CORBA Interface Repository so that clients can access the new objects statically or dynamically.

9. Build the clients that invoke IDL specified operations. The CORBA naming services will bind the client calls to the appropriate instance of customer objects in the legacy systems.

Wrapping Legacy Code (Functions). Object wrapping of legacy code is a feasible approach if the target legacy code can be invoked from another program such as a CORBA object server. For example, a COBOL subroutine written in 1972 can be invoked by a CORBA object server written in 1995. An important aspect of object wrappers is that they can also enhance the legacy code. For example, the object server could provide additional code that uses net sales to compute, say, projected sales provided additional information is available to the object server.

Wrapping Legacy Presentation. Object wrapping of legacy presentation may be the only option available to integrate legacy applications that are very old and unstructured. Basically, the object wrapper in this case is a layer on top of the screen scraper. Note that the object invocation must include all information that the user actually types during a terminal session (logon ID, password, key strokes, order number, etc.).

Figure 9.10 Object Wrappers for Legacy Systems

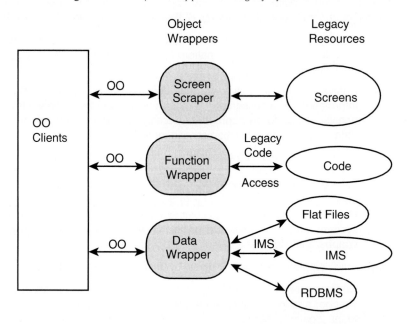

We have discussed different object wrapping implementation issues in Chapter 7 (e.g., wrappers for OSF DCE and Encina). The book by Mowbray and Zahavi [Mowbray 1995, Chapter 8] contains many detailed implementation examples about developing CORBA object wrappers for remote procedure calls, files, sockets, C API, Common Lisp, Smalltalk, Scripts, events, shared memory, dynamic queries, interprocess communications, macros, and headers. Off-the-shelf object wrappers are also commercially available (see Tucker [1997], Winsberg [1995] for a state-of-the-market review).

9.4.4.2 Integration Gateways—The Super Wrappers

Integration gateways integrate and synthesize object wrappers with various access technologies (screen scrapers, file transfer packages, database gateways, and application gateways) into a single framework (see Figure 9.11). These "super object wrappers" provide an OO view to the clients even though the needed information may be imbedded in IMS databases, indexed files, COBOL subroutines, 3270 terminal sessions, or a combination thereof. These integration gateways, henceforth referred to as *legacy integration gateways* to highlight the focus on legacy application integration, can provide standard OO APIs for client applications to invoke screen scraping, file transfer, database queries, and RPC function calls. It can also insulate the applications and end-user tools from any changes being made to the legacy applications. These wrappers can also, if needed, translate the requests and data between more than one host application and synchronize updates between the host applications. Theoretically, these gateways can also support intelligent features such as distributed query processing, distributed transaction processing, and automated selection of the best paradigm (RPC, RDA, queuing) for accessing data.

As expected, these gateways are complex and can be quite expensive to build. Few, if any, legacy integration gateways with the aforementioned characteristics are available commercially. The best approach is to build these gateways for specific purposes and then expand them gradually for additional capabilities/environments.

Figure 9.11 Integration Gateway

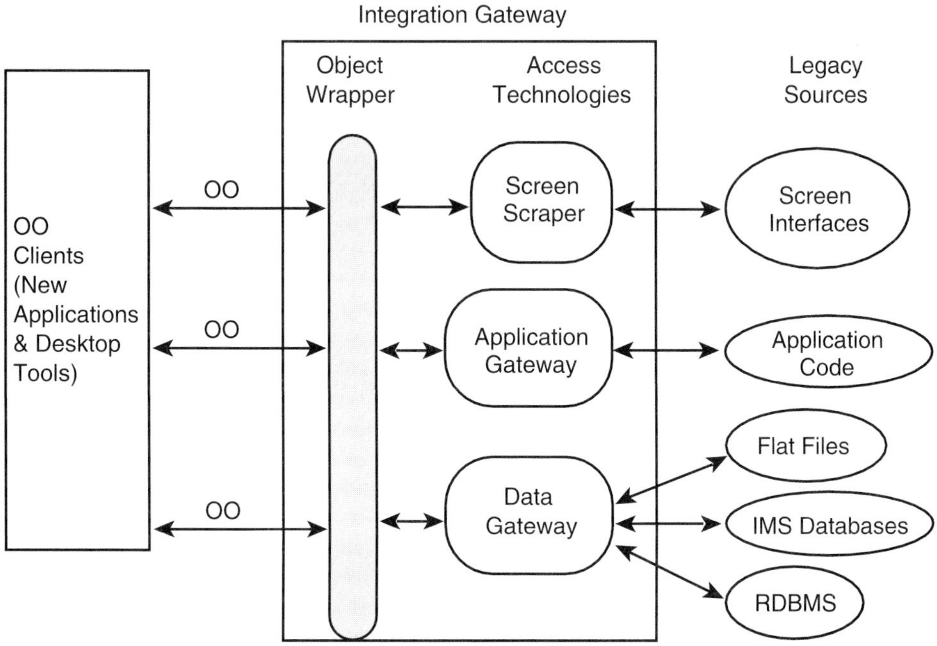

Some research in developing the legacy integration gateways has been reported [Wiederhold 1992]. For example, the TSIMMIS Project at Stanford is aimed at rapid integration of heterogeneous information sources that may be structured or unstructured [Chawathe 1994]. The DARWIN Project describes concepts of a legacy integration gateway for incremental migration of legacy systems [Brodie 1993]. Adapt/X Traxway, developed at Bellcore, is another example of a legacy integration gateway. We describe the concepts of a legacy integration gateway in the next section. Many of these concepts are based on the Bellcore Adapt/X Traxway product.

9.4.4.3 A Sample Legacy Integration Gateway (LIG)

Figure 9.12 shows a sample Legacy Integration Gateway (LIG). The LIG provides a collection of services to the LIG client applications through an Application Programming Interface (API), which supports an object-oriented paradigm. Examples of the services used by the LIG client applications are "retrieve customer address," "retrieve billing information about a customer," "create a purchase order," "update status of an invoice," and so forth. The LIG occupies the middle tier of a three-tiered physical architecture and acts as an agent and a server between the client business applications and existing legacy applications (i.e., host applications). Client business applications are mostly on workstations, and the host applications are mostly on mainframes.

Figure 9.12 A Sample Legacy Integration Gateway

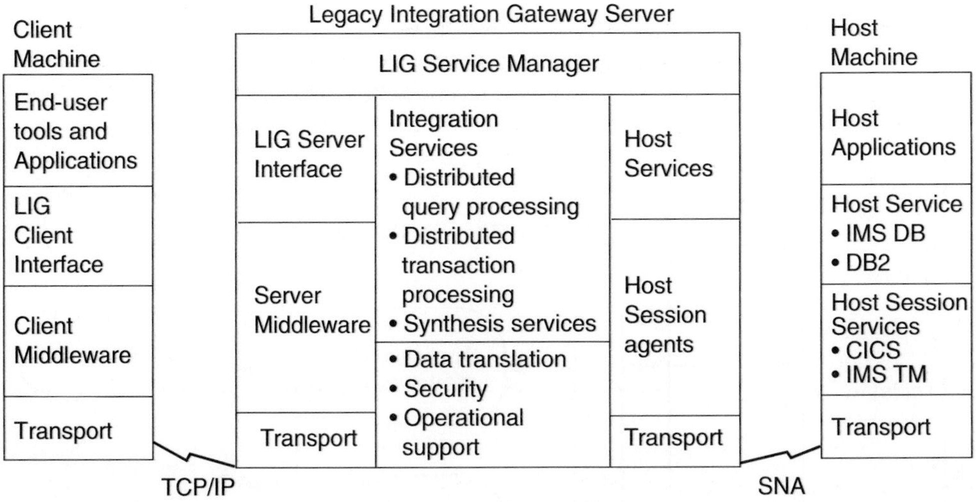

Client applications access host application data/functionality by issuing *service requests* (e.g., retrieve customer address) to the LIG. A service request is transported to the LIG machine by the client environment (typically a TCP/IP network). The LIG server converts each service request to *work units* (e.g., invoking IMS transactions or virtual terminal emulations to retrieve the customer address) needed to access the host application data/functionality. The work units are transported to the host applications over the legacy environment network (e.g., SNA, X.25). The main components of a LIG are described below.

The LIG is intentionally described at an abstract level so that different technologies can be used at the client side as well as the legacy application side. In practice, however, CORBA can be used for client interactions, thus facilitating a corporatewide API based on CORBA. Use of CORBA IDL as an enterprise API is discussed by Joder [1996]. Work on LIGs is also assuming CORBA and some products are beginning to use CORBA as a client side API. For example, the Bellcore Adapt/X Traxway gateway initially used OSF DCE but now uses CORBA for client interfaces.

LIG Client Interface. A LIG client application requests a specific LIG Service through a member function of a business object. The LIG client interface converts this call to a Remote Procedure Call (RPC) or CORBA invocation that will be sent to the LIG server machine. This interface checks security for the service, performs logging if needed, flattens the parameter objects, and builds an RPC.

LIG Server Interface. The LIG server interface communicates with the LIG clients through appropriate middleware (e.g., DCE/CORBA). Each LIG service interface is responsible for receiving a LIG service request, sending it to the LIG service manager for executing the service request, receiving the results from the LIG service manager, and sending the results back to the LIG clients.

LIG Service Manager. The LIG service manager is responsible for completing a LIG service that arrives at the LIG server machine. A service request from a LIG client may involve more than one back-end service (work units such as IMS transaction invocations) to be performed. In addition, work units within each service may be performed in parallel or may need to be performed serially due to some precedence relationships (e.g., the intermediate responses might constitute an input of the next work unit that must be done in order to partially or completely perform the service). The LIG service manager provides a mechanism to coordinate and monitor the progress of all work units related to a service request.

Integration Services. These services provide the logic for distributed query processing, distributed transaction processing, view integration, and other related activities needed to access information from different hosts and present it to the clients. We have discussed these topics in earlier chapters.

Data Translation Services. The purpose of the data mapper is to parse input messages and build output messages, where the input and output messages presumably have different message formats. This component allows data arbiter service developers to translate messages between client application format and host application format in a generic fashion. Typical examples of the host message formats are DSECT (Data Section or fixed-fielded block of characters), and line type (messages that are broken up into lines, delimited by carriage return).

Host Services. These service interfaces locate appropriate hosts and communicate with the host systems through a variety of interfaces. Examples of such interfaces are screen scraping interfaces, TCP/IP host interfaces, SQL interfaces, 3270 printer interfaces, and so forth.

Security Services. The security services provide for end-to-end authentication and authorization.Theses services deal with many difficult issues of security between heterogeneous systems. The LIG server itself must operate in a secure environment because the gateway itself presents a security exposure (it may have access authority to many back-end systems).

Operations, Administration and Maintenance Services. In the day-to-day production environment of LIG, a variety of operational, administrative, and maintenance (OA&M) features are needed. The purpose of this component is to provide the needed OA&M services such as LIG software installation, de-installation, and upgrade; LIG configuration management such as size of log files, memory pools, settings for logging and tracing, and specification of backup requirements; and other services such as startup/shutdown/backup/recovery services, and status monitoring and services, and browsing commands.

9.5   Web Gateways—Enabling Access and Integration through the Web

The technologies needed to access and integrate enterprise information with the World Wide Web consist of different types of "Web gateways." *Web gateways* bridge the gap between Web browsers and the legacy applications and databases. At present, the following approaches are used to develop Web gateways:

- Common Gateway Interface (CGI)
- Server Side Includes (SSI)
- Gateways as stand-alone servers
- Mobile code systems (Java gateways)

For legacy access, however, CGI and Java-based gateways are more prevalent.

9.5.1   Common Gateway Interface (CGI)

A CGI gateway is Web server resident program that can be invoked from the Web browsers (see Figure 9.13). A wide range of CGI-based gateways are commercially available. Most of these gateways at present are used for relational database access. However, some CGI-based screen scrapers (e.g., Apertus Enterprise Access) are also appearing in the marketplace. In fact, many database gateways and screen scrapers developed in the early 1990s are currently becoming Web-based by using CGI scripts. For legacy access, you may need to write your own CGI gateway program that invokes screen scrapers, data gateways, or procedure gateways of your choice. An example of such a CGI gateway is shown in Figure 9.13. We have discussed CGI previously (Section 4.2.3 in Chapter 4 and Section 7.4.2 in Chapter 7).

Figure 9.13 CGI Gateway for Legacy Data Access

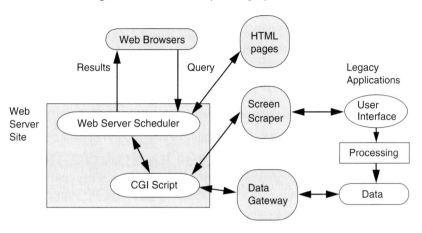

9.5.2   Java-Based Gateways

Java-based gateways run on the Web browser because Java applets can be imbedded in HTML pages and sent to the Web browsers where they execute. By using this approach, access to legacy applications and databases can be invoked directly from the browser. The Java applet can ask the user to issue a query and then send this query to a remote application or database (Figure 9.14). JDBC (Java Database Connectivity) allows Java programs to issue calls to relational databases. We have discussed Java-based gateways previously (Section 4.2.4 in Chapter 4 and Section 7.4.3 in Chapter 7).

Figure 9.14 A Java-Based Gateway

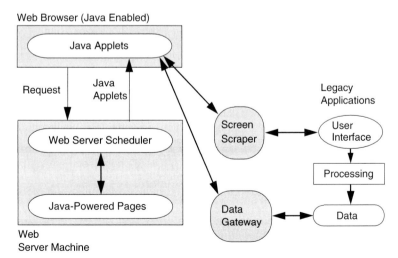

Note: The Java applets may have to go through the Web Server Machine
to access remote applications (this is a security restriction on Java).

You can use Java-based gateways to access/integrate legacy applications by coding some aspects of legacy application as Java applets. For example, the legacy user interface processing can be recoded as Java applets and thus used to integrate the legacy applications with the WWW. A limitation of Java-based gateways is that many Web browsers are configured to disallow direct remote connections from Java applets because this increases security risks. In these cases, the Java applets can only access the resources located on the Web server from where the Java applets were loaded. A Proxy server is needed on the Web server site that acts as a server to the browsers and as a client to the target application resources.

9.5.3 Using Web Gateways

Web gateways can be used to integrate the corporate information that contains HTML documents, relational databases, and legacy information sources. The Web gateways can directly invoke the access technologies such as screen scrapers or data gateways or utilize an object wrapper. A common technique is to use an object wrapper that can be invoked from a CGI gateway (see Figure 9.15). In addition to access from CGI gateways, the object wrapper can also be invoked from the Java applets residing in the Web browser (see Figure 9.15). In this case, the object wrapper is called from the CGI gateway as well as the Web browsers. The newly announced CORBA-enabled Web browsers can directly invoke the object wrappers if they are wrapped by using CORBA IDL.

It is best to develop the object wrapper so that it is invoked from different programs by using a single OO API. The distributed object technologies such as OMG CORBA and Microsoft DCOM are good candidates for object wrapping. In this case, the Web gateways, Java applets, or any other programs use CORBA or DCOM calls to interact with the wrapper. After performing front-end processing, the object wrapper accesses the appropriate surround technologies on an as-needed basis for different classes of legacy applications. A detailed discussion of using CORBA and the Web to wrap legacy applications can be found in Klinker [1996], Tucker [1997]. For a simple example, see the sidebar "Using HTML Tokens to Interface With CGI/CORBA: An Example."

9.6 A Procedure for Legacy Application Integration

Obviously, a large number of decisions need to be made to integrate legacy applications. We suggest a procedure which can be used to systematically understand the various issues, evaluate different approaches, select an appropriate strategy, and implement/deploy a solution based on the strategy. This procedure concentrates on four key steps:

1. Requirements analysis
2. Establish an overall solution architecture
3. Implement the solution
4. Deploy and support

Using HTML Tokens to Interface With CGI/CORBA: An Example

The following two pages show how some tokens "<# ... #>" in HTML pages are resolved into values by a CGI and/or a CORBA program. Basically, these tokens are detected by the CGI script or a CORBA program which then accesses, let us say, a database to return values to the browser for display.

HTML Page With Tokens

```
< HTML>

Customer named
<#customer.name#>
at present owes
<#customer.balance#>.
The customer phone number
is <#customer.phone#>
```

HTML Page With Values
From CGI and/or CORBA

```
< HTML>

Customer named
Warner Mach
at present owes
$200.00.
The customer phone number
is 212-555-1111
```

Figure 9.15 Integrated Access from the Web

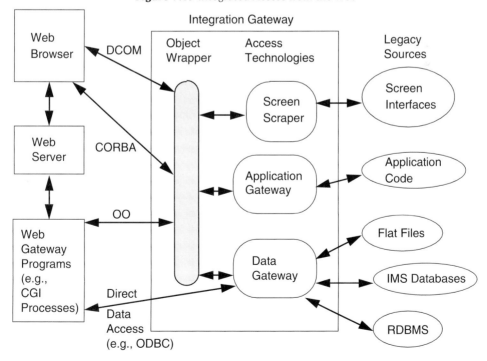

The discussion in this section assumes that an initial planning stage has concluded that integration of the given legacy application(s) is the right strategy (see Chapter 8 for a discussion of planning for legacy application reengineering). Our goal here is to proceed further by determining and implementing the most appropriate approach for accessing and integrating legacy applications.

9.6.1   Step 1: Requirement Definition and Analysis

The requirements gathered in this step are intended to drive the legacy access/integration. Consequently, these requirements augment the requirements collected during planning stage. The specific activities are as following:

1. Identify the legacy applications and data sources which need to be accessed and integrated.

2. Analyze and categorize the legacy applications into decomposable, semidecomposable, and nondecomposable.

3. Identify the client applications and/or tools which need to access the legacy information. In particular, you need to document the users of Web-based applications and services (number of users, where located, time frames when legacy information is needed, etc.).

4. Determine the appropriate access and integration requirements for each client application and tool. These requirements can be categorized in terms of remote data, remote function, and remote presentation access and integration. In particular, you should clearly understand why you need to integrate (keep in mind that integration technologies are harder and more expensive to build).

5. Understand and document management and policy issues such as cost limitations, time considerations, security considerations, conformance to corporate standards and infrastructures, and long-range considerations.

6. Specify operational requirements for legacy information access and integration such as performance requirements, interconnectivity and interoperability requirements with other applications and users, and portability and operability requirements of the solution approach.

9.6.2   Step 2: Solution Architectures

The solution architecture for each legacy information access/integration problem must answer the following key questions:

*   What type of access (i.e., access paradigm) is most appropriate?
*   Is integration needed or is access enough?
*   What type of integration technologies should be used, if needed?

The access paradigm can be a mixture of the following access paradigms: remote data access, remote function access, and remote presentation access. The exact approach is based on the requirements specified above and an evaluation of the trade-offs among the three approaches. The two key decision factors are (a) category of legacy application (i.e., completely decomposable, partially decomposable, not decomposable) and (b) type of resources that need to be accessed (i.e., data and/or functions). The following guidelines can be used to make this decision:

- If the main interest of the new applications and end-user tools is in accessing legacy data, then remote data access is an appropriate approach only if the legacy data are separable.

- If the legacy data cannot be separated, then access to a legacy function or legacy presentation may be necessary to access the required data.

- You may have to rely on screen scrapers (a legacy presentation access technology), to access the data of some really old legacy systems that are not decomposable at all.

Integration of legacy applications is used to extend the useful life of the legacy systems to leverage the existing investment in legacy systems. However, legacy application integration is a labor-intensive task with very few tools at the time of this writing. Basically, integration should be undertaken only if it adds significant *business value* beyond the information access (see Section 9.4.2 for pros and cons of legacy application integration).

You choose the most appropriate surround technologies that satisfy the requirements stated in the previous step. Examples of surround technologies are screen scrapers, database gateways, application gateways, object wrappers, and integration gateways. You should bind the solution approach by setting limits on what features will be included in the access technology and when these features will be needed. For example, each one of these technologies can provide different levels of support for

- Access to a single application, multiple applications on the same machine, applications across machines. Different surround technologies have different limitations in this area.

- Read or update capabilities. Many surround technologies only provide read access.

- Distributed query processing support. Some database gateways support distributed query processing on databases from the same vendor; others are beginning to support multiple vendor databases (e.g., Sybase OMNI Server allows joins between DB2 and Sybase databases).

- Distributed transaction processing. This implies that updates between different sites are synchronized. At present, this support is rare between different DBMS vendors

- Synthesis of results from multiple systems and paradigms. This allows combination of results from multiple hosts by using different paradigms (LLIG, LFA, LPA) and synthesis/integration of the results for presentation to the user. For example, this would allow extraction of information through a combination of screen scraping and IMS transactions interactions and a consolidated presentation of the results to the end users.

Table 9.4 summarizes the features of the surround technologies. As expected, the surround technologies with fewer features are less expensive and readily available off the shelf. At present, screen scrapers, bulk data transfer packages, and database gateways are widely available from different vendors. Most of the application gateways are homegrown and are sparse in the market. Integration gateways are an area of current and future work.

TABLE 9.4 : ACCESS (SURROUND) TECHNOLOGIES OVERVIEW

Access Technology	Access Paradigm Supported (RDA, RFA, RPA)	No. of Hosts Accessed	Read and/or Update Capabilities	Distributed Query Processing Capabilities	Distributed Transaction Processing	Synthesis of Results (View Integration)
Screen Scrapers	RPA only	usually one at a time	N/A	N/A	N/A	N/A
Bulk Data Transfer Packages	RDA for bulk data transfer	usually one at a time	read only from hosts	N/A	N/A	N/A
Database Gateways	RDA primarily	can be many	mostly read	primarily for same vendor	usually not supported	usually not supported
Application Gateways	RFA primarily, RPA possible	mostly one	read and update	usually not supported	usually not supported	usually not supported
Legacy Integration Gateways	RDA, RFA and RPA	many required	read and update	support required	should be provided	required

Figure 9.16 shows another view that can be used to analyze and assess the surround technologies by using the following two dimensions:

- **Type of legacy applications.** The legacy applications can be *"friendly"* to access (i.e., decomposable by using relational databases and clearly identified module interfaces), *"neighborly"* to access (i.e., semistructured by allowing access to only a few resources such as IMS databases) or *"hostile"* (i.e., monolithic by not allowing any access other than screen).

- **Type of integration needs.** The users may need the information to be tightly integrated (e.g., viewed seamlessly) or not integrated at all (e.g., appear as chunks that require different access mechanisms that are visible to the users).

This two-dimensional view can be used to visualize seven different scenarios and the most appropriate technologies. We can make the following observations from this analysis.

Scenarios 1, 2, and 3 require access only. Scenario 1 (remote access to relational databases from the Web) is becoming widely supported by numerous relational gateway products such as dbWeb, SQLWeb, WebLogic, dbKona, and so forth. It is best to use an ODBC- or JDBC-based gateway for flexibility. Scenario 2 (remote access to legacy programs from the Web) is

Figure 9.16 Technology Assessment

Type of Legacy Applications	Monolithic ("Hostile")	Scenario 3 (Web-based Screen Scrapers)	Scenario 6 (Presentation Wrapper)	Scenario 7 (Legacy Integration Gateways— Full Fledged)
	Semi-Decomposable ("Neighborly")	Scenario 2 (Homegrown Gateways)	Scenario 5 (Legacy Code Wrapper)	
	Decomposable ("Friendly")	Scenario 1 (Relational Gateways)	Scenario 4 (Data Wrappers)	
		Access Only	Partial Integration	Full Integration

Integration Level

largely being handled through homegrown gateways (remote function access gateways are rare). Scenario 3 (remote access to legacy presentation) is satisfied by invoking screen scrapers from the Web. Most screen scrapers are becoming "Web enabled" (i.e., they can be invoked from CGI gateways) and can be used to access legacy data through the remote presentation access paradigm.

Scenarios 4, 5, and 6 represent partial integration (i.e., integration within a class of application resources). Scenario 4 (integration of relational databases through the Web) can be supported by using existing data wrappers that provide access to multiple databases (e.g., Web interface to Sybase Omni Server). Scenarios 5 and 6 require integration at varying degrees of sophistication. The integration gateway is typically an object wrapper.

Scenario 7 needs full integration gateways. The gateways to satisfy this requirement are difficult to build and the implementation effort is substantial. To embark on this effort, it must be clear that there is enough business value to justify the investment. For the cases where there is a clear business need, this is a potential area of future work.

9.6.3   Step 3: Implement and Test

Implementation of integration solutions is dependent on the strategy chosen (legacy data access, function access, or presentation access). Detailed discussion of the implementation steps is beyond the scope of this book. However, the following steps are typical:

- Determine what will be bought and what will be implemented in-house. For larger problems, it may be better to choose an application gateway and then customize/expand it to meet organization needs

- Establish an implementation team

- Run a pilot if appropriate

- Conduct a detailed state-of-the-market analysis of the access technologies needed

- Prepare and send Request For Prices (RFP) for the access technologies

- Choose appropriate access technology suppliers

- Train staff for implementation (vendor-provided training can be beneficial)

- Acquire and install needed hardware/software and gateways

- Integrate and expand the access technologies

- Initiate development activities

9.6.4   Step 4: Deploy and Support

After the integration approach has been implemented, it needs to be deployed, supported, and managed like any other technology. In particular, the following issues need to be considered:

- Estimate time and cost needed for deployment and support

- Establish policies, procedures, and roles for deployment and support

- Analyze the organizational issues (staff estimates, training, end-user impact)

- Assign the support to an organizational unit

- Train staff for operation and support (many gateways need extensive support)

- Monitor for performance

- Monitor for next step, that is, seek feedback from users if and when the legacy applications need to be rearchitected and migrated

9.7   State of the Practice: Case Studies and Examples

Access and integration of legacy systems, especially through the Web, is an active area of work, although many efforts are relatively new. A few snippets are presented for a general understanding. To illustrate the main concepts, we will discuss two detailed examples that illustrate integration of IBM MVS mainframe-based applications with new end-user tools. These two examples represent a large number of legacy applications that are in operation today. Unfortunately, as you will see, these two examples are riddled with IBM mainframe jargon (I have tried to minimize it as much as possible).[2]

---

2. In my youth I was a systems programmer on IBM mainframe systems and installed IMS, SNA, DB2, and MVS. I learned this jargon intimately at that time. I am completely surprised that this jargon is still quite useful.

9.7.1   Short Case Studies ("Snippets")

Indiana University Uses the Web for Financial Reporting [Eckerson 1996]. Indiana University uses Netscape's Navigator browsers to provide access to financial information for approximately 1,000 financial managers and administrators on eight campuses. The Web browsers are used to query and review the financial data and can also extract and download needed data to the client side. The data extraction is achieved by using the Netscape browser "Helper Applications" that associates programs with different data types, including audio, video, text, and image. For example, by creating a new data type called "text/delimited" and associating it with a program such as Microsoft Excel, the users can directly load data into an Excel spreadsheet. The access to the financial data is achieved through a CGI gateway.

Lee Links Mainframe to Web [Simpson 1997]. Lee Printwear, a clothing manufacturer, developed a Web-based application to give its customers—wholesale distributors—up to date information on product prices and availability. The data, residing on MVS DB2, is accessed through a Microsoft Internet Information Server.

ABB Uses CORBA to Access/Migrate Legacy Applications [Konstantas 1996]. ABB, a large engineering firm in Europe, needed to deal with the huge embedded base of legacy applications. The legacy applications included several CAD-CAM programs and many large-scale Fortran programs dating back to the early 1970s. Konstantas describes how the legacy systems are being accessed and migrated by using CORBA. The objective of this project is to provide an interoperability layer between several heterogeneous legacy systems and new desktop clients.

Mortgage Company Surrounds Its Mainframe [Schatz 1995]. The Federal National Mortgage Association (known as Fannie Mae) wanted to accelerate mortgage origination by permitting inter- and extra-enterprise data sharing. The Fannie Mae corporate IS relied on mainframes and several fragmented PC applications. The time to process mortgage applications around 1990 was very long (sometime months) because the staffers were spending 80 percent of their time searching for data and only 20 percent analyzing them (mortgage processing is an intensely query and analysis task). Due to these delays, Fannie Mae was not popular with its customers and Congress and was losing significant market shares to its competitor (the Federal Home Mortgage Loan Association, known as Freddie Mac). Fannie Mae needed a facility that would allow loan originators to quickly query and analyze the data, but it did not want to forget the $100 million investment in its mainframe (MVS, COBOL, IDMS) systems. Their approach was to surround the mainframe systems with a layer of Sybase/Sun servers that housed data needed by loan originators. These data are fetched from the mainframe and are accessed by the Visual C++ clients residing on PC Windows desktops. An expert system is used for assessing the loans. This case study has been analyzed by Susan Cohen, president of the Aarons Group, who recognized it for its effectiveness in improving the mortgage approval process.

New York Stock Exchange (NYSE) Heads Off a Crash [Hayes 1995]. The NYSE faced a crisis on October 12, 1987 when the trading volume topped out at 608 million shares due to the congestion of their Tandem-based legacy system (the average trading volume at that time was 1.4 billion shares per day). NYSE invested $125 million to develop a three-tiered system where the Tandem machines became the third tier. In the middle tier, a number of HP machines extract and keep copies of Tandem data. The HP servers are accessed through a wide range of desktop tools, performing a variety of tasks. This system provides access to legacy data and improves the performance and flexibility of the platform. Basically, the legacy system was not retired; instead it was integrated with the new desktop tools through middle-tier machines. This platform is intended to support more than 2 billion shares per day.

Prudential Provides Access to Legacy Data [Fryer 1995]. Prudential Insurance Corp. maintains large volumes of customer data that is stored on 11 large-scale IBM 3090 mainframes, scattered from Los Angeles to New Jersey. These data, mostly in DB2 tables, need to be accessed by a large population of sales agents and other company staff personnel for analysis and reporting. Instead of replacing the mainframe legacy system, the company decided to use a legacy system access/integration approach. The worker PCs are connected to the mainframes through a data gateway from Sybase (i.e., Sybase MVS gateway).

Massachusetts "Motor Voter" System [Shibley 1995]. The Massachusetts Secretary of State's Office successfully designed and developed a "Motor Voter" system that offers voter registration at motor vehicle offices. This system makes it easy to register new voters and to update the existing voter lists as the voters change residences. The new system uses client/ server technology to integrate several existing local voter registration systems. The system uses PowerBuilder clients that are located in the 351 local offices and 36 registry of motor vehicle sites. Not surprisingly, the success of the project hinged on the active participation and cooperation of numerous politically autonomous stakeholders. This case study highlights the role of "organizational integration" in the success of integrating systems that cross organization boundaries.

University of Florida Reengineers via the World Wide Web [Roseen 1996]. The University of Florida changed its registration process by moving away from the old central registration system to a self-service system that uses voice response units and the World Wide Web. In the new system, the students do not have to wait in line at the start of each semester to register for courses, pay tuition, and buy books. Instead, they use the Web technology in a self-service mode by using their desktops. The student data and business logic are kept at the mainframe and the students register for courses and pay tuition through Web browsers. The Web browsers especially eliminate the user interface problems for on- and off-campus registration.

9.7.2   Detailed Example 1: Access/Integration of DB2 Applications

Many MVS-based applications that have been developed since the mid 1980s use the IBM DB2 relational database management system. The DB2 databases can be accessed through CICS or IMS transactions or through the TSO Program Development Facility (PDF).[3] Most DB2-based applications are decomposable from a database point of view because the DB2 catalogs provide enough information to authorized users to issue SQL calls. In some cases, the DB2 database administrators create views on the databases to facilitate multiple users. However, in some cases the DB2 applications can be viewed as semistructured or monolithic, thus forcing remote function or presentation accesses. This can happen due to the following reasons:

- The database administrators do not allow the end users to run ad hoc SQL against DB2 tables. This can be done by limiting the views and authorities of the end users.

- The number of DB2 tables can be very large and the end users need some help in understanding the schemas to issue queries. For example, many large-scale database applications have more than 300 tables. It is a nontrivial task for the end users to be able to know how to issue SQL statements to retrieve information about switches, customers, and trouble tickets in this situation.

To illustrate the issues and approaches to integrate DB2-based applications with desktop tools, let us consider a set of DB2 databases which support several legacy applications. We assume that these databases need to be accessed by a variety of end users for reports and ad hoc queries. We will use the methodology introduced above to analyze this problem and determine a solution approach.

9.7.2.1   Requirement Definition and Analysis

The DB2 databases need to be accessed from client applications and end-user tools from the following end-user environments:

- IBM PC DOS computer connected to a LAN server (e.g., Novell) or local controllers (IRMA boards). The LANs may be connected over a TCP/IP or an SNA network.

- IBM PC Windows computer connected to a LAN server (e.g., Novell) or local controllers (IRMA boards). The LANs may be connected over a TCP/IP or an SNA network.

- Apple/Macintosh computer connected to an Appleshare LAN server or directly connected to an SNA network. The Apple LANs may be connected over a TCP/IP or an SNA network.

- UNIX workstations (e.g., Sun, HP) connected to a TCP/IP LAN or corporate backbone.

- Web browsers on any of the above platforms.

Access paradigms may be a mixture of remote data access, remote function access, and remote presentation access. Remote data access may be needed for the following end-user

---

3. CICS (Customer Information Control System) is a very popular mainframe-based transaction processing system. The IMS (Information Management System) has two components: IMS Database (IMS DB) and IMS Transaction Manager (IMS TM). TSO (Time Sharing Option) is an on-line program development facility for MVS mainframe systems.

capabilities from end-user tools such as 4GL tools (e.g., Focus), report writers (e.g., Informix ACE Report Writer), and spreadsheets (e.g., Lotus):

- creation of views for different end users
- creation of indexes for improved performance
- running queries to understand data format and content
- running ad hoc queries and reports to answer specific questions and satisfy requests for information
- running queries to understand and diagnose application/data failures
- data conversion activities

Remote function access is needed from client applications which may invoke IMS transactions or CICS transactions to access DB2 data. Remote presentation access is primarily invoked through 3270 terminal emulations.

9.7.2.2 Solution Architecture

Table 9.5 shows the access technologies for access in place integration of DB2-based applications. Any of these technologies can be invoked through CGI or Java Gateways.

For remote data access, it is better to use open protocols or de facto standards which are supported by multiple vendors. Distributed Relational Database Architecture (DRDA) at present is the most appropriate solution because it is

- A de facto standard for DB2 access.
- A long-range potential solution to access DB2 data from Informix, Oracle, IBI tools (most of these vendors have already announced DRDA gateways).
- Implemented on LU6.2 which is currently supported over SNA (SDLC or IBM Token Ring) as well as over TCP/IP (IBM AnyNet feature).
- Independent of "a foreign server" on MVS because DRDA code is automatically included in DB2 release 2.3 and higher. Such servers are expensive (over $200,000) and require installation/maintenance support.

Microsoft's ODBC (Open Database Connectivity) is also a valid choice for DB2 access. For example, an ODBC program on a desktop can use ODBC drivers to send SQL requests to an ODBC to DRDA gateway.

For remote function access, CORBA wrappers are a promising option. Basically, the MVS code to be invoked is defined by using CORBA IDL. In addition, CORBA server code is written which receives calls from CORBA clients and invokes the legacy code.

OSF DCE, a widely accepted RPC-based middleware, is also an option for DB2 data access. Access of DB2 through OSF DCE RPC is approaching the production environment at the time of this writing. The IBM MVS DCE supports this access. Recall that OSF DCE does not at present support ad hoc SQL queries. Thus OSF DCE is not a suitable solution for DB2 access for ad hoc remote data access.

Queued Message Processing (QMP) is another potential candidate for remote function access. Access to DB2 data through QMP is currently supported through IBM's MQM product line. QMP needs special attention for ad hoc queries which may generate large messages in the message queue.

Remote presentation access is supported through a wide variety of screen scrapers that are commercially available from companies such as Apertus, Inc., Attachmate, Procomm, and so forth.

In this example, we are assuming that there is no need for integration of DB2 databases because adequate database gateways are available for DB2 (the business value of developing an object wrapper over DB2 is dubious).

TABLE 9.5 ACCESS TECHNOLOGIES FOR DB2 DATA ACCESS

Access Paradigms	Decomposable Application	Data Decomposable	Program Decomposable	Monolithic Applications
Remote Data Access	DRDA and ODBC	DRDA and ODBC	N/A	N/A
Remote Function Access	CORBA, OSF DCE RPC, and DB procedures	N/A	CORBA, OSF DCE RPC, and DB procedures	N/A
Remote Presentation Access	Screen crapers	Screen scrapers	Screen scrapers	Screen scrapers

Before getting into implementation, let us briefly review the DB2 data warehousing and data migration issues as the alternatives to access in place integration (this is only for sake of completeness).

A data warehouse can be established around MVS DB2 (many case studies indicate this option). If the decision support applications cannot meet performance requirements with MVSDB2 due to mainframe congestion, then a UNIX-based warehouse may be needed. The data can be extracted and downloaded by using FTP SQL which allows DB2 data to be extracted and downloaded to UNIX platforms. Specialized tools such as the PRISM Warehouse Manager can also be used to build this warehouse. The types of tools needed for the warehouse are dependent on the type of database used by the warehouse (Informix, Oracle, Ingres).

DB2 applications may be migrated ("downsized") to UNIX-based applications (e.g., Oracle) for cost savings and improved performance. This does require reprogramming and staff training. The migration gateways should make the transition transparent. Availability of DB2 on UNIX platforms and CICS on UNIX-RS6000 can make the transition easier.

9.7.2.3   Implementation and Deployment

Figure 9.17 shows a sample implementation strategy to access the DB2 data. The clients are identified as remote data access, remote function access, and remote presentation access clients. The remote data access clients can use proprietary or DRDA database gateways. The remote function access clients typically invoke IMS or CICS transactions on the mainframe to access DB2 databases. These transactions can be invoked by the IMS/CICS support for TCP/IP socket clients, DCE application servers, and CORBA wrappers. The remote presentation access clients access the DB2 databases through the MVS presentation services that can be invoked from a 3270 terminal or a screen scraper that emulates this protocol.

Note that these technologies are basically access technologies that will use many APIs to access the DB2 data. To integrate these APIs into a single OO API, the role of the CORBA object wrapper can be extended so that it can be wrapped around all other interfaces and APIs.

9.7.3   Detailed Example 2: Integration of an IMS Application

A large proportion of legacy data is stored in IMS databases. Reportedly 50 to 60 percent of legacy data in U.S. corporations are stored in IMS databases. IMS-based applications have the following properties:

- Application data are stored in IMS databases.

- IMS database schemas are specified through Database Description (DBD) and the programmer/user subschemas are specified through the Program Specification Blocks (PSBs).

- Applications use IMS DLI (Data Language Interface) calls to access and manipulate IMS data by using PSBs.

- IMS applications are written in COBOL, PL1, and C and execute under the IMS transaction manager as Message Processing Program (MPP) transactions or Batch Message Processing (BMP) programs.

The IMS database administrators create PSBs on the databases to facilitate DL1 calls. Most IMS applications are semistructured or monolithic, thus forcing remote function or presentation accesses. This is due to the following reasons:

- IMS does not directly support ad hoc queries (DL1 is not suitable for ad hoc queries). Many SQL-based tools have been developed which convert SQL to DL1 calls. Many performance and operability issues are related to the SQL to DL1 conversions.

- The IMS databases can be very complex and the end users need some help in understanding the schemas to issue queries even when SQL interfaces are available. For example, the TIRKS database structure is extremely complex. It is virtually impossible for the end users to be able to know how to issue SQL statements to retrieve information from this database.

Figure 9.17 DB2 Access Implementation Example

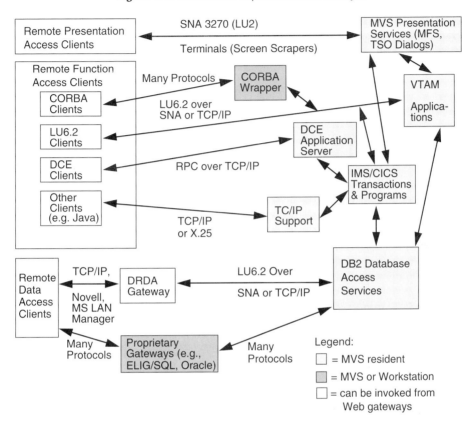

To illustrate the issues and approaches in IMS-based legacy data access, let us consider a set of IMS databases which support several legacy applications. We assume that these databases need to be accessed by a variety of end-user tools and applications. We will use the aforementioned methodology to analyze this problem and determine a solution approach.

9.7.3.1 Requirement Definition and Analysis

The IMS data are accessed through end-user tools residing on

- IBM PC DOS computer connected to a LAN server (e.g., Novell) or local controllers (IRMA boards). The LANs may be connected over a TCP/IP or an SNA network.

- IBM PC Windows computer connected to a LAN server (e.g., Novell) or local controllers (IRMA boards). The LANs may be connected over a TCP/IP or an SNA network.

- Apple/Macintosh computer connected to an Appleshare LAN server or directly connected to an SNA network. The Apple LANs may be connected over a TCP/IP or an SNA network.

- UNIX workstations (e.g., Sun, HP) connected to a TCP/IP LAN or corporate backbone.

- Web browsers residing on any of the above platforms.

The following capabilities are needed from end-user tools:

- running ad hoc queries and reports to answer specific questions and satisfy requests for information
- running queries to understand and diagnose application/data failures
- data conversion activities

Support is also needed for prespecified CICS/IMS transactions from client applications written in C, C++, COBOL, or 4GLs.

9.7.3.2   Solution Architectures

The access paradigms are remote presentation access, remote data access, and the remote function access. Table 9.6 shows the access technologies selected. The Web gateways (CGI or Java) can invoke these paradigms.

TABLE **9.6** ACCESS TECHNOLOGIES FOR ACCESSING IMS DATABASES

Access Paradigms	Decomposable Application	Data Decomposable	Program Decomposable	Monolithic Applications
Remote Data Access	SQL to IMS Gateways	SQL to IMS Gateways	N/A	N/A
Remote Function Access	CORBA, OSF DCE RPC, and DB procedures	N/A	CORBA, OSF DCE RPC, and IMS C/S	N/A
Remote Presentation Access	Screen scrapers	Screen scrapers	Screen scrapers	Screen scrapers

For accessing IMS data directly by using an RDA paradigm, virtually no open standards are available. DRDA at present is only restricted to DB2 access. Many proprietary gateways for IMS access from SQL have been announced over the last several years. An example is the EDA/SQL from Information Builders, Inc. EDA/SQL allows access to enterprise data, including IMS and DB2, from SQL clients located on UNIX, PC, and Mac computers, interconnected through TCP/IP and SNA networks. The main strength of EDA/SQL is that it is available on many hardware platforms and allows access to over 35 data sources on MVS and UNIX. The main weakness of EDA/SQL is that EDA/SQL software must be installed on every platform in the system—only those platforms and development tools supported by EDA/SQL can be used. For example, we found that EDA/SQL did not interoperate with a human resource application from PeopleSoft. EDA/SQL is also quite expensive. Some of these limitations may disappear as EDA/SQL adopts open standards (EDA/SQL has announced support for DRDA, OSF DCE RPC, and for ODBC).

For long-range access to IMS data, IMS Client/Server (C/S) is a good candidate. IMS C/S is highly advertised by IBM to transform IMS to the open client/server computing arena. The main features of IMS C/S, also known as "Open IMS," are

- IMS programs (MPPs as well as BMPs) will be able to directly interact with OSF DCE clients. The OSF DCE RPC will be the main exchange protocol.

- IMS clients will be able to run on different platforms (IMS APIs will become available on different platforms).

- SQL access to IMS will be supported through EDA/SQL.

For remote function access, CORBA and OSF DCE are good candidates. For CORBA, IBM's DSOM (Distributed Systems Object Model) will include IMS integration as a strategy. For DCE, MVS supports an Application Server (AS) to access IMS and DB2 data:

- Client issues RPC call.

- Application Server (AS) invokes an IMS transaction.

- No support for ad hoc SQL queries.

- OSF DCE does not directly support database services.

IMS Batch Message Processing (BMP) provides good capability to access IMS functionality. BMP programs at present can directly interact with TCP/IP sockets. Thus a TCP/IP client application can directly invoke a BMP program on the host computer. For remote presentation access, 3270 emulators are used.

We will develop a CORBA object wrapper that will encapsulate and integrate various IMS data access paradigms. The object wrapper will use the CORBA IDL to define operations on IMS data sources. IBM's DSOM provides the capabilities to run CORBA objects on MVS. Thus the IMS code will be invoked from the DSOM CORBA objects on MVS.

Let us briefly review the data warehousing and data migration issues as the alternatives to access in place and integration for IMS data.

"Native" IMS is not suitable for data warehousing because IMS data retrieval calls (DLI) cannot be issued from decision support tools. One approach is to use a database gateway (e.g., EDA/SQL) which translates SQL calls from decision support tools to IMS. However, a data warehouse can be established by storing IMS data in a relational database. The relational warehouse may be needed if the decision support users cannot meet performance requirements with SQL/IMS gateways such as EDA/SQL. The data can be extracted and loaded into a data warehouse by using FTP, or PRISM Warehouse Manager. The types of tools needed for the warehouse are dependent on the type of database used by the warehouse.

IMS data may be rearchitected and migrated to relational databases (e.g., Oracle) for cost savings and improved performance. This does require extensive reprogramming (IMS DL1 to SQL), database redesign (hierarchical to relational data model), and staff training efforts. Typical steps in rearchitecture and migration of IMS applications to relational database applications are (see Chapter 11 for details):

- Translate the IMS data model to a relational data model.

- Design the relational databases of the target system.

- Populate the target relational databases by unloading the IMS data and transferring them to the relational database.

- Determine how much of the existing application code can be eliminated by using data browsers, spreadsheet packages, and 4GL tools.

- Reprogram the remaining code by using embedded SQL.

9.7.3.3 Implementation and Deployment

Figure 9.18 shows an implementation strategy for accessing IMS databases. The clients are identified as remote data access, remote function access, and remote presentation access clients. The remote data access clients mainly use proprietary gateways that translate SQL to IMS (e.g., the EDA/SQL Gateway, the Ingres IMS Gateways). The remote function access clients typically invoke IMS or CICS transactions on the mainframe to access IMS databases. These transactions can be invoked by the IMS/CICS support for TCP/IP socket clients, DCE application servers, and CORBA wrappers. The remote presentation access clients access the IMS databases through the MVS presentation services that can be invoked from a 3270 terminal or a screen scraper that emulates this protocol.

These access technologies use many APIs to access the IMS data. To integrate these APIs into a single OO API, the role of the CORBA object wrapper can be extended so that it can be wrapped around all other interfaces and APIs.

9.8   State of the Market: Products and Standards

There are many proprietary off-the-shelf products in the marketplace that can enable integration of legacy applications. These products are frequently surveyed in trade journals. For example, the *Database Programming and Design Journal* periodically publishes a "Buyers' Guide" with a special section on gateways and middleware. A partial list of surround technologies designed specifically for legacy application integration includes products such as (listed alphabetically): ADDA/LegacyWare, Apple Data Access Language, Digital's Data Integrator, Gupta Technologies SQL Gateway, Informix DRDA Gateway, Information Builder's EDA/SQL, MicroDecision Systems Gateways, Netwise RPC Mainframe Gateway, Oracle Gateways, and Sybase Omniserver. Many other proprietary products have been announced and will continue to appear in the market. Analysis and discussion of these products are beyond the scope of this book.

Figure 9.18 IMS Implementation Example

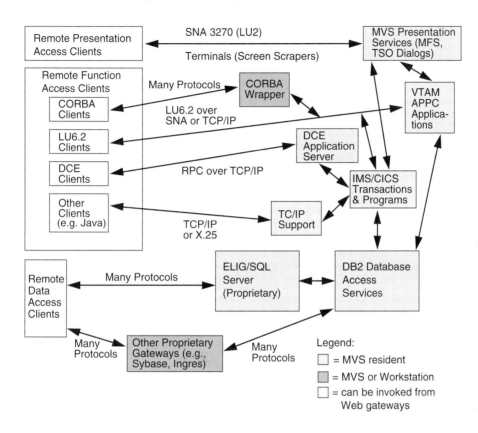

The middleware standards, discussed in Umar [1997], play a key role in application integration. In particular, formal and de facto standards such as CORBA, RPCs, ODBC, DRDA, and ISO RDA play key roles in developing portable and interoperable surround technologies. In addition, Gartner Group Research Notes analyze available products (see, for example, Burton [1996], and Natis [1996]) and the Patricia Seybold Group publishes special product analysis reports.

9.9   State of the Art: Research Notes

Integration of legacy applications with new applications and tools is an extensive undertaking. Research in developing integration methodologies and the tools to assist and automate the integration activities could have high payoffs.

Major areas of future research are the development and deployment of sophisticated surround technologies (mediators) that will integrate a diverse array of heterogeneous applications and tools of different vintages from different suppliers. These mediators will have to provide view integration, distributed query processing, and distributed transaction processing capabilities. The object-oriented technologies will play a key role in encapsulating and hiding the complexity of the heterogeneous data access. Interoperability and integration of various protocols (DRDA, ODBC, OLE/ActiveX, RPC, CORBA) will play fundamental roles. Research in gateways such as the TSIMMS project at Stanford [Chawathe 1994] and DARWIN project at University of California, Berkeley [Brodie 1993] are worth noting.

An interesting example of industrial research is the IBM BOSS middleware strategy that is based on extensive prototyping and research. BOSS is intended to support access and integration of IMS and other legacy applications through an integrated set of components such as DSOM (IBM's version of CORBA), Encina (a TP monitor), MQSeries (a message oriented software middleware product from IBM), OSF DCE, and Flowmark (an IBM workflow system) [Percy 1996].

9.10   Summary

Integration of legacy applications is a challenging task which requires review of user needs, business pressures, evolving standards and protocols, and an ever-growing potpourri of products from numerous suppliers. Due to the impact of the decisions on corporate business and the monetary investment, careful analysis of various trade-offs is essential. This chapter suggests a framework that segregates the application integration issues into three broad categories:

- Legacy Data Access—access of enterprise data, typically through ad hoc SQL, without invoking any enterprise functionality (e.g., business logic).

- Legacy Function Access—access of enterprise data through some existing functions (e.g., IMS/CICS transactions, procedures to be invoked through RPC).

- Legacy Presentation Access—access of enterprise data through some presentation services by invoking terminal emulator sessions.

This framework is used to survey and categorize the wide range of access-enabling technologies (commonly known as "surround" technologies) into object wrappers, screen scrapers, bulk data transfer packages, database gateways, application gateways, and host integration gateways. A methodology is outlined to approach the legacy application integration problem in terms of analyzing requirements, establishing solution architectures, implementation, and management/support considerations. Examples of how this methodology can be used to access DB2 and IMS data have been discussed. The framework and methodology presented in this chapter attempt to provide guidelines to approach the legacy application integration problem.

9.11 Case Study: Access/Integration for XYZCorp

The mainframe-based corporate Material Requirement Planning (MRP) system needs to be accessed and integrated with the new Web-based applications (e.g., the inventory manager, management planning system) identified in the XYZAICS initiative. The MRP system contains bill of materials (raw materials) information in IMS databases and outside vendor information in DB2 databases. In particular, an approach is needed to access/integrate the MRP application with the inventory management system. It is your task to access the mainframe databases (IMS and DB2) through the Web.

Hints about the Case Study

The solution to this project is strikingly close to the case studies presented in Section 9.7.

9.12 Problems and Exercises

1. Consider a legacy application of your choice. Develop the access/integration of this application with the WWW by using the four-step procedure described in Section 9.6. For each step, list the major decisions, the techniques/tools employed, and the final choices made by you.

2. Review, expand, and improve Table 9.2 to make it more general. What are the limitations of the access paradigm framework (i.e., remote data access, remote function access, remote presentation access)?

3. Expand Table 9.4 by adding existing products as examples.

4. Do a survey of the commercially available object wrappers and suggest a taxonomy to analyze the state of the market.

5. Do a survey, by using the Internet, of the Web-based gateways for legacy applications. Suggest a taxonomy to analyze the state of the market.

9.13 Additional Information

Enterprise/legacy data access has appeared in the literature under headings such as "universal data access," "open data access," "web access to legacy systems," and "dealing with legacy data." A variety of articles can be found in trade journals such as *Datamation, Database Programming and Design,* and *Data Management Review.* The issue of legacy systems is widely discussed in the literature. The papers by Mike Brodie [Brodie 1993], and [Brodie 1992] provide a good overview of legacy systems. The *IEEE Computer Magazine,* January 1995, is devoted to legacy systems and has many interesting articles.

Andrews, G., "Paradigms for Interprocess Interactions in Distributed Programs," *ACM Computing Surveys,* March 1991, pp. 49–90.

Bannister, D., "Trading Places (UNIX Connectivity)," *Connection,* June 16, 1993, pp. 14–15.

Bennet, K., "Legacy Systems: Coping with Success," *IEEE Software,* January 1995, pp. 19–23.

Bernstein, P., and Chu, D.W., "Using Semi-Joins to Solve Relational Queries," *JACM,* January 1981.

Brodie, M. L., "The Promise of Distributed Computing and the Challenge of Legacy Information Systems," in Hsiao, D., et al. (eds.), *Proc. IFIP TC2/WG2.6 Conference on Semantics of Interoperable Database Systems,* Lorne, Australia, November 1992.

Brodie, M. L., and Stonebraker, M., "DARWIN: On the Incremental Migration of Legacy Information Systems," Technical Memorandum, Electronics Research Laboratory, College of Engineering, University of California, Berkeley, March 1993.

Brodie, M. L., and Stonebraker, M., *Migrating Legacy Systems: Gateways, Interfaces & the Incremental Approach,* Morgan Kauffman, 1995.

Burton, B., "Data Interoperability," Gartner Group Conference, February, 1995.

Burton, B., and Hill, J., "IBI's EDA 4.0: A New Version, Another Strategy," *Gartner Group Research Note*, September 27, 1996.

Cerdingley, E., and Dai, H., "Encapsulation—An Issue for Legacy Systems," *BT Technology Journal,* July 1993, pp. 52–64.

Chawathe, S., et al., "The TSIMMIS Project: Integration of Heterogeneous Information Sources," Department of Computer Science, Stanford University, 1994.

Delligatta, A., and Umbaugh, R. E., "EUC Becomes Enterprise Computing," *Information Systems Management,* Vol. 10, No. 4, 1993, pp. 53–55.

Eberhard, E., "Information Warehouse: A User Experience," *Info DB,* Vol. 7, No. 2, 1993, pp. 6–12.

Eckerson, W., "Three Approaches for Accessing Legacy Data," Patricia Seybold Group's Open Information Systems, June 1994.

Eckerson, W., "Indiana University Uses the Web for Financial Reporting," *Open Information Systems,* Vol. 11, No. 2, 1996, pp. 37–45.

Ferrent, R., "BT's Information Warehouse," *Logistics Information Management,* Vol. 5, No. 4, 1992, pp. 42–43

Fryer, B., "Prudential Gets Healthy," *Information Week,* December 18, 1995, pp. 60–64.

Giordano, R., "The Information 'Where?' House," *Database Design and Programming,* September 1993.

Gotlieb, L., "Learning to Live with Legacy Systems," *CMA,* May 1993, pp. 10–11.

Hayes, M., "NYSE Heads Off a Crash," *Information Week,* December 18, 1995, pp. 59–60.

Inmon, W., *Building Data Warehouses,* John Wiley, 1993.

Joder, D., "Negotiating an Enterprise API," *Object Magazine,* October 1996, pp. 32–37.

Klinker, P., et al., "How to Avoid Getting Stuck on the Migration Highway," *Object Magazine,* October 1996, pp. 46–51.

Konstantas, D., "Migration of Legacy Applications to a CORBA Platform: A Case Study," *International Conference on Distributed Platforms,* Dresden, Germany, February 1996.

Lindstrom, F., "Re-engineering of Legacy Systems Using an Object-Oriented Technology," 4th International Workshop on Computer-Aided Software Engineering, Irvine, CA, December 1990, pp. 26–27.

Marchese, F., and Umar, A., "Client-Server Computing Through EDA/SQL: An Analysis," Bellcore TM-STS-022743, March 3, 1993.

Mayers, C., "Legacy Data Access," ANSA User Group Meeting, Cambridge, England, April 1994.

Moad, J., "Object Methods Tame Reengineering Madness," *Datamation,* May 15, 1995, pp. 43–48.

Mowbray, T., and Aahavi, R., *The Essential CORBA,* John Wiley, 1995.

Nadeau, M., "Remote Connections," *Byte,* June 1994, pp. 195–198

Nassif, R., and Mitchussen, D., "Issues and Approaches for Migration/Cohabitation between Legacy and New Systems," SIGMOD '93, International Conference on Management of Data, May 1993, pp. 471–474.

Nassif, R.; Zhu, J.; Goyal, P., "Basic Issues for Developing Distributed Applications Interacting with Legacy Systems and Databases," *Proceedings RIDE-IMS '93,* Third International Workshop on Research Issues in Data Engineering: Interoperability in Multidatabase Systems, Vienna, Austria, April 1993.

Natis, Y., "How to Survive the Middleware Tornado, Parts 1 and 2," *Gartner Group Research Note,* June 19, 1996.

Norvin, L., "Screen Scrapers Put a New face on Legacy Applications," *PC Week,* May 23, 1994, p. 94.

Nutt, G., *Open Systems,* Prentice Hall, 1992.

Ozsu, M., and Valduriez, P. *Distributed Database Systems,* Prentice Hall, 1991.

Percy, A., "IBM Communicates an Ambitious Middleware Vision," *Gartner Group Research Note,* July 18, 1996.

Reid, G., "Interfacing to Legacy Systems," *Object Magazine,* October 1995, pp. 46–51.

Ricciuti, M., "Terabytes of Data—How to Get at Them," *Datamation,* August 1, 1992, pp. 39–43.

Richter, J., "Distributing Data," *Byte,* June 1994, pp. 139–145.

Roseen, J., "University of Florida Reengineers via the World Wide Web," *Data Based Adviser,* June 1996.

Rosenberg, A., "All Together Now: Voice Mail, Fax and Email," *Bell Communications Review,* November 1995, pp. 60–64.

Rymer, J., "Database Interoperability," Patricia Seybold Group's *Distributed Computing Monitor,* October 1992.

Schatz, W., "Hourly Loan Approval For $1000 Less," *Client/Server Journal, Computerworld,* special issue, June 1995, pp. 26–27.

Schick, K., "The Key to Client/Server—Unlocking the Power Legacy Systems," *Gartner Group Conference*, February 22–24, 1995.

Sheth, A., and Larson, J., "Federated Database Systems for Managing Distributed, Heterogeneous, and Autonomous Databases," *ACM Computing Surveys,* September 1990, pp. 183–236.

Shibley, R., "Massachusetts Motor Voter: Roadmap for Participatory Change," *Open Information Systems,* 1995, Vol. 11, No. 5, pp. 22–25.

Simpson, D., "Are Mainframes Cool Again?" *Datamation,* April 1994, pp. 46–53.

Sneed, H., "Planning the Reengineering of Legacy Systems," *IEEE Software,* January 1995, pp. 24–34.

Taylor, F., *The Principles of Scientific Management,* Harper & Bros., 1911.

Thomas, G., "Remote Database Access Service Concepts," Bellcore Special Report, December 1993.

Thomas, G., "Databases in Distributed Systems," ANSA User Group Meeting, Cambridge, England, April 1994.

Thomas, G., and Chen, W., "Accessing Mainframe Data from TCP/IP Networks via the DRDA Protocol," Bellcore TM-STS-023460, October 11, 1993.

Tucker, M., "Bridge Your Legacy Systems to the Web," *Datamation,* March 1997, pp. 114–121.

Umar, A., *Distributed Computing and Client/Server Systems,* Prentice Hall, 1993.

Umar, A., *Object-Oriented Client/Server Internet Environments,* Prentice Hall, 1997.

Umar, A., and Marchese, F., "Client/Server in Heterogeneous (MVS, UNIX, PCs, Macs) Environments: Initial Analysis Results," Bellcore Memorandum, October 1992.

Waterson, K., "The Changing World of EIS," *Byte,* June 1994, pp. 183–191.

Wiederhold, G., "Mediators in the Architecture of Future Information Systems," *IEEE Computer,* Vol. 25, 1992, pp. 38–49.

Winsberg, P., "Legacy Code: Don't Bag It, Wrap It," *Datamation,* May 15, 1995, pp. 36–41.

10

Data Warehouses

10.1   Introduction

Simply stated, a data warehouse is a repository of information (data) for decision support. Data warehousing, initially popularized by IBM as an "Information Warehouse," is receiving a great deal of industrial attention at present. Many conferences and seminars are devoted to the planning, development, and deployment of data warehouses. The Gartner Group predicted in 1994 that data warehousing would become a strategic imperative, widely embraced by enterprises [Strange 1994]. This prediction has more than materialized with the data warehousing industry skyrocketing to a multibillion dollar industry. An IDC survey conducted at the end of 1994 indicated that 10 percent of the companies surveyed expressed an interest in data warehouses. At the end of 1995, the same survey indicated that 90 percent of the companies were interested in data warehouses.[1] By the end of 1996, data warehouses have become a norm in IT organizations with the average Return On Investment (ROI) on data warehouse projects estimated at 400 percent within 2.3 years [Robinson 1997].

---

1. Opening Remarks, IDC Data Warehouse Conference, August 12–15, 1996, New York.

Key Points

- A data warehouse is a repository of information (data) for decision support.

- Data warehouses are being established in many organizations to provide access to operational data by creating a repository instead of providing "universal" access to operational data through mediators.

- Data warehouses should be developed quickly by using the commonly available relational database technologies and associated tool set. Once a small data warehouse has been successfully developed and deployed, additional databases and users should be added gradually.

- Vendors have started offering data marts (specialized departmental data warehouses) as prepackaged solutions that can be set up in 60 to 90 days. The prepackaged data marts include everything from server software to development and access tools to consulting services.

- Relational database technologies, especially exploiting the parallel databases, will continue to play a key role in the data warehouses of the future

- Data mining applications have the potential for a pivotal role in data warehousing because they utilize statistical analysis and pattern recognition techniques to answer business questions.

- Web access to data warehouses is a natural area of growth.

- The need to integrate and access semistructured data (messages, reports, documents, software artifacts) within the framework of a data warehouse will grow and will transition data warehouses into true information warehouses.

This chapter presents an overview of data warehouse concepts, technologies, and development/deployment issues. In particular, the following sections will attempt to answer questions such as

- What is a data warehouse?

- Why is a data warehouse needed?

- Who uses the data warehouse?

- What are the key characteristics of a data warehouse?

- What are the architectural choices in developing a data warehouse?

- What type of enabling technologies are needed for data warehousing?

- How can you plan, develop, and deploy a data warehouse?

- What is the current state of practice in data warehousing?

When to Develop Data Warehouses and When Not To: A Legacy System's View

Data warehousing is a viable approach for enterprise data access, that is, instead of using surround technology ("mediators") to access enterprise data, the needed data are extracted and loaded into a data warehouse. This is an especially potent option if the data to be accessed for decision support are embedded in older (legacy) data management technologies such as IMS, VSAM, and ISAM. In general, the performance of mediators that allow access to nonrelational databases for extensive decision support (e.g., spreadsheets, data browsers, report writers) is less than satisfactory. [Newman 1996, White 1995, Ricciuti 1992].

A data warehouse is, in general, a good approach to deal with legacy data access if

- Demand for ad hoc queries and analysis is very high.
- The needed data are used for decision support (it is easier to provide decision support through a data warehouse).
- The surround technology for access in place is not efficient and does not meet the requirements of new users.
- The data do not change frequently (in such cases, the data warehouse needs to be synchronized with the back-end system frequently).
- Needed data are embedded in too many legacy systems (it is difficult to directly access 30 or so data sources and perform joins among them, etc.).

Data warehouses are not a good choice if

- Demand for data is low (access in place is better in this case).
- Most recent copy of data is essential (data warehouses give somewhat outdated view).
- Data change frequently in the legacy sources.

In general, data warehouses are useful in their own right because they support the decision makers in organizations. We are discussing here the appropriateness of data warehouses as a solution to the legacy data access problem.

10.2   What Is a Data Warehouse?

10.2.1 Overview

As stated previously, a *data warehouse* is a repository of information (data) for decision support (i.e., queries and analysis). The notion of a data warehouse was first introduced by Barry Devlin and Paul Murphy [Devlin 1986] with statements such as the following:

> To ease access to the data..., it is vital that all the data reside in a single logical repository, the Business Data Warehouse.

This concept was commercialized by IBM as an "Information Warehouse" in 1991 (see IBM Programming Announcement, September 11, 1991; and "Information Warehouse: An Introduction," IBM Manual GC26-4876). The IBM Information Warehouse strategy provides for direct access to operational data maintained by on-line systems and promoted the notion of "universal data access." This strategy was supported by a variety of protocols and data access mechanisms to be supplied by a multitude of vendors. However, the complexity and inadequacy of accessing non-relational data such as IMS data from SQL-based tools deterred many implementations of the Information Warehouse.

The term "Data Warehouse" was popularized by Bill Inmon [Inmon 1993] to emphasize the separation of *operational data* (the data that are used for daily transaction processing) from *informational data* (data used primarily by decision support users such as executives, analysts, and line managers). In many ways, a data warehouse is being used as a modern term for a collection of reporting systems. Data warehouses are developed primarily for Decision Support Systems (DSSs) rather than the traditional On-Line-Transaction Processing (OLTP) systems.

Figure 10.1 shows a conceptual view of a data warehouse. The basic components of a data warehouse are as follows.

Warehouse database that contains information to support corporate decisions. This logical database is the centerpiece of a data warehouse and is typically partitioned and organized by subjects (subject-oriented databases to reflect customers, prices, products, etc.). The warehouse database may be distributed to several sites (most corporations at present have one centralized data warehouse database). This database is primarily used for retrieval and typically contains

- Summary information (lightly summarized or highly summarized)
- Detailed data
- Historical data

Data sources that are used to populate the data warehouse. These databases typically consist of operational databases but may also include many other data sources such as external databases (databases that are external to the enterprise) and unstructured data (e.g., memos and meeting minutes).

Extract program that is used to load the data warehouse. The extract program may populate the data warehouse periodically (e.g., every midnight) or due to an event trigger (e.g., every time a customer's payment is received, the extract program sends this information to the data warehouse).

Metadata (data about data) define the informational data contained in the warehouse in user and/or business terms. Metadata help the users to issue business-related queries without having to know the physical intricacies of the data. Metadata present a comprehensive data dictionary and other data description and access information, based on a single, integrated data model.

Figure 10.1 Conceptual View of a Data Warehouse

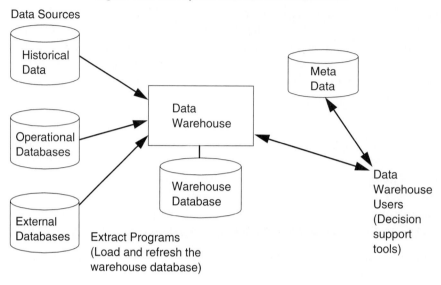

Users of data warehouses who employ a variety of decision support tools to access the data warehouse. Decision support tools typically include

- Report writers
- Data browsers
- Spreadsheets
- 4GL
- "Drill-down" applications
- Other planning and modeling tools

10.2.2 Definitions

*A **data warehouse*** is a repository of information for decision support.

*An **information warehouse*** is the same as a data warehouse.

*A **data mart*** is a regional data warehouse that may serve a region or a department of an organization.

Data sources are used as inputs to create a data warehouse. Data sources may be comprised of structured data (data stored in databases) or unstructured data (data contained in memos, diagrams, market reports, etc.).

Operational data are the data used to support the day-to-day operations of a company.

Informational data are the data used to support business decisions.

10.2.3 Examples

The following examples illustrate some sample data warehouses. We will describe more detailed examples in the section on case studies.

(1) A large bank pays $2 per card per month to VISA for the use of the VISA logo and services (i.e., $24 per year for every card holder) [Ferguson 1994]. The bank wanted to know

> How many VISA card holders from our bank did not use their VISA card last year?

The answer was 500,000. This meant that the bank paid $12 million to VISA for nothing (500,000 x 24 = 12 million). The bank canceled these customer cards and saved $12 million per year.

(2) A health care organization queries quarterly insurance claims for exceptions to the norm. The typical queries used are [Hott 1994]:

> Which doctors in California charge more than the national average for a broken leg procedure?
> Which doctors filed the largest number of claims during the last quarter?

A data warehouse answers these queries, resulting in improved cost monitoring.

(3) A materials director at Hughes Aircraft asked the following questions [Cooper 1994]:

> How many purchase orders were placed in 1991, 1992, and 1993 for the Sector, and what were the corresponding dollars?
> What are the top 10 purchased commodities and corresponding suppliers in the Sector?

The Hughes Aircraft operational data were spread over 8 computing platforms, interconnected through 7 types of networks, stored in 11 DBMSs, and owned by 630+ applications [Cooper 1994]. It was virtually impossible to answer these queries from the existing operational databases. A materials data warehouse was established with considerably improved materials management system.

(4) A retail department chain store tracks and analyzes sales by querying a store's data warehouse with questions such as the following [Hott 1994]:

> Which products in my store are selling most quickly?
> Which products stay in the inventory the longest?
> How does one store's profitability compare to the rest of the chain?

Answers to these queries help the retail store in establishing corporate directions.

(5) Many data warehouses are built around the concept of customer information for executive decisions. The example discussed in the sidebar "Importance of Customer Information: An Example Revisited" illustrates the issues raised for such an effort.

Importance of Customer Information: An Example Revisited

The following example of customer information was introduced in Chapter 5 as a sidebar and is based on the article "Cultivating An Information Culture: An Interview With Thomas Davenport," CIO, January 1995. Let us revisit this example from a data warehousing perspective.

An airline was flying a customer to Europe on business trips. The customer was not happy because he had lost his luggage a few times and the flights were typically late. So the customer stopped using the airline.

The airline did a lifetime profitability analysis of this customer and found that the airline had lost a potential $400,000 over the life of the customer (had he stayed with the airline). The airline also found out that there were several clues about his unhappiness (he had called the lost luggage department several times and had written complaint letters to the chairman),

Instead of developing a composite and complete profile of the customer history, each incident was treated separately and the customer was sent two free-drink coupons every time he complained.

What are the data warehousing implications of building a composite and complete customer information to avoid such situations. Here are the main ideas:

- A comprehensive data model with attributes to represent complete view of customer activities is needed.

- Access to information from different sources (luggage department, complaints department, flight information, etc.) is needed. Some of this information may be extracted and loaded into the data warehouse while other information may be just accessed from back-end systems (i.e., "virtual data warehouse").

- Powerful analysis tools including data mining are needed for studying the customer activities and cross relationships.

- Top management involvement is essential because individual departments may claim ownership of data (e.g., flight information)

10.3   Who Uses the Data Warehouse?

Data warehouses are primarily intended for a class of users we will call "decision support analysts" for a class of applications called Decision Support Systems (DSSs). A large body of management literature on decision support systems has accumulated since the mid 1980s (see, for example, the textbook by Turban [1993]). The focus of the decision support users is on informational data to drive the company and not on operational data to help in the day-to-day operation of a company. The users of data warehouses are typically business planners and strategists who issue queries such as illustrated in Table 10.1. Data Warehouse users ideally operate in an exploratory manner that is driven by the following principle [Peter Drucker, *Wall Street Journal,* December 1, 1992]:

Be Data Literate—Know What to Know

There are fundamental differences between the users of data warehouses and operational applications (see Table 10.2). The most important difference is that the DSS users operate in a discovery mode—they look at one piece of information to learn what additional pieces of information will be needed. The operational users are typically involved in the day-to-day operational systems such as order processing, purchasing, shipping, and inventory control. Due to this reason they tend to update data frequently and require an immediate response. In contrast, data warehouse users are usually managers and planners who browse through large quantities of data for ad hoc queries and forecasting applications that tolerate response delays.

Due to the differences in the users, the data characteristics of the decision support data are different from those of operational data (see Table 10.3). A data warehouse contains historical data that are summarized data, usually by subjects, for ease of queries. In many cases, the data warehouses are constructed from operational data by storing results of reports against operational data for later retrieval. In addition, data warehouses may contain additional information such as competitor data and unstructured data such as proposals, meeting minutes, and forecasting newsletters. In contrast, operational databases contain detailed data that are accessed and updated frequently to support the day-to-day business operations. The operational data are accessed by hundreds, and in many cases thousands, of workers who need subsecond response as compared to the warehouse data that are usually queried by a few users who can tolerate response time in the range of one to three minutes.

TABLE 10.1 EXAMPLES OF OPERATIONAL VERSUS DECISION SUPPORT QUERIES

Operational Queries	Decision Support Queries
How much credit is available to Mr. Jones?	Has Mr. Jones's credit limit increased in the last three years?
How many radios do we have on hand in the inventory?	What was the best month for radio sales?
How many claims did Dr. Dolittle file during the last month	Which doctors filed the largest number of claims during the last year?
What is the current salary of Sharon Walker?	How many raises has Sharon Jones gotten since she joined this company?

TABLE 10.2 OPERATIONAL VERSUS DECISION SUPPORT USERS

Operational Users	Decision Support (Data Warehouse) Users
Operate in predictable (nondiscovery) mode	Operate in discovery mode
Line workers and clerical	Decision makers and knowledge workers
High concurrency requirements	Low concurrency requirements
Update data frequently	Query data frequently
Stringent response time requirements	Relaxed response time requirements
Access small amount of data	Access large amounts of data

TABLE 10.3 CHARACTERISTICS OF OPERATIONAL VERSUS DECISION SUPPORT DATA

Operational Data	Decision Support Data (Informational Data)
Atomic (detailed)	Summarized
Application oriented	Subject oriented
Current, accurate as of the moment of access	Historical, represents values over time
Dynamic (updated frequently)	Static (updated infrequently)
Transaction driven	Analysis driven
Data updated in real time (no periodic reloads)	Data reloaded or updated periodically

10.4   Why Data Warehouses?

As corporations reduce the number of middle managers who generally provide and screen information, the remaining staff must be provided with a source of information needed to run the companies in the modern information-intensive competitive world. Some of this information is historical (archived) and the rest is embedded in the operational systems. However, operational data are not suitable for the ad hoc queries and analysis needed for decision support. Why? Here are some reasons [Poe 1996], [Radding 1995], and [Hackathorn 1995]:

- Access to operational data by a large number of users for reporting purposes, or even one user for a complex report, may interfere with the day-to-day operation of the on-line transaction processing applications.

- Operational data may be fragmented over multiple systems stored in diverse database managers requiring diverse access methods. In a large corporation, an analyst was assigned the task of producing a corporate report. He estimated three to five years with the following breakdown [Inmon 1993]:
    - To locate all data needed for the report: 9 to 12 months
    - To get access to the needed data: 15 to 24 months
    - To develop the report: Unknown effort

- Operational data may be legacy data that are embedded in IMS databases, flat files, and/or home-grown data management software. Access to legacy data through "surround" technologies such as database gateways for decision support is expensive and has serious performance implications.

- The reports generated from operational data are seldom developed in a manner where the next report can be developed from a previous report.

- Operational data do not include derived data such as summarized information and historical data typically needed by decision support users.

- Operational data do not typically include sophisticated indexes to quickly locate data for ad hoc access.

Because of these reasons, and the differences between the operational and decision support data discussed previously, most companies choose to build separate databases for warehousing applications. In addition, the following trends are facilitating separate data warehouses [Wright 1996], [Rist 1995], [Radding 1995], [Eckerson 1994], and [Strange 1994]:

- Transition to Client/Server. Many companies are building data warehouses to test the client/server systems. Data warehouses are being used as low-risk experiments with new technologies because many data warehouses are not mission critical.

- Cost Drivers. Due to the drop in the cost of disk drives and the maturity of relational database management systems (RDBMS) on mid-range computers, many companies are willing to store large amounts of data on UNIX-based RDBMSs for data warehousing purposes.

- Large Volumes of Data. Companies need to keep between five to ten years of historical data for accurate trends. These data, typically between 100 Gb (gigabyte) to 250 Gb are good candidates for data warehouses.

- Subject-Oriented Database Servers: A collection of subject-oriented database servers can be constructed and distributed to meet the needs of different user communities. For example, five different database servers for five different product lines can be developed instead of one large data warehouse. Subject-oriented databases are desirable for data warehouses and have become viable primarily due to the advances in client/server middleware.

● Integrated software. Many of the DSS packages for data warehousing are being linked to other work flow processes for increased end-user capabilities to take actions based on analysis. Some DSS tools are using OLE and other desktop application interface tools to link DSS applications with e-mail, spreadsheets, and other work flow packages.

10.5   Key Characteristics of a Data Warehouse

The key characteristics of a data warehouse are best defined in terms of the type of data stored in it and the tools to use the data.

10.5.1   Data Characteristics

Data in a data warehouse are [Inmon 1993]:

Subject oriented—the data are organized by subjects and not by applications. For example, operational systems for a retail store may be organized around order processing, purchasing, and sales. In a data warehouse, the data are organized by customers and products.

Integrated—different values and views are consolidated, that is, a single consistent view is created. For example, if credit limit is reflected as 10K or 10,000 in different operational systems, then one value, say 10K, is created in the warehouse.

Nonvolatile—the data in the warehouse are not modified.

Time variant—the data are summarized over a time horizon and time itself is usually represented in the data

In addition, the warehouse data are typically not mission critical. Moreover, the physical configuration of the data warehouse may be localized, centralized, or distributed.

Although data warehouses contain many important pieces of data, data warehouses should not be used for auditing purposes because they do not contain the complete picture (many fields to be audited may exist only in operational databases).

10.5.2   Tool Characteristics

Data warehouse tools are generally known as decision support tools. Basically, decision support tools are intended to help in setting business directions and fall into the following general categories.

Data Query and Reporting Tools. Data query and reporting tools provide a wide range of capabilities for decision support analysts. Typical capabilities of these tools include

● User screens that prompt users to type SQL statements and display results on the screen

● Point-and-click formulation of SQL statements.

Warehouses and the Web: A Good Marriage or a Meaningless Relationship?

Most data warehousing vendors at the time of this writing are announcing Web access to data warehouses (see Raden [1996] for examples). Is this a good match? The answer is yes for reasons such as the following:

- Web browsers are ubiquitous. Employees, customers, and business partners can access the information over the Internet or the Intranet by using Web browsers.

- The cost of Web browsers is negligible as compared to data warehouse access tools such as OLAP clients.

- The network cost and support can be uniform and can be outsourced.

- The issues of infrastructure compatibility and application access are minimized (everything needs to be compatible with a Web browser).

Due to these, and several other similar reasons that have made the Web popular, Web access to data warehouses should become a norm shortly. The issue of security needs to be addressed. The techniques to access warehouses from the Web are typically the following:

- Use Web browsers to invoke a CGI script that accesses the data warehouses and analyzes the results before sending them back to the browsers.

- Use Java applets that access the warehouse and then produce the analysis, charts, and mining pattern recognition at the browser site.

For most data warehouse applications the Java-based approach is much more appealing than the CGI-based tools because raw data are brought to the browser site and charts/diagrams/analysis are constructed and performed at the browser site.

- Query by Form (QBF) that displays a form that a user fills in. This form generates a SQL statement that is executed and displayed by the DBMS.

- Query by Example (QBE) that displays tables that the user can fill in multiple rows with examples of the desired data.

- Reporting and display capabilities for hard copies as well as different types of display devices.

A large body of query tools, report writers, and 4GL tools at present provide these capabilities. A significant class of these tools allow users to build SQL queries by pointing and clicking on a list of tables and fields in the database. Most of these tools are targeted for "power" users who understand relational database concepts. Examples of tools in this category are the common RDBMS tools, Q+E from Q+E Software, and Data Prism from Brio.

Logical Viewing and Presentation Tools. Instead of operations on tables, these tools present a logical or business-oriented view of data (e.g., customer object) and generate SQL queries based on operations on these objects. The results from these queries are also presented logically (sometimes through icons). In addition, these tools may hide the details of joins between tables from the end users. Some tools in this category (e.g., Business Objects) present the views by creating end-user-oriented aliases for tables and fields and then present these aliases through graphical objects. Other tools, such as MicroStrategy, may create metadata that identify the contents and the location of the data in the warehouse.

Executive Information Systems (EIS). These tools provide analysis capabilities that are tailored for executive decisions. A typical example of EIS is "drill-down" tools that allow executives to start at summary information and successively look at the details that make up the summary information. For example, an executive may first query a high-level information item (e.g., the total travel expense for the entire organization in 1997). The executives then "drills-down" to lower levels of details to understand what contributed to this expense. For example, if the travel expenses for 1994 were too high, then the executive would keep drilling-down until the main department or individual who is traveling too much is found. In addition to drill-down analysis, modern EIS tools offer analytical applications along functional lines such as financial analysis and sales and allow ad hoc queries against multidimensional databases, trend analysis, and detection. Other examples of EIS are problem monitoring and competitive analysis. Examples of EIS are Comshare's Commander and Pilot Software's Lightship. For a state-of-the-market review of EIS tools, see King [1996], Decker [1996], Ricciuti [1994], and Waterson [1994]. The sidebar "Intelligent Executive Information Systems" shows the integration of artificial intelligence and the Internet on EISs.

Intelligent Executive Information Systems

Developments in artificial intelligence and the Internet are being integrated into Executive Information Systems (EISs). The classic EISs have been based around drill-down applications. However, EISs have been gradually integrating desktop tools, groupware, and data warehouses. Now the Internet and intelligent agents are finding their place in EIS tools. The main trend is to replace a single drill-down tool with a collection of Web-based tools that employ analytical as well as AI tools operating around data warehouses and the general Internet resources. For example, modern EISs can include intelligent, autonomous, software agents to search for changes in data of interest to executives and identify patterns. These data may be located in the data warehouse, operational databases, or the public Internet.

The emphasis of intelligent agents for EISs should be more on organizational agents instead of personal agents, that is, a collection of interacting agents that know about the organizational rules and policies. These agents should have the capabilities to filter through e-mail, organize the results of search on the Internet, monitor news findings, issue queries to the data warehouses, support dialogs with the executives, and exploit the capabilities of the Internet to establish communications between groups of managers.

Sources: [King 1996], [Sauter 1997], and [Simon 1996].

Why Data Warehouses Are So Hot:
Promises and Pitfalls

Data warehouses are based on a very simple idea: If you need data, extract them and download to a site where you can easily access them. This extraction principle is especially appealing if you need to access data that are spread over different sites. In essence, data warehouses are popular because of the failure of the highly touted distributed database management technology [Simon 1996]. The legacy access middleware, discussed in the previous chapter, also has scaling and performance problems. Thus the organizations that desperately need access to data at different sites for decision analysis have accepted this extraction and access principle. After some initial problems, the data warehousing industry has matured significantly with solid return on investments. For example, an IDC survey conducted at the end of 1996 indicates that the average Return On Investment (ROI) on data warehouse projects was 400 percent within 2.3 years [Robinson 1997].

Promises and pitfalls of data warehouses have been debated for a while. For example, one of the earliest surveys, was conducted by Database Associates International in July 1993. This survey, based on feedback from 35 organizations implementing data warehouses, indicated that the key benefits of a data warehouse are (the number in parenthesis shows how many organizations chose the indicated key benefit):

- Better access to information (20)

- Better data quality (19)

- Competitive advantage (14)

- Reduce costs/increase productivity with IS (12)

- Empower user to directly access corporate data (12)

- Better performance and availability of informational and operational systems (3)

- Leverage existing client/server environment (3)

The obvious disadvantage of data warehousing is that it increases the duplication of data throughout an enterprise. Other risks and issues related to data warehouses are

- Cost justification

- Hardware, software, and staffing costs

- Education and training of the end user

- Management support

- Managing expectations of users and management

- Increased complexity due to duplicate data

Online Analytical Processing (OLAP). This class of tools was introduced by E. F. Codd to emphasize the analytical aspects of decision support tools [Codd 1993]. These tools are optimized for dynamic, multidimensional analysis of consolidated enterprise data for analytical functions such as forecasting. The main characteristics of OLAP tools are

- Data drill-down and data pivoting in multiple dimensions
- Complex calculations
- Immediate response
- Multiuser, client/server environment

E. F. Codd has proposed 12 rules of OLAP (see Table 10.4). The most important aspect of these 12 rules is the emphasis on multidimensionality (rules 1, 6, 9, 12). To support multidimensional analysis, multidimensional databases have been proposed. These databases extend the scope of relational databases (two-dimensional databases) to three dimensions and more. For example, the following three dimensions can be used for a sales database:

- Products
- Sales by month
- Sales by regions

A multidimensional database can efficiently store this information and allow three-dimensional analysis of this information (e.g., show product sales by regions, show product sales by month, show product sales by month and by region, etc.). More details about OLAP can be found in Codd [1993], Dorrian [1994], and Waterson [1994].

An area of considerable work is Web-based OLAP. The approaches to develop OLAP applications for the Web include off-line conversion of OLAP results to HTML, populating HTML templates with OLAP data on the fly, and Java applets/ActiveX components supporting OLAP. The Java/ActiveX approach is more appealing due to its flexibility and performance. Web-based OLAP tools are commercially available from vendors such as Arbor Software. A detailed discussion of Web-based OLAP can be found in Carickhoff [1997].

TABLE 10.4 THE 12 RULES OF OLAP (E.F. CODD)

1. Multidimensional conceptual view
2. Transparency
3. Accessibility
4. Consistent reporting performance
5. Client/server architecture
6. Generic dimensionality
7. Dynamic, sparse matrix handling
8. Multiuser support
9. Unrestricted cross-dimensional calculations
10. Intuitive data manipulation
11. Flexible reporting
12. Unlimited dimensions/aggregation levels

Data Mining. These tools use artificial-intelligence-based pattern recognition technologies in their data search algorithms or data visualization techniques to enable human pattern recognition. Data mining tools are more powerful than the traditional EIS tools that do little to recognize hidden relationships within data and have difficulties with elusive patterns. The coupling of artificial intelligence capabilities with decision support applications is an interesting area of future growth. See the sidebars "Mining the Data Warehouses" and "Sources of Information for Data Mining" for additional information.

10.6   Data Warehouse Architectures

The data warehouse view presented in Figure 10.1 is conceptual. In practice, the data warehouse can be architected in a variety of ways as shown in Figure 10.2 through Figure 10.4.

10.6.1 Localized Functional Warehouses ("The Data Marts")

The localized data warehouses, also known as the "data marts," are typically created by individual departments or divisions to support their own decision support activities (see Figure 10.2). These data marts may be created to support specific products (e.g., automobile parts) or functions (e.g., loan management) of individual departments, divisions, or regions. In some cases, data marts may be created for user populations with the same technical environments. For example, separate data warehouses for PC users, for UNIX users, and for MVS users could be created [Strange 1994].[2]

Figure 10.2 : Localized Data Warehouses (The Data Marts)

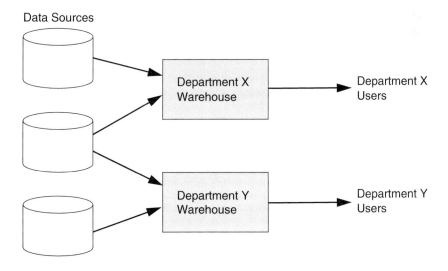

---

2. This option is not recommended because it leads to islands of technologies and should be used very rarely.

Mining the Data Warehouses

Data mining tools exploit a combination of AI and statistical analysis to discover information that is hidden or not apparent through typical query and analysis tools. Traditional database query tools are used to supply answers to simple questions, such as "How many VCRs were sold in New York during December?" OLAP (on-line analytical processing) tools go a step beyond the query tools and answer questions, such as, "compare sales relative to targets by region for the last three years." Data mining steps go further by finding patterns and inferring rules. Specifically, the data mining tools use a variety of underlying technologies such as neural networks, decision trees, statistical analysis, and machine learning to detect

- Associations (e.g., linking purchase of pizzas with beer)

- Sequences (e.g., tying events together such as marriage and purchase of furniture)

- Classifications (e.g., recognizing patterns such as the attributes of customers who will discontinue doing business with you)

- Forecasting (e.g., predicting future buying habits of customers based on past patterns)

Data mining has become a major growth area for data warehouses—a Meta Group report indicates that data mining tools and services will reach $800 million by the year 2000 [Wilson 1996]. Although the basic mining algorithms have been around for several years, the availability of massive amounts of corporate data in data warehouses have provided a rich field for these tools to mine. Data warehouses contain integrated, detailed, summarized, and historical data that can be mined to discover patterns of sales, customer buying habits, Lifetime Value (LTV) of customers, new customers likely to buy new products, demands on inventory, correlations between opening new stores and product sales, and so forth.

Although some capabilities provided by data mining can be provided by OLAP, the distinguishing feature of data mining is *knowledge discovery*, that is, data mining arrives at insights *automatically*. For example, suppose you have noticed a drop in the sales of your product and you want to know what the cause is. In most traditional analytical tools, you have to first form a hypothesis (e.g., product sales may be related to a price increase), translate your hypothesis into queries, and interpret/understand the results of the queries. A data mining tool, on the other hand, will scan the data warehouse and discover the correlations between product sales and other factors that you might have not thought about (sales might have dropped due to a competitor product, assuming this information is in the warehouse). The long-range goal of data miners is to behave in a manner similar to "military intelligence" (i.e., gathering useful information from snapshots, notes, maps, observations).

Sources of Information for Data Mining

Anand, S., et al., "EDM: General Framework for Data Mining Based on Evidence Theory," *Data and Knowledge Engineering Journal,* April 1996, pp. 184–224.

Brachman, R., "Mining Business Databases," *Communications of the ACM,* November 1996, pp. 42–48.

DePompa, B., "There's Gold in Databases," *Information Week,* January 8, 1996, pp. 52–54.

Edelstein, H., "Mining Data Warehouses," *Information Week,* January 8, 1996, pp. 48–51.

Inmon, W., "The Data Warehouse and Data Mining," *Communications of the ACM,* November 1996, pp. 49–51.

Mena, J., "Mining The Warehouse," *Data Management Review,* January 1997, pp. 41–45.

Parsaaye, K., "OLAP and Data Mining: Bridging the Gap," *Database Programming and Design,* February 1997, pp. 30–37.

Reeves, L., "Data Mining," *Data Management Review,* July-August 1995, pp. 92–94.

Communications of the ACM, November 1996, is a special issue on data mining and contains eight technical papers that explore different aspects of data mining (e.g., knowledge extraction, statistical inference, mining business databases, mining scientific databases, and mining data warehouses). Data mining heavily utilizes the AI work in knowledge discovery [Imielinki 1996], [Frawley 1992], [Matheus 1993], and [Piatetsky-Shapiro 1992].

The source data for these data marts usually come from the department's/region's operational databases. A small portion of the local warehouse data may come from "external" databases from other departments/divisions and companies. Once created, there is no coordination between the different data warehouses, even though the stand-alone data warehouses may submit data to the corporate site for consolidation and global reporting. The data in each stand-alone data warehouse are not likely to be consistent with corporate data or with data in other stand-alone data warehouses. This is primarily due to the differences in focus, level of detail, and end-user interests.

The primary advantage of data marts is that they can be developed quickly to serve the local needs without having to wait for the large corporate data warehouse. The obvious disadvantage is the proliferation of data warehouses that are not consistent with each other. In practice, stand-alone data marts can be used by organizations with very independent and "nonintersecting" departments as a starting point in an overall strategy for a centralized corporate data warehouse.

Data marts have become very big business because vendors have started offering data marts as prepackaged solutions that can be set up in 60 to 90 days. The prepackaged data marts include everything from server software to development and access tools to consulting services. The vendors such as IBM, Red Brick, Sybase, Oracle, and SAS Institute are offering data marts ranging in cost between $20,000 to $200,000 with a return on investment in the range of 400 percent [Robinson 1997].

10.6.2 Centralized Data Warehouse

The centralized data warehouse approach, shown in Figure 10.3, is the most common approach to building a data warehouse. This approach, popularized by IBM's Information Warehouse, advocates a large centralized warehouse database that adheres to a single, consistent enterprise data model. All operational and external data are copied and stored in the central data warehouse. The central warehouse may be used to populate individual data marts for improved performance and ease of access.

Figure 10.3 Centralized Data Warehouse

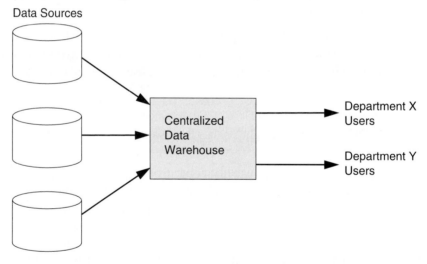

The primary advantage of this architecture is that the same consistent and complete data are utilized by all users. The users need to logon to one environment and are thus freed from having to worry about data stored in different platforms and environments (see the British Telecom case study later in this chapter). This approach also works well for enterprises where most of the processing is done at the corporate site. The main drawback of the centralized data warehouse is that it is very difficult to develop a global data model for most organizations (imagine building a global data model for General Motors!). It is also difficult to agree on a corporatewide level of detail and naming conventions. Organizations must also carefully manage the performance and end-user access to centralized warehouses to ensure that the users continue to rely on the centralized data warehouse.

This architecture is commonly implemented on MVS-DB2 platforms. IBM's Information Warehouse supports a variety of tools to support the centralized data warehouse approach. Examples of the Information Warehouse tools are

- Data Replication Server that extracts DB2 data by "scraping" the change logs and then sends the replicated data to target databases. The Replication Server extracts the data from logs based on some criterion (e.g., collect all changes made to a table after commit of each transaction).

- Data Propagator Relational, a set of copy tools that copy data to/from the DB2 family of products.

- Data Guide, a global data catalog, that allows end users to look up reports, queries, tables, files, and attributes.

- Visualizer Family of products for data query and data analysis, including multimedia information.

10.6.3   Distributed Data Warehouses ("The Virtual Warehouse")

Many data warehouses can be distributed in an enterprise in a manner similar to the file and database servers. These distributed data warehouses (distributed data marts) can be accessed by the end users through a "warehouse front end" as shown in Figure 10.4. The front end, a "data warehouse mediator," usually contains a global data dictionary that knows the location and format of the needed data and how to send the queries to the final destination. In some cases, the front end can send the requests directly to the operational databases, thus eliminating the need for some data warehouses. This approach also allows the creation of a *"virtual" data warehouse* that simply routes the user queries to the following data sources:

- Operational databases for detailed information

- Archival databases for historical analysis

- Data warehouses for highly and lightly summarized data

The virtual data warehouses essentially employ the read-only capabilities of distributed data management technology [Simon 1996]. Ideally, the virtual data warehouse should have the intelligence to automatically migrate the data from the data sources to the data warehouse. You can thus start with a small version of a data warehouse that automatically grows with use as needed data is transferred to it gradually. The data in the virtual data warehouses may be uniquely assigned or may be partially duplicated to improve performance and availability. A global corporate data warehouse can play a key role in this architecture. It can contain data that are common across the corporation. It may feed the local warehouses or may also be fed by local data warehouses.

Distributed data warehouses provide many benefits in terms of flexibility, performance, scaling, and load balancing. The main appeal of the distributed data warehouse is that it can be designed to match the topology of most organizations, that is, a corporate data warehouse at the corporate site and regional data warehouses (the data marts) at the branch offices. In this case, all local queries go to the regional data warehouses and all corporate queries go to the corporate data warehouse. In addition, different data marts may employ different technologies, for example, one data mart may use a specialized DBMS suitable for one type of subject.

Figure 10.4 Distributed Data Warehouse ("Virtual Data Warehouse")

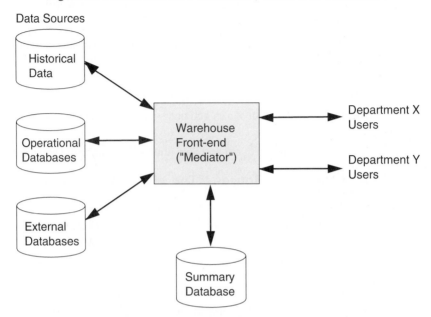

A potential disadvantage of this approach is that a global data model may still be needed to populate the warehouse front end. In addition, if the databases to be accessed through the front end are widely distributed, then significant performance degradation and service outages can occur. In general, distributed data warehouse design is complicated and requires considerable trade-offs in data distribution and query optimization such as:

- What data should be allocated where? Specifically,
    - What data should be kept in the corporate warehouse?
    - What data should be accessed directly from operational databases?
    - What data should be kept at the data marts?
- What queries should be routed to the corporate warehouse? The major options are
    - Route the queries for most recent information
    - Route for performance

These issues belong to the general class of distributed database design problems and will be discussed in the next chapter.

The distributed data warehouse approach is supported by the Hewlett-Packard Intelligent Warehouse. This product allows access to operational databases and also provides a metadata catalog. IBM supports distributed data warehouses by providing a warehouse front end (DataHub) and synchronization/refreshment of data between operational and data warehouse databases by a work-flow tool (Flowmark).

Operational Data Warehouses

Most data warehouses at present are developed for decision support (i.e., primarily read-only historical and summarized data for analysis and planning). These data can be out of synchronization with their data sources. However, in some business cases, there is a need for near-instantaneous access to the most recent operational data.

Operational data warehouses, also known as Operational Data Stores (ODSs), are intended to address this need. Ideally, these warehouses should store operational data to provide instantaneous access to end users. In practice, however, most vendors at present support ODSs by providing data extraction and load capabilities that extract source data changes as soon as they become effective and apply them to the ODS as soon as possible. In many cases, this involves "enabling" the source applications for this data exchange. Message-Oriented Middleware (MOM) is a commonly used technology in this arena.

10.7   Data Warehouse Design Issues

Design of a data warehouse involves a wide range of issues that include common database design activities such as database modeling, database normalization/denormalization, and database structure design. It is beyond the scope of this book to discuss the common database design activities. Interested readers should review the book, *Database Modeling and Design: The Fundamental Principles,* by Toby Teorey [Teorey 1994].

In this section, we discuss the issues that are somewhat unique to data warehouse design. In particular, we will attempt to answer the following:

- How to determine the granularity of data in the warehouse database
- How to partition the warehouse database
- How to design the database structures for warehousing

10.7.1 Granularity

Granularity refers to the level of detail. This is an extremely important issue in the design of a data warehouse because coarse granularity means less data and fine granularity means more data in the warehouse. The volume of data increases the disk space requirements, the number of indexes to be used, and the processor resources needed to manipulate the data. In addition, granularity greatly impacts the query capabilities of a warehouse. If the granularity is too coarse, then some queries requiring details cannot be generated from the warehouse, but if the granularity is too fine, then the performance of queries requiring summaries may degrade. Granularity forces a trade-off between the volume of data and the query capabilities. The following example, derived from Inmon [1993], illustrates the trade-offs.

In a telephone company, each phone call is recorded. Assuming 200 calls per month per customer and 100 bytes per record, 20,000 bytes per customer will accumulate per month. For a community of 100,000 customers, 20 million records would be accumulated per month and 2 gigabytes (Gb) of disk space would be utilized if each call record is stored in the data warehouse (low-level granularity). However, if a monthly summary record were created per customer in a data warehouse, then only 100,000 records would be created, requiring disk space of 20 million bytes (assuming 200 bytes per customer record per month). Table 10.5 summarizes the main trade-offs between coarse and fine granularity.

TABLE 10.5 IMPACT OF GRANULARITY ON WAREHOUSE DATA

Granularity	Records per Month	Record Size (bytes)	Number of Customers	Total Number of Records per Month	Total Size
Fine (each call is recorded)	200	100	100,000	20,000,000	2,000,000,000
Coarse (one summary record per month)	1	200	100,000	100,000	20,000,000

Now consider the following query:

> Did Warner call 313-555-2020 (his mother's phone number in Michigan) during the month of December?

The fine granularity warehouse will be always able to answer this question, albeit after thousands of I/Os (unless the right index is in place). However the monthly summary will not be able to answer this query unless each destination number called is somehow embedded in the summary record (not easily doable in a 200-byte record). Thus, the creation of summary records requires a great deal of thought and foresight.

Due to this difficulty in deciding the granularity and the expected impact on the data warehouse performance, it is common to design data warehouses with multiple levels of granularity. In the most general case, the following levels of granularity should be considered as a default for a warehouse:

- Detailed data for very short time periods (e.g., the current month). These data can be directly accessed from an operational system if feasible.

- Lightly summarized data for mid-range time horizons (e.g., the current year). These data, for example, could have one record per customer for each month of activity.

- Highly summarized data for longer horizons (e.g., the last two to three years). These data, for example, could have one record per customer for each quarter of a year.

- Historical archival data for very long horizons (e.g., more than the last three years). These data are usually archived to other media such as magnetic tapes and stored in off-site locations for disaster recovery. These data should rarely be accessed more than 5 percent. If accessed more frequently, this data could also be summarized and could have one record per customer for each year

In addition to these data, some "living sample" databases may exist in an enterprise. These databases are usually created for specialized statistical analysis and are extracted from archival data with some summary information added for statistical analysis. For example, a living sample database may be created for all the customers who live in Georgia when a company wants to rethink its business strategy in Georgia. These databases, in general, cannot be used for general-purpose decision support analysis.

The following pragmatic approach is suggested for handling the issue of granularity [Wright 1996], [Devlin 1994], and [Inmon 1993]:

- Develop a raw estimate of the number of rows of data and the disk space requirements of the data warehouse assuming that detailed data will be captured.
- If this requirement is manageable (100,000 rows or less), then build the data warehouse; else continue with the following steps.
- Concentrate on building a small, lightly summarized database in the warehouse.
- Determine the content of lightly summarized data by working with a few, even one, DSS analyst.
- Provide access mechanisms to the operational data when the lightly summarized data cannot handle the query (this is the "escape ratio" of the warehouse—the number of queries that had to go somewhere else to be satisfied).
- Be prepared to make adjustments quickly, learn from others, and do quick prototyping experiments if feasible.
- Closely monitor the queries and the escape ratios and work with the DSS analysts to understand what is going on.
- Gradually add more information in the warehouse, redesign the summary information, and add highly summarized data where needed. Pay particular attention to data warehouse escape ratios. In a well-designed data warehouse, the escape ratio should be less than 5 percent.

10.7.2 Partitioning (Fragmentation)

Partitioning, also known as fragmentation, refers to the breakup of data into separate physical units that can be managed independently. Each partition can be allocated to a dedicated database server machine and used as a data mart. The partitioning of data can be based on criteria such as

- geography,
- date,
- product type,
- numbers (e.g., first 200 items in physical unit 1, second 200 items in physical unit 2, etc.)
- organizational unit, or
- a mixture of the above.

For example, the following partitions may be created for a General Motors dealer data warehouse:

- Buick dealers in Florida
- Buick dealers in Michigan
- Buick dealers in California
- Chevrolet dealers in Florida
- Chevrolet dealers in Michigan
- Chevrolet dealers in California
- 1994 Chevrolet dealers
- 1995 Chevrolet dealers
- 1996 Buick dealers
- 1997 Buick dealers

The choice depends on the data warehouse architecture being chosen. For example, partitioning by geography and by organizational unit is more suitable for a localized or distributed data warehouse architecture. Partitioning by date is more suitable for a centralized data warehouse architecture, and partitioning by product type can lead to subject-oriented databases.

Most of the partitioning choices can be based on common sense, rules of thumb, and heuristics. Formal partitioning and clustering techniques based on statistical analysis (e.g. "clumping" discussed by Everret [1974]) and similarities based on fuzzy logic (e.g., "fusion" discussed by Negoita [1985]) have been published in the literature to represent the business entities that are needed in the data warehouse. We reviewed these techniques in an earlier chapter (Chapter 5).

10.7.3 Data Structures

The data in a warehouse are typically structured in one of the following manners:

- Simple cumulative. In this case the data in the warehouse are summarized by day, that is, activity by day 1, day 2, day 3, and so forth. The data warehouse loading program extracts all activity during a day, say by customer, and summarizes it for loading into the data warehouse.

- Rolling summary. This is a variation of the simple cumulative. This structure includes weekly, monthly, and yearly summary information in addition to the daily activity.

- Snapshot data. This structure directly represents the operational data that are not formatted or summarized before being loaded into the data warehouse.

- Cumulative snapshot data. The snapshot data from different operational databases may be merged and accumulated before being loaded into the data warehouse.

The simple cumulative approach is used most frequently and is a good starting point in designing the data structures for a data warehouse. The rolling summaries and snapshot data can be added gradually. In addition to these data structures, warehouse database structures need to be defined for efficient data access (e.g., indexing, denormalization, and joins need to be defined). Details of data structure design for data warehouse databases can be found in Poe [1996], Inmon [1995], Inmon [1993], and Teorey [1994].

10.8   Technologies for Data Warehousing

In the simplest case, a data warehouse can be created by loading a database (typically a relational database) and then accessing it by using commercially available report writers, data browsers, and spreadsheets. For a more realistic data warehouse, technologies need to be selected for

- Extraction and loading of data
- Database engine(s)
- Metadata facilities
- Data access technologies

10.8.1   Data Extraction and Loading Software

10.8.1.1   Basic Principles

The data extraction and loading software extracts needed data from source databases (operational systems, archival data, and external data sources) and populates the target data warehouse(s). The data are extracted and loaded initially into the data warehouse when the data warehouse is first created and afterwards to reflect the "deltas" of changes in the source data. Typical data extraction and loading software consists of the functionalities shown in Figure 10.5.

- **Selection (filtering) of needed data from the source databases.** This selection can be triggered by a schedule (e.g., every midnight) or by an event (e.g., update of some critical fields). The selection can be achieved through a predefined SQL statement for an RDBMS source database, or through a COBOL program, or through a 4GL tool such as Focus.

- **Transformation of data.** This includes the following data transformations before loading into the data warehouse:

    - Consolidation of data to present unified format, definition, and value. For example, a customer's credit limit may be represented as $12000, 12K, or 12,000. This program will choose one data format for the customer credit limit and store it in the warehouse.

    - Summarization. The data may be lightly or highly summarized before loading into the warehouse. In the simplest case, summarized data are generated by running SQL queries and storing their results in the warehouse. For example, if a company wants to analyze the monthly sale patterns, then the summarizing software would add up the sales and revenues generated by each product by month and store them in the data warehouse for ease of access. However, customized summary data may be generated by the extraction/load software.

    - Derivation. New data warehouse fields may also be derived by using other mathematical formulas such as averages, minimums, maximums, means, and standard deviations.

    - Conversion. Data from a source data format (e.g., IMS) may be converted to a target data format (e.g., relational). In many cases, the data are converted into a format that is acceptable for load utility at the data warehouse.

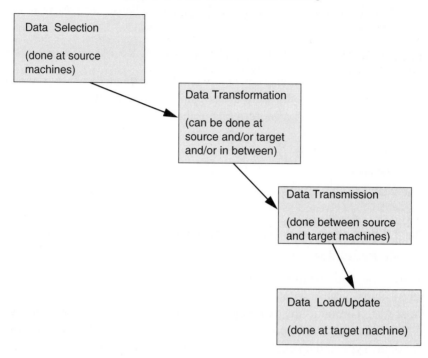

Figure 10.5 Data Extraction and Loading

- **Transmission of the data to the target site(s).** This is typically accomplished through bulk data transfer software, provided by almost all vendors. File Transfer Protocol (FTP), a bulk data transfer software package that operates in TCP/IP networks, is used most frequently for transferring files between heterogeneous computers (MVS, UNIX, PC-DOS, Mac) due to the popularity of TCP/IP. In some cases (e.g., the Platinum Data Warehouse tools), the data transmission between targets and sources is in real time by using a client/server paradigm. For example, the selected records may be sent to the data warehouse one at a time and processed before the next record is sent.

- **Data load/update.** The data are loaded in the data warehouse. The data warehouse database may be replaced entirely with the new data (*refreshed*) or selected values may be updated to reflect changes (*deltas*). Depending on the amount of data to be loaded, special techniques may be used to speed up the load process (e.g., bulk database load).

A variety of database extraction and load software is currently in use. Many companies have developed in-house tools for data extraction and loading. However, some off-the-shelf products such as the Prism Warehouse Manager from Prism Solutions, Extract Tool Suite from ETI, and Passport from Carleton are commercially available. In addition, many "replication servers" also provide the functionality needed for database extraction and loading [Fradkov 1996], [Stacey 1994], [Leinfuss 1993], and [Korzeniowski 1993]. The replication servers are in Umar [1997, Chapter 6]. A state-of-the-market review of the various data extraction and loading software can be found in Griffin [1996], [Wilson 1996], [Eckerson 1994], and [Kimball 1996].

Quality of Data Warehouses

The quality of data warehouses, that is, their accuracy (reflects correctness to real life), consistency (two or more things do not conflict with each other), currency (how recent is the information), and completeness (degree to which values are present in a data collection) is becoming of vital importance as organizations rely more and more on data warehouses. In one sense the issues of data quality in data warehouses are similar to other corporate databases (i.e., they involve data as well as process cleanup approaches). There are several unique issues such as the following:

- Quality of data as well as quality of metadata are important.

- Historical records usually do not have metadata (many changes have occurred).

- Data are not current—created through multiple sources of multiple vintages.

- Data "good enough" for operational systems may not be good enough for decision support (e.g., service order flowthrough analysis).

- Most problems occur for large and actively used information (e.g., customer information).

- A single, common key is needed for each entity in the warehouse.

- Data refreshes can (should be) be used for initial and periodic cleanups (e.g., reconciliation).

- Data life cycle can be assumed to start from warehouse load.

- Data should not change once they are in the warehouse.

Sources for additional information:

Bowen, B., "IT and Business Analysts Cooperate in Effective Data Warehouse Endeavors," *Client/Server Computing,* December 1995, pp. 72–78.

Burch, G., "Data Quality & Data Mining," *Data Management Review,* January 1997, pp. 22–33.

Celko, J., and McDonald, J., "Don't Warehouse Dirty Data," *Datamation,* October 15, 1995.

English, L., "Data Quality of Data Warehouses," *IDC Data Warehouse Conference,* August 1996.

10.8.1.2 Factors to Evaluate and Select Data Extraction and Loading Software

In order to choose data extraction and loading software, the following factors must be considered:

- Automatic code generation for extract programs in different languages (e.g., COBOL, C, PL1).

- Ability to extract, filter, transform, integrate, summarize and load data from a very diverse array of operational databases.

- Scalability to handle increased volume of data.

- Ability to capture the "delta" changes in the source databases based on a triggering mechanism.

- Bidirectional extract support so that the changes in data warehouses (if any) can also also submitted to the operational databases.

- Data transfer and loading times needed for high-volume bulk load.

- System administration capabilities to monitor and control the schedules of extractions and database loads.

- Cost, multiplatform support, and vendor support.

10.8.2   Database Engine

A DBMS is the main engine of a data warehouse. Relational database management systems (RDBMSs) are particularly suited for data warehouses. This is primarily due to the following reasons: the wide range of SQL-based DSS tools available in the market, the user-based and widespread experience with RDBMS technology in corporations, and the gradual improvement of RDBMS performance for heavy workloads. Most data warehouses at present are being developed around relational database management systems (RDBMSs). Many of the commercially available RDBMSs such as DB2, Informix, Oracle, and Sybase have been used in data warehouses.

Although RDBMS technology serves well as the database engine for a data warehouse, the following additional features are highly desirable:

- Support for storage and retrieval of unstructured data such as documents, graphics, and pictures. This support is currently available as BLOBs (Binary Large Objects) in most RDBMSs.

- Facilities for parallel query processing (see Section 10.8.2.1).

- Efficient storage and retrieval of multidimensional (e.g., three dimensional spreadsheets) information.(see Section 10.8.2.2).

- Capabilities for large index searches (see Section 10.8.2.3).

10.8.2.1   Parallel Databases and Parallel Query Processing

These databases exploit parallel processing hardware to maximize the DBMS performance. Parallel processing hardware at present falls into the following broad categories (see Figure 10.6):

- Shared memory, shared disk: In this configuration, multiple CPUs share the same memory space and disks.

- Shared disk: In this case, multiple parallel CPUs and memory units share the same disk.

- Shared connection: In this case, completely independent computers share a network connection. This is an example of distributed computing.

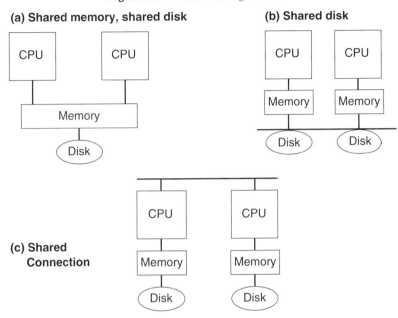

Figure 10.6 Parallel Configurations

Different RDBMSs have been designed to take advantage of these hardware configurations. In general, the parallel DBMSs that exploit shared-connection parallel architecture are well suited for data warehousing applications because complex SQL queries can be broken into small subqueries and each subquery can run in parallel on completely independent machines. For example, consider the following query:

> Produce the total sales of life insurance policies sold to senior citizens in the last three years.

This query could run much faster if it were subdivided into three subqueries (one for each year) and shipped to three databases (one for each year) on three parallel DBMSs with a shared connection.

A detailed discussion of this topic is beyond the scope of this book. Commercially available parallel DBMSs from different vendors such as IBM, Sybase, Oracle, Informix, and others with their suitability for data warehousing applications are discussed by Ferguson [1994]. A discussion of server hardware for data warehousing can be found in Appleton [1995].

10.8.2.2 Multidimensional Databases

Typically, a multidimensional database is a three-dimension spreadsheet. These databases capture and present data as arrays that can be arranged in multiple dimensions. Multidimensional databases present large amounts of data to users in a manner that is easily comprehensible. They also provide multiple indices for fast access to data. Many executive information systems such as Pilot Software's Lightship and Comshare's Commander use multidimensional databases. The main advantage of multidimensional databases is that they allow administrators to organize and view data along commonly viewed dimensions. This improves query processing and allows the users to navigate through the data warehouse easily. These databases can be used to answer queries that would be extremely difficult and cumbersome in SQL, such as,

> List the top five sales regions based on the percentage increase in revenues this year relative to last year.

Some work is proceeding in using RDBMS technology at the core of a multidimensional database. An example is the Microstrategy DSS Agent that presents a multidimensional view of data stored in a RDBMS. The main limitation of currently available multidimensional databases is that they usually cannot store large data amounts (typically more than 10 Gb of data) and have proprietary interfaces. More details about multidimensional databases can be found in Kimball [1996], Codd [1993], Dorrian [1994], and Ricciuti [1994].

10.8.2.3 Specialized DBMSs

Specialized database technologies have been developed and continue to be developed for large database applications such as data warehouses. Specific examples of such databases that can be used in data warehousing are

- Teradata, a database technology based on massively parallel processing and specialized indexing by Teradata corporation.
- Red Brick Warehouse by Red Brick Systems that is built for queries only (it eliminates the overhead of transactional updates) and fast indexes.
- HOPS database by HOPS International that attempts to provide mainframe performance on smaller machines by using indexing techniques, linear sorting algorithms, and file compression techniques.

In general, data warehousing tends to increase the size of databases, and data warehousing requirements will lead to very large databases (e.g., terabytes of data). Very large databases will require improvements in a mixture of technologies such as highly parallel query processing, improved techniques for large indexes, and hardware technologies such as RAID (Redundant Array of Inexpensive Disks). For a practical overview of very large databases, see Winter [1994].

10.8.2.4 Factors to Evaluate and Select DBMSs

In order to choose a DBMS for warehouses, the following factors must be considered:

- Ability to handle very large volumes of data that could be stored on multiple media with features for compaction
- Response time of queries and fast indexing facilities to improve query response times
- Capabilities for ad hoc queries as well as programmed interfaces
- Flexibility to handle operational as well as decision support users

- Open versus proprietary database structure, query languages, and tool interfaces
- Scalability to handle more users and increased volume of data
- Ease of managing the system and the tools to support adequate security, audit, and administrative features
- Monitoring tools to show when a database needs to be reorganized, which indexes are poorly structured, the number of joins between tables, amount of free space, and so forth
- Specialized capabilities for unstructured data, variable length data, lock management, compound keys, and index-only processing
- Fast loading times for high-volume bulk load and fast restore capabilities
- Cost, multiplatform support, and vendor support
- Installed base of the DBMS

10.8.3 Metadata Software

Metadata, data about data, serve as a directory and a catalog of the data warehouse (see Figure 10.7). Metadata are of fundamental importance for a data warehouse because of the heuristic and iterative life cycle of the data warehouse. In order to be effective, a data warehouse must be accompanied by powerful and accurate metadata. This is in sharp contrast to the role of metadata in the operational environments. In operational environments, metadata are almost an option for the users of the system because most of the work is routine transaction processing. However, users of a data warehouse have to rely on metadata to explore and navigate through the warehouse. Metadata can provide the following capabilities (the actual capabilities provided by metadata may vary widely):

- Data schema. Metadata show the names, the attributes, the keys, and the formats of warehouse tables.
- Semantics and data model specification. Metadata describe the business objects and properties represented by the tables and attributes. Metadata can store the data model of the data warehouse as an educational and reference aid (the analyst may want to understand how the physical database design was arrived at from the conceptual data model).
- Mapping of operational data to warehouse data. This mapping shows how the operational data were transformed to create the informational data. For each field in the data warehouse, metadata identify the source field(s) in the operational database(s), any conversions and derivations, name changes, logic to choose between multiple sources, and so forth.
- Common routines for summarization and access of data. Metadata can save DSS analysts a great deal of effort by storing the algorithms used to summarize or derive data.
- Predefined queries, reports, and spreadsheets. This information can be used to build new tools from existing tools.
- Extract history. Metadata should tell the analyst when data entered the warehouse and thus show the currency of the information being analyzed.
- Information about external and unstructured data. Metadata can contain information such as document ID, description of document, source of document, and so forth.

- Relationship to other metadata stores. This information can be useful to locate other sources of metadata, including diagrams and reports.

- Data location. For a distributed data warehouse, metadata may also show what tables are located where in the network.

Figure 10.7 : Metadata in a Data Warehouse

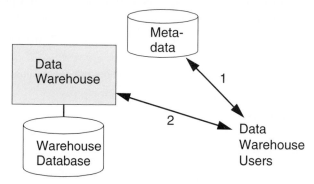

Steps in using a data warehouse:
1. Use the metadata to learn what queries to issue and how to issue the queries.
2. Issue the queries.

How many of these capabilities are actually developed in metadata depends on several factors such as the time and money budgeted for the warehouse, the level of use of the data warehouse (extensive metadata capabilities may not be needed for a data warehouse that is used rarely by a few analysts), and the long-range commitment of management to the data warehouse. The key question is: How much time and effort should be spent on developing metadata? The following examples illustrate the importance of metadata in a data warehouse.

- A DSS analyst from a telecommunications company is asked to list the number of switches in a particular geographical area. The data warehouse has more than 500 relational tables. The analyst first needs to find what tables contain these data and what fields can be used to formulate a query. It is virtually impossible to retrieve this information without metadata.

- A manager needs to know why the sales for a product were dismal in 1994. As part of the drill-down process to find this information, the manager needs to trace the sales summary for each region (stored in the data warehouse) to the detailed sales records of each sales representative (stored in the operational database). This tracing can be found in the metadata.

- A DSS analyst went to Hawaii for a month and stayed for a year (smart guy!!). On his return, he got his job back (lucky guy!!). Naturally, the first thing on his mind is to see how the contents of the data warehouse and the table structures have changed in this time period. Metadata come to his rescue.

- An executive needs to know if the correct Forbes article was used for market trends. This information can be found from the metadata.

Metadata can be, and in many cases is, stored in a relational database. However, it is important to store text, graphics, and other information in the RDBMS. At a minimum, the RDBMS must provide BLOB (Binary Large Object) support to qualify for metadata.

Commercially available software for metadata support is sparse. In many cases, the DBMS catalog is used as a starting point in creating metadata. Some products are beginning to appear. An example of a metadata product is the IBM Information Catalog that consists of APIs and other software that allow synchronizing of different metadata into corporate metadata.

10.8.4 Tools for Data Warehouse Access and Manipulation

A large number of tools can be used to access the data warehouse. As discussed previously, these tools fall into the following categories.

- Data Access and Reporting Tools
- Data Presentation and Analysis Tools
- Executive Information Systems (EIS)
- On-line Analytical Processing (OLAP) tools
- Data Mining

The DSS tools are becoming available from a diverse array of vendors on almost all computing platforms. The following factors can be used to choose appropriate tools:

- Ease of use of the tools.
- Flexibility to handle different types of queries (ad hoc, predefined queries, and structured report writer.
- Capabilities for novices as well as power users.
- Scalability to handle multiple users concurrently.
- Integration with other tools and desktops through DDE and OLE.
- Metadata support.
- Installed base of the tools.
- Access from remote clients.
- Security services to assure that unauthorized users do not access the data warehouse.
- Cost, multiplatform support, and vendor support.

An interesting example of tool selection for data warehousing is presented by the OFFCO RFP. OFFCO is a fictitious office supply retail company created by Database Associates,

Inc. for creation of a data warehouse RFP. The RFP is submitted to several vendors for response. Results of the RFP are published in DB/EXPO proceedings. The technical requirements of the RFP are

- Open systems—ability to interchange hardware and software products from multiple vendors
- Distributed computing—locating data and processes according to business requirements
- Scalable processes—hardware capabilities sized as needed with no impact on applications
- Local autonomy—all database servers capable of independent operations
- Relational databases—RDBMSs required for data warehousing

The results presented in DB/EXPO 94 consist of ODBC, SQL Access Group (SAG) language definition, Prism Data Warehousing tools, and Sybase RDBMS and network interconnect products. More details about this RFP can be found in Sherrett [1994].

10.8.5   Middleware to Access the Data Warehouse

Data warehouses represent a good example of the client/server paradigm. In fact, several enterprises have developed data warehouses as a first experiment in developing client/server applications. The DSS tools described previously typically reside as clients on desktops. The SQL statements generated by these tools are routed to the appropriate data warehouse server by the client/server middleware. Client/server middleware for data warehouses needs the following capabilities

- Client middleware that handles the DSS tool call, converts it to an appropriate format, connects to the data warehouse server, and so forth.
- Database server middleware that handles client tool calls, submits them to the database engine, builds the response, and routes them back to the client.
- A database front end that may be useful to route queries in a distributed data warehouse.

The client/server middleware is extensively discussed in Umar [1997]. For a data warehouse, Remote Data Access (RDA) that sends remote SQL statements is the most frequently used client/server interaction paradigm. In addition, database RPCs may be useful in data warehouses to invoke canned reports. The choice of the appropriate middleware software and the appropriate protocols depends on the target database and the DSS working environment. The C/S protocols that are potential candidates for accessing different target data warehouse databases from the PC-, UNIX-, and Mac-based DSS analysis tools are shown in Table 10.6 We can make the following observations from this table:

- ODBC may be used widely to access data warehouse databases from different database vendors.
- DRDA may be used in centralized data warehouses to access DB2 data from client tools from different vendors.
- Proprietary exchange protocols from different C/S vendors such as EDA/SQL, Informix, Oracle, and Sybase may be used.

This picture is changing quickly as more data warehouses access tools become Web-based. These tools use server-based (e.g., CGI) or browser-based (e.g., Java) gateways that access the data warehouse databases.

TABLE 10.6 CLIENT/SERVER MIDDLEWARE FOR DATA WAREHOUSE ACCESS

	MVS-DB2 Warehouse	UNIX-RDBMS Warehouse	PS2 RDBMS Warehouse
PC Client	1. DRDA for exchange protocol 2. ODBC for API	1. DRDA for DB2 on UNIX 2. Proprietary exchange protocols for other RDBMSs 3. ODBC for API	1. DRDA for DB2 on PS2 2. Proprietary exchange protocols for other RDBMSs 3. ODBC for API
UNIX Client	1. DRDA for exchange protocol 2. Proprietary for API	1. DRDA for DB2 on UNIX 2. Proprietary exchange protocols for other RDBMSs 3. Proprietary for API	1. DRDA for DB2 on PS2 2. Proprietary exchange protocols for other RDBMSs 3. Proprietary for API
Mac Client	1. DRDA for exchange protocol 2. Proprietary for API	1. DRDA for DB2 on UNIX 2. Proprietary exchange protocols for other RDBMSs 3. Proprietary for API	1. DRDA for DB2 on PS2 2. Proprietary exchange protocols for other RDBMSs 3. Proprietary for API

10.9   A Procedure for Data Warehouse Planning and Development

10.9.1 Overview

A data warehouse prototype can be created quickly by extracting needed information from operational data, storing results of some reports in the data warehouse for quick access to summary data, giving access to the warehouse by using off-the-shelf data browsers, and synchronizing the warehouse data with operational data once a week. However, as the size and use of data warehouses grow, several issues arise that require a systematic methodology. For example, according to a 1996 Data Warehouse Institute survey of 21 data warehousing project managers about their most difficult challenges, methodology was the third biggest challenge (technology and education were the other two). Examples of the issues are

- How to plan for a successful implementation of a data warehouse
- How to get management commitment and get the users involved
- What information to store in the warehouse at what level of granularity
- What architecture to use (centralized, localized, distributed)
- How to design the metadata
- How many warehouse "servers" to have and where to locate the servers
- How frequently the data should be refreshed
- How to select appropriate software products

Brokers for Data Warehousing

Data warehouses, especially data marts, can benefit from the broker architectures for data synchronization. Consider a situation where three data marts need to be fed by four data sources (see figure below). The data can be fed/synchronized by using point-to-point middleware. However, this approach works only for a small number of participants. In large-scale systems, a broker is needed to mediate between clients (data sources) and servers (data marts). Although the best-known implementation of the broker architecture is the Object Request Broker (ORB), for data warehouses message brokers are more appropriate.

A message broker delivers messages between disparate applications, including legacy applications, mainly by using Message-Oriented Middleware (MOM).

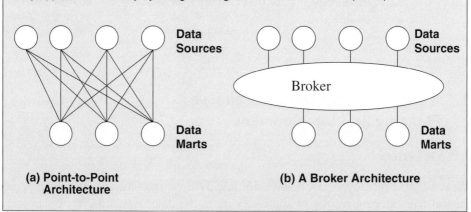

(a) Point-to-Point Architecture

(b) A Broker Architecture

Different methodologies to address these and other issues have been developed. For example, Griffin [1997] describes the methodologies used by different vendors such as Evolutionary Technology Incorporated, Information Builders, NCR, and PRISM Solutions. The procedure shown in Figure 10.8, based on a synthesis of different published approaches,[3] can be used to systematically address these issues. This methodology should be exercised in iterations where the first iteration builds a prototype that is refined in later iterations. There is general agreement that it is not a good idea to spend more than three to four months in the first iteration and show quick results to upper management before proceeding with the next iteration [Griffin 1997], [Newman 1996], [Devlin 1994], [Inmon 1994], [Inmon 1993], [Hott 1994], and [Witte 1994]. The risks of failure in large-scale data warehousing projects are many. For example, a consumer products manufacturer spent $3.5 million over several years to build a corporatewide data warehouse and failed [Eckerson 1994]. In general, one subject data warehouse should be created in the first iteration, followed by more subject databases in subsequent iterations.

The methodology shown in Figure 10.8 is based on the extensive data warehouse plan presented by Haisten [1994] with extensions based on Griffin [1997], and Inmon [1994]. This approach proceeds in the following overlapping steps described later:

1. Management Planning

2. Requirement Gathering

3. Data Modeling

4. Design and Implementation

5. Deployment and Support

Key Guidelines for Successful Data Warehouses

- Plan for the warehouse based on scope (corporate, departmental).

- Build a small data warehouse (usually a data mart) to discover more needs and to show quick benefits to users and upper management.

- Develop a data model that gives a complete view of business data . Mining of an incomplete data warehouse is of very little value (you may discover nothing!).

- Growth and flexibility should be the main drivers in architecture and design.

- Visit user sites with similar suites of tools to see how everything works together (packaged tools from different vendors do not necessarily work well together).

- Invest in maintenance and support services because many well-architected projects fail in the maintenance and support phases.

---

3. Methodologies about data warehouse development have been published by different vendors, consulting firms such as Sentry Technology Group, and consultants/educators [Griffin 1997], [Inmon 1994], and [Haisten 1994]. Basically, all have generic activities such as planning, requirements gathering, data modeling, and design. The difference is on emphasis (e.g., some suggest cross-functional teams while others recommend discovery through prototyping).

Figure 10.8 : Data Warehouse Planning and Development Procedure

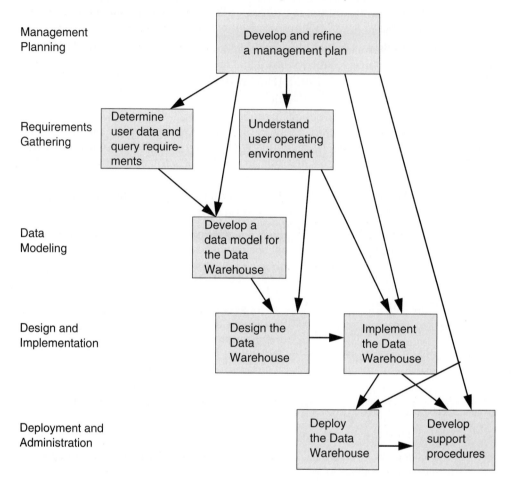

10.9.2 Step 1: Management Planning

Appropriate management planning is mandatory for a data warehouse that is used for corporate decision making. Planning must include business justification, development of a project plan, involvement of business and IS managers, and clear assignment of roles/responsibilities of the warehousing project. Specifically, a planning document should be created that contains

- Definition, description, and scope of the data warehouse
- Business drivers for developing the warehouse
- Identification of source systems and target users
- The primary users of the warehouse and what business decisions they will make by using the warehouse

- The key players and stakeholders in the warehouse and their roles and responsibilities
- What type of policies and procedures will be used to administer the warehouse (e.g., how frequently the warehouse will be populated, what the metadata will show)
- A schedule for the development, deployment, and support of the data warehouse

Development of a management plan itself is an iterative process that requires several management reviews and adjustments. While developing a management plan, the following guidelines should be considered:

- The data warehouse effort must be driven by business managers and not the IS managers. For example, one technique used is to ask a business manager to define a few queries that will be worth a million dollars or more and then develop a data warehouse around these queries [Hott 1994].

- A great deal of attention needs to be paid to the quality of data being delivered to the users. Otherwise, the business decisions being made will not be very effective.

- Commitment needs to be from the business as well as IS management to deliver the right data to the right users at the right time.

- The decision-making authority should be pushed to the people who have adequate tools to make decisions based on the most relevant information.

- If possible, the data warehouse project should be managed with co-project managers from business and IS areas.

A detailed cost justification for a data warehouse often cannot be done a priori because the real benefits may not be known or even anticipated at the moment of warehouse construction. In general, the first iteration of the data warehouse should be small enough to build and large enough to show business value. Data warehouses should be built iteratively and quickly with a great deal of cooperation and discussion about the business value between the warehouse users and the warehouse designers. The costs to implement a data warehouse depend on the size of the effort. Table 10.7 shows typical cost figures for a phased data warehouse implementation.

10.9.3 Step 2: Requirements Gathering

This activity concentrates on understanding and documenting the warehouse user requirements. The traditional requirements need to be modified for data warehousing. It is important to limit the time spent on gathering the user requirements. Unlike traditional systems, not all the requirements of a decision support system can be ascertained ahead of time. Only after the users start using the warehouse do they really begin to understand what kind of information they need and in what format. Practical approaches to gather requirements vary somewhat. For example, Evolutionary Technology Inc. suggests building a data warehouse quickly to uncover needs, while NCR and Information Builders concentrate on focus groups and user interviews. The following checklist should be used as a guideline for requirement gathering, no matter what approach is used:

- Information needs of the user:
  - detailed data
  - summary data and derived data
  - existing data (what, where, in what form)
  - data currency requirements (how frequently data need to be synchronized)
  - understand and categorize users' expertise into novice and experienced

- Query processing needed
  - determine between 5 to 10 critical queries (concentrate on the queries that could save business millions of dollars)
  - reports needed, how frequently needed (collect current reports to get insights)
  - decision support activities needed (drill-downs, analytical models)
  - metamodel needs

- User environment to be supported
  - number of users
  - type of users (e.g., managers, planners)
  - type of workstations (PCs, Macs, UNIX, Xterminals)

- Interconnectivity requirements
  - connectivity of data warehouse to other applications
  - other users who may, indirectly, benefit from the data warehouse
  - network connectivity issues between the users and the data warehouse

- Management and support requirements
  - security requirements for access to the warehouse data
  - budget and time restrictions
  - policies, standards, and standard operating environments

TABLE 10.7 COST ESTIMATES FOR DIFFERENT PHASES OF A DATA WAREHOUSE IMPLEMENTATION (SOURCE [DEVLIN, 1994])

Project Phase	Time Frame (Typical Start and End)	Typical Implementation Cost	Typical Hardware/ Software Costs
Proof of Concept (Prototype)	Month: 0–4	U.S. $25K	Less than U.S. $50K
Version 1: Focus on One Key Business Area	Month: 3–13	U.S. $1,000K to $1,500K	U.S. $100K to $1,000K
Version 2: Add the Next Business Area	Month: 9–18	U.S. $600K to $800K	U.S. $100K to $500K
Version 3: Expand to Next Business Area	Month: 17–18	U.S. $400K to $800K	U.S. $100K to $300K

A good starting point in this activity is the analysis of existing reports and other data sources for decision support. The analysis of current data sources leads to a better understanding of the Present Method of Operation (PMO) for decision support. After this, the limitations of the PMO and the desired capabilities of the Future Method of Operation (FMO) can be well understood and cataloged.

10.9.4 Step 3: Data Modeling

A data model represents the view of data at several levels of detail. The high-level data models are represented by the typical Entity-Relationship-Attribute (ERA) diagrams. The lower-level data models represent the physical database design information such as table layout, primary keys, indexes, and so forth. The data modeling for a data warehouse is primarily concerned with identifying and representing the business entities that are needed in the data warehouse in terms of an ERA diagram. Detailed discussion of ERA modeling is beyond the scope of this book (a brief overview was presented in Chapter 5). Basically, development of an ERA-based data model involves the following steps:

1. Define entities (the principal data objects about which information is to be collected)

2. Identify relationships (the real-world associations) among entities

3. Identify and develop attributes (characteristics of entities)

4. Represent this information by using an ERA diagram

In case of a data warehouse, the existing corporate data model for the operational system is a good starting point (if one exists). From this data model, the data model needed for the warehouse can be developed by deleting the entities not needed in the warehouse (i.e., removing purely operational data), by adding needed attributes (e.g., time), and by adding the derived data entities needed for the warehouse. It may also be desirable to perform "stability" analysis on the data model before proceeding with the physical design. The stability analysis separates the data into groups based on their tendency to change. For example, stability analysis of a data model may create the following data groups:

- Seldom changing data (e.g., once or twice a year)
- Sometime changing data (e.g., once or twice a month)
- Frequently changing data (e.g., several times in a day)

Although the principles of data modeling are straightforward, the practice of building a data warehouse data model is nontrivial. This is primarily due to the coordination and agreements needed between different information owners. In practice, development of a data warehouse model may need to be completed in several steps and may need top management support or involvement of some dedicated people who are devoted to the notion of a global business data model as a basis for a corporate data warehouse. The modeling process must include users as an essential part of the loop. It is important to review the model with the users, resolve definition issues, and challenge old misconceptions (data models may reveal aspects and practices of business that some users are not aware of).

10.9.5 Step 4: Design and Implementation

This step is concerned with the technical details of designing and implementing the data warehouse. Design of a data warehouse involves the following steps already discussed in Section 10.7

- Granularity
- Data partitioning
- Data structure design

In addition, the data are allocated to the candidate data servers, depending on the desired data warehouse architecture. For example, in a centralized data warehouse all data partitions are allocated to the central site. On the other hand, in a subject-oriented distributed data warehouse, we can allocate each partition to a separate data server. In a more generalized distributed data warehouse architecture, the data allocation can be viewed as a File Allocation Problem (FAP) which has been discussed very heavily in the computer science literature. We reviewed the theory of data distribution and the available FAPs in Chapter 6. However, sophisticated allocation algorithms may not be needed for data warehouses. The common allocation strategies are

- Allocate all warehouse data to one server
- Allocate one partition (i.e., subject database) to one server uniquely
- Replicate the heavily used data to a few servers to improve performance and availability
- Replicate the entire data warehouse to a few sites

The allocation trade-off can be represented in terms of the following pluses and minuses:

+ Performance (data distribution and replication improves performance)

+ Availability (data redundancy improves availability under failures)

– Synchronization cost (data replication increases this cost)

– Hardware cost (more servers increase hardware costs)

Because data warehouses are primarily read-only, synchronization costs are minimal. In addition hardware costs are dropping steadily. Thus in the case of a warehouse, many duplicate copies can be created to improve performance and availability.

The issue of selecting the data warehouse tools also needs some attention. Allocation of the tools to a user workstation gives users a great deal of independence but can increase software license costs. The data warehouse tools can be allocated to an "application" server to which many users logon to access the warehouse. The application server approach has the benefits that it reduces costs, allows dumb terminals, X terminals, and the new breed of network computers to use the data warehouse and also provides better security and administrative controls.

Once the overall design of the data warehouse has been established, then the following implementation activities are undertaken:

- Choice of the subject databases. Once again, it is best to start with a small implementation effort which may focus on one subject database for one division or department.

- Selection of data warehouse tools. The data extraction and loading, the database engine, and the data access tools need to be carefully selected. The discussion of these tools in Section 10.8 and the factors to be considered for evaluation and selection can be used in this step. It appears that no single tool will be adequate for all data warehousing needs. Thus tools with open interfaces are more desirable. The tools must also take into account the user experience.

- Acquisition and installation of hardware/software. This step can progress gradually as a small warehouse is gradually expanded. This avoids investing in major hardware/software acquisition and installation before business value is demonstrated.

- Monitoring and tuning the data model and the warehouse. The data warehouse needs constant monitoring and tuning to improve query response. The tuning can consist of [Wright 1996, Hott 1994]:
  - denormalizing the data model to reduce the number of joins
  - creating summary data needed frequently and storing them in the warehouse
  - moving data to faster servers or duplicating data to improve query performance
  - designing better indexes and spreading the data to multiple disks (e.g., put data for one month on one disk) to reduce disk contention
  - handling the failure of a portion of the warehouse
  - maintaining the performance of queries as the data volumes scale upwards

- Purging the warehouse data. If the data are not being used in their present form, they should be purged by using one of the following techniques:
  - data are transformed from one level of the warehouse to another
  - data are retrieved in case they are needed in future (some summary and derived data generated especially for the warehouse may be needed in the future)
  - data are physically deleted from the warehouse

- Evaluation of new DBMS technologies as candidates for replacing the existing data warehouse DBMS. This may happen if the size of the data warehouse grows to the point where the existing DBMS technology cannot be "tuned" and serious alternatives need to be considered.

10.9.6 Step 5: Deployment and Administration

This step concentrates on

- Deployment of the warehouse at the appropriate site(s)

- Operation and support of the warehouse

- Administration of the warehouse

Deployment includes population of the data warehouse database from the data sources. This involves extraction, transport, conversion, and population of the warehouse. We have discussed this topic previously (see Section 10.8). Deployment also includes the installation of any hardware/software to provide access to the data warehouse in a production environment.

Operation and support assure smooth and consistent operation of the data warehouse. They specifically involve issues such as help desk support, user training, backup/recovery, hardware/software upgrades, performance monitoring, security monitoring, and so forth. The activities are similar to the typical database administration and control activities, and are crucial to the real-life survival of data warehouses (see Strehlo [1996] for examples). The main differences are:

- Quality of the data warehouse needs to be monitored and improved continuously (see the sidebar "Quality of Data Warehouses").

- Performance monitoring and analysis are essential due to the ad hoc nature of queries (ad hoc queries that impact performance seriously must be analyzed quickly).

- Version control and synchronization need to be done for data plus the metadata.

- Metadata maintenance is crucial (metadata are much more important for warehouses).

- The size of the database is very large (backup and recovery may take extra time). As organizations increase the granularity and historic span of data in the data warehouses, the data warehouse size is becoming a major issue.

- The users are typically managers (there is little time for training).

- Use is primarily read-only (data can be reorganized/reloaded on an as-needed basis).

Administration is concerned with setting and enforcing policies and procedures for the data warehouse. In particular, this entails setting policies for data access, establishing the frequency of data synchronization, maintaining an inventory of the data warehouse information (this is typically assisted by the metadata), deciding when to upgrade the underlying hardware/software of the warehouse, and overseeing the data warehousing future plans.

10.10   State of the Practice: Case Studies and Examples

Many data warehouse case studies are appearing in the literature. For example, the International Data Warehousing Association (IDWA) regularly publishes data warehouse case studies (see, for example, "Warehousing: What Works," published by IDWA at the end of 1996 that contains discussion and lessons learned from 22 case studies). Similarly, *Client/Server Computing* includes special sections on "Data Warehousing Directions" several times per year (see, for example, the December 1996 issue) that include numerous case studies. It is not possible to describe all case studies in this chapter. A few case studies are described to highlight different aspects of data warehousing.

10.10.1 IBM Shifts to Data Marts

Source: Radding, A., "Monoliths Are Out," Sentry Market Research Report on Data Warehouse Directions, *Client/Server Computing,* December 1996, pp. S27–S28.

IBM introduced and promoted the concept of a global, enterprisewide data warehouse. However, the user demands and the difficulties in building large-scale global data warehouses that serve the entire organization from a central site seem to have changed IBM's mind. At the time of this writing, IBM operates, or is developing, more than 80 data marts. Why? Like many other large corporations, IBM could not afford to wait while it built a global data warehouse. In far less time, IBM had multiple data marts up and serving customers.

10.10.2 ReliaStar Financial Data Warehouse for Competitive Advantage

Source: Appleton, E., "Use Your Data Warehouse to Compete," *Datamation,* May 15, 1996.

ReliaStar, a publicly held $16.7 billion insurance and employee benefits company based in Minneapolis, needed to do something to stay competitive. The key to the growth of the company is the 9,000 independent agents who sell for ReliaStar. However, independent agents—which by definition have the right to sell any firms's products—are up for grabs by other competitors such as other insurance companies and banks entering this market. The key idea is to have these agents do more business with ReliaStar as compared to the competitors.

Naturally, agents are attracted to firms that make selling easy. Most of the business conducted by insurance companies is paper intensive, requiring agents to conduct business over phones with multiple forms, call backs, and voice mail. The basic strategy of ReliaStar is to make the life of these agents easy so that they find it less painful and more profitable to do business with ReliaStar than other competitors. ReliaStar also needs to attract new agents.

This is being accomplished through a data warehouse application called ReliaStar Connection. This application allows the agents to quickly access policy, pricing, customer, and other information quickly without any telephone calls. The warehouse also supports analysis and productivity tools for the agents. The warehouse infrastructure consists of a mainframe DB2 database in Minneapolis that is accessed from agent PCs over a WAN. The analysis tools reside on the PCs and mainframes. The warehouse supports a "virtual" environment that allows access of data from multiple sources instead of duplication of everything.

10.10.3 3Com's Data Warehouse

Source: Eberhard, E., "Information Warehouse: A User Experience" *Info DB,* Vol.7, No. 2, 1993, pp. 6–12.

3Com Corporation is a California-based manufacturer of global data networking products. Networking is a fast moving, very competitive industry requiring fast response to varying global market conditions. Like many other similar industries, 3Com has experienced problems in using its data. Here are some examples:

- Top-level executives demanded that reliable sales and marketing information be available to make production decisions.

- Monthly sales reports obtained from different departments did not match.

- Reports were more suitable for operational day-to-day support instead of trend analysis and decision support.

- The business analysts needed an informational environment that integrated well with the desktop tools they were already using—spreadsheets, word processors, and data browsers.

- IS professionals were spending most of their time on writing one-time reports of sales and marketing for business analysts.

- Many reports were too general purpose and larger than the analyst needed for any single analysis.

3Com developed an information architecture that consisted of separating the operational systems (currently running on HP platforms) from a data warehouse (a new system developed on DB2). The data warehouse is accessed from IBM PCs, Macs, and Sun workstations through SQL browsers, spreadsheets, and an EIS.

An initial prototype of the data warehouse was established for proof of concept as well as internal marketing of the concept. The prototype tested the technical as well as administrative aspects of the new environment and measured the impact of the data warehouse traffic on the corporate backbone. The prototype was accepted for production after four months. A production methodology was followed that included a team of IS and business analysts, hiring an experienced data modeler to lead the data modeling effort, rewriting the extract/load program, extensive data warehouse design effort to build summaries and views, implementation of on-line help, and development of a training program.

The data warehouse was implemented in five months. The data warehouse consisted of 5.5 Gb of data. Due to the data warehouse, top managers can access recent sales information, business analysts have discovered some shifts in business practices, and requests for paper reports have decreased significantly. Several direct quotes from 3Com management are reported in the case study to indicate management satisfaction. It is noted that the data modeling effort and the summarization process could have been initiated during the prototyping process.

Comments. This case study represents a very common approach taken in developing data warehouses. The lessons learned from this undertaking are typical of many other data warehousing projects (e.g., complete separation of operational and decision support systems is essential, starting with a small prototype is a good idea, development of a sound data model is essential, and proper hardware/software estimates are important before embarking on large-scale production).

10.10.4   British Telecom's Data Warehouse

Source: Ferrent, R., "BT's Information Warehouse," *Logistics Information Management,* Vol. 5, No. 4, 1992, pp. 42–43.

British Telecom (BT) has established a data warehouse for its Group Logistics and Group Procurement divisions. The warehouse is a single centralized database that contains all the data needed to support the management and delivery of BT's supplies in the UK.

The primary business objectives of this data warehouse were to provide stock visibility to all parts of the organization and thus reduce stock, reduce lead times, and increase efficiency by reducing paperwork. To meet these objectives, BT embarked on a three-year task of separating data from operational systems and developing a data model for the logistics and procurement business functions. The project required an investment of roughly $4.5 million and required involvement of 124 BT staff members.

The implemented data warehouse is not used as an extract database—it involves real-time updating of the database. The data warehouse resides on an MVS-DB2 mainframe. It handles 850,000 orders per month, holds information on 73,000 item records and 100,000 contracts with 26,000 suppliers, and dispatches goods to more than 10,000 customer delivery points. The database is divided into three categories: reference databases (for item, customer, supplier); transaction databases (orders and purchase orders), and application databases (stock, contracts). Outside suppliers are connected to the data warehouse through Electronic Data Interchange (EDI)—this allows switching of orders to outside suppliers if a needed item is not available in BT inventory.

This project has reportedly caused a $600 million reduction of stocks, a reduced requirement for inventory warehouses,[4] reduction of repetitive clerical activities, better cost control, and reduced lead time for some products (e.g., delivery time cut from 10 days to 3.5 days for chloride batteries). The biggest benefit to BT is that the data are held in one central site and not in multiple locations. This provides total stock visibility, facilitates switching of orders to the most appropriate stock holding location, and enforces standardization to allow systems accessing the data to be organizationally independent.

Comments: This case study shows implementation of a centralized data warehouse. Unique features of this case study are:

- More business benefits due to centralization of information for total stock visibility. The benefits of centralization are not usually mentioned these days.

- Long range (three-year) effort as compared to short (3 to 4 months) data warehousing efforts.

- The data are updated (most data warehouses are retrieval only).

---

4. Let us not forget, there are warehouses other than the data warehouse!!!

10.10.5   Banc One's Transition to Data Warehousing

Source: "Rightsizing: Re-engineering Information Systems through Client-Server Technology—Case Studies," *Sun Microsystems, 1993.*

Banc One is a Columbus, Ohio-based bank holding company. Banc One provides a wide variety of services, including branch banking, mortgages, loans, and credit cards. The Risk Management department, a subsidiary of Banc One, is responsible for all strategic and tactical decisions regarding risk or profitability of credit card accounts. This department supports the main decisions for approving/declining credit card accounts, increasing/decreasing lines of credit, reissuing existing credit cards, creating feasibility studies of the bank's future credit card activities, and forming the bank's credit card policies within each state.

The Banc One computing environment consisted of three IBM mainframes running MVS operating systems, CICS transaction managers, and flat files. The Risk Management department relied primarily on more than 60 "canned" plus ad hoc reports produced by using the SAS Institute tools. The mainframes were overloaded, so these reports were run at night as batch jobs, causing the following problems:

- The reports were not suitable for risk management and required 15 employees to reenter report data into PCs so that it could be properly analyzed.

- The canned batch reports took two days (one day to produce report and another to enter the information on PCs) and the ad hoc reports took anywhere from one to six weeks (this depended on the type of report).

- Producing these reports was expensive (average cost per ad hoc report was $2000 and $300 for canned reports).

Due to these problems, the Risk Management department had to make decisions with incomplete or outdated information. The computer communication platform used by Banc One to speed up risk management decisions and to reduce computing costs had the following main components:

- A database server which was connected to the mainframes through SNA 3270 links. This server resided on a Sun computer and used an Informix database manager.

- Three Sun application servers which ran SAS, Informix spreadsheet, and 4GL tools and word processors.

- Thirty Sun workstations for risk management analysts.

- A TCP/IP network interconnected the Sun computers. As stated previously, the database server was connected to the three mainframes through 3270 SNA links (an SNA 3270 link emulates a computer as a 3270 terminal connected to an IBM mainframe).

The application architecture consisted of the following:

- Historical profile of each customer was stored on the database server. These data were extracted once a month from the mainframes and showed the credit history of each customer. In addition, daily financial activity of each customer (purchases, cash advances, payments, etc.)

was downloaded daily from the mainframes to the database server. This database kept information in summary format for quick reporting and thus served as the "information warehouse" for financial risk analysis.

- The application processing logic for risk analysis was performed on the three application servers with SAS and Informix-4GL tools. The SAS programs were moved from the mainframes to the application servers (SAS runs on both mainframes and UNIX Sun computers).

- The user interface processing was done on the 30 Sun workstations.

When this platform and application architecture was announced, it encountered tremendous resistance because it represented a major change in computing practices. The department convinced upper management by demonstrating that the bank was spending an additional $5,000 to $10,000 a day by not making the transition (the proposed configuration cost was reportedly $600,000 as compared to $2 million per year for the mainframe system). Upon approval, a four-month pilot project was initiated, and a UNIX administrator and a UNIX developer were hired. After the pilot, the new system was completed and deployed in a month. Currently operational, this application architecture has allowed the Risk Management department to increase its canned reports from 60 to 100 and facilitated more ad hoc queries with SAS and Informix on-line query facilities. Other applications, such as processing credit card applications, are being considered for client/server application architectures.

Comments: The main idea in this case study is that the mainframe data were replicated and stored in a mid-range server dedicated for the Risk Management department. In many similar cases, the management has found that periodic downloads of data to dedicated departmental servers for decision analysis is a good business decision. Another computer hardware and another database manager could be used instead of the Sun Informix DBMS configuration used above. What is generally needed in these situations is an environment which provides a wide range of decision analysis tools such as 4GLs, on-line query processors, report writers, spreadsheets, and data browsers. Most DBMS vendors at present are providing such tools.

10.10.6 Short Case Studies ("Snippets")

- Freeman [1997] reports about construction of an extremely large scale (terabytes) data warehouse by Mastercard International. This data warehouse, built in 150 days, is intended to provide portfolio information to its more than 22,000 customers (member financial institutions). The data warehouse uses Oracle7 on NCR 3600 enterprise servers with 350 disk drives. A proprietary program is used in loading the data and extensive OLAP tools are used for analysis.

- The "Data Warehouse Directions" supplement of the October 1996 issue of *Client/Server Magazine* has four data warehouse case studies. The case studies include France's Telecom's data warehouse to support hundreds of decision makers, Bristol-Myer's data warehouse for a consolidated view of managed care facilities and doctors, Cole Taylor Bank's data warehouse for better customer service and cross-selling, and a manufacturing company's data warehouse for faster access to better customer and market data.

- The Spring 1996 *Newsletter* of the International Data Warehouse Association describes five case studies of data warehouses. The case studies describe HBO's data warehouse to support sales and marketing, fraud detection at the Canadian Imperial Bank Corporation through a warehouse analysis tool, Epsilon's reliance on automatic generation of extract programs to reduce costs, Centra Health's data warehouse for improved patient care, and a distributed data warehouse developed by Bull for a French rental/sales company.

- Source Informatics, a Phoenix-based pharmaceutical firm, has implemented a data warehouse that contains 2 terabytes of data culled from 34,000 retail pharmacies. The data warehouse was initially installed on an IBM mainframe using DB2. It was converted to an Oracle-based system. Web access to this warehouse is being provided through DSS Web from Microstrategy, Inc. *Source:* "Healthy Gains at Source Informatics," *Client/Server Computing*, December 1996, pg. S16.

- Duncan Witte [Witte 1994] describes two case studies with different business uses and technical environments but with identical design and development principles for successful implementation. The first case study describes a data warehouse for the Atlantic Richfield exploration and production operations. This data warehouse required extraction of data from many large databases such as DB2, IMS, Oracle, Model 204, and so forth. The second case study describes a pricing and marketing data warehouse for the Brookhaven Grocery Company, a regional grocery store chain in Lousiana, Texas, and Arkansas. This data warehouse required extracting data from VSAM files only. In both cases, the same design approach (build a prototype, get users involved, expand the warehouse gradually, etc.) was used with success. The lessons learned are typical.

- Barry Devlin [Devlin 1991] describes the experience of implementing a data warehouse for IBM Europe. This case study contains a good description of overall IBM Europe informational strategy and data architecture and technical details of the design and implementation decisions. The case study concludes with lessons learned and future directions. An interesting observation is made about how the designers of operational systems and the data warehouse interacted with each other, that is, the DB2-based operational system designers worked much more closely with the data warehouse designers than the IMS-based operational system designers. Incidentally, the data warehouse was implemented on a DB2 platform.

- Brooks and his colleagues [Brooks 1992] describe how three companies (Alabama Power Company, Southern Services Company, and DECO) transformed two materials management applications into a data warehouse application. Most of the information in this paper focuses on the advantages/disadvantages of client/server applications. However, it does show how data warehouses are used as a first step into client/server applications.

- Mary Cooper [Cooper 1994] describes the experience of building a materials data warehouse for Hughes Aircraft. This data warehouse was created to answer questions such as, "what are the top 10 selling materials?" that required months to answer. A standard data warehouse infrastructure was created based on DB2 and UNIX/Red Brick DBMSs, Clear Access and Business Objects as access tools, Prism Warehouse Manager, and Sybase Open Client/server environment.

Additional data warehouse case studies are described in various vendor announcements (e.g., PRISM Corporation's *Data Warehouse Newsletters*) and conferences such as DB/ EXPO and IDC Data Warehousing Conferences. Many short case studies are also appearing in trade journals such as *InfoWorld*.

10.11 State of the Market

Data warehouses have become big business with more than 90 percent of companies involved in this effort in 1996, according to IDC. Many tools to support the massive development and management of data warehouses are appearing in the market from database vendors, software suppliers, computer hardware/software firms, and special-purpose data warehouse suppliers. For example, a Sentry Market Research report on data warehouse directions published in *Client/Server Computing Magazine,* October 1996, lists over 70 vendors that supply data warehouse data acquisition tools (e.g., data extractors, data cleaning tools, data replicators), data access tools (e.g., report writers, query analyzers, OLAP, data visualizers, data miners, data access middleware, forecasting), data management (e.g., data warehouse and data mart design tools, automation of data warehouse building), and consulting/support services. The *Data Management Review Magazine* has a monthly section that reviews data warehouse tools.

State-of-the-market analyses are published regularly by consulting groups such as the Gartner Group, Forrester Research, Patricia Seybold, and IDC. These tools and services will mature with time. General market trends appear to be:

- Web interfaces to data warehouses will become a norm in data warehouse access tools.

- Data mining applications will play a key role in data warehousing.

- The need to integrate and access semistructured data (messages, reports, documents, software artifacts) within the framework of data warehouse will grow and will transition data warehouses into true information warehouses.

- Data marts will grow as prepackaged data warehouses but will need to be synchronized frequently with a central data warehouse.

- Relational database technologies, especially exploiting the parallel databases, will play a key role in the data warehouses of the future.

- Sophisticated metadata capabilities will be needed and will be developed.

- OLAP techniques will outweigh multidimensional databases (Gartner Group).

- Data warehousing vendors will keep developing homegrown methodologies as part of consultation and education services.

10.12 State of the Art: Research Areas

Data warehouses are essentially large databases for decision support. Thus most large database research issues are applicable to this area. Potential specific research areas are

- Virtual data warehouses to integrate data warehouse databases with semistructured information located in different locations in different formats. This may require development of an "information integrator" that operates as an agent of the data warehouse for information retrieval.

- Data quality of the warehouse. This requires development and customization of extensive tools for data warehouse cleaning and purification.

- Data mining applications for sophisticated knowledge discovery.

- Utilization of intelligent agents in data mining and executive information systems

- Automated construction of metadata models.

- Design of distributed data warehouses with intelligent work-load migration algorithms.

- Operational data stores that will provide instantaneous access to most recent operational data.

10.13 Summary

In summary, a data warehouse is a repository of information for decision support. The interest in data warehouses has been fueled by the difficulties in providing "universal" access to operational data. To provide access to these data and other data needed for decision support, data warehouses are being established in many organizations. Decision support questions, if asked in a typical operational environment, would require several weeks to answer. The analysts need to know: what applications to access data from, in what format the data are located, how to access the data, and so forth.

Data warehouses can be, and should be, developed quickly by using the commonly available relational database technologies and associated toolsets. The first warehouse should concentrate on one or two subject databases to demonstrate business value and technical feasibility. Once a small data warehouse has been successfully developed and deployed, additional subject databases and users should be added gradually. As the size and use of a data warehouse grows, many technical as well as management issues discussed in this chapter will need to be considered.

10.14 Case Study: Data Warehouse for XYZCorp

A corporate data warehouse is planned within the scope of the XYZAICS initiative. This data warehouse will keep information about XYZCorp products, customers, and services for decision support. The data warehouse will extract and store information from a wide variety of data sources. The management is especially interested in using Web technologies and "advanced" data mining, analysis, and modeling techniques. You have been asked to develop this data warehouse.

Hints about the Case Study

The procedures discussed in Section 10.9 could be used to design and develop this warehouse. The architectural and design issues discussed in Sections 10.6 and 10.7, respectively, should be reviewed.

10.15 Problems and Exercises

1. Consider a decision support application of your choice. Develop a data warehouse for this application by using the five-step procedure described in Section 10.9.

2. Suggest a taxonomy to analyze the state of the market. For each step, list the major decisions, the techniques/tools employed, and the final choices made by you.

3. Discuss the new sets of security, privacy, and data quality issues and problems being introduced by the widespread use of data warehouses.

4. Some people contend that there are no differences between database design and data warehouse design. Do you agree or disagree? Justify your answer.

5. Conduct a survey of the Web-based data warehouse tools, especially data mining.

10.16 Additional Information

The paper by Devlin and Murphy [Devlin 1986] gives the initial thoughts on data warehousing. The books by Poe [1996], Kimball [1996], Inmon [1993], and Inmon [1994] provide a great deal of information about designing and using data warehouses. In many ways, design of a data warehouse involves the fundamental principles used in modeling and designing any relational database application. Several industrial reports from consulting groups such as Gartner Group, Sentry Technological Group, IDC, and Patricia Seybold have been published on data warehouses. Many conferences such as the DB/EXPO and IDC Data Warehousing Conferences are devoted to data warehousing. Frequent articles and short case studies appear regularly in trade journals such as *Data Management Review, Info World, Open Systems Today,* and *Database Programming and Design.* The Data Warehousing Institute publishes numerous case studies, guidelines, and analyses regularly.

Alur, N., Richards, D., Winsberg, P., et al., "Data Warehouse in Practice" *InfoDB,* Summer 1993, pp. 9–17.

Anand, S., et al., "EDM: General Framework for Data Mining based on Evidence Theory," *Data and Knowledge Engineering Journal,* April 1996, pp. 184–224.

Appleton, E., "The Right Server for Your Data Warehouse," *Datamation,* March 15, 1995, pp. 56–58.

Barth, P., "Real User Solutions: Getting the Most out of Data Warehousing," DB/EXPO 94, New York, December 1994.

Brooks, D., Neilsen, E., Reagan, R., "Improved Materials Management through Client/Server Computing," *Proceedings of the American Power Conference,* 1992, pp. 976–981.

Carickhoff, R., "A New Face for OLAP," *Internet Systems,* January 1997, pp. 24–29.

Codd, E. F., Codd, S. B., and Salley, C. T., "Providing OLAP (On-line Analytical Processing) to User-Analysis: An IT Mandate," E. F. Codd & Associates White Paper, 1993.

Cooper, M., "Data Warehouse Experience at Hughes," DB/EXPO 94, New York, December 1994.

Decker, S., "The Executive Information System," *Data Management Review*, October 1996, pp. 62–67.

Devlin, B., "Data Warehouse Implementation Experience in IBM Europe," *Proceedings SHARE Europe Spring Meeting,* April 1991, pp. 229–247.

Devlin, B., "The Business Case for Data Warehousing," DB/EXPO 94, New York, December 1994.

Devlin, B. A., and Murphy, P. T., "An Architecture for a Business and Information System," *IBM Systems Journal,* Vol. 27, No. 1, 1986.

Dorrian, J., "Multidimensionality: An Emerging Model for Data Analysis," DB/EXPO 94, New York, December 1994.

Eberhard, E., "Information Warehouse: A User Experience," *Info DB,* Vol. 7, No. 2, 1993, pp. 6–12.

Eckerson, W., "Data Warehouses," *Open Information Systems,* Patricia Seybold Group, Vol. 9, No. 8, August 1994.

Everret, B., *Cluster Analysis,* Heineman Educational Books, London 1974.

Ferguson, M., "Data Warehousing and Parallel Computing," DB/EXPO 94, New York, December 1994.

Ferrent, R., "BT's Information Warehouse," *Logistics Information Management,* Vol. 5, No. 4, 1992, pp. 42–43.

Fradkov, S., "Data Replication," *Data Management Review,* October 1996, pp. 18–21.

Frawley, W., et al, "Knowledge Discovery in Databases: An Overview," *AI Magazine,* Fall, 1992, pp. 57–70.

Freeman, E., "Birth of a Terabyte Data Warehouse," *Datamation,* April 1997, pp. 80–84.

Friend, D., "An Introduction to Multidimensional Database Server Technology," Pilot Software White Paper, 1993.

Gelman, A., Kobrinski, H., Smoot, L., Weinstein, S., "A Store-and-Forward Architecture for Video-on-Demand Service," International Conference on Communications, 1991, pp. 842–848.

Giordano, R., "The Information 'Where?' House," *Database Programming and Design,* September 1993, pp. 54–61,

Griffin, J., "Avoid Data Warehousing Migraines," *Datamation,* August 1996, pp. 74–77.

Griffin, J., "Methodologies For The Future," data warehouse supplement, *Client/Server Computing,* February 1997, pp. S5–S7.

Hackathorn, R., "Data Warehousing Energizes Your Enterprise," *Datamation,* February 1, 1995, pp. 38–42.

Haisten, M., "Planning A Data Warehouse Project," DB/EXPO 94, New York, December 1994.

Hott, D., "Designing a Data Warehouse," DB/EXPO 94, New York, December 1994.

Imielinski, T., and Mannila, H., "A Database Perspective on Knowledge Discovery," *Communications of the ACM,* November 1996, pp. 58–64.

Inmon, W., *Building Data Warehouses,* John Wiley, 1993.

Inmon, W., *Using Data Warehouses,* John Wiley, 1994

Inmon, W., "Data Warehouse Success Requires Development Automation," *Application Development Tools,* March 1995.

Kelly, S., and Hadden, E., "Data Marts: The Latest Silver Bullet," *Data Management Review,* January 1997, pp. 16–17.

Kimball, R., *The Data Warehouse Toolkit: Practical Techniques for Building Dimensional Data Warehouses,* John Wiley, 1996.

King, D., and O'Leary, D., "Intelligent Executive Information Systems," *IEEE Expert,* December 1996, pp. 30–35.

Korzeniowski, P., "Replication Gains in Distributed DBMS," *Software Magazine,* April 1993, pp. 93–96.

Leinfuss, E., "Replication Synchronizes Distributed Databases Over Time," *Software Magazine,* July 1993, pp. 31–35.

Matheus, C., et al., "Systems for Knowledge Discovery in Databases," *IEEE Transactions in Knowledge and Data Engineering,* December 1993, pp. 903–914.

Negoita, C., *Expert Systems and Fuzzy Sets,* Benjamin Cummings, 1985.

Newman, D., "Data Warehouse Architecture," *Data Management Review,* October 1996, pp. 34–41.

Piatetsky-Shapiro, G., and Matheus, C., "Knowledge Discovery Workbench for Exploring Business Databases," *International Journal of Intelligent Systems,* Vol. 7, 1992, pp. 675–686.

Poe, V., *Building a Data Warehouse for Decision Support,* Prentice Hall, 1996.

Radding, A., "Support Decision Makers with a Data Warehouse," *Datamation,* March 15, 1995, pp. 53–56.

Raden, N., "Warehouses and the Web," *Information Week,* May 13, 1996, pp. 80–86.

Ricciuti, M., "Terabytes of Data—How to Get At Them," *Datamation,* August 1, 1992.

Ricciuti, M., "Multidimensional Analysis: Winning the Competitive Game," *Datamation,* February 15, 1994.

Rinaldi, D., "Metadata Management Separates Prism from Data Warehouse Pack," *Client/ Server Computing,* March 1995, pp. 20–23.

Rist, R., "Building a Data Warehousing Infrastructure," *Data Management Review,* February 1995, pp.42–44.

Robinson, T., "One Data Mart To GO?" data warehouse supplement, *Client/Server Computing,* February 1997, pp. S11–S13.

Romberg, A., "Meta-Entities: Keeping Pace with Change," *Database Programming and Design,* January 1995, pp. 54–58.

Sauter, V., *Decision Support Systems,* John Wiley, 1997.

Saylor, M., "Data Warehouse on the Web," *Data Management Review,* October 1996, pp. 22–30.

Sherrett, C., Lee, G., Mizola, P., "Real Application Workshop: Building and Accessing the OFFCO Data Warehouse," DB/EXPO 94, New York, December 1994.

Simon, A., "Beyond the Data Warehouse," *Database Programming and Design,* December 1996, pp. 42–26.

Stacey, D., "Replication: DB2, Oracle, or Sybase," *Database Programming and Design,* December 1994, pp. 42–51.

Strange, K., "Data Warehousing—Passing Fancy or Strategic Imperative?" *Gartner Group Report,* October 1994.

Strehlo, K., "Data Warehousing: Avoid Planned Obsolence," *Datamation,* January 15, 1996, pp. 32–36.

Teorey, T. J., *Database Modeling and Design: The Fundamental Principle,* 2d ed., Morgan Kaufman, 1994.

Turban, E., *Decision Support and Expert System: Management Support Systems,* 3d ed., Macmillan Publishing, 1993.

Waterson, K., "The Changing World of EIS," *Byte,* June 1994.

White, C., "The Key to a Data Warehouse," *Database Programming and Design,* February 1995, pp. 23–25.

Wilson, L., "The Tool Box Is Half Empty," Sentry Market Research Report on Data Warehouse Directions, *Client/Server Computing,* December 1996, pp. S21–S23.

Winter, R., "The Future of Very Large Databases," *Database Programming and Design,* December 1994, pp. 26–32.

Witte, D., "Real User Solutions: Experiences in Data Warehouses," DB/EXPO 94, New York, December 1994.

Wright, G., "Developing a Data Warehouse," *Data Management Review,* October 1996, pp. 31–33.

11

Migration Strategies

533

11.1   Introduction

This chapter concentrates on the issues, approaches, and tools associated with migration of legacy applications to more modern Web-based architectures. In particular, we concentrate on gradual migration of large-scale mission-critical applications. The "cold turkey" migrations that involve complete rewrites and replacement of legacy applications are not viable in many cases due to the reasons discussed in Chapter 8 (i.e., a better system must be promised, business conditions do not stand still to allow for new developments, specifications for legacy systems rarely exist, legacy application rewrite efforts can be too large to easily manage, and rewrite of large legacy applications may take long enough to make the rewrite itself legacy at completion).

A survey conducted by the Business Research Group in 1994 indicated that 64 percent of the respondents did not want to undertake migration of legacy systems because of cost and technical difficulties [Chepetsky 1994]. Due to these reasons, we primarily focus on gradual migrations. Migrations, gradual or not, make sense in some cases and not in others (see the sidebar "When to Migrate and When Not To"). Typical examples of application migration include MVS-COBOL-IMS applications to Web-based object-oriented client/server architectures, UNIX-C/C++-RDBMS, or Windows-SQL server environments. In many cases, only the user interfaces of existing applications are being migrated to the Web.

Gradual migration of large-scale applications involves a mixture of activities such as data migration, application code conversion, reengineering of user interfaces, and portability of application components. Application migration is a tedious, expensive, and time-consuming effort that must be managed carefully. If done correctly, migration can produce significant payoffs. However, if not done correctly, migrations can result in "migraines" for the management, cause business disruptions, and turn off users. It is our objective to maximize the benefits and minimize the risks by answering the following key questions:

- What are the main concepts and categories of application migration (Section 11.2)?

- Why is user interface migration (typically from text-based to GUI/OOUI) so popular and what are the pertinent issues and approaches (Section 11.3)?

- When and how is data migration a viable approach and what type of tools and techniques are available for data migration (Section 11.4)?

- How can a complete application be migrated gradually by using the migration gateways that isolate the end-users from the migration activities (Section 11.5)?

- What are the special features of "system" migration where groups of applications are transitioned from one platform to another typically as part of "mainframe unplugs" (Section 11.6)?

- Can an approach be developed which allows IS staff to systematically approach the legacy application migration problems and maximize the chances for success (Section 11.7)?

Key Points

- Application migration is an expensive undertaking that may take anywhere between 6 months to 2 years. It must be properly justified and planned.

- Application migration should be considered for applications that are expected to support critical business functionality for long time periods.

- Legacy applications can be migrated either partially, fully, or as a collection of applications on a platform (e.g., mainframe unplugs).

- Dual applications (legacy application being migrated and the replacing application) are typically supported over the period of migration.

- The effort needed to migrate depends on the architecture of the legacy application, that is, if the application is decomposable, semidecomposable, or nondecomposable.

- Tools and "migration gateways" are needed to enable application migration.

- OO technologies can play a key role in migrations by using object wrappers around the legacy components being transitioned.

- For a successful migration, the technology, the people, the plan, and the process must be paid attention to.

11.2   Migration Concepts and Strategies

Migrations take place between an existing *(source)* system to an intended *(target)* system. The source systems in our case are legacy applications that may be characterized as completely decomposable, semidecomposable (data or program decomposable), and monolithic nondecomposable (see the side bar "Categories of Legacy Applications"). The target systems in our case are OCSI applications which have the characteristics we have described earlier in this book (i.e., applications can be viewed as a set of objects, with well-defined interfaces, that can be distributed across a network, and accessed from Web browsers). The whole motivation of migration is to reengineer the source legacy applications that are inflexible and hard to maintain to the newer target OCSI applications that are flexible and scalable.

Migration of legacy applications is an expensive and risky undertaking. The costs and bene-fits of this venture must be carefully weighed. When should an application be migrated and when not? The sidebar "When to Migrate and When Not To" discusses the key reasons to make such a decision. Once a decision to migrate an application has been made, the next step is to determine one of the following migration strategies:

- Partial application migration

- Complete application migration

- System migration (retiring the mainframe)

Partial application migration transitions only a part of the application. For example, it may be necessary to migrate only the user interface (see Section 11.3) or the data (see Section 11.4) of a legacy application. Partial migrations are useful only when parts of the legacy application are sources of trouble and discontent. For example, most users do not know or care about how an application is internally structured—they see only the user interfaces or need access to the legacy data. In many cases, however, the entire legacy application may need to be migrated due to the expense and loss of opportunity associated with the mainte-nance and support of a legacy application. We discuss full application migration in Section 11.5. System migration (mainframe unplugs), discussed in Section 11.6, may be needed if all applications from one computing platform (usually a mainframe[1]) are migrated to another platform (e.g., UNIX). Many corporations have successfully used this option to retire their mainframes (usually smaller IBM 4381 computing platforms). The key steps needed to rearchitect and migrate legacy applications to exploit the latest technologies for long-range flexibility and growth requirements are as follows (we will go through an expanded version of this in Section 11.7):

1. Establish business and technical requirements that will drive and guide the migration projects.

2. Establish a migration architecture that selects the best migration approach. In particular, decompose/partition the host application and choose parts (p1, p2,...,pn) of the application to be migrated in the next few years. In many cases, the user interfaces are migrated first (i.e., migrate the text-based user interfaces to desktops and replace them with GUI technology).

3. Migrate these parts to the target (future) application:

    – Iteratively install the target platforms (computers, GUI workstations, networks, intercon-nectivity devices, etc.).

    – Design the target interfaces, applications, and databases and allocate the components to the right places

    – Use a gateway to mediate between the legacy application and the target application.

---

1. This practice is also prevalent in UNIX to Windows NT conversions.

When to Migrate and When Not To

Migration of legacy applications is a good strategy if

- The target legacy application is supporting a long-range business function that requires frequent modifications and functional enhancements. In most cases, legacy applications are inflexible and expensive to modify. The continuous cost of maintaining an old system can be crushing.

- The target legacy applications cannot satisfy the growing business needs easily (i.e., if the changes in the application are needed quickly). Legacy applications cannot be modified/extended quickly. This is not a cost issue; this is a timeliness issue which may jeopardize competitive edge. For example, if you need to change your billing systems quickly (e.g., weekly) to attract new customers, but your billing system needs three months for each change, then it is time to say a tearful goodbye to your billing system.

- The strategies of surrounding these applications or setting up data warehouses are not enough (remember surrounding an already overloaded application increases its workload). In particular, numerous interfaces to new applications are not easy to implement and manage. Once again, the legacy applications are typically difficult to interface with new applications.

- Other business drivers exist such as initiatives to replace mainframes, corporate adoption of client/server architectures, and reengineering of applications to meet new business needs.

Migrations, in general, are expensive, technically difficult, and time-consuming undertakings. This investment should not be undertaken if

- The target applications serve a business function that is being phased out (i.e., the time to migrate may be longer than the expected life of the application)

- The main value provided by the application is access to its data (i.e., its business logic is of low value). In this case, access in place (i.e., legacy data access) or data warehousing should be considered (see Chapters 9 and 10).

- The target application is too large and too heavily used. In this case, it is difficult, if not impossible, to complete the migration because it takes a great deal of commitment and money for a long time. Off-shore reengineering shops may help [Dedene 1995].

- Management commitment to complete the migration does not exist.

- Additional head counts or budget for migration are not available.

11.3 User Interface Migration to the Web

Reengineering of user interfaces is an appealing approach for many legacy applications. In essence, the character-based user interfaces (e.g., the 3270 displays) are replaced with a Web browser or other GUI/OOUI services to make the legacy systems more user friendly. The main advantage of this approach is that the usefulness and the life of the legacy application are extended considerably without a major rewrite of the entire application. This approach is especially effective for those applications that contain useful business logic and associated data services but do not appeal to the user community due to the old-style user interfaces. Migration to Web browsers is appealing because Web browsers are ubiquitous and increase the usability of legacy systems. For example, Boeing's IT managers reportedly reach 20 times more customers with their new Web-based parts sales system than they did without it [Varney 1996]. In addition, Web access to legacy systems is maturing quickly because dozens, perhaps even hundreds, of middleware vendors are working on the Web to enterprise systems mediators [Tucker 1997]. Approaches used for user interface migration consist of (see Figure 11.1):

- "Wrap" the legacy user interface by using a screen scraper
- Replace the legacy user interface with a Web or other modern GUI interface

Wrapping. Screen scrapers, described in Chapter 9, can be used as a quick and dirty way for surrounding (wrapping) the existing legacy user interface. The Web browsers (through a CGI gateway, for example) or other GUI program issue calls to the screen scraper that in turn invokes the legacy user interface operations. Many screen scrapers with Web interfaces are commercially available to support this paradigm. This approach is useful when the user interface processing of the legacy system cannot be separated from the rest of the code (i.e., the application is not decomposable). This approach does not necessitate *any* code change in the legacy application. However, the major drawback is that the performance experienced by the GUI users is not good due to the extra processing and handshaking between the GUI, screen scrapers, and the legacy user interface. Issues related to wrapping legacy code were discussed in Chapter 9. A detailed discussion of using CORBA and the Web to wrap legacy applications can be found in Klinker [1996].

Categories of Legacy Applications

Completely decomposable (all components are well structured and separable). These applications are friendly to migration efforts.

Data decomposable (data services are well structured and have well-defined interfaces). These applications are semifriendly ("neighborly") to migrations.

Program decomposable (program modules are well structured and have well defined interfaces). These applications are also semifriendly ("neighborly") to migrations.

Monolithic (unstructured applications with intermixed data, program logic, and user interface processing). These applications are hostile to migrations.

Figure 11.1 Approaches for User Interface Migration

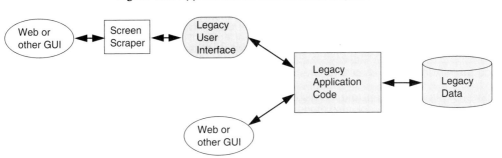

Replacement. The replacement approach is much more desirable because it completely eliminates the legacy user interfaces. In addition, this approach can also enhance and provide additional user interface capabilities that might not have been envisioned in the original application. However, this approach is primarily useful when the user interface processing code is not intermixed with the business rules and data services code. User interface replacement requires a considerable effort for applications that do not have separable user interfaces. Developers of the new interface must understand how the legacy interface was conceived and implemented, and what constraints are inherent in the old interface that cannot be violated. In large-scale systems with thousands of screens, this can be a nontrivial effort (this is essentially a reverse engineering task where developers have to pore over thousands of lines of COBOL code that "snakes" through screen handling, processing logic, and data access functions). Good tools for automatic or semiautomatic reengineering of user interfaces are needed to minimize this effort. An example of such a tool is AUIDL (Abstract User Interface Description Language) that was developed at the Computer Research Institute of Montreal [Merlo 1995].

In practice, a mixture of the two approaches can be used as a gradual user interface reengineering strategy. For example, a screen scraping wrapper can be developed initially to produce a Web-based GUI for increasing the end-user acceptability. With time, the screen scraper and the legacy screens can be retired without showing significant impact on the users. While this mixed gradual strategy can be very useful for large mission-critical applications, this strategy exposes you to several risks. First, this approach involves considerable throwaway code (i.e., the screen scraping code is developed first and then thrown away). Secondly, this approach may deter the developers from taking a fresh and fundamentally different approach to user interfaces. Finally, this approach may introduce many points of sabotage by knowledgeable users who could modify the local code during transition (many practitioners do not properly protect the code that is throwaway). Due to these reasons, the user interface reengineering process should consist of the following steps [Merlo 1995]:

1. Understand the original system and extract the code fragments that deal with user interface processing. This may be quite difficult if the user code is not decomposable.

2. Convert the extracted code into graphical specifications in terms of screens. If the extracted code is not available, then develop the graphical specification by walking through the screens.

3. Introduce improvements to the interface. Focus on the features that will enhance the usability and life of the legacy application.

4. Generate a new graphical user interface.This could be developed as a wrapper around a screen scraper.

5. Integrate the new interface into the original system. This may involve gradual steps.

11.4   Data Migration

11.4.1   Overview

Corporations in the United States reportedly spend more than $4 billion a year on different forms of data migration.[2] Data migration involves movement of data from one format/platform to another. In practice, data migration may include a wide range of issues such as data conversion (e.g., from a nonrelational to a relational database), data transformation (e.g., creation of summaries and views), data movement (e.g., movement of mainframe databases to UNIX platforms), and data allocation (e.g., determination of the locations where the data will be assigned and if redundant copies are needed). Typical examples of data migration are

*   IMS databases to Oracle, DB2, Informix, and Sybase

*   Focus system (a popular fourth-generation language) to DB2

*   Lotus Notes to/from SQLBase, SQL Server, and other RDBMSs

*   IMS, DB2, and VSAM to a data warehouse

*   Movement of data from one database server to another (this may involve data replication)

Data migration may be motivated by application migration (e.g., downsizing/rightsizing of mainframe legacy applications to cheaper platforms), database rearchitectures (e.g., IMS to DB2), adoption of client/server paradigm (e.g., allowing client applications and end users to access remote databases), data warehousing (e.g., facilitate decision support users), "data bridging" (e.g., linking of different applications through a common database), and reengineering of applications to meet new business needs. Specifically, data may be moved from one platform/format to another due to reasons such as the following:

*   In several cases, data migration is easier than application migration. For example, a viable use of legacy systems is to migrate data and use mainframe as a "client" [Gartner Group Briefing, July/ August 1994].

---

2. This expenditure is quoted by many data migration tool vendors (e.g., Evolutionary Technology, Inc.).

- Cost of new platform may be cheaper in terms of hardware, software license fees, staff time, and so forth.

- The database on the new platform may have better tools for application development and/or administration. Thus it may be quicker and cheaper to develop and maintain new applications around the new platform.

- For improved performance, it is usually better to dedicate a database server for each database instead of several databases sharing a mainframe. This strategy is commonly used for "subject" databases where each subject database is allocated to a dedicated server.

- The new platform may provide better and easier data access and manipulation tools.

- Changes in organizational policies and/or changes in business directions may necessitate the use of new platforms. For example, a corporate decision to focus more on UNIX instead of MVS for future applications may influence this choice.

However, data migration is a tedious, expensive, and time-consuming activity that must also be carefully managed. In particular, the issues of how existing applications will deal with data migrated to new platforms is of key importance. Successful migration of data and applications requires analysis of business drivers, expected benefits, and potential pitfalls. Specifically, the following factors must be kept in mind:

- One-time costs incurred due to the data migration effort. Examples of these costs are
  - Training costs for programmers, end users, technical support staff, operators, and administrators.
  - Redesign and reconstruction costs for database redesign, software conversion, and database repopulation.
  - Replacement/upgrade costs for database management system, hardware upgrade, and operating system upgrade.
  - Administrative costs for planning, operational procedure conversion, and documentation.

- Expected recurring benefits for users/developers gained from migration. Examples of these benefits are
  - Performance benefits in terms of response time, communication traffic, local I/Os, and so forth.
  - Improved availability.
  - Improved flexibility in developing new applications.
  - Improved tools for end users.
  - Better data access tools.
  - Improved development tools.

- Expected recurring benefits for administration and support. Examples of these benefits are
  - Ease of administration through improved tools.
  - Data security improvements.
  - Backup/recovery facilities.
  - Help desk and quality of technical support (it is almost impossible to get technical support for really old data sources).

The factors discussed can be converted into a checklist and used as a basis to analyze and evaluate various data migration efforts. If needed, these factors can be converted into a cost-benefit evaluation model (see Umar [1990] for an example).

The focus of this section is on migration of large and mission-critical enterprise data with primary attention to data conversion, data transformation, data transfer, and data allocation. In particular, this section will attempt to answer the following questions:

- What are the main concepts, issues, and approaches in data migration?
- What type of tools and techniques are becoming available to aid data migration projects?
- How does data allocation relate to data migration?
- What type of data allocation tools and techniques can help during the data migration projects?

11.4.2 A Framework for Categorizing Data Migration

Conceptually, data migration consists of the following logical functionalities shown in Figure 11.2 (we have used this framework to describe data replication and warehouse extraction tools):

Selection (filtering) of needed data from the source databases. The selection can be achieved through a predefined SQL statement for an RDBMS source database, or through a COBOL program, or through a 4GL tool such as Focus. The selection criteria may be null (i.e, extract an entire database) or they may be based on complex rules (e.g., choose the customers with good credit rating, choose the prices that have changed in the last 12 hours).

Transformation of data. This includes conversions of data formats and data models. For warehousing, this includes data consolidation (unification of different values), summarization, and derivation (generation of new fields).

Transmission of the data to the target site(s). This is typically accomplished through bulk data transfer software, provided by almost all vendors. It is assumed that the target site(s) have been selected by using a data allocation procedure. File Transfer Protocol (FTP), a bulk data transfer software package that operates in TCP/IP networks, is used most frequently for transferring files between heterogeneous computers (MVS, UNIX, PC-DOS, Mac) due to the popularity of TCP/IP.

Data load/update. The data are loaded at the target machines. The target data may be replaced entirely with the new data (*refreshed*) or they may update selected values to reflect changes (*deltas*). Depending on the amount of data to be loaded, special techniques may be used to speed up the load process (e.g., bulk database load).

These functionalities may be used differently by different forms of data migration. For example, some data migrations may require extensive data transformations while others may use very sophisticated data selection rules. For purpose of analysis, we propose that data migration falls into the following broad categories (Table 11.1 shows the typical functionalities used in these categories of data migration).

Figure 11.2 Data Migration Functionalities

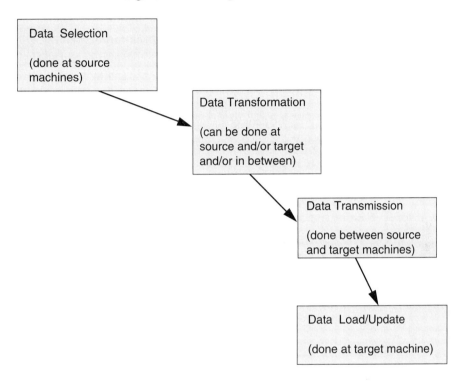

Data Downsizing. In this case, mainframe databases are moved to cheaper computing platforms. As a result, entire database(s) are migrated permanently (one hopes!) after some conversions. As shown in Table 11.1, data downsizing/rightsizing commonly requires simple data selection rules (usually an entire database or partitioned data are migrated), some data conversions (e.g., IMS to relational), bulk data transfer between source and target machines, and re-creation of records (data refreshes) at the target machines.

Data Reallocation. Databases from existing sites are reallocated to new sites to improve performance and/or availability and to reduce costs (e.g., an Informix database is moved to a faster Informix database server machine). The existing database(s) may be partitioned and distributed to several sites. Data reallocation may result in data duplication. However, it rarely involves data conversion. As shown in Table 11.1, data reallocation commonly requires simple data selection rules (usually an entire database or partitioned data is migrated), no data conversions (e.g., one Oracle database is moved from one database server to another), bulk data transfer between source and target machines, and re-creation of records (data refreshes) at the target machines.

TABLE 11.1 FUNCTIONALITIES FOR DIFFERENT DATA MIGRATION CATEGORIES

Data Migration Categories	Data Selection	Data Transformation	Data Transmission	Data Load/ Update
Downsizing/ Rightsizing	Simple	Some format and data model conversion	Bulk data transfer	Usually refresh (re-create new records)
Data Reallocation	Simple	No or minimal conversion	Bulk data transfer	Usually refresh (re-create new records)
Application Rearchitecture	Moderate	Some format and data model conversion	Bulk data transfer	Usually refresh (re-create new records)
Data Warehousing	Complex	Extensive summa- ries, derivations, consolidations	Bulk data transfer or C/S exchanges for interactive delta updates	Refresh or deltas
Data Bridges	Complex	Format and data model conversion	C/S exchanges	Usually deltas

Application Rearchitecture. The existing applications and databases are reengineered and transformed into a C/S model. This also includes permanent movement of data from the existing to the new format. As shown in Table 11.1, application rearchitecture commonly requires moderate data selection rules (usually segments of data are migrated), some data conversions (e.g., a database is redesigned for C/S interactions), bulk data transfer between source and target machines, and re-creation of records (data refreshes) at the target machines.

Data Warehousing. Data from operational systems are extracted and stored in a database exclusively for decision support. We discussed this topic extensively in Chapter 10. As shown in Table 11.1, data warehouses commonly require complex data selection rules (usually data are extracted from many operational databases), extensive data transformations, bulk data transfer plus C/S exchanges between source and target machines, and re-creation of records plus delta updates at the target machines.

Data Bridging. Data bridges are used to link applications that use the same or related databases on different platforms. Data bridges keep track of the changes between the different databases. As shown in Table 11.1, data bridges commonly require complex data selection rules, some data transformations, C/S exchanges between source and target machines, and delta updates at the target machines.

11.4.3 Data Migration Technologies

The technologies for data migration fall into the following broad categories:

- Database unload/reload utilities
- Automated data conversion tools
- Data propagators and replication servers
- Migration gateways

11.4.3.1 Database Unload/Reload Utilities and Customized Coding

These utilities provide the simplest mechanism for data migration. Data from a source database are unloaded into a sequential file, the sequential file is transported to the target database environment where it is reloaded. Virtually all commercially available DBMSs provide database unload/reload utilities. Some DBMSs write special information in the unloaded sequential files to improve the reload performance. Unfortunately, this feature introduces problems when data from one vendor DBMS need to be migrated to another vendor DBMS. A few DBMS vendors write the unloaded file in a common exchange format that can be reloaded by another vendor DBMS. Due to these difficulties, users may need to develop their own utilities for database unload/reload.

The database unload/reload approach is used widely for data migration because it allows virtually any-to-any data migration. However, this technology does require a great deal of programming and administrative work, especially if the data models of the source and target databases are different (e.g., IMS to DB2). In addition, these tools are only useful for data refresh. Use of customized programs for data migration is an extremely expensive undertaking because many extract and reload programs in COBOL, PL1, C, and other programming languages have to be written and maintained. This expense is expected to increase as hundreds of data sources in large organizations are being targeted for migration due to the pressures of data downsizing/rightsizing, application rearchitectures, data reallocations, data warehousing, and data bridging. Better tools are needed.

11.4.3.2 Automated Data Conversion Tools

These tools go a step beyond the database unload/reload utilities and attempt to automate the data conversion from one data model to another. Although many different data model conversions can be imagined, a great deal of research and development has been concentrated in the following directions:

- IMS to relational data model. This work concentrates on the heavily used IMS databases and attempts to aid the migration of IMS databases to relational databases that may reside on a diverse array of platforms (mainframes, minicomputers, and desktops). This effort is largely fueled by the application reengineering, migration to C/S architectures, and data downsizing decisions made by several organizations [Meier 1994], and [Umar 1990]. Some products such as the IBM Data Propagator convert IMS databases to DB2 and vice versa.

- Object-oriented to relational data models.This work is motivated by combining/bridging the object-oriented model with the commercially mature RDBMS technology. One approach used is to develop compilers that convert the object model into SQL code that can be used to generate relational tables. An example of this approach is presented by Blaha [1994] that combines OMtool, an object-model editor, with Schemer that converts the object model into SQL code.

As mentioned previously, manual data conversion is an expensive undertaking because it requires a great deal of work. To automate this process, a great deal of industrial attention is being paid to data conversion tool sets that automatically generate data extraction/conversion programs. The code generators typically reside on PCs and UNIX workstations and generate COBOL, C, and other programming language code that is later compiled and executed at the source machines for data extraction. The code generators usually provide a graphical user interface that is used to specify the various data sources, selection criteria, transformation rules, and target databases. The users of the generator do not usually require any programming skills. The code generators not only generate the extraction programs, but they also produce execution scripts and job control languages for the entire data migration effort. In addition, maintenance aids are generated for collection of metadata.

A wide variety of automated data conversion tools are becoming commercially available. Examples of such data conversion tools are Prism's Warehouse Manager, Evolutionary Technology's EXTRACT, and Platinum's Warehouse Toolset. A particularly interesting tool is the DBStar Migration Architect that discovers data integrity rules from the data sources (ISAM, VSAM, IMS) and uses these rules to design and populate the new relational databases. These and other tools provide varying degrees of capabilities. Table 11.2 shows the factors that can be used to evaluate data conversion tool sets.

11.4.3.3 Data Propagators and Replication Servers

This software goes beyond the automated data converters by providing facilities for synchronizing the migrated data periodically. The work in this area assumes that data migration is not a one-time effort; instead data migration is assumed to be a gradual process that requires several synchronizations between source and target databases. The tools in this category may include a wide range of capabilities such as the extraction of deltas, data conversions, synchronous and asynchronous updates to multiple copies, and summarizations for data warehouses. An example of such a product is the IBM Data Propagator [Meier 1994]. The commonly available data replicators from Sybase and Oracle, discussed in Umar [1997, Chapter 6], also provide these capabilities. In addition, many data converters that initially focused on entire database refreshing are beginning to provide add-on features for extracting deltas and just updating the target databases with the deltas.

TABLE 11.2 EVALUATION MATRIX FOR DATA CONVERSION TOOLS

Evaluation Criteria	Product 1	Product 2
Source data supported (e.g., IMS, VSAM, ISAM)		
Target data supported (e.g., DB2, Oracle, Informix)		
Ease of use (LAN/response time with concurrent users, user GUI interface, training requirements)		
Data dictionary capability (ties to IEF, ability within metadata to evaluate usage of data attributes, etc.)		
Productivity aids (e.g., generation of scripts, JCL created)		
Extraction capabilities (ability to select records/fields, computations performed such as sums and averages)		
Automatic conversion code generation capability (quality of code generated, completeness of code generated, efficiency of generated code)		
Operability (environment needed for tool operation, that is, PCs, UNIX workstations)		
Vendor maturity (strength of company, market position, etc.)		
Product maturity (product reliability, product direction)		
Product support (based on other client feedback and customer service contracts, technical support, help desk support)		
Metadata capabilities (completeness, extensibility, manageability of business rules, availability of generic metadata that can be customized)		
Product documentation/user guide (quality and ease of use of the document)		
Price (initial and maintenance)		

11.4.3.4 Migration Gateways

In many cases, data migration is a long-range undertaking where the data from one format are gradually migrated to the target format. This is especially true if the databases are being used very heavily and the end users cannot be "shut down" during migration. Migration gateways provide the software module which isolates users from migration from existing to future databases. These gateways enable data migrations gradually and can insulate the users from any changes being made to the underlying system. For example, the same user interface may be invoking new modules and databases. On the other hand, new GUIs may be accessing legacy data. Users do not know if the legacy, the new system, or a combination is supporting a given function. Migration gateways will be discussed in Section 11.5.5.

11.4.3.5 Synthesis of Data Migration Tools

In practice, a mixture of the aforementioned tools are used in most data migration projects. The general strategy should be to use automated data conversion tools as much as possible and use customized coding only if necessary. The data propagators/replication servers should be used for periodic data synchronization. Data migration gateways should be used to isolate end users from long-ranges gradual migrations. Table 11.3 shows what tool strategies should be used for different data migration problem categories.

11.4.3.6 Data Allocation/Reallocation Strategies and Tools

Data allocation/reallocation are important aspects of data migration, that is, where to put the data after migration, where to move the data for improved response time performance, or should a replicated copy be created for certain user populations. Data allocation is also an important step of database design in distributed environment (see Chapter 5). Figure 11.3 shows the different drivers for data allocation/reallocation in distributed environments.

Figure 11.3 Data Allocation/Reallocation Drivers

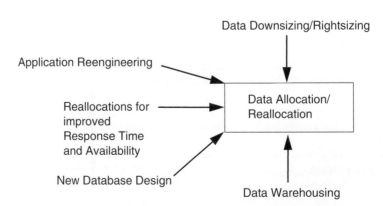

TABLE 11.3 TOOL SUITABILITY FOR DATA MIGRATION CATEGORIES

Data Migration Categories	Data Unload/ Reload Utilities and Customizing Coding	Automated Data Conversion Tools	Data Propagators and Replication Servers	Data Migration Gateways
Downsizing/ Rightsizing	Should be used rarely	Should be used as much as possible	Should be used for deltas	Should be used for gradual downsizing/rightsizing
Data Reallocation	Used frequently	Used only if conversion is involved	Replication servers used for data synchronization	Used rarely
Application Rearchitecture	Should be used rarely	Should be used as much as possible	Should be used for deltas	Should be used for gradual rearchitecture
Data Warehousing	Should be used rarely	Should be used as much as possible	Should be used for deltas	Not used
Data Bridging	Should be used rarely	Should be used as much as possible	Should be used for deltas	Not used

Data assignment involve decisions such as data partitioning (fragmentation), data clustering, and data allocation. We have discussed these topics in Chapters 5 and 6. Instead of repeating this discussion, let us present the following approaches as a summary of data assignment:

- **Common Sense:** In this approach, the datasets are allocated to the computers based on intuition and rules of thumb. This approach is appropriate if the number of candidate computers is small and also if the need for accuracy is low.

- **Trial and Error**: In this approach, an initial data allocation choice is made based on intuition and then the performance and other objective functions are measured through experiments. If the desirable results are not obtained, then the datasets are moved to other sites and the experiments are repeated.

- **Predictive Models**. This approach is conceptually similar to the trial and error approach. The main difference is that analytical and/or simulation models are used instead of the actual allocation and experimentation with the database. The analytical model discussed in Chapter 6 can be used in this approach.

- **Optimization Algorithms.** These algorithms, described in Chapter 6, can be used to automatically determine the data allocations that will minimize given objective functions. This approach is typically useful for a large number of computers where there is a need for some degree of accuracy.

- **Mixtures.** The above approaches can be mixed in a variety of ways to solve data allocation problems.

Table 11.4 shows how these approaches can be used based on two problem parameters: number of candidate computers, and the accuracy of results required. As shown in Table 11.4, common-sense approaches can be used for small problems which do not require very accurate results. However as the size of the problem as well as the accuracy requirements grow, the need for more formal approaches increases. As stated previously, however, a mixture of approaches can be, and are, used. A pragmatic data allocation procedure for solving data migration as well as distributed database design problems consists of the following steps:

Step 1: Use intuitive analysis to narrow down choices and to eliminate unsuitable solutions.A qualitative decision table helps the user make major high-level decisions.

Step 2: If a candidate solution is found, then go to step 4, else proceed.

Step 3: Use a simple allocation algorithm to determine a candidate solution. Depending on the need, any of the allocation methods described in Chapter 5 can be used here.

Step 4: Do a quick paper and pencil analysis of the candidate solution to estimate the response time by using the response time estimation method described in Chapter 6.

Step 5: Based on this analysis, allocate the datasets to the computer(s) and perform actual measurements and experiments.

Step 6: If the results are satisfactory, then stop; else go back to step 1. If the problem is too large, then a detailed optimization algorithm may be employed, if needed.

TABLE 11.4 SUGGESTED APPROACHES FOR DATA ALLOCATION

	Small Number of Candidate Computers	**Large Number of Candidate Computers**
Low Accuracy Requirements	Use Common Sense	Use Trial and Error Method
High Accuracy Requirements	Use Predictive Model	Use Optimal Allocation Algorithms

The key point is that the judgment of the analyst plays a pivotal role. This hierarchical approach allows the analyst to gradually use more sophisticated tools for more complicated problems. Based on his/her judgment, an analyst may decide to terminate this procedure at any step if enough information has been gained to make a good decision. This procedure can be used at the core of a knowledge-based decision support system for distributed resource allocations.

11.5 Complete Application Migration

11.5.1 Overview

In many cases, complete legacy applications need to be rearchitected and migrated to an OCSI environment. This strategy is especially useful for legacy applications that will continue to support mission-critical business functions for a long time. In such cases, partial migration approaches may not be enough. Complete application migration is best achieved through a gradual migration plan that systematically moves components of the legacy application to the target platform. The gradual migration plan shown in the sidebar "Legacy Application Migration Steps" presents a general framework that can be customized for different situations. Basically, the plan consists of 11 steps that are grouped into stages such as legacy application decomposition, target application design, target platform installation, migration, and cutover. We will discuss these steps as we go along.

The migration may take several years for large-scale mission-critical applications. This implies that methods and tools must be provided to use the legacy applications while they are going through transitions. OO technology can play a central role in migrations by providing object wrappers [Emerich 1996], and [Joder 1996]. The notion of a *migration gateway,* a superobject wrapper, is very useful in this context because it can enable gradual migration by insulating the users of the legacy application from changes being made to the application. We will introduce a few examples of migration gateways in the next few sections and then discuss the general capabilities of migration gateways in Section 11.5.5.

Application architectures play a pivotal role in these activities. For the purpose of this discussion, we will use the legacy application categories described earlier (decomposable, semidecomposable, and monolithic). The discussion in this section is largely based on the work by Brodie and Stonebraker [Brodie 1993], and [Brodie 1995]). Interested readers should refer to Brodie [1995] for additional information.

11.5.2 Highly Structured (Decomposable) Application Migration

Highly decomposable applications are easiest ("friendliest") for migration because each component has well-defined interfaces. Thus each component of the legacy information can be replaced gradually during the migration process. The migration process can proceed in the following directions (or a mixture):

- Migrate the legacy database first
- Migrate the legacy database last

> ## LEGACY APPLICATION MIGRATION STEPS [Brodie 1995]
>
> **Legacy application decomposition (sequential steps):**
>
> 1. Incrementally analyze the legacy application.
>
> 2. Incrementally decompose the legacy application structure.
>
> **Target application design (parallel steps):**
>
> 3. Incrementally design the target application interfaces (user, foreign application)
>
> 4. Incrementally design the target application code.
>
> 5. Incrementally design the target database.
>
> **Target environment installation (sequential steps):**
>
> 6. Incrementally install the target environment.
>
> 7. Incrementally create and install the migration gateway.
>
> **Legacy application migration (parallel steps):**
>
> 8. Incrementally migrate the legacy database.
>
> 9. Incrementally migrate the legacy application code.
>
> 10. Incrementally migrate the legacy interfaces.
>
> **Cutover:**
>
> 11. Incrementally cutover to the target application.

Database Migration First. You can migrate the legacy database first and then convert and migrate the application code and user interfaces. The specific techniques used for data migration have been discussed previously (Section 11.4). This approach is especially useful if newer applications need to access the legacy data. Thus by migrating the databases to a target platform (the target database), the new end users and applications can start accessing the legacy data, in addition to the legacy application. A migration gateway is needed to allow the legacy application code to access the new target database. This gateway must provide "target data gateway" functions by translating the legacy database calls to the target database calls (see the right-hand side of Figure 11.4). This migration approach and the migration database are called "forward" migration and gateway, respectively, by Mike Brodie [Brodie 1995]. After the database has been migrated, the application code and user interfaces can be migrated on an as-needed basis until the entire application has been migrated. At that time, the migration gateway is retired.

Database Migration Last. The database can be migrated last by first migrating the user interfaces and the application code. This approach works well for the situations when the users are tired of the old legacy user interfaces and/or "new and improved" business functionality needs to be added quickly to the legacy application code. This approach also works well if the legacy database is too large to be converted in one step. The user interface and some of the application code can be converted first while still using the legacy database. The migration gateway used for this strategy acts as a "legacy data gateway" because it converts the new database calls to the old database calls (see the left-hand side of Figure 11.4). This migration approach and the migration database are called "reverse" migration and gateway, respectively, by Mike Brodie. After the application code and user interfaces have been migrated, the legacy database can be migrated gradually on an as-needed basis until the entire application has been migrated. At that time, the migration gateway is retired.

Figure 11.4 Migration of Decomposable Applications

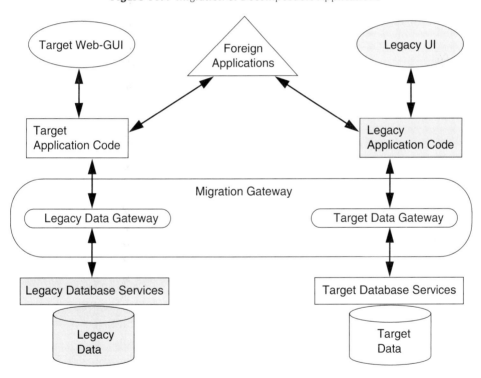

In many real-life situations, a mixture of the two strategies can be used. For example, portions of the database may be migrated first and some of the user screens (hopefully the most frequently used ones) may also be translated at the same time. In these cases, the forward as well as reverse features of the migration gateways are used throughout the migration process. This represents the situation shown in Figure 11.4 where parts of application are legacy (gray) while the others are already converted to target platforms. Once the application has been completely converted, then all the legacy components and the migration gateways should disappear.

11.5.3 Semidecomposable (Program Decomposable) Applications

For semistructured program decomposable applications, the data cannot be directly accessed—they can be only accessed by invoking predefined functions on the data because program code is decomposable. Many existing legacy applications fall into this category. Migration of these applications is harder than the decomposable applications. In particular, the migration gateways have to operate at a higher level (i.e., between the user interface and application code) as compared to the lower-level database gateways used for decomposable application migration. (See Figure 11.5). Because the user interfaces and the application code can be separated for this category of application, we can only decide whether to migrate the use interface or the application code first. Thus, the migration process can proceed in the following directions (or a mixture):

- Migrate the user interface first
- Migrate the application code first

Figure 11.5 Migration of Semidecomposable Applications

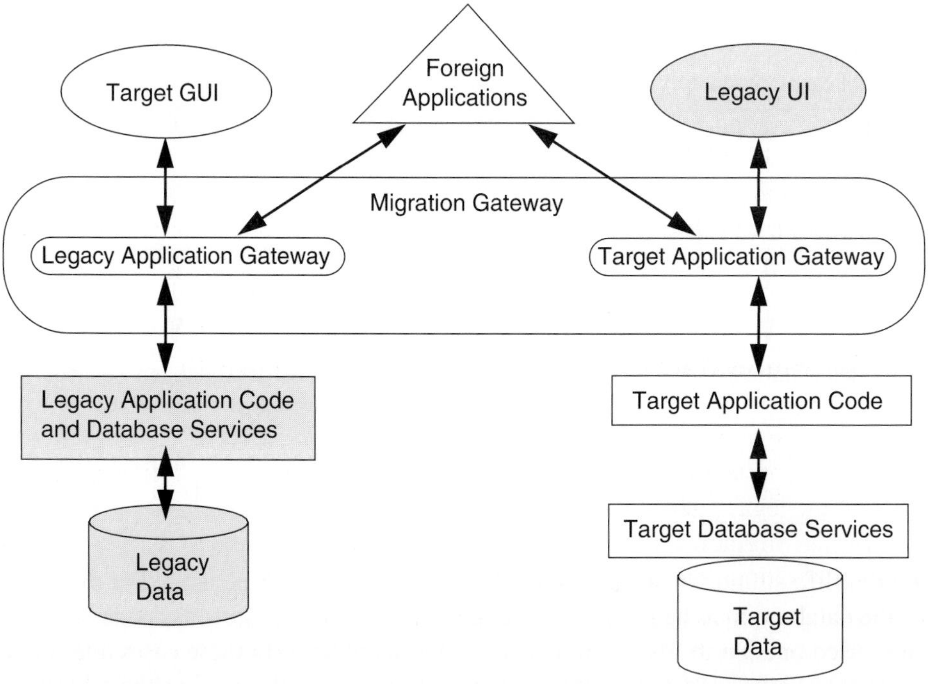

The user interfaces can be reengineered and migrated first to improve the end users' exposure to the application. The migration gateway must provide the ability to invoke the legacy application code from the new GUI processing programs (the left side of Figure 11.5). If the application code is migrated first, then the end users continue to use the existing legacy user interfaces during the migration process. The migration gateway in this case would invoke the new target application code from the legacy user interface processing programs. Naturally the two approaches can be intermixed during the migration of large-scale mission-critical applications.

11.5.4 Unstructured (Monolithic) Applications.

These applications are usually old applications that do not follow any structured methodology. In general, these applications are hardest ("hostile") to migrate. The main approach used in this situation is to insert a migration gateway between the end users and the legacy application to hide all the migration details (see Figure 11.6). Basically, all users and foreign applications first access the migration gateway (this may involve a gateway logon sequence). After this, the migration gateway may invoke the legacy application or the target application components. The migration gateways for this migration basically encapsulate the entire application and thus are quite difficult to build. In addition, the migration gateways for unstructured applications are used in full force until the entire legacy application has been converted. This is in contrast to the migration gateways for the earlier situations that retire gradually as more legacy functions migrate to the target platforms. An example of such a gateway is the Adapt/X TraxWay gateway developed at Bellcore.

Many large-scale applications may have an architecture that is a combination of decomposable, semidecomposable and monolithic. These categories can also be instrumental in determining a migration strategy for such hybrid applications. The best approach is to separate the pieces that need to be migrated first and then introduce a migration gateway that allows, as much as possible, a gradual migration with minimal exposure to the end users.

11.5.5 Migration Gateways—Technologies for Migration

Gradual application migration is a long-range undertaking where different components of the legacy application are rearchitected and transitioned to the target platform. This is especially true if the legacy applications are being used very heavily and the end users cannot be ignored during migration. Migration gateways provide the software modules that enable application migrations gradually and can

- Insulate the applications and end-user tools from any changes being made to the legacy applications. For example, the same user interface may be invoking new modules and databases. On the other hand, new GUIs may be accessing legacy data. Users do not know if the legacy, the new system, or a combination is supporting a given function.

- Translate the requests and data between the mediated components. For example, the user interface calls are translated to the target database and application calls.

Figure 11.6 Migration of Nondecomposable Applications

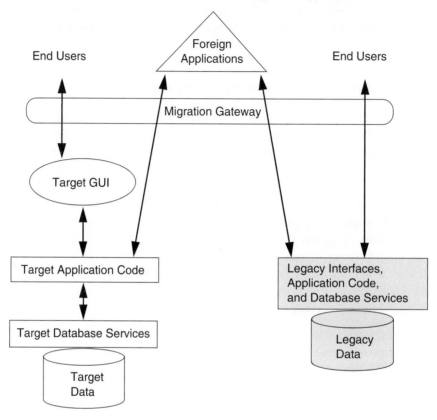

- Coordinate update synchronization between the legacy and the target system databases. For example, this feature may include the replication servers and/or two-phase commit software.

- Support intelligent features such as distributed query processing and distributed transaction processing.

- Support automated selection of best paradigm (RPC, RDA, queuing) for accessing data.

- Provide security, logging and other administrative features The host integration gateways can be used for enterprise data access or for migration of legacy applications.

These gateways are essentially the same as the legacy integration gateways discussed in Chapter 9. As a matter of fact, a legacy integration gateway can be used to integrate back-end legacy applications and facilitate gradual migration of these applications. The complexity of these gateways naturally depends on the category of legacy application being migrated (migration gateways for monolithic applications are much more complicated than the ones for completely decomposable applications). The DARWIN Project describes concepts of a migration gateway for incremental migration of legacy systems [Brodie 1993]. Bellcore's TraxWay is another example of a gateway that can be used for application migration. Figure

11.7 shows a conceptual view of a CORBA-based migration/integration gateway. We have discussed the main characteristics of this gateway in Chapter 9. This gateway would provide a common API based on CORBA IDL (see Joder [1996] for discussion).

Figure 11.7 A Migration/Integration Gateway

Client Machine	Host Integration Gateway Server			Host Machine
	Host Application Support Services			
End-user tools and Applications	CORBA Objects	• RDA support • RFA support • RPA support • Distributed query processing	Host Services	Host Applications
CORBA Clients				Host Services • IMS DB • DB2
CORBA Middleware	CORBA Middleware	• Distributed transaction processing • Synthesis services • Data translation • Security and Operational features	Host Session Agents	Host Session Services • CICS • IMS TM
Transport	Transport		Transport	Transport

11.6 System Migration—Mainframe Unplugs

11.6.1 System Migration Concepts

A growing number of companies have successfully migrated all applications from their mainframes and eventually unplugged their mainframes. Many of these unplugs have occurred on smaller IBM 4381 mainframes running fewer than two dozen applications [Eckerson 1994]. Many of these migrations, also known as "mainframe downsizing," have resulted in replacement of IBM mainframes with AS/400s and/or UNIX platforms.

System migrations are intensely parallel activities where many applications are migrated in parallel. Consider, for example, a medium-sized corporation that runs a dozen applications on an IBM 4381 machine. Let us assume that the company finds that it will save significantly by migrating these applications to a UNIX platform if the migration can be accomplished in one year. This company finds, like many other companies, that it takes between six months to an year to migrate each application. In this case, it is intuitively obvious that the dozen applications will have to be migrated in parallel.

System migration moves all applications and databases from one computing platform (usually a mainframe) to a target computing platform (AS/400, UNIX platforms, Windows NT).

System migration can provide the biggest dividends, but it is a risky undertaking. The techniques for system migration consist of

- Sliding (rehosting)
- Rearchitecting

Sliding (also known as rehosting). This basically transfers applications from one platform (host) to another without changing the functionality or architecture of the source applications. Consider, for example, a mainframe-based sales reporting application that uses a terminal host model by using a DB2 database and COBOL application programs. This application can be transferred to a UNIX platform (e.g., an IBM AIX or HP UX) system that also uses DB2 and COBOL (DB2 and COBOL are both available on a UNIX platforms at the time of this writing). With minor modifications, this application can be "slided" from a mainframe to UNIX platform. This approach is one of the quickest and cheapest for unplugging mainframes. The main time-consuming efforts are staff training and testing. After the applications have been rehosted and the conversion "blues" are over, the applications are examined for rearchitecture and functional enhancements. Rehosting can be accomplished by using the following techniques:

- Recompilation and testing of the application on the new platform. This may require some changes to the application code (for example, COBOL programs usually require conversion of its ENVI-RONMENT DIVISION statements when COBOL programs are migrated from one platform to another).

- Emulation of the initial host code on the new host. For example, CICS/MVS applications can be transferred to OS2 and AIX environments by using the CICS for OS/2 and CICS/6000.

- Replacement of mainframe application with a vendor-supplied package. For example, a mainframe order processing application can be replaced with a UNIX-based order processing package if it satisfies the requirements.

Rearchitecture. System migration is a good opportunity to rearchitect the classical terminal host applications to OCSI architectures. This strategy requires extra effort but can have long range benefits because the new architectures may better satisfy the growing business needs. Rearchitecture, if chosen, requires starting from scratch with requirement gathering and project planning as the first steps. Rearchitecture involves a combination of data architectures, application software architectures, and user interface reengineering. We have discussed these issues extensively in previous chapters (Chapters 5 and 6) and in this chapter.

11.7   A Procedure for Migration

Many technical as well as organizational factors need to be kept in mind for migration of large and mission-critical applications. Due to the implications of rearchitecting and migration of mission-critical applications, the following pragmatic rule of thumb should be used:

> Time life of the reason for migration should be longer than the migration itself.

In other words, let us assume that you initiate a two-year application migration effort with the primary reason of hardware cost savings. However, if the hardware cost savings disappear in six months due to vendor prices, then you have a very tough year and half ahead of you. Other measures, listed in the sidebar "Cautions for Migrations," should be considered before launching a migration effort.

A systematic procedure, described in this section, is needed to allow the various trade-offs to be evaluated and proper courses of action to be taken. This procedure, based on a synthesis of my own experience with the experiences reported by Brown [1996[3]] and Brodie [1995], is primarily intended for the migration of large and mission-critical corporate applications. Many of the procedure steps can be simplified for smaller and less-critical applications. The procedure consists of the following steps:

1. Establish and analyze business and technical requirements that will drive and guide the migration projects.

2. Establish a migration architecture that selects the best migration approach.

3. Acquire or build the software needed to enable migration, (for example, migration gateways).

4. Migrate the selected application components to the target application.

Cautions for Migrations

Here are some notes of caution while undertaking migrations [Mowbray 1996, Brown 1996, Hess 1995]:

- Migrations from mainframe-based legacy to distributed computing changes not only the technology but also the IS organization, that is, the roles and jobs of IS staff change due to migration. Thus your staff skills need to migrate with the technology.

- The work load of the legacy system continues during migration.

- There is very limited, if any, additional head count or budget for the transition.

- The most successful transitions are based on focused results—a few strategic applications that deliver significant value to the business.

- Migration is more an art than science—it is difficult to predict and manage because each migration project has its own unique nuances.

- To succeed, it is important to develop a detailed time line with risk analysis.

---

3. Brown [1996] reports experience of managing a project that gradually migrated 11 insurance legacy applications to OO applications.

11.7.1 Step 1: Business Analysis and Migration Planning

It is important to clearly understand the business drivers and specify why the migration is taking place. The following steps provide a good starting point:

- Assess Business Goals: It is important to identify the goals and objectives of application migration and understand its role in the short-term and long-term goals of the IS organization. It is important to ask questions such as: What is the primary driver for application migration (cutting cost, improving customer service, business process reengineering, data warehousing, etc.)? Is there a primary champion of this migration?

- Analyze the applications to be migrated. The legacy applications (a1, a2,...,an) that will be migrated need to be analyzed in terms of the business processes that are supported by these applications. An impact matrix which shows the business processes, new applications, end-user tools, and databases that access or feed into/from the legacy applications may be needed.

- Assess readiness for migration. The human and organizational factors play a key role in mission-critical application migration projects. In many cases, data migration and user interface migration precede the entire application migration and can thus impact job assignments and staffing. User interface migration especially has end-user and organizational implications.

Based on the business analysis, a go/no go decision is made. A migration plan is developed if a "go" decision is made. A migration plan includes information such as the following [Brown 1996], and [Eckerson 1994]:

- Gradual versus quick migration. A gradual migration plan is needed if the applications to be migrated are large, used heavily, and are based on older technology (IMS, flat files) and thus may require extensive conversion.

- Main steps of migration. The main steps, the deliverables, and time lines are assigned.

- Staff assignments.The roles and responsibilities of internal IS staff as well as external consultants and systems integrators are specified.

- Project management. The main milestones, budgets, policies, and procedures are specified.

For large and mission-critical applications, it is necessary to define the requirements that drive the data migration task and must be satisfied by the migrated database. These requirements are specified after interviewing the producers as well as users of legacy information. It is important to start with an existing model of the application being migrated. In addition, it is important to develop an understanding of the following operational requirements before proceeding:

- Size information (number of users who will access the legacy database, database size)

- Response time (average, worst case) requirements of the users

- Scaling and growth requirements

- Security requirements

- Availability restrictions

- Connectivity needed from user sites (e.g., from PCs, Macs, UNIX)

- Interoperability and interfaces with other (existing/proposed) systems

- Backup/recovery needs and disaster handling

- Policy restrictions (e.g., standards and policies to be followed, application control, and auditing restrictions)

11.7.2 Step 2: Develop and Justify a Migration Architecture

To develop a migration architecture, you decompose/partition the legacy application and choose parts (p1, p2,...,pn) of the application to be migrated in the next few years. In many cases, the user interfaces are migrated first (i.e., migrate the text-based user interfaces to desktops and replace them with GUI technology). Data migrations are also a good starting point if the new systems need quick access to legacy data. Development of a migration architecture involves several decisions such as the following:

- What application components should be migrated and where should the migrated components be allocated to?

- How will the migrated components fit within the information architecture of the organization?

- How will the existing/new users and applications access the migrated components (interconnectivity and interoperability)?

- What will be the impact of migration on the IT infrastructure?

The first step is to identify the applications that can be moved entirely to smaller machines without splitting.The following applications may not be good candidates for migration to small platforms:

- Large database applications that are shared by thousands of users

- The applications that are closely tied to other mainframe applications and databases

- The applications that require strong central security and control

- The applications that require around-the-clock availability

Next, the major migration options are specified. For most applications, the following options are viable:

- Migrate user interfaces only

- Migrate data only

- Migrate complete applications

- Migrate groups of applications

- Mixtures of the above

Factors used in evaluating the options include total cost of conversion, hardware cost, software cost, end-user training costs, response time implications, scaling and growth requirements, and other factors specified as migration requirements. Table 11.5 shows a matrix that can be used as a basis to choose the most appropriate migration strategy.

Connectivity (how the migrated applications/database will be accessed from remotely located client end-user tools and applications), and interoperability (how the new applications/database will interoperate with other new and/or existing databases in the system) are of key importance. We have discussed these issues in Chapter 9.

The information architecture after migration is mapped to the underlying computer-communication platform (IT infrastructure) and trade-offs are evaluated (too much data on one site, backup sites, too much processing on one site, performance, potential network bottlenecks, security, and availability exposures). As a result of this analysis, the platform could be modified (e.g., bigger machines, more machines, redesign of network). This may require detailed analytical analysis of performance trade-offs due to data allocation and even the use of an optimal resource allocation algorithm.

TABLE 11.5 INTUITIVE ANALYSIS OF MIGRATION STRATEGIES

Solution Options / Evaluation Factors	User Interface Migration	Data Migration	Complete Application Migration	System Migration (Mainframe Unplugs)
Migration cost				
Hardware/ software cost				
End-user training cost				
Flexibility Gains				
Performance				
Availability				
Manageability and control				
Security				

11.7.3   Step 3: Implementation

This phase involves issues such as the following:

- Where exactly will the migrated components be assigned (partitioned, replicated, etc.)?
- What type of migration tools and techniques will be employed?
- What type of implementation logistics will be needed to support the migration?

The migrated components can be assigned to a wide range of computing platforms. For example, the user interfaces can be allocated to desktops, the application can be allocated to mid-range computers, and databases can be kept at the mainframes. We have discussed detailed algorithms for resource allocations in Chapters 5 and 6.

The migration tools, as discussed earlier in this chapter, include reverse engineering tools, data transformation tools, replication servers, and migration gateways. The factors to be used for evaluating these tools include the application components being migrated, legacy applications supported, the target application supported, degree of automation provided, price, infrastructure restrictions, vendor support, and so forth. See the appropriate sections on user interface migration, data migration, and complete application migration for more details.

Implementation logistics for migration are dependent on the strategy chosen (user interface migration, data migration, complete application migration, system migration). Detailed discussion of the implementation steps is beyond the scope of this book. However, the following steps are typical:

- Determine what will be bought and what will be implemented in-house. For larger problems, it may be better to choose a basic migration gateway and then customize/expand it to meet organization needs.
- Establish an implementation team.
- Run a pilot if appropriate.
- Conduct a detailed state-of-the-market analysis of the access technologies needed.
- Prepare and send requests-for-prices (RFPs) for the access technologies.
- Choose appropriate migration/reengineering technology suppliers.
- Train staff for implementation (vendor-provided training can be beneficial).
- Acquire and install needed hardware/software and gateways.
- Integrate and expand the migration technologies.
- Initiate development activities.

11.7.4 Step 4: Deployment and Support Considerations

After a migration approach has been implemented, it needs to be deployed, supported, and managed like any other organizational activity. In particular, the following issues need to be considered:

- Estimate time and cost needed for deployment and support
- Establish policies, procedures, and roles for deployment and support
- Analyze the organizational issues (staff estimates, training, end-user impact)
- Assign the support to an organizational unit
- Train staff for operation and support (migration gateways need extensive support)
- Monitor the performance and progress of the migration process
- Seek feedback from users about the performance of the resulting product

11.8   State of the Practice: Examples and Case Studies

Many migration efforts were initiated in 1992 and 1993 when C/S technology was new and very popular. Although a few case studies tout successful migration of applications, the actual results of the migration tide have been somewhat mixed. In fact, several companies have halted or postponed the migrations. For example, an *Information Week* reader survey conducted at the end of 1995 indicated that 80 percent of the survey respondents had to reevaluate, cancel, or pull back from client/server migration projects [DePompa 1995]. Perhaps this is why very few migration case studies are appearing at the time of this writing (most case studies are on legacy access and/or warehousing). Here is a sample of a few case studies and a detailed migration example.

11.8.1 Short Case Studies ("Snippets")

Hewlett Packard's Migration to Client/Server Architecture [Ross 1993]. HP initiated an effort to move its terminal-host legacy information systems to client/server applications in 1989. The migration from legacy terminal-host applications to this C/S application architecture took two forms: leverage and design from scratch. HP decided to leverage the operational applications and decided to redo the obsolete applications. During this migration, HP invested in hardware, software, telecommunications, and staff training. New skills for developers as well as data center staff were needed. In addition, standards and guidelines were developed for development methodologies and platforms. We reviewed this case study in Chapter 8.

Keyport Life Insurance Co., a Boston-based insurance company, initiated a four-year downsizing effort in 1989. The effort concentrated on migration from two mainframes to an Ethernet-based PC environment. They expected cost savings of $1.5 million out of a total IS budget of $5 million. They encountered many hidden costs that were not thought of initially. In addition, the PC-LAN environment was not as mature as the mainframe for administrative policies and procedures (e.g., change control), and security became a major problem. Backup/recovery took too long (backups over Ethernet with a personal computer took 5 hours nightly, 10 hours weekly, even with two tape backup units). The migration effort encountered several obstacles such as culture shock, staff retraining, and lack of application software and application developer tools. *Source:* "Dirty Downsizing," *Computerworld,* special report, August 10, 1992.

Textron Financial Corp., in Providence, RI, downsized from an IBM 3090 mainframe to LANs with Microsoft SQL Server. A new real estate application was developed on the LAN and showed shorter development cycle (6 months compared to 12–18 months). However, many functions from the mainframe could not be moved to LANs because they were too complex and/or too large. A few functions did move successfully, such as the bulk of an inventory system that was moved to a 75-user LAN. The customer information was kept on a mainframe DB2 database that was accessed through a gateway. A major observation was that the role of MIS changed to system integrators as compared to traditional analysts. Finally, there were no indications of major cost savings. *Source:* Korzenioski, P., "Many Different Paths to Get to Downsizing," *Software Magazine,* January 1993, pp. 81–85.

Migration through Off-Shore Reengineering. Dedene and DeVreese [Dedene 1995] describe how two large-scale legacy applications from Sidmar Steel and Catholic University of Leuven, both from Belgium, were reengineered by using off-shore software houses. We described the experience with Sidmar Steel in Chapter 8. The interested reader should review the original source for information about the Catholic University conversion. Basically, the results of this experience are positive, suggesting that off-shore software houses are good candidates for application migration.

Oil Driller Replaces Mainframes [Brandel 1995]. Global Marine, Inc., a Houston-based oil driller, decided to replace its IBM mainframe system with a UNIX-based client/server environment to initially reduce cost but also to provide more flexibility and to reduce development time. A three-year detailed plan for migration was developed with a clear definition of goals and risk analysis. The migration, initiated in 1992, was completed in 1995 when the mainframe was unplugged and the two-tier UNIX-based client/server system took over. The new system consists of Sun servers running Sybase databases that are accessed by PCs running PowerBuilder clients. The analysis of this case study by Dr. Lewis Leesburg, Director of IS Research at UCLA, gives high marks to this migration for improving the quality of service and the corporate bottom line. However, the migration ran into several problems such as lack of adequate C/S tools, problems with business partners, and resistance from the users (they did not want to generate their own reports).

Holstein Association Puts the Mainframe to Pasture [Rinaldi 1994]. Holstein Association is a Vermont-based company that maintains records on more than 17 million cattle. The company kept its records on an IBM 4381 system. The management decided to transition away from mainframe to meet the demands of increased workload (e.g., 353,000 new animals added to the database in one year), to improve service to its 50,000 members, and to increase the productivity of internal staff. The new platform is a pair of HP servers with Informix databases. The main challenge was to provide access to the mainframe and the HP servers during the transition period. The staff spent much more time on this issue than budgeted. Another issue was that the corporation was used to a great deal of handholding by IBM.

Migration from OSI to CORBA [Eckert 1996]. The ISODE package provides e-mail and directory services on an ISO platform (see http://www.isode.com for a description of ISODE). Eckert describes the experience of migrating the ISODE-based External Reference Manager (XRM) of a multimedia mail system to CORBA. This case study describes the technical aspects of migrating to CORBA with discussions of the communication paradigm (RPC to object invocations) and changes in IDL.

11.8.2 A Detailed Example: Migration of a Project Management System

In an electronic component corporation, a companywide Project Management System (PMS) facilitates three functions: project creation, project tracking, and electronic transmission of the project information to project managers for status review. Typically, there are three categories of data associated with projects:

- Administrative data that contain information such as project number, organization responsible, the manager's name and phone, funding source, funding level, major customer(s), planned completion dates and various other project administration indicators.

- Text data that typically contain descriptions of the project work, its basic assumptions, and expected benefits.

- Status information that describes the financial status (e.g., the amount of money spent), and progress status (e.g., milestones completed, open issues, etc.).

The initial PMS was an IBM mainframe MVS-DB2 application which provided displaying, updating, and printing capability of project information over an SNA network. The project number was used for validation within other internal financial systems on MVS. The initial PMS system maintained a table of access security (project security table). Support staff could only access their authorized project information through this security table. Figure 11.8 gives a high-level functional view of the initial system. The PMS system accessed the project data and security tables stored on MVS. The main users of this system are the company comptrollers who send the information to the project managers. Initially, project managers did not have a direct way to review and/or update project information. The initial process was to download project information to the comptroller department's computers (PCs). Then the project information was transferred to the project managers through e-mail (some project managers use PCs, the other use UNIX platforms). After a project manager had reviewed and updated the project information associated with the project, the comptroller support staff received a copy through e-mail and then updated the MVS PMS for the official information and printing.

Figure 11.8 Initial Project Management System

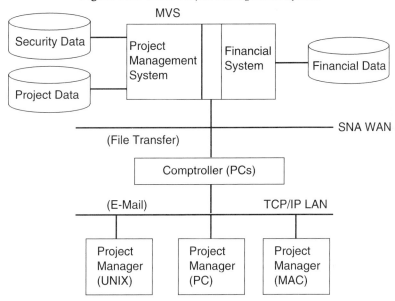

Step 1: Business Drivers and Requirement Definition

With increasing responsibilities of the project managers and reduction in the number of comptroller support staff, there was a need to provide a mechanism that would allow all the project managers to track their project information on-line directly. There were about 300+ project managers who resided in 10 regions of the company. Each region has a comptroller. The main requirement was to support the 300+ project managers directly with minimal or no intervention from the comptrollers. The following statements provided additional information:

- Security and confidentiality of project information were crucial requirements. In the initial PMS system, support staff could only access their authorized project information through a security table. It was up to the support staffs to distribute the project information to the responsible project managers. An equivalent security system would be needed, that is, as a policy, the project security table would provide the security for auditing any future system.

- Size of the project information database was about 800 Mb.

- Each region had different local software packages (e.g., Microsoft Word, etc.) to manage their project information. Some of these packages ran on UNIX-based word processors, some ran on

Mac-based word processors, and others ran on PC-based word processors. Before updating the MVS PMS system, all word processor macros had to be filtered out to first obtain a plain data file. This was a very time-consuming task for the support staff. This task had to be eliminated.

- Organizational and strategic pressures forced reduction of the operating cost by 20 percent. This could be accomplished if mainframe CPU and DASD usage were reduced by migrating to cheaper platforms. The comptroller support staff was part of the company overhead and this overhead was being reduced. Thus any solutions had to consider reduction of the comptroller staff. The organization feels that the future of the business systems will move from expensive mainframes to cheaper microcomputers without loosing performance.

Step 2: Development of a Solution Architecture

Based on an initial analysis of the problem, a task force identified the following viable options:

1. Keep the initial configuration intact (i.e., do not change anything).

2. Keep the project data and PMS system on MVS and provide access to them from terminal emulation software from the project manager's desktop.

3. Keep project data and PMS on MVS and provide access to project data from client tools located on the project manager's desktop.

4. Move most of the project data and PMS to a UNIX platform and provide access to project data from client tools located on the project manager's desktop.

These options were evaluated against the key business drivers and requirements stated in Step 1. Figure 11.9 summarizes the results of this analysis.

The task force proposed to move most of the project data and PMS software MVS to a UNIX environment and use the client/server architecture between the UNIX server and desktops (configuration 3). This solution was chosen even though it increased initial operating cost (had to buy a UNIX machine and C/S middleware software) and raised some security issues. However, the proposed solution provided maximum flexibility to the project managers. They ran their own tools, bypassed the comptrollers, and made the PMS system available directly to the project managers.

The main motivation for migrating the PMS data and programs away from MVS was to reduce MVS workload. For example, if the 300+ users were allowed to logon directly to MVS PMS system through terminal emulations or C/S middleware (instead of the 10 comptrollers who initially logged on to MVS PMS), it could cause response time problems for PMS as well as other users of MVS (the MVS system supports many other production systems). In addition, setting up 300+ users to access the SNA network required additional hardware and software. With technical staff reductions at the central mainframe site, the increasing number of users could have created additional support bottlenecks.

Figure 11.10 shows a conceptual view of the proposed solution. According to the proposed architecture, a project manager can directly display, update, or print the official project information. The client software may run on UNIX workstations, PCs, MACs, and

Figure 11.9 Intuitive Analysis of Migration Strategies

Evaluation Factors (Information Requirements)	Keep the Initial Configuration	Project Data and PMS on MVS, Direct Access from Desktops through Terminal Emulations	Project Data and PMS on MVS, Direct Access from Desktop Clients	Move Most of the Project Data and PMS Functionality to UNIX and Access UNIX from Desktop Clients
Give more control to project manager	−3	−1	2	3
Eliminate intervention by comptrollers	−3	3	3	3
Support 300+ users directly	−3	−2	−1	2
Flexibility and growth for each project manager's needs	−3	−1	2	3
Reduce operating costs	3	2	1	0
Enforce security	3	3	2	1

Legend: + 3 means that the requirement is satisfied very well by this configuration

− 3 means that the requirement is not satisfied very well by this configuration

LAN servers. The administrative data, text data, and status information are migrated to a UNIX machine. A copy of the administrative data will be maintained on MVS to provide interface with other MVS-based financial systems through a very simple Project Tracker on MVS (this system only supplies project administration data to other systems). Due to the complexity of maintaining dual database synchronization, the MVS database for the text description and status information will not be maintained. The UNIX-based PMS will interface with MVS for project number validation. The following processing steps were proposed:

- All users will invoke a client which will access the PMS system on UNIX. The UNIX PMS database will have the entire project description. The MVS PMS database only keeps valid project administration information (especially project numbers).

- If a new project is to be initiated, then the UNIX PMS will access the MVS project database for creation of a new project with associated administrative data (e.g., project number). This administrative data are sent back to the UNIX server and stored in the PMS UNIX database.

- If an existing project description needs to be reviewed or updated, then only the UNIX PMS database is accessed. There is no need for MVS database access.

- If a project is to be deleted, then the UNIX server will access the MVS database and delete the project administration data from MVS. The project is then deleted from the UNIX PMS database.

The proposed solution satisfies the requirements stated in Step 1. This solution also attempts to eliminate the involvement of the comptrollers and puts the project information directly in the hands of project managers. The initial cost to set up the new UNIX client/server application requires a one-time upfront charge which involves hardware, software, and the database management system. The operational cost savings will take place thereafter.

Figure 11.10 Proposed Project Management System

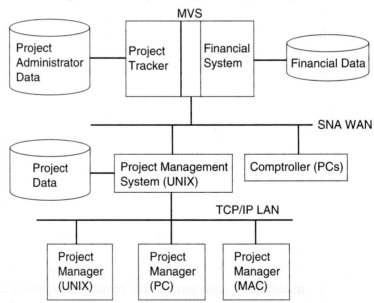

Step 3: Detailed Design and Implementation

Rough data partitioning and clustering were done before allocation (see Chapter 5 for a review of data partitioning and clustering). The data to be allocated were partitioned by regions because very few projects cross regions. Thus, 10 data partitions were created. The need for clustering data between two regions arose because these two regions had several common projects. Thus the 10 partitions were reduced to 9 datasets (d1,d2,...,d9), where d9 is the clustered dataset from two regions. Although there are many computers in each region, each region designated a database server for the regional project database.

The data allocation problem is to allocate the datasets d1, d2,...,d9 to regions r1,r2,r3,...,r10. The following issues must be addressed:

- Should all datasets be allocated to one UNIX machine dedicated to project management?
- Should the datasets d1,d2,...,d8 be allocated uniquely to the regions r1, r2,...,r8? Is there a need for some data redundancy among these regions?
- Where should d9 be allocated? Should it be allocated to r9, r10, or both?

After some quick paper and pencil analysis, the first strategy was used because one UNIX machine could easily handle 300+ users plus house the 800 Mb of project information. The UNIX machine is dedicated to this purpose and is henceforth referred to as the Project Management Server. The response time of each project manager is primarily a function of the data transmission time (the Project Management Server is a very powerful machine and is very lightly loaded). The Project Management Server is accessed through a TCP/IP Ethernet LAN (the transmission rate is 10 Mbits per second at maximum). This would satisfy most performance requirements. However, if the TCP/IP LAN has significant network traffic and the project management server is used more frequently, then the server hardware should be upgraded and the network should be segmented for improved performance.

The PMS database will maintain the security access table and will be transparent to the MVS PMS system security. Furthermore, there will be additional security to authenticate each client. Since most of the users are linked to the TCP/IP LAN, the C/S middleware needed to connect the end-user tools to the remotely located PMS database must use the TCP/IP communication protocol. The TCP/IP connection will need to be installed for those users who do not have a TCP/IP connection. The project management server must also interact with the MVS project tracker for validation since the project number is created on MVS, and the project number interfaces with other existing MVS financial systems for validation.

The key point of this case study is that an MVS project database is migrated to UNIX based on the systematic methodology presented in this chapter. This case study shows how the business drivers were documented and how the decisions were made to conform to the business drivers. The result of this analysis produced a solution in which the project data are migrated to a UNIX machine with a copy of project administration information kept at MVS for interfacing with other mainframe-based systems. The project managers could review and update the project status data by using their own desktop tools. However, they could not create new projects or delete existing projects without coordination with the mainframe system.

11.9 State of the Market: Products

A wide range of tools for assisting in application migration have become available. These tools can aid in partial application migration activities such as user interface and data migration, complete application migration, and system migration (mainframe unplugs).

The tools for user interface migration include a wide range of screen scrapers such as Apertus Enterprise Access from Apertus, IRMA/QuickApp from Attachmate, Rumba from Wall Data, WCL from Multi Soft, and Client Builder from Client Soft. In addition, several object wrappers such as Odaptor from Hewlett-Packard, PARTS CICS from Digitak, and CL/7 from Century Analysis may be of some help. For data migration, data extractors and converters such as the Data Propagator from IBM, PRISM Warehouse Manager from PRISM, EXTRACT from Evolutionary Technologies, and Platinum Data Transport from Platinum should be reviewed. In addition, DBStar's Migration Architect could be very useful because it analyzes legacy data to determine data schema, creates logical and physical schema, and assists in data migration. If data migration also involves data cleanup, then data cleanup tools such as Integrity from Vality and Enterprise/Synch from Apertus could be used.

For full migration, the migration gateways play a key role. Examples of the commercially available gateways that can be used in this area are the Adapt/X TraxWay from Bellcore, EDA/SQL from Information Builders, and Data Integrator from Digital Equipment Corp. In addition, the database gateways from database vendors such as Informix, Oracle, and Sybase can be especially useful for migrating decomposable applications. In addition, a variety of tools that analyze existing application code and do reverse engineering are invaluable in understanding the existing legacy applications and rearchitecting them. An example of such a tool is the Legacy Workbench from Knowledgeware that analyzes COBOL code quality, restructures programs, and identifies business logic for reuse.

For system migration, emulators that mimic one computing platform on another are very popular. Examples of such tools are the IBM CICS/6000 and CICS for OS2 that emulate the CICS/MVS calls. System migration can essentially use all of the partial or full application migration tools since system migration involves migration of several applications, usually in parallel.

Brief discussions and comparisons of the aforementioned tools appear in periodicals such as *Datamation, Database Programming and Design , Byte,* and *Computerworld.* In particular, *Software Maintenance News* publishes a comprehensive reengineering tools survey.

11.10 State of the Art: Research Notes

Research in the following areas could have long-term payoffs:

- Methodologies for evaluating trade-offs and streamlining the migration process
- Tools to assist and automate the migration activities

An example of research in methodologies includes the legacy- and reuse-based software life cycle proposed by Ahrens and Prywes [Ahrens 1995]. The essence of this approach is that legacy software processing can become a key catalyst for transitioning to a reuse-based approach if domain and software knowledge can be extracted about the reusable components of legacy systems. Harry Sneed [Sneed 1995] proposes a way to quantify the costs and prove the benefits of reengineering over other alternatives. He proposes a five-step planning process that starts with an analysis of the legacy system and ends with contract negotiation. Research on structural redocumentation that can be used to understand the architecture of large-scale legacy applications has been reported [Wong 1995]. In fact, many of the software reengineering papers focus on reverse engineering that can be of direct value to the migration of legacy applications [Arnold 1993], and [Chikofsky 1990].

The main need for research in tools is in the area of migration gateways. Ideally, a migration gateway should be available to provide transparent migration of decomposable, semidecomposable, and nondecomposable applications. Most of the gateways at present are at the database level (i.e., they translate SQL to non-SQL or vice versa). A CORBA-based migration gateway with the capabilities listed in Section 11.5.5 can be very helpful at present. In addition, there is a need for better specification extractors (the tools that generate specifications from code), architecture extractors (the tools that will extract application architecture from code), and generally speaking, reverse engineering tools.

11.11 Summary

Gradual migration of legacy applications is receiving a great deal of industrial attention because it allows rearchitecture and systematic transitioning of legacy applications that need to serve the long-range business goals of an organization. Application migration involves a wide range of issues such as data reengineering (e.g., from nonrelational to a relational database), code reengineering (e.g., transformation of a monolithic application to a collection of objects), and user interface reengineering (e.g., conversion from text to graphical user interfaces). This chapter has focussed on migration of large and mission-critical applications. We introduced a conceptual framework that can be used to categorize and analyze different aspects of application migration and discussed the main tools and techniques that are becoming available to aid the application migration projects. A methodology is developed, and illustrated through an example, which allows IS staff to systematically approach the application migration problems and maximize the chances for success.

11.12 Case Study: Migration for XYZCorp

The XYZCorp management has agreed to initiate migration of the order processing application. This application is a UNIX-based flat file system that was developed in the 1980s to receive orders, verify them, and send them to the mainframe for shipping/receiving and billing purposes. You have been asked to produce a detailed migration plan for the rearchitecture and transition of the order processing application to a Windows NT platform and employ an OCSI paradigm. What specific steps and tools/techniques will you employ in this migration?

Hints about the Case Study

The four-step migration procedure described in Section 11.7 can be used in this case study. It is best to convert the database (flat file to relational databases), the programs (C to C++), and the user interfaces (text screens to Web-based GUI) of this application.

11.13 Problems and Exercises

1. Consider a legacy application of your choice. Work through the migration details of this application by using the four-step migration procedure described in Section 11.7. For each step, list the major decisions, the techniques/tools employed, and the final choices made by you.

2. Review, expand, and improve Table 11.1 to make it general for any data migration.

3. Complete Table 11.2 to evaluate some of the data conversion products.

4. Complete Table 11.5 for a specific case.

5. Review and analyze a migration gateway that is commercially available.

11.14 Additional Information

Literature on legacy application migration has grown steadily since 1992. Relevant literature appears under headings such as "legacy migration," "application/system downsizing," "software reengineering," and "reverse engineering." In particular, the book by Brodie and Stonebraker [Brodie 1995] contains detailed discussion about gateways, interfaces, and implementation approaches for incremental migration of legacy applications. *Object Magazine*, October 1996, is a special issue on migration strategies and has many articles on how to use the object technologies for successful migrations. *IEEE Software,* January 1995, is a special issue on legacy systems and contains several informative papers. Similarly, *Communications of the ACM,* May 1994, is a special issue on software reengineering with many interesting articles. The Patricia Seybold Group's special report on mainframe migration strategies [Eckerson 1994] contains a great deal of practical information. In addition, the collection of papers on software reengineering [Arnold 1993] and the *Reverse Engineering Newsletter* edited by Mike Olsem should be reviewed.

Ahrens, J., and Prywes, N., "Transitioning to a Legacy-and-Reuse-Based Software Life Cycle," *IEEE Computer,* October 1995, pp. 27–36.

Arnold, R., ed., "Software Reengineering," *IEEE CS Press,* 1993.

Bennett, K., "Legacy Systems: Coping with Success," *IEEE Software,* January 1995, pp. 19–23.

Blaha, M., et al., "Converting OO Models into RDBMS Schema," *IEEE Software,* May 1994, pp. 28–39.

Brahmadathan, K., and Ramarao, K., "On the Design of Replicated Databases," *Information Sciences,* Vol. 65, Nos. 1 and 2, 1992, pp. 173–200.

Brandel, M., "Oil Driller Is Afloat and Ready for the Next Boom," *Client/Server Journal, Computerworld,* special issue, June 1995, pp. 26–27.

Brodie, M. L., "The Promise of Distributed Commuting and the Challenge of Legacy Information Systems," in Hsiao, D. et al. (eds.), *Proc. IFIP TC2/WG2.6 Conference on Semantics of Interoperable Database Systems,* Lorne, Australia, November 1992, Elsevere North Holland, Amsterdam 1993.

Brodie, M. L., and Stonebraker, M., "DARWIN: On the Incremental Migration of Legacy Information Systems," Technical Memorandum, Electronics Research Laboratory, College of Engineering, University of California, Berkeley, March 1993.

Brodie, M. L., and Stonebraker, M., *Migrating Legacy Systems: Gateways, Interfaces & the Incremental Approach,* Morgan Kauffman, 1995.

Brown, B., "Leading a Successful Migration," *Object Magazine,* October 1996, pp. 38–43.

Buckles, B. P., and Harding, D. M., "Partitioning and Allocation of Logical Resources in a Distributed Computing Environment," General Research Corporation Report, Huntsville, Alabama, 1979.

Casey, R. G., "Allocation of Copies of a File in an Information Network," *Summer Joint Computer Conference 1972,* AFIPS Press, Vol. 40, 1972

Chepetsky, S., "Migrating Legacy Apps Key to C/S Computing," *Client/Server Today,* July 1994, p. 8.

Chikofsky, E. and Cross, J., "Reverse Engineering and Design Recovery: A Taxonomy," *IEEE Software,* January 1990, pp. 13–17.

Chu, W. W., "Optimal File Allocation in a Multiple Computer System," *IEEE Transactions on Computers,* October 1969, pp. 885–889.

Coulouris, G., and Dollimore, J., *Distributed Systems: Concepts and Design,* Addison Wesley, 1989.

Dedene, G., and DeVreese, J., "Realities of Off-Shore Reengineering," *IEEE Software,* January 1995, pp. 35–45.

DePompa, B., "Corporate Migration: Harder Than It Looks," *Information Week,* December 4, 1995, pp. 60–68.

Eckerson, W., "Mainframe Migration Strategies: A Framework for Moving from Mainframes to Open Systems," *Open Information Systems,* Patricia Seybold Group, Vol. 9, No. 5, May 1994.

Eckert, K. P., "From OSI to OMG: Experiences from the Port of an ISODE-based Application to OMG/CORBA Concepts," *Computer Communications,* Vol. 19, 1996, pp. 4–12.

Edelstein, H., "Lions, Tigers, and Downsizing," *Database Programming and Design,* March 1992, pp. 39–45.

Emerich, M., "The Impact of OT on Legacy and Migration Strategies," *Object Magazine,* October 1996, pp. 44–45.

Everret, B., *Cluster Analysis,* Heinemann Educ. Books LTD., London, 1974.

Finckenscher, G., "Automatic Distribution of Programs in MASCOT and ADA Environments," Royal Signal and Radar Establishment, London, 1984.

Gray, J., "An Approach to Decentralized Computer Systems," *IEEE Transactions on Software Engineering,* June 1986, pp. 684–692.

Hess, M., "Transition to New Computing Environment," Gartner Group Briefing, February 1995.

Jain, H., "A Comprehensive Model for the Design of Distributed Computer Systems," *IEEE Transactions on Software Engineering,* October 1987, pp. 1092–1104.

Joder, D., "Negotiating an Enterprise API," *Object Magazine,* October 1996, pp. 32–37.

Kleinrock, L., *Queuing Systems,* Vol. 2, John Wiley, 1976.

Klinker, P., et al, "How to Avoid Getting Stuck on the Migration Highway," *Object Magazine,* October 1996, pp. 46–51.

Larson, R. E., et al., "Distributed Control: Tutorial," IEEE Catalog No. EHO 199-O, October 1982.

Meier, A., et al., "Hierarchical to Relational Database Migration," *IEEE Software,* May 1994, pp. 21–27.

Merlo, E., "Reengineering User Interfaces," *IEEE Software,* January 1995, pp. 64–73.

Mowbray, T., "Introduction: Migrating Legacy Systems to OT," *Object Magazine,* October 1996, p. 31.

Nitzberg, B., and Lo, V., "Distributed Shared Memory: A Survey of Issues and Approaches," *IEEE Computer,* August 1991, pp. 52–60.

Ozsu, M., and Valduriez, P., "Distributed Database Systems: Where Are We Now?" *IEEE Computer,* August 1991, pp. 68–78.

Patrick, R. L., *Application Design Handbook for Distributed Systems,* CBI Publishing Co., 1980.

Radding, A., "Dirty Downsizing," *Computerworld,* August 10, 1992, pp. 65–68.

Ramamoorthy, C. V., Garg, V. and Prakash, A., "Programming in the Large," *IEEE Transactions on Software Engineering,* Vol. SE-12, No. 7, July 1986, pp.769–783.

Ramamoorthy, C. V., and Vick, C. R., *Handbook of Software Engineering,* Van Nostrand, 1984.

Ricciuti, M., "Universal Data Access!" *Datamation,* November 1, 1991.

Ricciuti, M., "Here Come The HR Client/Server Systems," *Datamation,* July 1, 1992.

Rinaldi, D., "Putting the Mainframe to Pasture," *Client/Server Computing,* November 1994, pp. 35–40.

Ross, W., "Hewlett-Packard's Migration to Client/Server Architecture," in *Distributed Computing: Implementation and Management Strategies,* Prentice Hall, 1993, ed., Khanna, M.

Sneed, H., "Planning the Reengineering of Legacy Systems," *IEEE Software,* January 1995, pp. 24–34.

Teorey, T. J., Charr, J., and Umar, A., "Distributed Database Design Strategies," *Database Programming and Design,* April 1989.

Teorey, T. J., and Fry, J. P., *Design of Database Structures,* Prentice Hall, 1982.

Tucker, M., "Bridge Your Legacy Systems to the Web," *Datamation,* March 1997, pp. 114–121.

Umar, A., "The Allocation of Data and Programs in Distributed Data Processing Environments," *Ph.D. Dissertation,* Univ. of Michigan, 1984.

Umar, A., *Object-Oriented Client/Server Internet Environments,* Prentice Hall, 1997.

Umar, A., and Teichroew, D., "Computer Aided Software Engineering for Distributed Systems," *Proceedings of IEEE Region 10 Conference on Computer Communications,* Seoul, Korea, August, 1987.

Umar, A., and Teichroew, D., "Pragmatic Issues in Conversions of Database Application Gateways," *Information and Management Journal,* Vol. 19, 1990, pp. 149–166.

Umar, A., and Teorey, T. J., "A Generalized Approach to Program and Data Allocation in Distributed Systems," *First Pacific Computer Communication Symposium,* Seoul, Korea, October 1985, pp. 462–472.

Varney, S., "IS Takes Charge of Customer Service," *Datamation,* August 1996, pp. 46–51.

Wohl, Amy, "Is Downsizing Right for You?" *Beyond Computing,* IBM Publication, August/September 1992, pp. 10–11.

Wong, K., et al., "Structural Redocumentation: A Case Study," *IEEE Software,* January 1995, pp. 46–54.

Woodside, C. M., and Tripathi, S. K., "Optimal Allocation of File Servers in a Local Area Network Environment," *IEEE Transactions on Software Engineering,* August 1986, Vol. SE-12, No. 8, pp. 844–848.

Wreden, N., "The Ups and Downs of Downsizing," *Beyond Computing,* IBM Publication, August/September 1992, pp. 12–15.

Glossary of Acronyms

ACM	Association of Computing Machinery
AI	Artificial Intelligence
API	Application Programming Interface
APPC	Advanced Program to Program Communications
ANSI	American National Standards Institute
ATM	Asynchronous Transfer Mode
BISDN	Broadband Integrated Services Digital Network
BSP	Business System Planning
BPR	Business Process Reengineering
CAD	Computer Aided Design
CAM	Computer Aided Manufacture
CBX	Computerized Branch Exchange
CCITT	The International Telegraph and Telephone Consultative Committee
CDPD	Cellular Digital Packet Data (a standard for wireless networks)
CGI	Common Gateway Interface (an interface for developing gateways for the World Wide Web)
CICS	Customer Information Control System—an IBM mainframe transaction manager
CLI	Command Level Interface (command level API for SQL)
CORBA	Common Object Request Architecture
CPU	Central Processing Unit
CSMA/CD	Carrier Sense Multiple Access/Collision Detect
DBMS	Database Management System

DCE	Distributed Computing Environment
DCP	Distributed Computing Platform
DDBM	Distributed Database Manager
DDBMS	Distributed Database Management System
DDL	Data Definition Language
DDTMS	Distributed Data and Transaction Management System
DIS	Draft International Standard
DML	Data Manipulation Language
DNA	Digital Network Architecture
DOD	Department of Defense
DRDA	Distributed Relational Database Architecture (from IBM)
DS	Directory Services
DTM	Distributed Transaction Manager
DTMS	Distributed Transaction Management System
DTP	Distributed Transaction Processing
ES-IS	End System to Intermediate System
FAP	File Allocation Program (Procedure)
FDDI	Fiber Distributed Data Interface
FEP	Front End Processor
FMS	Flexible Manufacturing System
FTAM	File Transfer, Access, and Management
FTP	File Transfer Protocol
GSM	Global System for Mobile Communications
GUI	Graphical User Interface
HTML	Hypertext Markup Language
HTTP	Hypertext Transfer Protocol
IEEE	Institute for Electrical and Electronic Engineers
IIOP	Internet Inter-ORB Protocol (a CORBA protocol supported by all CORBA vendors)
IMS	Information Management System—IBM DB/DC system on mainframes
I/O	Input/Output
IP	Internet protocol
IPC	Interprocess Communication
ISDN	Integrated Services Digital Network

ISO	International Organization for Standardization
IT	Information Technology
JDBC	Java Database Connectivity
LAN	Local Area Network
LDBMS	Local Database Management System
LLC	Logical Link Control
LU	Logical Unit—an endpoint in the IBM SNA environment
MAN	Metropolitan Area Network
MAC	Medium Access Control
Mbps	Million bits per second
MHS	Message Handling Service
MIME	Multipurpose Internet Mail Extension
MIPS	Million Instructions Per Second
MOM	Message Oriented Middleware
MMS	Manufacturing Messaging Specification
MVS	Multiple Virtual System—operating system on IBM's mainframes
NAS	Network Application Support—DEC's open architecture
NBS	National Bureau of Standards
NCP	Network Control Program—a component of IBM's SNA
NCA	Network Computing Architecture (from Oracle)
NFS	Network File Services—SUN Microsystem's File System for Networks
NIST	National Institute of Standards and Technology
NLM	Network Loadable Module (A Novell Netware feature)
NM	Network Management
NMS	Network Management System
OCSI	Object Oriented Client/Server Internet
ODBC	Open Database Connectivity (a Microsoft standard for database connectivity)
ODP	Open Distributed Processing (ISO Model)
ODIF	Office Document Interchange Format
OLAP	Online Analytical Processing
OLE	Object Linking and Embedding (a Microsoft specification for distributed objects) s
OODBMS	Object-Oriented Database Management System
OOPL	Object-Oriented Programming Language

OSF	Open Software Foundation
OSF DCE	OSF Distributed Computing Environment
OSF DME	OSF Distributed Management Environment
OSI	Open System Interconnection
PU	Physical Unit (used in IBM's SNA)
RDA	Remote Database Access
RPC	Remote Procedure Call
SAA	System Application Architecture, IBM's "Open" Environment
SDLC	Synchronous Data Link Control—Layer 2 Protocol in IBM's SNA
SQL	Structured Query Language
SMDS	Switched Multi-megabit Data Service
SNA	System Network Architecture—IBM's Network Architecture
SNMP	Simple Network Management Protocol —TCP/IP Network Management Protocol
SONET	Synchronous Optical Network
SSI	Server Side Includes (an interface used in the World Wide Web)
TCP/IP	Transmission Control Protocol/Internet Protocol
TCP	Transmission Control Protocol
UDP	User Datagram Protocol
URL	Universal Resource Locator
VT	Virtual Terminal
VTAM	Virtual Telecommunications Access Method—a component of IBM's SNA
WAN	Wide Area Network
WWW	World Wide Web

Index